The Rose of
Martinique

Also by Andrea Stuart

SHOWGIRLS

ANDREA STUART

THE ROSE OF MARTINIQUE

A Life of Napoleon's Josephine

MACMILLAN

First published 2003 by Macmillan
an imprint of Pan Macmillan Ltd
Pan Macmillan, 20 New Wharf Road, London N1 9RR
Basingstoke and Oxford
Associated companies throughout the world
www.panmacmillan.com

ISBN 0 333 73933 7

A CIP catalogue record for this book is available from
the British Library.

Typeset by SetSystems Ltd, Saffron Walden, Essex
Printed and bound in Great Britain by
Mackays of Chatham plc, Chatham, Kent

For my loved ones

CONTENTS

List of Illustrations

Section II

Endpapers and all inside illustrations courtesy of The Bridgeman Art Library, with the exception of 1, 7, 8, 16 and 27: Roger-Viollet; 2: Collection Musie de la Pagerie; 6 and 18: the**art**archive.

PREFACE

I was initially drawn to Josephine through a sense of personal identification. We were both born in the Caribbean, descendants of plantation dynasties; we were both brought to the Old World in mid-adolescence and had to find our way in a society brutally different from that we had left behind. It seemed to me that this background and these experiences had a profoundly formative impact on Josephine the woman, and that by neglecting them we risk misunderstanding her entirely. The fact that Josephine and Napoleon were both immigrants, for example, explained for me the intensity of that bond which so many commentators have described as improbable. So it was the little-explored story of Josephine's early years that attracted me to her as a subject. But the more that I discovered about her, the more I was swept away by her dramatic and tumultuous life.

As a biographical subject Josephine has benefited from our enduring fascination with her illustrious second husband, Napoleon Bonaparte. There have been nearly sixty biographies written about her in the two centuries since her death. (A definitive biography of Josephine is therefore impossible; I offer this only as a general biography with a new accent.) Many of these books, however, have been written by Napoleon enthusiasts whose real interest lay in finding a new angle from which to approach Bonaparte. Others have been motivated by the desire to explore the fascinating times in which Josephine lived. In many ways, then, Josephine still feels like undiscovered territory. Unusually among her biographers, my interest in Napoleon grew out of my fascination with Josephine and not the other way round.

But the 'immortal Josephine' deserves our interest in her own right. Her life, even more than Napoleon's, gives us a picture of the terrible vicissitudes of her time. She managed to be at the forefront against every important backdrop of her era's turbulent history: from the slave plantations of the West Indies, which bankrolled Europe's rapid cultural, intellectual and economic development, to the decaying of the ancien régime, so ably captured by Choderlos de Laclos in *Les Liaisons Dangereuses*; to the Revolution itself, from which she barely escaped with her life; and then to be rescued from the decadence of post-revolutionary Parisian life by 'the colossus of the age', Napoleon Bonaparte. Whether at the Tuileries, Fontainebleau or Malmaison, Josephine played a central role in the new imperial court, contributing equally to its aesthetics and atmosphere.

After five years of what Virginia Woolf described as the 'donkey work' of biographical research and writing, Josephine's allure remains undimmed for me. Rather than being simply a foil to her illustrious husband, Josephine has emerged as a uniquely modern woman: a migrant whose charm, adaptability and style enabled her to negotiate her way through dangerous and unpredictable times.

The completion of this book would not have been possible without the support and encouragement of a great number of people. My first debt is to my editor, Georgina Morley, whose faith in the book has been unwavering and whose fortifying lunches kept my spirits up when my energy flagged. The enthusiasm of my wonderful agent, David Godwin, kept me buoyant when my nerve would otherwise have failed. I would also like to thank my copy editor Talya Baker, whose painstaking efforts have improved the manuscript immeasurably, and everyone at Macmillan who took Josephine to their hearts and saw her through with such tender care. Thanks are also due to my fellow Josephine-phile Elaine Hutchison, for the help she gave me with the first chapter, and the Society of Authors for their generous support. Also I would like to thank Elizabeth Murray, Elizabeth Cartmale Freedman and Emily Zahn for generously sharing some useful information on Napoleon.

My research has taken me on some interesting travels. In Martinique, where I began my research, I was met with great kindness. My dear friend Alissandra Cummins, director of the Barbados Museum, pointed me in the right directions. Thanks are also due to Lynn-Rose Beuze, Conservateur des Musées Régionaux, who provided contacts and important information; Liliane Chauleau at the Archives Départementales for her cooperation and help; Mlle Montjoly at Le Musée de la Pagerie for her material on the La Pagerie plantation; and Simone Rose Rosette and Emile Hayot, who provided information and hospitality in equal measure. Above all, I am indebted to Alex Calmont at the Bibliothèque Schoelcher, whose help went way beyond the call of duty. In France I am indebted to the staff at the Bibliothèque Thiers and to Bernard Chevallier and all of his team at the Musée de Malmaison, who provided me with unlimited access to the chateau and its archives. A great big thank you to Dr Catinat and Jean Abou who helped to augment my research in France with such charm and efficiency.

My special gratitude goes to my parents, Kenneth and Barbara Stuart, and my siblings, Lynda and Steven, who in their different ways have been essential in making this book possible. Thanks to my many friends and advisors, including Matt Seaton and Marybeth Hamilton, whose early comments were very useful; Janice West, Rebecca Arnold and Boyd Tonkin, for their regular contribution of relevant texts; Claire Barratt, for her technical expertise; and Philippa Brewster, whose insightful comments and thoughtful editorial suggestions have been invaluable as always. Special thanks to Norman Track and my dear friend and fellow Josephine enthusiast, Sandra Gulland, who travelled this ground before me and who has been unfailingly generous with her material and sources. My gratitude also to my friend Sigrid Rausing, whose helping hand allowed me to complete this book. Above all my thanks to Tara Kaufmann, whose intelligent criticism, editorial contributions and unstinting support have made this the book it is.

We are shaped and fashioned by the things we love

GOETHE

One

CHILDHOOD

Love for an island is the sternest passion: pulsing beyond the blood,
through roots and loam, it overflows the boundary of bedrooms, and
courses past the fragile walls of homes . . .

PHYLLIS ALLFREY

AT THE HEART OF A glittering archipelago that encircles the waist of the
Americas lies the birthplace of Empress Josephine. Today the island of Martinique is a bustling French *département*. It is as much a part of France,
theoretically, as Loir-et-Cher or the Pas de Calais, except that it is thousands
of miles away from the mother country, set in the turquoise of the Caribbean
Sea. The human mosaic that is its populace tells a complex story of slavery
and settlement. The racial melange of its people derives from Africans and
Amerindians, white planters and indentured Indians who replaced slaves in
the cane fields, as well as Chinese and Syrian merchants.

The island's geography is as variegated as its people. Shaped like one of
the exotic butterflies that so abundantly populate its foliage, Martinique is a
voluptuous island, its rolling hills interspersed by verdant valleys. Mangoes
and pineapples flourish here without any human encouragement. Bananas
grow upwards, swollen and yellowing towards the sun, and fat green bread-
fruits cling heavily to the trees. In the north, dense lush forests are decorated
with ferns and orchids. This luxuriant herbage is counterpointed in the south
by vegetation typical of any dry zone: cactus and brush. Indeed, Martinique
is like two islands in one. The side bordering the Atlantic is steep and subject
to a heavy surf. The other coastline, which is fringed by the Caribbean Sea,
is as smooth as an azure rug.

Martinique has a lurid, swashbuckling history. Enticed by tales of an island populated 'entirely by women', Christopher Columbus dropped anchor in 'Matinino' in 1502. By then the island's original population, an Amerindian tribe called the Arawaks, had been massacred by the more warlike Caribs. The latter coexisted relatively peaceably with the first trickle of Europeans. Western arrivistes could be divided roughly into two categories, the desperate and the damned: people fleeing from justice, soldiers fed up with fighting, sailors who came and never left. All the newcomers were dismayed to discover that this particular paradise was prodigiously populated with snakes.

The French officially claimed the island in the 1630s and the colonial race began in earnest. Intoxicated by the promise of the New World and the fabulous wealth to be found there, settlers came from far afield: from France mainly, but also from England, Ireland, Spain, Portugal and later Italy. Adventurers with titles of nobility newly bought or forged, and younger sons hoping to earn the fortunes they could not inherit, joined the recidivists, vagabonds, beggars and prostitutes that the French authorities sent to the island as *engagés* to work out their prison terms in exchange for their freedom. These new migrants were dreamers and gamblers all, flush with hope, dazzled by the possibility of reinventing their lives.

But the islands were lawless. Pirates and privateers, with their histories of murder, violence and shipwrecks, dominated both the commercial and military lives of the colonies. Clad in their signature garb of leather waistcoat and gold hooped earrings and wielding well-honed machetes, this international cast of reprobates terrorized the daily life of the region and indelibly wrote themselves into the Caribbean's colourful mythology. These were the golden days of piracy, the most unpredictable and dangerous of times. The 'brotherhood of the coast' counted amongst its members men like the Englishman Bonnet, who claimed that he had taken to the sea to escape a nagging wife, and the French nobleman De Grammont, who killed his sister's seducer in a duel; they fought alongside the likes of Monbars (the 'Exterminator'), and the 'Emperor of Buccaneers', Sir Henry Morgan.

By the eighteenth century Martinique's flourishing trades, legal and illegal, had turned it into a thriving colony. The Caribs had been almost totally exterminated. Slavery, introduced more than a hundred years earlier, had been stepped up in order to meet the demand for sugar, the 'white gold' that had enriched Caribbean islands beyond all expectation. Martinique's geographical position as gateway to both South and North America guaranteed its military importance and gained it the nickname the 'pearl of the Antilles'. Its two largest cities, Saint-Pierre and Fort-Royal, were the most cosmopolitan in *Les Isles du Vent* – the Windward Islands – a playground and meeting place for traders, travellers and military men alike. It was no wonder that, in a treaty concluded with Britain in 1763, when presented with the choice between holding on to Canada (which Voltaire famously dismissed as 'a few acres of snow') or to the commercially and strategically important 'sugar islands' including Martinique, Santo Domingo and Guadeloupe, the French chose the latter.

Josephine's family story is intricately woven into the tapestry of Martinique's history. Pierre Bélain d'Esnambuc, the founder of French power in the Antilles, who had taken possession of the island on behalf of Louis XIII in 1635, was one of her ancestors. She was also a descendant of Guillaume d'Orange, a courageous and audacious leader, who was responsible for protecting the colonials from Carib aggression in 1640 and who played a crucial role in defending Martinique during the Dutch Navy's attempt to take the island in 1674. Six generations on, a descendant of both these men – Rose-Claire des Vergers de Sannois, daughter of a prosperous plantation dynasty – married Joseph-Gaspard de Tascher de La Pagerie.

The marriage was not one that her father, Joseph-François des Vergers de Sannois, would have regarded as a social coup. The groom's father, Gaspard-Joseph, had arrived on the island in 1726 with nothing but his certificate of nobility to commend him. His pedigree was impressive enough: his ancestors included a Tascher who had endowed a monastery in 1142 and another who had been a crusader in 1190. But Gaspard himself was made of less impressive stuff and he didn't particularly prosper in Martinique. Despite a promising marriage to a plantation heiress, he had not been able to consolidate his position and ended up working as steward on a number of plantations, living off the good will of his powerful connections. His reputation on the island was so poor – in spite of his constant boasting about his noble descent – that the father of one of his daughters' suitors hesitated to agree to marriage because of 'the loose living of her father and the public disorder of his affair's.'[1]

Des Vergers de Sannois père had an equally noble pedigree, the bulk of the family originating in Brest, but his roots on the island were considerably longer than those of the Tascher family, as long as the history of settlement itself. He was a true Creole, the name given to those of European descent born in the colonies. (The slaves called them *bekés*, an Ibo word which, derived from the phrase 'whites found under the leaves', had derogatory connotations of low or illegitimate birth.) The Sannois family had numerous plantations scattered throughout the region; their holdings on Martinique alone were worth 60,000 livres*, in addition to which they had substantial cash savings. As the putative head of one of the oldest and most renowned families on the island, he was a *grand blanc*, one of the elite caste of plantation dynasties who intermarried and interrelated, dominating island life through their virtually unimpeded power. (The *petits blancs*, many of them the poor white descendants of *engagés*, worked largely as sailors, petty administrators and tradesmen.)

Were it not for the dangerously advanced age of Rose-Claire, M. de Sannois would probably never have considered the union. But at twenty-five she was – by the terms of the island nobility – virtually unmarriageable. No doubt Rose-Claire, who had never left her small island, was seduced by the young Joseph-Gaspard de Tascher de La Pagerie, with his easy manner and veneer of sophistication acquired during his five years at the French court, where he had been a page to dauphiness Marie-Josèphe de Saxe. But her father was not. Still, the young man had a good military reputation; he had become the first lieutenant in the coastal artillery on his return to Martinique and had distinguished himself in the military skirmishes of the island. This was small consolation for the Sannois family, but against the fear of remaining without an heir her reluctant parents agreed to the marriage.

The couple's first child was born in Martinique on 23 June 1763 and five weeks later the robust baby girl was christened at the tiny white church in Trois-Îlets where her parents had married two years earlier. The Capuchin friar who conducted the service wrote in his records, 'Today, 27 July 1763, I baptized a little girl aged five weeks, born of the legitimate marriage of Messire Joseph-Gaspard de Tascher and Madame Rose-Claire des Vergers de Sannois'. The child was put forward for baptism by her maternal grandfather and her paternal grandmother. Her given name was Marie-Josèphe-Rose de Tascher de La Pagerie. After the ceremony, which had been attended by a large gathering of family and friends, Rose – or little Yeyette, as she had been dubbed by her mulatto nurse, Marion – was, as tradition demanded, taken on a tour of neighbouring plantations where she was fêted, kissed and complimented, and numerous items were added to her layette.

After the celebrations the little girl returned to the extraordinary place where she had been born. The plantation, or as it is called l'Habitation de la Pagerie, now a museum, is situated in the south-west of Martinique in the

---

*A livre at the end of the eighteenth century was worth about £43 today.

tiny hamlet of Trois-Îlets, which takes its name from the three miniature islands that adorn its bay. Until it was hit by a hurricane, the town's vista was dominated by the small white church in which little Rose was christened. To the west of Trois-Îlets lies the plantation, nestling on a little plateau in the middle of a slim, funnel-shaped gorge. Its setting, wrote one observer, seems a 'haven of peace'.[2]

Known in the area as 'Little Guinea', after the African origin of most of its slaves, L'Habitation de La Pagerie was and is a place of exceptional natural beauty. It is not difficult to understand the passionate attachment Rose's family had for it. They felt that they had literally carved their new life out of the wilderness. In order to subdue this land and claim it, they had waged an unceasing war against nature. Almost as quickly as her ancestors cut and cleared, burnt and built, the vigorous vegetation of the island went about sabotaging their work; splitting walls, dislodging stones and destroying foundations. Every inch of the plantation's five hundred hectares represented a victory to Rose's family, a monument to their will, a symbol of their tenacious ability to prevail in the most impossible of circumstances.

The 'great house' at La Pagerie was a relatively modest affair. As was the tradition, it was built on slightly raised land so that the planter could keep a continuous eye on his investment. It was a simple, one-storey building, white and wooden and airy, covered with tiles and perched on a foundation of large squared stones. Inside the house was equipped with an eclectic mixture of traditional French furniture and pieces constructed in the Americas. The rooms were scented by blossoms cultivated on the property: tuberoses, jasmine, immortelles. Around three sides of the house ranged a *glacis*, a type of covered veranda with slatted railings which the young Rose spent much time peering through.

Immediately surrounding the house was a neat shady garden, dominated by large tamarind, mango and frangipani trees, their flowers and foliage almost obscuring the house. To the extreme right and left were the outbuildings, including the kitchen which served the great house. A hedge of hibiscus, roses, immortelles and acacias surrounded the entire domestic compound. It is easy to imagine Rose as a little baby being walked by her nurse up and down 'palm alley', which extended to the right of the house. This honour guard of gigantic palm trees rose like Roman columns on either side of the road, their verdant fronds interlaced to make a giant canopy; it remained one of her favourite places.

As the months passed, Yeyette's plump little legs carried her further around her family's plantation. The true majesty of La Pagerie was not its architecture but its land. It was set in a valley dramatic with slopes and gullies and giant ceiba trees, about which Josephine would often reminisce. The voluptuous hills were interspersed with green pastures and savannahs and field after field of green sugar cane. Here on rolling grassy land cows and sheep endlessly grazed. The sugar cane rippled continuously in the breeze, creating a song that never ceased, and enclosed the factory and the dwelling houses 'like a sea'. Visible through the gaps in the foliage was the iridescent blue of the Caribbean water.

The area was originally cultivated by the Caribs, so by the time Rose's family settled there it was already richly endowed with fruits and vegetables. On the slopes of the hills grew a mixture of coffee, cocoa, cotton and cassava, while the abrupt and precipitous mountain sides were covered to the summits with luxuriant hardwood forests. At the edges of the plantation, always threatening to encroach, was the dreamscape of the rainforest. Here tangled vines and serpentine lianas concealed ravines and hung their garlands around anarchic vegetation. Sustaining all of this was the river La Pagerie, which ran like a vital artery through the body of the property. Sometimes sluggish and noxious, sometimes meandering and sweet tasting, at other times dangerous and swift with unpredictable currents, it is really numerous rivers rolled into one; today it is known as 'the River with Five Names'.

Viewed from the summit of the hills of Lamentin, L'Habitation de La Pagerie is even more spectacular. The plantation is bordered on three sides by a range of hills that spread out, gradually losing their green to the misty blue of the sky. The highest peak, Carbet, is wrapped in a headdress of vapour. On the fourth side the property slopes down to the bay of Trois-Îlets. From this vantage point the funnel-shaped valley is reminiscent of some giant natural amphitheatre. Every slope and gully is cloaked in foliage. The air is fresh with salt, sweet with the scent of tropical flowers. The sense of peace is absolute. It is no wonder that Rose, buffered between hills and sea, felt so safe here. Her family's land stretched as far as the eye could see; to a young girl it must have seemed like the entire world.

In the days of Rose's youth La Pagerie was indeed a world, an enclave complete unto itself. Like most plantations it was a self-sufficient community, as self-contained as any small town, sustained largely by what was grown on the property and by the hunting and fishing yielded from its own lands. It had its own carpenters and ironmongers, its own flour mill and sawmill and a tiny hospital. While the cane crop provided the backbone of the plantation's economy, La Pagerie also sold the small amounts of coffee, indigo and cotton cultivated on its slopes. It even produced its own honey and polish, much sought after in the district, derived from the large colony of bees that thrived amongst its myriad varieties of vegetation.

The La Pagerie family ruled like despots, absolute monarchs of all they surveyed, and little Rose was brought up with the privileges of any royal heir. She was surrounded by loving relatives and courtiers, including her mother and father, her grandparents de Sannois, her aunt, nicknamed Rosette, and her sisters, Catherine-Désirée, born 11 December 1764, and the youngest girl, Marie-Françoise (known as Manette), born in early September 1766. She was watched over by her much loved nurse, Marion, and her young helpers, Geneviève and Mauriciette, who bathed and dressed her, pampered and cosseted her. Brought up amidst slaves who were exclusively occupied with fulfilling her every desire, Rose was typical of many Creole children, who were often characterized as 'excessively capricious'.[3]

By her own admission it was a 'spoilt childhood'. From a very early age she was blessed by a sense that she was loved and appreciated and beautiful. Despite this she managed to remain a sweet-natured child of enormously appealing appearance. With her large, amber eyes and luminous complexion, little Yeyette was a delicious sight. Her chestnut hair, meticulously curled, glistened golden in the island's bright sunshine. Her skin, burnished by the sun, glowed. The 'pretty Creole', as her neighbours called her, had an irresistible charm even in her infancy. Everyone adored her, particularly her usually stern grandfather. She was like a kitten; alternating between an appealing timidity and insatiable curiosity, agility and hunger for life.

The peace of Rose's life at La Pagerie was rudely shattered on 13 August 1766 when a hurricane hit the island and did not relent for two days. Three-year-old Rose was asleep in her little wooden bed during the first indications of the storm: a gentle obscuring of the horizon on the north-west side of the island. Then the night abruptly fell into profound darkness. The tropical sky, normally lit by moon and stars, was enveloped by black, bursting clouds and lashed by rain. The smells of sulphur and bitumen, produced by the combination of electricity and moisture, befouled the air.

Rose, bundled in her nurse's arms, fled the house along with her heavily pregnant mother, her father, her sister Catherine and a handful of domestic slaves, to take refuge on the first floor of the *purgerie* ('sugar-drying house'). Winds of over one hundred miles per hour swept across the island; the earth trembled and flames spurted from its breast. Rivers burst their banks. The sea was no less intimidating: the waves were so high they seemed to merge with the clouds. The moans and cries of the drowning were obliterated by the noise of the surf. 'It was', said one survivor, 'a horrendous turmoil; a terrible fury of water, fire and wind. It seemed as if nature itself was coming to an end.'[4]

Nothing could withstand the hurricane's rage. The island's crops of sugar, indigo, bananas and cocoa were entirely lost; trees were ripped out by their roots; men and cattle were thrown into the air. A cabin boy was lifted from the deck of a ship and deposited unharmed on dry land. Houses were prised open and roofs lifted off like corks being pulled from bottles. In the town of Trinité, near Trois-Îlets, the force of the hurricane, 'almost as if in defiance of God', detached a church from its very foundations, lifted its walls and threw them back down in pieces. 'When it was over a woman was found crushed to death, her two children sleeping peacefully in her arms. Another family escaped death by using the door of their home as a raft and clung on till they could be rescued.'[5] Altogether 440 people died and 580 were injured; countless were made homeless and the economy was devastated. Beholding the aftermath, according to one report, many in the population, soaked and shivering, fell to their knees and prayed for the clemency of God.

When the exhausted and bleary-eyed La Pagerie family emerged they were confronted with a scene of total devastation. The slave quarters, constructed of fragile bamboo, had been entirely swept away. The cane crops and much of the rest of the plantation's vegetation had been levelled. The pastures were strewn with the corpses of cattle, and in the river floated the bodies of those slaves who had not managed to find a safe haven during the storm. The earth was strewn with the skeletons of trees, and much of the family's property: clothing, crockery, bits of furniture. Nothing was left of the great wooden house. Only the *purgerie*, where they had sheltered, and the stout stone-built kitchen remained intact. It was a disaster from which the plantation would take decades to recover.

After the shock had subsided, the work of reconstruction began. The entire island was mobilized to clear debris, replant crops and nurse the injured. At La Pagerie they rebuilt the slave quarters, the laundry and the dovecote. The upper floor of the *purgerie* was converted into a family abode and a veranda was built along the south side. These rather uncomfortable and makeshift domestic quarters were intended as a temporary arrangement, but because of financial problems and Rose's father's inertia they were to remain the family home for the rest of her childhood.

The economic devastation wrought by the hurricane was only exacerbated by the death of grandfather de Sannois six months later. The family
had anticipated a generous legacy, but the machinations of a corrupt notary
meant they inherited only debts. Rose's dowry, already depleted, now disappeared completely. Money was to remain a worry throughout her childhood.
At first Rose was too young to fully appreciate the implications of this. The
family's precarious finances became more of an issue as she grew older and
had more contact with the highly materialistic and competitive plantation
families. But at four years old the lack of certain comforts barely impinged
on her daily life. Her experience was of an affectionate, loving environment,
buffered by the planters' life of apparent ease; a leisure made possible by slave
labour.

Life slowly returned to normal. The family, which had been famous for
its hospitality, resumed entertaining. The loss of the house precluded formal
balls and dances, but the large, lavish lunch parties – which were traditional
on the island to celebrate Easter, Christmas and birthdays and to honour
important visitors – were still possible. An army of slaves would labour for
days, cooking, baking and cleaning, to feed up to three hundred guests. The
food was laid out, usually on long trestle picnic tables covered in white linen
and decorated with the exotic flowers grown on the plantation. Typically the
fare was a mixture of French and island specialities: fine French wines were
offered as well as *ti ponch*, the island version of rum punch; roast meats and
saucissons were served with local delicacies like crab soup, sweet potato
and fricassée of turtle; pastries were provided alongside tropical fruits like
mangoes and guavas. If the weather was particularly hot the company was
fanned by slaves with huge fans made from lengths of bamboo and ostrich
feathers, or they retired indoors – into rooms that were darkened against the
heat and light – for the afternoon siesta.

This style of entertaining, which became known in the islands as 'creoli-
zing', was relaxed and leisurely, and guests sometimes lingered for days. But
these great social occasions were few and far between. On most days no
visitors came and Rose and her sisters were expected to make their own
amusements. Plantation life tended to be insular and isolated, and La Pagerie
was no exception. It was difficult to reach, accessible overland on horseback
or by carriage only by treacherous and rudimentary roads in an era when
most travel was laborious and slow. And so – with the exception of an
occasional visit from the curate on his donkey – the family and its slaves were
left largely to their own devices.

Were there a painting depicting Josephine's childhood, its palette would resemble that of Gauguin, who first acquired his taste for bright shades on a visit to Martinique in 1887. This was a world of primary colours: the cobalt blue of the sky, the searing gold of the sun and splashes of red provided by sunsets and tropical flowers. Interspersed with these dominant pigments was the full range of the spectrum: pinks, purples, oranges, yellows, whites and infinite hues of green; provided by tropical plants like orchids, bougainvillea, scarlet flamboyant trees, hibiscus and amaryllis. The plantation was gaudy with colour; the air thick and wet and scented with honeysuckle, jasmine and frangipani.

In the background, but shaping all their lives, was the agricultural enterprise that was the plantation's raison d'être. Life at La Pagerie was ruled by the rhythms of sugar production. The plantation's dwellers were woken every morning by the slave master blowing his conch shell to summon the slaves to work. Cane could be planted at any time of year and the reaping of one crop was often the signal to plant again. So the slaves worked ceaselessly: digging ditches, planting, harvesting, clearing and then beginning again. (One of the emblematic symbols of the Caribbean remains that of women carrying the bundles of cane on their heads to be pressed.) The extraction of the juice was an urgent affair lest the canes begin to rot, so slaves worked up to eighteen hours a day, first to transport the canes, then to extract the juice and manufacture the raw sugar. The sugar mill was like a scene from Dante's inferno. Here near-naked slaves laboured in the glow of the flames and the roaring noise and terrible heat of the boiler room to transform the recently pressed juice into a thick, dark syrup. At these times the air of the plantation, always slightly sweet because of the growing cane, was heavy with the cloying scent of burnt sugar.

Rose adored sweet things. She haunted the cane fields in the hope of being given a section of fresh cane, cut and peeled, so that she could chew and suck the sweet juice from the fibrous cane husk. Many years later she would grow sugar cane in the greenhouses at Malmaison so that her grand-children could experience her childhood love. But at La Pagerie the cane juice was just the first delight. There was also *le sirop*, when the recently pressed juice was transformed into a thick dark syrup, then the dark treacly molasses, then the raw crystalline brown sugar, before it was refined into the final exportable product. Rose's sweet tooth left a lifelong legacy: a cavity in her front left incisor which prompted her to develop her distinctive smile, broad and beguiling but with her teeth resolutely covered.

But the process of 'civilizing sugar' only intermittently encroached on her daily life, which was centred around her family and a handful of slaves who were carers and companions. It was a childhood conducted in the open air, with a freedom of movement encouraged by the loose, cool, cotton clothes that were the fashion for colonial children. Here in their own natural theme park the girls discovered trees, flowers and fruits, and watched black finches, blue herons or any of the twenty-five other species of birds that inhabited the plantation. They had races and played catch or hide-and-seek. There were hives to scrutinize, lizards to torment, endless places to explore or to retreat to or to fall in love with. The plantation was an intensely evocative place and its images sank deeply into the child's mind, reappearing in the gardens she created many years later in France.

It was a physically active childhood. Rose went riding on her little Spanish pony or walking in the hills. Long journeys were taken by palanquin, a kind of hammock decorated with fringes and bird feathers and carried by slaves. There were excursions to the sea for fishing parties, trips in the small, quick canoes known as pirogues or swimming in the shallow bathing spots in the bay, which are now called 'baignoires de Joséphine' in her honour. She danced alongside the slaves as they celebrated their days off in marathon dance sessions of release and pleasure sometimes lasting from sunset to sunrise. As an adult she would recollect primarily the *sensations* of her childhood: the intense quality of light, the warmth of sun-baked skin, above all the feeling of being light, free, unencumbered. 'I ran, I jumped, I danced, from morning to night; no one restrained the wild movements of my childhood.'[6]

Little Guinea had so many magical places guaranteed to stir a child's imagination. There were mysterious places, like the curious water tank built out of three tiers of rock one hundred years earlier by the Caribs, whose cryptic carvings could be found repeated on stones throughout the island. There were peaceful places, like the river's shady bathing pools in which semi-precious stones could sometimes be found glittering in the river bed. Accompanied by her beloved nurse Marion or her sisters and friends, Rose would bathe here, then sit on cool, mossy stones and chat or dream. There were exciting places, hills and ravines and dark places in the tropical forest, which she explored despite the attendant dangers of snakes, tarantulas and scorpions underfoot. Here Rose and her sisters would play and prowl and dream and rummage on the borders of their small world.

The physical texture of her days was very different from that of a child brought up in France. She jumped from scorching paving stones onto damp, cool grass; savoured the bitter taste of the golden-skinned June plums, with their prickly seed inside; breathed the smells of sun-baked stones mingled with those of vanilla and eucalyptus leaves; felt the darting surprise of tiny shoals of mercurial fish that flashed silver past her feet as she swam in the clear Caribbean water. At dusk she watched the fiery red-and-yellow sunset, chased fireflies as they floated like miniature lamps in the tropical night and fell asleep to the sound of the cicadas and tree frogs whose symphony accompanied the day's descent into darkness.

'Night', one traveller said of Martinique, 'has the luminosity of the supernatural.'[7] For a little girl raised on the folk tales of her black nurse, this was particularly true. The night was a procession of phantoms: the breeze shook the trees like castanets, the cane rustled, the fruit bats whistled in the dark. Vegetation that seemed innocuous in the sun became frightening and grotesque under the moon's diaphanous rays. The tree that in the daylight was simply a tree became a being, one of those zombies the islanders called *tim-tims*, or the ghostly *moun-mos*. These eerie sensations were only heightened by the noises from the slave village. As the family sat sedately indoors, playing cards, singing or talking, the slaves' fires were all that was visible to the main house. But the sound of their singing and the murmurs of their story telling wafted through the clear evening air. Night was the slaves' time, their only real period of leisure, so all their living was done then. It was then that the masters felt least secure about their investment. It was the time of revolts and mysterious disappearances which heightened the strained atmosphere and made the night even more disturbing and curiously exciting for an imaginative little girl like Rose.

So much of who she was – and would become – was forged here, in the exotic sensory splendour of her birthplace. It was a world that had to be apprehended through the body, not through the intellect. It helped to account for her mainly sensual intelligence and her highly evolved aesthetic judgement. Her style was reminiscent of that of the mulatto women who brought her up: opulent and highly seductive, just as it was their contagious Creole accents that inflected her beautiful voice with its appealing island lilt. Even her carriage, for which she would become so renowned in France, was like one of the 'Caribbean Venuses' of the islands, who walked, remarked one observer, as if they were 'floating across sand', slowly and languorously, their heads held perfectly upright.

In later life Rose tended to depict life in Martinique as a pre-Lapsarian paradise. But there was already a serpent in this garden of Eden: slavery.

Many biographers have been disposed to give her family the benefit of the doubt in relation to their treatment of slaves, describing them as 'benevolent protectors'. But there is no evidence to suggest that La Pagerie was any better or worse than other plantations or that the family had pioneered a utopian scheme to eliminate exploitation from plantation life. Had they done so, this would have been so unusual that it would certainly have been recorded in the accounts of the period. Brutality was an intrinsic part of plantation life and no child, however privileged or protected, could escape its ugliness or its savagery.

La Pagerie was a place of disturbing contrasts. The family compound, with its pretty gardens and shady trees, overlooked thirty-eight squalid little huts that constituted the slave quarters. Here in dark, airless hovels with the beaten earth for a floor and beds of straw or animal hide, 150 men, women and children slept and ate, lived and died. Here was also home to many of the young slaves who were Yeyette's childhood playmates: Maximin, Ti-Medas, infirm since birth, and one-legged Bocoyo. But at the end of the day the La Pagerie sisters returned to their enchanted life in a world of meticulously maintained grace and beauty, and their companions returned to that other, dark, world of deprivation and suffering.

The sight of slave gangs working in the cane fields, half naked under the searing sun – backs bent under the lash, sweat pouring from their bodies – which so disturbed and awed new visitors to colonial territories, was a part of everyday life for Rose. As they advanced side by side through the sugar cane, working with a collective rhythm, they seemed, to one observer, 'as formidable as a phalanx of infantry'.[8] But the crop was harvested at the cost of beatings and brutal suppression. The slaves' cries and groans punctuated the air. They worked from sunrise till sunset, six days a week, all year round. On their day of rest they were expected to work on their own plot of land. Overcome by overwork, disease and a lack of food, death seemed a blessed release. 'The whip', wrote the fervent abolitionist Victor Schoelcher, is the 'soul of the colonies'. It is 'the clock of the plantation: it announces the moment of waking up and of going to bed; it marked the hour of work; it also marked the hour of rest . . . the day of his death is the only one in which the negro is allowed to forget the wake-up call of the whip'.[9]

In the early, most brutal, days of slavery, the average life expectancy of a slave in many colonies was a dismal twenty-five years. The *Code Noir*, instituted by Louis XIV and enacted in 1685, was designed to lay out the structure of colonial society. It purported to ensure human and civilized social structures; in fact, it encoded brutality. Beatings, brandings and being burnt alive were accepted punishments for a sliding scale of offences. There were few, if any, legal or social constraints on the more bizarre cruelties that have been recorded and which nearly always went unpunished. Slaves were covered in honey and staked out on anthills to be stung to death; other planters preferred inserting gunpowder into offenders' orifices and then igniting it. One visitor to the island was horrified to discover that just prior to dinner his charming hostess had had her cook thrown alive into the oven and watched impassively as he screamed and burned to death. His crime? An infraction regarding washing the dishes.[10]

Slavery did not exist just on the master's lands; it lived in his house and pervaded the intimate relationships of his household. About one quarter of the slaves at Little Guinea worked as domestics: valets, laundresses, nurses, cooks, cleaners. They were inevitably entangled in the family's daily life. The atmosphere of the plantation house was not unlike that of a royal court, with the plantation owners in lieu of a royal family. They saw it not only as their right but also as their duty to meddle in their charges' lives: dispensing advice and punishment, even interfering with their sex lives, since any child begat at Little Guinea was their property. Slaves, in order to obviate the powerlessness of their situation, acted like courtiers: collecting information, lobbying for position and status. Everybody scrutinized everyone else. There were endless bickering, gossiping and rumours. Intrigue was rife. Underlying this was a continuous undercurrent of fear and suspicion. Slaves knew that their very lives were dependent on the whims of their owners. The owners wondered whether every acquiescent, smiling face might provide the Judas kiss; whether the nurse who cared for their children, or even their own illegitimate offspring, might become the purveyor of ground glass or the wielder of a knife in the dark. (In 1806 Rose's mother did prosecute one of her servants for an alleged attempt to poison her.)[11]

Sex made the already intense atmosphere of plantation life even more heated. It was widely accepted, and expected, that male plantation owners would take liberties with their slaves. As a result, women like Rose's mother were often expected to live with their fathers' and husbands' concubines as well as their illicit offspring. It was no wonder that Creole women had a reputation for vindictiveness in relation to their female slaves, for these women, their most constant companions, were also their rivals.

The slave system, which encompassed sexual and reproductive compulsion, created a hidden history in every plantation family. The La Pagerie family was no exception. A question mark hung over the racial origins of Rose's grandmother Mme de Sannois, née Catherine Brown. On an island where individual pedigrees were minutely scrutinized to avoid the 'horror' of miscegenation, her antecedents remain shrouded in mystery. More concrete were the queries about the paternity of many of the mulatto women who worked in the house, like Rose's nurse, Marion. Was she fathered by Blanque, the overseer? grandfather de Sannois? Joseph? Or some other white man from some other plantation? There was little doubt about the paternal identity of the pretty mulatto slave Euphémie, who eventually accompanied Rose to Paris: it was widely accepted that she was the illegitimate daughter of Joseph de La Pagerie. But in the morally askew world of the colonies, family could also be property; Rose's half-sister was also her slave. Even within the home, slavery distorted human relationships and warped affectional ties.

What did a sensitive little girl like Rose make of this profoundly ambivalent place with its juxtaposition of beauty and savagery? She once declared, 'I was always careful to cover with a favourable veil those faults [in the slave] which did not affect me personally.'[12] Her own compassion towards the plantation's slaves was never in doubt, and they reciprocated with a fierce loyalty that would be useful when she returned to the island years later. But the cruelty of her world was inescapable. Rose learned early to compartmentalize her feelings, exercising great kindness while closing her eyes to wider cruelties – a skill that would serve her greatly in later life.

Rose was born in a complicated place during a tumultuous time. As one of the most strategically placed and valuable sugar islands in the region, Martinique was a favourite pawn, continually being passed backwards and forwards between Britain and France in the endless wars for economic and tactical supremacy in the Caribbean. According to family lore, Rose was still in her mother's womb when Mme de La Pagerie, accompanied by two slaves, climbed the hills of the plantation to watch the terrible battle raging in Fort-Royal's harbour in which her husband was fighting. For three nights the guns roared and blazed in what would prove to be a watershed victory for the French troops and the islanders caught up in the fallout of the Seven Years War. Three months before Rose's birth, Martinique was returned to France after almost a decade of occupation. Rose thus avoided being born a British subject by as slim a margin as Napoleon – born on the island of Corsica which had recently been recaptured by the French – would avoid being born Italian.

Peace arrived in the form of the 1763 Treaty of Paris, but it came at enormous cost. During the years of blockade and enemy occupation the island's planters had accrued huge debts and their plantation incomes had fallen to less than one-third of operating costs. Those estates which had not been razed by fire had been so seriously neglected that many of the buildings were in total disrepair, while their fields and pastures had all but reverted to wilderness. At Trois-Îlets, the situation was compounded by a malaria epidemic as well as outbreaks of dysentery and yellow fever that ravaged both the black and the white populations.

A series of natural disasters exacerbated the terrible economic effects of the initial blockade. Martinique seemed to be conspiring against its own recovery. A few months after Rose's birth, the island was infested with ants unwittingly imported with a cargo of slaves from Africa. In neighbouring Barbados these had already caused such extensive damage that plans had been drawn up to evacuate the island. In Martinique the ants consumed almost all the vegetation, even the pastures on which the animals grazed. The trees were so thickly smothered that birds did not dare alight on their branches. Even the island's fearsome serpents were defenceless against the marauders, which ate them alive in their relentless march across the island. Travelling in great armies, the ants managed to cross streams by forging bridges from the innumerable dead bodies of those which had gone before. Despite the best efforts of the islanders, who organized hunting parties to burn the ants in their millions, for a time they seemed unstoppable. Such was the threat to householders that little Yeyette was constantly guarded by slaves, who were stationed at the foot of her cot as she slept.

Just two years later the great hurricane of 1766 further devastated the island. Even worse, Mt Pelée, the island's volcano, was in murderous mood throughout Rose's childhood. With terrifying regularity it smoked and spewed ash, tossed blazing scoriae and dribbled lava, keeping the populace on tenterhooks, never letting them forget its deadly threat. The earth tremors, endemic to the island, seemed to grow even more frequent. When it finally did erupt, in 1902, Mt Pelée completely destroyed the town of Saint-Pierre, killing its entire population of twenty thousand people in ten minutes and covering the island in ash. The only survivors were a tailor returning to the town on his donkey and a drunkard who was protected from death by the underground jail cell in which he had been incarcerated. He was later employed by P. T. Barnum as a wondrous curiosity displaying his magnificent lava burns, the only living testament to Mt Pelée's awesome destructive power.

Martinique housed another volcano – the institution of slavery itself. It rumbled and festered beneath the society's surface, putting pressure on its fault lines, constantly threatening to erupt and destroy everything in its path. The difficulty of a small minority ruling over a population ten times its size caused ceaseless concern. The systematic brutality of the slave system, designed to keep slaves obedient and fearful, could not assuage all the colonialists' fears. They worried about uprisings and the possibility of being poisoned in their own homes; they feared that the *marrons*, runaway slaves who had fled to the hills, would raid their plantations and murder them in their beds. Perhaps their guilt, however well suppressed or unacknowledged, added another noxious ingredient to the pressure cooker that was slave life. Certainly the intense paranoia and hatred was contagious. Governor Fenlon wrote in 1764, 'I arrived in Martinique with all the prejudices of Europe against the harshness with which the Negroes are treated', but after a short stay he declared that 'the safety of the whites requires that the Negroes be treated like animals'.[13]

The anxieties of planters in islands like Martinique were heightened by the burgeoning abolitionist movement, which they feared might boost slaves' hopes and incite them to rebellion. In the second half of the eighteenth century the critics of slavery were becoming more vocal. In England the movement gained ground massively after 1765. In France it had been boosted by philosophers and writers like Montesquieu and Rousseau, whose book *Le Contrat Social* condemned slavery and whose ideas fuelled an enthusiasm for the exotic and associated images of the 'good savage'. The romance of this ideal was given a further fillip by Aphra Behn's novel *Oroonoko*, about a noble African prince sold into slavery. Originally published in 1699, the novel was hugely popular throughout the eighteenth century. The great Diderot – the driving force behind the ten volumes of *L'Encyclopédie*, which appeared from 1765 to 1772 and featured discussion of the main ideas and philosophical debates of the day, with contributions from all the important French writers of the time – also attacked slavery, as did the chevalier de Jaucourt, whose book on slavery and the treatment of blacks was fervently condemnatory.

The abolitionist debate that ensued in France was fuelled by the publication of the abbé Raynal's *Histoire philosophique et politique des établissements et du commerce des Européens dans les deux Indes*, published in 1770. He joined with other voices like Condorcet and the English economist Adam Smith, who under the pseudonym Joachim Schwarz published *Réflexions sur l'esclavage des Nègres*, which criticized the viability of the slave system and put forward a plan to end slavery within seventy years. This debate would eventually lead to the emergence of the Society of Friends of Negroes, founded in February 1788 by Brissot and Mirabeau and modelled on the English organization founded by Granville Sharp and Clarkson. It attracted high-profile members like Lafayette, Clermont-Tonnerre, le duc de La Rochefoucauld-Liancourt, Trudaine and Lameth, who committed themselves (despite the enormous difficulties) to immediate abolition of slavery and an end to the slave trade.

In the turbulent years leading up to the French Revolution the anti-slavery issue was discussed with increasing passion. In many ways the slave societies of the Caribbean were 'but a garish exaggeration, a crazy caricature, of the ancien régime in France'.[14] In Martinique, as well as in mainland France, a tiny privileged minority viciously exploited the majority, preserving through patronage the best positions for themselves. They considered themselves vastly superior to both the labouring class and the vigorous, emerging mercantile middle class. In both societies, the most cosseted and spoilt members, overburdened with leisure and money, indulged in a degree of decadence and heedless cruelty that shocked the world. The colonists in Martinique and the aristocrats in France were Nero fiddling while Rome burned, ignoring the cauldron of unrest that boiled beneath them. It was no wonder that, comparing the two societies, the revolutionary Mirabeau accused them both of sleeping on the edge of Vesuvius.

The peculiarities of colonial life created a complex and volatile society. The colonists felt profoundly misunderstood by outsiders, whom they believed did not appreciate the uniquely dangerous circumstances in which they lived. The result was a sort of siege mentality and a feverishly independent spirit. Armed with their formidable economic power, they battled constantly with the metropolis for the right to run their own affairs. 'God', they crowed, was 'too high, and France too far' to control their behaviour. The island developed a network of arcane and abstruse social rules, most of which were underpinned by paranoia about race. Freed men of colour were not allowed to wear certain clothes, jewellery or haircuts, so that they would not be confused with whites; certain names belonged exclusively to white families, in order to avoid the terrible slander of being taken for a 'coloured'.

This intensity of repressed feeling, combined with an excess of leisure, created a decadent society. Drinking and prostitution were endemic, as was the widespread and overt sexual exploitation of female slaves that so scandalized visitors to the island. Gambling had also reached epidemic levels: stories reverberated around the island about daughters sold into marriage or entire plantations changing hands after one night at the tables. The inhabitants bet on everything: cards, dice, cockfights, even battles between snake and mongoose which took place in secret venues. Duelling had reached such a pitch that the casualty rate on this tiny island with a Creole population of less than ten thousand sometimes rivalled that of Paris. In the period 1779–80 there were seventeen deaths in as many months as a result of duels.

This unique society shaped the temperament of the Creole community. They were seen as coarse, clannish, impatient and – according to one observer writing in the year of Rose's birth – 'violently attached to their pleasures'. Their leisured, affluent lifestyle fuelled a tendency towards ostentation and supported their tradition of lavish hospitality. The benevolence of the climate, the beauty of the island and the relaxed pace of life encouraged the 'liveliness of their imaginations' as well as their intense physicality; in particular 'the pronounced elegance' of the women. But the 'same conditions that endowed them with these advantages impeded their progress.' Indulged from their infancy, growing up with a battery of slaves to perform the simplest task, Creoles were 'indolent' and had 'little ambition'. In later years, Rose would exploit these ideas about Creoles to her own advantage, taking refuge in her supposed 'native indolence' to avoid doing things she did not want to do. But there was truth in these stereotypes too. Rose was in many ways an exemplary Creole, 'vivacious, pleasure-loving, sensual and wilful',[15] and it is almost impossible to imagine her emerging from any other society.

Rose's mother was also a typical Creole: fiercely protective of her family and passionately attached to her island. Her relationship with the island was a kind of love affair. Martinique was in her blood. Her forefathers had struggled to conquer and keep it. This battle with the land, the dynamic of defeat and victory, of submission and subjugation, made their relationship with the island a kind of romance. The island's beauty and its profound sensuality also played a part: Mme de La Pagerie's response to it was visceral. Its physicality makes visitors gasp and the hairs rise on the back of the neck. Its dangers and uncertainties only added to the piquancy of the affair. Hers was a fleshy, irrational kind of love; an *amour fou*. Nothing, she believed, compared with the beauty of her island. To her, the threat of separation from this place seemed like a kind of death. She would never leave.

By contrast, Rose's father longed to escape. Much to his wife's annoyance, he was forever comparing the parochial social life of Martinique with the glamour and sophistication of the French court. Unlike his wife, whose roots on the island were over a century long, he was the first generation of his family to be born on the island – hardly a Creole at all. For him the island's charm had begun to pall. The wonderful scenery that had once exhilarated him had become familiar and even monotonous: a little greener in the wet season, a little browner in the dry. He found the climate inhospitable. The humidity and heat exacerbated his recurring bouts of malaria and rheumatism.

The work was dull too. While Joseph was not averse to striding around La Pagerie in his white frock coat with its shiny buttons, nankeen jodhpurs and gold-topped cane, the planter's uniform, he found that running a plantation did not suit his nature. The challenge and excitement of founding the plantation was over; what was left was merely maintenance, the meticulous and tedious work of overseeing the overseer, looking over the shoulder of the bookkeeper, double-checking finances and contracts.

But most unbearable of all was the solitude. An intensely sociable man, Joseph had enjoyed the conviviality of the court and the camaraderie of his army days. But La Pagerie was socially isolated because of its geographical position and the limitations of the era's transport – there were only his wife and daughters, and one or two white employees who didn't live on the premises, to provide an appropriate audience. The 'loneliness of plantation life' was a recognized syndrome throughout the sugar islands, as a letter written by one depressed planter to his brother in France demonstrates: 'nowhere does time pass more slowly or with so much suffering'.[16] Joseph was not alone in preferring the incessant bustle of Fort-Royal, with its harbour full of ships and its streets full of merchandise. There he gambled and drank, dreaming of resurrecting his buried dreams in France, dividing his time between his black mistress and his tumbler of rum.[17]

Whether Joseph married Rose-Claire for love or to bolster his precarious finances and social position is unclear, but the marriage was in trouble virtually from the start. There was already something a little defiant and defensive in the tone of a letter Rose-Claire wrote to a relative on the occasion of Rose's birth: 'Contrary to our hopes, it has pleased God to give us a daughter . . . my own joy has been no less great. Why should we not take a more favourable view of our own sex? I know some who combine so many good qualities that it would seem impossible to find them all in any other person.'

A couple of years later, while pregnant with their final daughter, her expression of her fears was all too explicit: 'I hope with all my heart that this will be the little nephew that you desire; perhaps that will give his father a little more love for me.'[18] In the years that followed, Joseph disappeared with increasing frequency. Although he was at La Pagerie during the hurricane and for the birth of their third child, he spent more and more time at the family's other plantation, Paix-Bouche in St Lucia, or in the capital. She wrote bitterly, not long after, 'He spends his time in his charming Fort-Royal. He finds more pleasure there than he does with me and my children.'[19]

In Joseph's defence his brother wrote, 'He means well . . . he loves his family, above all his children, but he must be pushed.'[20] But Joseph could not come to terms with plantation life. His sporadic and inept management only exacerbated the devastation wrought by war and natural disasters on the financial well-being of the plantation. Under his guiding hand La Pagerie diminished to almost half the size it had been during its heyday, when it boasted 322 slaves and produced up to 700 kilograms of sugar each year. His wife was left to pick up the pieces. For a woman who was described as 'extraordinary for her industriousness and the firmness of her character',[21] the situation must have been extremely frustrating. She was hampered by his erratic involvement, alternately laissez-faire and hysterically overactive. It would not be until after his death, many years later, that she would be free to put the estate back onto a profitable footing.

The profits were always there to be had; La Pagerie's sugar played its own part in the burgeoning transatlantic trade that was enriching the developing imperial powers. The ships that carried La Pagerie's harvest had previously stopped in Africa, where they bought newly captured slaves in exchange for tobacco, gold coins, handkerchiefs and coral necklaces. Transported in such horrific conditions that up to one-third of the slaves habitually died in transit, the living cargo was sent on to French ports like Nantes, La Rochelle, Saint-Malo and Bordeaux, where the ships took on essential supplies destined for the Caribbean. Here they finally unloaded their abused charges, who were sold, branded and broken; then they returned to Europe laden with tropical produce including the 'white gold' that enriched all who touched it, except of course the slaves who sacrificed their lives for it.

It would have been impossible for Rose to remain unaware of her parents' marital problems. As the estrangement between the couple grew, her father's absences became longer. When he was at home he was a loving, if occasionally irascible parent – depending on the state of his health and how much he had had to drink. But it was Rose-Claire who was the dominant parent, a constant reliable influence that the girls could count on. We know a fair amount about Rose's relationship with her parents from the letters that she exchanged with them throughout their lifetimes. With both, the correspondence is loving and warm; though her letters to her mother possess a tinge of awe that she clearly doesn't feel for her father.

Rose, the eldest, was close to both her parents; she must have grown adept at negotiating the tension between them, sympathizing with both parties without jeopardizing the love of either. It was a skill that would prove useful later on. Throughout Rose's life she was a consummate 'pleaser', capable of navigating turbulent times and political factions without offending either side, sustaining people's affection in the most difficult of circumstances. There would be another legacy from her parents, an important but paradoxical one: she inherited both her mother's passionate attachment to the island, and her father's equally intense desire to escape it.

France was dangled before her throughout her childhood. Nurtured on tales of her father's five glamorous years at court – the King on his golden throne decorated with its fleurs-de-lis, the hunt with the royal family, the multi-coloured spectacle of the fireworks on the birth of the dauphin – Rose also had more concrete enticements. Just before her third birthday her father's sister Marie-Euphémie-Désirée de Tascher, known to her family as Edmée, wrote offering to educate Rose in France. The family was delighted; a French education was what every Creole family dreamed of for its children. Her mother replied, 'She shows great promise and I hope that in two years' time you will help her to take advantage of it.'[22] In the years that followed, the plan to send Rose to France was scuttled temporarily by the financial problems caused by the hurricane and by the death of grandfather de Sannois. But the family was still expectant, as a letter from grandmother de Sannois, written in the year approaching Rose's fifth birthday, indicated: 'I am truly not in a position to send her – But I do not despair of being able to accomplish what you wish.'[23]

Although Rose loved life on the plantation, the picture that her father painted of France was so glorious that Martinique must have seemed dull in comparison to the imagined life over the seas. But her father had now taken over the finances of the plantation and he was not of a decisive disposition. His wife, nonetheless, remained hopeful. But over the next few years no amount of familial pressure seemed capable of rousing him from his inertia. A cousin wrote to Edmée in 1775, 'I think he will not decide at the moment on making the voyage to France. His reason is that it requires a great deal of money and this is what he lacks: he has this in common with many other good folk. I have told him that if he is not sending her, then I have three girls who are ready to make the journey.'[24] And so Rose grew up with the promise of France always before her but somehow tantalizingly just out of reach.

At seven Rose was struck down with smallpox. For several days the family feared for her life. But the little girl rallied and mercifully was left unmarked by this often disfiguring disease. After a lengthy convalescence, the question of her education came to the fore again. Her mother was worried. 'Beautiful and good child,' she declared, 'your character and your heart are excellent but your head . . . oh! your head!'[25] Had she been brought up in France, her mother felt, she would have learned by example and overcome the Creole 'repugnance for learning', but as it was, Rose was uninterested in academic matters. Something had to be done.

At ten, in 1773, Rose was sent away to school. After an arduous journey by carriage and canoe ferry, accompanied by her nurse, she arrived in her father's playground, Fort-Royal. Founded in 1638, the town – later renamed Fort de France – had grown up on a swamp beside the sea. Today crabs still crawl out of its gutters. In the decades before Rose's birth it emerged as the island's capital rather than the larger, more densely populated town of Saint-Pierre. Its position meant that the stagnant water occasionally caused terrible smells, and outbreaks of fever were a constant problem. There was a canal, which people traversed by gondola or small boat. Amidst its dwellings, great and small, were shops, brothels and the careenage. It had its '*quartier misérable*' where the very poor lived, and a small colony of lepers. Later there would be town police to stop fighting in the bars and prevent horses galloping in the streets. In time, a market was established to rival that of Saint-Pierre, where women in their *bambouche* headdresses sold imported monkeys and parrots, as well as coconuts, bananas and mangos, iguanas and fish.

Rose's new school, Maison de la Providence, was right in the heart of this steamy, bustling town. It was housed in an imposing white building, flanked by two villas, and surrounded by a courtyard, outbuildings and meticulously landscaped gardens. Founded in the year of Rose's birth by the formidable Father Charles François, prefect of the Capuchin order in the Antilles, the school also provided a home for a select number of indigent women. Its raison d'être, according to its founder, was to counter the 'indolence' and 'depravity' inspired by too much proximity to black people, and to prepare 'young girls from good families' for their future destinies as 'wives, mothers and mistresses of plantations'. 'In our school we want to imprint our students with that sense of modesty, grace, softness, discretion and love of work and of God, those qualities', wrote the Father, 'that are the best ornament of their sex and the guardian of all the virtues'. As a result the curriculum of *Les filles de la Providence* was dominated by religious studies.

Rose dressed in red-and-blue striped cotton uniforms like all the other girls. They awoke at five and began their day with two hours of prayers and meditation. Any academic pretensions that Father François had started out with had been relaxed in the years since the school had opened, and its goals had become altogether more worldly and practical. Classes started promptly at seven and were supervised by the formidable Mother Superior and her team of teachers largely imported from France. There were lessons in penmanship, basic arithmetic, geography, drawing and embroidery. Rose's parents paid extra for dancing lessons from Francis, *maître de ballet et premier danseur* of the theatre Saint-Pierre, and for painting lessons from a local artist.

But it was not all hard work. Rose and her special friend Yves enjoyed three breaks a day and two days off per week (Wednesday and Saturday afternoons), so there was lots of time for shared confidences and crushes, and the endless gossip about other *beké* families and trivia about fashionable French life that had such cachet at any colonial girls' boarding school. The girls were also allowed one day trip into town each month and Rose spent most of this time with old Mme de La Pagerie, her grandmother, or with her father's commander at the port. It was less an education than a finishing school, more concerned with narrowing the mind than broadening it, and it produced young girls who returned home, grumbled one observer, with 'frivolous tastes and heads stuffed with romantic nonsense'.[26]

So it was that Rose returned home at the age of fourteen, dreaming of France and hoping that, despite her lack of dowry, her parents would be able to arrange a marriage. While she waited, she attempted to settle back into her old life. But it was difficult; she had grown used to the conviviality of school. One of the few distractions from the monotony of plantation life was the occasional ball, held on neighbouring plantations or at Government House in Fort-Royal. These were a slightly old-fashioned pastiche of what happened in France. Accompanied by a slave orchestra, the visitors milled around in the night air until it was cool enough to go inside. Torches lit the lawn, while the house slaves stood in attendance watching their long shadows across the illuminated grounds. Sometimes there would be fireworks or a performance by a travelling theatre group, who were always much in demand on the island. Handkerchiefs fluttered around the perspiring dancers and the scent of the tropical flowers that decorated the rooms perfumed the air.

Despite its airs and graces, Martinique was still a rather rough-and-ready society. It had not been that long since the settlers were struggling against the land and the Caribs in their own version of the Wild West. It was a commercial society, not a cultured one, and conversations centred around shipping problems, crop rotation and the buying and selling of slaves. In contrast to Paris – where, Rose had heard, women held a uniquely influential role in the exquisitely refined world of aristocratic society – Martinique was a male-dominated laager, breeding a coarse social life which repelled all but its aficionados. One visitor, referring to the crudity of its manners and the paucity of conversation, concluded, 'It is a sad society, that of the Creoles'.[27]

Nor could anyone living in Martinique fail to notice the ambivalence with which the metropole regarded its colonies. They had all seen the derisory caricatures of red-faced, rum-swollen planters abusing their slaves. The families who occupied this separate world were never allowed to forget that they were mere colonists, who should not dare to claim true kinship with the mother country. For Rose, Martinique was always a place she was going to leave, while France was a place of alchemy. She believed in it the way a seminary novice believes in the sacraments. She dreamt of flight, of a life transformed into one of luxury and glamour.

To complicate life further, fighting had returned to the region. In 1777 the War of American Independence was under way and Martinique, the principal through-port for commerce between France and the revolting colonies, was inevitably drawn into the conflict. Martinique's governor, General de Bouillé, was in an invidious position. The island was not officially at war but its feelings about the historic enemy, England, were unequivocal. Despite a warning from the English governor of Barbados that Martinique should not under any circumstances harbour 'the rebels, pirates or others' who engaged themselves in the conflict, corsairs were already using the island as an illegal hideout in between their maritime forays against the British troops. (The governor revealed his own allegiances by approving the building of a pirate vessel called *Le Serpent à Sonnettes* in Fort-Royal's harbour.) The treaty signed between France and the United States, 'of commerce, friendship and alliance', only heightened the tension in the region. As a result, Britain took the island of St Lucia in December 1778. France garrisoned over 2,000 troops on Martinique and it became the Caribbean centre of French operations and assistance to the Americas.

It was around this time that le comte Montgaillard, serving in Martinique, met the girl who would eventually become Empress Josephine. 'She was', he remarked, 'suffused with grace, more seductive than beautiful, but already remarkable for the litheness and the elegance for her size; dancing like a fairy, amorous as a dove and possessing a thoughtlessness, a coquettishness, which we no longer see, but which astonishingly has remained unchanged in the colonies, a certain capriciousness and extravagance, even though the family in real life lives in mediocrity.'[28]

Even in her youth, this portrait implies, Rose possessed the charms that would captivate the colossus of her age. Whether Montgaillard's acuity was the result of exposure to the potent Josephine myth which evolved in later years, we will never know, but what is indisputable is that even the faults indicated by the comte appealed to Napoleon. He would meet Rose at a point in her life when time had tempered her thoughtlessness. As to her coquetry and capriciousness, he adored the former and indulged the latter.

With such nascent allure, it is no wonder that legend has fabricated for Rose any number of adolescent romances. Only one seems likely to be true: a brief idyll with a young man of Scottish Jacobite descent, known only as William K. Separated after a few months by disapproving parents, the star-crossed lovers were not to see each other again until her deathbed, when she was too ill to recognize him. Less likely are the reminiscences of men like General Tercier who, alluding to a supposed love affair with the teenage Rose, wrote tantalizingly in his memoirs, 'She was young then; so was I . . .'[29] His insinuation was only one among scores of tales perpetuated by men hoping to enhance their own amorous reputations by association with one of the most desirable female figures of their age.

One day, probably in 1777, Rose and two friends decided to go and see the local sorceress. Euphémie David was in many ways typical of the obeah women or sorceresses who were influential across the island. They might be dismissed by outsiders as charlatans but on a plantation it was impossible to entirely disbelieve in their powers. Their medicines often worked where European medicine failed, and their spells and potions were sought after by Europeans and Africans alike.

David lived alone in the hills near Little Guinea, in a tumbledown shack whose path was bordered by huge lilies, *amaryllis gigantea*, a flower that Josephine loved. Inside her hut was the normal paraphernalia of her profession: herbs drying, containers with unidentifiable objects, and various crude receptacles. The girls entered the hut with trepidation. After they had slipped her a few coins, the old mulatto questioned each in turn and then took the first one's hand. Her fate was not to be 'in the theatre of the world', she pronounced. She would marry a planter and lead a happy and prosperous life in the colonies. The second girl, a distant cousin of Rose's called Aimée Dubucq de Rivery, had an altogether more sensational reading. She was told that she would be kidnapped by pirates and sold into a seraglio in 'a grand palace' across the seas. After many privations she would bear a son who would ascend to a throne. But, David concluded, 'at the very hour when you know your happiness is won, that happiness will fade like a dream, and a lingering illness will carry you to the tomb.'

The final reading was hardly less exciting. The old woman told Rose that her palm revealed two marriages. The first would be to a young blond man connected to her family. He would take her to Europe, but the marriage would not be happy. After many tribulations, David continued, she would remarry, and this second marriage would be to a 'dark man of little fortune'. But he would become celebrated, 'covering the world with glory' and making her 'greater than a queen'. 'But', she concluded, despite all this, 'you will die unhappy', and 'regret frequently the easy, pleasant life of Martinique'.[30]

The fantastic quality of this story and the unreliability of its source has led many to dismiss it as a fable. But Rose would refer to the prophecy in newspaper interviews[31] long before she could have anticipated becoming empress, as would others of her acquaintance. If it or something like it did occur, this perhaps accounts for Josephine's sense of destiny, since no Creole girl, brought up in the superstitious and magical world of the Caribbean, could ever discount such a prophecy. As to her friends: the first did indeed spend her life as chatelaine of a plantation and her cousin Aimée's life was to become as contentious and extraordinary a legend as Josephine's own.

A visitor to Martinique once wrote about young Creole girls: 'She is a bird in a cage who vaguely aspires to liberty but without suspecting the perils of that liberty once it happens.'[32] He could not have described Josephine's fate better had he known her.

The primary architect of Rose's marriage was her aunt Edmée. Her motives were not entirely altruistic. For over two decades she had been romantically involved with François de Beauharnais, governor of Martinique and the other islands of the French Caribbean. When they met, Beauharnais was in his forties, married and no innocent in the ways of love or indeed of the world – he had conferred upon himself the title of marquis ten years before the King saw fit to make it official. Edmée was nineteen years old,

tall and blonde. She was also intelligent, ambitious and as determined as her
brother Joseph was feckless and dreamy. She knew that neither her father nor
her brother could be relied upon to protect her interests and that her fate
was in her own hands.

Initially Edmée contrived to make as favourable an impression on his
wife as she did on the marquis, and she was soon invited to take up the role
of the marquise's companion, sharing the official residence at Government
House. The development of the relationship between Edmée and the marquis
did not seem to disturb this amicable arrangement in any way. The only
troublesome aspect was Edmée's single status, and so the marquise set about
searching for a husband for Edmée, one who would be happy to attach
himself to their curious ménage à trois.

The most likely candidate emerged in the handsome form of Alexis
Renaudin, a King's Musketeer who had recently arrived on the island.
Ignorant of Edmée's situation, Renaudin was eager to marry her. However
his father, a hugely successful planter at Lamentin, was troubled by the
rumours about Edmée and the marquis and by the public reproaches made
against her for 'having frequently abused her influence with M. and Mme de
Beauharnais to obtain favours from them which excited the liveliest complaints'.[33] The Renaudin family had secrets of its own, however. Alexis had
just recently been released from the fortress prison of Saumur, accused by his
father of trying to poison him. This combination of obstacles – adultery,
troubled family relations and community opinion – did not bode well for
the union, and no sooner were Alexis and Edmée married than they began
to drift apart.

Meanwhile, Beauharnais's career was in crisis. In 1758 the British fleet
attacked Guadeloupe, the neighbouring island that also fell under the marquis's jurisdiction. The lieutenant in command on the island sent desperate
pleas for help, but none was forthcoming. Governor de Beauharnais had a
clear duty to respond, and the ships available to do so, but there was a more
pressing matter for him to attend to: the wedding of his mistress to Alexis
Renaudin. It was only after the celebrations were over, some three months
later, that he finally sailed to the island. It was too late. After the death of
many of its defenders, Guadeloupe had finally capitulated just one day before
Beauharnais arrived. The governor did not hesitate: he instantly turned tail
and returned to Martinique, abandoning Guadeloupe to its fate.

The scandal soon broke. An anonymous pamphlet, *Lettres sur la prise de
la Martinique par les Anglais*, accused the governor of sacrificing Guadeloupe

to his amorous arrangements. Beauharnais furiously denied the allegations, compounding his deplorable behaviour by sending reports to Paris that blamed the brave lieutenant and officers of Guadeloupe for the island's downfall. Gradually the full story emerged and the marquis was recalled to France in disgrace.

He managed to linger on in Martinique for months, in order to be near his beloved Edmée. Alexis soon discovered what the whole of Martinique already knew; violence flared and separation swiftly followed. He sailed for France to sue for a legal separation. Edmée initially went home to her parents, but soon followed her husband, accompanied by two slaves, Charlotte and Arthemise, in order to secure a financial settlement. Hot on both their heels came her lover and his wife, the ever-patient marquise. In their precipitous haste to follow Edmée, they left their youngest son, Alexandre, in the care of Edmée's mother.

In France, the muddled Beauharnais ménage slowly settled into a permanent arrangement. Little Alexandre finally returned home in 1765 at the age of five. The marquis, with the help of influential friends at court and in the Admiralty, managed to clinch both a promotion to commodore and a hefty pension of 10,000 livres for his years as governor, a fortune when the average tax bill was 1,300 livres per capita in this period of high taxation. Mme de Beauharnais conveniently retired to her family's country property, leaving the door open for Edmée, who had temporarily taken up lodgings at one of the numerous convents in the capital devoted to sheltering ladies having marital difficulties. That this solution was perfectly amicable to both women is supported by the warm correspondence they shared until Mme de Beauharnais's death in 1767. Since Edmée's estranged husband lived for another three and a half decades and divorce didn't really exist in France, marriage was impossible. So the lovers simply moved in with each other. The ensuing scandal focused not on their adultery – Parisian society was used to that – but on their audacity in sharing a home.

The situation remained static for almost two decades. But then Edmée realized it was time to look to the future. In 1777 she was thirty-eight and her lover was an infirm sixty-two. Without the protection of marriage, which – in light of Renaudin's robust health – seemed a very long way off, Edmée knew that the marquis' death would leave her in penury. However, she had raised her seventeen-year-old stepson Alexandre from childhood; and he 'loved her like a mother'.[34] Why not arrange to keep him and his inheritance close, within her own family? She decided to arrange his marriage to her niece and god-daughter, Rose, who had finally reached marriageable age.

Edmée's letters to her brother's family took on a new urgency. One of her nieces, she wrote, should be sent over as soon as possible to marry Alexandre, whom she described glowingly as having 'an agreeable face, a charming figure, wit, genius, knowledge; and, what is beyond price, all the qualities of soul and heart are united in him: he is loved by all round him.' Rose's parents were less impressed with the thought of 'his charming figure' than with the prospect of his substantial private income. What was more mysterious was why Alexandre should want one of the La Pagerie daughters. That they were Creole was no obstacle; indeed it was a positive boon. Many mainland aristocratic families had been fortified by the huge dowries that Creole brides usually brought with them. But Rose had no dowry. In reality both sides had their reasons: Alexandre was too young to come into a large inheritance from his mother's side of the family unless he married.

But there was one terrible hitch, revealed in a letter from the marquis to Joseph de La Pagerie. 'I should have much desired that your eldest daughter were some years younger: she would certainly have been preferred, since I have been given an equally favourable account of her. But I must confess that my son, who is only seventeen and a half, thinks that a young woman of fifteen is too close in age to him. This is one of those occasions when wise parents are forced to bow to circumstances.'[35] After all her dreams, Rose was being passed over. Instead, the marquis requested her sister Catherine who, unbeknownst to those in France, had recently died of yellow fever. So Joseph wrote to say that he would bring his youngest daughter, eleven-year-old Manette, to France as soon as the weather was mild enough to travel.

Rose, normally so easy-going, railed and begged, quarrelled and cried. She clung to her dream with a previously unsuspected tenacity, shocking her father into making new representations on her behalf. 'The oldest girl, who has often asked me to take her to France, will I fear be somewhat affected by the preference which I appear to give to her younger sister', he wrote. 'She has a very fine skin, beautiful eyes, beautiful arms, and a surprising gift for music. She longs to see Paris and has a very sweet disposition. If it were left to me I would bring the two daughters instead of one, but how can one part a mother from both her remaining daughters when death has just deprived her of a third?'[36]

But it was not left to him. Timid Manette contracted a fever, which her mother felt was prompted by the threat of separation from her family. Joseph was left with only one possibility, the daughter that Alexandre had specifically not wanted: Rose, the eldest. As providence would have it, the situation on the other side of the Atlantic was getting more desperate. The marquis's health was deteriorating and he feared that Alexandre's guardians might talk the boy out of the marriage. Her aunt wrote, 'We leave you to be guided by Providence which knows better than we do what is good for us . . . but we must have one of your children. Come with one of your daughters or with both of them, but hurry.'[37] The letter was followed swiftly by one from the marquis enclosing an authorization for the marriage banns to be published in Martinique. Alexandre's name had been filled in but the space for the name of the bride had been left blank. It seemed that Rose was destined for France, after all.

Fearful that Alexandre might be swayed by machinations within the Beauharnais family, Edmée urged immediate departure. But Joseph's indifferent health and customary indecisiveness led to a long delay. True to form, he did not seem able to collect himself sufficiently to make the necessary arrangements; six months after he had received authorization to publish the wedding banns they had still not been called. It was not until 11 April 1779 that the priest of Notre-Dame de la Martinique finally announced the banns of marriage between Alexandre-François, chevalier de Beauharnais, and Marie-Josèphe-Rose de Tascher de La Pagerie.

Joseph's difficulties in making and executing plans were exacerbated by external obstacles to a speedy departure. Martinique had been drawn into the fallout from the American struggle for independence. As France's base in the region, Martinique had played a surreptitious role from the beginning of the conflict, but it was now official: Britain and France were at war. St Lucia, where Joseph had spent so much of his time ostensibly overseeing one of the family's plantations, was under British occupation and Martinique was under siege. The war was not the only threat to the journey. The Atlantic crossing was always perilous and the hurricane season was swiftly approaching. People often disappeared at sea.

Rose did not leave for France until September 1779. The small party – Rose, Joseph, her aunt Rosette, and her maid and half-sister Euphémie – sailed in the naval store-ship *Île de France* as part of a convoy of ships escorted by the frigate *Pomone*. What must she have thought, as she stood on the deck of the ship, with its delicate shrouds and fluttering ensigns, amidst the movement and bustle of departure – this child-woman who had packed her dolls along with her meagre trousseau? What excitement and fear she must have felt as she watched her beloved island recede slowly from view. She was leaving behind a beloved homeland, and a family grieving the death of one daughter, the illness of a second and the departure of a third to set out for an unknown future in a strange, new land. A girl with a less intense sense of her destiny might well have been daunted.

It would prove to be a hazardous, miserable, three-month voyage, prolonged by terrible storms and constantly threatened by enemy attack. But at its start the journey was beautiful. The ship sailed over banks of white sand, cutting through the Caribbean waters with their floating vegetation, rare fish and transparent molluscs, reflecting such a diversity of colours in the incandescent light of midday that it must have seemed as if the ship was cutting through a sea of jasper. Rose must have watched the waves and marvelled at the sea's coral depths, her cheeks burning, her hair tousled by the wind, her mind overwhelmed. What did she feel as she watched the last of the Caribbean's prodigious sunsets building in the sky or enjoyed the last of the superb nights that the region offered, floating on a sea aglow with phosphorescence, while the mountains of Martinique, her island, could still be discerned, faintly outlined by the light of the moon?

Two

ARRIVAL

She is not pretty, she wears no rouge.

SAINTE–BEUVE

ROSE MUST HAVE ARRIVED IN the Old World filled with passionate yearnings she could not fully articulate, even to herself. She was fifteen years old, moving to a country she had never seen to marry a man she did not know. But her fear would have been tempered by anticipation. France was the country of her father's reminiscences, the place of his golden hours. Perhaps it would provide glamour and romance for her, too; maybe it would become the source of her own glittering memories.

But whatever buoyancy had attended her departure had long since been wrung out of her by the rigours of a horrendous voyage. The Atlantic crossing was traditionally long and arduous, but hers on the *Île de France* was made worse and more protracted by terrible weather conditions. The ship was buffeted by roiling seas and seemingly endless storms that threatened the craft so severely that much of the travellers' baggage was irreparably damaged by water. On at least ten separate occasions they genuinely despaired for their lives. The terror of their three months at sea was intensified by the constant threat of the British fleet, with whom France was once again at war. They also feared sharing the same fate as Rose's cousin Aimée, who had been captured by pirates just the year before.

By the time the ship docked in the great port of Brest on 12 October, the party was exhausted and bedraggled. This travel fatigue must have made Rose's first vision of France even more disorientating and overwhelming. Instead of the technicolor hues of the Caribbean, she was confronted with the pallid skies of a French autumn. Instead of the warmth of the sun on her skin, there was a damp chill. And all those white faces! Rose would never have seen so many Europeans in one place in her entire life. Brest itself was an intimidating sight. Located 310 miles west of Paris, it was one of the two major bases of the French Navy, dwarfing the ports that she would have been familiar with in the Caribbean. Partially excavated from rock, Brest stood on one of the largest and best protected deep-water bays of the European seaboard. Its deep scalloped bay, surrounded by hilly promontories, opened onto the ocean through a deep and narrow pass. The port was also home to the notorious prison hulks of Brest, sinister in appearance and notorious by reputation, which were only closed in the nineteenth century when Devil's Island and the penal colony of French Guiana were established.

It was this 'dung heap' of a town (in Alexandre's words) that greeted Rose's party on their arrival and became their home for several days. Since, in the hustle and bustle of leaving, M. de La Pagerie had, with his usual feyness, neglected to inform Mme Renaudin of their departure from Martinique, the first she heard of the trip was when she received a note on 20 October, eight days after their arrival, saying that the party had arrived at the port. She immediately set out, accompanied by Alexandre, but, despite their haste, it would still be another few days before they arrived in Brest.

The family reunion must have felt strained. They were there to plan a wedding, but the key players had not seen each other for almost two decades. Appraising glances would have been exchanged along with embraces; old family ghosts would have disturbed the air. When Mme Renaudin had last seen her brother and sister they were young and vigorous and full of hope. Now Joseph was a querulous invalid and Rosette was a middle-aged spinster, sly and sharp tongued. From their perspective, Edmée too had changed. In the place of the young Hellenic beauty they remembered was an intimidatingly elegant woman of a certain age. Alexandre, whom they had last seen as a plump-limbed toddler, was now a young man. Meanwhile, the newcomers to this passion play, Rose and Euphémie, were miserable, still tired and fraught by travel.

Joseph's health continued to deteriorate and he was forced to take to his bed. The delay gave Alexandre ample opportunity to scrutinize his bride-to-be. She was not what he had expected or, to be blunt, what he wanted. Like most French men of that age, Alexandre's ideas about Creole women were the product of a complex mythology that had built up around the islands in his epoch. Eighteenth-century France was awash with paintings depicting '*la belle créole*', lounging in charming *déshabille* or bathing naked, attended by her black or mulatto slaves. Travellers' tales reinforced the popular fantasy of Creole women as almost oriental in their sensuality, as seductive as any courtesan. One reported, in lascivious detail, on the supposedly everyday costume of Creole women, whose breasts 'spilled out' of transparent muslin peignoirs. Another enthusiastically described the effect these ephemeral garments had on the viewer, as awakening 'the idea of a voluptuousness, made only more seductive by the nonchalance that characterizes all their actions'.[1] Without a doubt, these images were less the product of real experience than the fevered fabrications of writers and artists, but they were so potent that even travel agents simultaneously exploited and popularized them in the commercial notices they designed to induce adventurers to visit the 'magical' islands.

The Creole women with whom Alexandre was actually acquainted were Creole in name only. They might have been born in the islands, but these daughters of the great plantation families had been sent to France early to be educated, visiting their island homes only occasionally. (Hence Mme Renaudin's eagerness to have her nieces receive a mainland education.) Having acquired a Parisian patina, these heiresses were the brides of choice for aristocratic families in search of fortunes. They were regarded as infinitely preferable to the rich but bourgeois daughters of financiers, since they were nobility, if only minor nobility. And of course some of the island mystique still clung to them. Many considered them more beautiful than 'French women of the old soil', with their 'dark diamond eyes' and 'passionate' natures. They were 'the rulers of the court and the capital', instantly recognizable for the 'provocative languor of their walk . . . and for their natural elegance, universally imitated but never surpassed'.[2]

Instead of the bird of paradise of his dreams, or the polished Parisian Creoles with which he was familiar, what Alexandre got was Rose: plump, provincial, adolescent Rose, bare faced, in her démodé clothes, with an accent so thick it could be cut with a knife. Neither she nor her husband-to-be had any inkling that one day she would become an essential pillar of that very Creole mythology by which he – and the rest of France – had been so thoroughly seduced. Alexandre's carefully phrased letter to his father couldn't hide his disappointment: 'Mademoiselle de La Pagerie may perhaps appear to you less pretty than you had expected, but I think I may assure you that her amiability and the sweetness of her nature will surpass even what you have been told.'[3]

Rose, by contrast, was bowled over by her fiancé. Alexandre was exactly the sort of young man that she and her school friends had fantasized about back at the convent. He was a type that was regarded as exceptionally attractive during the period. Not particularly tall, he was nonetheless 'handsomely built' with wide-set, intense blue eyes, a long curved nose and full lips. His hair, meticulously coiffed and powdered, was pulled back into a neat bow at the nape. In an age where the most romantic of all occupations was the army, he was a soldier. His natural assets were heightened by his captain's uniform: white with silver-grey buttons and facings. Most impressive of all was his manner. At nineteen, Alexandre was already an impressively worldly young man, supremely confident and supernaturally elegant; a true champion in the game of life.

Alexandre was as much a product of his sophisticated and cosmopolitan education as Rose was of her rudimentary, colonial one. After his return from Martinique, he had been sent to the Collège de Plessis in Paris, where his elder brother François was already a pupil. Later, when Alexandre reached the age of ten, a tutor was hired to educate both boys. His name was Patricol and he was an elderly teacher of mathematics with a passion for Enlightenment philosophers such as Rousseau. Pedantic and rather self-important, he was nonetheless a profoundly important figure in the life of both the Beauharnais boys. He was particularly influential for Alexandre, perhaps in part as compensation for the boy's disjointed relationship with his own father.

After a few years, Patricol took the pair to Germany to learn the language. The trip was an important one for young Alexandre, who became markedly more independent. In 1775 their beloved tutor was offered a new post with the two nephews of Louis-Alexandre, duc de La Rochefoucauld, one of the most famous members of the French nobility and a star of Enlightenment circles, who numbered amongst his friends the likes of Voltaire, Lafayette and Benjamin Franklin. It was too enticing a proposition for Patricol to turn down, and it was arranged that Alexandre would follow the tutor to his new job. He spent the next few years dividing his time between the duc's grand Parisian hotel and the chateau of La Roche-Guyon, some fifty miles down the Seine from the capital.

Alexandre was now firmly ensconced in the household of one of the greatest aristocratic families of France and also at the centre of the nation's liberal intelligentsia. In these glittering circles he witnessed and participated in the debates that would eventually fuel the Revolution. The duc de La

Rochefoucauld was a leading light in the worlds of politics, the sciences and the arts. He was a founder member of the Société des amis des Noirs, the first anti-slavery organization in France, and had been the translator of the text of the Constitution of the thirteen American states. Four years before the French Revolution, the city of New York awarded him honorary citizenship. He was a member of the Academy of Science and had served as president of the Royal Society of Medicine. He had addressed the *parlement* of Paris, reminding the King of the rights of the French nation. This exciting and sophisticated milieu had a profound effect on Alexandre's social and intellectual growth.

Not all Alexandre's adolescent role models were as exemplary as the duc. His tutor related with disapproval the deleterious influence of the Hurault brothers on the fifteen-year-old. These young men, whom Alexandre had first met in Martinique, had, Patricol reported, been regaling Alexandre with their 'garrison adventures' and impressing him with their cavalier attitudes to women and war: 'What astonishes me most in him, and greatly displeases me, is the extreme care that he takes to hide, and the ease with which he disguises, the feelings of his heart. His eyes do not interpret them. No blush ever mounts to his cheek . . .'[4]

It was a revealing remark. Though still an adolescent, Alexandre was developing the inscrutability of the seasoned politician he would eventually become, as well as the skills of a hardened roué. His ability to deceive and dissemble – and to do so with neither embarrassment nor remorse – would have a terrible effect on his marriage. His cynical, rather predatory attitudes – particularly in relation to women – were later noted by his friend the marquis de Bouillé. Alexandre's vigorous romantic pursuits, he wrote, 'flattered his ego and occupied him almost exclusively'.[5] A Casanova, who was more interested in conquest than sentiment, Alexandre's women represented just so many 'trophies of war'. He often 'recounted his good fortune with women' and proved his boasts by compiling lists of 'the titles and other attributes of the ladies'. Bouillé – who was a decade his junior, and who had become his confidant at an impressionable age – felt that Alexandre's 'frivolous' attitude to the opposite sex was so pernicious that it had a detrimental effect on his own romantic happiness in later years.

At the age of sixteen Alexandre won a commission in the Sarre infantry regiment, which the duc commanded. By the spring of 1777 he was serving with his regiment at Rouen. Despite the demands of army life, he managed to find time to enjoy the romantic distractions available in the busy garrison town. In October of that year he was granted leave. He spent his first fortnight at the duc's chateau in La Roche-Guyon and then joined his father and Mme Renaudin at Noisy-le-Grand. It was on this visit that she revealed the marriage plans that could simultaneously give him financial independence, ensure her own security and transform Rose's life.

The wedding plans continued to unfold despite the substitution of Rose for her terrified baby sister. The revelation that Alexandre had fallen in love with a married woman from Brittany only added impetus to Mme Renaudin's plans. On 25 August Alexandre wrote to her, 'The day after tomorrow I am going into the country with one of my friends – It is at the home of the wife of a sub-lieutenant in the navy, a charming woman . . . I count on spending two days there and in that short space of time I shall do everything possible to succeed . . . Perhaps, by the time this letter reaches you, I shall be the happiest of men . . .' A few days later, his letter was triumphant: 'I will not conceal it from you: your chevalier has tasted happiness. He is loved by a charming woman who is the object of all the aspirations of the garrison of Brest and the district . . . Her husband, who left three days ago, told me that he was under orders to be away for three weeks. I hope with all my heart that nothing will oblige him to return early . . .'[6]

Even more peculiar than a man very publicly in love continuing to arrange a marriage to another woman was the curious complicity that existed between Alexandre and his father's mistress. For he shared with Mme Renaudin the details of his conquest. He explained that this was because she was like a mother to him. But he did not treat her much like a mother figure. Very few young men would confide these romantic details to their mothers, nor would they include an explicit letter from their mistress, as Alexandre did, so she could 'judge the choice that I have made'. But the intimacy of Alexandre's relationship with Mme Renaudin and his strong desire to please her at least partly accounts for his willingness to go along with the wedding plans.

After several days of rest and recuperation, M. de La Pagerie had rallied sufficiently for his doctor to declare him well enough to travel. However, Mme Renaudin, worried about the possible effects of the long journey to Paris on his health, took the precaution of arranging for him to see a notary in Brest before his departure. Here he signed a document which gave his consent to the marriage and gave Mme Renaudin full powers to act on behalf of himself and his wife. She now had the right to appoint as dowry whatever sum she thought appropriate, and for this purpose she also had the right to designate, bind or mortgage all property belonging to M. de La Pagerie and his wife. Mme Renaudin could now breathe easily: the marriage was well and truly in her hands and she could now turn her attention to organizing the journey to the capital, the cost of which she was underwriting.

In recognition of M. de La Pagerie's still fragile state of health, the trip was planned in easy stages. The little caravan set off on 2 November. It must have been a magical journey for Rose, despite her tendency towards carriage sickness, as they watched France unfold before their eyes. They covered about thirty miles a day, staying in some towns for an entire day to allow M. de La Pagerie to catch up on his rest. It was a sufficiently leisurely pace to allow the young couple to get to know one another. Mme Renaudin's letters to the marquis were optimistic. She wrote that Rose 'has all the feelings that you could wish her to have toward your son, and I have observed with the greatest satisfaction that she suits him . . . He is busy, yes, very busy with your daughter-in-law.' Another letter, three days later, crowed, 'things are constantly getting better and better.'[7]

This was not entirely wishful thinking. The fiancé himself began a letter to his father with the words 'The pleasure of being with Mlle de La Pagerie . . . is the sole cause of my silence.'[8] Certainly, Rose was transfixed by her elegant husband-to-be. She had never before met a young man like him. His self-assurance was like a magic shield that surrounded him; no situation seemed to be beyond his command. Surly innkeepers immediately became eager to please him; he always knew the correct wine; no amount of travelling marked or creased his impeccable uniform. In his turn, Alexandre couldn't help but be flattered by Rose's naked adoration and large lovelorn eyes. In a rather patronizing way he enjoyed her company; she flattered his already lofty self-regard. But he was also acutely aware that she was simply not presentable in the fashionable society in which he was determined to make his mark.

Rose's excitement must have intensified to fever pitch as the travellers finally approached the vast, gated city of Paris, in all its 'limitless grandeur and scandalous luxury'. The approach into the city, lined with fine trees, was magnificent. But what would have struck her first was the smell. Paris may have been 'the capital of the world', the centre of science, arts, fashion and taste – but it was also 'the centre of stench'. It was said that the putrid odour of the city could be 'smelt three leagues away' and that its heavy, fetid air was so thick that it could be seen. So vile was its atmosphere that many first-time visitors were overcome by nausea and some even fainted.

Dominated by the smell, the journey across the capital would have passed in a great sensory blur. As their cabriolet bounced and jostled over cobbled streets, Rose was surrounded by buildings so tall they seemed to disappear into the sky; narrow, dirty streets without pavements; terrible traffic jams. She had never seen so many people: beggars and soberly dressed administrators, milkmaids and porters. A stream of posters advertising everything from lost cats to entertainment spectacles flashed past her eyes. The noise was deafening. The vendors' cries and oaths, the constant burble of the street, all melded together into what sounded like another, totally unfamiliar language.

Eventually the travellers drew up in front of the house in rue Thevenot. Situated on a rather narrow street, in a district that had once been ultra-fashionable but now was rather faded, it was a tall, thin, two-storey house with an imposing front door guarded by the stone head of some unidentified goddess. The house had originally belonged to the marquis's grandmother, and had only recently become the home of the marquis and Edmée, who had abandoned their fashionable apartment in the rue Garancière in its favour especially so that the young couple could live with them. This aloof house, with its decadent trio of occupants and its surroundings of decaying grandeur, stink and noise, was Rose's new home.

As soon as the party had unpacked and got settled, Mme Renaudin resumed the wedding plans. There was the wedding contract to be settled, the trousseau to be ordered and guests to be invited. The wedding banns, which had already been called three times in Martinique eight months earlier, were published in the first week of December. Taking no chances, Mme Renaudin arranged for them to be read in three separate parishes: at Noisy-le-Grand where the wedding was scheduled to take place, as well as at Saint-Sulpice, which she had just left, and Saint-Sauveur, where they had just moved. On 9 December she petitioned and obtained the right to dispense with further banns.

The next day the marriage contract was signed 'in the apartment which M. de La Pagerie occupies in the home of the Dame de Renaudin', in front of several witnesses including the couple's fathers, Alexandre's brother François and the abbé Louis-Samuel Tascher. (He was a distant relative of Joseph's and his chosen proxy in the event that his health, which had once again taken a turn for the worse, prevented him from attending the wedding.) The bride's father promised a generous dowry of 120,000 livres, from which the

cost of her trousseau was to be deducted. This contribution had been calculated on the basis of the paper worth of the properties in the Indies and, as
was known by all parties, was more illusory than real. Joseph had barely been
able to pay for their passages to France, after all, so there was no possibility
of him raising this magnificent sum. The real amount that Rose was expected
to receive was a much more modest 6,000 livres per annum, the five per cent
interest that her father had undertaken to pay on the outstanding sum. Had
this materialized it would have been still sufficient to subsist in comfort at a
time when the average royal tax receipts were 1,400 livres.

Rose's contribution to the marriage was the presents and furniture that
she had received from relatives and friends. These were valued at 15,000
livres, though no plans were ever made to bring them over from Martinique.
Alexandre brought the income he had inherited from his mother and grandmother, the very substantial annual sum of 40,000 livres derived from their
estates in Santo Domingo and family lands in France. By far the most
substantial contributor to the marriage was Mme Renaudin, who gave Rose
the house at Noisy-le-Grand and all its furnishings, as well as a claim on a
large sum of money that she hoped to recover on the death of a relative.
However, since Mme Renaudin maintained a life interest on all these endowments, Rose was not able to use them.

The wedding finally took place on 13 December. It was not a particularly
fashionable event, rather a sober, suburban affair held at the small, cold
church in Noisy-le-Grand. To celebrate the occasion, the groom – with his
customary audacity – conferred upon himself the title of vicomte, to which
he was not yet entitled. The Beauharnais clan was out in force and Alexandre
was surrounded by a large number of supporters, including numerous cousins,
his tutor Patricol, his brother François and many of his army friends. Poor
Rose was virtually on her own. As they had feared, her father's health had
precluded the possibility of him attending the ceremony. Instead, Rose was
given away by the abbé who, although a relative, was not someone she knew
with any intimacy. There was no mother-of-the-bride, no sisters or friends
to prepare her, exclaim over her dress, listen to her fears or dry her tears.
The only female support was provided by her aunts Rosette and Edmée, to
neither of whom she was genuinely close. Her inscription, childlike and
uncertain, is the only female signature in the marriage register. Married life
had begun.

Three

MARRIED LIFE

France, a country where it is often useful to display your vices,
and always dangerous to reveal your virtues.

CHAMFORT

IMMEDIATELY AFTER THEIR MARRIAGE THE young couple established themselves at the rue Thevenot. The Beauharnais's hôtel (the term used for a
privately owned mansion) stood in that part of the city lying between the
Grands Boulevards and Les Halles of today. The area had not been truly
fashionable since the reign of Louis XIV, when there had been a court at the
Louvre and the Tuileries. By 1779 the tall, noble houses that lined its
dark, sunless streets, with their high garden walls and wrought-iron railings,
embodied a faded grandeur. The mansion itself was something of a mauso-
leum: enormous, claustrophobic and cold, with an imposing entrance hall
and sweeping reception rooms, decorated with chandeliers, tapestries, paintings and gilded furniture. A grand staircase led to the family's ill-ventilated
but capacious bedrooms and then on to the mansarded attic, which housed
the servants. The stone house was impossible to heat; cold in winter, stifling
in summer. The road outside was so narrow that carriages could not turn
around in it; and it had a smelly gutter running down its centre. For Rose,
arriving in winter, life at rue Thevenot must have felt like a kind of imprisonment, conducted largely indoors, in chilly airless rooms ministered to by
silent grey-faced servants. It could not have been more different from her
outdoor life in Martinique, surrounded by the riotous beauty of nature, with
its bright sunlight and soft tropical air.

For the sixteen-year-old Rose it must have been as if a veil had fallen,
obscuring everything she had ever known. Everything in this new country

was unfamiliar, exciting, threatening. There was so much to learn, so much to get used to; it was almost like being reborn. She carried with her a freight of expectation with regard to France and she was not yet quite sure how the reality would match up. She didn't realize that soon she would find herself baffled by everything, from the weather to the people. Why was the sky grey, not blue? Who were these actresses that everyone gossiped about over dinner? And what was the appeal of this man Mesmer who claimed to heal people with electricity? Even their attitudes to royalty were different from what she had expected. It was not that the King and Queen weren't liked; they were still popular, as France's involvement in the struggle for American independence had been successful. But there was none of the reverence that her father displayed. Instead it was fashionable to complain about one's duty at court or jest about the King, a good fellow, 'despite looking like a peasant shambling behind a plough'.[1]

But there was no time for nostalgia; Rose had a city to learn. Paris, 'the capital of Europe', was in 1779 still a semi-medieval, fortified city state where the King's executioner carried out public tortures and traffic was occasionally interrupted by horse and hounds pursuing a stag into the heart of the city. How extraordinary this vast inconvenient metropolis must have seemed to Rose, brought up on a small island like Martinique. Even from her apartments she could hear the roar of the city, the clatter of hooves and coaches, the rolling of wheels on cobbled stones. Gradually the inexplicable cacophony outside her windows began to make sense. Now she could distinguish the cries of the milkmaids in their saucy red braces; the perambulating dealers of rags, brooms, old irons; the apple and orange pedlars with their large trays; and the city's twenty thousand water sellers.

'Paris is the finest theatre in the world', declared the nineteenth-century journalist and statesman Jules Bastide. Throughout the day, street performers – jugglers, rope-dancers, sleight-of-hand artists and quacks – drew audiences, competing with the wandering cobblers, running porters, floor polishers, book stalls, trinket shops and sweetmeat sellers for attention. The city never seemed to sleep. The working day began just after midnight, when market traders and farmers rattled by in their rickety carts, journeying to the capital to sell their vegetables, fruits and flowers. Just after dawn they were followed by bakers, lemonade- and coffee-sellers and other itinerant pedlars of food to feed those who would soon enter the city. Their cries animated the early morning, while hairdressers – armed with combs, curling tongs and hair powder – rushed around the city to prepare their clients for the day. By early morning the city streets were teeming with a mixture of livestock going to market, dancing masters in their cabriolets, fencing masters in their *diables*, coaches ferrying people backwards and forwards to the provinces and young men of fashion perched in their speedy, large-wheeled whiskies.

Navigating the city on foot was a nightmare, noted Arthur Young, an English traveller: 'The streets are very narrow, and many of them crowded, nine-tenths dirty and all without foot-pavements . . . Walking in Paris is a toil and a fatigue to a man, and an impossibility to a well-dressed woman.'[2] Another menace for the pedestrian was the Parisians' habit of relieving themselves even in the middle of busy thoroughfares. 'The women,' reported Hester Thrale, a literary hostess and writer who visited Paris in 1775, 'sit down in the Streets as composedly as if they were in a Convenient House with the doors shut.'[3] Those travelling *à pied*, usually sensibly attired in black, acquired great dexterity – jumping nimbly out of the way, or plastering themselves against walls to avoid being squashed. The situation was exacerbated by carriage dogs, usually Great Danes, running ahead of their owners' vehicles knocking down almost as many people – including the writer Rousseau – as the vehicles themselves. But even those like Rose who travelled by carriage had a hard time. The traffic problems 'rendered the streets excessively dangerous'. Over 200 people were killed each year in street accidents. All was made even worse when it rained. Then the population was splattered with the city's notorious mud, a noxious mixture of sewage, excreta and dirt. It was scraped up regularly, collected and used as fertilizer. But there was still a deep layer of it, rendered into a stinking paste by each downpour.

The all-engulfing stench provided its own map of the city: the excremental odour of the fullers' and tanners' workshops near Rose's home; the vile smell of urine at the Palais de Justice, the Louvre, the Tuileries and the Opéra; and, the epicentre of stench, Montfaucon in the north of the city, where sewage reservoirs and slaughterhouses stood side by side. These odours mingled with smells from a thousand other sources: butchers' shops, cemeteries, hospitals, drains. Rose grew able to identify them all, a skill that came to all those who lived in the city. As the famous chronicler of the city Louis-Sebastien Mercier said, 'If I am asked how anyone can stay in this filthy haunt of all the vices and all the diseases piled one on top of the other, amid an air poisoned by a thousand putrid vapours, among butchers' shops, cemeteries, hospitals, drains, streams of urine, heaps of excrement, dyers', tanners', curriers' stalls . . . if I am asked how anyone lives in this abyss, where the heavy, fetid air is so thick that it can be seen, and its atmosphere smelled, for three leagues around . . . I would reply that familiarity accustoms the Parisians to humid fogs, maleficent vapours and foul-smelling ooze.'[4]

These conditions meant that many found Paris unbearable. One British diplomat concluded, 'It is the most ill-contrived, ill built, dirty stinking town that can possibly be imagined.' Another, scornful of the city's visual attractions, remarked, 'upon the whole, it is one of the most dreary and gloomy Cities I have been in'. Yet Paris continued to attract visitors from all over the world, for it was also 'the capital of pleasure'. As Gouverneur Morris, an American, wrote: 'I have seen enough to convince me that a man might in this City be incessantly employed for forty years and grow old without knowing what he had been about.' He concluded that pleasure was the great business of the French capital. A man in Paris, he wrote, 'lives in a sort of whirlwind which turns round so fast he can see nothing'.[5]

It was a mercy that the capital offered such diversions, since its streets provided Rose with most of her few distractions in the early months of her marriage. No doubt she had expected her new life to be made up of a glorious round of private suppers, balls, theatres and masquerades, but the reality was much less glamorous. Her social life was confined largely to Alexandre's immediate circle of friends and family, and her dreams of being presented at court proved to be in vain. Her husband's family, despite its social pretensions, was not quite aristocratic enough to warrant that honour.

An early opportunity to enter Paris society arrived in the form of the flamboyant and vivacious Fanny de Beauharnais, who was connected to the family through her own marriage (to the marquis's brother) and that of her daughter (to Alexandre's brother). Aunt Fanny – as the entire family called her – was warm-hearted, elegant and pretty. Married young into a disastrous union, she had separated from her husband and now devoted her energies to love affairs, a literary career and running an influential salon. Her writings demonstrate allegiance to both the sentimental pre-Romantic movement and the gallant light poetry of the school of Dorat. She wrote ceaselessly: poems, pamphlets and a novel entitled *Blinded by Love*.

But it was as hostess of what was later described as 'probably the most important salon in Paris on the eve of the Revolution'[6] that Fanny gained fame and influence. Contemporary reports describe her sitting 'enthroned, on her silver-and-blue settee, over-rouged, a chaplet of pink rosebuds sprinkled on her powdered hair', among her devotees, an eclectic group of 'men of the world and men of letters, though the worth of the latter was very uneven'.[7] They included sentimentalists and reformers: men like

Cubières, Restif de la Bretonne and the chronicler Mercier, whom one decrier dismissed as 'the triumvirate of bad taste'. Not everyone enjoyed the salon at rue du Bac: one visitor found the atmosphere so smoky and stuffy – Fanny detested fresh air – that there was more coughing than conversation.

Still, to Rose it must have seemed the height of sophistication. Unfortunately she did not make a good impression at the salon: she lacked the necessary social skills, had few opinions on art or politics and was too shy to be witty. Aunt Fanny was genuinely fond of Rose, and happy to introduce her into her gatherings. But Alexandre was mortified by his young bride's gaucheness and increasingly left her at home.

One popular diversion that Rose was allowed to share with her husband was freemasonry, but here too he grew increasingly disinclined to have her as his companion. Intensely fashionable at the time – among women as well as men – freemasonry offered a number of Parisian lodges, whose names were usually associated with moral virtue. Alexandre and Rose joined *La Triple Lumière*. Although the lodges were later associated with the political dissent that brought down the monarchy, at this stage they were simply exclusive clubs that provided the privileged with the opportunity to dress up in fancy dress, flirt and participate in the performance of 'silly penitences for peccadilloes that the lodge deemed punishable'.[8] Once again, Rose failed to shine.

When Alexandre rejoined his regiment, Rose's world became even more circumscribed. The days were long at rue Thevenot, with only the company of her older relatives – her still-invalid father, her father-in-law and her aunt. She had no friends in Paris, and her distraction was long drives through the city. It was said that she kept the pieces of jewellery her husband had given her in her pocket and played with them, showing them off to acquaintances like a little girl. Missing her husband, Rose complained to Alexandre that his letters did not arrive frequently enough. This earned her a sharp reprimand: 'Rely on my fairness, and do not poison the pleasure which I take in reading what you write by reproaches which my heart does not deserve.'[9]

It is hard to build a picture of Rose at this time. She hated writing letters, so we have few first-person accounts of her life at this point. The adult woman she would become was forged through trial and experience: at this stage she was very young, unformed and lacking in confidence and opinions. Surrounded by adults who were big personalities, ambitious, confident and in tune with their world, she became overwhelmed, drowned out by their noise. She moved like a wraith through this transition between two lives, no longer the Caribbean princess but not yet a Parisian woman. She seems to have been eager to please, desperate to be loved, clingy and possessive. Yet Alexandre's complaints in his letters to her – and the paucity of her letters to him – suggest she also demonstrated an almost adolescent sullen rebellion. She was, after all, still only sixteen years old.

Alexandre had not totally given up hope of moulding his bride into a woman worthy to be his wife. Although she exasperated him, he found her adoration endearing and grew quite sentimental about her in her absence. He was, however, determined to change her, and many of his letters to her would appear to have been written by a teacher, not a lover. On 26 May 1780 he made clear his determination to eradicate her shortcomings: 'I am delighted at the desire to improve yourself which you have demonstrated to me. Such a taste, which one can always fulfil, brings pleasures which are always pure, and has the precious advantage of leaving no regrets in the one who heeds it. By persisting in the resolution you have you will acquire knowledge that will raise you above others and, combining wisdom with modesty, will make you an accomplished woman.'[10]

Rose was only too aware that she was not the sort of woman that Alexandre, or Paris, admired. She was not à la mode: the simple Creole style to which she was accustomed was not yet fashionable in France. Parisian women in the late 1770s were so be-looped, be-ribboned and be-plumed that they looked like great, ambulating beds. Their elaborate dresses, made of heavy ruched and embossed fabrics, were buttressed by corsets, petticoats, and wide panniers (a kind of hip pad), creating an impressive width and bulk. So unwieldy were these garments that sitting down in them was a 'cross between docking a boat and parallel parking'.[11] This intimidating effect was heightened by the fashion for '*garniture*': flowers, fringes, ribbons, gauzes, pompoms, even garlands of rope. Perched atop all this were theatrically white faces and magenta cheeks framed by towering hairstyles – sometimes a couple of feet high – combed over an artificial pad of horsehair, held together with pins and pomades and a wide range of ornaments, including fruit, flowers, even glass pigs. Some of these hairstyles were so high that women had to kneel or sit on the floor of their carriages to accommodate their hair. Once concocted, these arrangements could not be easily disturbed and wig scratchers – long ivory or bone sticks with a tiny stylized hand at the end – were useful for scratching the vermin that often nested within them. One hairstyle, popular the year before Rose arrived, conceived to celebrate the success in June 1778 of the French Navy frigate *La Belle-Poule*, consisted of an imitation of the frigate itself, complete with masts, riggings and guns.

Parisiennes were expected to be not only elegant, but also able to hold an interesting conversation, speak with the right accent and display impeccable manners. Rose possessed none of these attributes. Nor had she – despite her natural grace – learned to dance well. In an age where the ability to dance was considered of supreme importance, this was considered a terrible short-coming. In the decades immediately before the Revolution, the cult of feminine 'charm and graces had reached unprecedented heights'. Parisian women were a unique breed, according to Thomas Jefferson, who noted that 'the ease and vivacity of their conversation gives a charm to their society to be found nowhere else'.[12] Another commentator agreed that because women in Paris are 'accustomed from early days to reflect, they are freer and more enlightened than anywhere else . . . They have the strong character of a man combined with the fine feeling of their own sex'.[13]

In contrast to the Martiniquan plantocracy, where it was definitely believed that women should be virtuous rather than clever, Rose had moved to a society that rewarded women of outstanding intelligence and unabashed sensuality. In Paris 'the supreme talent', according to Mercier, 'was to be amusing'. The female stars of the final hours of the ancien régime were stylish, intelligent women whose love lives were as intricate as their conver-sation. Stéphanie de Genlis, a great admirer of Alexandre, was one such woman. Pretty and elegant, she presided over a salon held in the Palais Royal, the residence of her royal lover, the duc d'Orléans. Here she entertained a learned and decadent group of dissenters who gathered to discuss politics, flirt and witticize.

Her great rival was Germaine de Staël. She was the only child of the Swiss financier Jacques Necker, the linchpin of the French Government's financial strategy during the decade that preceded the Revolution. Necker's wealth and social prominence guaranteed his daughter's social position, but it was her own gifts that consolidated her reputation. A gifted writer and polemicist, she was one of the outstanding female intellects of her age; she would also emerge as one of the most important *salonnières* of her generation. With her swarthy complexion, bulbous lips and prominent nose, Germaine was by no means beautiful (Gouverneur Morris thought that she 'looked like a chambermaid'), but she was imposing. And once she opened her mouth and focused her large luminous eyes on someone, all thoughts of exterior disadvantage disappeared. The force of her personality and her charm were irresistible.

At the age of seventeen she had declined the much envied opportunity to marry William Pitt, the young British Prime Minister, because it would have meant abandoning her beloved country. She explained later, 'The universe is in France; outside it, there is nothing.'[14] To continue to enjoy 'the heavenly noise of Paris', she settled for the much less enviable catch of Eric-Magnus de Staël, then attached to the Swedish embassy in Paris. The marriage negotiations took several years, during which she extracted an assurance that the king of Sweden would never recall him from the city; and he was promoted to ambassador, created a baron and given access to the Necker millions. After the wedding she would describe her husband thus: 'he is the only convenient choice for me because he will not make me unhappy for the simple reason that . . . he cannot trouble my feelings.'[15]

It was to the salons of these women that Alexandre took his young wife. Unlike Martinique, with its desultory exchanges about crop rotation and slave prices, in Paris the art of conversation was an established and valued commodity. Conversation, argued Mercier, had been perfected in Paris to a degree unequalled anywhere else in the world: 'It is an exquisite diversion that can belong only to an extremely civilized society which has instituted precise rules that are always observed.' The ideal conversation, according to Mme de Staël, was 'effortless, unaffected, relaxed and smooth'. It was an art, and could be learnt once the individual had eliminated bad habits like interrupting, showing off or being pedantic. Reminiscing about the effect of a good conversation, Germaine wrote from her exile in Switzerland some years later, 'it is a certain manner of acting upon one another, giving mutual and instantaneous delight . . . of displaying the understanding in all its shades by accent, gesture, look; of eliciting, in short at will the electric spark. In France,' she concluded, 'conversation is not . . . merely the means of communicating ideas, sentiments and transactions . . . it is an instrument that Frenchmen are fond of playing, and which animates the spirits like music among some people and strong liquor among others.'[16]

Rose was understandably overawed by the totally unfamiliar 'atmosphere of the Parisian salons, where wit, intrigue and intellectual cross-fertilization were stimulated by a constant supply of new faces drawn from literature, science and the arts'.[17] These salons were at the centre of Parisian social and intellectual life. In a single session, according to the comte de Ségur, conversation could cover subjects of the greatest diversity: 'the *Esprit des Lois* and the tales of Voltaire, the philosophy of Hevetius and the operas of Sedaine or Marmontel, the tragedies of La Harpe and the licentious tales of the abbé de Voisenon, the discoveries in India . . . and the songs of Colle . . .' as well as sharing gossip and arranging romantic liaisons. Alongside the frivolity and intrigue still integral to salon life there was also an atmosphere of intellectual brilliance and social flexibility. The salons provided one of the few effective outlets for free expression of ideas, frustrating to some extent the otherwise formidable censorship of the ancien régime. It was the salons that nurtured and gave refuge to the growing forces of political opposition, social protest and general intellectual dissent.

Political opinion was divided between those who favoured a republic based on the American model and those who preferred a British-style consti-tution. Alexandre and his circle – the dissolute comte Mirabeau, Talleyrand, who would later serve Napoleon, and Louis de Narbonne, who would eventually serve as a minister during the Revolution – were associated with the latter. Their aspirations were expressed by Mercier when he cried, 'Where is our great Charter, the basis of the government of England and formerly the basis of ours? Where is our Habeas Corpus, of which the English are so justly proud?' The 'Americans' were led by the idealistic young Frenchmen who had volunteered to fight for the romantic cause of American indepen-dence. Men like Lafayette, the wealthy noble who achieved a generalship in Washington's army, Rochambeau, hero of Saratoga, and the duc de Castries. For them, America was a utopia and American visitors like Benjamin Franklin and Thomas Jefferson were heroes, fêted and flattered wherever they went.

In the waning years of the ancien régime, women had considerable influence. It took hard work to become a *salonnière*, plus skills that had to be learned, often by acting as an apprentice in established salons. It required extraordinary tact, organization and hard work: circulating material, facilita-ting conversation, pulling in the reticent, stopping the flow of the loquacious, so all could shine. But for many women the effort was worth it. The salons provided a unique opportunity to achieve fame, power, education and self-expression. In an age where ambition was considered a dubious quality in a woman, the salons provided an outlet. By personifying the *'service idéal'* associated with Rousseau, women had a chance to reshape the social forms of their day.

'Women accustom us to discuss with charm and clarity the driest and thorniest of subjects,' remarked Diderot. Others were less enthusiastic about women's input. 'In the salons,' Rousseau railed, 'men try to please women and in so doing they become womanish, effeminate . . . Unable to make themselves into men, the women make us into women.' He felt the city had a corrupting effect on women: 'I should never take my wife to Paris, still less my mistress.' Many foreigners agreed, identifying French women as Europe's most dangerous species and deploring their astounding social and political influence. As Scotsman David Hume fumed, the French nation 'gravely exalts those whom nature has subjected to them, and whose inferiority and infirmities are absolutely incurable.' It was no wonder that France was known as 'the woman's country'.

Rose had flown her little island only to end up drowning in the drawing rooms of *Les Liaisons Dangereuses*. The novel, published in 1782 and written by a forty-one-year-old army officer called Choderlos de Laclos, summed up the glamorous, libidinous, even decadent world in which Rose now found herself. The book was an immediate *succès du scandale*. Described as 'an outrage to the morals of the whole nation,' this shocking, cynical novel caused matrons and bishops to express disgust. A copy with blank binding was rumoured to have been ordered for the Queen's private library. The first edition sold out within days. Public excitement was intensified by the belief that the novel was a roman-à-clef. 'Keys' identifying the chief characters circulated busily. When Laclos admitted that the book was based on people he knew, the speculation grew further.

A remorseless exposé of the debauched sexual mores of French high society, *Les Liaisons Dangeureuses* provided its author with an *entrée* into the circles that he described. Written in epistolary form, its main characters, the marquise de Merteuil and the vicomte de Valmont, have been described as 'professional profligates' who made sexual intrigue a business from which they derived profit and pleasure. In the novel love was war, and fidelity merely an obstacle to be overcome by lies and false promises, even by coercion if necessary. Seduction was a victory enjoyable only if the game was as prolonged and subtle and as vicious as possible. As Valmont declared: 'Let her yield herself, but let her struggle! Let her have the strength to resist without having enough to conquer; let her fully taste the feeling of her weakness and be forced to admit her defeat.' For Valmont, his seduction of the virtuous Mme de Tourvel was a 'battle' and she was the 'enemy'.

Les Liaisons Dangereuses had particular personal relevance for Rose, since a number of historians believe that Alexandre was the model for the libertine Valmont.[18] This was not impossible, although it was an honour claimed by many male *galants*. Alexandre and Laclos had served together in the army and become friends. More significantly, Alexandre's own behaviour was notorious. His friend Bouillé noted his 'fondness' for collecting and displaying 'trophies' wrested from his romantic conquests; most of Alexandre's liaisons were less about love than about notching up more tributes to his virility. Like all roués, Alexandre was insufferably vain, and could be truly gratified only by knowing that his love affairs were public knowledge.

In contrast to poor, gauche Rose, Alexandre had all the attributes a fashionable young seducer required: looks, wit and impeccable social skills. An astute broker of his capital of charm and elegance, he was an ambitious young man, determined to make sure that everyone knew him and that he was welcomed everywhere. At balls and receptions he moved effortlessly through the social landscape: delighting the city's renowned beauties with his wit and clever compliments, entertaining his young military comrades with barrack-room gossip and risqué jokes, taking the time to win over suspicious chaperones and mothers with just the right mix of familiar but polite chatter, and impressing visiting dignitaries and diplomats, high-ranking officers and aristocrats alike with his erudition and intellectual opinions.

True, some were offended by his presumptuous arrogance, others by his penchant for boasting of his female conquests. Still, he remained a highly sought-after escort who left a trail of broken hearts across the city. An accomplished and zealous flirt, like Laclos's anti-hero, Valmont, Alexandre preferred older women, particularly those who were experienced or already married, because they were a greater challenge. They demanded all his seductive strategies; he could be more ardent and forward in his approaches, utilizing the more daring moves in his arsenal of gallantries without being met by shows of outraged modesty.

His greatest triumphs took place in the ballroom. Watching him on the floor – every muscle tensed, his legs and arms gracefully poised, his heels tapping rhythmically across the floor – many a heart was lost as women imagined themselves clasped in his expert arms. Even Marie Antoinette was smitten, insisting – despite the fact that he was not of the highest circles – that Alexandre be included in many of the most exclusive gatherings. 'In an age when dancing was considered an art, he was thought – with some reason – to be the finest dancer in Paris'.[19]

No man was ever more at home on a dance floor; one of his contemporaries wrote that it was impossible to imagine him 'elsewhere than in a quadrille'.[20] Alexandre believed in dancing. He understood its social potential as well as its sensual possibilities. Never one to ask only the beautiful or rich women to dance, he was careful to please all the ladies. He was just as happy to take an ardent spin across the floor with some elderly duchess as with some dewy-skinned debutante. 'Dancing', he once wrote, 'is . . . a universal remedy against all ills.'[21] Unlike those frigid men of fashion who arrived at balls late and left early, or those who self-consciously shuffled their feet as though dancing was some tedious obligation, he threw himself into dancing with abandon, with a kind of inspired elation.

This was a man who left the ballroom flushed and exhausted but also totally exhilarated. He always had enough spare energy for one last penetrating look, the kind that set fans fluttering and inspired pounding hearts and breathless sighs, or even precipitated an amorous tryst at dawn's first light. Whether he felt offended that his social position was so reliant on his performance on the dance floor, or feared that his glories would fade after the ball was over, is unknown. What is clear is that in the choicest Parisian society he staked out a unique niche: ladies' man, social ornament, clever conversationalist, but most of all wonderful, indefatigable dancer.

While Alexandre danced and debated and flirted, Rose was usually left at home because he was embarrassed by her. In society she seemed gauche, awkward and ignorant and she drove him mad with her clingy possessiveness. 'She wants me to occupy myself in society solely with her; she wants to know what I say, what I do, and what I write . . .'[22] When she did mingle it was obvious that she had no witty turns of phrase, a provincial outlook and outmoded, ill-informed ideas about politics and relationships. For a man with as inflated an ego as Alexandre to have a wife who reflected so poorly on him was unbearable. Even her good qualities − her loving manner, her beautiful large eyes − were forgotten in his chagrin. Her lack of social elan made her seem plainer than she actually was, and certainly Rose did not yet look her best: she had a bit of puppy fat and did not look comfortable in the ornate dresses of the era. It should not have been an entirely unexpected problem, since, as le comte Montgaillard wrote, 'the ignorance of Creoles was almost proverbial'. Warming to this thesis, the comte continued, 'We all know *grandes dames* of that origin who, while perfectly established in the highest ranks of society, could barely read, far less write.' Rose was no exception. 'Ignorant like most Creoles,' wrote Napoleon's valet Constant, 'she had nothing or nearly nothing to contribute to a conversation.'[23]

These ideas about Creoles persisted throughout Rose's life in France,

colouring her public image. The 'islands' were a 'magic word' in the metropolis, conjuring up images of exotic locations, heroic adventures and endless
riches. It was a myth that held some truth. France had been massively
enriched by its colonies, and it was not just the merchants and traders who
reaped the fabulous commercial benefits of the 'white gold', they filtered
through to much of society: 'At the end of the eighteenth century, in every
house where one was received by distinguished people, where elegant, select,
lavish parties were held, you could search for and find the wealth of the
colonies.'[24]

This commercial impact translated into political influence: Creoles were
said to 'rule the crown and the city'. They were 'highly prized at the court
of Marie Antoinette' and their influence on French cultural life was profound.
By the middle of the eighteenth century, *littérature exotique* was a huge craze,
inspired by Rousseau and travel accounts like that of the Dominican friar,
Father Labat, entitled *Voyage to the French American Islands*. Writers and
painters such as Sainte-Beuve, Chateaubriand and Lethière, as well as their
artistic heirs, Gauguin and Baudelaire, fell in love with the exoticism of the
islands and in turn converted their audiences. The literate public devoured
lurid tales of love and adventure set against backdrops of tropical landscapes
and eternally blue skies and animated by pirates and Indians. Seduced by the
enchantment of life in the Antilles, many believed that the 'existence of
whites in the tropics was aesthetically privileged'. In fashion, furnishings,
even daily life, Creoles set the tone. The truly 'refined' sent their linen back
to Martinique to be laundered, so that it could acquire the unique, fresh
scent of the salty, tropical air; and wine was regularly sent on a couple of sea
journeys to the Antilles and back in order to be aged.

This confection of myths and mores influenced the French perception
of Creole living. Creoles were believed to be rich and privileged but also
'indolent', 'ignorant', 'spendthrift' and 'lacking in ability'. These blithely
prejudiced ideas about Creoles were widespread during the period and Rose
would fall victim to them throughout the time that she lived in France.
Ironically, the terms used to denigrate Creoles were not dissimilar to the
stereotypes that Creoles ascribed to their slaves.

Rose found herself in a society that she neither understood nor was
understood by. She must have been bewildered by these new expectations
which were so very different from those of her island home. In Martinique
Rose was part of a 'nobility of the skin'; her European heritage a symbol of
her social privilege. But once in France she was one among millions; her

white skin did not confer any special favours. Even more startling was the fact that some individuals of colour had acquired a social prominence she could only dream of.

There was the chevalier Saint-Georges, whom Napoleon's minister Talley-rand once described as being 'the most accomplished human being I have ever met'. Born in Guadeloupe, the product of a relationship between a French aristocrat and an African woman, he became known first as one of the greatest fencers in France and later as one of the most talented musicians of his time. A violin virtuoso, composer and director of the Concert des Amateurs, his orchestra was present at every fashionable occasion. Apart from his musical ability and prodigious physical gifts, 'the divine mulatto' was famed for his wit and charm; he carried a jewelled cane to which he added another gem every time he made a new conquest. His talents made him a great favourite at the court of Marie Antoinette, but his background made him sympathetic to the Revolution, and in 1792 he commanded a troop of black soldiers. One of these soldiers was another prominent black figure: Thomas-Alexandre Dumas. The son of a French marquis and a beautiful slave woman, he was born in Santo Domingo and travelled to France a few years after Rose. Known as the 'black devil', he was a famously strong fighting man who began his military career as a Royal Dragoon and ended up serving under Napoleon as a general in Egypt. Capable of bending a musket with his bare hands, he would carve his unique place in history as the father of the novelist Alexandre Dumas.

Accomplishment was highly valued in France and Rose had to become accomplished. Horrified by the void that he had discovered in his wife's education, Alexandre decided to play Pygmalion. Writing to his seventeen-year-old wife, Alexandre, only three years her senior, revealed that the first time he met her he had formulated a plan 'to recommence your education and repair by my zeal, the first fifteen years of your life which has been so tragically neglected'.[25] To this end he provided her with a work plan that he had developed with the aid of his confidants Patricol and Mme Renaudin. It involved reading the works of good poets, learning by heart various treatises on the theatre and studying history and geography. He even hired a dance instructor.

In Alexandre's absence Rose dutifully set about her homework. Writing to her husband, she reassured him that she was indeed trying to educate herself. He wrote back congratulating her: 'By persisting in the resolution which you have taken, the knowledge which you will acquire will raise you above others and, combining learning with modesty, will make you an accomplished woman.'[26] It was a surprisingly patronizing and pompous letter for a young man to write to his young bride, and was only the beginning of the many long, boring letters he would send her giving her instructions like a schoolteacher manqué. Little did he know it was all in vain; his methods of teaching were not for her. Rose was not suited to learning by rote; everything that she learned was gained through conversation and observation.

Alexandre clearly expected his wife to be grateful for his efforts to mould her. He assumed she would be obedient and eager to follow his instructions. It did not occur to him that she might feel profoundly hurt, that he might confirm her fears that her husband was ashamed of her. It was hard enough being away from the magic circle of love and support at La Pagerie, to feel so out of her depth, so judged and found wanting. But his efforts to educate her served to further undermine Rose's confidence. Her response was what we would call today 'passive aggressive'; she expressed her feelings of rejection and resentment by appearing to be acquiescent, even as it became evident over time that she studied infrequently if at all.

In July 1780 Alexandre had to rejoin his regiment. His departure distressed Rose, while his letters to her expressed a mixture of frustration and ambivalence that was becoming characteristic of their relationship. Alexandre may have been a cynical roué, but he could be sentimental and self-indulgently romantic. He was also fond of Rose; a fondness that persisted throughout their rocky marriage and beyond. He was flattered by her adoration and charmed by her innocent sweetness, even though it was associated with a naivety and lack of sophistication that he found infuriating. This affection, and the lavish courtesy expected of a man of his class, help explain the lush outpourings of the letters he wrote her at this time. In his first missive after arriving at his destination, Brest, he declared, 'If I could embrace you as I love you, your plump little cheeks would tingle.'[27] In his next letter, he reassured her: 'Yes, my heart, it is really true that I love you . . . there is nothing I desire more than the peace of our household and the tranquillity of domesticity.'[28]

Alexandre's words were not matched by his actions, however. These letters do not provide proof of marital passion so much as evidence of Alexandre's epistolary prowess. Letter-writing was considered an essential accomplishment for a fashionable man or woman of that era. A stylish letter was a performance of seduction and persuasion, a demonstration of energy and clarity, a chance to show off fetching expressions of sentiment or an unfailing sense of the *mot juste*. Alexandre's letters seem rather florid and insincere to twenty-first-century readers, but would no doubt have been well received by their eighteenth-century counterparts.

That made it all the more important that Rose, too, learn to write letters. Alexandre was determined to teach her how, and grew increasingly frustrated by her unwillingness or inability to cooperate. At the end of August he returned to his favourite topic: 'You do not tell me about your talents. Are you still cultivating them, my dearest? . . . I should like you always to send me the first draft of your letters. I find there are, perhaps, some faults in your expression.'[29] He also wrote to Edmée, making clear his suspicion that Rose's writing was not all her own work, and lobbying for her support in his efforts to determine 'what is to be done about my wife's letters'.[30]

Aunt Edmée was indeed helping Rose who, despite loving Alexandre and valuing his letters to her, simply refused to reciprocate. As in her later relationship with Napoleon, her refusal to write created considerable marital tensions and seems perverse. Rose would become a competent letter-writer; it is hard to know whether, at this stage, she desisted through lack of confidence or in order to avoid and resist Alexandre's hectoring. Maybe this was an early expression of her strong instinct to avoid unpleasantness; maybe it was a forewarning of the skills she would develop in passive power-play.

Above all, though, the letters between them at this time make clear how terribly mismatched this young couple were. Rose had been nurtured on the fevered romantic obsessions that swamped her small island school and had arrived in France with fairy-tale notions about marriage and fidelity. Alexandre had been raised with very different views. As Louis XVI's mother once lamented, the higher ranks of the French nobility considered it downright uncouth to love one's wife: 'One can still find faithful couples among the inferior classes but among persons of quality I don't know a single marriage of reciprocal affection or fidelity.' In Alexandre's circles, the handful of women who clung to their virtue were ridiculed as 'rustics'. 'It was not fashionable', commented the prince de Ligne, 'to be a good father or a good husband.'

For the upper classes in France, marriage was an economic arrangement that often yoked together people of very different temperaments. Since there was little personal choice involved in these arranged marriages, many men and women felt free to dispose of their affections as they wished. Alexandre's own parents lived apart amicably (divorce was not yet permitted in France) while pursuing their own interests and sexual arrangements. This was a commonplace arrangement. Mme de la Tour du Pin recorded a conversation with Mme de Staël in which Germaine made clear her astonishment at the former's readiness to cater to her husband's wishes. She said in amazement, 'It seems to me that you love him as a lover.'

Yet the salons of *Les Liaisons Dangereuses* were beginning to be influenced by new, Enlightenment ideas. Alexandre himself, the very model of the practised womanizer, was deeply attracted to the 'home and hearth' ideals of Rousseau. Alexandre embodied paradoxical forces in his personality, but also in the culture of the time, that allowed this libertine to avow sentimental attachment to romantic ideals, just as he combined revolutionary principles with a fierce attachment to aristocratic privilege. He liked the idea of being in love with his wife, and never more so than when she was many miles away. He was a product of two epochs: his intellectual preferences were for the Enlightenment ideals of fraternity, equality and companionate love, while his behaviour owed far more to eighteenth-century mores of institutionalized inequality and strict separation between marriage and romance.

Alexandre agreed with the views expressed by Patricol, who insisted, 'It isn't the same to be a wife as it is to be a mistress; the former is a companion for life who should aim to inspire those sentiments of friendship that are solid and durable, not those of love which are temporary.'[31] Alexandre wanted more from a wife than 'an *objet* who has nothing to say to me', which is how he once described Rose. As he complained to Edmée, how could his 'tender heart love a woman incapable of filling those long intervals between the effusions of affection'? But these sophisticated ideas were lost on his wife, who could offer love and sexual passion in profusion, but was incapable of providing the cultured companionship he craved.

Rose had met Alexandre when she was at the cusp of sexual awakening. He was her first lover and she valued and enjoyed the 'effusions' he so easily dismissed. Her intense possessiveness and jealousy demonstrated that she was in his sexual thrall. Naive and inexperienced, she was thrown off balance by the power of the erotic sensations she discovered with her husband. In her marriage she experienced all the passion and jealousy of first love and, even if she had wanted to, she did not know how to repress the intensity of her feelings.

Alexandre was, in any case, still infatuated with someone else. He had married, according to his friend Bouillé, '*contre coeur*' – against the wishes of his heart – and Rose's resentments were fuelled by the suspicion that her

husband was still seeing his mistress. Hers had been a crowded marriage from
the start. The married lady from Brittany, 'the charming woman' about
whom he had written so rapturously to Edmée years before, was still in his
life. Her name was Marie-Françoise-Laure de Girardin de Montgerald, and
she was married to Alexandre-François Le Vassor de la Touche de Longpré.
Laure de Longpré was a Creole herself, a distant relative of Rose's family on
her mother's side. She was Alexandre's first love, about whom he wrote,
'Until this moment I have misunderstood my sentiments; whether because
my sensibility was not sufficiently developed or because I have until now
attached myself only to persons incapable of inspiring a violent passion. I
have never experienced true love. The object who reveals it to me for the
first time is so virtuous and so tender that it is with the deepest despair that
I see the moment approaching when I must part from her for a long time.'[32]

Laure was twenty-nine years old when the relationship began, eleven
years Alexandre's senior and the mother of a small daughter. Her second
child, born in the same year of Rose's marriage, was almost certainly Alexandre's. The baby was christened Alexandre, an act of chutzpah that was only
possible because of the coincidence that her lover and her husband shared a
first name. Elegant, fashionable and sophisticated, she was just the sort of
woman that one imagines Alexandre would have fallen for. Given to violent
mood swings, she knew how to play the game of love. She was complicated
enough to sustain his interest, and dramatic enough to heighten his prema-
turely jaded palate with her capricious behaviour. That she was also a little
neurotic was evidenced by her habit of always carrying a candle with her
that she nibbled compulsively.

Laure de Longpré was the shadow that perpetually haunted Rose's marriage. In her most jealous moments she must have been filled with defeated
rage at the thought of the two lovers discussing her, even before her wedding;
perhaps deciding on her because Laure did not consider her a threat. And
she was not a threat: Laure's charms were still irresistible to Alexandre, who
found his wife's so easy to resist. Later Laure would loom ever larger in
Rose's mind, a dangerous figure whose machinations would eventually destroy
her marriage.

Alexandre visited Rose and the family in Paris during December, but he
stayed only briefly. After a short turn of duty he decided not to return to
Paris but went instead to La Roche-Guyon, to the La Rochefoucauld clan
(and perhaps to his mistress). News soon followed that Rose was definitely

pregnant, and Alexandre wrote to Mme Renaudin that he was trying to reorganize his duties in order to be at home for the birth in August or September. 'My greatest desire would be gratified if I could manage to be present at the accouchement of Madame de Beauharnais. Even though the conditions should be very hard I will certainly take my leave.'

The rapprochement brought on by the news of the pregnancy was short-lived. Lamenting the state of his marriage, Alexandre explained to Patricol that he had initially believed that the couple could be happy. But when his plan to 'commence' her education was met with 'such indifference and so little will to learn' he gave up, convinced that he was wasting his time. Alexandre read her reluctance to change as a personal rejection: 'If my wife really loved me, she would make the effort . . . to acquire the qualities which I admire and which would bind me to her.' He retaliated by resuming what he described as his 'bachelor existence'. This, he explained to Patricol, was not really what he wanted, since he still preferred 'the happiness of a home and domestic peace' to the 'tumultuous pleasures of society'.[33]

In response, Patricol, who obviously believed that the relationship was worth salvaging, made some sensible suggestions. Perhaps Alexandre was being somewhat impatient and intolerant? After all, not everyone was suited to such a dry programme of study. Perhaps a 'new system' was required. Instead of trying to sustain his wife's education on his own, he should consider enlisting the entire household. If they were willing to read the selected material aloud to her she was much more likely to absorb it. The teaching team – including Edmée and Rose's father – was assembled and another assault was made on Rose's ignorance. As part of this campaign poor Rose was expected to read four volumes of abbé Vertot's formidable *Roman History*. Whether she did indeed do so remains unknown. As she was now six months pregnant, she justifiably had other things on her mind.

Friends and family were worried about the troubled marriage. Patricol wrote to Edmée urging her to suggest that Rose curb her jealousy, which he felt was damaging both partners. He also suggested that Rose be persuaded to change her strategy in relation to 'tender-hearted' Alexandre: 'brusqueness and bossiness are two of the worst ways to attract to her a husband whom she loves'. He concluded rousingly, 'Do everything, madame, which your zeal and affection dictate, and I have no doubt that we shall succeed, you and I, in reuniting the two spouses whose happiness is so inseparable from our own.'[34]

Rose's first child, a boy, was born on 3 September 1781. He was baptized

Eugène-Rose the following day at the church of Saint-Sauveur. His mother was eighteen and his father was twenty-one years old. It was Alexandre's second child, but he was nonetheless delighted, and for a while the couple's relationship was warm and affectionate. As the novelty of the new baby wore off, so did Alexandre's good behaviour, and the domestic atmosphere deteriorated. Edmée suggested that Alexandre take a trip abroad. On 1 November he left on a tour of Italy, from where he wrote self-pitying letters about the 'parties and public illuminations' he was missing in wintry Paris.

When Alexandre returned from the terrible deprivations of his Italian tour the following July, the household had changed dramatically. Both Rose's father and Aunt Rosette had gone back to Martinique, leaving Rose even more isolated than she had been before. She was almost desperately grateful to see her husband again, and Alexandre, in his turn, found that Edmée's remedy had worked: absence had indeed made the heart grow fonder and he seemed, in Rose's words, 'enchanted to find himself with her again'. The sense of a new start was buttressed by the move to a new home. Leased in Alexandre's name, not his father's, the new residence, on the rue Neuve-Saint-Charles in a more fashionable district near the church of Saint-Philippe-du-Roule, was the first home Rose could truly call her own, and in this brief oasis of calm she became pregnant once again.

Then, with little warning, Alexandre was gone again. Soon after his disappearance Rose received a letter that was, by turns, defensive and accusatory. According to Alexandre, his actions were mature and responsible: 'Will you pardon me, my dearest, for having left you without saying goodbye, for having gone away . . . without having told you again, a last time, that I am all yours? . . . Love for my wife and the love of glory both hold the most absolute sway in my heart. If I yield to the latter, it is for your future good and for that of your children . . . I therefore submit patiently to all the reproaches with which you so unjustly and pitilessly overwhelm me . . . Credit me with sufficient sense to know how to conduct myself and sufficient conscience not to forget my duties as father and husband.'[35]

Alexandre did have some justification for his sudden departure. As the War of American Independence continued, French soldiers were needed to meet the English threat in the Caribbean. To that end, Alexandre applied to his old family friend, the marquis de Bouillé, now governor of the Windward Islands, for a position as aide-de-camp. In his support he submitted a glowing reference from his protector, the duc de La Rochefoucauld, describing him as 'a young man of upright character, possessing wit and a great desire to learn'. Unfortunately, Bouillé had left for his post in the islands before Alexandre's request arrived. Not to be discouraged, Alexandre decided to go to Martinique as a volunteer.

Typically, the military ambitions that now agitated Alexandre's mind had only overwhelmed him after prolonged exposure to the hearth and home he claimed to crave. He was young, vain and restless; domestic life bored him and made him feel trapped and resentful. Unable to admit these contradictions even to himself, it was little wonder that he found a reason to escape.

Writing from Brest, where he awaited his ship, Alexandre's letters to Rose reflected the extravagant mood swings that his ambivalent feelings about domestic life inspired. In the first of eighteen letters addressed to Rose from the port, he declared his distress that there was no letter from her awaiting his arrival, accused her of indifference to his feelings, and demanded to know how he could be so forgotten. When he discovered that she had indeed written to him, he did not scrap his accusing letter but merely added a short thanks in a postscript demanding that she help him obtain the official permission he needed to depart.

The permission finally arrived, but Alexandre had to wait until a convoy of ships was ready to leave. Much to Rose's distress, he then wrote to tell her that Laure de Longpré's father had died in Martinique, and that she had joined him in Brest in order to board the same boat out. Even this development did not shame Alexandre into silence: 'Since, having two servants, you cannot send even one to Paris for the days when the mail leaves, I shall address myself to others for news of the state of your health and that of your son. Farewell, madame.'[36]

The words poured from his pen; accusatory and often contradictory. This manufactured ire against Rose may have been Alexandre's way of coping with the guilt he felt about his ill-treatment of his wife. By convincing himself that she was the one who was neglectful and indifferent, the blame for their troubles would be hers not his. In his next letter he wrote, 'The courier has arrived and there is nothing that I had expected. My God! What business have you that prevents you from giving me this pleasure? This neglect is inconceivable . . . Ah! but your feelings are shallow. Real love has never existed in your heart . . . If, as I begin to fear, our marriage turns out decidedly badly, you will have only yourself to blame.'[37]

The epistolary melodrama continued, as Alexandre projected onto Rose his own ambivalent and mercurial feelings. Sometimes he was repentant, full of 'a thousand pardons' and endless protestations of eternal devotion from 'the most devoted of husbands'. At other times he was belligerent, accusing her of coldness and even implying that she might be unfaithful. Amidst this barrage of complaints, accusations, protestations and instructions, Alexandre never allowed her to forget the 'cruel sacrifices' he was making or the 'terrible deprivations' he was suffering.

A brief lull descended in October, when Alexandre begged Rose to forgive him 'a million times' for the terrible 'injustice' of his accusations. He wrote lovingly, making reference to the new arrival who he assumed, wrongly, would be another son. 'Kiss my dear little Eugène with all your heart and guard his little brother . . . When will I next see them!' In another he wrote sympathetically, 'You are ill, my dear wife, and I am not beside you to care for you and, if it be possible, to share your ailment . . . If you suffer, if your body fatigued with pregnancy causes you some discomfort, then the torments of the spirit are my share.' He ended with a request that she count Eugène's little teeth and 'kiss him as you kiss your husband, with the same tenderness'.[38]

But the whining soon resumed. Once again she was silent, not sufficiently sensitive to his needs. Such were his crosses, Alexandre implied in one letter, he was looking forward to oblivion: 'Amidst the risks of war and of the seas, where I go to seek death, I shall without sorrow and without regret see a life taken from me whose moments will have been reckoned only in misfortunes. Adieu!'[39]

Alexandre's departure was now scheduled for 8 November. The convoy departed on time, only to be once more delayed off the harbour at La Rochelle. This only gave him time to stew. His unhappiness was evident in the final letter he dispatched to his wife before the aptly named *Venus* finally departed on 21 December:

> *I hoped to receive further news from you; but I have hoped in vain . . .*
> *The dinghy has just arrived, and there is not a word from you! Is it possible*
> *that you refuse this consolation to a poor husband who does nothing but*
> *toss back and forth without making any progress towards his destination?*
> *Ah, unhappy absence! How many troubles you cause me to foresee! For*
> *the rest, if your inconstancy is inevitable do not keep me in ignorance, so*
> *that I may never see you again. Adieu! Forgive my letter, but I am*
> *furious.*[40]

Four

ALEXANDRE IN MARTINIQUE

. . . and in trust I have found treason.

ELIZABETH I

ROSE HAD A MERCIFUL BREAK from Alexandre's histrionics until February 1783, when she received a truculent letter condemning her 'indifference' to his suffering on this perilous journey, while she stayed behind in the 'midst of pleasures'. Since Rose was now seven months pregnant, and she was isolated with the ailing marquis and Aunt Edmée, 'pleasures' were few and far between, but Alexandre didn't allow this to spoil his rhetoric. Conveniently forgetting his moonlight flit, his mistress and the financial muddle in which he had left his wife, he had rewritten history, casting himself as the victim of her capricious neglect. As his journey passed, he magnanimously decided to forgive her, so as not to deprive himself of 'the sweet pleasure of saying I love you'. He continued that he had worked hard to convince himself that 'you love me a little'. Despite this largesse, Alexandre couldn't resist ending the letter on a spiteful note, remarking that he had played lotto with Laure de Longpré during the long days of the journey: 'I was often bored by the game but amply recompensed by the pleasure which I derived from the company.'[1]

The *Venus* docked in the turquoise waters of Fort-Royal on 21 January 1783 and Alexandre immediately set off to visit his in-laws at Trois-Îlets. He was profoundly disconcerted by what he saw as he travelled across the island. Alexandre had not seen Martinique since he was five years old. Instead of the Rousseauesque paradise of 'noble savages' that many Frenchmen eulogized during the Enlightenment, he was confronted with the realities of a slave society: crude conditions and impoverished people. 'The morals,' he wrote to Rose, 'the multitude of people of colour, in their indecent costumes, their manner of living, their dwellings, the appearance of libertinage, all this has amazed me.'[2] The state of the La Pagerie plantation was also something of a disillusionment. Far from his dream of a white mansion and a retinue of perfectly drilled, impeccably uniformed servants, he found the family still living in the ramshackle ruins of the *purgerie*, camping cheek by jowl with their bedraggled slaves. Rose's father had still not found the money to repair the damage wrought by the hurricane.

Alexandre's account of the rendezvous with his wife's family was buoyant. 'All is well,' he wrote from Trois-Îlets, 'your father is busy with the crop, your mother loves and always misses you.' He reassured her that sixty-five-year-old grandmother de Sannois was still hearty for her age; but that Rose's pretty sister Manette was 'sadly marked by her illness'. Whether Alexandre remembered that it was Manette who was originally intended to be his bride, and counted his a lucky escape, is not known. He did have hopes – until he saw her – of marrying her off to an army friend. But now her looks were ravaged, and her infirmity meant that the family was even less willing to part with her, even had there been the money to provide a dowry. So instead of matchmaking, Alexandre put his efforts into trying to convince Manette to undergo the newly fashionable treatment of inoculation for the disease which had so debilitated her. He also satisfied his in-laws' hunger for information about Rose's well-being. 'They were delighted to have news of you', he told Rose, and the portrait of her that he had taken with him had evoked happiness in 'all their hearts'.[3]

Alexandre's reception at Trois-Îlets was probably more muted than his letter suggests. Rose's father had only recently returned from France, and he had seen with his own eyes the unhappy beginnings of her marriage, which he had no doubt recounted to his formidable wife. Whether Alexandre detected a chilliness in his in-laws' manner, or whether he preferred less rustic pleasures, his stay at the plantation was short. In less than two days he had returned to Fort-Royal, claiming that he had business to undertake.

Whatever reservations the La Pagerie family might have had about their son-in-law, he was the toast of the capital. His urbane charms bowled over Rose's aunt and uncle, the baron and baronne de Tascher. The latter wrote a letter to Mme Renaudin gushing, 'Ah, the charming boy, God grant that my son will resemble him in every way, if he does I will ask nothing more of him and I will be the happiest of women!'[4]

Alexandre was disappointed to discover that there was little prospect of him seeing military action. The American campaign was all but finished; peace negotiations had begun in London the week before his arrival. The disgruntled glory-hound wrote to Rose that, should he fail to gain his commission, 'I would find my consolation in the pleasure of seeing you again, and of returning to embrace you the sooner; love would compensate me for being deprived of glory.' After these stirring words of love, Alexandre reverted to the endless task of wife-improvement, instructing her on how to bring up the son that he had barely seen. It was important that she be firm with Eugène, he lectured, lest he be spoilt by an 'excess of maternal love'. Rose must also be vigilant about herself: 'I recommend that you keep busy: this will counteract the indolence which has always been the primary cause of your neglect of your duties.'[5]

The avuncular tone of this letter was not entirely insincere. There were times in Alexandre's confused mind when he really did care for his wife; his mixed signals only added to Rose's emotional confusion. He was possibly also feeling rather guilty. Since he had taken up residence in Fort-Royal, his vigorous pursuit of a number of local beauties had provoked lively gossip. When the young swain's amorous adventures concluded with him resuming, very publicly, his affair with his mistress, Laure de Longpré, the town was scandalized: he was after all a married man whose wife was a local girl.

By the third week of April, Alexandre's friendliness towards Rose had been replaced by the old aggression. In a welter of ambivalence, guilt and resentment, fuelled, no doubt, by his own bad behaviour, a new series of letters commenced. Once again he accused her of neglecting him: 'I recall my darling that you once predicted that I would be able to tell if you were being unfaithful to me by your letters . . . well it has been three months since I have heard a single world from you . . . I have promised myself not to write you any more. Vain promises! They are like those which you made to think of me . . . I assume that you are in good health because of the letter you sent to Mlle de La Pagerie . . . me I get nothing . . . Embrace my beloved son for me. Take care of his future and may he think for a moment of a husband who loves you and will love you all your life . . .'[6]

Rose had indeed been writing to all of her loved ones except Alexandre. On 29 April he fired off yet another letter of accusation. 'Finally I have no doubt of your inconstancy! With my own eyes, I have seen the proof! Yes, with my own eyes, I have seen that you have written to your parents, and me, I alone have been forgotten.' But it was not just the absence of letters that had sent him into a fury. It was also the remarks that Rose had made about him in a letter to her aunt Rosette, which Rosette rather maliciously had allowed Alexandre to read. 'You did not speak of me,' he raged, 'except to say that you have cured yourself of the intense feeling you once held for me.'

'This', he continued, 'has accounted for the obstinate silence that you have maintained since I departed from France . . . proof of your change of heart is indicated to me in this conduct . . . Each letter, I always say, will be the last. But each time, my heart has forgotten my sermons and I take up the quill with verve whenever the occasion presents itself. But no more', he thundered. He would no longer tell her anything else about his plans. 'Should you want information about me,' he concludes melodramatically, 'my father will always know my news and through him, if you are curious you can find out which country I'm living in . . . I am abandoned.'[7]

But of course this was not Alexandre's last word. Letter followed letter like rounds fired from a gun. Still Rose did not respond. She did not send him a single line during his sojourn in Martinique. Her reasons were numerous. She was probably fed up with sending letters that were criticized and corrected by a husband eager to 'improve' her. She had almost certainly been kept informed of his continuing liaison with Laure de Longpré. Tired of his infidelities and accusations, Rose had — whether through guile or exhaustion — hit upon the one weapon guaranteed to upset her husband most: silence. Alexandre was incited to fury by her lack of response. Even worse, Rose neither explained nor justified her silence. Jealousy, rage, passionate entreaties, Alexandre could cope with, but nothing wounded his lofty self-regard more than indifference. Even without the provocation of his affairs, the ceaseless bullying of his letters would have been reason enough to disregard him. In any case, Rose, with a new baby and a young child, and isolated with her invalid relatives, had other problems to worry her. Alexandre's precipitous departure had left her in great financial difficulty. She had spent a great deal on presents to be transported by Alexandre for the family in Martinique and had to pay the costs of her accouchement and the christening.

Amidst a hailstorm of Alexandre's angry letters, Rose's second child, a girl, had been born on 10 April. She was christened Hortense-Eugénie: Fanny stood as godmother, and the ten-year-old Robert Gaspard de Tascher stood in for Rose's father. News of the birth was immediately dispatched to the family in Martinique, but even then Rose did not write directly to her husband. Worn out by the birth, hurt and disappointed, she found it easier to ignore him. The longer she remained mute, the more he blustered, bullied and beseeched. As he wrote on 10 May 1783, 'You know my character, boiling, torrid, my desires are lively as are my sentiments and passions.' And although he raged, she refused to supply even the slightest 'consolation' or provide him with any news of his family. With characteristic hysteria he concluded, 'They speak of a forthcoming war against the Emperor [of Austria]. May God grant that it take place, that I may serve in it, and that I may find there the end of a life that has become such a burden.'[8]

Alexandre's overwrought emotional state probably explains the behaviour that followed. When the news of Hortense's birth reached Martinique in June, Laure de Longpré maliciously suggested that since the child had been born two weeks early she could not have been fathered by Alexandre. Laure's motive for this slander was possibly rooted in her family's long-running feud with the Tascher de La Pagerie clan, as well as in romantic rivalry, despite the fact that Laure had recently begun a romance with the man who was to become her second husband, the Franco-Irish soldier Arthur Dillon. However fallacious Laure de Longpré's theory, she had given Alexandre a concrete focus for his fury against his wife.

Ever since his arrival in the Caribbean, Alexandre had been stoking his grievances against Rose, complaining about his wife to all who would listen. At first he lamented to her aunt, the baronne Tascher, about Rose's lack of education. Now the news of the birth had provided him with fresh impetus to attack her. Accompanied by Laure, Alexandre sought to make a case for a separation; the pair scrambled around the island for dirt on Rose. Her family were understandably outraged, and her mother wrote indignantly to Alexandre's father, the marquis de Beauharnais, 'I would never have thought that he would have let himself be led around so, by Mme de Longpré . . . She has turned his head so completely, he does not know what he is doing.'[9]

In his search for scandal Alexandre returned to Trois-Îlets and interrogated the plantation slaves. Caught between bribes and threats, the slaves were terrified. In a society where to fail to say what a white man wanted to hear could lead to beatings or even death, it was a testament to the slaves' fondness for Rose that only one was induced to slander her. 'Little Sylvester' had been only five years old when Rose left Martinique, but Alexandre persuaded him to invent a series of unlikely allegations. His punishment was inevitable. As

Rose's mother wrote to her later: 'I still have him chained up, but he is well fed.'[10]

Alexandre even accosted a house slave called Brigitte, whom he accused of knowing about Rose's past and of concealing various letters. She was offered numerous enticements to reveal tales of Rose's supposed sexual misbehaviour but to no avail. In a statement to Rose's parents, she declared that 'M. le vicomte used all his means to extract something unfavourable about the conduct of my mistress, and he was angry when I protested without ceasing that of all the people that I know, there was not one I more esteemed, cherished and respected.'[11] Alexandre was so angry that he had threatened to kill the poor woman if she revealed the conversation to her master or mistress. On discovering that Alexandre had attempted to corrupt their slaves in order to wage a campaign of slander against their daughter, Joseph exploded with rage. In an unusually clear-sighted and acute letter that arrived in France seven months after the incident, he recounted the blazing row that followed: 'This then is the fruit of your journey and the noble campaign that you were to have waged against the enemies of France: it has been confined to making war upon the reputation of your wife and the tranquillity of her family.'[12]

In the midst of these machinations, Alexandre fell ill with typhus. He spent his convalescence in the home of the Turons, old enemies of the de La Pagerie family. To celebrate his return to health he seduced Mme Turon, the wife of his host. Revealingly, despite his very public muck-raking against Rose, Alexandre was still egotistical enough to expect his mother-in-law to visit him in the home of his new mistress. To his extreme annoyance she refused, remarking acidly, 'I would have found myself very much out of place in such society.'

The explosion that had been brewing finally arrived in the form of a letter delivered to Rose by her old enemy, Laure de Longpré. One can imagine the scene: an impeccably dressed Mme de Longpré arriving at the house in Noisy-le-Grand where the Beauharnais family had repaired to spend the summer months. After an exchange of icy pleasantries, the mistress handed over a letter to the clueless wife. Absorbed with her two infants, Rose could not have been prepared for what she read in its pages. She knew virtually nothing of the dramas that had taken place in Martinique because her family, in an effort to protect her from the truth, had carefully kept them from her.

The letter from Alexandre was dated 8 July. 'If I had written in the first moment of my rage my pen would have scorched the paper and you would have thought in hearing all my abuse that it was in a moment of bad humour or jealousy that I was writing to you; but it is more than three weeks since I discovered what I will now reveal to you. In spite of the despair in my heart and the fury which suffocates me, I will contain myself, I will tell you coldly, that you are in my eyes the vilest of creatures.'

He knew, he thundered 'in the greatest details' about her 'abominable conduct' in her birth country. He knew about her affairs with various men in Martinique. He knew about the people she had employed to keep her secrets, the content of the letters to her lovers. 'As to repentance, I do not even ask it of you, you are incapable of it: a creature who . . . can take a lover into her arms when she knows that she is promised to another, has no conscience; she is beneath all the sluts in the world.'

Continuing his self-righteous assault, he declared that she had deceived her family as they slept, and he had heard that she also had an affair with a man in Santo Domingo on her way to her wedding in France. 'You alone have abused an entire family and carried shame and ignominy onto a foreign family of whom you are unworthy.' After this 'infamous and atrocious behaviour' how could she could expect anything but the problems which had arisen in their domestic life? And what, he declared, 'shall I think of this last child, arriving eight months and a few days after my return from Italy? . . . I am forced to accept it, but I swear to all the heavens that it belongs to another; it is a stranger's blood that courses through its veins! The child will never know my shame, and I vow here that she will never learn, either in the arrangements for her education or in those of the household, that she owes her life to an adulterer.'

He concluded:

> *Never, never shall I put myself in danger of being so abused again . . .*
> *have the decency to take yourself to a convent as soon as you receive this*
> *letter: this is my last word and nothing on this entire earth will make me*
> *withdraw it. I will see you once and once only on my arrival to Paris, to*
> *discuss practicalities . . . but, I repeat, no scenes and no protestations . . .*
> *You will persist in denying, I know because from your earliest years you*
> *have been in the habit of deception . . . I am already on guard against all*
> *your efforts, and I will be careful always to arm myself against vile*
> *promises, which would be contemptible as they are false.*[13]

What must Rose have felt when she read this savage litany of abuse, accusations and threats? Rose knew Alexandre's imputations were false, but she must have wondered where he had heard such lies. As to his claim to have found evidence of immorality before her marriage, who could have slandered and betrayed her so completely? How could her own husband believe such lies? Even more than the imputations against her character, it was the tone of his letter that was so shocking: full of hatred and contempt. Perhaps she had hoped that her apparent indifference to his series of letters would shame him into examining his own behaviour. Instead she was facing the terrifying prospect of being turned out of her home and losing her husband and family.

To Rose's intense relief, Alexandre's entire family rallied round her. To her credit, and theirs, they never questioned her innocence. More than any others, these people, her intimate family circle, knew, and felt guilty about, Alexandre's terrible failings as a husband. They knew that the accusations about Hortense were false. When would Rose, isolated at home, without money or friends, have had the opportunity to be unfaithful? But Alexandre was unmoved by their entreaties. Secure in his own 'virtuous conduct' he wrote to Rose, with the self-absorption that he had elevated to an art, to declare that he would arrive in Paris by October, 'if my health does not succumb to the exhaustion of the journey, added to my terrible state of mind'. His grief, he reported, had forced him to take to his bed – he did not mention that the bed was shared with Mme Turon – and the letter concluded, 'believe me madame, of the two of us, you are not the more to be pitied'.[14]

As Rose tried to come to terms with the allegations, accounts of Alexandre's scandalous conduct began to arrive from Martinique. A letter from her mother gave full account of his 'horrible behaviour': how Mme de Longpré had planted the seeds of doubt; how he had abused their hospitality; how he had attempted to bribe the slaves. Her mother continued, 'my darling daughter . . . all those who know you and all your friends are full of indignation for what has been inflicted upon you; this abominable outrage . . . Come back to your little country,' she urged, 'our arms are always open to welcome you . . . and console you for the injustice you have suffered.'[15]

She also sent a sternly worded letter to Alexandre's father, the marquis. 'I would never have thought that the vicomte, our son-in-law, would have caused us such unhappiness . . . During his stay here he has been very inconsiderate. He has passed his time . . . with numerous women . . . behaving in a dissipated manner . . . being led around by Mme de Longpré.' She continued by revealing how he had corrupted her slaves and abused their home. 'Such totally base conduct and vile methods, how can this be the behaviour of a man of culture and good birth? . . . It is hardly possible that my daughter can stay with him, unless he give sincere proof of a complete change . . . I ask you in the name of all the love you have for her, how can she continue to live with a husband who is so extremely weak as to use money to cover his shame and buy the dishonour of his wife?' Pleadingly she added, 'Oh my poor daughter . . . send her to me so she can mingle her tears with those of a loving mother . . . Send her to me, monsieur, and I will give her new life.'[16]

Meanwhile, Alexandre had departed the island. His ship, the *Atalante*, finally arrived at Rochefort on 15 September. He immediately wrote to Rose in that combination of bullying and self-pity which was so uniquely his own: 'I discovered with astonishment from your father's letters that you are not yet in a convent.' But there was no point in her hoping that he had changed his mind, he cautioned. Despite 'his illness', provoked, he added, by the 'terrible sadness' she had caused him, he remained resolute. How could they live together after what he had discovered? He would have been 'tortured by the perpetual images of the wrongs of which you know I am aware'. Warning that the interventions of his father and her aunt were only hardening his resolve, he concluded that she had only two options: 'return to the Americas . . . or go to the convent . . . no attempt, no effort, no approach that they try will move me'.[17]

In this alone he was true; he was indeed obdurate. Alexandre went to great lengths to avoid the imprecations of his friends and family. After his arrival in France he eschewed the family home for that of a relative of Mme de Longpré. When he finally arrived in Paris in late October, with the exception of a request to see his son, Eugène, Alexandre continued to avoid the rue Neuve-Saint-Charles and its inhabitants, moving into a house owned by the duc de La Rochefoucauld. His entire circle worked for a rapprochement between the couple but to no avail. Everyone tried to reason with him: his father, his brother, even the duc de La Rochefoucauld himself. At no time did he see Rose, or communicate with her. As time went by it became clear: she had no choice but to comply with Alexandre's wishes. On 27 November 1783 she left for the convent.

Five

THE CONVENT

It is by style that we are saved.

HENRY JAMES

ROSE MOVED INTO THE CONVENT of Panthémont in the last week of November. She was accompanied by her aunt Edmée (for moral support) and by Eugène; Hortense was left behind with her wet nurse.

Entering a convent did not mean that Rose was condemned to a life of chastity, frugality and piety; this was not a religious order of the sackcloth-and-ashes variety. Since the beginning of the Middle Ages it had been an established custom for well-born Frenchwomen – widows, spinsters, spurned wives – to rent lodgings in Parisian convents. (Indeed, it remained so well into the nineteenth century.) Reassuringly for Rose, Aunt Fanny had chosen this option after the disintegration of her own marriage. Since the Church owned around one-fifth of the capital's real estate, these establishments were numerous – there were around 200 in the 1780s – and offered accommodation ranging from the basic to the luxurious.

The convent of Panthémont was a typical example. Under the energetic patronage of its abbess, Marie-Catherine de Béthisy de Mézières, the convent had been converted into a fashionable retreat for women of the best society who, like Rose, had had to leave their homes. Situated in the aristocratic neighbourhood of the faubourg Saint-Germain, on the rue Grenelle, opposite the entrance to the rue des Bohèmes, the convent was set in beautiful gardens, surrounded by ivy-covered walls. Its grounds encompassed a newly restored chapel, the residential buildings and a teaching block; the convent, like most establishments of its kind, also doubled as a school for young women. Despite its fashionable location, board costs were reasonable: only 800 livres per annum, and accommodation costs for its thirty or so secular residents ranged from 300 livres for a single room to 1,200 livres for six-roomed apartments, with their own kitchens, on the first floor of the main building. Apart from formal attendance at chapel, the boarders were subject to no special discipline. They were not required to take vows and could come and go as they pleased and receive visitors when they chose.

It was here, in these beautiful and peaceful surroundings, that Rose set about rebuilding her shattered life. Whatever her heartbreak over a husband she still loved, and a marriage that – at the age of twenty – was irrevocably over, she knew the situation must be settled: the children's future must be safeguarded. Her options were limited. The legal constraints on women's lives were summarized in the *Encyclopédie*: 'According to the old and new laws,' it explained, 'the married woman is submitted to her husband, that is, she is in his power, so that she must obey him.' If she did not fulfil her duties he could correct her 'with moderation'.[1] Husbands had recourse to the law to punish their wives for any real or suspected infraction of her sexual duties – as Alexandre had planned to do – but Rose had no legal right to act against his infidelities. In order to sue for a separation (divorce was not yet legal), women must prove a cumulative and often humiliating case of neglect and abuse while men could simply present cursory evidence of infidelity. The process of pursuing their rights through the law courts was so tortuous that many women were deterred from taking action. But Rose, aflame with justifiable indignation, was adamant, courageous and determined. With Mme Renaudin's guidance, she acted with speed and efficiency. Overtures were made to the Crown, so that the process for an official separation could begin, and within a couple of weeks an appointment was made with an official of the Châtelet, the court of justice in Paris.

Alexandre, meanwhile, still refused to come anywhere near the family home, taking up residence instead at the duc de La Rochefoucauld's hôtel in the rue des Petits Augustins, where he hoped to kickstart his military career by convincing the duc to appoint him his aide-de-camp. He did find time to visit the daughter whom he had only recently denounced as belonging to someone else. Mme Renaudin received a letter from the village curé at Noisy-le-Grand that read, 'M. le vicomte has come to see Mademoiselle his daughter . . . He did not call on me, because of his travelling companions, but sent his apologies. He paid the wet nurse for two months, gave his daughter jewellery from the fair, and left, seemingly very satisfied. It is said he is amusing himself greatly in Paris.'[2]

On Monday morning 8 December 1783 Rose met the court adjudicator Louis Joron in the guest parlour on the second floor of the convent. Here she presented her formal complaint 'against le sieur Beauharnais, her husband'. The product of the meeting was a long, meticulous and unhappy document, in which Rose laid out her sufferings. She told Joron of her arrival in France, her wedding, her hopes for the marriage. She documented Alexandre's frequent absences, from which the official calculated that in two years and nine months of married life, Alexandre had spent a miserly ten months with his wife. She told him sadly of Alexandre's 'great dissipation' and of the trip to Martinique that had led to their separation. She presented for the adjudicator's perusal those two final letters from Alexandre, with all their atrocious accusations, insults and threats. She added that, despite the support of various respectable people – including her father-in-law, who stressed her innocence – 'he will persist in his resolution not to live with her any more'. Consequently she had applied for a legal separation of 'body and habitation'. Joron's sympathies were with the appealing and ill-used Rose. His report concluded, 'It is not possible for the complainant to submit to such indignities. She would be lacking in what she owes herself and her children, exposing herself to a most terrible fate.'[3]

On 3 February 1784 the provost of Paris issued the first response to her complaint. It ordered that she should remain at the convent until the legal process had been resolved. Alexandre was ordered to pay maintenance for his children, wages for Euphémie (who was caring for Eugène), and other sundry costs that Rose had previously been carrying. Alexandre's response was typically vindictive. Despite now being substantially richer than his father (he had inherited Pyvart de Chastullé, a plantation in Santo Domingo, from his mother's family), he insisted that the family home be sold. This behaviour only undermined Alexandre's case further, especially since he also pursued Rose for the jewellery she had been forced to sell when he abandoned her in France without financial support. In particular, he hounded her for the medallion that she had sold in desperation to pay for Hortense's birth and christening. As she wrote to a friend, 'I was obliged to my debtors, the birth was arriving . . . and I couldn't raise the expenses of the baptism . . . M. de Beauharnais must know that I have nothing and need everything, but since money is not my God this is not what concerns me most.'[4]

While the wheels of justice continued to grind slow, Rose was harried with financial worries. In a letter to one of her creditors she explained why she had not settled her account. 'Since his [Alexandre's] return from

Martinique he has rejected nearly all the bills submitted to him, promising to pay them only if I would recognize that these bills were correct. I would not have refused if the merchant had actually delivered the merchandise and the worker had done his work; but these things did not remain in my possession; M. de Beauharnais sold everything as soon as he arrived in Paris. He should know better than anyone what has become of this furniture.'[5]

Alexandre's decision to banish Rose to a convent was meant as a punishment. But it turned out to be an important watershed in her development. For the first time since arriving in France she was surrounded by her peers, women who were in similar circumstances to her own. The women's collective vulnerability and shared experiences were great social levellers and created an intimacy that in other circumstances would never have existed. Instead of being judged and found wanting, as she had felt with her husband and in the competitive environment of the salons, her companions genuinely liked and approved of Rose. 'She was interesting', remarked one of her cohabitees, and they found her story touching: a beautiful young woman, with adorable children, victimized by a barbarous husband. They admired the fact that she had not fallen apart and that she was facing the future bravely, despite its uncertainties. It was amongst these women that Rose developed her first real friendships in France.

Rose's time at Panthémont was the most profitable part of her education. Initially the convent was simply a refuge, a peaceful haven from the turbulence of an unhappy marriage. But eventually the tranquillity of convent life and the support provided by the other boarders and the nuns began to have a healing effect. At a time of life when her personality was still molten, the peace of convent life was liberating, providing her with the space in which to develop her own character. Separated from her husband and isolated from the loving support of her own family, Rose could find out how she functioned as a separate being. She finally had the time to discover who she was and become aware of her own identity. The convent became a place where she could first discover and then reinvent herself.

Like an actress learning a part, Rose studied the women who surrounded her in order to learn how to be *une vraie Parisienne*. During the daily life of the convent, her meetings with the residents in the corridors, in the parlours, on the way to the chapel, Rose watched her companions. She had a wide variety of feminine archetypes to study: her fellow-boarders included conservative matrons and cosmopolitan ladies about town, provincial nobility and the grand bourgeoisie. She noted their gestures, watched their movements, listened to their voices and studied their small talk. She observed how they entered rooms and how they left them; how they greeted people and how they took their leave. She sought the secrets of their effortless ease, their apparently natural grace. She scrutinized how they dressed and how they applied their make-up, even how they arranged their hands.

She came to understand how these women constructed their beauty, particularly in a society where natural prettiness held little charm. In Paris 'a woman was like a diamond', according to Mercier; not beautiful 'till it has been cut and polished and set in its full brilliance'. Rose eventually became expert at these feminine arts, but at this point she was still a neophyte, only beginning to appreciate the constant effort needed to keep abreast of changing fashions. The convent provided her with an apprenticeship of sorts to this community of women who shared recipes for beauty potions and swapped tips about maquillage in order to create the fashionable look: chalk-white face, red cheeks, magenta lips. They taught her how to darken brows and lashes with burnt cork or lampblack, how to use gunpowder to scrub the teeth white. Like her new friends, Rose would become addicted to rouge. (It was said that by 1781 French women used 2 million pots of rouge annually.) Her dress sense improved with exposure to the fashion bibles like the *Cabinet des Modes* and *La Galerie des Modes et Costumes Français* that her companions reverently studied. At the convent, Rose began to understand that femininity was a performance and beauty a craft.

It was not an easy craft to master. The ancien régime was a milieu with elaborate social mores. To move elegantly, for example, was 'the ultimate status symbol'. But in contrast to our rather straightforward modern views about movement, eighteenth-century ideas were convoluted. So Rose's natural grace was not enough. Even simple activities like entering a room or exiting it, sitting, passing people on the street or having a cup of tea were highly embellished, ritualized and self-conscious, as choreographed as any dance. A woman was expected to carry her head artfully, her arms curving gently away from the torso, not dropping straight down at the sides like those of servants or rustics. She had to walk 'swimmingly',[6] feet turned out, as if gliding along on a set of casters. Whatever the discomforts of her viciously boned corsets, she must walk with steps shorter than a man's and without jostling her skirts. All without ever appearing awkward, stiff or inelegant. All these movements had precise standards of performance that had to be learned, and required time and practice to perfect.

The other social arts were just as demanding. The importance of verbal skills could not have been more clearly impressed on Rose than by her disastrous early experiences in Parisian society. She had learned, to her cost, that the requirements for good conversation were as stringent as those for elegant carriage. By observing women at the convent she gradually mastered the art of greeting acquaintances with the right degree of formality or familiarity, of speaking softly and in a low voice, of listening attentively and intelligently, of knowing when to interrupt with tact or respond with a witty double entendre. More important still were the subtle, non-verbal skills: the fluttering use of the handkerchief, the subtle deployment of the fan. The latter, an accessory that could 'express a thousand moods', was considered as dangerous a weapon in a woman's hands as a sword was in a man's.

One can become stylish through instinct, osmosis or effort. Rose's style emerged as a result of all three. She naturally possessed some of the raw materials: a beautiful voice, an empathetic nature and a bewitching way of moving. In the convent she assimilated the aura of the boarders amid whom she lived, and she slowly began to understand the unwritten codes of the elegant society she had entered. But her style was mainly the product of her own hard work. Although not an intellectual, Rose learned quickly through observation and instinct. This quality, in conjunction with the extraordinary adaptability that was evident throughout her tumultuous life, allowed Rose to achieve by herself what all Alexandre's bullying and books never could: her transformation into a woman à la mode.

The forces of fashion also conspired in Rose's favour. The panniered dresses and terrifying hairstyles that had prevailed on her arrival in France were now somewhat démodé, worn only in the most formal of circumstances. In their place came a style that suited Rose much better, especially now that she had grown up a bit and her face and figure had lost their youthful puppy fat. The new look was captured in Vigée-Lebrun's painting of Marie Antoinette which had caused such a sensation in the salon of 1783. It featured the Queen in a straw hat and a simple white gown, reminiscent of the plain muslin dresses favoured by Creole women, who had carried the look from the colonies to the court. Rose looked charming and felt comfortable in this new style. At last her native style was seen as an asset; at last she could feel confident in her femininity and in her burgeoning sexuality.

Rose's stint at the convent was not the nadir of her life, as Alexandre had assumed it would be. Instead it taught her how to present herself with elegance and provided her with greater social ease and confidence. It was during this time that the stylish, charming, graceful woman who would eventually be renamed Josephine began to emerge.

The acrimonious atmosphere between the estranged couple intensified in early 1785 when Alexandre forcibly kidnapped Eugène from the convent. Rose immediately wrote to the provost of Paris demanding that the authorities force Alexandre to return the three-year-old. Her request brought matters to a head and the warring couple were summoned to appear at the Châtelet. On 5 March 1785 the dispute was finally settled in the study of Maître Trutat, notary of Paris. Rose was totally vindicated. Unable to provide a shred of evidence to sustain the charges that he had made against his wife, Alexandre was forced to accept an out-of-court settlement. 'The said Vicomte de Beauharnais recognizes that the Vicomtesse, his wife, has pleaded with just cause; that he was wrong to write the said lady the letters of 12 July and 20 October of which she complains, and which he admits were inspired by the passions and anger of youth.' He regrets 'all the more having given way to these passions because on his return to France, the testimony of the public and her father-in-law was all to her advantage. He realizes that his conduct warrants the separation that the lady Vicomtesse de Beauharnais desires.' It continued, 'That since both parties want to avoid disagreeable publicity' and because Rose wanted to 'give the strongest proof to her two children of her maternal feeling', she has decided 'to accept the offer which has been made to her'.[7]

The terms of the settlement allowed Rose to live wherever she chose and to enjoy revenues from her dowry and whatever else might fall to her. Alexandre had to meet all legal costs and make her an annual allowance of 5,000 livres. There was no further nonsense about Hortense's paternity, she was to remain with her mother until marriage and Alexandre was to pay an additional 1,000 livres a year for the child's upkeep. Eugène was to be brought up by his father, as was the custom of the time, but he would remain with his mother until he was five years old, and spend summers with Rose thereafter. And so ended four years of married life. Rose was just twenty-one.

Six

FONTAINEBLEAU

We laughed and danced our way to the precipice.

MADAME DE LA TOUR DU PIN

IGNORANT OF THE EVENTS HOVERING on the horizon, France in the middle of the 1780s was optimistic and buoyant. There was a tangible energy for change, for seizing the future and bending it to the collective will. In the arts and the sciences fresh innovations gave people a renewed sense of possibility and hope for the future. Enlightenment ideals had ignited both popular and intellectual thirst for reform. With what one historian aptly described as 'the collective masochism of the French aristocracy',[1] many members of the nobility, including Rose's estranged husband, now devoted themselves to the social transformation that would eventually deprive them of power.

It was into this febrile, fast-paced world that Rose emerged, blinking, finally an adult. Caught up in a tumultuous relationship and isolated in the elderly Beauharnais ménage, her own tribulations had prevented Rose from fully engaging with the changes in her adopted city. Now, finally, the marriage was over. The settlement had left her comfortably off and in control of her destiny for the first time. Whatever her lingering heartaches, she had refashioned herself into a true *Parisienne*, acquiring a nucleus of friends of her own to guide her through the unnerving social and political whirl that was pre-revolutionary Paris.

Rose remained in the city for several months after the settlement. She kept on her rooms at the convent out of necessity, since the house in rue Neuve-Saint-Charles was no more; Alexandre had sold the furniture and cancelled the lease. The family's other home, at Noisy, had been sold by Aunt Edmée, according to the rights given her in the wedding contract.

Undoubtedly the unhappy memories associated with both residences meant that neither would have appealed overmuch to Rose. Her independent little apartment at the convent in the heart of Paris was much more enticing.

Rose's rebirth seemed to be echoed in the city around her: Paris was going through a massive building boom. 'Huge blocks of dwellings rise from the ground as if by magic,' wrote an awed Mercier, 'and new districts of the most magnificent houses take shape. The building mania gives an air of grandeur and majesty to the city.'² He calculated that one-third of the city had been rebuilt in the previous two decades. The building fever lifted the city's energy levels, a concrete proof of public optimism. Thomas Jefferson, who arrived in 1784, was entranced by the ever-changing panorama of the capital, 'every day enlarging and beautifying'.³

The Palais Royal was a microcosm of the city's new spirit. Opened in 1784, it was the brainchild of Louis XVI's first cousin Philippe, the duc d'Orléans, fondly known during the early months of the Revolution as 'Philippe Égalité'. The Palais Royal was like a giant shopping mall, a conveniently located assemblage of delights, including gambling dens, shops, cafés, bookstalls, lace makers, lemonade sellers and strolling players. Visitors could ogle the magic-lantern or shadow-light shows, or frequent brothels. It was, according to Mercier, 'an enchanted place, a small city enclosed in a large one. A prisoner could live here free from care for years with no thought of escape.'⁴ In this 'quotidian carnival of appetites' all classes of people mingled unselfconsciously. Women of fashion like Rose promenaded alongside courtesans; soldiers of distinction enjoyed themselves alongside the humblest farm officials. The social mix of the Palais Royal had never been seen before. It was an embodiment of the newly emerging democratic spirit of the city; its exuberant energy seemed to sum up the spirit of the times.

The mood for change was evident not just on the ground but in the air. Balloon-mania gripped France. The most famous flight was put on by Étienne Montgolfier on 19 September 1783, when his blue taffeta balloon decorated with golden fleurs-de-lis was released into the air above the royal palace at Versailles. It carried in its basket three passengers: a sheep named Montauciel (Climb-to-the-sky), a duck and a rooster. To the delight of its immense audience (more than 100,000 people), it drifted for eight minutes before landing in the woods a few miles beyond the chateau. The animal aeronauts survived unscathed. So extraordinary was the spectacle of such flights that they provoked intense emotion in those who beheld them. On one occasion at Saint-Cloud the entire crowd, watching a balloon passing overhead, fell to their knees with their hands clasped as if in prayer. In another case, balloonists landing in a field were confronted by peasants who, convinced they were extraterrestrials, forced them to undress to prove they were human. Balloonists became national heroes, their exploits eulogized in ballads and captured in portraits. People supported balloons as today they support football teams; women even wore miniature balloons woven into hairstyles. It was a craze that gripped men and women, rich and poor; a truly democratic spectacle that elicited enormous popular support. There was the sense that they were witnessing a genuinely liberating event. People felt it was an 'augury of a free-floating future', argues the historian Simon Schama; things that had previously been unthinkable now seemed possible.[5]

Underneath the surface elation, complex and dangerous undercurrents lurked. The French Revolution was now only a few years away. Years of fatalism were being overridden by Enlightenment preoccupations with scientific progress, social reform and a new sense of possibility. The success of the balloonists proved that scientists could even conquer the air. Why then could society not overcome all its ills? And much was perceived to be wrong. The King's financial support of the American War of Independence, greatly acclaimed at the time, had drained France's coffers and now the country was on the verge of bankruptcy. There was a general perception that the King was ineffectual and the Government corrupt. It had become fashionable to scorn life at court and to be rude about the royal family. The King was referred to as 'the Locksmith' because of his fondness for tinkering with mechanical objects, and even more cruelly as 'the Fat Pig'. But it was Marie Antoinette who bore the brunt of popular hostility. Scabrous pamphlets about her proliferated, and were devoured by privileged and poor alike. They depicted her as an extravagant, depraved woman presiding over a decadent and greedy court. Innumerable pornographic publications were also printed, showing 'the Austrian' in a ceaseless round of grandiose feasts and orgies with both men and women. Simultaneously presented as Machiavellian and empty-headed, increasingly seen as 'the foreigner', Marie Antoinette became the scapegoat for the Government's inadequacies and the country's problems.[6]

The profound economic, political and commercial shifts in the years immediately preceding the Revolution had a great impact on social behaviour in the capital. 'Ladies no longer escorted each other or rose before greeting', wrote the disapproving marquise de Crequy. 'People said "women" instead of "ladies" and "men of the court" instead of "nobles". The greatest ladies were invited to supper and mixed with the wives of financiers.'[7] Many felt that this breaking down of class barriers and social mores was just one more sign that the ancient social and political structures were collapsing.

The repercussions of these social shifts were particularly important for women. All of a sudden new social spaces were opened up to them. Theatres, opera and concerts were now part of the beau monde, places where women could go on their own or with men other than their husbands. Even Marie Antoinette was a devotee of the theatre and attended performances without the King. In the atmosphere of tallow and sweat and dust, women enjoyed performances of operas and plays that explored issues pertinent to their lives: love, adultery and divorce. But it was not just the performances that drew women like Rose to the theatre and made them passionate devotees; they also adored 'its subtly erotic atmosphere', enjoying the 'conversations, flirtations, assignations and love notes, which had become an accepted part of the theatre-going experience'.⁸

Nothing summed up the new *zeitgeist* better than a play that Rose saw many times: Beaumarchais's *Marriage of Figaro*. When it opened on 21 April 1784 at the Théâtre-Français, fist fights broke out as huge crowds battled for seats. Despite attempts to suppress it (the author was imprisoned in the prison of Saint-Lazare), the play was the greatest theatrical success of the decade. The story of a wily servant who gets the better of his master, the play made fun of *grands seigneurs*, while celebrating the ordinary man. Its incipient arguments about equality expressed newly emerging sympathies, assuring the play's popularity with those in the rowdy *parterre*. Less explicable was the play's popularity with the *grand monde*, whose responses to it were decidedly masochistic, observed the baronne d'Oberkirch: they 'smacked themselves across their own cheeks; they laughed at their own expense and what is even worse they made others laugh too . . . strange blindness!'

Enjoying the distractions of the city, Rose lingered in Paris as long as she could. But life there was expensive and she missed her family. Eventually she and the children joined Mme Renaudin and the marquis at their new home in Fontainebleau. Situated thirty-seven miles south-east of Paris, near the forest of the same name, Fontainebleau was a rather sleepy hamlet when Rose moved there. (It became a popular summer resort in the following century, when it attracted Parisian holidaymakers in droves.) The house that the marquis rented on the rue Montmorin was more modest than their previous residences, though it had stabling capacity for twelve horses. But it was pretty and Rose liked it well enough to have some furniture sent over from Martinique to furnish her apartments. She maintained her rooms at Panthémont as a handy pied-à-terre for her occasional visits to the capital.

Domestic life had its normal upheavals. The marquis was now a frail seventy-two, and everyone was concerned about Edmée's mysterious stomach complaint. As per the separation agreement, a year after Rose had settled in the town, Eugène, aged five, went to live with his father in Paris. Alexandre enrolled the little boy in the pension run by M. Verdière on the rue de Seine. Rose missed him acutely but was kept abreast of his doings by regular letters from Alexandre. She in turn replied with tales about little Hortense. This epistolary exchange was not a rapprochement; Alexandre and Rose would never again live as man and wife. But it was evidence of the genuine affection they both felt for their children.

Sadly, Alexandre's new-found maturity did not extend to his financial commitments. His dedicated pursuit of the pleasures of the capital was eating into the financial legacy that he had received on his marriage. As a result he was often late in paying Rose's allowance. There was further bad news from Martinique. More out of necessity than confidence the marquis de Beauharnais had appointed Rose's father administrator of his Caribbean estates. With Joseph's customary flair for mismanagement the Beauharnais revenues began to fall sharply and consistently. Despite a barrage of letters interrogating his business practices and giving him instructions and suggestions, the situation did not improve, and the marquis's proceeds were reduced to an irregular trickle. This made it even more difficult for Rose's father to send his desperate daughter even a part of the 5,000 livres she had been promised on her marriage.

The family's money problems were exacerbated by the wider economic situation. In 1786 the King had been informed by his minister Calonne that the country was in a dire financial crisis. Blaming his political rival, Necker, for mismanagement, Calonne explained that all credit was exhausted and radical change was the only alternative to bankruptcy. His proposals for fiscal reforms included the replacement of the existing tax system with a Universal Land Tax and the introduction of stamp duty, as well as freer grain trade and the abolition of internal customs and barriers. The Assembly rejected his reforms and in April 1787 Calonne was dismissed. Various compromises were debated while the Government sought to raise urgently needed loans.

The difficult economic conditions impacted profoundly on the little household in Fontainebleau. In his heyday the marquis had enjoyed an annual income of 150,000 livres. By the early 1780s he was receiving a modest pension of only 12,000 livres, and sweeping state cuts now reduced this to the miserly sum of 2,800 livres. With growing assertiveness Rose confronted their financial problems. She wrote to the Minister of War to complain about the treatment of her father-in-law. Though this effort was in vain, she was more successful when she did battle with the Government's tax officer in November 1785. Explaining that she was now separated from her husband, Rose succeeded in reducing the inflated demand by half to thirty livres. Other financial battles arose as a result of Alexandre's fecklessness. One creditor wrote to Rose requesting payment for jewellery that Alexandre had purchased for some other woman.

Their financial woes were somewhat alleviated by the arrival, in the spring of 1787, of baron Tascher, Rose's paternal uncle, who brought money from her father. It was not all that Joseph had promised, but it gave Rose hope that more would follow. 'I have received, my dear father, the money order of 2,789 livres 6 sols 8 deniers that you sent via my uncle, all my thanks. This makes me hope that you are seriously occupied with trying to provide me with more considerable sums.' Clearly mortified about having to pressure her father for funds, she continued, 'You know well enough, my dear father, to be quite sure that were it not for a pressing need for money, I would speak of nothing but fond feelings for you . . . I embrace you with all my heart.'[9]

In June 1786 Rose's life was disrupted by the birth of a mystery child. The little girl, baptized Marie-Adelaide d'Antigny, was initially rumoured to be Rose's illegitimate offspring. The gossip probably arose because both Rose and Mme Renaudin took such an interest in the child, appointing a M. Calmelet as trustee of her affairs, a role he also played for Hortense. Later Rose would organize Adèle's marriage and pay for her trousseau, and Edmée would bequeath her an annual income of 300 livres in her will. Rose's involvement in Adèle's life inevitably generated a great deal of talk. But her behaviour had a simple explanation: she believed the child was Alexandre's, the product of a liaison with an unknown married woman. Years later Alexandre's paternity would be confirmed, but since neither he nor the child's mother took any interest in her, it was left to Mme Renaudin and Rose to take responsibility for her well being.

Rose had something of a ready-made social life in Fontainebleau. Aunt Fanny had a home there, as did the Cecconi sisters and their father, who had been so supportive during the stormiest days of her marriage. The abbess of Panthémont had also introduced Rose to her nephew, the vicomte de Béthisy, colonel of the Royal Picardy Grenadiers. She had made the acquaintance of the marquise de Montmorin and her son, who was governor of the castle and colonel of the Flanders regiment and who had the curious distinction of being the only one of his subjects whom Louis XV had held at the baptismal font. The company was not scintillating; Fontainebleau was rather old-fashioned in its interests. Whereas Parisians talked enthusiastically of the need for fiscal and constitutional reform, in Fontainebleau the talk revolved around rather passé gossip about the court. Still, life passed amiably enough; there were private theatricals to act in or organize and card parties to attend, as well as the occasional ball.

Fontainebleau's role as a royal seat shaped Rose's social activities during the hunting season. She became acquainted with various officers of the King's household, such as François Hüe, chief clerk of the rivers and forests and of the royal hunt. A jolly big-nosed man, his devotion to the King would eventually land him in prison. In addition to the officials permanently stationed there, Rose also got the chance to meet some of the nobility that descended on the town during the season. For centuries, through the reigns of the Valois and Bourbon kings, it had been the greatest of the royal hunts. But it too had been affected by the country's economic difficulties, and the event was not quite as extravagant as it had traditionally been. Though there were fewer spectacles and games, the hunt was still a glittering affair, and within this glamorous circle Rose got the chance to practise her new-found charms. She began to shine. Much to the annoyance of her estranged husband she, not he, had been given permission to discreetly follow the hunt, a privilege that corresponded to rank. Always a great animal lover, Rose avoided the kill throughout her life. Instead she took pleasure in other aspects of the hunt: the champagne breakfasts, the sound of the trumpets, the sight of the beaters, the galloping through the beautiful shady forests as the hunt moved from lodge to lodge. In the autumn of 1787 the marquis wrote to Mme Renaudin, who was visiting Paris: 'The vicomtesse went boar hunting yesterday. She was soaked to the skin, but perfectly happy and had a bite to eat after changing her clothes.' Although not allowed to approach the King or go to the balls given in the palace, Rose enjoyed herself, completely unaware that she would one day preside over this royal seat as the consort of France's ruler.

Occasionally, too, there were visits to Paris. Rose stayed first at the convent, and then, when her lease expired, at the home of the banker Denis de Rougemont, who was an old friend of the Beauharnais family. These trips gave her the opportunity to see her beloved Eugène and to enjoy the capital's more lively social scene. Here, as in London, the table talk revolved around the Affair of the Diamond Necklace, one of the most notorious scandals of the century. The unwitting star of this complex scandal was Marie Antoinette. Its plot, worthy of the most implausible melodrama, revolved around a sting perpetrated on the vain and gullible cardinal de Rohan. Ever eager to ingratiate himself with the Queen, the cardinal was convinced by a band of schemers that she wanted a rather vulgar diamond necklace, made up of 647 diamonds, weighing 2,800 carats and worth a million and a half livres. The cast of this little *drame* included a self-styled magician called Cagliostra and an adventuress called Jeanne de la Motte, who claimed to be descended from royalty. The action included a moonlight rendezvous between the cardinal and an ash-blonde *grisette* picked up in the Palais Royal, disguised in white muslin to impersonate the Queen. Believing that he had received the go-ahead for the purchase, Rohan advanced substantial sums of money for the necklace; meanwhile the real jewellery had been broken into parts and was being fenced across the Channel.

When the whole affair came to light, amidst the deafening cries of outraged creditors and indignant jewellers, all the participants managed to engineer public sympathy for themselves, except for poor Marie Antoinette. This despite the fact that she had not wanted the necklace in the first place, and had been attempting to improve her public image by making serious attempts to curb her ostentatious spending. But what seemed like an amusing sideshow would prove to be one of the nails in the coffin of the ancien régime. The public believed that Marie Antoinette's greed had caused the situation in the first place, and its cast of corrupt charlatans and venal aristocrats seemed a perfect symbol of a régime ridden by corruption. More even than empty coffers, famished peasants and grumbling artisans, it was – according to Napoleon – the real beginning of the French Revolution and the end of the French monarchy.

At the time, however, Rose, like most of her peers, was not overly concerned with the political situation; she was too busy enjoying her independence and her new-found confidence. This was boosted by a number of admirers, including the chevalier de Coigny, a gentleman twenty years her senior and with a colourful past. (He had lost his father in a duel and had been a suitor of Lady Sarah Lennox.) He would later become one of the most active agents of the Bourbons, and Rose would save his head during the years of the Consulate. Another beau was a married, older man, the comte de Crenay, a brigadier in the cavalry, who had begun his military career serving Louis XVI's father in the Royal Guard.

Despite the apparent serenity and pleasures of her new life, Rose suddenly and unexpectedly decided to return to Martinique. To fund the trip she turned to her friend Denis de Rougemont, who advanced her 6,000 livres, borrowed 1,000 livres from her aunt and sold her harp, depriving herself of one of her favourite pursuits. As soon as the money was assembled, Rose gathered up Hortense and Euphémie and departed for Le Havre. There she rented a small house from a Creole acquaintance, where the trio waited the entire month of June to find an appropriate ship. On 2 July 1788 they sailed for the islands.

Seven

RETURN OF THE
NATIVE

Myself, I know that exiles feed on hope.

AESCHYLUS

WHAT PROMPTED ROSE'S HASTY DEPARTURE for Martinique? What could have induced her to undergo the interminable Atlantic crossing that she so loathed, with all its attendant dangers and deprivations? It was certainly highly unconventional for a young lady to consider such a journey unescorted by a husband, father or brother. Her actions seem particularly rash as she left with insufficent funds, a skeleton wardrobe and a five-year-old in tow. In the Caribbean, speculation about her motives still swirls. Some thought that Rose was in pursuit of a man she had met before her marriage who was now stationed in Fort-Royal. Her daughter Hortense later suggested that she was in flight from love, specifically her enduring feelings for Alexandre, and sought a remedy in the 'temporary situation of a voyage'.[1]

It was also suggested by one biographer that 'Rose . . . was pregnant and wanted to hide her illegitimate swelling'.[2] In Martinique there is still talk of a child, while in neighbouring Dominica the belief is that Rose became pregnant after arrivng back in the Caribbean and prolonged her stay in order to give birth there. But if this was the case, would Rose really have moved from broad-minded Paris – and the capable and worldly guidance of Mme Renaudin, who could be guaranteed to fix such a situation with discretion and efficiency – to the prying eyes of Martinique, where her every move would be scrutinized and gossiped about?

Money was almost certainly a motive. In the months since their divorce

Alexandre had exacerbated Rose's anxiety over her finances with his irregular payments, contestations over her dowry and squabbles over their joint property. As a result, Rose was in the uneasy position of being more or less reliant on her Aunt Edmée and the marquis to supplement her income. Since both were in delicate health, this dependency made Rose insecure. And since Rose was aware that she was receiving less from the La Pagerie coffers than was her due, she may have felt that her physical presence might provoke her work-shy father to generate greater funds on her behalf.

Rose had other reasons to return, as her daughter Hortense explained in her memoirs: 'The position of my mother, although brilliant, did not allow her to forget her country, or her family. She had left behind an ageing mother whom she wished to see again one more time.'[3] Always protective of her mother's reputation, Hortense's description of Rose's situation at this time as 'brilliant' was an exaggeration. But it was true that Rose was worried about her relatives. She knew of her father's and sister's ill health, and had written to various friends in Martinique expressing her concerns for her mother. Less tangible, but perhaps just as important, is the possiblity that after all Rose had recently endured, she was overcome with that profound homesickness that sometimes overwhelms migrants; that longing for familiarity, love, security, for what has been left behind.

It was a long journey, made fraught by the resumed hostilities with England, and by a near-miss with another vessel at the place where the Seine empties into the Channel. Their ship, the *Sultan*, eventually docked in Martinique on 11 August 1788. It was the middle of the rainy season, when the island was at its hottest and most humid. Rose was so excited about returning to La Pagerie that she didn't stop in Fort-Royal to enjoy the hospitality of her aunt and uncle Tascher. One can only imagine Rose's feelings as she traversed the azure bay, felt the familiar salt-spray of the sea on her face, and saw once again the three tiny islands that gave Trois-Îlets its name.

At the dock, the trio were hustled into the family's carriage to make the short journey home. They found the plantation somewhat changed since Rose's departure. The great house had finally been rebuilt a couple of years earlier, so that it was no longer necessary to camp upstairs in the *purgerie*. The new house was similar to the original one, wood on a stone foundation, with a neatly tiled roof. Rose and Hortense were settled into one of the five bedrooms to the right of the house. But the rest of the plantation was still ramshackle and shoddy. It had been almost ten years since Rose had last seen

Little Guinea, and much had altered – not least Rose herself, who had left a parochial girl and returned a fashionable young lady.

Their reception was rapturous. Desperate to get a look at the prodigal daughter, all the slaves were there to greet her, including her old nurse, Marion. Rose found that her concerns for her mother's health were groundless: Mme de La Pagerie was older certainly, but as indomitable as ever. However, her father's health had deteriorated to a shocking degree. Her grandmother de Sannois had died, and her beautiful younger sister Manette had, as Alexandre had recounted, been sadly disfigured by the disease that had plagued her for years, which some have suggested might have been scurvy.

After the emotional reunion, Rose settled into the sedate pattern of island life. She remained there for over two years, back in her heart's home, in the talismanic enclave that gave her such a deep sense of security. Once again she awoke in rooms flooded with light and listened to the rippling sound of the wind rushing through cane. She sat again beside the river, bathing in its cool, clear water, and walked through the lush groves of frangipani and bougainvillea, enjoying the sweet-scented air.

Her sojourn in Martinique allowed Rose to share with her precious daughter the experiences of her own tropical childhood. It is easy to imagine mother and child strolling over Little Guinea's rolling grounds, the scent of the rich, warm, damp earth in their nostrils, the blinding sunlight assaulting their eyes. Occasionally the pair would have stopped, the dark chestnut head bent over the small blonde one, to examine an unfamiliar flower or one of the technicolor butterflies for which the island is justifiably famous, or to watch a dust-coloured lizard darting through jade-green grass, even as the sadness and the deprivation of slavery hovered like persistent ghosts, just beyond the charmed circle of their beauty and privilege.

Hortense had only one vivid memory of her stay in Martinique, one that spoke volumes about her mother's own upbringing. One day, watching her grandmother count money, the little girl got it into her head that the piles of copper pennies were hers to dispose of. Gathering the money into her skirt, she set out with one of the house servants to dispense the coins to the slaves on the plantation, as she had seen her mother do. She returned to a household in turmoil: her grandmother furious, the slaves quaking in fear lest they be blamed for the money's disappearance. Once the little culprit had been identified, Mme de La Pagerie's response was so stern that Hortense, who up until then had 'never shed a tear, nor been rebuked by a harsh word', never forgot it. 'The humiliation I suffered from the mistake was so intense that . . . since that far-off day, I have never told a lie or thought to embellish the truth.'[4]

In the main, though, life was uneventful. There were a few local visits to friends and neighbours, like the Marlets, who lived in the plantation adjacent to La Pagerie. Apart from these social events, Rose also had the opportunity to reacquaint herself with the real work of the plantation, and confront again the slave system, with its curious divisions of labour, working for the prosperity of her family. She may even have attempted to examine the finances in order to understand the fluctuations of the funds she received in France. In fact, the Pagerie plantation should have been doing rather well during these years. From the 1783 Treaty of Versailles and the American War of Independence France had won from England certain colonial concessions that had improved the economy of Martinique and that of the other sugar islands. But there was no evidence of prosperity in the account books at La Pagerie; Joseph simply did not have the skills to take advantage of the new commercial climate.

Rose would also have been drawn into anguished speculation about the fate of her cousin Aimée Dubucq de Rivery, who had apparently disappeared while making the treacherous Atlantic crossing. The family were concerned that she might have been captured by pirates. Her fate, as recounted in countless novels and works of non-fiction, turned out to be even more lurid. Not only had she been kidnapped by Barbary pirates, but she had been transported to Algiers, where she was auctioned into the harem of Turkish Sultan Selim III. The blonde and blue-eyed Creole beauty soon emerged as the ruler's favourite concubine, gaining the title of the Sultane Valide as the mother of his heir, Mahmoud II, who remained in power until 1820. Historians remain divided about the veracity of this fabulous life story. Some sceptics have favoured an equally lurid explanation for her disappearance: that poor Aimée was murdered by a covetous relative and buried secretly on the grounds of the family plantation. Whatever happened in reality, the legend of Aimée Dubucq de Rivery consolidated the exotic mythology associated with Creole women that so shaped public perceptions of Josephine.[5]

As time passed, the now sophisticated Rose grew discontented with the rather limited pleasures of Trois-Îlets. By 1789 she was spending more and more time sampling the worldly distractions of Fort-Royal. As port commander, her uncle Robert Tascher was responsible for entertaining the government officials and naval officers from the ships anchored in the town's harbour. Rose attended his various soirées and balls, especially enjoying those held at Government House. She discovered that social life on the island had become more urbane while she had been away. As one historian, writing about the social behaviour amongst the more privileged Creoles in the years immediately preceding the Revolution, observed: 'the prodigality of the tables was unbelievable, and the toilettes of the women surpass all description'.[6] To her surprise, in order to compete with the local beauties Rose was forced to send back to France for her formal dresses. Describing her during this time one old acquaintance wrote, 'That lady, without being precisely pretty, nevertheless was attractive because of her style, her gaiety and her good heart. Most preoccupied with procuring the luxurious enjoyments of her era, she found that her attractiveness gave her certain advantages . . . She defied public opinion rather overtly . . . As her funds were limited and she loved to spend, she was often forced to draw on her admirers' purses.'[7]

But underneath this surface tranquillity, disquiet was growing in Martinique. The ripples of unrest that would culminate in the French Revolution were spreading out from the mother country and reaching the shores of its colonies. Martinique was already a divided society, characterized by overlapping struggles between slaves seeking freedom, free coloureds fighting racial discrimination and the colonial elite seeking political independence. As one historian noted, 'All dreamed of nothing but a favourable transformation of their situation: the planters wanted to augment their power, the "free coloureds" wanted to acquire all the rights of citizens, and the blacks, their freedom.' In few societies 'can the ideals of liberty, equality and fraternity have seemed as dangerous as they did in these plantation societies, founded as they were on bondage, inequality and prejudice'.[8]

The first manifestation of dissent was in a new spirit of resistance amongst the slave population. Isolated and uneducated though they were, it was impossible to keep all news of popular unrest from them. They discovered that America had already begun the process of outlawing slavery; that in France public debates about abolition were under way between philanthropists and planters; and that during the American War of Independence the marquis de Bouillé, governor of Martinique, had established companies of men of colour whose participation in that conflict had bolstered their claims for equal rights. This information leaked into the slave population in myriad ways: some black people had returned to the Caribbean after being allowed to mix in Parisian taverns and public places; some who had learned to read and write had seen pamphlets and leaflets in the possession of their masters; some had overheard snippets of conversation in taverns or at dinner tables.

They circulated the information they had gleaned, and the slave population grew more and more aware of the possibility of emancipation, fuelling the growing clamour for liberation.

Events in the mother country, meanwhile, were accelerating. In July 1788, whilst Rose was crossing the Atlantic, a hailstorm had whipped across much of western France, ravaging wheat crops and causing the price of bread to rise sharply. The political situation was as tumultuous as the weather. The marquise de Sade, wife of the infamous marquis, observed, 'We've been in an uproar of scandals, fear, promissory notes, bankruptcy, joy, rebellion . . .'[9] The King, attempting to resolve the nation's economic crisis, had tried to levy a new stamp tax. An already hostile parliament argued that the right to do so belonged exclusively to the Estates General, a representative assembly founded in the fourteenth century. This body, which included clergy and nobility as well as commoners, had not met since 1614. Louis recessed parliament and arrested two dissenting leaders. All of the nation's regional parliaments declared solidarity with the Parisian Assembly and the fate of the ancien régime was sealed. In the following months, anti-royalist demonstrations spread throughout the country, supported by all classes of society. By the third week of June, the clergy came out in support of the Third Estate, which represented ninety-eight per cent of the population. Renamed the National Assembly, it gained widespread support. Furious, Louis ordered the Estates General meeting place closed. Finding the doors barred, the Assembly reconvened to the nearest possible site – a tennis court. What followed was the infamous Oath of the Tennis Court, when delegates swore not to adjourn until they had produced a constitution for France.

The King ordered his Royal Guard to disband the Estates General. The Third Estate protested, and progressive nobles like General Lafayette and the comte de Mirabeau lent their support to the deputies. Louis, facing further insubordination from his own troops, secretly hired sixteen extra regiments, made up largely of Swiss and German mercenaries. But it was his sacking of Necker, the popular Finance Minister who had given millions of his own money to alleviate France's financial problems, that was to be the last straw. News of his dismissal spread throughout the capital. On 12 July 1789 tens of thousands of people carrying busts of their hero and that of the popular Philippe Égalité, the King's cousin, marched through the streets. Mobs grabbed ammunition from the Hôtel de Ville, while the newly formed National Guards were massing. Two days later, on 14 July, the mob marched on that symbol of royal despotism, the Bastille prison. The Revolution had begun.

In the Caribbean, slaves interpreted the French Revolution largely through its willingness to debate abolition and the colonial question, and they embraced it in this light. But this sometimes fostered misunderstandings. Slaves believed that the Revolution was anti-slavery long before it actually was. (The revolutionaries often encouraged these misunderstandings, presenting reforms as being more significant than they really were, in order to garner support.) Certainly the Revolution's threat to Caribbean slavery was both ideological and political. In the realm of ideas, it proclaimed an inspirational doctrine of liberty and equality, which belatedly came to include anti-racism, from 1792, and then anti-slavery, from 1794. The Revolution weakened the white power structure of the colonies by causing conflict, whilst the war split the population into factions.

By the time revolution broke out on the streets of Paris in 1789, angry colonists and alarmed officials were complaining that anti-slavery literature was circulating in the British and French West Indies, attracting the excited attention of slaves. Incautious table-talk by colonists, dockside conversations with newly arrived seamen and overly optimistic letters from slaves abroad were further sources of information and misinformation regarding anti-slavery. Like Chinese whispers, they spread amongst the slave population, and Caribbean blacks were more aware than ever that cracks were appearing in what formerly had seemed to be the impenetrable structure of white rule.

An official in Martinique wrote, 'All the writing in favour of freedom of blacks . . . ends up with us. The masters who talk indiscreetly in front of their slaves, they communicate with their friends; there lies the origin of all this ferment.'[10] The ideas of freedom fomented in the heads of the slave population. A rumour spread across the region that an emancipation law had been passed in France and Louis XVI had proclaimed their liberty. This erroneous belief was created in part by Necker's speech of 5 May 1789, in which he said, 'The day is coming where . . . you will extend a look of compassion . . . on the unfortunate people who are victims of the barbarous slave trade.'[11]

However naive it might seem, enslaved men and women were willing to believe talk of abolition, not only because it fulfilled their deepest aspirations but also because contemporary developments combined to give it an air of plausibility. Both before and after the 1789 attempts to reform the slave trade, the planters' negative press signalled to the slaves that they had potential allies. Reports of the initial phases of the French Revolution also encouraged the slaves' expectations of radical change. Though the news of the July uprising took months to reach the island, the new mood in France swept through the Caribbean. Martinique was the first of the islands to explode into conflict.

Trouble began with minor insubordination among slaves. It escalated on 31 August into a full-blown revolt in the city of Saint-Pierre, where slaves, armed with machetes and hoes, went on the rampage. Agitation spread, and among the white population there was general fear of 'grand carnage'. By May 1790 the island was seething with unrest. News from Fort-Royal only increased the fear in sleepy Trois-Îlets. Rose's uncle baron Tascher, the port commander, was taken hostage during negotiations with rioting slaves. The insurgents had also seized the fort and threatened to bombard Fort-Royal.

It was the hurricane season; the atmosphere was oppressive and humid, intensifying the sense of threat. Whereas the disturbances in France were only distant rumours to Rose, the troubles in Martinique seemed to be encroaching ever nearer. Martinique was a small place. Every story was retold and its ramifications discussed, and the white population's paranoia was soon at fever pitch. Rose, fearful for Hortense, decided it was time to leave the island.

Late summer 1790 found Rose at Government House in Fort-Royal, a guest of the governor. She spent her time attempting to negotiate their passages back to France. One day, accompanied by Hortense and Euphémie, she started across the Savannah (the rectangular grassy square around which Fort-Royal was designed, and where her statue is now erected). She was familiar with every inch of this ground. She had crossed it virtually every day when she was at boarding school, and in her subsequent stays in the capital. But all of a sudden their stroll was interrupted by a cannon shot landing at their feet. Terrified and panicking they ran into a ship's captain who offered them passage on his frigate, the *Sensible*. Rose immediately accepted, and, without luggage or the opportunity to bid farewell to the family, set off in haste for the ship.

Rose's feelings on her journey back to France must have been ambivalent. The Martinique of her memory had been easier and more idyllic than the island ever was in real life. And the hostility of the slaves – the majority of the population – perhaps made Rose feel that she didn't belong, had never fully belonged, to her island. But perhaps it was not so much the island that had changed, but Rose herself. She was too much of a Parisian now to be able to fully readjust to Martinique's slower rhythms and its lack of urgency. It was like swapping the Comédie Français for some small provincial theatre.

Had she stayed, she would always have felt as if she were missing something. Hers was the migrant's dilemma: she didn't fully belong to her new life, but had changed too much to ever go back home.

As the ship moved out to sea, the rebellious slaves attempted – unsuccessfully – to fire on the retreating vessel. On board, too, conditions were difficult. Rose was forced to plunder the ship's store to supplement her non-existent wardrobe. This lack of appropriate attire was a game to little Hortense, the pet of all the other travellers, who delighted in the makeshift shoes created for her by the crew.

Meanwhile, back in Martinique, the response to the slave uprising was prompt and brutal; an indication of the fear that it inspired in the slave-owners. The slaves involved were arrested, and the ringleaders sentenced to be publicly beaten to death, their severed heads displayed on posts at major crossroads on the island, their bodies jettisoned as roadside rubbish. Rose would have been unaware of this as the ship crossed the Atlantic. When she landed at Toulon several weeks later, she was unaware too that she would never see her homeland again.

Eight

REVOLUTION

In that time of horrible memory every French person
was either an accomplice or a victim.

COMTESSE DE BOHM

THE *SENSIBLE* ARRIVED IN THE deep, sheltered bay of Toulon late in the evening of 29 October 1790. Rose, Hortense and Euphémie were bedraggled and exhausted. It had been a stormy, fifty-two-day crossing culminating in a near-collision in the Straits of Gibraltar during which the ship nearly ran aground and capsized. But as soon as they had regained their land legs, the trio began the arduous 500-mile journey to the capital. They found a country transformed. Every village through which they passed was marked by the momentous events of the Revolution. Relics of the summer celebrations of the first aniversary of the fall of the Bastille, 'the great federal day', lingered everywhere: towns were still festooned with drooping banners, battered triumphal arches and faded window-garlands. Most had erected 'patriotic altars' with the inscription, 'the citizen is born, lives and dies for the nation'. In every public square and village green stood the ubiquitous 'trees of liberty', decorated with the cap of liberty and tricolour ribbons, symbolizing that community's commitment to the Revolution.

Paris too had changed. There was a heap of rubble where the Bastille had once stood and ominous graffiti was scrawled on walls. The most startling legacy of the summer of 1789 was the presence of Lafayette's National Guard, cocky young men who strutted through the streets sporting revolutionary cockades, intimidating potential opponents and maintaining good revolutionary order. The atmosphere of 'hope and joy' that had animated the city since late 1789 had grown a little stale, but Revolution was still very much the fashion. Thomas Jefferson recorded that the city, once 'gay and thought-less', had become 'a furnace of Politics' where 'men, women and children talked of nothing else'.[1] 'Republicanism is absolutely a moral influenza,' wrote another visitor, 'from which neither titles, palaces, nor even the diadem can guard their possessor.'[2] In the salons women like Stéphanie de Genlis – displaying an early example of radical chic nestling in her plunging cleavage in the form of a pendant made of a polished piece of Bastille stone – fervently debated the Republic. The brightly coloured wall posters that decorated the city now advertised the promises of the various political factions. On the streets, hawkers sold revolutionary souvenirs, including miniature Bastilles and clay busts of revolutionary heroes like Lafayette and Marat. In the cafés, the populace could choose from any of the dozen new pamphlets and 335 newspapers printed daily that now flooded the capital. Their fiery rhetoric fuelled the diatribes of coffee-house orators, street-corner demagogues and casual conversation.

Convinced that the 'fraternal millennium' had finally dawned, foreigners flocked to the city in order 'to drink at the fountain of freedom'. Despite the destruction and violence of the fall of the Bastille, there was still, for many, 'a sense of something utterly new coming into being, some fresh, immense possibility of political life, a new community of hope'.[3] As Words-worth wrote of 1790, the year that Rose returned, ''Twas a time when Europe was rejoiced, France standing at the top of golden hours, And human nature seeming born again.' Tourists and sympathizers like Wordsworth 'eagerly picked up pieces of stone from the prison rubble to bequeath to their children' and 'Bastille keys were carried across Europe as the insignia of Revolution; Chateaubriand even took one to the governor of Newfoundland, while another reached Jefferson's house in Virginia'.[4] The revolutionary wind had begun to blow. No one then knew the extent of the devastation this particular hurricane would wreak.

At the centre of this unfolding drama stood Alexandre. During Rose's sojourn in Martinique he had virtually abandoned his military career to further his political one. When Louis XVI had called the historic meeting of the Estates General in the summer of 1789, Alexandre, along with all those with political ambitions, decided to stand for election. He was selected as a deputy to represent Blois, his ancestral town, and joined the forum of the Estates General. There he allied himself alongside his mentor, the duc de La Roche-foucauld, and other liberal nobles. When that June the Estates General unilaterally reconstituted itself into a permanent body with the power to make laws and renamed itself the National Assembly (sometimes known as the Constituent Assembly), Alexandre's circle was euphoric.

These were heady days for Alexandre, as they were for all his young compatriots, fired with passionate zeal for the Revolution. They were Plato's philosopher-kings, shaping the great agendas of revolutionary thought. They were the liberal elite who were going to pry the country out of its long wallow in the muddy sty of tradition. They were going to liberate the world from superstition and inequality, and deliver in its place a golden age of brotherhood and reason. Change was no longer a dream: Frenchmen now felt they had the chance to end the deadlock of privilege, raise the poor out of misery and end all kinds of slavery. The idea of a future that could be shaped was a new intoxication. History had become something they could almost grasp in their hands.

Alexandre and his fellow deputies, busy drafting the much longed-for constitution, had had their idealistic debates interrupted by the pivotal events of 14 July. The catalyst for this explosion of violence was provided by two rumours: the first that the King intended to suspend the National Assembly, the second that he planned to exile Jacques Necker, the financier in whom the people had genuine confidence. When the armed mob of 100,000 men and women stormed the Bastille, murdering its governor and releasing its inmates, far from the deputies at Versailles being upset, Alexandre and his comrades were overcome with joy, crying out in glee and throwing their hats in the air.

The euphoria of this watershed moment was somewhat dimmed by the months of rioting and violence that followed. These reached a climax on 5 October when angry women gathered at the Hôtel de Ville to protest about the price and scarcity of bread, then set out for Versailles to confront the King. By the evening the palace was under attack and numerous members of the Royal Guard had been killed. Engulfed by the hungry and angry of Paris, the King agreed to approve the Declaration of the Rights of Man and the abolition of feudalism. The terrified royal family was escorted back to the capital by a drunken mob bearing the heads of the guards on pikes, and then consigned to virtual imprisonment at the Tuileries. The violence precipitated the first wave of emigration: many of those who could afford to leave fled the country, taking with them tales of brutality and disorder. But others firmly believed that the bloodletting was a necessary benediction of change and that the Revolution was all but over.

During these tumultuous months Alexandre's status grew. In November 1789 he was elected as one of the three Secretaries to the Assembly; one month later he was appointed to the military committee. He proposed an ambitious project: the democratic reorganization of both the army and the militia. His plan, which suggested the King be deprived of military command, brought him into conflict with his devoutly royalist elder brother, also a deputy, and François became known as 'Beauharnais without amendment' to distinguish him from his brother.

Alexandre was active in shaping the agenda of revolutionary thought. He spoke and wrote on subjects as disparate as universal male suffrage, the abolition of privileges, a new criminal code inspired by English jurisprudence, education, the press, religion and the plight of the Jews. These great ideological discussions of the first National Assembly formed the climax of the eighteenth-century Enlightenment. They led to sweeping and fundamental changes that were embodied in a number of radical decrees. During the first six months of 1790 the National Assembly passed laws for the suppression of primogeniture and solely masculine inheritance, abolition of a hereditary nobility, the sale of Church property and the establishment of a civil constitution for the clergy.

The liberal nobility seemed determined to surrender its privileges. Alexandre and his comrades, including the vicomte Matthieu de Montmorency, Prince Victor de Broglie, the duc d'Aiguillon, the marquis de Montesquiou and the duc d'Orléans, tripped over one another in their enthusiasm to deprive themselves and their caste of the rights that had long preserved their wealth and power. Titles were abolished. Military, government and Church positions were no longer the preserve of the well born, and their pensions and salaries were opened up for inspection by the Assembly. Careers in the Church, an established alternative for the aristocracy, lost their lustre as tithes were banned and priests were restricted to one benefice, so dramatically reducing their income.

By the time Rose returned to France in October 1790, the antics of the National Assembly had become the nation's favourite entertainment and its deputies had become stars. Alexandre, who had been elected president of the Assembly in the month of Rose's return, was one of its most glittering prizes, particularly admired for his passionate oratory. His personality was ideally suited to this role; as his friend the marquis de Bouillé wrote, 'M. de Beauharnais possessed energy, a stubbornness of disposition, a depth of intelligence, a longing to win fame, and an overpowering ambition.' Bouillé felt that Alexandre's political aspirations were fired by wounded pride and the frustrated ambitions typical of many members of the petty nobility. 'These disadvantages tormented his vanity, and perhaps contributed to his decision to ally himself with the enemies of the court and join with the voices of the Revolution.'[5]

Alexandre's new political role was immensely gratifying to his considerable ego. 'To be a deputy was quite à la mode', remarked baron Frenilly. He characterized the delegates as the sort of men who were 'eager for agitation and noise . . . To be surrounded, listened to and believed' was, he felt, 'what they really wanted.'[6] The Assembly, which had relocated to the former riding school of the Tuileries, rivalled the theatre in popularity, despite the pervasive smell of horses and urine. It had become one of the fashionable places to see and be seen. Women like Rose and Aunt Fanny queued to watch the debates, scrutinize each other's outfits and swoon over the orators. Deputies like Alexandre 'were welcomed everywhere and fêted everywhere as the masters and arbiters of France'.

Bouillé's assessment of Alexandre was a bit harsh, reflecting the jaded views of a conservative looking back with the wisdom of hindsight. Without doubt Alexandre enjoyed the attention; he was nothing if not vain. But he was also genuinely committed and impassioned. Politics and Enlightenment ideas had fascinated him since boyhood, and their transformation into revolution had given meaning to a life that might otherwise have been squandered on an endless round of dissipation and meaningless pleasures. Like others, he was swept along in the vision of a new age, intoxicated by the free exchange of ideas. As Germaine de Staël rhapsodized, 'One breathed more easily, there was more air in one's chest and an unlimited hope for unfettered happiness had forcefully taken hold of the nation, as it takes hold of men in their youth, with illusion and without caution.'[7]

Alexandre's political prominence changed Rose's life, too. She was now married to a celebrity. Even in sleepy Fontainebleau, where she was staying, his name provoked a frisson of excitement. But there was little time to bask in his reflected glory, for shortly after her return she received news that her father had died. (He would be followed a year later by her ailing sister, Manette). Her grief prompted a few reclusive weeks, but it was soon clear to her that the shifting sands of the Revolution made social rehabilitation necessary and desirable.

Rose had good reasons to flee the safety of the suburbs. The domesticity of her little haven in Fontainebleau was beginning to feel constraining. The health of both the marquis and Aunt Edmée was deteriorating and their social life was even more limited than in the past. Rose was an attractive single woman who was perhaps ready to move on from grieving for her failed marriage. She definitely wanted to be near Eugène, who was currently enrolled at the Collège d'Harcourt in Paris. She had also found a good school for Hortense there; not yet eight, she was sent to the Abbaye-aux-Bois, which was run by Bernardine sisters. It was a happy family reunion, since Rose was close to both her children, and she wanted to give Hortense and Eugène the opportunity to be together again after two years apart.

No doubt Rose, like everyone else, also wanted to be in the city where history was being forged. Momentous events were happening and she wouldn't have wanted to sit them out in some backwater. Her husband's social position made the city more alluring: the couple might be estranged but they were still married, and the name Beauharnais now opened many doors. Rose visited the city with increasing frequency, staying at the home of her brother-in-law, François de Beauharnais, in his residence in the rue des Mathurins. Within a few months she had largely shifted her base to Paris.

In order to survive in this new revolutionary environment, Rose needed to reinvent herself once again. With the extraordinary adaptability that characterized her throughout her life, she confronted the challenge of refashioning herself as a *citoyenne* (citizenness). There was a lot to learn: a new revolutionary language was emerging, new phrasings were coined and old words were yoked to strange new meanings. (As Arthur Young wrote,' 'Making a constitution is a new term they have adopted . . . as if a constitution was a pudding to be made by recipe.') The working people of Paris were calling themselves sans-culottes, (without breeches). The word 'aristocratic' no longer applied to a class but to anything that was counter-revolutionary: hence aristocratic food, books, plays, modes of speech and hairstyles. Its opposite, 'patriot', no longer referred to a lover of the country but to a devotee of the Revolution. So it was possible to be an 'aristocratic' maid or a 'patriotic' duke. (Or would have been had hereditary titles not been abolished in the summer of 1790.) In December 1790 an article in the *Mercure* suggested the banning of the singular *vous*. Soon after, Rose noticed that even the flower girls were addressing her as *tu*, rejecting *vous* as aristocratic. With the introduction of *tutoiement* it seemed that the final social distinction had fallen. But more change was still to come. By autumn 1792 everyone was addressed as *citoyen* or *citoyenne*. Rose's enthusiastic adoption of revolutionary behavioural codes offended some of her acquaintances, who found her just a little too adaptable: 'She was not at all averse to following the requirements of the times,' sniffed one contemporary, 'and those times required one to flaunt the language and the behaviour of the common people.'[8]

Rose also needed a new wardrobe: most of her clothes had been left behind in her hasty departure from Martinique and those that survived were now unsuitable. For it was in fashion that the order of society was most visibly turned upside down. By the summer of 1790 the *Chronique de Paris* was already urging that distinguishing marks of rank such as expensive 'aristocratic' fashions should be banned. Extravagant displays of jewellery and costume were out. The only embellishments encouraged were 'patriotic' ones, like Mme de Genlis's locket of Bastille stone, fans depicting the feast of the federation, or, later, guillotine earrings. Women were encouraged to demonstrate their patriotic zeal by wearing native fabrics of comparative simplicity, and the fashionable colours were the red, white and blue of the tricolour. The clothes themselves were simple: a jacket and skirt, accompanied by a matching gilet, with a shawl draped around the shoulders. The intricate coiffures of the ancien régime had given way to simple, unpowdered styles adorned by patriotic headwear such as bonnets '*à la Bastille*' or the '*bonnet à l'américaine*'. Fashion magazines of 1791 and 1792 show how the overcast mood in politics and society is reflected in dress. 'Simplicity in dress is fashionable, as well as a corresponding sobriety in manners; it is no longer the vogue to have a "pleasant, soft or frivolous air", but to have a "firm manner, a head held high, a brisk walk, a little chatter" . . .'[9]

Creoles like Rose were in an ambivalent position during the Revolution. Those from the sugar colonies had traditionally been associated with wealth and privilege, and therefore met with some hostility, especially as the Revolution became increasingly radical. Rose's friend Mme Hosten, an ardent revolutionary, decided to leave the city when she was abused on the street by a hostile crowd who cried that she should 'take her indigo and her sugar-loaves with her and go back where she belonged'. Rose made the sensible decision to describe herself as an 'American', a general term for people from either the Antilles or the American continent. It avoided the connotations of wealth and conservatism associated with 'Creole' and evoked all the republican dreams of the New World.

Rose's own political feelings were rather tepid. She had been raised by her conservative, colonial parents to be a royalist, but her marriage to Alexandre and exposure to his Enlightenment circles had had an impact. By the dawn of the Revolution she was inevitably associated with her husband's views, and was described by a contemporary as a 'constitutional monarchist'. Whether she would have owned this categorization or not, Rose certainly enjoyed the stimulation of the privileged political circles in which her estranged husband moved, even while apparently eschewing any strong opinions of her own. Hiding behind her languorous Creole mask, she once drawled, 'You know, I'm too indolent to take sides.' In an age where the political landscape was shifting so rapidly, and where the wrong political allegiance was potentially fatal, this was probably a judicious position to take. Certainly it was true that Rose had little interest in the grand ideas and theories of the period. As her friend Mme de Rémusat wrote about her in later years, 'Her attention wandered from any discussion of abstract ideas.' All her life she would be more interested in people than in politics. She was an instinctive political chameleon who found it expedient to exploit her own indifference to traverse the great political shifts of her era.

Alexandre was at the pinnacle of his revolutionary career in 1791 as the president of the Assembly. He was in the chair on the morning of 21 June when reports came in that the royal family had fled the city. Alexandre's announcement was a model of understatement: 'Messieurs, the King has fled during the night. Let us proceed to the order of the day.'[10]

The royal plot to flee revolutionary France (organized in part by Marie Antoinette's lover, Count Fersen), seemed jinxed from the start. Unable to extricate herself from some interminable court ceremony, the Queen arrived late at the midnight rendezvous. Travelling in a lumbering green-and-black Berlin with a white velvet interior, the royal family – disguised as servants – made slow progress as they trundled through north-western France. A broken harness had to be mended; the courier lost his head. By the time the royal party arrived in the 'miserable little town' of Varennes, they were two hours behind schedule and the entire country was on the alert. Their escape attempt was ultimately foiled by a lowly ostler who confronted Louis XVI with a coin bearing his image and asked him whether he was King. Intercepted at last, the royal family had travelled 165 miles from inept beginning to blundering end.

The flight of the King enraged the populace. They felt betrayed; the King had 'deserted his post'. The National Assembly was put on red alert. Crowds tore through the Parisian streets smashing shop and inn signs that bore the fleur-de-lis. Some joker posted a sign outside the Tuileries saying

'House to Let'. Six thousand angry people surrounded the royal party on the first stage of their journey home. The next day, escorted by three representatives from the National Assembly and a contingent of troops, they began the journey towards the capital. As they approached Paris, the mood became funereally sombre. A widely posted sign warned, 'Anyone who applauds the King will be beaten, anyone who insults him will be hanged.' On a day of blazing heat, the King re-entered Paris. The Berlin, filled with choking dust from the road, revealed through a window the lined, harried face of Marie Antoinette. Silent, sullen crowds lined the route. Their hats remained firmly on their heads as a sign of disrespect and displeasure.

This was a watershed moment for Alexandre. He was the master of the hour, organizing the pursuit of the fugitives and overseeing their capture, arrest and return. He also presided over a remarkable 126-hour session of debates that began with the King's flight and ended with news of the royal party's capture on 27 June. Alexandre reacted to the collective hysteria with coolness and firmness. He wrote to his father, 'I am overwhelmed with fatigue, but I found the energy and courage in the hope that . . . I could serve the public good and maintain the peace of the realm.'[11]

The King's flight was a turning point of the Revolution, polarizing the situation irrevocably. The constitutionalists, or Feuillant party (named after the former convent in which they met) were inextricably associated with the king and thus defended him, but for many, like the young Napoleone Buonaparte (as he was still called), the monarch's betrayal undermined the idea of a viable active constitutional monarchy and they converted to republicanism. In the Assembly, moderates like Lafayette found their stars waning. They were opposed by an increasingly vociferous 'left', those who had crossed the floor to sit on the left of the podium. The 'left' was made up of an uneasy coalition between the Girondists (so named because of the region from which they came) and the Jacobins, who took their name from the working-men's club where they met. (In the Assembly the latter were nicknamed the 'Mountain' because of their habit of sitting high up against the wall to the left of the president.) The Jacobins were led by a formidable triumvirate: the scrofulous Jean-Paul Marat, founder of the extremist journal *L'ami du peuple*, who had long since named Louis and Marie Antoinette enemies of the people; the mighty orator Danton, unmistakable for his battered face – he had been trampled by pigs as a child – which he described as having 'the rough features of liberty'; and the cold, cat-like Robespierre, who never appeared without his hair impeccably coiffed and powdered. It was to this radical faction that Alexandre now allied himself.

The political tension increased on Sunday 17 July 1791 when a peaceful gathering on the Champs de Mars to sign a republican petition was fired on by the National Guard. When the smoke cleared there were more than fifty dead and hundreds injured; martial law was proclaimed. The authorities were fearful of retaliatory violence from the populace, and over the next couple of weeks they went after extremist leaders. Danton fled to England; Robespierre and the other Jacobin leaders went into hiding in Paris; militant clubs were harassed and radical newspapers suppressed. By the end of the month the situation had settled down somewhat, although the King was now routinely referred to by the gutter press as 'Louis the false' or 'the Fat Pig', while Marie Antoinette was dubbed 'the Austrian she-wolf'. Alexandre was elected president of the National Assembly again on 31 July 1791, and he guided the Constitution to its completion. This gave the King the right of veto, confiscated all church property and ensured a single legislative Assembly elected by about three-quarters of adult males. On 14 September, when the King pledged his oath of allegiance to the new Constitution, those in the Assembly and those on the streets cried out, 'The Revolution is ended!' and celebrated with fireworks and parties.

At this time, Alexandre's political importance was such that his portrait was hung alongside that of Robespierre in that year's Salon, the annual exhibition of the nation's best art. Rose found herself married to the de facto ruler of France. His children, Eugène and Hortense, recalled that the crowds in Fontainebleau, where they stayed during their school holidays, would call to them, 'There go the dauphin and the dauphiness!'[12] But Alexandre's triumph was short-lived. In a rather short-sighted move by the Constituent Assembly, the first-wave members made themselves ineligible to stand for subsequent legislatures, and he would never again hold such an exalted position.

Rose passed most of the summer of 1791 in Fontainebleau with her children. In October she moved to a hotel at 43 rue Saint-Dominique, where she shared costs with its owner, her friend Mme Hosten. The two women had much in common: they were both Creoles born and brought up in the Caribbean, their husbands were absent and both had children. Marie-Françoise Hosten-Lamotte was a mother of three: two sons currently in St Lucia and a daughter of thirteen, Désirée, who would become very close to

Hortense. The two girls spent much of their time devising little theatricals to perform for their mothers. Mme Hosten introduced Rose into the wider Creole circles in Paris and also some of the royalist ones in which she had a toehold. She frequently invited Rose to spend weekends at her country house in Croissy.

This friendship became Rose's emotional anchor and lasted throughout the Revolution. Although history has depicted Rose as a woman who lived for and through men, in reality she valued female friendship and nurtured and sustained loyal relationships with women.

In retrospect, the middle of a Revolution seems a strange time for Rose to launch herself as an independent woman on the Parisian scene. But at the time it made sense. The atmosphere in the city was so calm that many believed the Revolution was over. Baron de Frenilly wrote in the spring of 1791 that 'A sort of halt or truce appeared to have taken place in the Revolution – the mass of citizens said: "All's well! The Revolution is over; let us enjoy ourselves and rest." A foreigner might have thought that France was the most peaceable country in Europe . . .'[13]

Life was full of hope for Rose. Her children were at school; she was free of the constraints imposed by the presence of her formidable husband; she was totally independent. The ambitions she had nourished for such a long time – to frequent good society, to dress in the latest fashions, to taste luxury, to ornament the salons of Paris about which all the world talked, to see a court of admirers at her feet, to enjoy all the pleasures that ancien-régime society had offered – seemed on the brink of satisfaction. But this brilliant, colourful, amiable society was in its last act. The winter season of 1791–92 was, according to one observer, as 'joyous and brillant as though people were accumulating joy to last them all the time they were to sorrow . . . We continued to dance as they do in camp on the eve of a battle; and Paris gave herself up to games and pleasures.'[14]

In her attempt to enter this dying world Rose found that the recent upheavals had worked in her favour. The turmoil of the Revolution, and its resultant emigrations, meant that society was slightly more fluid than previously. The bourgeoisie mingled with those of good birth and the doors of the great were opened to Rose. She became close friends with princesse Amélie of Hohenzollern-Sigmaringen, who lived with her brother, the prince de Salm-Kyrbourg, in a magnificent hotel, now the palace of the Légion d'Honneur. She was one of the few women in Paris who still preferred to gossip about fashion and love rather than politics. A rather shallow woman, she would later offer Rose and Alexandre proof of a friendship that was enduring and profound.

The prince de Salm also proved a loyal ally. German by birth but long resident in France, his wealth and nobility had earned him great favour at court. But his reputation was dubious. It was said that he had once worn a concealed breastplate during a duel – very dishonourable – and had attempted to stab his adversary once he was on the ground. Thomas Jefferson concluded that he was 'a prince without talents, without courage and without principles'. In 1789 the prince started moving to the left and his magnificent mansion became a gathering place for constituents like Alexandre. The Hôtel de Salm, a building destined to become a Paris landmark, was inspired by the neoclassical designs of Rousseau. It combined the suave elegance of the French hôtel with the monumental grandeur of the antique world. Situated on the Left Bank, it is dominated by a Roman triumphal arch, framing an inner courtyard surrounded by a colonnaded peristyle. It was in these magnificent surroundings that Rose and Alexandre spent much of their time during the early months of the Revolution.

They also paid numerous visits to Aunt Fanny's latest salon, her third, which had relocated to the beautiful hôtel in rue Tournon previously occupied by the duc de Brancas. Her Friday gathering was described as 'the egg of the National Assembly'. Here the seeds were nurtured which would fertilize public opinion and produce the fruits of liberty. Her 'brilliant and lively circle' included her lover, the poet Cubières, luminaries such as the encyclopedist Marmontel and the author Choderlos de Laclos, famous hostesses like Mme du Deffand and Mme d'Houdetot and a sprinkling of well-known and highly decorative young beauties. The Rose who descended the grand marble staircase that led to Fanny's blue-and-gold apartment was not the timid girl who had been so intimidated in her earlier years. She had metamorphosed into a glittering butterfly who flitted with ease through this illustrious company. Both sexes found her seductive and gracious. Men admired her amber eyes, her flawless skin, the perfection of her arms, the sensual aura that radiated from her person. Women enjoyed the sweetness of her manner.

It was in this varied milieu that Rose met all the stars of the Revolution. They included the comte de Mirabeau, who once declared that his ugliness was his greatest weapon (he would die after a vigorous ménage à trois with two beautiful opera girls and posthumously be exposed as a royalist spy); Talleyrand, the aristocratic bishop turned revolutionary who would play such an influential role in the career of her second husband; and Lafayette, hero of the War of American Independence and founder of the National Guard, whose pompousness was such that he was once described as a statue in search of a pedestal. The latter held 'American dinners' on Mondays, to which he invited any representatives of the American government currently visiting the city, from Jefferson to Franklin. On these occasions everyone spoke English and talked of events past and present in America, land of the free and democratic. Rose even formed an attachment to Charlotte Robespierre, who gave her a small miniature of herself as a token of their friendship. For Germaine de Staël, Parisian society from 1788 to 1792 was a golden age. 'Those who lived at that time cannot prevent themselves from admitting that one has never seen both so much life and so much intellect anywhere else.'[15]

Because of their overlapping social circles, it was inevitable that Rose and Alexandre would meet frequently. As a result, some of her more sentimental biographers have claimed that the couple were rapturously reunited during these years. In one particularly sweet story little Hortense – dressed in a miniature costume '*américain*' – is said to have brought the two together for a candle-lit dinner at the home of one M. de Montmorin. But Rose and Alexandre were not reconciled. Without doubt the détente that they had reached before her departure for Martinique was sustained. Their genuine concern for their children helped to ensure this. But there is no evidence that the pair ever cohabited again.

Alexandre's romantic life was as frantic as ever; his political prominence only aided his pursuit of the eligible women of Paris. Rose too had her romances. And why not? She was twenty-seven years old, very publicly separated from her husband, whose own affairs were notorious, and free to do as she pleased. She was linked first with Scipion du Roure, a young and handsome naval officer, whom she had met on board the *Sensible* during the crossing from Martinique. With his 'Roman features, his elegance and his gallantry',[16] he was said to be captivating. Many years later Horace de Viel-Castel would claim that his father, then an officer in the Dragoons, had had an affair with Rose before her marriage to Napoleon. There were others; a long list of men boasted that they had sought and obtained her favours. It is not altogether clear how many of these claims were fuelled by the desire of her male contemporaries to brag of a romance with one of the great beauties of the age, but certainly Rose enjoyed a number of dalliances at this time.

In later years Rose's reputation was battered by accusations of *galanterie* (easy morals) and gold-digging. But these slurs were usually made by Napoleon's enemies, who hoped to besmirch his standing by destroying hers. Others wished to enhance their own romantic status. (Almost every man who crossed her path, even in childhood, would claim her as a lover.) Many of her own biographers, writing from the perspective of the austere morals of the Victorian age, have felt it necessary either to censor Rose or to protect her, by editing accounts of her life according to their own agenda. It is hard, amongst all this misinformation, to get a clear picture of Rose's love life. But it is safe to assume that fewer men bedded her than claimed to have done, and that this is more than some people would have liked. Rose was a woman of her age and class and, like her famous contemporaries Germaine de Staël and Mme de Genlis, she was a passionate and sensual woman at a time when sexual pleasure was celebrated rather than repressed.

Rose was not the only woman to be emboldened by the turbulence of the times. In many ways Paris seemed a good place to be female. France was the only country in Europe where '*la question des femmes*' had been consistently debated for many years. The terms of the debate had been laid down by women like Marie le Jars de Gournay, the adopted daughter of Montaigne. Fiercely independent, she eschewed 'feminine' frills and furbelows and refused to adopt the submissive or ingratiating manners associated with traditional female behaviour. The author of *Égalite des Hommes et des Femmes* (1622) and *Grief des Dames* (1626), she was a relentless campaigner against any notion that women were 'naturally' inferior.

In the later years of the ancien régime, at the time of Rose's arrival in France, the position of women was still a topic of sustained and intense interest. Rose was no intellectual but she could not avoid getting caught up in these debates, especially since Aunt Fanny was one of the era's most fervent advocates of women's rights. As early as 1773 she had published a short pamphlet on the subject, addressed, 'To all those who think, salute!' Once the idea of political and social equality had been conceived, it could not fail to lead to the demand for equal treatment for women. As the marquis de Condorcet concluded in 1790, 'Either not a single individual of the species has any true rights or else all have the same . . .'

Condorcet was not a lone male voice in supporting female emancipation. Significant thinkers like Jeremy Bentham, Frederich Schlegel and Theodor Gottlieb von Heppel were among the men who helped to propagate the movement. French feminism was deeply entangled with the ideologies of the Revolution. The Dutch émigré Baroness Etta d'Aelders had published a tract suggesting that women's clubs should be set up to help the Revolution. By 1791 Olympe de Gouges published her answer to the Declaration of the Rights of Man, entitled *Déclaration des droits de la femme and de la citoyenne*, which demanded civil and political liberty for women. It stated unequivocally, 'Woman is born free and her rights are the same as those of a man.'[17]

On the streets, women were fully involved in revolutionary activism. It was a woman, Théroigne de Méricourt, who led the storming of the Bastille. Dressed in her man's clothes, plumed hat and swirling blood-red cape, the magnificent 'she-soldier' and idol of the political clubs seemed to many the archetype of a sexually and politically liberated woman. De Mericourt, who had been born into a well-to-do family and become a successful court-esan, was also highly visible on the 'Day of the Market Women', the march to Versailles that escorted the King back to the royal residence. Three years later, seated on her jet-black horse, she led a company of women in the assault on the Tuileries.

As Théroigne de Méricourt stalked the streets, so Manon Roland domi-nated the salons. The wife of a serious-minded and much older civil servant, Jean-Marie Roland de La Platière, she was a self-taught intellectual who – writing usually under her husband's name – worked behind the scenes shaping and influencing revolutionary policy for moderates of the Girondist party. She was passionate about the revolutionary cause: 'We can be regenerated by blood alone,' she wrote. For a brief, heady moment, dangerous women like these emerged and thrived. Sharing the limelight were women like Pauline Léon, the chocolatier's daughter who led the Society of Revolutionary Republicans, a radical and combative faction that made its rowdy presence felt on the Parisian streets, and her compatriot in arms, the statuesque actress Claire Lacombe, who always signed her name, 'Lacombe, free woman'.

The efforts of this diverse group of highly visible women helped to draw the concerns of the neglected female onto the revolutionary agenda. By the end of 1792, after vociferous debate, the age of marriage without parental consent was lowered from thirty to twenty-one and marriage was made into a civil contract. Divorce became obtainable by mutual consent. There were even plans to appoint women as civil servants. France had become the centre of women's aspirations for emancipation. Unsurprisingly Mary Wollstone-craft, author of the celebrated *Vindication of the Rights of Woman*, was initially a fervent supporter of the Revolution and attracted to the ferment of possi-bilities that was Paris; she moved there in December 1792.

★

But months before Wollstonecraft arrived the political scene had begun to darken. On 12 April 1792 France declared war on Austria. The fear of invasion forced the pace of internal conflict, prompting a flurry of political explosions. Five days later the guillotine was wheeled out for the first time. On 20 June a mob invaded the Tuileries and held the King hostage for four hours, forcing him to wear the red bonnet of liberty and drink the health of the nation. On 25 July the duke of Brunswick – who had been leading Austrian and Prussian troops through a series of easy victories against the disorganized and poorly armed French troops – issued a manifesto declaring that he was fighting to restore the power of the King and the Church and threatening to lay waste to France in punishment for the Revolution and to execute the entire population of Paris if the royal family was threatened again. The proclamation was in every newspaper and pamphlet. People could talk of little else and there were calls for the King's immediate abdication.

By August, house searches – or 'domiciliary visits' as they were known – led to thousands of arrests. Designed to generate the maximum fear, they were normally conducted late at night or in the early hours of the morning by ten or more people invading the victims' home with guns, sabres and pikes. Crowds roamed the streets singing the revolutionary anthem, '*Ça Ira*' ('It Will Go On') with its inflammatory lyrics including the line 'We shall hang all the aristocrats.' The atmosphere in the city became so threatening that Rose withdrew her children from school to keep them with her.

On 9 August the tocsin – the bell of alarm – rang out from the churches. Aware that something terrible was about to happen, much of the population hid indoors. The next day crowds gathered early for a mass attack on the Tuileries. Accompanied by the cry 'No aristocrats! No priests! No veto', they marched to the palace. The result was a scene of total carnage. Over five hundred of the King's Swiss National Guard were massacred, their bodies clubbed and stabbed, their genitals hacked off and fed to the palace dogs. The royal family escaped death only because they took refuge in the Assembly building. This bloody insurrection, which became known as the 'Second Revolution', had far-reaching repercussions. The King was suspended from his functions and the royal family were imprisoned in the grim fortress of the Temple, situated in an ancient district not far from the Bastille.

By autumn 1792 the threat of a 'patriotic war' seemed to be terrifyingly near. With the rallying cry of '*le patrie en danger*', Paris was transformed into an armed camp. The streets were the scene of frantic activity, echoing to the sound of marching feet and beating drums. It was widely believed that the enemy was only a few days from the city. The rush to join up was captured in Watteau's painting, *Departure of the Volunteers*, but the new recruits feared leaving the city unprotected. Beset from without, the paranoia switched to 'the enemies within'. Danton's warning that 'there are traitors amongst you' reverberated around the city. The populace feared the counter-revolutionaries, refractory priests, and hidden saboteurs at large within the city. They feared that aristocrats would make common cause with the criminals and take over.

This paranoia about traitors focused on the prison population. Revolutionary rags warned the populace that 'the prisons are full of conspirators . . .', suggesting that the city needed to be purged of all the 'venal priests, gilded aristocrats, diseased whores and court lackeys'.[18] This concern was not without reason: the prisons were intensely overcrowded and their security was lax. Within their walls the atmosphere was tense. Outside, the air stank with fear, anger and the odour of conspiracy. Paris was a powder keg about to blow.

It exploded on 2 September, when the ringing of the tocsin was again the signal for the mob to vent its bloodlust. That morning the volunteers began to gather, then the prisons were attacked. As Rose and her little family cowered indoors, near enough to two prisons to hear the screams and cries, groups of men and women rushed the jail gates armed with muskets, hatchets, pikes, knives, scythes and all the makeshift weaponry of the streets: axes, sabres, even carpentry saws. Once inside, the mob set up ad hoc tribunals and released prisoners with applause and embraces or subjected them to the 'axe of vengeance'. Around 1,600 people were massacred. Amongst the dead were children as young as eight, who proved peculiarly difficult to despatch – 'At that age it is hard to let go of life.'

At the prison of La Force Mme de Lamballe, the alleged lesbian lover of Marie Antoinette, was hacked to death. Her head was placed on a pike and paraded past Marie Antoinette's window so that she could see the macabre remains of her dead friend. The city seemed indelibly splattered with blood: its gutters ran red, its walls were stained scarlet, and women crossing the public squares would find their feet slipping in earth made boggy with blood. No longer could the violence that had plagued the Revolution be described as incidental, an unfortunate by-product of political change. The heads on pikes, the massacres, the beheadings, or indeed the lynchings, stabbings and fatal beatings that fell into the category widely described as 'popular justice', were now a significant feature of daily life. The population had to come to terms with the fact that bloodshed was intrinsic to the Revolution, at its very centre; as the historian Simon Schama puts it, 'It was the source of its energy.'[19]

The September Massacre was a turning point for many. Sickened by the bloodshed, a new wave of emigrants sought sanctuary abroad. Aunt Fanny fled to Italy, while many others went to England, Germany and America. To the revolutionary-minded, the aristocracy's willingness to leave the country rather than submit to a change of government revealed that their real home-land was their class rather than their country. This perception hardened existing antagonisms, radicalizing the Revolution yet further.

Amongst those planning to leave were the friends of Rose and Alexandre, the prince of Salm and his sister Amélie. They offered to take Eugène and Hortense with them; Rose gratefully accepted. They planned to retreat to their estate at Saint-Martin in Artois and wait there for an opportunity to leave France. The children were told only that they were going on a country holiday. Eugène was delighted at the prospect, but little Hortense was miserable; at nine years old she had rarely been separated from her mother. She wrote a beseeching note to which Rose replied, 'I was very pleased with your letter, my dear Hortense; I am touched by your regrets at being away from your mother; but my dear it is not for long. I hope that the princess will return in spring, or I will come and collect you . . . I am so sad at being separated from you . . . I love my little Hortense with all my heart. Hug Eugène for me. Goodbye my child, my little Hortense; I embrace you with all my heart and love you dearly.'[20]

But the reunion came sooner than even Rose had predicted. Alexandre was furious when he heard that Rose had sent the children away. His position in the revolutionary hierarchy had already been made precarious by his older brother, François, who had joined the émigré army under Condé. He feared that if his own children emigrated he would be totally compromised. He insisted that the children be returned immediately. In probably the only unselfish act of his life, the prince de Salm brought the children back to Paris. This act of kindness would have fatal consequences for the prince, who never again got the chance to flee the city. On their return Alexandre insisted that Eugène go to school in Strasbourg, where he was now stationed. Hortense, whose school, like most of the convents in the city, had been closed, would be taught at home by her mother's paid companion, Mlle de Lannoy.

In September 1790 the new *République française* was declared. The popu-lace's celebrations were dampened by unease over the fate of the royal family, still imprisoned in the Temple. Fear hung over the city like a pall. Two months later, on 26 December, the trial of Louis XVI began. The King was accused of treason, a charge supported by the discovery of secret documents purportedly linking him with counter-revolutionary forces. The guilty verdict, delivered on 15 January, was a foregone conclusion. What was vigorously debated, however, was his sentence. After much heated argument and by the slimmest of margins, the newly founded Republic chose regicide.

The execution was scheduled to take place on 21 January in the place de la Révolution, to which the guillotine had recently been moved. People began collecting the night before, when a dusting of snow had fallen. By the following morning there was a huge crowd, excited and solemn, despite the freezing temperatures. While many supported the sentence, all were awed by the momentous event they were about to witness: the execution of a king.

At 10.15 a.m. a closed carriage made its way through the crowd. Louis was wearing grey breeches, grey stockings, a pink waistcoat and a brown silk coat, his hair carefully coiffed. As soon as he stepped out he entered into an altercation with Sanson the executioner, who wished to tie his hands. With his hands free, the King ascended the high platform, crossed himself, pulled off his coat and waistcoat and began speaking – 'My people, I die an innocent man' – before his voice was drowned out by the roll of the drums. His head was placed in the guillotine's lunette. The noise of the crowd swelled to a roar and then fell silent. Sanson signalled to his son, the blade fell, and the crowd bellowed as Louis's head rolled into the basket. Souvenir hunters dipped their handkerchiefs in the blood while the executioner – as was his privilege – launched an immediate auction of the King's effects.

The execution of the King hurtled the country into a new frenzy of insecurity. On 1 February England declared war on France and a series of laws against 'enemy aliens' was promulgated in Paris, beginning with special registration and passport requirements. On 5 February there were food riots in the city, and three weeks later the first loyalist rising in the Vendée began. On 15 April, with growing fears of enemies both abroad and at home, the Committee of Public Safety was instituted. Now the Revolution was threatened by both war and civil war.

France was also having trouble with its sugar colonies. In Martinique, just after Rose's departure, an alleged plot by the population classified as 'coloured' (those of mixed race) was discovered and violently put down by the authorities. On the island of Santo Domingo the countryside was burning. The slaves were in armed revolt, fighting for their freedom. Fierce opposition was provoked by a proposed decree that would emancipate the 'coloured' population in the colonies. At the National Assembly a representative of the settlers declared that his compatriots would never take the law 'from the grandson of one of our slaves. No! Rather die than assent to this infamy . . . If France sends troops for the execution of this decree, it is likely that we will decide to abandon France.'[21] But full rights were given to 'coloured' men in 1792. In August 1793 the Martiniquan settlers called the Republic's bluff: rather than submit to emancipation of their slaves, they delivered the island to Britain. The National Convention nonetheless abolished slavery in all of France early in 1794.

All of this had its repercussions within the little household at rue Saint-Dominique. Rose was in financial difficulty. She had spent her early life and then her marriage in need of money, and now she was again. The Revolution had proved economically crippling for many of her contemporaries; Aunt Fanny had been forced to pawn her jewels in order to survive, and now Rose was in trouble. The busy social life she had adopted on her return to France, along with her love of luxury, stretched her modest income to the limit. The annuities that Mme Renaudin had been guarding for her had been largely swallowed up by debt. Rose's father had died insolvent and his widow had been forced to bargain with her creditors in order to save the plantation; Rose's pension was diminished substantially. And this income as well as Alexandre's own funds from his own family plantations was often disrupted because the turmoil in the Antilles had seriously interrupted the flow of money to France.

But since her stay at the convent Rose had begun to realize her own power and resourcefulness, and how these could be translated into the money she needed and wanted. Along with a number of friends, she engaged in a little illicit dealing with Belgium, where certain commercial items from Paris were strongly sought after. The prize was a not inconsiderable amount for the time, but although this kept her afloat for a while, it did not last long; with Rose, money never did. Throughout her life, the disorganization of her financial affairs was such that, no matter what her resources, she was always in debt.

Alexandre's situation was also cause for concern. After the heights of leading the National Assembly, his career had taken some dangerous turns. When the Revolution declared war on Austria in the spring of 1792, Alexandre dramatically announced himself ready to 'fly to the frontier'. Since he was now ineligible for re-election this was not quite the heroic sacrifice that it appeared; the army was now the only option left to him. In August 1792 he was appointed chief of staff to the Army of the Rhine and was based in Strasbourg. By March 1793 he was in command of a division, and by the end of May he had full command of the Army of the Rhine.

Alexandre's meteoric rise through the army hierarchy was largely as a result of the disarray within the republican ranks. Many of the upper echelons of the French Army were now émigrés. This created opportunities for young men of talent and ambition, notably Napoleone Buonaparte, to rise swiftly through its ranks. But the same conditions that created these opportunities also created grave problems for the Revolutionary Army, which was inconsistently led, chronically disorganized and ill-equipped. Despite these disadvantages, it initially achieved a number of successes, including that of Valmy in late September 1792, which halted the Austrian advance towards Paris. This was followed by victories at Savoy and Nice. Parts of the Netherlands and Belgium were annexed and forced to pay levies for their 'liberation'.

It was in this frenzied atmosphere that Alexandre took up his command. Sadly, like his father, he was no great shakes as a soldier. Instead of concerning himself with his army, he spent most of his time drawing up a rigorous training programme and writing lengthy dispatches to be read aloud to the Convention and published in the official journal, the *Moniteur*. So stirring were these articles that he was eventually offered the position of Minister of War. Astutely he declined the position, which was something of a poisoned chalice that had destroyed the career and lives of all who had occupied it.

Alexandre's appointment as commander-in-chief of the Army of the Rhine coincided with severe reversals in the Revolutionary Army's fortunes. In March 1793 General Dumouriez, supreme commander of the Republican Army, defected to the enemy. In the same month General Custine, Alexandre's commanding officer and also an erstwhile aristocrat, was forced to retreat from Mainz, leaving 20,000 men trapped. Despite his many victories on behalf of the Revolution, Custine's failure led to his transfer, arrest and eventual beheading. These military setbacks provoked widespread hysteria and brought down the Girondist Government, which was accused of complicity with the traitorous generals. By the summer of 1793 the enemy was deep inside French territory and a state of national emergency was declared.

In this intensely paranoid atmosphere, Alexandre's glorious missives –

which had so impressed the former regime – cut little ice with the suspicious Jacobins. One of their earliest reforms was to send out 'representatives on mission' to investigate the conduct of armies in the field. The report on Beauharnais was decidedly ambivalent. It celebrated his strong ties to the local Jacobin club. As president of the Strasbourg Society of the Friends of Liberty, Alexandre quickly gained a reputation as the most ardent defender of liberty on the north-east frontier. He charmed political visitors and even offered a prize of 300 livres for the best essay on the most appropriate means of developing public spirit in Alsace. The report was decidedly less enthusiastic about his morals, lamenting the public scandal he provoked by 'spending his days wooing prostitutes, and his nights in giving balls for them'.

Alexandre was so busy with politicking and promiscuity that, unsurprisingly, he was neglecting his military duties. This became evident in June 1793 when Mainz, under siege from the enemy, requested reinforcements from General Beauharnais and his 60,000 men. Despite issuing constant reassurances that the Army of the Rhine was on its way, he dawdled. When Mainz fell the following month, Alexandre, in a move reminiscent of his father's behaviour in Guadeloupe, criticized the 'cowards who had capitulated', urging the Convention to decapitate the traitors and send their heads to the king of Prussia. Then, as the enemy marched on France, he abandoned his command altogether, citing ill health, and unilaterally promoted a subordinate in his place. In his letter of resignation Alexandre anticipated the suspicion that would fall on him as a former aristocrat. 'In these times of revolution,' he lamented to the Convention, 'when treason is becoming so frequent and the ex-nobles always seem to be the leaders in plots to destroy liberty, it is the duty of those who, though stained with this hereditary taint, have liberty and equality graven upon their hearts, to proclaim their own exclusion.'

This high-minded sacrifice was precipitated less by principle than by fear. Alexandre was aware of the increasing criticism of his noble background and his military ineptitude, and also of of his incessant skirt-chasing. In the newly fastidious climate of the times – a mood set by Robespierre, the 'Virtuous One' – Alexandre's libertinism was particularly distasteful; a legacy of ancien-régime decadence that should be eradicated. The representative on mission agreed, suggesting that Alexandre's resignation be accepted forthwith, since 'General Beauharnais by his own admission has neither the strength nor the moral energy necessary in a General of the Republican Army.' In the

margins of this report were added the chilling words: 'In my opinion, Beauharnais should be arrested.'[22]

On 21 August, the day after it passed a decree forbidding anyone of noble
birth to hold a military commission, the Convention accepted Alexandre's
resignation. A later decree demanded that all officers who either had been
dismissed or had resigned must confine themselves to their estates. By the
time the notorious Law of Suspects was passed in September, Alexandre's
arrest was almost inevitable. Holed up in the family chateau, La Ferté Beauharnais, near the town of Blois, Alexandre made a great show of attending
Jacobin Society meetings and collecting nervous testimonials to his republicanism. In a letter to his father he virtuously asserted ' . . . my brain is not
lazy. It tires itself in projects for the good of the Republic, even as my heart
overflows in efforts and aspirations for the well-being of my fellow-citizens.'[23]

Through the summer and autumn of 1793, the helter-skelter pace of
political change continued. The Committee of Public Safety, waging a fierce
war on the eastern borders of France, had become obsessed with its own
security at home. On 10 July Danton was removed from the committee after
a fierce internal power struggle with Robespierre. Three days later Marat
was assassinated in his bath by Charlotte Corday. Throughout September the
committee tightened its hold on the Parisian population, adopting a series of
emergency measures that restricted people's rights to gather together and to
move freely around the city. These culminated in the suspension of the
Constitution and the establishment of what was, in effect, a military dictatorship led by Robespierre and Saint-Just.

During this frightening period, Rose spent much of her time, according
to her friend Mme de Rémusat, 'busying herself with helping as many people
as possible and although her reputation for conduct is questionable, that of
her sweetness, her grace and the gentleness of her manner is not'. She had
learned to be a skilful networker. Through her husband she had gained access
to revolutionary circles, and her own background as both a Creole and an
aristocrat gave her access to their enemies. Armed with her own distinctive
physical charm and her opportunistically apolitical attitude, she was able to
navigate the maze of radical revolutionaries, Bourbon spies, foreign visitors,
financiers and Caribbean lobbyists, picking up friends, flirtations and useful
contacts along the way.

By autumn 1793 the revolutionary Terror was under way and being
executed with impressive bureaucratic efficiency. In addition to house searches, the '*terroristes*' demanded that citizens put a notice on their front doors

indicating the number of residents inside. Anyone could be denounced at any time, without any real evidence, which kept the population fearful and divided. Guillotinings took place daily. In justification Saint-Just declared that 'the Republic consists of extermination of everything that opposes it'. In the Revolution's need to 'purify' French society against the 'fanatics' of Christianity and the monsters of federalism, the entire country was in flames. In the Vendée, where civil war raged, General Westermann put down those hostile to the Revolution with spectacular brutality, proclaiming: 'There is no more Vendée, citizens, it has perished under our free sword along with its women and children . . .'[24] By the middle of 1794 the pacification of the Vendée was complete. The most notorious massacres took place in Nantes where prisoners were trussed and loaded onto leaking flat-bottom barges. Up to 4,800 were drowned in these vertical deportations.

In Paris the population was paralysed by the anticipation of violence and the experience of terror. Many felt it was safer to stay at home than go out where an injudicious remark, gesture or choice of dress might evoke the wrath of passers-by. Those who did venture outside no longer wore red, white and blue; the new colour of choice was grey, because it drew as little attention to the wearer as possible. (By the spring of 1793 fashion had completely died. It would be four years before the fashion magazines resumed publishing.) A display of interest in anything so frivolous as clothing could endanger life. 'Even cleanliness was seen as counter-revolutionary', wrote the eighteenth-century poet Helen Maria Williams. 'Men who appeared in a clean shirt were in danger of being accused of being a scented fop.' Even one's choice of perfume was a statement of political allegiance. Smearing one's head with *pomade de Samson* [*sic*] was an affirmation of patriotic convictions, while 'impregnating your ruffle and handkerchief with essence of lily or eau de la Reine'[25] was to brave banishment or the guillotine.

The Revolution's determination to replace the visual reference points of the old France, to create a new 'empire of images',[26] caused upheaval in all areas of people's lives. The plays they loved were revised and references to royalty and aristocracy were eliminated; on their playing cards the queen of hearts was transformed into 'Liberty of Arts', while the king became a 'sans-culotte General'. There were even proposals to abolish the titles of chess pieces. Once-familiar street names were changed, making it impossible to direct anyone around the city: the rue Monsieur de Prince became the rue Liberté, the place de la Croix-Rouge became the place de la Bonnet-Rouge, Notre-Dame became the Temple of Reason. The churches people had once worshipped in were despoiled, the statues disfigured. Blacksmiths broke down chapel railings, stonemasons effaced noble titles from carved epitaphs. Saints, angels and archangels were removed from niches and burnt or smashed. To further separate France from the Church, the Gregorian calendar was replaced by a republican calendar, which began on 22 September 1792, the date the Republic was proclaimed. This gave the populace one day off every ten days, plus five or six 'complimentary days' tacked on at the end of the year: a considerably heavier workload. Confused people could be heard asking each other 'What's today in real days?' The result was a disorientated, even alienated populace. Parisians found themselves strangers in their own city; foreigners in their own land.

The Law of Suspects had rendered Rose's presence in her apartment in rue Saint-Dominique perilous. Not only was she highly visible on the capital's social scene, she was also one of those 'former nobles', one of those 'wives', one of those 'friends of the nobility' specifically proscribed in the edict. She decided to move to Croissy, since suburban towns tended to be less dangerous than either major cities or country chateaux, where revolutionary violence raged. In towns like Croissy the revolutionary edicts were less likely to be applied with zealous fervour. In this idyllic backwater the Revolution had been embraced with enthusiasm but applied with restraint. This was largely due to the efforts of Rose's acquaintance Jean Chanorier, a retired tax collector and the town's former mayor. Under his astute guidance, Croissy was steered away from the excesses that had overwhelmed so much of the country. Rose felt safe here, or as safe as it was possible to feel in these terrifying times.

Maison Rossignol suited her perfectly. The rent was the reasonable sum of 1,200 livres per annum to be divided with her housemate, Mme Hosten, and she already knew its previous tenant, Mme Campan, a former lady-in-waiting to Marie Antoinette who still resided in the village. The house was situated just off the town's main road, in a beautifully landscaped garden scattered with trees. From the narrow terrace that ringed the house and the windows of the salon, Rose could look out at the wooded hillsides of Rueil, and spy the turret of Croissy church and the heights of Mont-Valerien. A little meadow sloped gently down to a towpath lined with lilac hedges which followed the path of the river Seine, which at this point doubles back on itself, like some shimmering ribbon. Opposite the house, across the tops of the trees, Rose could see Malmaison, the house she would grow to love, nestled in its vast gardens and parks.

On 26 September 1793, two days after moving in, Rose presented herself to the municipality as was required by law. There she made the required declaration that she had taken up residence in the village. Her visit was recorded by the secretary, who awarded her the much-sought-after 'certificate of citizenship' that warranted that she was not an aristocrat on the run. The document makes no mention of Hortense, but three days later a note was added in the margins that the 'citoyen Eugène Beauharnais aged twelve years' would be joining his mother in her new residence.

Determined to settle her household into a model of republican rectitude, and in response to the Convention's dictum that all children should learn a trade, Rose arranged for her two children to take up apprenticeships. Eugène was apprenticed to a country carpenter, Jean-Baptiste Cochard, who would soon became the national agent of the 'commune'. This was a stroke of good fortune because his revolutionary status provided her household with much-needed credibility at a point when the family was acutely vulnerable. Hortense, meanwhile, was apprenticed to a dressmaker who conveniently happened to be her governess, Mlle de Lannoy.

Although Rose was careful not to draw attention to herself, there was some low-key socializing. She spent discreet but enjoyable evenings hosted by M. Chanorier in his elegant chateau, accompanied by Mme Hosten and her friend Mme Campan, who was staying with her landlord, M. Bauldry. There she met the former abbé Maynaud de Pancemont who had narrowly escaped being killed in the massacres at Les Carmes prison; and Charles de Vergennes and his family. The nephew of a prominent minister of Louis XVI, Vergennes had been a revolutionary enthusiast in the early days and was a former commander of the National Guard. But sickened by the Revolution's sanguinary excesses, he had retreated to Croissy with his family.

His daughter Claire was a special friend of Hortense. Her memoirs recall frequent visits to the Beauharnais home, where the two girls played dressing-up with Claire's jewellery and shared their childhood dream of being 'the mistress of a huge treasure'. Claire, who later married a general and became a lady-in-waiting at Napoleon's court, particularly admired Rose: 'Her limbs were flexible and delicate; her movements were easy and elegant. La Fontaine's words could not be more aptly applied than to her: *"et la grace, plus belle encore que la beauté"*.'[27]

Rose might have remained safe had she stayed quietly in Croissy and waited out the revolutionary storm. But she never could resist an appeal for help, especially if it came from someone very dear to her like her aunt Fanny. Her daughter Marie had been arrested because her estranged husband François – Alexandre's brother – was an émigré army officer; this despite the fact that she had long since divorced him and was living happily with a handsome man of mixed race in a model republican ménage. Marie's daughter, Hortense's friend Émilie, had already appealed in vain to the Committee of Public Safety for her mother's release. Now Fanny and Émilie begged Rose to add her voice to their appeals. Rose returned immediately to the apartment in the rue Saint-Dominique (now de-canonized and called simply rue Dominique) and began to lobby her contacts.

The city to which Rose returned was a different place from the one she had left. Long gone were the rambunctuous, noisy streets of the early Revolution; now the populace cowered indoors, concentrating on simply surviving. The brothels were closed, dancing was forbidden and food shortages were endemic. Morale had plummeted to a new low following the shameful trial and subsequent execution of Marie Antoinette on 16 October 1793, in which she was accused of aiding and abetting foreign powers and conspiring to provoke civil war within France, as well as sexually corrupting her own son. People had become frozen with fear, not just of the authorities but also of each other. They were frightened of being denounced, of being accused of treason, foreign plots, corruption or worse; everyone seemed to be accusing everyone else. Knowing that almost any action – a glance or smile, displaying too much enthusiasm or not enough – could be construed as 'unpatriotic', people avoided social interaction as much as possible. In company they play-acted the role of the perfect revolutionary subject in order to safeguard their own lives. They publicly rejoiced at the execution of relatives or friends. Wives denounced their husbands to the Tribunal, and husbands their wives; mothers offered their sons to National Justice, children betrayed their parents.

Rose, like all of Paris, heard the terrible stories of women hustled to the guillotine straight from childbirth, suckling their newborns until the tumbril arrived; of the people who had slipped and fallen in the blood of their comrades, only to be dragged to the guillotine by their pinioned arms; of the Committee's insistence on guillotining a corpse, lest he 'escape' his sentence; of the severed heads that were presented for the crowds to bay at; of the dark, recurring tales of cannibalism. She learnt of the terrible fates of many of her friends and acquaintances. The duc de Clermont-Tonnerre,

Alexandre's fellow revolutionary noble, had been chased by a mob, then was shot and his body thrown from a second-floor window; Louis de La Roche-foucauld had been dragged from his carriage, stoned, then dismembered with hatchets and sabres, in front of his wife and mother; Condorcet had apparently poisoned himself rather than risk capture and the guillotine. As Pierre Vergniaud, the Girondin orator, mourned, 'The revolution, like Saturn, is devouring its own children.'

The very nature of the city, with its great gate and formidable wall guarded by sixty barrier towers, intensified the revolutionary experience. Its physical containment exaggerated the claustrophobic dominance of the Terror. The psychological stresses provoked by rumours, vendettas, mob scares and violence built up like steam in a pressure cooker, in a manner impossible in a modern city, where there are innumerable routes of escape. For the inhabitants of revolutionary Paris, the very fortifications that once had made them feel safe and secure now trapped and imprisoned them. In these months the city felt like some vast, inescapable Petri dish, breeding vituperation, violence and fear. Nothing and no one seemed safe from the Revolution's destructive flame. (Hence the sad tale of Évariste Fragonnard, who destroyed as many of his father's beautiful paintings as he could, denouncing them as decadent. Or the fate of the *chiens de Poitou*, a breed of dog favoured by the aristocracy. The sight of these animals enraged the populace, who attacked them in the streets.)

When Rose spoke about these 'terrible, terrible' times in later years, she did not elaborate on the psychological impact they had on her. But it is hard to imagine that she escaped the profound disturbances which beset her contemporaries, many of whom reported a litany of psychological and physical disorders including nightmares, sleeplessness, anxiety and depression. The pervasive atmosphere of violence, even in the early days of the Revolution, reduced the painter Élisabeth Vigée-Lebrun to a condition of nervous despair: 'A thousand sinister noises were coming at me from all sides; finally I lived only in a state of anxiety and profound melancholy.'[28] As the Revolution grew more unpredictable and bloody, the situation worsened. Mary Wollstonecraft, in the city at the onset of the Terror, found herself psychically disturbed. 'Death,' she wrote mournfully,' 'in so many frightful shapes has taken hold of my fancy.'

Her malaise was shared by many. Over time the practical hardships of survival, the constant spectre of violence, the daily encounters with fear, resulted in widespread psychological distress. The city's asylums were filled to the brim with ever-increasing numbers of shattered souls. Despite his belief in the regenerative social effect of the Revolution, Philippe Pinel – a doctor with an interest in the nascent science of clinical psychology at the infamous Bicêtre asylum – admitted that it had wrought intense mental as well as bodily disturbance in many of his patients. By 'disorganizing' the senses and 'massively stimulating the passions', he argued, the Revolution was literally driving people mad.[29]

Women particularly suffered from the dissonance between revolutionary promise and revolutionary reality. The cause of women's rights, so optimistically embraced at the start of the Revolution, had been trampled in the dust. Condorcet, one of the most ardent and prominent feminists to be active in revolutionary politics, was arrested when the Jacobins achieved power. Young Charlotte Corday's murder of Marat – a misguided attempt to obtain support for the besieged Girondists, many of whom had been sympathetic to feminism – gave weight to the Jacobins' anti-feminism, allowing them to claim that the assassination was the result of allowing women to meddle in the affairs of men. They pointed to the more extreme women's revolutionary clubs as violent and out of control, and moved swiftly to repress them.

Women who had been revolutionary activists were now characterized as 'monsters', 'whores' and terrible mothers. They were 'bacchantes', 'bold women who no longer blush', 'libertines without morals or virtue'. Some argued that they weren't even women at all but 'men-women', hermaphrodites who deserved no quarter. Olympe de Gouge, accused of 'having forgotten the virtues that belong to her sex', was guillotined in November 1793, the same month as Charlotte Corday. Manon Roland, who had also 'forgotten the virtue of her sex' and as a result become 'a monster in every respect', was arrested and bravely faced her death in the same month. The other female stars of the Revolution fared little better. On 2 April 1794 (13 Germinal by the revolutionary calendar) the Committee for General Security ordered the arrest of Claire Lacombe, who endured an extended imprisonment. Théroigne de Méricourt was beaten almost to death by a posse of Jacobin wives and driven irrecoverably insane. For women the promise of the Revolution had been virtually extinguished; the job would be finished by Napoleon. '*Liberté*, personified by Delacroix as Marianne, may have been female, but somehow on the way to *Égalité* she lost out to *Fraternité*, the brotherhood of man.'[30]

★

If women's collective revolutionary dreams had disintegrated, the lives of many individual women had nonetheless been transformed. In these years Rose had begun to explore her entrepreneurial abilities, discovering that – like her mother – she rather enjoyed doing business. More importantly, Rose had begun to realize the significance of her social contacts and her ability to network. She had been influenced in this by the example of women like Germaine de Staël. Unlike de Staël, however, her interventions were on behalf of others rather than in pursuit of her own political power. In a dangerous time, when many were too frightened to act on others' behalf for fear of compromising their own safety, Rose was willing to take risks to stay true to her values of decency and compassion.

She was confident that her interventions could make a difference. She knew everyone, and she had successfully helped many people already (including Anne-Julie de Béthisy, cousin of the abbesse de Panthémont and niece of an acquaintance in Fontainebleau, the marquise de Moulins). So she did not hesitate to come to Fanny's aid, and she set about attempting to lobby her contacts personally to secure Marie's release. Through her friend Bertrand Barère, secretary to the Committee of Public Safety, she made repeated requests for a personal meeting with Guillaume Vadier, the fearsome president of the committee. In the hardening political climate, this proved futile and her sister-in-law remained imprisoned in Sainte-Pélagie.

With no other recourse, Rose sent a cleverly crafted letter that simultaneously defended both her sister-in-law and her husband, whose situation had become precarious.

Lapagerie Beauharnais to Vadier, Representative of the People: Greetings, esteem, confidence, fraternity. Since it is not possible to see you, I hope that you will read carefully what I enclose here. Your colleague has told me of your severity, but at the same time he has told me of your pure and virtuous patriotism; and that despite your doubts about the loyalty of ex-nobles, you are always interested in the unfortunate victims taken in error.

I am persuaded that in reading this letter your humanity and your sense of justice will take into consideration the situation of a woman unlucky in all regards, but to be associated with an enemy of the Republic, Beauharnais the elder, that you know and who, in the Constituent Assembly, was in opposition to Alexandre your colleague and my husband. I would be very upset, Citoyen-Representative, if you confuse in your thoughts Alexandre with the elder Beauharnais. I can put myself in

your place: you have the right to doubt the patriotism of former nobles,
but it is within the realms of possibility that amongst them may be found
ardent friends of Liberty and Equality. Alexandre has never deviated from
these principles: he has constantly held the line. If he was not a republican,
he would have neither my esteem nor my affection. I am an American and
I know only him of his family and if you would permit me to see you I
would dispel your doubts. My household is a republican household: before
the Revolution my children could not be distinguished from sans-culottes,
and I hope that they will be worthy of the Republic.

I write to you honestly as a sans-culotte of the mountain [the extreme
Left] *... I do not ask either favour or grace, but I appeal to your*
sensibility and your humanity on behalf of an unfortunate citoyenne.

If I have been misled about her and the situation she finds herself in,
or should she appear to you to be suspect, I beg you to disregard what
I've said, since I, like you, would be inexorable, but do not make a mistake
about your old colleague. Believe that he is worthy of your respect ...

Goodbye, esteemed citizen, you have my entire confidence ...[31]

Rose's assertions that she was 'of the mountain', that she did not know
her husband's family, that her children had always been brought up as sans-
culottes were ludicrous. But the tone of her letter was clever. The reminder
that she was 'an American' evoked the Republic's finest aspirations. But the
political situation was too far gone even for those dreams. Nothing could
halt the juggernaut that was the Terror. Rose received no reply, and Marie
remained in prison. Rose had drawn attention to herself in a uniquely
dangerous time.

Alexandre's fate was a foregone conclusion. Despite his protestations of
innocence, the assiduously collected votes of confidence, and certificates
of revolutionary club memberships, he was denounced early in 1794. It was
inevitable: the Law of Suspects specifically listed men like him: 'all public
functionaries suspected or removed from their functions by the National
Convention or its commissioners and not reinstated'. Despite courageous
local protests on his behalf, Alexandre was arrested in March at his chateau
in Loir-et-Cher. He was taken to the prison at the Luxembourg, then
transferred on to the prison of Les Carmes, protesting all the while that his
arrest was a mistake. Rose exhausted herself trying to help him: scurrying
around the city, meeting or writing to every old friend; even copying out

testimonials to Alexandre's republican zeal in order to strengthen his case. But her efforts were to no avail; the arrest warrant was not revoked.

Alexandre's arrest sealed Rose's fate. An anonymous note sent to the Committee for General Security denounced her and her housemate, Mme Hosten. The sinister document claimed that the Hosten woman's dwellings, both at Croissy and in Paris, were a 'gathering place for suspected persons', and specifically named some of the individuals who supposedly gathered there: Calone and Vergennes père and his elder son. 'Beware', it concluded, 'the former vicomtesse, wife of Alexandre de Beauharnais, who has many connections in the offices of the ministries.'[32]

On 19 March Charles de Vergennes and his son were arrested. A month later, under the provisions of the Law of Suspects, the arrests of 'Beauharnais, wife of the former general, rue Dominique no. 953' and her friend Mme Hosten were ordered. The next day, very late on what would have been Easter Sunday, 21 April 1794, their apartment was searched by three members of the revolutionary committee. Despite the terror that these domiciliary visits were designed to evoke, Rose kept her head and remained cool and pleasant. She managed to make an unusually favourable impact on the committee's representatives, citoyens Lacombe and Georges, who – far from sending papers supporting the allegations – reported that 'after the most scrupulous search we have found nothing contrary to the interests of the Republic; on the contrary, a multitude of patriotic letters which can only commend the citoyenne'.[33] Despite this surprising support, their orders were clear: to seal the papers in the domicile and conduct the citizen to prison. Fearing that her facade of bravery would crack, Rose insisted that the children should be left to sleep. Entrusting them to the care of their governess, Mlle de Lannoy, she said, 'I could not bear to see them cry. I should not have the strength to part from them.'[34]

Nine

IMPRISONMENT

I know nothing so cruel as to wake up in a prison cell in a place where the most horrible dream is less horrible than reality.

JACQUES-CLAUDE BEUGNOT

ROSE AWOKE THE FOLLOWING MORNING on a thin straw pallet in a cramped and fetid dormitory at the notorious Les Carmes. Her captors had originally planned to deposit her at the cells set up in the convent of the English Ursulines but it was full. Instead she had been sent to the jail on rue Vaugirard where her husband had already been languishing for a month. Rose had not been lucky. Les Carmes was once aptly described as an Augean stable, and of the fifty or more places of detention operating in Paris, it was certainly one of the least salubrious.

This erstwhile convent of the Carmelites had been used as a prison since August 1792 when foreign invasion had threatened France. The following month, during the notorious September Massacres, over one hundred of its inhabitants – largely priests – had been hacked to death within its confines. When Rose arrived two years later the walls, ceilings, stairs and cobbles were still stained with blood. Conditions within Les Carmes were vile. The smell in the prison was mephitic. The reek of unwashed bodies mingled with that of the latrine buckets placed along the length of the prison's dark and airless stone corridors. Women like Rose, traversing their length, learned quickly to pick up the hems of their skirts so as to avoid the overflow from these buckets, which created a foul-smelling slime across the floor.

The dormitories at Les Carmes were cramped, often sleeping as many as fourteen. Rose shared her vermin-infested cell on the first floor with the duchesse d'Aiguillon, Delphine Custine and a number of other women. It was a long rectangular room, overlooking the garden. The windows in the cell were barred three-quarters of the way up, so the women existed in a perpetual twilight. Like the rest of the building, the room was either boiling or freezing. In the summer the humidity was such that the women were forced to wring out their linen by midday. Rose and a couple of other women laboured to keep their room clean, one of her companions remarked: 'The other prisoners could not be bothered to make the effort.'[1]

The atmosphere in the prison was demoralized and desperate. Unlike the Luxembourg, where aristocratic prisoners created a miniature ancien régime – bringing in inlaid furniture to decorate the large, airy rooms, dressing up in elaborate clothes, gambling and staging theatricals – at Les Carmes none of these indulgences was tolerated. The prison had not been a palace, it was gloomy and squalid, and there was nothing to distract its inhabitants from the terrible imminence of death. Sapped of spirit, both male and female prisoners neglected their appearance: the women sat listless in deshabille, their hair cropped up to the nape of the neck in anticipation of the executioner; the men lounged around in shirt sleeves, without stockings or cravats, their heads tied in handkerchiefs, their faces unshaved.

The inmates' days were punctuated by the bell that had been used to summon the Carmelite nuns to their prayers. The prison population was segregated: the men, shepherded from their side of the building down the main corridor, had their dinner in the refectory first, followed by the women. The food was mediocre, but the prisoners were provided with a half-bottle of wine and as much bread as they wanted. Men and women mixed for only a few hours a day in the courtyard, where they could breathe fresh air and walk under the open sky and where their blinking eyes could adjust to the light. There everyone mingled together, walking and talking, the men playing cards or backgammon.

It was during these periods of recreation that the Revolutionary Tribunal sent its representatives to collect fresh victims. When the Tribunal's cart entered the forecourt, the entire prison was alerted. Once the victim's name had been called, it was the tradition that they should raise an arm, compose their face, make a simple goodbye and depart with the minimum of fuss. Those left behind wished them good luck and waved goodbye with as little display of feeling as they could manage. 'The same blade was suspended over every head and anyone spared on one occasion did not assume they would survive more than one day beyond those whom they saw departing.'[2] This grisly ritual took place every day, with the exception of décadi, the tenth day – the revolutionary calendar's equivalent of Sunday, when the guillotine took a day off.

The prison population at Les Carmes reproduced France in miniature. All professions, all backgrounds, all ages were condemned to live together, rubbing up against one another as they awaited death. They included women in their eighties and adolescent boys. Cabinet-makers, laundresses and dentists slept alongside grand-dames, generals and deputies. Celebrities like the abbé de Boulogne and the former minister Destournelles mingled with maids and tobacconists. Rose also encountered many familiar faces: women she had met at the convent, close friends like the prince de Salm, who had been trapped in Paris after he had kindly returned Eugène and Hortense from his country house in Saint-Martin; and of course there was her dear friend Mme Hosten, arrested on the same warrant as herself; and her daughter Désirée, at fifteen already married and pregnant.

And of course there was Alexandre. What a strange, sad meeting it must have been. Rose had not seen him for some months, probably not since his triumphant appointment to the Army of the Rhine. But whatever regrets or residual bitterness existed between them could not survive the threat of the guillotine. Romance was long since over but their fates were still irrevocably intertwined. As his wife, his defence was hers and they worked together to collect the necessary testimonies, justifications and certificates of good citizenship. Here in Les Carmes they finally achieved the perfect détente, gossiping about prison life, working towards their joint defence, above all worrying about their two children left vulnerable in a dangerous time.

Nine hours after Rose's arrival at the prison she and Alexandre joined forces to send letters of reassurance to their children. Rose's note was simple: 'My darling little Hortense, it breaks my heart to be separated from you and my dear Eugène; I think ceaselessly of my two darling children whom I love and embrace with all my heart.' Alexandre wrote to Eugène: 'Think of me, my child, think of your mother and give all your effort to your studies and work well.' To them both he added, 'Your mother and I are sad not to be able to see you. The hope of embracing you and the pleasure of speaking to you soon consoles us.'[2] The worried parents were allowed to receive one reply, then all correspondence was banned.[3]

Immediately after his mother's arrest Eugène – who in the absence of his father, had taken on the role of paterfamilias – had gone to see Jean-Lambert Tallien, a prominent revolutionary figure and friend of the family, to beg him to intervene on Rose's behalf. As his sister recounts, 'He would have been willing to help us but was already powerless to do so. Terror had frozen every heart.'[4] Hortense and Eugène also attempted to see their mother immediately after her arrest. However, the jailer Roblâtre would not allow them to visit, nor would he pass on letters. Even when they added a line such as 'your children are in good health' to the inventory lists pinned to the small articles that they brought in for her, the jailer would cross the words out. The children resorted to writing the lists themselves, so she would know by their handwriting that they were well. An even more ingenious plan was hatched with the unwitting help of Rose's ugly and bad-tempered pug, Fortuné. One day when the children were at the gates of the prison arguing in vain to be let in, the dog slipped through the gates and ran to his mistress. She eventually discovered the note that had been secreted under his collar, a method of getting messages to Rose that was used from then on.

The children had remained at the rue Dominique under the care of Mlle de Lannoy and a few staff. The little household was supported by money from Martinique channelled via a banker in Dunkirk. The children spent time with the princess Hohenzollern, the sister of the prince de Salm. She was living under house arrest with her nephew and a young English girl in her care. As the children played together they were unaware that the large crowds they could see assembling in the distance around the place Louis XV were actually gathering around the guillotine.

The history of the guillotine tells its own story of the Revolution. In December 1789 Dr Joseph-Ignace Guillotin, an ex-Jesuit and physician, and a deputy of the National Assembly, proposed a reform of capital punishment that he felt would be in line with the egalitarian principles outlined in the Declaration of the Rights of Man. He argued that decapitation, which was instantaneous and painless, should replace the barbaric practices of the ancien régime. The 'machine', as it was generally known, went into sporadic use for the first time in April 1792 at the traditional site of public executions on the place de Greve. In the third week of August of that year, it was moved to the place du Carousel, in front of the Tuileries.

For a populace that had been used to the altogether more baroque practices of the ancien régime – the penitentiary processions, the loud public confessions, the climactic jump of the body on a gibbet – the guillotine was a terrible anticlimax. 'It was the business of a minute,' remarked one disappointed observer, 'the blade descends, the head vanishes, the body is immediately stuffed into a basket. The spectactor sees nothing, there is no tragedy for them.'⁵ (Even the appearance of the machine was unprepossessing; a big window with a blade at the top.) In the past, only the nobility had enjoyed the privilege of getting their heads cut cleanly off. For everyone else executions were long, drawn-out and very bloody. The public executioner Charles-Henri Sanson and his sons were masters of all manners of torture and they took pride in their work. Crowds flocked with picnic baskets, chose their spot and settled down to watch what was essentially a popular entertainment. Criminals were broken on the wheel or drawn and quartered (horses were harnessed to each limb and whipped until the man was torn apart). Some were burned alive, while others were hung slowly, their bodies writhing and twisting in the air. Sometimes flesh was pulled off their bones as they screamed; sometimes boiling oil or sulphur were applied to wounds or they were tormented with hot pokers or rods. Under the ancien régime, execution was a theatrical production of pain and anguish in which the King's executioners took their bows like musicians and the audience went home exhausted and purged by the intensity of the spectacle.

The guillotine offered none of this catharsis, but as the symbol of revolutionary justice it was regarded with affection by the populace, who initially flocked to see the 'machine' at work. A seemingly endless stream of macabre nicknames emerged: the 'patriotic razor', the 'widow', the 'reign of the guillotine', the 'argument of the guillotine'. Parisian slang was equally eloquent about the experience of being guillotined: to 'bob their shoulders', 'give them a fast trim', 'teach them the second dance you do lying down'. The guillotine was familiarized, domesticated and commodified: miniature guillotines were made into paperweights, children's toys and even hair ornaments and earrings.

Despite its painlessness and its speed, the guillotine was particularly upsetting for the nobility. Ancient tradition respected class distinctions by allowing them a different kind of execution from the *petit peuple*. It was also ritualistic, with ornate swords and dress codes that satisfied their sense of distinction. In contrast, the entire process of the guillotine was a profound humiliation: the crude shift they were forced to wear, the violent shearing of the hair, the horrible and very public place of execution, the indecent nudity as their garments were torn to expose their body to the blade. (Like her cellmates, Rose cut her own hair to eliminate at least this part of the shaming procedure.) All of this was a unique affliction for a class which depended on 'the tight control of the body-image and emotions for their worth as a class and as individuals'.⁶ If the guillotine frustrated heroic role playing by the aristocracy, they worked hard to compensate by attempting to observe as rigid a code of conduct as they could muster.

The guillotine didn't change just the nature of the experience but also the scale on which capital punishment occurred. Its speed meant that it was possible to kill people at a rate unimaginable before the Revolution. Between March 1793 and August 1794 14,080 death sentences were carried out. As the Terror engulfed the country, the very characteristics that had been celebrated in the guillotine – its efficiency, its rapidity, its lack of discrimination – began to scare people. No one used pet names for the guillotine any more; people stopped attending executions. The guillotine had been turned against them, and this emblem of their Revolution was now seen as voracious, insatiable, even vampiric.

Rose found the ordeal of prison life very difficult. For those who were waiting to see if they had drawn 'the winning number in the lottery of Saint–Guillotine' the hours passed in terrible idleness. They endured the daily threat of being taken away never to return, the steady loss of acquaintances and friends, the haunted nights and the deprivations of prison life. All of this reduced Rose to a wreck who wept ceaselessly, endlessly laying out her tarot cards in the hope of a reprieve from her stars. The air was thick with images of death, and the terrible enemy loomed over her like a fog.

She could not comprehend the unspoken code of behaviour which demanded that aristocratic men and women went to the guillotine with their hauteur intact. Perhaps when she entered the prison she was unaware of the unspoken taboo against weeping, pleading, exhortations for salvation. Unable to repress her own fear, she might have attracted disapproval and reproof. Nor could she understand why the highest praise was reserved for those who were able to maintain a calm, even stony, indifference in the face of death, those who went to the guillotine as though they were off to attend a ball at Versailles.

She did not understand that underneath the aristocracy's froideur simmered a hysteria born of the intense collective humiliation that death by the indiscriminate guillotine represented to their class. This desperate indifference, when it could be mustered, was the only psychological retaliation they could achieve against their persecutors. By hiding their feelings, they felt they were depriving the mob of satisfaction in their demise and scoring the only victory left to them. Not brought up in the same milieu, or sufficiently steeped in the same values, these subtleties passed Rose by. In extremis she could not keep up the pretence of being a *Parisienne*. She was an outsider, her 'class was not her country'. Rose did not want to die with dignity; she wanted to live.

The prisoners were menaced not only by the threat of the guillotine; as paranoia spread in the city, they feared that the September Massacres would be repeated, and that this time they would be the victims. They also worried that they would be accused in one of the numerous 'prison conspiracies' that the authorities periodically trumped up in order to dispatch a large number of prisoners to the guillotine so as to soothe public anxieties about the threat of the burgeoning prison population.

During the last months of the Terror, conditions in the prisons worsened and the jailers at Les Carmes became more ferocious. One morning, for example, a warden entered the women's cell and took Rose's bedlinen in order to give it to another prisoner. Her cellmate, the duchesse d'Aiguillon, challenged the guard, demanding to know whether it would be replaced by something better. 'No,' he replied with a horrible smile, 'she would not be needing it, since she would soon be on her way to the Conciergerie and then on to the guillotine.' Rose later recalled the incident herself, adding, 'At these words my companions in misfortune were driven to cry out. Eventually tired of their endless lamentations, I told them that their sadness was senseless, that I could not die, because the prophecy said I would be Queen of France.'[7] During these terrible times, Rose wavered between abject fear and the hope that the strong chain of predestination would save her from death.

Delphine de Custine, daughter-in-law of Alexandre's erstwhile superior in the Army of the Rhine, General Custine, and famous society beauty, wrote that, despite the weeping, Rose was 'extremely seductive in her way of speaking, her manner had inimitable charm and in the prison she had conquered all hearts.' Another of her closest friends in prison, the English-woman Grace Elliott, the mistress of the duc d'Orléans, was enraptured by Rose. 'She is one of the most accomplished and one of the most amiable women I have ever met,' she wrote in her journal. Their only area of friction was politics: Rose she felt had been a 'constitutional' but now 'there was no one in the world less Jacobin, or who had suffered as much by Robespierre and the reign of terror.'[8]

Mercifully, both Rose and Alexandre found distractions. In the dramatic context of the Revolution, where the pressure of imprisonment was com-bined with the constant fear of death, the desire to live and to love was intensified. Alexandre was madly in love with Delphine de Custine. Rose's cellmate, a blonde beauty with remarkable aquamarine eyes, had arrived at Les Carmes not long after Alexandre. She had been married to Armand de Custine, a general, who had been guillotined just before her imprisonment. When she arrived at Les Carmes, defiantly dressed in mourning although it was considered unpatriotic to mourn the death of an enemy of the Republic, she made a conquest of many hearts. She was already acquainted with Alexandre; they had many mutual friends on the Parisian scene. In prison their relationship developed into an intense affair. Delphine had never loved her husband, though she regarded him as a 'dear friend', and Alexandre became her first love. Alexandre also fell genuinely in love, dubbing her the 'queen of Roses'. He wrote to her with the sort of unreserved ardour that Rose could only dream of inspiring in him. In a letter to Delphine's brother Elzéar, Alexandre describes him as 'brother to a divinity'; for Delphine it was Alexandre 'that was in her heart'.

They were open with Rose about their relationship. But it did not matter, she too had met someone. At twenty-six, General Hoche was five years her junior, tall and well built. He had an open, sympathetic face and even features, virilized by a scar shaped like a comma between his eyebrows; all framed by a mass of curly, black hair. 'Hoche', according to Elliott, 'was a very handsome young man, with a very military appearance, good humoured and very gallant.' Rose would have been attracted to him even if he had not been handsome, because he was brave and comforting. Hoche radiated authority. A devout republican, he was the son of a kennel-man and had enjoyed a meteoric rise through the military ranks by his own merit. Even in prison he maintained an inspiring bravado. As he wrote to an acquaintance: 'My health is good, always gay, happy and innocent. Nothing is as agreeable as a good dinner when you are hungry. Vive la République.' As a postscript he added, 'I'm sending you tomorrow my dirty linen.'⁹

Hoche's romantic situation was more complex than Rose's. He had married a lovely sixteen-year-old, Adelaide Dechaux, only eight days before he was carted off to prison by the authorities, who were suspicious of popular generals and hard on unsuccessful ones. And he was in love with his child bride. But the shadow of the guillotine loomed over him, and in these uncertain hours it seemed pointless to resist the seduction of the beautiful Creole. The diversion that the relationship afforded both of them allowed them to forget their situation. He made Rose feel strong. There were other benefits to the affair. As a VIP prisoner, Hoche had his own room, fine wines, liqueurs and good food. He shared these comforts with his new friend. Their affair was furious and brief. Twenty-six days after the pair had met, they were separated, when the general was sent to the Conciergerie to await news of his fate.

The atmosphere at Les Carmes, like that in the other revolutionary prisons, was a kind of 'amorous frenzy'. 'Everywhere', reported one witness, 'the sound of kisses and cries of love resonated around the sombre corridors.' At Les Carmes this was made possible by the lax security within the prison. There were no bars to separate prisoners; the jailers simply locked the access to the corridors. With minimal effort or a little bribery it was easy to arrange an assignation. 'Thanks to darkness and loose clothing', the nights were alive with the sounds of 'the crowning of love's tenderest wishes.' 'Married couples rediscovered their partners, lovers redoubled their passions.' These pleasures were sometimes disrupted by tales of the outrages of the Revolutionary Tribunal at which lovers would 'lapse into silence or regard each other with anxiety, but then they would embrace with renewed ardour; exploiting the chance to forget in each other's arms.'[10]

In mid-May, Eugène and Hortense attempted to intervene once again on their mother's behalf. Their letter to the Convention said:

> Innocent children appeal to you, citoyens-representatives, for the liberty of
> their beloved mother, who can be blamed for nothing but the misfortune
> of having entered a class to which she has shown that she considered herself
> a stranger, since she has never associated with any but the best patriots,
> the most excellent members of the Mountain . . . Citoyens-representatives,
> you will not permit the oppression of innocence, patriotism and virtue.
> Give back life to these unfortunate children, whose age is not fit for sadness.
>   Signed Eugène Beauharnais aged twelve,
>   Hortense Beauharnais aged eleven[11]

But the Convention was deluged with such pitiable entreaties. There was no response. However, political shifts a few weeks later gave the family hope that both Rose and Alexandre would be released. The Convention, prompted by Robespierre, had eschewed atheism and now recognized the existence of a supreme being and the immortality of the soul. In celebration of this, Robespierre instituted the Feast of the Supreme Being on Sunday 8 June 1794. It was widely believed that on this great day Robespierre would proclaim himself dictator, grant an amnesty to all prisoners and re-establish order and religion. Public hopes for an end to the bloodshed were given credence when they heard that the guillotine had been wheeled away and that there would be no executions that day.

In her memoirs Hortense recounts how the family's maid told her she must make herself smart because her father and mother might be released from prison and she might be allowed to go and kiss them. Dressed in a white lawn frock with a wide blue sash, her shoulder-length hair meticulously curled, the eleven-year-old went to the Tuileries to watch the spectacle designed by the painter David. Half a million people – most of the population of Paris – watched as the bands played, choruses were sung and flowers were tossed in the air. Women dressed as nymphs danced, children marched and doves were released. Then the members of the Convention filed down a long wooden staircase that had been erected near the central hall and led to the garden.

A solitary figure walked in front of the procession, the only one whose hair was powdered: Robespierre. Hortense strained to hear what he had to say, hoping to hear him declare the amnesty. But not a single word was audible. The deputies drew near the great central basin in the garden which had been drained dry and where various wooden statues representing Atheism and other 'fictions' had been placed. Torch in hand, Robespierre set them alight. In an instant everything had been destroyed and eddies of smoke and flame rose skyward. Then a rogue spark set fire to Hortense's dress. With difficulty the flames were extinguished and the hysterical little girl was taken home. 'To add to the trials of this day nothing was said about freeing the prisoners and it left me sad and suffering instead of in the joy I had expected.'[12]

One day, recounted Hortense, an unknown woman called at rue Dominique. She had in her possession a note in Rose's handwriting giving her leave to collect the children. Mlle de Lannoy reluctantly gave her permission. The woman led Eugène and Hortense to a residence situated opposite Les Carmes. Then a window in the prison opened and their mother and father appeared. Surprised and delighted, Hortense cried out. Her parents made a hasty sign for them to be quiet but it was already too late, a sentry had heard her cry and given the alarm. The woman bundled the children quickly away. A few days later the prison window was boarded up. It was the last time that the children would see their father.

Time ran out for Alexandre towards the end of July. On the twenty-first of that month his name was called and he was sent to the Conciergerie, the 'vast amphitheatre of death', for interrogation and trial. Knowing that he would be executed, he arranged to send an Arab necklace, to his inamorata Delphine, which she kept all her life, and he wrote his final letter to Rose.

4 Thermidor Year II
the one and indivisible
Republic

*It appears from the sort of interrogation to which a fairly large number of
detainees was subjected today that I am the victim of villainous calumnies
brought against me by several aristocrats, so-called patriots, at present in
this house. Presuming that this infernal machination will follow me to
the Revolutionary Tribunal, I have no hope of seeing you again, my friend,
nor of embracing my dear children.*

*I shall not tell you of my regrets: my tender affection for them and the
brotherly attachment that binds me to you can leave you in no doubt as
to the feelings with which I take leave of life.*

*I also regret leaving a country that I love and for which I would have
given my life a thousand times over. Not only shall I not be able to serve
her, but she will see me torn from her bosom, supposing me a bad citizen.
This frightful idea does not allow me not to urge you to speak well of
me in the future: work to rehabilitate my memory, proving that a life
entirely devoted to serving one's country and to the triumph of liberty and
equality must in the eyes of the people repulse hateful calumniators, who
have been drawn above all from the class of suspect people. This work
must be postponed, for in the revolutionary storms a great people fighting
to destroy its chains must surround itself with justified mistrust, and no
more fear of forgetting a guilty man than striking an innocent one.*

*I shall die with a calm that nevertheless allows me to feel the dearest
affections to the last, but with that courage that characterizes a free man,
a pure conscience and an honest soul whose most ardent wishes are for the
prosperity of the Republic.*

*Farewell, my friend, console yourself with my children, console them
by enlightening them, and above all teaching them that it is on account
of virtue and civic duty that they must efface the memory of my execution
and recall my services to the nation and my claims to its gratitude.*

*Farewell, you know those whom I love, be their consoler and by your
care make me live longer in their hearts.*

*Farewell, for the last time in my life, I press you and my dear children
to my breast.*

Alexandre Beauharnais[13]

★

On 23 July Alexandre appeared before the Revolutionary Tribunal as part of a job lot of forty-nine. They included assorted ci-devant nobles (whose titles the Republic had suppressed), one Charles Harrop aged twenty-two of London, two curés, assorted artisans and numerous servants. Forty-six of them, including Alexandre, were instantly declared guilty. The next day he went to the guillotine in the place Louis XV, renamed place de la Nation, alongside his friend the prince de Salm, the square visible from the home of the princess Hohenzollern where his children played. When Rose heard about the death of her husband she collapsed completely and was so ill that she was confined to her dormitory. Rousing herself only to comfort his lover, Delphine, she remarked to another cellmate, 'I was very fond of my husband.'

It is not clear how Rose escaped Alexandre's fate, but, according to the biographer Ernest Knapton, the evidence points to the name of Delperch de la Bussière. A bit-part actor who was employed during the Revolution by the Committee of Public Safety, he is said to have been responsible for the disappearance of more than a thousand documents regarding prisoners, including Rose, which led to the postponement of their trials. His method was literally to eat each page of the incriminating files. That Rose felt herself in his debt was obvious when, at an 1803 benefit performance for the actor at a Parisian theatre, she sent him a purse of one thousand francs*, with the words 'in grateful remembrance'.

Rose was also saved by the epic shifts of events. A few days after Alexandre's execution, Robespierre fell, cannibalized by his own Revolution. The news reached the prisoners at Les Carmes in an unusual manner. A woman standing outside the prison began to gesticulate furiously to attract their attention. Then she began a curious mime. First she shook her dress, then she picked up a rock and displayed it. Over and over again she repeated these strange actions. The prisoners began to guess. 'Robe?' 'Pierre? 'Robespierre?' Satisfied, the woman nodded vigorously. Then in a universally recognizable gesture she drew her index finger slowly across her throat. The grisly charade was over. Robespierre was dead.

---

* The franc was introduced in 1795 in place of the livre, which disappeared from circulation by 1799.

Ten

THERMIDOR

*One must have lived through them to realize how far one can
go astray in times of social upheaval.*

TALLEYRAND

THE MOMENTOUS EVENTS THAT CULMINATED in Robespierre's demise led
directly to Rose's release ten days later. The catalyst for both events was fear.
Sickened by the sanguinary excesses of the Terror, and alarmed that they
were the next to be purged, a number of revolutionaries – including Paul
Barras, Joseph Fouché, Jean-Lambert Tallien and Louis-Stanislas Fréron –
decided it was time to get rid of Robespierre. The Thermidoreans, as they
came to be known, began secretly to lobby the moderate deputies of the
Convention. Arguing that there was no need to continue the Terror, and
playing on the pervasive fear of being next in line for the guillotine, they
cemented a workable coalition against the 'Incorruptible'. On 26 July Tallien,
according to contemporary lore, received a dagger and a letter from his
imprisoned mistress, the ravishing Thérésia Cabarrus. The message taunted
him for not having the bravery to rescue her: 'I die in despair at having
belonged to a coward like you.'

Motivated, it was said, by shame and love (but more likely by fear for
his own neck), Tallien led the attack for the conspirators the following
day. Waving his lover's dagger, he interrupted Robespierre's address to the
Convention with the repeated cry, 'Down with the tyrant! Down with
the dictator!' Emboldened by this gesture, the deputies turned on Robespierre, demanding his arrest. In the ensuing confusion, Robespierre and his
henchmen took refuge in the Hôtel de Ville. Later, Barras and his men
stormed the building. Couthon, one of Robsepierre's acolytes, threw himself

from his wheelchair and hid beneath a table; his brother Auguste jumped from a window; Robespierre managed to shoot himself in the jaw before he was dragged away. His most fanatical disciple, Saint-Just, was the only one to remain calm. On 10 Thermidor jubilant Parisians thronged the streets to see the man who had sent so many to their end take his turn on the scaffold.

The news of Robespierre's death inspired wild elation in the city. In the streets complete strangers fell on each other, hugging and kissing, weeping and laughing in 'convulsions' of joy. The authors of the Incorruptible's fall – Tallien, Fréron, Barras et al. – were treated as heroes: men lifted their hats to them, market women offered them flowers, and young people kissed their coat tails. 'It seemed that one breathed more freely', exulted one observer, as if the crushing weight of anxiety and fear that had gripped the populace had suddenly been lifted. A newspaper crowed: 'We are free . . . our thoughts, our intentions, will no longer be poisoned; our mistakes will no longer be turned into crimes; the interior of our homes will at last be a safe refuge from spying and denunciation.'[1]

It was into this jubilant atmosphere that Rose was released on 6 August 1794, after three and a half months' imprisonment. She was amongst the first batch of prisoners to be liberated from Les Carmes. Her benefactor was, according to her son Eugène, her old friend Tallien, the hero of the hour. Too frightened to intercede when her children had petitioned him, he was now in a position to act on Rose's behalf. When she received the news that she was to be released, Rose fainted. But she quickly recovered herself, behaving with her customary charm, according to a fellow inmate, when her companions applauded the wonderful news. After many embraces and exchanges of well-wishes, she walked through the prison gates 'amid the good wishes and blessings of the whole establishment'.

She emerged into a ghost town. Paris immediately after the fall of Robespierre was a nightmarish vision of neglect and vandalism. The walls were splashed with mud and refuse; grass was growing up between the paving stones. So many fleurs-de-lis had been chipped off the fronts of buildings that the city looked 'besieged and battered'. Crosses had been ripped from every church steeple. The statue of Liberty on the place de la Révolution had been painted pink and was hanging off its pedestal. Most disturbing of all for recently released prisoners were the streets. Once so noisy and congested, they were now eerily silent, due to the lack of vehicles on the road.

Nonetheless, those first few days of freedom must have been like waking from a nightmare. Amidst the delight and relief of being liberated, of seeing her children and being reunited with her family and friends, were the smaller miracles of being alive and free: clean sheets, decent food, and nights uninterrupted by her cellmates' stifled weeping or the scratching of the rats that terrorized the prison. But there were adjustments to be made. Rose's health was shattered and she had the shadowed, haunted eyes of all the recently released. For one observer meeting her then, her suffering was all too evident. Rose, he said, was 'very thin, drawn . . . and much exhausted through her life of privations'.[2]

Just as debilitating were the invisible psychological scars of the past few desperate months. Rose had looked into the abyss. Like most, she had hoped – even assumed – that confronted with the guillotine she would have gone to her death bravely, even defiantly. But in reality she had been afraid, terribly afraid. Now, like many in her situation, she suffered shame and guilt at having survived. Whether she suffered the symptoms of trauma – sleeplessness, sudden rushes of terror, flashbacks – remains unknown. But the health problems that she did admit to in the period following her release – migraines, nervous exhaustion, problems with her menstrual cycle – were physical proof that she had not escaped the experience unscathed.

Rose's hidden wounds paralleled the injuries that the Revolution had inflicted on the psyche of the entire country. With its unrelenting momentum, its emergencies and exigencies, it had proved as punishing to minds as to bodies. The disruption, uncertainty and violence of the Revolution had represented a ruinous physical and psychological struggle for the entire populace. You didn't need to be an active combatant to be wrecked by it; even on the home front it had shattered constitutions and ruined lives. People were haunted by what they had seen and heard – violence, death, even cannibalism, and so the Revolution had created a profound rupture in the social body of the country. No one had emerged from the revolutionary experience unaffected; everyone had lost something cherished: a loved one, an ideal or a long-held dream.

But there was no time for recuperation or reflection, not for France, not for Rose. It must have swiftly dawned on her just how difficult her situation was. Brutally widowed, her world in tatters, she was thirty years old, penniless, with two children to support. Funds from Martinique were a problem: after five years of civil war the island was once again in the hands of the British. Mme de La Pagerie, who had allowed the plantation to be used as a base for royalist rebels, was very short of funds. Even had she been able to raise some

La Pagerie: it was in this vibrant world, with its vivid juxtapositions of beauty and brutality, that Rose grew up.

A typical eighteenth-century Caribbean plantation, where slaves worked in harsh conditions to produce the 'white gold' that enriched European empires.

Eighteenth-century Paris, the 'capital of the world' and the 'centre of stench'.
The streets smelled so bad that first-time visitors would often vomit or faint.

Place de l'Apport de Paris, Grand Châtelet. The 'limitless grandeur and scandalous luxury' of the city coexisted with widespread poverty and deprivation.

Alexandre de Beauharnais, Rose's first husband. He combined love of privilege and luxury with revolutionary politics, rampant libertinism with a sentimental attachment to family life, and love of learning with studied superficiality. He once described Rose as 'beneath all the sluts in the world'.

The execution of Louis XVI. The act of regicide – at a time when kings were believed to be appointed by God – sent shock waves across Europe and was a watershed in France's revolution.

Les Carmes, where Josephine was imprisoned during the Revolution. This former convent was one of the filthiest and most degrading prisons in Paris: its walls were stained with blood, its floor swam with ordure, and its inhabitants lived in a state of perpetual fear.

Lazare Hoche, Rose's lover and fellow prisoner – handsome, gallant, good-humoured, but also married. Hoche supported Rose through her darkest hours. Many felt that, had he been available, she would have married him in preference to Napoleon.

Paul Barras, Rose's wily and decadent protector. Sophisticated, cynical and brilliant, he was said to have 'all the vices of a king, without having a single one of the virtues'.

Thérésia Tallien, 'an angel who lacked only wings'. Rose's close friend and social accomplice, Mme Tallien personified the values of contemporary femininity: intelligent, revolutionary, sexually alluring. She is portrayed here in one of the daring Thermidor fashions that she and Rose did so much to popularize.

ci-devant Occupations — or — Madame Talian and the Empress Josephine dancing Naked before Barrass in the Winter of 1797 — A Fact!

Josephine was a frequent target of the English caricaturist Gillray's scabrous attacks. This one, published in 1804, the year of her coronation, reads, 'ci-devant Occupations – or – Madame Talian and the Empress Josephine dancing Naked before Barrass in the Winter of 1797 – A Fact! Barrass (then in Power) being tired of Josephine, promised Buonaparte a promotion, on condition that he would take her off his hands; – Barrass had, as usual, drank freely, & placed Buonaparte behind a Screen, while he amused himself with these two Ladies, who were then his humble dependents. – Madame Talian is a beautiful Woman, tall & elegant; Josephine is smaller & thin, with bad Teeth, something like Cloves, – it is needless to add that Buonaparte accepted the Promotion and the Lady – now – Empress of France!'

The Tuileries, the Emperor's first official residence. Josephine hated its lack of privacy, gloomy atmosphere and dark corridors.

Josephine. This informal portrait anticipates the Romantic style that would emerge two decades later.

money, it would have been hard to get it to her desperate daughter, since the British fleet controlled all traffic to and from the Antilles.

How to survive? This was the challenge that now confronted Rose. Forced to scrabble around for funds, in desperation she approached an old family friend, the ci-devant marquis de Caulincourt. An unemployed lieutenant-general renowned for his affability and generosity, the marquis was having his own financial troubles. Nonetheless he introduced Rose to his contacts at the Bourse and is thought to have drawn on three of his own annuities in order to help her. Whether the relationship between the pair was an actual romance remains unclear. A remark that she later made to a friend, in which she included the marquis in a triumvirate of possible husbands, implies that Rose thought of him as a serious suitor. Certainly at fifty-four he was still an attractive man, with expressive black eyes, chestnut hair and an imposing bearing. And there is little doubt that he felt some *tendresse* for his young friend, so perhaps Rose instinctively knew that the relationship might have gone further had she allowed it. As it was, the marquis remained married to the wife who had borne him five children and the two families remained on good terms. The marquis's sons went on to do well under Napoleon's patronage and madame la marquise became one of Rose's closest confidantes during the Empire.

Another potential avenue of financial salvation lay in resurrecting the painful past and obtaining access to her confiscated goods. As a result of the cloud that hung over her guillotined husband's reputation, her own property remained under seal. Knowing that by clearing Alexandre's name she could both honour his last request and alleviate her family's financial difficulties, she worked with a will, rallying all her contacts, charming and cajoling them by turn. When Jean Debry, a member of the Convention, mentioned Alexandre positively in a speech, Rose sensed an ally. She wrote to thank him for his defence of 'a virtuous republican who had perished because of his aristocratic background'. Promising to enclose a copy of Alexandre's final letter to her, she described touchingly the plight of a man, who 'had consecrated his entire life to the Revolution'. Continuing persuasively, she argued the case of a patriot who, even under the shadow of the guillotine, 'when a man had little interest in hiding his true feelings, continued to express the ardent love of his country which he never ceased to feel'.[3]

Meanwhile Rose lived on credit and the kindness of friends. In need of an apartment of her own, she moved to the nearby rue de l'Université. Her servants offered to work for nothing and the faithful Marie de Lannoy lent Rose her life savings. She also borrowed 50,000 francs from Aunt Edmée. But the loan was in *assignats*, the unstable paper currency instituted by the Revolution. The populace loathed this newfangled innovation, preferring the old-style gold livres, and they trusted it even less after its value began to plummet. So speedily did the *assignat* decline that prices altered daily, and householders tried to shop as early as possible in order to beat the afternoon's price rises.

Soaring costs and deflation of currency caused great hardship. Millions were plunged into poverty, although others took advantage of the financial chaos to make quick fortunes. 'The capital of the world resembles a bazaar', remarked one observer, with everyone involved in frenzied buying and selling. In private residences, auction houses, even sidewalks, people displayed the detritus of ruined lives: paintings, church ornaments and family jewels hawked to the perusers, by the greedy and the desperate. In the former aristocratic quarters the scale of the tragedy was startlingly evident. Fine residential hôtels were a picture of melancholy, neglect, abandonment and depreciation: the Hôtel de La Rochefoucauld had become a warehouse, with a public bath in its cellars; the Hôtel de Conti a horse market; and the Hôtel de Salm, where Rose had spent so many nights dancing and dining, was now all lit up for the parties given by its new parvenu owner.

While Rose's financial troubles were exacerbated by the perilous state of the economy, her daily life was made more difficult by the conditions in the city. Its streets were a nightmare to negotiate. Pigs and dogs foraged in the filthy streets amidst the multiplying hordes of beggars, prostitutes and criminals mingling with the desperate citizenry and the thousands of refugees who had begun to flood in from all over the country. At first there were no carriages around and hacks were able to charge exorbitant prices. To add to the citizens' confusion, the street names were constantly changing and housing was repeatedly renumbered. A special card was required in order to circulate in the vicinity of the National Convention and passports were shown at every section boundary, sometimes at every road. On Rose's passport she is described as having 'orange eyes' and her age has been reduced by three years.

The streets were also dangerous. The 'relief and joy' that had immediately followed Robespierre's execution had given way to rage and a violent desire for revenge. By the late summer of 1794 the streets of Paris were awash with pamphlets, songs and vaudevilles triggered by the death of the tyrant. 'Throatcutters, your last hour has arrived', balladeers sang triumphantly. Print sellers hawked their wares on street stands, with cries of 'Jacobins, the assassins of the People!' and 'Hang the Jacobins, they are scoundrels!' Window displays in the shops between the Palais-Royal, rue Saint-Jacques and the seat of the National Convention at the Tuileries were brimming with vehement images dramatizing the Incorruptible's fall.

In the theatres the 'hideous monsters' and 'frightful cannibals' were being exorcized in a host of spectacular new productions. Posters on every lamp post beckoned with the promise of such spectacular productions as *Robespierre in Hell!* Theatrical patrons who did not display sufficient enthusiasm were dealt with by Fréron's own shock troops, the 'Gilded Youth', who shouted and shoved until intimidated audiences joined them in the royalist anthem, '*Réveil du Peuple*' ('The Awakening of the People'). Dressed in their high-collar coats with gilt buttons, their lower faces engulfed in oversize cravats, and armed with long, knobbly cudgels, these young men – mainly the offspring of artisans and tradesmen guillotined during the Revolution – terrorized the streets in their quest to wreak revenge on the Jacobins. Busts of revolutionary heroes were smashed and Marat's decaying body was dragged from the Panthéon and thrown into a sewer.

If this violent political factionalism was not enough, the city was also in the grip of a crime wave. In Paris alone, it was estimated that there were fifteen organized brigand gangs with chiefs, passwords, storehouses and fences. There were murders in the theatres and robberies in the middle of the day. City officials warned that it was 'of the utmost urgency that the Government exercise the most severe vigilance against robbers and assassins. At night one no longer dares to go out alone . . . and beyond the barriers . . . it is even worse.'[4] In 1795 Tallien's 'cottage' was attacked and all the windows smashed, and not long after his wife was set upon by thieves as she got out of her carriage. The next year a new criminal threat emerged: a brilliant and masked group of bandits known as the 'Company of Avengers', whose membership was confined to persons of fashionable appearance and deportment. These killers for hire varied their prices according to the fame of the target and the difficulty of the enterprise.

Social order had disintegrated. People had lost control over their lives; there were no certainties, no loyalties, no assurances. In a desperate attempt to reassert some pattern and meaning into their world, they searched for answers in mysticism and occultism. Paris was awash with prophets, magicians, seers, fortune-tellers, bowl-gazers and mystics. Cults mushroomed all over the city, each with their secret meetings, passwords, signs and rituals. Although the scene had lost many favourites of the ancien régime – like the magnificent Sicilian charlatan Cagliostro, who claimed to have been born in Egypt a thousand years before, and Franz Mesmer, whose claim to cure illness through the use of 'animal magnetism' was taken very seriously by the aristocracy – those seeking answers were more than compensated by the entry of many others. The formidable Mme Lenormand, whose ample form strained her brightly coloured Grecian robes, maintained that Rose became her client at this time and remained so until her death. This claim was denied by Rose's friends. But during his sojourn in St Helena, Napoleon would confirm that Rose did indeed believe in soothsayers, and consulted them regularly – if furtively – throughout her life.

At least one of Rose's anxieties had been solved by her prison passion, Lazare Hoche, who had been released from prison two days before her. The couple had resumed their affair almost immediately. Despite loving letters pledging eternal devotion to his 'little wife' back in Thionville, Hoche had not rushed to rejoin the ever-patient Adelaide once he was released. His excuse was an order from the Committee for Public Safety. The reality was his renewed affair with Rose, after four anguished months apart. His wife, who was young but not stupid, recruited friends and family to pile on the pressure for a marital reunion. But Hoche found excuses, pleading first ambition and then poverty. This bought him a few more days to devote to Rose, whom he described in a letter as 'the delightful widow of his comrade'.

Newly appointed commander-in-chief of the army on the coast of Cherbourg, and aware of Rose's worries about both money and her children, he offered to take Eugène on campaign with him. This was a godsend for Rose, who had been frightened that her restless adolescent boy would either fall victim to, or become involved with, the packs of young men who were battling it out on the streets. Eugène was delighted. He liked and admired Hoche, who had become part of the family, and he had nurtured military ambitions ever since his time living with his father in Strasbourg. Despite Rose's anxieties, the plan solved two problems: it provided her son with a trustworthy protector and it gave her a link to a man she still desired.

Perhaps Rose hoped that he would marry her. Divorce, made legal during the Revolution, was very à la mode and Hoche's new, young bride, both 'provincial and inexperienced', probably did not seem an invincible rival. But Hoche was genuinely torn between his adoring wife and his elegant, experienced mistress, and seemed unable to reach a decision. With the sudden news of his military appointment, however, his priorities instantly shifted. Romantic life slipped into second place. He wrote to his wife to demand that she set out with the indispensable equipment for his campaign – that is, his guns and sword – to take leave of her 'unlucky husband'. Their reunion renewed Hoche's feelings for her.

By 1 September he had taken up his command in Caen. He was still in contact with Rose, however, exchanging letters that discussed Eugène's welfare as well as their feelings for each other. These letters have largely disappeared, but the efforts to which Rose would later go to recover them from Hoche suggest there was enough incriminating evidence in them to make her nervous. In lieu of these precious letters, others would attest to the intensity of her feelings for Lazare. One intimate wrote, 'Of all the men she liked, Hoche was the one whom she loved the most.'[5] But le comte Montgaillard said, 'Endowed with the most attractive looks, Hoche inspired the strongest desires in Mme Bonaparte. But a little time before his death, he did not hide his repugnance that the relationship inspired in him, since Josephine would not stop asking for money.'

In her search for support, Rose also turned towards home. In November the first letter that she really believed would get through was dispatched to her homeland. The joy of being in contact with her family again illuminates each line:

> *A person who is leaving for New England has agreed to transport this letter to you. I will be very happy if it manages to give you the news that your daughter and your grandchildren are well. Without doubt you have heard of the misfortunes that have befallen me. I've been widowed for four months! My only consolations are my children and you, my dear mother, for my support. My most ardent wish is that we will be reunited one day, and I hope very much that circumstances will serve to realize that. Goodbye my darling mother; accept my loving embrace and that of your grandchildren: a day doesn't pass that I don't speak of you and that I am not filled with the urge to see you. Goodbye again, my darling mother.*
> *Your daughter who loves you with all her heart.*
> *[P.S.] . . . Greetings to all the slaves on the plantation . . .*[6]

Though this first letter did not actually mention money, as Rose's financial crisis deepened so her letters became more desperate. In the first of two letters written in December 1794 she wrote, 'As for your poor daughter, she exists and so do her children, though they have had the bad luck to lose their father. I had reasons to be attached to my husband, whose loss I regret; my children now only have my support and I cling to life only to make them happy.'[7] She went on to explain that she had for the previous couple of years been surviving on advances made to her by Jean Emmery, a banker long associated with the La Pagerie family. She now owed the banker such considerable sums that she felt she was 'in danger of taking advantage of him'. That same month Rose wrote her mother again, explaining that she had arranged for Hamburg financiers MM. Matthiessen and Sillem to get the funds to her, should her mother be able to send any.

In January 1795, no funds forthcoming, she wrote once more, revealing all her fear and desperation:

> *I hope that you have received the tender expressions of your poor Yeyette and that of her children; she really needs support from you; her heart is battered and she has been deprived for a long time . . . You have without doubt been apprised of the misfortunes that have befallen me along with my children, and we have no other hope of existence but your generosity . . . Without the care of my good friend Emmery and his associate I don't know what would have become of me. I know your affection too well to have even the least doubt that you will provide me with the means to live, and that you will recognize and pay off what I owe to M. Emmery . . .*[8]

The plaintive requests finally had their effect. Despite her own straitened circumstances, Mme de La Pagerie managed to send some funds to ease her daughter's distress. It was not enough to allow Rose to relax, however. In her struggle to keep her poor little family afloat, Rose discovered resources she did not know she had, initiating a whole series of measures in an attempt to salvage her situation. With admirable persistence she again petitioned the Committee for General Security to remove the seals from her sequestered possessions at rue Dominique. Persuaded by Rose's influential friend Tallien, the Committee finally agreed in February 1795, describing it as 'an act of justice'.

The winter of 1794–95 was abnormally severe. The Seine iced over as did the Channel around the northern coastline. Vital transport routes were blocked and neither food nor fuel could reach Paris. Having already suffered a disastrous harvest, the people grew desperate. They chopped up their own furniture for firewood; trees in the city and beyond were completely culled.

People had to queue for almost all essentials: candles, meat, wood, dairy produce, sugar, salt, soap, oil, even wine. A thriving black market flourished around all these precious goods, further inflating their costs. Driven to extremes, people ate unripe corn, mouldy vegetables and rotten fish and meat. Some were seen stuffing their mouths with grass from the public gardens. 'Cries of despair' reverberated in the streets and some unfortunates begged to be shot rather than perish of hunger. Gaunt cats and emaciated dogs, 'transparent carcasses' turned loose by their owners, roamed the town, savage and ferocious. Wolves prowled at the gates of Paris.

But it was the bread situation that was the most eloquent index of popular misery. Outside the city's bakeries the lines began to form at about one in the morning. Women and children stood all night in freezing temperatures for a meagre ration of one-quarter of a pound of black bread, which was delivered at seven o'clock. Those lucky enough or strong enough to fight their way to the front received their portion; others were turned away empty-handed after their long and desperate vigil. Once acquired, the bread – a concoction made of pea and chestnut flour distributed to bakeries by the Government – was uniquely unappetizing. 'Many a time when this fake bread was brought to me,' wrote the baron Frénilly, 'I threw it against the wall, where it remained sticking, and not even my dog would approach it.'[9] Those lucky enough to obtain ordinary white flour would have it covertly baked by a few brave pastry cooks; and they would then meet in secret to eat it. In those times, Frénilly continued, 'it was indiscreet, an unheard-of impoliteness, to go to dinner at a friend's without taking your own bread . . .'[10]

It was a measure of the desperation of Rose's financial position that she was one of the few people exempted by friends from this new social rule. Her terrible experiences brought some advantages; Rose discovered that she was very à la mode. 'It was the height of good manners to be ruined,'[11] wrote Frénilly, ' . . . to have been suspected, persecuted and, above all, imprisoned. Without the last qualification,' he explained, 'there was neither salvation nor consideration for you in society. People greatly regretted that they had not been guillotined, but said they were to have been released the day after, or two days after, 9 Thermidor . . .' To demonstrate his point further, the author recollected his shame at a 'victims' luncheon' where he had 'to bear the affront of being the only one present who had not been in prison'.[12]

'But it is impossible to die of hunger with more gaiety', Frénilly acknowledged. For despite the deprivations of that terrible winter, the Parisian population threw themselves frenziedly into their pleasures. The theatres were full and new ones seemed to open daily. The prostitutes, who had disappeared during the Terror, were back and doing roaring business; some twenty thousand of them, according to one official, 'swarming like ants' in the streets, and 'flooding' the city, much to the 'shame and scandal of the Government'. Above all else, though, the people danced. Rich and poor, privileged and humble, pious and brazen: everyone went dancing – in barns and in cellars, on the tombstones in Saint-Sulpice cemetery and even on the bloodstained cobbles at Les Carmes.

Paris was in the grip of a 'bacchanalian epidemic'. By 1797 there were 600 dance halls in the city. Parisians danced in order to forget, in order not to think, in order to remember that they were alive. 'They longed for the noise, the lights, the heat, the pleasure of moving their bodies,' wrote one witness, for 'the entire disordering of the senses' that these events provided. Some found the 'dancing reaction' disturbing, to them it 'was demented, neurotic and frankly lascivious . . . sudden, impetuous, terrible'.[13] For Rose this reaction to imprisonment probably didn't seem so alien: it was not unlike the dance marathons of the slaves back in Martinique, their orgies of release and forgetting.

The nation's compulsive pleasure-seeking was undoubtedly a product of the spiritual vacuum caused by the sudden cessation of the Terror. Mercier explained the behavior of his fellow citizens thus: ' . . . in revolutionary times the customariness of danger, the sacrifice of private ties and the sentiment of public ill, makes them reckless of life.' In the days of continuous slaughter and perpetual peril, austerity and repression had allowed no room for dalliance. After the months of fear-stricken silence in shuttered homes, people now felt it was enough just to be alive and free. Death had been so much a part of daily life that they had become inured to it. Exhausted by a protracted period of weeping, they turned to laughter again, even though they were still suffering. Seeing nothing to look forward to and nothing to look back on, Parisians focused on the sheer enjoyment of the moment. The present was everything, and distractions and comforts justified the day. Napoleone Buonaparte, newly arrived in the city, remarked, 'Everyone appears determined to make up for what they have suffered; determined too, because of the uncertain future, not to miss a single pleasure of the present.'

In the end Rose was pulled back from the brink of ruin by the qualities that had always sustained her: her charm and her intense sociability. It was her new circle of friends that rescued her during these difficult months. They centred around her benefactor, Tallien, and his lover, Thérésia Cabarrus. Rose had known Tallien since he was a hungry young journalist at the beginning of the Revolution and his assistance around the time of her release had brought them back into contact. He was a rather handsome man but not particularly intelligent. His parents had been doorkeepers at the home of a marquis, whose bastard he was assumed by many to be. Twenty-seven years old, he had enjoyed various jobs during his adolescence – lawyer's runner, printer's devil – before publishing a paper and becoming active in the Revolution. A failed assassination attempt in September 1794 increased his fame and political position.

Thérésia Cabarrus, his lover, was the daughter of a Spanish nobleman. An extraordinary beauty, tall, with brown eyes and beautiful, silky black hair, she was, according to one admirer, 'an angel who lacked only wings'. Married at fifteen to a French marquis, she had been imprisoned during the Terror in La Force, one of the most formidable jails in Paris. The exotic toe rings that she favoured covered the scars caused by rat bites she had received there. It was she, even more than her soon-to-be-husband, who had captured Parisians' collective imaginations after Robespierre's demise. Despite Tallien's active participation in the coup of 27 July, the populace felt it had been her beautiful head on the block, and it was her acerbic note that had pushed the conspirators into action. (Besides, who could resist the romantic tale of the endangered beauty, the dagger and the smuggled note?) Now, at twenty, she was dubbed '*Notre-Dame de Thermidor*' ('Our Lady of Thermidor') and had become a 'symbol of freedom recovered'. Tallien and Thérésia provoked hysteria when they appeared in public together. In his memoirs Étienne Pasquier, a recently released prisoner himself, described a visit by the couple to the Odéon theatre: 'Having navigated the press of fans outside, the Talliens found upon entering the theatre that the entire audience were standing on chairs and benches, where the ovation was prolonged into more applause and cries of love.'[14]

Despite an age difference of ten years, Rose and Thérésia quickly became close friends. (Rose referred to her friend affectionately as 'little one'.) The two women had a great deal in common: they had both suffered imprisonment and deprivation; they were both trying to navigate the uncertain waters of post-revolutionary Paris; they both had a love of luxury and pleasure and enjoyed beautiful clothes and glamorous parties. The complicity between Rose and Thérésia was mirrored in the close friendships between other society women of the times. Mme Récamier, after meeting Mme de Staël, declared, 'from then on I thought only of her'. Germaine was equally smitten: 'It seemed to me when I saw you that to be loved by you would satisfy destiny.' She went on, 'I love you with a love surpassing friendship.'[15] These romantic friendships between women had been in fashion before the Revolution. This was illustrated in Rousseau's novel *La Nouvelle Héloïse*, in which the passion between Claire and Julie often threatens to overshadow the story's heterosexual relationships. After the fall of Robespierre, romantic female friendships became fashionable again. In large part this was because women's relationships with men had been disrupted by execution, emigration and the new divorce laws. Many women came to rely on each other for the intimacy, stability and sometimes also sex that they had previously obtained from men. Rose was certainly a good friend to Thérésia, attending most of her gatherings and acting as witness to her wedding. The marriage was a happy day for Tallien, who adored Thérésia. Her motivation was rather more pragmatic: she was ambivalent about her new husband but knew that she needed a protector, especially since she was four months pregnant. As she later wrote, 'When you traverse a tempest, one can't always choose which plank to grasp.'[16]

The ceremony was followed by a huge party held at her famous home, La Chaumière. This attractive cottage lay at the end of an alley that ran perpendicular to the Champs-Élysées, which then was a wooded country area. It was decorated just like a cottage on the stage of the *opéra-comique*, painted in oils, decorated with unpolished wood and entirely surrounded by flowers. But its rustic exterior belied the luxury of the interior. Thérésia's salon was one of the most lavish in the capital. Fashionably decorated *à la antique*, it was full of Roman columns, frescoes depicting mythological scenes and Etruscan vases. The main salon was dominated by an indoor fountain from which Neptune, armed with a trident, glowered out at the room. Even more luxurious was Thérésia's bedroom: designed around a huge mirror and a statue of Thérésia herself modelled as a bathing Diana, it was dominated by her bed, an epic construction, draped in yellow with bronze cherubs on each corner.

At La Chaumière Rose met the most influential mercantile and political figures in the city. Soon she was on intimate terms with all of the deputies: Fréron, Sieyès and Louvet; and men who dominated the financial world, like Perregeaux and Ouvrard. The latter had begun the Revolution as a lowly accountant for a grocery store in Nantes and, through skilful profiteering, had emerged as perhaps the richest man in France; he lent money to Rose on occasion. A lavish spender, in the dining room of one of his chateaux fountains of punch, almond milk and other exotic drinks played continuously.

These new rich mingled with the young generals, like Bernadotte, Hoche and Buonaparte, as well as with great performers like the singer Garat and the actor Talma and with the beauties of Paris. Of these 'enchantresses who charmed history',[17] the most prominent were Rose and Thérésia. But they were ably supported by the likes of Mme Récamier, the wife of a rich banker, famous for her shawl dances and her bedroom, 'the most beautiful in Paris'. She possessed, according to Chateaubriand, 'the double enchantment of the virgin and the lover'.[18] There was also Mme Hamelin, a witty and wild young Creole, whose face one contemporary compared with that of a bulldog. Despite her jolie-laide looks, her 'magnificent black hair, the waist of a nymph, the foot of a child, and extraordinary grace' made her irresistible to many. There was the Italian beauty Mme Visconti and the wayward and ravishing Aimée de Coigny, about whom the tragic poet André Chenier had written his famous work, *La Jeune Captive*. These women, 'the reigning divinities of fashion and beauty',[19] shared similar histories: arranged marriage at an early age, after which they had sought partners who were capable of fulfilling their considerable social and political aspirations. They also satisfied a current taste for the exotic: all but Récamier were foreigners, with dark, dramatic looks.

Rose also enjoyed the company of more demi-mondaine characters, like her great friend the actress-courtesan Julie Carreau, from whom she would soon rent a house. She also enjoyed the company of the actress La Racourt, who shared her passion for plants. The great tragedienne, who entertained in her gilded and carved salon with its blue marble mantelpiece, preferred men's clothes and a good stout walking stick, and lived openly in sapphic bliss with one of Marie Antoinette's former ladies-in-waiting. Her private life was considered so shocking she was eventually denied a consecrated burial.

It was in this milieu that Rose met the man who would substantially improve her situation: Paul Barras. The strategist behind the overthrow of Robespierre, Barras had succeeded Tallien as president of the National Assembly and emerged as one of the most visible and prestigious of the deputies in the Convention. That winter Rose sent him a graceful little note. On the pretext of drawing his attention to a 'sans-culotte volunteer wounded in fighting for the Fatherland', she mentioned that she had not had the pleasure of seeing him for a long time. Then, reproaching him gently for 'abandoning an old acquaintance', she invited him to visit her in the rue de l'Université.[20]

A vicomte by birth, Paul de Barras was the scion of a noble and very ancient family from Provence. One of his forebears had fought in the Crusades and was involved in the medieval courts of love; another ancestress had been canonized. He was a sophisticated and well-travelled man who had managed to traverse the Revolution and come out on the winning side. An unrepentant regicide, his only defence was that 'Times of war are not moral times.' As well as being a brilliant politician, Barras was also a decadent roué, a cynical profiteer, profligate, crooked and treacherous. As one foreign diplomat remarked, 'he would throw the Republic out of the window tomorrow, if it did not pay for his dogs, his horses, his mistresses, his table and his gambling'.[21] He was, according to another contemporary, 'a veritable pirate . . . holding in his hand all the cut-throats, Septembrists [people involved in killing in the September massacres] and massacrers of the Republic'.

At forty he was an attractive man, tall and vigorous, 'with a sarcastic mouth, piercing green eyes and an easy manner'. It was rumoured that he had acquired 'equivocal tastes' in India, where he had fought against the British, and enjoyed the company of handsome young men as much as that of beautiful women. Many of his political colleagues disapproved of his circle.

> Barras did nothing but surround himself with the most villainous leaders of anarchy, the most corrupt of aristocrats, lost women, ruined men, the movers in business, the agitators, the mistresses and the minions. The most infamous of debauchees were regulars in his household. Truth meant nothing to him, wickedness was just a game to him. He is as untrustworthy as he is amoral; in politics he is without character and without resolution. While he always mouths the language of the patriot, that of the sans-culotte, he surrounds himself with the most extraordinary splendour. He has all the appetites of an opulent prince, generous, magnificent and dissipated.[22]

Another politician was more succinct but just as disapproving: 'Barras had all the vices of a king, without having a single one of the virtues.'[23]

Against the backdrop of that terrible winter, Rose's decision to contact Barras made perfect sense. Hunger haunted her and she feared for the future of her children. Even had there been the opportunity for employment, which there was not, she would not have been qualified. As an aristocratic woman, she had been prepared for no occupation but marriage. So she played the cards she had been dealt and traded on the only commodities she then possessed: her beauty and her grace. Since Barras preferred his women to have the elegance and grace of the ancien régime, Rose was exactly his type. She was also useful. As a revolutionary regicide he was persona non grata in circles that Rose could move in with impunity, so she provided him with useful contacts. With a wife tucked away somewhere in the south of France, he offered none of his partners marriage or fidelity, but he did provide them with witty company, the power of his patronage and financial support. Rose's friendship with Barras developed swiftly and 'around May or June, Rose de Beauharnais', according to a contemporary, 'was admitted into Barras's harem.'

It was a sophisticated affair. As Barras's official mistress, Rose's credit was much improved. She acted as his hostess at the Luxembourg and at his country residence in Chaillot, where she met everyone of influence. She entertained him at the rue de l'Université and at Croissy. She had managed to hold on to the house there, largely through his good graces, since he was now paying the rent on the property and would continue to do so until he bought the chateau de Grosbois in May 1796. Pasquier, another Croissy dweller, wrote,

> We had as neighbours Mme de Beauharnais. Her house was adjacent to ours; she only visited it rarely, once a week, in order to entertain Barras and the numerous people who made up his entourage. In the mornings we watched the arrival of baskets of provisions, then the mounted soldiers began to circulate on the road from Nanterre to Croissy, as the young Director would soon arrive on his horse. The house of Mme Beauharnais had, as was the custom with Creoles, a certain apparent luxury; but alongside this superfluity many of the necessities were missing. Meat, game, exotic fruits overwhelmed the kitchen – we were then in the epoch of huge food shortages – and at the same time, it lacked saucepans, glasses and plates, which she had to borrow from our modest little household.[24]

Lurid tales have evolved about these evenings at Croissy. The imaginative historian Guy Breton described them as one long debauch: during the soup course, according to Breton, Rose, Mme Tallien and Mme Hamelin retired to their boudoirs and returned completely nude. On her entrance, 'Thérésia dipped the tip of her breast in Barras's champagne glass.' During the meat course, Rose gave Barras a love bite. During the salad, Fortunée Hamelin – wearing only a tiny serviette – titillated her audience with a 'little aphrodisiacal dance'. During the dessert, Mme Tallien, on her hands and knees, 'imitated the undulations of an African panther'. By the 'cheese course Rose was sitting on Barras's knee'. After the meal, according to Breton, the proceedings degenerated into a full-blown orgy. 'The future Empress enticed the future Director onto a couch', where 'like any concerned hostess she saw to the well-being of her guest'. In the meantime, Mme Tallien was entangled in front of the fire with one of the handsome bodyguards she always travelled with 'in case of any trouble' and Mme Hamelin savoured the last mouthful of her dessert before joining in. The action continued into the early hours, until Rose and her guests fell asleep on the floor at sunrise.[25]

True or not, it was largely Rose's relationship with Barras that led to this kind of story. Barras's taste for, and indulgences in, saturnalia in all forms, was well documented, and as his mistress it was assumed that Rose enjoyed the same sorts of sexual excesses. But in later years, during the Consulate and the Empire, Rose, now renamed Josephine, displayed no taste for such bacchanalian goings-on. But who is to say what is right or wrong for those attempting to stay afloat in such precarious times? Barras himself later contributed actively to her reputation of waywardness, out of mischief and revenge. After the 1789 coup of Brumaire, which brought Napoleon to power and removed Barras from it, he, feeling betrayed by his protégée and ex-lover, viciously slandered her reputation. In his memoirs he claimed that Rose exploited all the 'ruses' and 'the services of the courtesans' in her relationships. Her allure was about 'consummate cunning and artifice', he said, ' . . . she derived none of her attractions from nature, but everything from art, the most refined, the most provident, the most improved art ever called into requisition in the exercise of their profession by the harlots of Greece and Paris'.[26] His ignoble attack continued with a blistering series of accusations. She was so insatiable, he claimed, that she had affairs with various black men as well as with his servants. He also claimed, rather contradictorily, that her sexual relationships were motivated only by monetary practicality, not by pleasure; unlike Mme Tallien who was spurred on by 'feminine enjoyment', Rose's 'libertinism', he claimed, 'sprung merely from the mind, while her heart played no part in the pleasures of her body; in a word, never loving except from motives of interest, the lewd Creole never lost sight of business although those possessing her might suppose she was conquered by them and had freely given herself . . .' He concluded that 'she would have drunk gold from the skull of her lover'.[27]

That many of her contemporaries saw Rose as a *femme galante* is attested to by a rather unlikely source: a satire called *Zoloé et ses Deux Acolytes ou Quelques Décades de la Vie de trois Jolies femmes* sometimes attributed to the marquis de Sade. The infamous writer had served as an army officer in the Seven Years War. Not long after his return he had spent the next twelve years of his life imprisoned at the Vincennes and then the Bastille because of his notorious sexual escapades. Released during the Revolution, Citoyen de Sade had become something of a celebrity as a result of his stirring pamphlets and his powerful oratory. After the Terror his fame was enhanced by the publication of numerous pornographic classics, like *Philosophy of the Boudoir* and *Juliette*.

As a distant cousin of Barras, de Sade had reason to be interested in his circle. He was also furious with his powerful relative, who had refused to intervene on his behalf when, despite his years of active revolutionary service, he found his name on the list of proscribed émigrés. Barras's reasons were simple. Despite their common reputation as notorious libertines, he disapproved of his relative's sexual sadism. 'According to his way of thinking, the pleasures of the senses do not consist of reciprocally agreeable sensations but are based on the imposition of the greatest possible pain . . . To acquire disciples, to strengthen them in their criminal ways, he tried to demonstrate, in the novelistic genre . . . that the evils of the world are reserved for those whom we call virtuous and the crowns of felicity are bestowed on the vicious; that it has been thus since Adam and will always be thus.'[28]

The result of de Sade's resentment of his cousin and his fascination with Rose was, some believed, the roman à clef about *Zoloé*. Though it wasn't published until 1801, this scandalous little tome was marketed as a 'true story of the end of the last century'. The novel, which included scenes of secret orgies held in a pleasure house, excited a great deal of attention, not least because the principal characters were so easily recognizable. Josephine was clearly the Zoloé of the title: an 'American by origin', Bonaparte was the baron d'Orsec (Corse), Barras was Sabar, Mme Tallien was Laureda and Mme Visconti was Volsange.

The portrait of Rose is unmistakable.

Zoloé came from America and possessed colossal estates in the Colonies . . . even at the age of fifteen her studied coquetry and her great wealth brought her many admirers. Her marriage to le comte Barmont [Beauharnais], a favourite of the court, did not drive away these admirers, who swore more ardently than ever not to be gainsaid;

and Zoloé, the susceptible Zoloé, could not bear to disappoint them. From this marriage came a son and a daughter, who today share in the good fortune of their illustrious stepfather . . . now on the verge of her forties, she tries to live as though she were twenty-five. Her rank attracts a swarm of courtiers, and, up to a point, provides a good substitute for the charms of youth. To a fine mind, a character yielding or proud according to circumstances, an insinuating manner, an amazing subtlety of dissimulation, and every quality of seduction, is allied a mad desire for pleasure, a hundred times stronger even than Laureda's, together with the greed of a moneylender. The money she gets she spends with a gambler's fervour; her unbridled luxury would swallow up the income of many provinces'.[29]

Today most opinion leans away from de Sade as author of *Zoloé*, but whoever wrote this naughty little piece, there would have been a certain justice in the era's most emblematic writer taking on the era's most emblematic woman. In any event, there was something of his two great heroines in Rose. Like Justine, left penniless in an unfamiliar environment, the more she clings to her virtue, the more it is assaulted by the corrupt and the privileged. With her huge, appealing, liquid eyes, she is woman as eternal victim, punished because she is vulnerable and poor, but above all because she is a woman. Juliette is the direct opposite of her sister. An adventuress, she targets the powerful and influential, using her sexuality for financial profit and libidinal satisfaction. Combined they made a perfect portrait of Rose, who was both victim and predator; shifting between vulnerability and strength; submissiveness and assertion; yielding and resistance. She had learned how to survive and develop the skills to cope, while still longing for someone to protect her.

This depiction of Rose would gain the marquis de Sade Napoleon's undying enmity. As First Consul, he would have de Sade imprisoned at Sainte-Pélagie, from where he was transferred to the Bicêtre and then on to Charenton, where he would remain locked up for virtually the rest of his life.

Was Rose really a courtesan? It depends on how one defines the term. 'The courtesan is, in fact, a woman whose profession is love, and whose clients may be more or less distinguished,' wrote historian Joanna Richardson. 'Though she sold herself for material gain and did not have the security of being a wife, the courtesan was at least free to choose and refuse her lovers.'[30]

Certainly some of this applied to Rose. She was free to choose her partners. But love was not her 'profession', though it was, at this desperate time, her most saleable commodity. Rose's dilemma was most akin to that of the heroine of one of her favourite novels, Daniel Defoe's *Roxana*, who, when she is widowed with children and faces starvation, adopts the maxim, ''Tis better to whore than to starve'. Settling her children on their grandparents, Roxana becomes a kept woman. The novelist presents the reader with a predicament: what else could she do?

The plight outlined in the novel is the lack of resources. If the ideal widow is, by implication, one who venerates her husband's memory and lives a quiet, chaste, retired life, the novel provides a vivid picture of the dilemma that confronted eighteenth-century women without a private income, without a man to support them, in a society where female earning power was limited. In a struggle in which the odds were stacked against the lone woman, the author argues that as long as she had youth and some physical attraction, these liaisons were a recourse and a resource that could not be neglected. As the same author wrote in *Moll Flanders*, 'Vice came in always at the door of necessity, not at the door of inclination.'

It was not just women who had lost husbands and family fortunes who were trying to make their way in the city after the Revolution. The divorce laws introduced in 1793 had resulted in a flood of newly single women. Of the many separations which followed, fewer than one-tenth were by mutual consent. Both men and women took advantage of the new legislation, putting one another aside with alacrity. (Thérésia, for example, would divorce her husband Tallien in 1797.) As one observer wrote, 'The general licence of opinions and morals, the divorce laws, domestic independence, so many barriers overthrown, so many prejudices destroyed, have only served very much to increase the number of precarious unions substituted for marriage, and those to favour the sudden growth of a new population.'

Of these 'precarious unions', Rose's relationship with Barras was typical. Expediency and pressing debt led many women in these years into casual arrangements with affluent men. A century and a half later, Simone de Beauvoir would capture the complexities of the courtesan's position. Unlike the prostitute, the high-class hetaera, she argues, can achieve a degree of recognition, freedom and even power. But insecurity never goes away. 'No man is absolutely their master. But their need of man is most urgent. The courtesan loses her means of support if he ceases to feel desire for her. The beginner knows that her whole future is in men's hands; even the star, deprived of masculine support, sees her prestige grow dim.'[31] It was this predicament that dogged Rose: how long could she sustain this situation after her beauty faded and she became, in the words of a famous courtesan, 'a yellowing pearl'?

In the spring of 1795 Rose's financial fortunes were enhanced by another source. The bankers Emmery & Vanhee (of Dunkirk) and Matthiessen and Sillem (of Hamburg), in liaison with Rose's friend Rougement, 'assured to her' several thousand livres from the islands. Later that spring she held a family council designed to help sort out finances with respect to Hortense and Eugène. Her business advisor, Calmelet, who had safeguarded her finances while she was in prison, and Raguideau, her legal advisor, were present. On their recommendation Rose borrowed 50,000 livres from Mme Renaudin, who had sold the house in Fontainebleau in exchange for a more modest residence. She was given power-of-attorney over the revenues due to the children from Alexandre's properties in Santo Domingo. Rose was also compensated for the horses Alexandre left in Strasbourg and for the books sequestered in the library at La Ferté, as well as receiving 10,000 livres for the furniture sold by the Government.

For the first time in many months Rose was able to exhale. In that first summer after the Terror, she, accompanied by Mme Tallien – who was recovering from the birth of Rose's god-daughter and namesake Rose Thermidor – threw herself into the newly fashionable outdoor life. They took part in the craze for horse racing, riding, swimming and chariot racing and took promenades in the fashionable boulevard des Italiens. Ostensibly a product of the craze for all things Hellenic, these vigorous pursuits were yet another reaction to the trauma of the Revolution. The city was like an invalid recovering after a long illness; its inhabitants wanted to rediscover their senses, to feel their bodies again.

The other indulgence was food. After months of starving, Parisians now gorged and swilled to the extent of their means. Up and down the boulevards new eateries sprang up in response to the new craze for eating away from home. Small restaurants and pastry and sausage shops emerged alongside more upmarket establishments staffed by famous chefs of the ancien régime, like Véry, Méot and Beauvilliers. Here wealthy patrons were treated to delicacies like partridge pâté, wild boar and the newly created dish, lobster Thermidor. As one observer wrote, 'The hearts of the greatest number of rich Parisians have suddenly transformed into gullets, their sentiments are no more than sensations, their desires, appetites . . .'[32]

But it was the dance craze that continued to be the most obvious expression of the new sensuality. As someone who had lost an immediate relative to the guillotine, Rose was eminently eligible to attend the enormously smart and aristocratic '*bal des victimes*'. On entering the ballroom, men had to salute by bobbing their head in the manner of a victim as he bent to be guillotined. Some of the women adopted the *coiffure à la victime*, hair cropped to simulate the cut received by victims on the way to the scaffold. Others wore dresses not unlike the shifts in which the doomed were transported to the guillotine. These were appliquéed with the red lace called *croisures à la victime*, or they wore a red ribbon around the throat symbolising the cut of the guillotine blade. Though these macabre recreations scandalized those abroad, they were in their own way a form of collective mourning: an attempt to both memorialize and exorcize the Terror.

Rose and her friends also attended the 'high society' subscription events held at places like the Hôtel de Longueville, where the patrons watched quadrilles danced by black maidens, and then watched themselves dancing, reflected in the huge mirrors, to the accompaniment of Hullin's syncopated horns. Or they went to 'that enchanting spot', the Hôtel de Richelieu, where 'a hundred goddesses scented with perfumes, crowned with roses, float about in Athenian gowns'. Here women like Rose and Thérésia threaded their way through the appraising clusters of spectators, 'shining in the crowd like soft illuminations of light', on to dance floors where the strangely silent spectators – usually male – watched the dancers – mostly female – as they danced the night away, oblivious, as if in a trance. Rose enjoyed making an appearance at these events. On one occasion she sent a note to Thérésia so they could coordinate their outfits for greater impact: 'I will be wearing on my head a red headkerchief, à la Creole, with three kiss-curls at my temples. It will be harder for me to carry off and more natural for you, because you are younger, and if not more beautiful, incomparably more fresh. You see I do justice to everyone . . .'[33]

Above all Rose enjoyed being able to afford the new fashions. In contrast to the modest and sober outfits that had been politically expedient during the Revolution, the new styles were flamboyant and exhibitionist. Inspired by the mania for the Graeco-Roman, with its connotations of artistic excellence and political liberty, fashionable women discarded corsets and adopted sleeveless transparent tunics, sandals and belts clasped by cameos. Their jewellery was also inspired by antiquity: bracelets, earrings, pendants and medallions were engraved, sculpted or painted with historic or mythological scenes. Since their dresses had no pockets to spoil their line, women attached tiny taffeta purses to their belts. Designed to carry nothing more than a handkerchief, a tiny mirror, a container of rice powder and a theatre programme, these bags were often embroidered with the initials of their lover du jour.

There were many variations on the theme. Fashionable women, according to Mercier, appeared as 'nymphs, female sultans, savages; once a Minerva, another time a Juno . . . another time a Eucharis'. Thérésia made the news arriving at Ranelagh dressed as Diana the Huntress, her bosom 'half nude', with a jewel-studded quiver and short tunic 'revealing her alabaster thighs'.[34] Rose's friend the Creole Fortunée Hamelin was reputed to have walked for a bet the length of the Champs-Élysées in a shift that bared her breasts. Another infamous wager illustrated both the slightness of the era's fashions and the risqué behaviour of its women. One night at La Chaumière, Mme Tallien wagered one of her male guests that the whole of her costume, including bracelets and cothurnus (half-boots), would not weigh more than two six-franc pieces. Scales were brought in by a servant and she stripped in front of the thirty or forty people present. She won the bet.

Though a bit more conservative than her contemporaries, Rose looked beautiful in this Grecian style of dress, which was so reminiscent of the Creole shifts of her youth. Her preference was for white dresses of a muslin so fine that it had to be woven under water. In these styles she was draped, not dressed; the effect was voluptuous and sculptural. The sleeves of the garment, gently puffed at the top, gripped her arms gently; the neckline scooped scandalously low over the breasts and the fabric fell from under the bosom like the drop from a sheer cliff.

These styles outraged many. One of the Parisian papers declared that 'some thoughtless females indulge in the license of freedom rather too far, and shew their persons in a manner offensive to modesty'. Another declared that 'the man of delicacy' could not help but be put off by this unwarranted display of 'unwrapped wares'. Still another commentator complained that these women, hair coiffed *à l'enfant* with little tight curls, their arms a little too red, nude up to their shoulders, dresses cut up to their armpits, their feet shod in sandals, white and pink flowers to titivate, their mouths coloured with rouge, their faces covered in rice powder, 'resembled enormous dolls, made by a mechanic who also wants to be a confectioner'. The rumour that these *provocatrices* (meaning Rose and friends) dampened their garments with water to make them even more clinging only worsened their reputations.

It was these daring, stylish women, known as the *merveilleuses* (the marvellous ones) who would be featured in the pages of a new fashion magazine the *Journal des Dames et des Modes*. But just in case the less sophisticated of his readers, amazed at the daring nature of some of the outfits, accused him of using ladies of dubious virtue as models, the editor reassured them of the social status of his muses. 'It is they we will follow in spectacles, to balls, on walks, it is their clothes that we'll copy . . .'[35] Of these women, Mmes de Beauharnais, Tallien and Récamier – known as the 'Three Graces' – were the most famous. Despite the terrible vicissitudes of her life, Rose had transformed herself into not merely a fashionable woman, but a fashion celebrity. She was one of the It Girls of her day. And every alteration of her toilette was noted by the style-conscious all over the metropolis. As one Parisian newspaper declared: 'An event! Alteration in the style of hair-dressing affected by Mesdames Tallien and Beauharnais!'[36] Another journal concluded: 'Mme Tallien, Mme de Beauharnais, Mme Récamier and Mme Hamelin, pursuing the current fantasies of Graeco-Roman dress and decoration . . . are of more consequence than all five armies on the five fronts.'

In the late summer of 1795 Rose had decisions to make about her children. Eugène had returned from his army stint with Hoche and his mother now enrolled him in the Collège Irlandais, an academy for young men. Hortense had been staying with the marquis and Mme Renaudin in Fontainebleau, but this was not an arrangement that could continue indefinitely. Her daughter had to be educated, and in a far more sophisticated manner than Rose's own Creole childhood had allowed. So when Rose discovered that her old friend from Croissy, Mme Campan, the erstwhile lady-in-waiting to Marie Antoinette, was opening an exclusive academy for young ladies very near to Eugène's school, she organized an interview immediately. Mme Campan was happy to come to a financial arrangement that allowed Hortense to enrol at the Institut National de Saint-Germain.

Family matters settled, that August Rose moved into her new home, at 6 rue Chantereine. She had rented the property – courtesy of Barras – from her friend, the actress Julie Carreau, who would soon marry the actor Talma. It was situated in the Chaussée d'Antin, which had recently become fashionable because of its proximity to the theatres, restaurants and Champs-Elysées. The area had originally been marshland; it had been reclaimed by developers, who had sold the land on to big bankers, rich bourgeoisie and nobles of the old regime as well as a smattering of distinguished actors who built charming little houses or 'follies'. Originally a small country lane, rue Chantereine was so named because of the songs of reinettes (frogs) still to be heard there.

The house was set in a rectangular courtyard, and flanked by a coach house on the right and a stable on the left. The ground floor was dominated by a large drawing room arranged around an elegant stone fireplace and lit by two high French windows. It led on to the garden and was adjacent to an oval dining room, which connected to the basement by a small ladder. The basement included a cellar, a kitchen and a box room. The sleeping quarters were on the first floor. As soon as she took up occupancy, Rose endeavoured to stamp her own personality on her new home. She sought to combine a light-filled Caribbean feel with the Graeco-Roman influence of the new Directoire style. So she kept Julie Carreau's Pompeii-inspired fresco of gods and goddesses in the dining room and added the sheer muslim curtains that were fashionable in Martinique. She covered the chairs with sky blue nankeen, and dotted around the house ornaments inspired by antiquity, including an Etruscan silver urn and a little bust of Socrates. Despite these fashionable touches, however, sharp eyes noted that in the dining room there were almost no spoons or cups, and just three plates were displayed in the glass-fronted cabinets. But Rose's flair veiled her relative poverty with an illusion of luxury: her exquisite taste and the glorious arrangements of flowers from her little garden charmed all visitors.

In autumn 1795 the Directoire was established in an attempt to restore some sort of political equilibrium to the country. Based on a fragile alliance of moderate republicans and constitutional monarchists, it was designed to provide a bulwark against dictatorship. The executive and the legislature were separated and power was divided between the Council of Ancients (or Elders) and the Council of Five Hundred. Five Directors presided over this system, including Rose's lover, Barras. Almost immediately he emerged as the most powerful of his four colleagues. 'King Barras' would become the emblematic figure of the administration. He was the only one of the Directors to hold onto his post for the four years of the Directoire. His official apartments on the first floor of the Palais du Luxembourg, beside the famous Rubens gallery, were the most luxurious and the best appointed and the official costume suited his dignified frame better than it did his co-Directors. In his draped scarlet coat embroidered in gold, and with his glittering ceremonial sword, he looked every inch the 'king' that people had dubbed him.

Barras was to preside over a period as marked by venality and corruption as any period in French history. The age of the Directoire has been compared with post-communist Russia, but a more evocative marker is perhaps Weimar Germany. It was characterized by a dizzying social fluidity, during which new elites emerged and old ones were forgotten, sweeping away the traditions and certainties of the past. A free-falling economy combined with an almost demented entrepreneurialism; desperate social conditions were juxtaposed with a hysterical hedonism; crime spiralled alongside a desperate sexual decadence. The fabric of social cohesion seemed entirely destroyed. As the gap between the *Gros* and the *Maigres* (the Swollen and the Empty Bellies) widened, society's gaiety masked great despair. The police complained that 'the luxury is shamelessly at odds with the most excessive poverty, and the orgies of debauch are renewed and prolonged in the presence of unfortunates whose emaciated hands seek a painful existence in the gutters'.[37]

Even before it was officially installed, the Directoire was under attack. The first of a series of attempted coups d'état, known as the Vendémiaire (5 October) uprising, erupted in 1795 when royalist factions rebelled against the recently declared 'Constitution of year III', which favoured leftist republican candidates for the new legislative bodies. Barras successfully delegated the suppression of the dissident factions to his new protégé, a young soldier called Napoleone Buonaparte.

It was around this time that Rose met the man who would transform French history and her own life. Like so much about Napoleon, the story of his first meeting with Rose has been mythologized. Known as 'the legend of the sword' the tale goes something like this: after the celebrated day of Vendémiaire when Napoleone quelled popular unrest with that infamous 'whiff of grapeshot', a public announcement was issued that unauthorized weapons must be surrendered to the authorities. An official visit to the Beauharnais house demanded the surrender of Alexandre's sword. Outraged, Eugène objected to the seizure, only to be told that any complaints must be taken up with the current commanding general of Paris, Napoleone Buonaparte. Arriving at his office, the fifteen-year-old gravely and persuasively argued that he be allowed to keep this important military legacy of his father, a deceased republican hero. Profoundly touched, Napoleone relented. So impressed was he by the young man's manner, one version of the tale goes, that he asked to meet the mother of this remarkable youth. In another version it was Rose, in appreciation of Napoleone's generosity, who asked to meet the commander. Neither version is true. The reality was much more prosaic. As Bonaparte, looking back from exile in St Helena, recalled: 'It was chez Barras that I saw my wife for the first time, she had a great influence on my life and in my memory she is always dear.'

Much has been made of the 'improbability' of their relationship, but in reality 'the Creole' and 'the Corsican' had a great deal in common. For a start, they were both outsiders. Like Rose, Napoleon was an islander, born in Corsica on 15 August 1769. His homeland, like hers, was a pawn in the colonial games of European nations, with a profoundly ambivalent relationship to the mother country. In addition, both Napoleon and Rose were French citizens by a very slim margin. Just as the British had returned Martinique to France only three months before Rose's birth, so Napoleon only narrowly avoided being born Italian, since Corsica had reverted to France just a few months before he was born. Both Rose and Napoleon were hot-blooded creatures: neither would ever become used to the cold and damp of northern France; hence the fact that Napoleon is nearly always pictured standing as close to a fireplace as possible. (As Emperor he complained that he couldn't share his second wife's bedroom because of her Austrian habit of sleeping with the windows open.)

Though by no means rich, the Buonapartes, like the La Pageries, were of good, solid stock, well known on their island. Rose and Napoleon both had a strong mother ('strict but tender', according to Napoleon) and a weak, disorganized father. His happy, family-centred childhood was disrupted when Napoleone was sent to school in France at the age of nine. Like Rose, he had found it hard to settle into French life, but instead of bewilderment Napoleone, ensconced in the military academy at Brienne, coped by becoming belligerent. When he was taunted by school mates for his strange accent and foreign manners, he cried out, 'I'll make you French pay for this.' Despite this defensive posturing, the young Napoleone was nonetheless ambitious and his army career thrived. At sixteen he elected to join La Fère, a well-regarded artillery regiment stationed at Valence, the nearest garrison town to Corsica. And in 1788 he was posted to Auxonne, whence he went to Paris, where he spent much of the Revolution.

It was on a visit to Paris that he had his first sexual encounter, an event he described as a 'philosophical experience', but which appears to have been a curt and rather sordid event. Strolling through the arcades of the Palais

Royal on a November night in 1787, he chanced upon a half-dressed, half-frozen *fille de joie*. Engaging her in conversation, he took her to his small – but warm – room and discovered her sad story. She had fallen in love with an army officer, who had brought her to Nantes and then abandoned her. This desertion had precipitated her squalid existence; as she explained to the naive young man, 'one must live'. She stayed till dawn. It was the first night that Napoleone had ever spent with a woman.

His first and only real relationship had begun a few months after his exceptional military performance at Toulon when, as a young artillery major, he recaptured Toulon from the royalists on behalf of the Revolution in late 1793. Through his brother Joseph, Napoleone met Désirée Clary in Marseille, where his family had settled when they fled Corsica. She was the younger daughter of a well-to-do merchant family, and Joseph was courting her elder sister, Julie. Each girl was blessed with a generous dowry of 100,000 livres, which alone might have piqued Napoleone's romantic interest. But the sixteen-year-old Désirée had additional charms. Sweet-natured, conciliatory and affectionate, she was quite an attractive girl, with a fine nose and nicely shaped mouth, despite slightly bulbous eyes and a tendency to plumpness.

Recalled to Nice in April 1794, Napoleone was put in command of military planning for the proposed campaign against Italy. His salary allowed him to set up a home for his family in Antibes. Joseph, now married to Julie Clary, was included in the household. Lucien, who had married the local innkeeper's indigent sister, was most definitely not. (Indeed, the Buonaparte family would never tire of trying to break up this happy union.) Désirée came to Antibes for a holiday, but nothing developed there between her and Napoleone.

The fall of Robespierre changed Napoleone's prospects for the worse. Napoleone's friendship with Augustin Robespierre, younger brother of the Incorruptible Maximilien, led to Napoleone being put under house arrest. He later denied his friendship with Augustin in order to save his own skin, proving his own maxim that 'men are moved by two motives only: fear and self-interest'. Reintegrated in the army but without his command, Napoleone began courting Désirée with more seriousness. In his first letter to her, dated 24 Fructidor (10 September), he tellingly renamed her – as he would later do Rose – deciding unilaterally that Eugénie sounded more romantic than her given name. His letters to the 'good Eugénie', however, are very different from the passionate outpourings with which he would later deluge 'Josephine'. Despite his claim to have 'taken her virginity', his letters to

Désirée seem the product of a platonic relationship: affectionate yet curiously reserved.

Sometimes he lectured her on his pet subjects: army placement, household management and social protocol. At other times he enjoyed playing the mentor: instructing her on how to dress and how to improve her piano playing. The lack of romance in his letters was so marked that Désirée gently reproached him for his *'froideur'*, asking him to write more frequently and more passionately. He responded angrily, defending himself against 'the injustice of her reproaches' and brutally went on to supply some complaints of his own.

Despite Napoleone's brusque manner and his rather unsavoury appearance, the innocent, impressionable Désirée fell for him. In part this was because their courtship took place against the backdrop of the Terror, when death was a constant companion – and the young girl had endured the loss of her father and the threatened arrest of her brother, whose life Napoleone had helped to save. But Désirée's feelings were also a product of her own intense nature. He was her first suitor, she believed herself in love, and she wanted to be married like her sister. The duchesse d'Abrantès, recalling Désirée, remarked that she ' . . . loved prodigiously everything that was melancholic and romantic. Then the word was unknown. Since then we know what it is and its resemblance to madness is less obvious.'[38]

Her family was not enthused. Her mother remarked, 'I already have more than enough Buonapartes in my family.' Despite this resistance, the couple thought of themselves as unofficially engaged. And Napoleone wrote with some feeling on 11 April 1795 22 Germinal year II, 'Your portrait is engraved on my heart.' After a brief reunion they were parted again by the demands of his career. Utterly miserable, Désirée occupied her time daydreaming, playing the piano and writing him letters. One tear-stained missive included the words 'The hour for our promenade approaches, but my friend is not here to find me. Ah! how I regret that we have to be apart . . . Each instant that you are far from me pierces my heart . . .'[39]

By the end of the following month, Napoleone was in Paris, accompanied by John-Paul Marmont, another young officer and Andoche Junot, a Burgundian who served under him at Toulon. Since he was a general on half pay, he had little money. They took up modest lodgings near the place des Victoires and dined frequently and gratefully with a family friend of the Buonapartes from Corsica: Mme Permon. An attractive woman in her forties, she had provided a haven for the young Napoleone on his days off from the

Royal Military School. He was such a familiar face at the Permons' that her young daughter Laure (who later as the duchesse d'Abrantès served at his Imperial court) nicknamed him – much to his annoyance – 'puss-in-boots' because of the way his skinny legs looked in his oversized boots. Perhaps because he was so at home at the Permons', he eventually asked the well-to-do widow for her hand. Amazed and a bit amused, the diplomatic Mme Permon elegantly declined, citing her age as the reason.

With the exception of his time with the Permons, these early days in Paris were one of the lowest points in Napoleon's life. He divided his time between attempting, rather futilely, to make contacts with prominent figures and wandering forlornly around the city. In a letter to his brother Joseph he declared that life had little meaning left for him and he wouldn't move out of the way if he were about to be run over by a carriage. His letters to Désirée were equally gloomy. Urging her to write more frequently, he lamented that her letters to him provided one of the few 'instances of happiness' in his 'uncertain and unhappy existence'.

It was in the hedonistic summer of 1795, when Rose and Thérésia were gallivanting around the city, that Barras introduced Napoleone into his social circle. But it is unlikely that Rose would really have noticed him. In a city awash with Republican Army officers, he was just another uniform, devoid of the reputation or outstanding masculine beauty that made a man like Hoche stand out. As one contemporary remarked, 'Who is this General Buonaparte? Where has he served? Nobody has ever heard of him.' Indeed, as the financier Ouvrard noted, 'of all those present . . . Barras's little protégé as [Buonaparte] was derisively known . . . was perhaps the least noticeable and the least impressive.'[40]

In his early days in Paris, Buonaparte was indeed an unprepossessing sight. The duchesse d'Abrantès described with distaste this small, sickly man with 'his thin angular features, long unwashed hair and jaundiced complexion'. That he was clad in a 'worn, ill-fitting uniform' did not improve matters. His friend Bourrienne, while acknowledging that 'he was badly dressed and a bit grubby', focused more on Buonaparte's rather unfortunate manner. 'His character was cold, often sombre. His smile was false and he often grinned at the wrong time.' In addition, he was 'given to inappropriate outbursts of laughter which did little to endear him to others'. This lack of social skills hindered his entry into this glittering Parisian milieu. Much to Napoleone's frustration, he could not impress these people, despite the scope of his vision and his undoubted military potential. To them, as Mme de

Chasteney wrote, he was just 'a little general who was unhesitatingly dubbed a fool by all those who knew him'. Undoubtedly this was a profound blow to the self-esteem of a man who was already having an unhappy time in the city.

But as the summer wore on the tone of his letters began to change. Barras had taken General Buonaparte to 'the salons of Mme Tallien, Mme de Staël . . . and to several other houses where he dined and was made welcome'. Here he was exposed for the first time to women with real social and political influence, like Mme Tallien, Mme Hamelin and Mme Récamier, and of course the woman of his destiny: Rose de Beauharnais. Napoleone was bowled over. More and more, he began, rather tactlessly, to enthuse about the wonders of Parisian women to his lover: 'Beautiful as in old romances and as learned as scholars . . . Their toilette, the fine arts and their pleasures take up all their time. They are philosophers, lovers, courtesans and artists . . . all these frivolous women have one thing in common, an astonishing love of bravery and glory . . .'[41]

In retrospect, many have questioned the young hero's desire for this decadent, older femme fatale. At the time, however, the mystery was why she would have been interested in him. When Napoleone met her, Rose was the star, her every movement discussed, her every outfit dissected. For during these post-revolutionary years Rose truly came into her own. Her phenomenal adaptability, which allowed her to adjust to new mores and cope with constant change, served her well. She seemed to epitomize what this period was all about, with its passion for spontaneity, its love of the exotic and its relentless pursuit of pleasure. Rose was both a product and an emblem of the prevailing zeitgeist.

One simply has to imagine Napoleone's first sighting of her to understand how she would have affected him. The setting: one of those 'luminous nights' of Barras's. An impeccably decorated room in the Palais de Légalité (the politically correct revolutionary alternative name for the Luxembourg) or his glorious country house: gilded and opulent, a bastion of *haute luxe*, where crystal chandeliers twinkled in the lamplight and white flowers spilled from vases in breathtaking profusion; tables laden with exquisite food and drink – the sort of luxuries the rest of the city only dreamed of; the room suffused with the sounds of privilege – the delicate clink of silver cutlery against fine porcelain, the tinkling of a piano or the rippling of a harp, the murmur of refined voices muted by damask and brocade; candles or torches flickering, beautiful, musk-scented women floating by in their Grecian robes. Napoleone a bit player only, watching from the sidelines, awkward, tolerated but largely ignored. Rose luminescent, at the very epicentre of the action; courted by everyone, popular, charming, at ease. She would have represented everything he wanted to be and everything he wanted to have.

When they actually met it was, unsurprisingly, an unequal contest. Buonaparte may have been the genius on the battlefield but in the drawing room it was Rose who was the prodigy. She was an accomplished seductress who had mastered all of the skills necessary to ensnare and persuade. The 'perfection of her gestures', the 'Creole elegance' of her movements, the soft depth of her voice entranced others. Rose seemed to know exactly when to bestow her enigmatic, close-mouthed smile or gently touch her companion's arm; she had the ability to listen so that the recipient felt they were the centre of her world. In her hands a fan was a deadly weapon. So when Napoleone eventually had a conversation with Rose, it is no surprise that he was instantly lost. 'I was not insensitive to the charms of women,' he would later explain, 'but until then I had not had good fortune with them; and my character rendered me timid before them. Madame de Beauharnais is the first to have reassured me. She said flattering things about my military talents, one day when I found myself placed next to her. Her praise intoxicated me; I addressed myself only to her . . .' After that evening he admitted, 'I followed her everywhere; I was passionately in love with her.'

Not surprisingly, Désirée's letters to Napoleone became more anxious. 'How could you think for a moment that I am no longer in love with my Eugénie, and continue to think of her . . .', he consoled her. But the truth was that Napoleone was dazzled by the new milieu in which he found himself, and by the 'unequalled' pleasures of Paris, with its spectacles and balls, that he heedlessly raved about in the same letter. Désirée's intuition that he was growing apart from her was all too accurate. She tried a new tactic. She stopped writing for a time, until he eventually responded to her silence. Though he was in love with Rose, he was not sure of a positive outcome; he had to maintain the relationship with Désirée until he was sure what would happen. But she was no longer the object of his affections. In a letter to his brother dated 9 November he adds a postscript instructing him to embrace Désirée. She was no longer his 'good Eugénie'.

Around this time, Rose wrote her first letter to Napoleone. As with so many of the letters of their courtship, some of it was later censored by her zealous children. In this case the date has been obscured so as to avoid the accusation that Rose was chasing the hero of Vendémiarie. It reads, 'You no longer come to see a friend who is fond of you. You have quite forsaken her. This is a mistake, as she is tenderly attracted to you. Come to lunch with me tomorrow, septidi. I want to see you and to talk to you about matters of interest to you. Good night, *mon ami, je vous embrasse.*' It was signed, 'the widow Beauharnais'.[42]

The tone was perfect: playful, light, teasing; it succeeded in reassuring the general of her interest in him, as well as dangling a tempting titbit of self-interest before him with the phrase 'matters of interest to you'. Napoleone couldn't reply fast enough. In a letter dispatched the same evening he wrote, 'I cannot imagine the reason for the tone of your letter. I beg you to believe that no one desires your friendship as much as I do, no one could be more eager to prove it. Had my duties permitted it, I would have come in person to deliver it. Buonaparte.'[43]

Their dance had begun. Napoleone was so awed by Rose, and his sense of her unattainability, that he assumed it would be a long courtship. But as he explained in the memoirs from St Helena that he customarily dictated in the third person, 'When Mme de Beauharnais invited him to visit her he was struck by her extraordinary grace and her irresistibly sweet manner. The acquaintance was shortly to ripen into intimacy.' That 'intimacy' was to inspire some of the most beautiful love letters of the eighteenth century. The first of these, dated December 1795, commemorated their first night together:

> *I awake filled with thoughts of you. Your image, and the intoxicating*
> *pleasures of last night, allow my senses no rest. Sweet and incomparable*
> *Josephine, how strangely you work upon my heart! Are you angry with*
> *me? Are you unhappy? Are you upset? . . . my soul is broken with grief,*
> *and my love for you forbids repose. But how can I rest any more, when I*
> *yield to the feeling that masters my inmost self, when I quaff from your*
> *lips and from your heart a scorching flame? Yes! One night has taught me*
> *how far your portrait falls short of yourself! You start at midday: in three*
> *hours I shall see you again. Till then, a thousand kisses,* mio dolce
> amore: *but give me none back, for they set my blood on fire.*[44]

This letter, its date altered by Hortense and Eugène so that it appeared to be written after their marriage, was, one suspects, the night of Napoleone's real erotic awakening. If losing his virginity had proved somewhat disappointing, Napoleone was now plunged into the tumult of sensuality that had engulfed Rose so long ago on her marriage to Alexandre. Rose was a seasoned voluptuary, and the inexperienced young general was beguiled and bewitched. All of his preconceived ideas about love (merely 'a social feeling') and dismissive remarks about the French ('entirely absorbed by eroticism') were shattered. It was his turn to be *bouleversé*, thrown over by the power of erotic love. She was his very own tropical Scheherazade, who had awakened his senses and overwhelmed him with physical passion.

She appealed to him in many ways and represented so much of what he longed for. She seemed to him *une vraie Parisienne*, a legitimate member of the aristocracy: an insider, comfortable in the world that intimidated him. Unlike the unsophisticated Désirée, who adored and looked up to him, Rose represented a challenge. This drew a man like Napoleone, who loved difficulty and risk and for whom pleasure and danger were never far apart. Older, elusive, capricious, luxury-loving, she was the sort of female rouée that he couldn't resist trying to conquer. 'The artificial woman, the coquette whose only preoccupation is to subjugate the stronger sex,' wrote one of his biographers, 'appeared to him like an enemy whom he wished to make capitulate.'[45]

Romantically and sexually out-gunned, it was no surprise that Napoleone quickly proposed. Unusually for him, on this occasion his motivation was primarily emotional. There were also pragmatic justifications for following his heart, however. The one person that he consulted, Barras, strongly recommended the marriage. 'You have rank, the talent to become a hero; but you are isolated; without fortune, without relations; it would be best if you married; that will give you confidence.' In St Helena, Napoleon admitted that Barras had done him a 'good turn' when he advised him to marry Rose. 'He pointed out that she belonged to both the old regime and the new, that the marriage would give me "consistency", would make people forget my Corsican name, would make me wholly French.'

There may also have been some financial motivation. The couple's only serious premarital quarrel occurred when Rose discovered that Napoleon had been probing into her financial affairs. (He had apparently visited her notary and inquired about the family's West Indian properties.) That money was not his motivation in marrying her, as he tearfully argued at the time, is borne out by the incandescent passion of his love letters during this period and the early days of their marriage. As his friend Marmont attested, 'When General Bonaparte fell in love with Mme de Beauharnais, it was love in all the power and strength of the term. It was apparently his first passion and he felt it with all the vigour of his nature.'[46]

It was Rose, not Napoleone, who was full of doubt. She delayed giving him an answer throughout the winter. She consulted everyone: family, friends and acquaintances, many of whom felt she was marrying beneath her. One of these was the rather Gothic figure of Raguideau, her advisor. 'One of the shortest men I think I ever saw in my life,' according to Bourrienne, Raguideau was also cursed with an outsized head and a hump, but he was one of the most trustworthy and reliable figures in Rose's life. He felt that marriage to Buonaparte was not a sensible plan. 'Why not marry an army contractor,' he suggested, 'who can give you all the money you could need?' It was certainly true that Napoleone had no money, and a general was always a gamble: military promise aside, he could be killed or fall out of political favour, both of which would leave her financially desperate. 'Far more sensible to marry a statesman like Barras or a financier.'

Raguideau was particularly dismayed when he surveyed a draft of the marriage contract. Learning from past experience, Rose had made sure that she had custody and control of both her children, but financially it was not a generous proposal. It stipulated that there should be no community of goods of any kind, that neither would be responsible for the debts of the other, and that Buonaparte would settle upon his wife the measly annual sum of 1,500 francs. Napoleone's contribution to the marriage contract, or rather lack of it, prompted Raguideau's caution: 'this man brings you nothing but his cloak and his sword'. Far from being offended by this statement, Napoleone declared that Raguideau's advice was honest and shrewd and that Rose should entrust her affairs to him. His only revenge would come many years after Rose had signed the offending document, at the height of his glory, during the Imperial coronation when he reputedly turned to Raguideau and asked, 'What do you think of my cloak and sword now?'

Her daughter was not enthusiastic. Hortense, who met Napoleone at a dinner Barras held at the Luxembourg, recalled, 'I found myself placed between my mother and a general who, in order to talk to her, kept leaning forward so often and with so much vivacity that he wearied me and obliged me to lean back. Thus in spite of myself I looked attentively upon his face, which was handsome and very expressive but remarkably pale. He spoke ardently and seemed to devote all his attention to my mother. It was General Bonaparte . . .' Hortense noted that every time she returned home from her boarding school, the general's attention to her mother had become 'more assiduous'. Frightened that Napoleone would 'take her away from them', both literally and emotionally, Hortense begged her mother not to marry him.[47]

Rose was not in love with Buonaparte. He wasn't even her type. She preferred more traditionally handsome men, and those with charm and a certain ease of address, like Hoche or her erstwhile husband. Nor did Napoleone transport her senses. Never the most sensual of men (he later boasted in relation to his mistresses that, excluding the preliminaries which he frequently 'dispensed with', he was often finished within three or four minutes), Napoleone did not have the sexual finesse to compete with her more experienced lovers. Even had he done so, Rose had learnt through bitter experience the difference between passion and love. She was disquieted by his intensity and perhaps a little suspicious of it, remarking uneasily that 'Bonaparte is in adoration before me as though I were a divinity . . . his love for me is a kind of a cult.'

Maybe she wondered if Napoleone – who had read Goethe's tale of doomed love, *The Sorrows of Young Werther,* seven times in his youth – was enjoying playing the role of the impassioned lover a little too much. She knew she was not a paragon, and she also knew that their relationship had not yet evolved to such a point of intimacy or intensity that it deserved such lavish investments of feeling. As she explained to Barras: 'I admire the courage of the general, I'm impressed with his breadth of knowledge across all topics, about which he speaks equally well . . . but I am frightened I avow of the influence that he seems to want to exercise over all that surrounds him. Nonetheless,' she admitted, 'his gaze has something singular about it that fascinates me.'

Perhaps it was the final split with Hoche that ultimately decided her. He had been recalled to Paris at the end of December 1795; his defeat of the rebels meant that the civil war in the Vendée was considered to be over. Named commander-in-chief of the Army of the West Coast in preparation for a projected disembarkation in Ireland, Hoche lingered in Paris despite his wife's advanced pregnancy. It seemed he could not get Rose out of his mind. He could not have avoided knowing what everyone in Paris was gossiping about: that Rose was Barras's mistress. What enraged him were the attentions of Napoleone, the young man who had created so many excuses not to serve under him in the Vendée. That Napoleone also thought of him as a threat was made clear one night at the home of the financier Ouvrard. Buonaparte, in an uncharacteristically playful mood, pretended to be a fortune teller, and began reading various guests' palms, including that of Mme Tallien, 'inventing a thousand follies'. When he came to Hoche, his mood darkened; taking his hand, he said disagreeably, 'probably out of jealousy: "General, you will die in your bed." Hoche flushed angrily at this, the ultimate slur for a soldier, and Mme de Beauharnais changed the subject.' Affronted by the existence of his rivals, Hoche nonetheless lingered in Paris until early January, when the birth of his daughter prompted him finally to return to his wife's side. The divorce that Rose had hoped for was never mentioned. Fearful of a future in which she might end up worn out and with nothing, she finally accepted Napoleone's proposal.

Biographers have claimed that Napoleon renamed Rose in order to forget her lurid past. But this tendency to re-invent his lovers was in evidence before Rose entered his life: he had renamed Désirée, who had no past to obliterate. (And we must bear in mind that it is around this time that Napoleon renamed himself, removing the final 'e' from his first name and the 'u' from his surname to make it more French, a lead that his family followed.) Freud's explanation for the name 'Josephine' is altogether more novel and centres on Napoleon's eldest brother, Joseph: 'In the Corsican family, a sacred tenet very particularly preserved is the privilege of the eldest . . . therefore the eldest brother is the natural rival.' This elemental hostility leads to a subconscious desire for 'the death of the rival, to do murder'. The young Napoleon is beset by the longing to 'Eliminate Joseph, to take the place of Joseph, to himself become Joseph.' But the hated rival is also profoundly loved. So these contradictory feelings of love and ambition, resentment and repression, become part of the complex subconscious matrix that motivates the great man, that becomes an essential part of his psychological landscape.

   The denomination Joseph(ine) was therefore decisive for Napoleon, according to Freud. 'By virtue of the name he could transfer to her a part of the tender feelings he reserved for his eldest brother.' She in turn becomes essentially enmeshed in the complexes that fuel his vaunted ambition. But while his feelings of love for Josephine de Beauharnais were obsessionally centred around the name, this didn't, Freud emphasizes, represent a real identification with the person that was Joseph. 'The eldest brother had become more a symbol of Napoleon's own myth and motivation. Thus when guided by realistic, worldly motives he repudiates the much loved Josephine, he dooms himself.' He has betrayed his own inner mythology, according to Freud, and his decline – in part an act of self-punishment – becomes inevitable.[48]

★

Josephine's second marriage was very different from her first. Instead of a church service, it was a civil ceremony, as befitted her husband's position as 'General Vendémiaire', saviour of the Revolution. Nor was it a family affair. Josephine had not dared tell her children of her marriage plans, so they were not included in the party. Neither did she invite the marquis and Aunt Edmée. Napoleon, too, had none of his familiars present. His brother Lucien explained their absence by citing their mother's disapproval: 'Our mother was not happy with the marriage of her son the general with the ex-marquise (*sic*) de Beauharnais. The principal and only reason she shared with us was, that she was too old for her son and could not give him children.' Josephine – perhaps because of her own ambivalence about the occasion – did not invite any of her female friends. Instead she was accompanied by Calmelet and Jean Tallien.

The ceremony took place at the once glamorous Hôtel de Mondragon. It was a curious venue at which to celebrate one of 'the more glorious events in French history'. Situated in a tiny road off the avenue de l'Opéra, this beautiful eighteenth-century residence had been seized during the Revolution and transformed into the town hall of the second municipal district of the Paris canton. A room on the second floor had been allocated for civil marriages. There was still some evidence here of the hôtel's former glory: a marble fireplace, large gilt mirrors and the delicate Louis XV panelling, but the room, like the rest of the building, was sorely neglected. As Josephine recalled years later, the dingy, crudely furnished room was lit by a single, half-hearted candle flickering in a tin sconce.

The bride, wearing a white muslin gown with a tricolour sash and an enamelled medallion engraved with the words 'To Destiny', given to her by Bonaparte, arrived to this decaying splendour punctually at eight o'clock on the evening of 9 March 1796. Barras, one of Napoleon's witnesses, arrived shortly after. But there was no sign of the groom. The minutes turned into hours. There was nowhere comfortable to sit; and with increasing ill-temper the weary registrar finally went to bed, leaving the ceremony to one of his underlings, who hobbled about gamely on his wooden leg. Finally, at almost ten o'clock, Napoleon bounded up the marble staircase accompanied by his aide. Carried away with his plans for Italy, he had lost track of the time. This would set the tone for their entire relationship. No matter how great Napoleon professed his love to be, it would always come second to his military ambition.

Errors so abound throughout the marriage certificate that only the chaos of the times has prevented its legality being challenged. Josephine's age, which had been something of a moveable feast since the Revolution, becomes twenty-nine, since her year of birth is given as 1767 instead of 1763. In order that the newly-weds would appear to be roughly the same age, Napoleon had gallantly made himself eighteen months older, giving his birthday as 5 February 1768 instead of 15 August 1769. Since none of the proper documentation could be reached in the colonies, all this information went unquestioned. Napoleon gave the address of the town hall as his home address, even though he was lodging at 20 rue des Capucines. His aide, the only witness, was under age and therefore not legally eligible to fulfil the role and the one-legged Lacombe apparently was not legally entitled to conduct the marriage.

After the ceremony the tired couple returned to the house at 6 rue Chantereine. As Bonaparte explained to visitors later, it was not a romantic night. 'See this fellow,' he said, indicating Josephine's dog, Fortuné. 'He took possession of Madame's bed on the night I married her. I was told frankly that I must either sleep elsewhere or share the bed with him. Not a very pleasing alternative! Take it or leave it, I was told.' Proving that 'the darling creature' was indeed 'less accommodating' than Napoleon, the ill-tempered canine had promptly bitten his human love rival on the shin. Josephine, no doubt aggrieved that she had been left to cool her heels at the altar for almost two hours, probably felt it served him right; while Bonaparte, who had never liked dogs, would from then on like them even less.

Eleven

ITALY

The great ambition of women is to inspire love.

MOLIÈRE

IT WAS A BRIEF HONEYMOON. The day after the ceremony the newly-weds drove out to Saint-Germain to see Eugène and Hortense. Josephine, displaying a singular lack of nerve, had already begged Mme Campan to break the news of the marriage to the children. In her memoirs, Hortense recounted how the stalwart headmistress had listed the advantages of marriage to the new General-in-Chief of the Army of Italy, a man who could also become Eugène's protector. She had also stressed the desirability of Napoleon's background: 'In Corsica, his family is old and honourable and to all points of view, this alliance seems fitting.'

Despite Mme Campan's preparatory efforts, the bride and groom found Eugène reserved and Hortense weeping in fear because she thought her new stepfather would be very strict. Napoleon exercised all his charm to win them over, visiting their classrooms and strolling through the gardens with them. He melted even the austere manner of Mme Campan when he arranged to have his virtually illiterate sister Caroline enrolled at the school. He simultaneously arranged to send his younger brother, Jérôme, to join Eugène at the Collège Irlandais. Napoleon undermined his success only at the very end of the visit, when he gave Hortense one of his infamous pinches on the ear, almost bringing her to tears again.

That evening Napoleon wrote to the president of the Directoire, Letourner, to officially inform them of his marriage. He was unaware that the Directors had already decided to withhold Josephine's passport to travel: they did not want their 'young hero' distracted from his military tasks by his wife's fragrant charms. The following day, 11 March, was devoted almost exclusively to preparations for Napoleon's departure. The bell rang ceaselessly, meetings were held in the drawing room, maps of the Alps were consulted in the study. In the evening a carriage drew up outside the house and Napoleon wrapped his new bride in his arms, kissed her passionately and promised to see her soon. Then, accompanied by Junot and Chauvet, paymaster of the Army of Italy, he was gone – just two days after his midnight marriage – to take up command of that army. He took with him 8,000 livres in gold louis, 100,000 livres in bills of exchange, a promise from the Directors for reinforcements and, close to his heart, a miniature portrait of his beloved wife.

As soon as he had departed Napoleon began writing to his 'incomparable Josephine'. What followed was a series of love letters, some of the most notably passionate and lyrical of the eighteenth century. Courier after courier was despatched, as the letters – sometimes two a day – poured into 6 rue Chantereine. Napoleon's letter-writing style may have been vulnerable to accusations of self-consciousness, but the sincerity of the content cannot be impugned. Written with all the abandonment of intimacy, his letters are the quintessential expression of the lover's confusion: a tumult of longing, desire, paranoia and sensuality; a veritable cascade of sensation, passion, despair, imagined jealousies and sexual frustration.

The first was written on 14 March 1796 from the Chanceaux Post House between a change of horses:

> *Every moment separates me further from you, my darling, and every moment I have less power to bear our separation. You are the ceaseless object of my thoughts; I exhaust my imagination in thinking of what you are doing. If I see you unhappy, my heart is torn, and my grief grows greater. If you are happy and lively amongst your friends, I reproach you for having too soon forgotten our sad parting three days ago; then you must be fickle, and henceforth stirred by no deep emotions. So you see I am not easy to please; but my dear, I have quite different sensations when I fear that your health may be affected, or that you could be upset; then I regret the haste with which I was separated from my darling . . . If I were asked how I slept, I would first have to receive a message that you had had a good night. The ailments, the passions of men influence me only when I imagine them touching you, my darling. May my star, which has always preserved me in the midst of great dangers, surround you, enfold you,*

even while I face my fate unguarded. Ah! be not gay, but a trifle melancholy; and especially be free from worries, as your body from illness . . . Write me, darling, and at great length, accept the thousand and one kisses from your most devoted and true lover. Bonaparte.[1]

On 20 March Napoleon stopped en route to see his mother in Marseille. He had some apologizing to do. Knowing that they would disapprove, Napoleon had not had the courage to invite any of the Bonaparte clan to his wedding. Madame Mère was not amused. She had heard about Josephine from her other sons and had not liked anything that she had heard. An older woman? An extravagant fashion-plate who already had two children? She would have much preferred the virginal Désirée Clary, whose youth made her more likely to be malleable and whose childbearing years were still in front of her. Nonetheless she accepted the charming letter Josephine had sent with as much enthusiasm as she could muster and, with Napoleon standing at her shoulder dictating, was even induced to write a reply.

Despite the intoxication of new love, Napoleon did not neglect his life as a warrior with a reputation to prove. His first task on arriving at headquarters in Nice on 27 March was to meet his senior officers. Berthier, the eldest, at forty-three, had been born into the officer class and served in the American War of Independence before the Revolution. Despite his unruly appearance, with wild, frizzy hair, he was a born organizer and a natural chief of staff. Then there was Kilmaine, originally from Dublin, who was in charge of the cavalry; Masséna, an ex-smuggler, whose wiry frame and beaky nose made him look like an eagle; and Augereau whose own chequered past as a watch salesman and dance teacher did not make him any less of a disciplinarian with his soldiers. The latter pair, who both coveted command, resented the youthful Napoleon and sniggered behind his back when he passed around his cherished miniature of Josephine.

His soldiers were also a challenge. But Napoleon, despite his awkward manner and his 'puny and sickly looking' appearance, was already beginning to display that magnetic charisma with which he would inspire his men to an almost fanatical loyalty. He is said to have declared, 'Soldiers, you are naked and malnourished; though the Government owes you much, it can give you little. The patience and courage you have displayed in the midst of these obstacles is admirable, but they procure you no glory; no fame shines upon you. I will lead you into the most fertile plains in the world. Rich provinces, great cities will lie in your power; you will find there honour,

glory and riches. Soldiers of the Army of Italy, do you lack the courage
or the constancy?' Historians have subsequently questioned whether this
pronouncement was ever really made, but he certainly said or did something
inspirational. For what is incontestable is that, even with his unique leadership
abilities still in embryo, Napoleon managed to motivate the disillusioned men
of the Army of Italy to efforts of which they had never previously imagined
themselves capable.

Despite these military exertions, Napoleon could not get Josephine out
of his mind. On 30 March 1796 he wrote,

> *I cannot pass a day without loving you; a night without longing to hold*
> *you in my arms; I cannot even drink a cup of tea without cursing the*
> *glory and the ambition which keeps me from the soul of my existence. In*
> *the middle of business, at the head of my troops, reviewing the camps, my*
> *adorable Josephine is the single object in my heart, occupation of my spirit,*
> *absorbs my thoughts. If I leave you with the speed of the torrential waters*
> *of the Rhône, it is only that I may return to you sooner. If, in the*
> *middle of the night, I arise in order to work, it is only to speed the days*
> *before the arrival of my beloved . . .*[2]

Historical record has focused on Napoleon's passion for Josephine, rather
than on her love for him. This tendency has been fuelled by the absence of
Josephine's own letters to read and examine. But the only reason why we
have Napoleon's passionate outpourings is because Josephine meticulously
filed and kept each of his letters in a be-ribboned box, which was discovered
by a footman after her death; those written from her to him were either lost
or discarded.

That she did write to him, and with some passion, is evident in one of
his responses, on 3 April:

> *I have received all your letters, but none has affected me like the last. How*
> *can you think, my charming one, of writing me in such terms? Do you*
> *believe that my position is not already painful enough without further*
> *increasing my regrets and subverting my reason? What eloquence, what*
> *feeling you portray; they are fiery, they inflame my poor heart! My*
> *incomparable Josephine, away from you there is no joy — away from you*
> *the world is a wilderness, in which I stand alone . . . You have robbed me*
> *of more than my soul; you are the only thought of my life. When I am*
> *weary of the worries of my profession . . . when men disgust me, when I*

am ready to curse my life, I put my hand on my heart where your portrait beats in unison. I look at it, and love is for me complete happiness; and everything laughs for joy, except the time during which I find myself absent from my beloved.

By what art have you learnt how to captivate all my faculties, to concentrate in yourself my spiritual existence — it is witchcraft, dear love, which will end only with me. To live for Josephine, that is the history of my life. I am struggling to get near you, I am dying to be by your side; fool that I am, I fail to realize how far off I am, that lands and provinces separate us. What an age it will be before you read these lines, the feeble expressions of the fevered soul over which you reign. Ah, my winsome wife, I know not what fate awaits me, but if it keeps me much longer from you it will be unbearable — my strength will not last out . . . the thought that my Josephine might be ill; and, above all, the cruel, the fatal thought that she might love me less, blights my soul, stops my blood, makes me wretched and dejected, without even leaving me the courage of fury and despair . . . to die without your love, die in uncertainty of that, is the torment of hell . . . My unique companion! You whom fate has destined to walk with me on the painful path of life! The day on which I no longer possess your heart will be that on which parched Nature will be for me without warmth and without vegetation. I stop, dear love! my soul is sad, my body tired, my spirit dazed, men worry me — I ought indeed to detest them; they keep me from my beloved . . .[3]

His next letter, written from Albegna, is reflective: his friend and military colleague has been killed. His mind 'distressed' and 'in need of consolation', he muses to his beloved:

What does the future mean? The past? What are we ourselves? What magic fluid surrounds and hides from us the things that it behoves us most to know. We are born, we live, we die in the midst of marvels; it is astounding that priests, astrologers, charlatans have profited by this propensity, by this strange circumstance, to exploit our ideas, and direct them to their own advantage. Chauvet is dead . . . I see his ghost; it hovers everywhere, it whistles in the air. His soul is in the clouds, he will be propitious to my destiny. But, fool that I am, I shed tears for our friendship, and who shall tell me that I have not already to bewail the irreparable. Soul of my life, write me by every courier, else I shall not know how to exist . . . Sleep consoles me; it places you by my side, I clasp

*you in my arms. But on waking, alas! I find myself three hundred leagues
from you . . .*[4]

Some have argued that Napoleon was too much of an egotist to be capable
of love. Family feeling, yes, argued the duchesse d'Abrantès, but not love.
This judgment seems a bit harsh. The youthful Napoleon was not the same
man as the cynical megalomaniac he would become in middle age. In later
years he became solipsistic, more in love with power than he could ever be
with any individual. But as a young man he was vulnerable, inexperienced
and intensely romantic. There is no doubt that Napoleon was bowled over
by his feelings for Josephine; and this first real experience of physical passion
hit him with hurricane force. Like many a first-time lover, he was as much
in love with love as he was with Josephine herself. The youthful Napoleon
had revealed his template for ideal love in his unfinished novel, *Clisson and
Eugénie*, written some time between 1789 and 1795. It tells the story of a
young man who is already a successful warrior, but whose soul remains
unsatisfied. He achieves a brief interlude of domestic bliss but then is recalled
to battle. When Eugénie's letters eventually peter out, he is left to seek death,
expiring, 'shot through with a thousand wounds'.

Josephine, beautiful and elusive, fitted the script perfectly. Her unattainability only heightened her desirability for Napoleon, who was titillated by
the prospect of the elusive and the difficult. That Josephine remained something of a figment of his imagination is evident in Napoleon's letters, in
which he is clearly bewitched by his own romantic rhetoric. When Josephine
does not respond in the way he wishes, he chastizes her; she is not playing
her part. Thus the youthful Napoleon is seduced by the idea of 'women', a
'sensuality of the mind', as the French historian Masson puts it, rather than
by Josephine herself.

If Napoleon threw himself into the part of the tormented lover, Josephine
slotted into her role as femme fatale with equal ease. During the early days
of their relationship she teased and tormented him, sometimes lavishing him
with attention, at other times ignoring him. Sometimes she went so far as to
mock his sexual prowess behind his back, giggling with friends that Bonaparte
was *bon-à-rien* (good at nothing). Like Zola's Nana a century later, Josephine
exulted in her sexual power: she was often capricious, and occasionally cruel.
In a delightful reversal of the powerlessness she had experienced in her first
marriage, Napoleon's adoration allowed her to play the temptress, the spider
who enmeshed her hapless male victims in a shimmering web.

His love for her was also fuelled by the image of himself that she reflected back to him. The fact that she had been pursued by men he admired and competed with – who had lost out to him – only increased her desirability. She symbolized the social status that he aspired to, and his capture of her flattered his ego and his sense of amour propre. But his uncertainty about his real status in Josephine's life is evident in the manner in which he addressed his letters. Despite their marriage, the first letters of the campaign were addressed to the citoyenne Beauharnais, then to citoyenne Bonaparte care of citoyenne Beauharnais, then to Mme Bonaparte care of citoyenne Beauharnais.

This uncertainty may explain the accusatory tone of some of his missives. Napoleon's complaints about her letter writing must have provoked a sense of déjà vu for Josephine, whose first husband had similarly chastized her almost two decades earlier. Her letters were not passionate enough, their style was not sufficiently fulsome. 'You called me *vous*!', he thundered in response to her first letter. '*Vous* yourself! Ah, wicked one, how could you write that letter. And then, from the 23rd to the 26th is four days. What were you doing, since you were not writing to your husband? Ah, my dear, that *vous* and those four days make me sorry not to possess my old indifference. Woe to whosoever may be the cause of it. *Vous! Vous!* What will it be in a fortnight!'

A couple of weeks later she was still not responding as he wished. It was not just the content of her letters, it was also their lack of frequency. 'No letters from you. I get one only every four days. Whereas, if you loved me, you would write twice a day. But you have to chat with your gentlemen callers at ten in the morning and then listen to the idle talk and silly nonsense of a hundred fops until an hour past midnight. In countries with any morals everyone is at home by ten in the evening. But in those countries people write to their husbands, think of them, live for them. Goodbye, Josephine, to me you are an inexplicable monster.' But he could not resist adding, 'I love you more each day. Absence cures small passions but increases great ones.'

As with Alexandre, Josephine's style continued to disappoint. On 7 April Napoleon wrote,

> . . . *I am not happy with your last letter; it was as cold as if it had sprung merely from friendship. I did not find within it the fire that illuminates your gaze, or which I have sometimes believed I have seen there. But how insanely infatuated I am! I found your earlier letters weighed too heavily*

on my soul. The disorder they provoked gave me no rest, overwhelmed my
senses. I desired cooler letters but these gave me the chill of death. Not to be
loved by Josephine, the thought of finding her inconstant . . . but I am
forging troubles – there are so many real ones, there is no need to
manufacture more! You cannot have inspired a boundless love without
sharing it, for a cultured mind and a soul like yours cannot requite
complete surrender and devotion with the death blow . . . Don't speak to
me of your villainous stomach. I hate it . . . Adieu, until tomorrow, mio
dolce amore . . . PS A kiss, lower, lower, lower than your heart.[5]

Napoleon was thinking of love but he was also making war. His troops under
Augereau were victorious at Millesimo on 24 Germinal (13 April). But at
this point in the campaign failure alternated with success. Where the failures
were concerned, Napoleon was astute enough, however, to dissimulate in his
reports to the Directoire. Unaware of this, Barras – full of enthusiasm for
his protégé – wrote officially to Josephine on 2 Floréal year IV (21 April
1796): 'Accept, amiable citoyenne, my sincere compliments on the success
obtained by your husband: nearly four thousand enemies are imprisoned or
dead. He didn't stop there, and quickly we received details of the battle.
General Bonaparte has perfectly lived up to the confidence of the Directoire
and the opinion that it holds of his talents, which have so significantly
contributed to the victories of the good army of Italy . . .'

There were no letters from Bonaparte to Josephine from 7 to 23 April.
However, on the 23rd he wrote to Barras informing him of his achievements.
'Up to the present time, I have engaged in six battles with the enemy. I have,
in ten days, taken 12,000 prisoners. I have killed 6,000 men, captured 21
colours and 40 cannon. You see that I have wasted none of my time and
lived up to your confidence.' At the end of the letter he added beseechingly,
'I desire greatly that my wife join me.'[6]

On 24 April, in a letter addressed 'To my sweet love', Napoleon wrote,

You have had many days without writing to me. What have you been
doing? Yes, my good, good darling, I am not jealous, but sometimes a
little anxious. Come quickly. I warn you: if you are late, you will find me
ill. The exhaustion and your absence are too much to bear. Your letters
provide the basis for my daily happiness, and my happy days are not
frequent. Junot bears 22 flags to Paris. You should return with him, do
you understand? . . . should he return without you, I will suffer grief
without remedy, inconsolable unhappiness, constant anxiety. My adorable

love, he will see you, he will breathe on your temples. Perhaps you will
even accord him the unique and priceless pleasure of kissing your cheek, and
I, I will be alone and very far away; but you are about to come, are you
not? You will soon be beside me, on my heart, in my arms, over my
mouth. Take wings, come quickly but travel carefully . . . Napoleon.[7]

As his friend and aide Marmont explained:

> General Bonaparte, occupied as he was by the grandeur of his
> schemes which he confided in me and of his future, was nonetheless
> at the time preoccupied by feelings of a different nature; he thought
> ceaselessly about his wife. He desired her, he awaited her with
> impatience: she, on her side, was more occupied with enjoying the
> triumphs of her husband, in the excitement of Paris, than with
> rejoining him. He spoke frequently of her and of his love, with the
> effusion, ardour, and the delusions of a very young man.[8]

On 12 April Napoleon had his first victory at Montenotte. Nine days later
he requested, yet again, that the Directoire allow his Josephine to join him.
During the negotiations of the armistice of Cherasco his willingness to sign
was, according to some, predicated upon article five – known as '*l'article de*
Josephine' – which guaranteed safe passage for his beloved by the shortest road
from Paris. He wrote to Josephine saying he had prepared lodgings for her
in Mondovi and Tortoni as well as left 200 louis for furnishings. He chose
Joachim Murat, a devoted disciple, to be her escort. On 6 May, the day that
Murat was scheduled to arrive in Paris, Napoleon went on a trip to inspect
military placements. His mood was anxious, according to Marmont. 'The
delays that Josephine threw in the way of her departure tormented him
terribly and he succumbed to paroxysms of jealousy and superstition which
were strong in his nature. So when he discovered that the glass protecting
the miniature of Josephine, which always accompanied him, was broken, his
face paled, his manner became extremely agitated, and the impression of
profound sadness descended around him; "my wife is either very ill or
unfaithful." '[9]

On Murat's arrival in Paris he endeavoured to discover from Josephine
whether she was involved with someone else. She denied this, claiming to
be ill. The symptoms she reported were suspiciously akin to those of a
pregnancy. Informed by Murat, Napoleon wrote to her ecstatic: 'I long to
know you carrying children. It must give you a majestic respectable look.'

Napoleon later discovered, to his great distress, that the piratically handsome, black-curled Murat had boasted of an improper dalliance with Josephine – 'barely decent details, fit only for a hussar officers' mess'. Though false, Murat's claim – probably the product of braggadocio and the desire to be associated with one of the celebrated beauties of the age – would be held against him by Napoleon for the rest of his life.

Many of Josephine's biographers have dismissed her symptoms, and the subsequent claims of pregnancy, as a ploy to avoid joining her husband in Italy, but it is possible they were more than a delaying tactic. Josephine complained of these ailments – headaches, fevers and menstrual irregularities – over a period of several months, long after there was any pretence at delay. It is possible that at nearly thirty-three she, like many women who had been imprisoned during the Terror, was suffering from the symptoms of premature menopause brought on by trauma and loss.

Much has been made of Josephine's reluctance to join her husband, but in the circumstances it was understandable. She had been married for just two days but had been effectively single for more than a decade. She had grown used to managing her own life, not organizing it around a husband. The thought of being separated from her children, from friends like Mme Tallien and from her beloved Paris for an indeterminate amount of time seemed too painful to bear. And the four months after Napoleon's departure were a particularly pleasurable period in the city. 'Life in Paris', according to Mathieu Molé, who would eventually become a minister under Napoleon, 'was very pleasant at this time . . . most of the émigrés had returned home and were filling the gap which their absences had left in society. Everybody was trying hard to forget the sufferings of the past. Misfortune seemed to have left a stain which everyone was anxious to remove as quickly as possible.'[10]

Family matters also diverted her. There were frequent visits from Hortense and Eugène and there were two family weddings to plan for and enjoy. After almost half a century together, the marquis de Beauharnais and Josephine's aunt Edmée Renaudin were getting married. The tenacious M. Renaudin had died, leaving his widow finally free to marry her now eighty-two-year-old lover. Four months after Josephine's own wedding, on 20 June 1796, the happy occasion was held, after which the elderly couple purchased a new home nearer to their grandchildren. The other family wedding was that of Françoise de Beauharnais, Aunt Fanny's daughter and the estranged wife of Alexandre's elder brother, François. She was marrying the man with whom she had been living for some time, a handsome mixed race divorcee named Charles Guillaume Castaing, who had saved her from the guillotine. Her daughter Émilie, who had been greatly traumatized during the terrible years of the Revolution, was to join Hortense at Mme Campan's.

Meanwhile in Italy, after the fall of Piedmont, victory followed victory for Napoleon. Ensconced in the Milanese palace from which the Austrian Archduke Charles had recently fled, Napoleon wrote to the Directoire triumphantly: 'The Tricolour flies over Milan, Paiva, Como and all the towns of Lombardy.' At Arcola he was almost killed when his horse was shot out from beneath him and he was thrown into a swamp. He was rescued with only seconds to spare. A Directoire spy provided a vivid portrait of the young hero not long after this fateful event: 'haggard, thin, the skin clinging to his bones, eyes bright with fever'.

As Napoleon's representative in Paris, Josephine's life became more pleasant with each of his victories. Verses written in her honour were submitted to the newspapers and she was recognized and applauded wherever she went. Much to her gratification, her credit with merchants was now better than ever, and she displaced her friend Mme Tallien as the star of the city's balls, dinners and galas. At a ceremony to celebrate the captured standards that Junot had presented to the Directoire on Napoleon's behalf, she was greeted with wild approbation. On 'one of the loveliest days of May', Josephine and her companions descended the great staircase of the Palais du Luxembourg accompanied by martial music and cries of 'Long live the Republic!' The sight made a fetching tableau: Josephine on the right; Junot – in his splendid hussar uniform – playing the escort; Mme Tallien on his other arm. The poet Arnault compared Josephine, Thérésia and Juliette Récamier, in their garlands of flowers, to the 'three months of spring reunited to celebrate victory'. Awed at the sight the crowd roared, '*Vive le général Bonaparte!*', '*Vive la citoyenne Bonaparte!*' A female spectator shouted that she was 'Notre-Dame-des-Victoires!' ('Our Lady of Victory'), and this title endured until her death, indissolubly associating her with the military success of her husband.

Largely as a result of Josephine's own prominence and influence, the Directoire was thoroughly 'creolized'. Her supporting players were Creole friends like the jolie-laide Mme Hamelin, whose insouciance bewitched the city. Exotic women were very much in fashion: when British caricaturists depicted Directoire beauties it was with African features and black frizzy hair.[11] The Directoire's love of the Creole was obvious in all areas of aesthetic life: the deceptively simple white dresses were reminiscent of those favoured in the colonies; and the headkerchief tied à la Creole, which Josephine had helped to popularize, was now the height of fashion. The Creole influence extended beyond fashion, however. Émigrés returning from the Americas brought back new trends in furnishing and decorations, while Creoles popularized food and drinks such as Martinique's ti-punch, a lethal rum cocktail that Josephine served to her delighted guests at rue Chantereine.

On 15 May the 'young conqueror' entered Milan in triumph. He made a rousing speech that promised an end to tyranny. 'Thought has become free . . .' No doubt the Milanese hoped that Napoleon would be a benevolent protector; he was of Italian descent, he spoke Italian, loved the country's music and art and had gathered around him Italian historians, philosophers and scientists. But these optimistic expectations did not prevent him from looting from the city twenty of its greatest masterpieces, including works by Correggio, Titian, Raphael and Michelangelo. In spite of the Directoire's disapproval, Napoleon unilaterally assumed authority and arranged truces with the dukes of Parma and Modena and the king of Naples, guaranteeing peace with France and protection from Austria – at a price.

By the end of May Napoleon, now master of Lombardy, was still waiting for his beloved wife. He wrote, 'Without you I am of no use here. I will leave the pursuit of glory and serving the *patrie* to others; this exile suffocates me; when my beloved is ill, I cannot coldly calculate how to beat the enemy . . . My tears drop on your portrait; it alone is always with me.' But the Directoire still denied compassionate leave; he was not going to enrich their coffers playing the lovesick swain in Josephine's boudoir. As the couple's reunion continued to be delayed, Napoleon's letters grew even wilder. His theories about her apparent reluctance changed with every missive. He wondered whether she was merely indifferent to him. 'Should I accuse you? No. Your conduct is your destiny.' But most consistently of all he feared that he had a rival: 'Have you taken up with some stripling of nineteen?'

Inundated with Napoleon's frenzied letters, Josephine diagnosed his behaviour as 'delirium'. Her friend the poet Antoine Arnault, to whom she had shown these letters, described them as being 'characterized by the most ardently passionate feeling. Josephine was amused by the sentiments which were not exempt from expressions of jealousy. I can still hear her reading a passage, in which there was evidence of the anxieties about a potential rival that so clearly troubled him. In the letter her husband said, "If it was true, you have reason to dread Othello's fist!" I can still hear her say with her Creole accent, "He is funny, Bonaparte!" '

Josephine's brutal treatment of Napoleon clearly illustrates the power balance in their relationship at that time. It also reveals how far Josephine had travelled from the romantic, innocent girl she had been. Once again, she found herself married to a man who did not share her views on conjugal life. But this time it was she who was the world-weary cynic and he the romantic idealist. She had been trained out of her teenage sentimentality by the ridicule of her decadent first husband, who had dismissed her ideas about fidelity and companionate married love as unsophisticated and provincial. Subsequent painful romantic experiences and exposure to the ideas of the brittle, decadent milieu she inhabited had completed the transformation. Her stint in Les Carmes taught her that life was short and that happiness had to be seized; it didn't matter whether or not relationships lasted, one must take one's joys where one could. By the time she met Napoleon, according to one of her French biographers, Josephine was a 'woman without illusions',[12] grateful for the benefits that the marriage could provide her but expecting little more. She was sceptical of the ardour expressed in his letters and bemused and amused by their tone.

Napoleon and Josephine's marriage, like so many epic love affairs, was a drama of poor timing and missed opportunities. She began the relationship a disaffected cynic, unwilling to fully commit herself, while he was the young romantic, head over heels in love. As his ardour cooled to a more realistic level, she would grow secure enough to remove the mask of the blasé sophisticate and allow herself to fall in love. He by this time had become cavalier with her feelings. She would eventually fall so utterly in love with him that Byron's line from *Don Juan* could have been written of her: 'Man's love is of man's life a thing apart / 'Tis woman's whole existence'. Josephine would eventually embrace the companionate model of family-centred life that had originally inspired her as a very young woman and which Napoleon also shared. She would find happiness in the cosy domesticity that she had once been so inclined to despise.

But, for now, Napoleon's fear was well founded; there was someone else. His name was Hippolyte Charles. They had met in the middle of April, when Charles had accompanied Napoleon's old friend General Leclerc to Paris in order to pay his respects to the young conqueror's wife. Despite the fact that he was almost ten years her junior, Charles pursued Josephine with impressive energy. She was captivated. Writing to Talleyrand, she declared, 'We are smitten, Mmes Récamier, Tallien, Hamelin have all lost their heads, the man is so gorgeous. He dresses with such impeccable taste . . . I think that there is no one in the world who arranges a more perfect cravat.'[13]

The consensus was that Charles was indeed a very attractive man (although one dissenter sniffed that he looked like 'a hairdresser'). He was a 'Mediterranean type', according to one contemporary, slightly shorter than average (the same height as Napoleon, around five feet six inches), with a well-muscled physique and small hands and feet. He had a handsome face: fine-featured with a rounded chin and passable teeth, piercing blue eyes, and olive skin that tanned easily to a deep brown. His features were framed by perfectly styled jet-black hair, moustache, sideburns and beard. An impeccable dresser, he was a picture of elegance in his sky-blue uniform, red belt, Hungarian trousers, boots of beaten Moroccan leather and a curved sabre in a sheath of leather and silver, decorated with a bristling dragon breathing flames of gold.

He was the sort of man who flourished in drawing-room society. Women adored him and he was easy in their company. 'He was', remarked one female contemporary, 'utterly charming, with the impeccable manners of a hussar . . . and great elegance.' He took an active interest in fashion and complimented women adroitly. He always knew the latest gossip and had for each conversational sally some clever riposte. 'It was impossible to find a more comic man,' commented the duchesse d'Abrantès.[14] His practical jokes were of the vulgar slapstick variety, thoughtless and silly, and included pouring glue into General Junot's sabre and dressing up as a Creole and prancing round Josephine's salon. Mostly he was famous for his quips and puns, which so entertained Josephine that she would choke with laughter, covering her 'terrible teeth' with a handkerchief.

M. Charles was more than just 'a card', he was also an honourable man. Born in Romans, in the Drôme, he had enlisted, aged nineteen, as a National Guardsman in the early days of the Revolution and had fought at the Battle of Valmy. He acquired the nickname *l'Éveillé* ('the lively one'), because of his ability to raise his companions' spirits. 'I have never known a better comrade, or a better-humoured one', wrote a fellow soldier. In later years, despite his lack of funds, he never attempted to capitalize on the valuable love letters he had received from Josephine, and he insisted on his deathbed that his family burn the letters so they would not fall into the wrong hands.

Josephine's biographers have been divided over Hippolyte Charles. A vocal minority claim that the correspondence between him and Josephine is a fabrication, forged for financial gain or to sully Napoleon's reputation.

They seem unable to believe that Josephine could prefer an insignificant adjutant to the great Emperor. But in 1796 Napoleon was not yet the legend he was to become. And he was not – unlike Charles – a handsome man, with the kind of ease and charm that appealed to women. Nor would he ever be. Despite the claims of the more fervent Napoleonists, who maintained that Napoleon was as 'great a lover as he was a warrior', Bonaparte himself knew this was not the case. 'I have never been a lover,' he wrote to his brother, and the ease of his later romantic conquests would be the product of his fame and achievement rather than his skills of seduction.

Why did Josephine have an affair with Charles? It is possible that, fearing the onset of an early menopause, she felt compromised in her femininity and was reassured by the attentions of a young, charming man. Certainly she was not the romantic idealist her husband was. As a *vraie Parisienne*, she kept her romantic and married life separate and saw taking a lover as perfectly acceptable. And Hippolyte Charles was the perfect candidate. Unlike Napoleon, who did not know how to speak to women and was ill at ease in their company, Charles was debonair and easy-going. He was a romantic *amuse-bouche* – appealing to look at, titillating to the taste buds: an enjoyable diversion before she got to grips with the main course.

It was also possible that her affair with Charles represented Josephine's rebellion against the constraints of her new marriage. She had been alone for ten years and now found herself with an increasingly controlling and intense husband. Perhaps this little affair was a stab at autonomy, an act of self-assertion. She may have already realized that to be Napoleon's consort was no small burden, with all that it entailed of loneliness, and a life of strenuous new duties, often in alien countries, away from family and friends, with, as often as not, no husband near to come between her and the power-hungry schemers. Josephine, a woman who had experienced love as a ceaseless drama, was now entering into marriage with the 'master of upheaval'. Is it any wonder she hesitated before she walked into the flames?

Charles was not the only obstacle preventing Josephine's reunion with her husband. A letter to Napoleon from the Directors, dated 21 May, makes it clear that they had been blocking her departure behind the scenes: 'It is with great reluctance that we yield to the desire of citoyenne Bonaparte to join you. We were afraid that the attention you would give to her would distract you from attending to the glory and safety of your country. Hence we had long resisted her wishes . . . We hope that the myrtle with which she will crown you will not detract from the laurels with which you have already been crowned by victory.'

Even after the permission for travel had been granted, there were further delays. Then Josephine's letters to her husband stopped. Napoleon was desperate: 'I received a courier who left Paris on 27 May, and I have had no response, no news of my *bonne amie*. Could she have forgotten me, or have forgotten that there is no greater torment than not to have a letter from *mio dolce amore*? They gave me a great fête here; five or six hundred elegant and beautiful figures sought to please me; none had that sweet and music-like countenance which I have engraved on my heart. I saw only you, I thought only of you!' Then he added, 'Your pregnancy, how goes it? I imagine constantly that I see you, with your little round belly – it must be charming!'[15]

By June Napoleon was distraught: 'All my couriers arrive without any letters from you . . . When you do write, the few words you send me never express anything profound . . . You have never loved me . . . My heart has never felt anything mediocre . . . You have inspired in it a passion without limits, an intoxication which you only degrade.'[16] The next letter verged on the hysterical: 'Josephine, where will this letter be delivered? If at Paris my misfortune is definite; you no longer love me. I would have nothing to do but die . . . All the serpents and Furies are alive in my breast and I'm already only half alive . . . I hate Paris, women and love . . . This situation is terrible . . . and your behaviour . . . But should I accuse you? No. Your conduct is your destiny. So amiable, so beautiful, how can you be the instrument of my despair . . .'[17]

The same day, in a letter to Barras, he reiterated the point: 'I am desperate. My wife is not coming. She has some lover who is keeping her in Paris. I curse all women . . .' The following day he wrote to his brother Joseph in the same mood: ' . . . I am in despair. My wife, all that I love in the world, is ill . . . You know that I have never been in love before, that Josephine is the first woman that I have adored . . . I love her to the point of fury, and I cannot rest until I'm near to her. If she doesn't love me any more, there is nothing more for me to do on this earth'.[18]

Despite Napoleon's suspicions, it is unlikely that he had specific knowledge about Hippolyte Charles. The affair was so new that it had barely had time to become a rumour. But Napoleon's accusations of infidelity provided his tortured mind with a legitimate explanation for his wife's neglect. His anxieties continued to spiral as the campaign against Austria moved to a new climax. Though he had joked in an earlier letter that she should take a lover if she was feeling low, he now firmly retracted it: 'You know very well that I could never bear it if you took a lover – much less seriously suggest one to you. To see him and to tear out his heart would be one and the same thing . . . A million kisses on your eyes, your lips, everywhere.'[19]

In the letters sent as he marched through Genoa, Tuscany and Rome, during the siege of Mantua, and while he entered Modena and Bologna, Napoleon's distress at Josephine's continued absence is apparent. On 15 June he wrote, 'My life is a perpetual nightmare. A disastrous presentiment impedes my breath . . . I no longer live; I have lost more than life, more than happiness, more than repose . . .' Later, having heard that she was ill, he was filled with remorse:

> *Forgive me, my sweetheart. Love has inspired me to abandon reason . . .*
> *In five days I can be in Paris, and on the twelfth back with my army.*
> *Without you, I can be of no value here . . . when my beloved is in pain,*
> *I cannot coolly calculate victory . . . Remember that there has never been*
> *a love like mine, it will last as long as my life . . . I am nothing without*
> *you . . . All my thoughts are concentrated on your alcove, in your bed,*
> *on your heart. Your illness is on my mind night and day. Without appetite,*
> *without sleep, without interest in friendship, glory, country . . . Should*
> *you be in danger, I warn you, I shall leave at once for Paris. My presence*
> *will conquer the disease . . . I have always been able to impose my will*
> *on destiny.*[20]

On 26 June he wrote, 'For a month, I have received nothing from my good friend but two letters of three lines only. Is she having affairs? Does she feel no need to write to her good friend?' Then his mood took a new turn, and he wrote angrily, 'You were supposed to leave on 24 May, idiot that I was, I expected you in June. As if a pretty woman could abandon her habits, her friends, her Mme Tallien, a dinner with Barras, a performance of a new play, and the dog Fortuné, yes, Fortuné! You love all of these more than you love your husband . . . Adieu, my good friend. A kiss on your mouth, another on your heart and another on your little belly.'[21]

It was now six weeks since the Directoire had granted Josephine permission to travel, and Napoleon's threats to return to Paris were making the Government extremely nervous. They couldn't risk compromising the success of the Italian campaign because Mme Bonaparte would not give up the joys of the capital. This point was brought home forcefully to Josephine and her travel arrangements were expedited. As a broad hint, Barras planned a farewell dinner for her at the Luxembourg, after which he dispatched her to Italy, looking, according to Antoine Arnault, 'as though she were going to a torture chamber'.

She travelled in the first carriage of a convoy of six vehicles, accompanied by Hippolyte Charles, Napoleon's brother Joseph, his aide Junot, and her pug, Fortuné, sporting a new leather collar with two little silver bells and a small silver name tag with 'I belong to Madame Bonaparte' engraved on it. Among those following in the later coaches were Désirée Clary's brother Nicholas, the duke of Serbelloni, and Josephine's pretty maid, Louise Compoint. The convoy was escorted by a detachment of cavalry and was led by one of Napoleon's most faithful soldiers, Moustache. The travellers stopped briefly in Fontainebleau so that Josephine could say goodbye to Aunt Edmée and the marquis. Here their party was joined by Antoine Hamelin, husband of her Creole friend Fortunée, who travelled in his own post-chaise. He claimed that Josephine had borrowed 200 louis which she promised to return to him on arrival in Milan.

Always a martyr to travel sickness, Josephine complained of headaches, stomach upsets and the heat as the convoy made its stately way south. At each relay stop, according to Hamelin, Josephine and Hippolyte Charles, and Mlle Louise and Andoche Junot enjoyed adjoining suites. Joseph, smarting from a 'painful souvenir of his Paris love affairs' (a nasty venereal disease), remained alone, editing his novel. Via Lyon, Chambéry, le Mont-Cenis and Turin, the journey Napoleon had expected to take twelve days took eighteen. The mood of the journey should have been cheerful, according to Hamelin, as Junot kept them laughing with his robust military wit. But 'the little Charles' had taken to jealous sulking whenever someone else was shown any favour. On their arrival, the party drove through the streets of the city to be met by an ecstatic Napoleon and an escort of militia.

The couple's reunion was played out against the backdrop of the beautiful Serbelloni palace, 'a pile of pinkish, crystal-flecked granite that sparkled like sugar-candy in the sun', that was now serving as the Army of Italy's headquarters. With its huge columns, beautiful grounds, ornate French furniture and magnificent marble galleries decorated with Italian works of art, it was a fairy-tale setting. Napoleon's desire for his wife was so intense it was, according to Hamelin, embarrassing. 'He loved his wife passionately,' he wrote. 'From time to time he would leave his study' where he was working on military plans, 'in order to play with her as if she were a child. He would tease her, cause her to cry out, and overwhelm her with such rough caresses that I would be obliged to go to the window and observe the weather outside.'[22]

Napoleon organized a number of events to celebrate Josephine's arrival. The most impressive of these, a grand ball given by the duke of Serbelloni, was attended by all the great Milanese beauties. Mme Visconti, the Italian beauty who had conquered the heart of Paris and whose portrait by Gérard still hangs in the Louvre, arrived draped in a bandeau of red velvet, on which 'Viva Bonaparte' was embossed in diamonds. All this female pulchritude made no impact on Napoleon, who, according to one guest, 'established his position behind the chair of his wife and would address his conversation to no one else'.[23]

But the reunion was almost as short as the honeymoon had been. After four days Napoleon was gone. Despite her husband's naked adoration, and the lavish entertainments put on for her pleasure, Josephine was in morose spirits. In a letter to Mme Tallien she complained, 'I had the most difficult journey possible. I was 18 days en route. I had a fever on mounting the carriage and was sad besides. The fever is over but the sadness still endures.' Despite her misery, Josephine's immediate concern, as she explained to her friend, was to set up a household. 'Arriving in Milan, the municipality treated me like an archduchess and not like a republican. They lodged me in the most beautiful house in Milan. They had made up my household of 30 domestics, five cooks . . . I took the liberty of dismissing all of them and recreating my little household at rue Chantereine.' Despite these endeavours, Josephine pronounced herself bored: 'I hardly see Bonaparte at the moment. He is very occupied with the siege of Mantua . . . I am dying of boredom here in the middle of the superb fêtes given for me. I never cease to miss my friends of Chaillot [the Talliens] and the ones at the Luxembourg [Barras] . . .'[24] She also missed her family. In a letter to her daughter she wrote, 'I cannot wait, my dear Hortense, for the time that I can embrace you, and assure you of the love, the most tender love of your mother, a mother who loves you most dearly . . . Bonaparte embraces you. He is sending you a 'queen's chain', and I'm sending you a necklace and antique earrings . . . Your brother has still not arrived; I await him with impatience. Adieu, I embrace you with all my heart and love you so much . . .'[25]

The arrival of friends like Mme Hamelin, who had come to join her husband Antoine, helped to assuage some of Josephine's ennui. But the swelling Parisian presence caused shock waves amongst the population of

Milan. The women of Josephine's circle – wives and mistresses of French army entrepreneurs and government officials – were a particular source of outrage. Journals complained of their 'immodest behaviour; arms, bosom, shoulders, all are uncovered. The arrangement of their hair is a scandal – sown with flowers and feathers, and the whole crowned with little military helmets from which locks of untidy hair escape. They even have the effrontery to dress in tunics revealing legs and thighs barely hidden by flesh-coloured stockings. Their manners match their clothes: arrogant talk, provocative looks, and meat eaten on Fridays.'

Meanwhile, Josephine was growing alarmed at her husband's intensity. His adoration began to reveal depths of obsession and possessiveness that may have disturbed her. She wrote with dismay to a friend, 'My husband doesn't just love me, he worships me. I fear he will go mad. It is impossible for him to be happy if I am not by his side . . .'[26] Napoleon's letters to her bear this assertion this out. The first, dispatched after their brief reunion, was as passionate as ever:

> *I received your letter, my adorable love. It filled my heart with joy . . .*
> *Since I left you, I am always sad. My happiness is to be near to you.*
> *Without ceasing, I replay in my memory your kisses, your tears, your*
> *charming jealousy. And the charms of the incomparable Josephine create*
> *a perpetual flame alive and scorching in my heart and in my senses . . . I*
> *thought that I loved you but now that I have seen you again, I love you*
> *a thousand times more . . . Millions of kisses, even to Fortuné, despite his*
> *meanness . . .*[27]

The following day, he wrote again.

> *I received a letter from Eugène, that you sent me. For my part I will write*
> *your adorable offspring, and I will send them some jewellery. Assure them*
> *that I love them as if they were my own children . . . I am very anxious*
> *to know what you are wearing and what you are doing, I was in Virgil's*
> *village, on the borders of a lake, in the moonlight, and not for an instant*
> *did I stop thinking of Josephine . . . I am all about Josephine, and I have*
> *no pleasure or happiness except in her society . . . I have lost my snuff*
> *box, can you choose me another and have something pretty inscribed in*
> *it with your hair . . .*

The next day, he confessed that he opened some letters addressed to her when the courier brought them to his headquarters. 'Although this seems a perfectly ordinary action to me, and you gave me permission the other day, I fear this may vex you and that would upset me . . . I am guilty; I ask your pardon. I swear it is not from jealousy – certainly not. I have too high an opinion of my adorable love for that. I should like you to give me complete permission to read your letters. Then I will have no remorse or fear.'[28]

On 21 July at half past eight in the evening he wrote in meditative mood:

> *I hoped to have received one of your letters before this evening. You know, my dear Josephine, how much pleasure they give me, and I am sure that you have the same pleasure in writing them . . . What are you doing at this hour? You're sleeping, of course. And I am not there to breathe in your scent, contemplate your grace and overwhelm you with caresses. Far from you, the nights are long, dull and sad. Near to you, I regret that it is not always night. Goodbye, beautiful and good, totally incomparable, totally divine. A million loving kisses, everywhere, everywhere.*[29]

Napoleon was now in Castiglione, and in anxious mood. Mantua remained uncaptured behind him while the Austrian army was poised to descend from the Alps. Nonetheless he wrote to Josephine on 24 July instructing her to join him at Cassono. She left Milan immediately, accompanied by Hamelin and his friend Monglas, both still hoping for Napoleon's patronage. On her arrival, Napoleon's tension was palpable, despite his pleasure in seeing her. His concerns about the campaign distracted him but did not prevent him from wanting her near him. The trio moved on to Brescia where they stayed for two days, and then carried on to Verona. Here they lodged in a residence that the exiled Louis XVIII had stayed in a short while before. The pleasure of following in the footsteps of royalty was short-lived. As Josephine sat with Hamelin on the balcony after lunch taking coffee and enjoying the idyllic view of the Adige flowing beneath them and the foothills of the Alps ahead of them, she noticed white flecks against the hillside. They were the white uniforms of the Austrians, who had outflanked Napoleon's General Masséna and were advancing on the town.

The soldiers in question were under the command of Wurmser, the veteran Austrian commander-in-chief. Although worried for Josephine's safety, Bonaparte was unwilling to send her back across unsecured territory to Milan. He decided to send her to Peschiera, halfway between the two. As the party made a hasty departure, Josephine heard gunfire, which must have reminded her of that terrible flight from Martinique. This time, however, it was not the roar of cannon but the repetitive crackle of musketry, accompanied by the sight of Austrian soldiers collapsing to the ground.

The commander of Peschiera, General Guillaume, was – according to Hamelin – a man of 'little brain' and he was thrown into confusion by the arrival of the commander-in-chief's wife. He pointed out that the surrounding area was infested with Austrian soldiers and the town was under constant threat. Mme Bonaparte should leave immediately; he could not guarantee her safety. Josephine stood her ground, refusing to leave until she received new orders from her husband. It was a difficult evening. While Josephine lay fully clothed on her bed awaiting news from Napoleon, the rest of the party watched anxiously from the town's ramparts as nightfall brought the menacing sight of the fires of Austrian bivouacs illuminating the dark sky.

News of the Austrian advance on Peschiera reached Napoleon that night. Junot was dispatched immediately with a letter instructing Josephine to make her way to Castelnuovo. When he arrived the next morning with a detachment of dragoons, Junot ordered the party to ready themselves immediately. They made a hasty getaway through the only town gate that remained open. But a few leagues down the road the party was confronted by the sight of an Austrian gunboat on the lake. As it opened fire in their general direction, Junot vaulted from his horse and stopped the carriage. He bundled Mme Bonaparte and her maid, Louise Compoint, into a ditch running parallel to the road. Soon smoke obscured the embankment and the two women, guided by Junot, scrambled along the ditch until they could safely re-enter their vehicle and continue their journey.

Passing through Densanzano, which had seen fighting the evening before, Josephine was confronted with the terrible detritus of war: bodies of the vanquished lay twisted and broken in the fields on either side of the road. During these trials, according to Hamelin, 'Madame Bonaparte did not display one moment of weakness. Her only thoughts and worries were for the life, the glory, of her husband. This woman, so futile, so occupied with pleasures . . . was to metamorphose into a chaste heroine.' He marvelled that 'it is really true that the adaptability of women's emotional make-up renders them capable of playing, in good faith, every role'.[30]

Josephine maintained her composure until they arrived in Castelnuovo and she saw her husband, who met them outside the peasant cottage where he had set up headquarters. Finally able to abandon control, she flew into his arms sobbing. 'I promise you, my darling,' he consoled her, 'I will make

Wurmser pay dearly for your tears.' Napoleon's chivalrous reassurance was bravado: his victory against the Austrian was at this point by no means assured. There was still much work to be done and Bonaparte asked Hamelin to escort Josephine to Tuscany. He had signed a treaty with the grand duke who presided there, a man whom he considered honourable. Josephine would be safe there while they waited for the situation to improve. He handed over money for expenses; five minutes later the party were packed into their carriages and ready for departure.

They had not journeyed far when Josephine glanced through the window and noticed the colonel in command of the regiment of dragoons that was acting as her escort. He was citoyen Milhaud, who had been 'the representative of the people' to the Army of the Rhine during the Revolution. She remarked wryly to Hamelin, 'You see how bizarre my destiny is. That man who is here to protect me is the same one who denounced and then hounded my first husband, Monsieur de Beauharnais, to the guillotine.'

For the next ten days Josephine and Hamelin moved through the Tuscan region. Their arrival in each town was met with ambivalence. Nobody wanted to snub Josephine if her husband was going to prevail; nobody wanted to risk fêting her if he was to be defeated. Not sure which way the wind would blow, in Lucca she was anointed with the sacred oil reserved for kings and in Livorno she was met with suspicion. In Florence she stayed with the governor with whom Napoleon had already made a treaty. While she was there, intruders broke into the mansion where she was staying in an attempt to check whether she was secretly travelling with the body of her husband who, according to local rumour, had been killed in battle.

After the watershed battle of Castiglione on 5 August, Josephine and Hamelin were escorted to the rendezvous point at Brescia by thirty hussars under the command of her victorious husband. When they arrived that evening they were greeted by a note instructing them to carry on to Creomone, where Bonaparte was waiting for them. Claiming the lateness of the hour, Josephine insisted she was too tired to continue and demanded to stay the night in Brescia. She was given the apartment that had previously been occupied by her husband, while Hamelin was assigned one that had housed Napoleon's aide-de-camp. After settling in, Hamelin returned to her suite, where a table had been laid for a late supper. He noticed immediately that the table was set for three. The addition to the party was none other than Hippolyte Charles. The meal finally over, the men made to return to their rooms. A 'languishing' voice called Charles back from the door. Later, just before he settled down to sleep, Hamelin returned to retrieve the hat and pistols he had left in the antechamber outside her bedroom. 'A grenadier posted outside the door denied me entry . . . I understood that the heroine of Peschiera had reverted to the *femme galante* of Paris.'[31]

The next day they joined Bonaparte at Corona. Hamelin's protection of Josephine was finally rewarded with the post he sought: military agent with the legation at Ferrara. They all then returned to Milan. After another brief but passionate reunion, Bonaparte again took leave of his wife to pursue Wurmser, in the hopes of driving him completely out of Italy. Almost as if he sensed her misdeeds with Charles, his letters complain about her lack of love. 'Your letters are cold', as cold as if 'we had been married for fifteen years'. On 31 August he wrote to Josephine, who had returned to Milan, 'You, to whom nature has given sweetness, amenability, all that is pleasing, how can you forget him who loves you with all his heart?'[32]

On 3 September he continued: 'No letters from you. This is really making me anxious . . . I wait every day for the courier to bring me your news.' Two weeks later he continued with his lament of neglect: 'I write you, my good love, very often, and you write little . . . You are mean and ugly, very ugly, above all you are shallow. It is evil, to deceive a poor husband, a tender lover! . . . Adieu, adorable Josephine. One of these days the doors will burst open noisily, like those of a jealous lover, and I will be in your arms . . .'[33]

In early September Josephine took advantage of the duke of Serbelloni's departure for Paris to send another batch of letters and presents to friends and family. Hortense and Eugène received endless gifts, there were sausages and cheeses for Tallien, a length of crêpe and some Florentine straw hats for Thérésia, and coral trinkets for her god-daughter Thermidor. For Barras there was a case of liqueurs and a note reassuring him of her continued loyalty. In another to Hortense she declares, 'how much I love you. I divide my feelings for you with Eugène, my darling daughter, I love both of you to distraction'.[34]

To Mme de Renaudin, she wrote:' M. Serbelloni will tell you, my dear aunt, of the manner in which I have been received in Italy, fêted everywhere I went, all the princes of Italy have given me fêtes, as did the grand duke of Tuscany, brother of the Emperor. Ah well, I prefer to be humble and living in France. I have no love for the honours of this country. I'm very bored. It is true that my health contributes greatly to my sadness; I am so often indisposed . . . I have the most amiable husband it is possible to encounter.

My needs are his. He is every day in adoration before me, as if I was a divinity; it is impossible to be a better husband . . .'[35]

Slowly it was becoming clear to Josephine what measure of man she had married. He had none of the aristocratic elegance of her first husband or Barras, nor did he possess the unabashed sensuality of the handsome Hoche or the facile charms of Charles. He was not displayed to advantage in the drawing rooms of Paris. But here, in the field, directing his men, dealing with French war commissioners, being courted by grovelling supplicants, he shone. His immense presence and position also worked to Josephine's advantage. Delegates from the principalities of Italy, the kingdom of Naples, the Papal states and the archdukedom of Tuscany, all came to play court, and they did not usually arrive empty-handed. Fearful of massive indemnities, and hoping that Josephine's influence might soften her husband, they overwhelmed her with gifts. The kings of Naples gave her a pearl necklace, the Pope gave his 'Daughter-in-God' a collection of antique cameos. In turn, she assumed the role of mediator, a role that would grow with Napoleon's power.

On 21 November 1796 Napoleon wrote,

> *I am going to bed, my little Josephine, my heart full of your adorable image, and upset to have to spend so much time away from you. But I hope that in a few days, I will be more happy . . . to give you proof of the ardent love that you inspire in me . . . You know well enough that I cannot forget your little visits. You know very well, the little black forest . . . I kiss you there a thousand times and I wait with impatience for the moment I can be there again . . . To live in Josephine is to live in the Elysian fields! . . . Kisses on your mouth, your eyelids, your shoulder, on you everywhere, everywhere!*[36]

The overt eroticism of Napoleon's language shocked many. After reading some of his letters, the novelist Prosper Mérimée told Josephine's grandson Emperor Napoleon III, 'He can talk of nothing but kisses, kisses, everywhere and upon portions of the anatomy not to be found in any dictionary of the Académie Française.' Napoleon's upbringing in garrisons and battlefield was obvious, he spoke the language of 'the army camp'. His nicknames for her pudendum, which in St Helena he compared with Trois-Îlets, are numerous: 'the little black forest', 'little Oscar', 'little Quiquette', and 'the baron de Kepen'. Of course, these letters were not designed for public consumption.

Hasty, colloquial, clearly written in the heat of desire, they vibrate with passion and sensuality. His pen covered the paper feverishly; words were crossed out, passages underlined, at some points so emphatically that the paper is almost torn where he had stabbed it for emphasis. Despite Hortense's judicious censorship, this correspondence lifts the veil on the inner sexual world of a passionate couple.

How did Josephine provoke this erotic delirium? An entire book has been dedicated to her boudoir skills.[37] Some of her charms were intrinsic. Napoleon adored her perfect figure, with its high, pert breasts, tiny waist and perfect hands and feet. He believed that she possessed 'the most beautiful cunt in the world'. He loved the way she moved, the sensual roll of the hips, so unhurried and graceful a product of her childhood in the islands. She was his tropical Scheherazade, whose 'enchanting voice', deep and musical, with a gentle Creole lilt, bewitched him, both stirring him to desire and lulling him to sleep. Her skin was described by the baron de Coston as 'luminescent in its fineness'. Napoleon recalled it in a fit of erotic nostalgia many years later: 'What skin!' he exclaimed.

But Josephine's allure was also cultivated. By the time she met Napoleon she was a sexually experienced woman, though not quite the hardened courtesan Barras portrayed – and her *éducation amoreuse* was well advanced. Napoleon on the other hand was virtually a virgin. And he was grateful for a woman who could guide him and make him feel confident. She knew how to please and was good at 'affecting pleasure'. Napoleon would remember with satisfaction her movements in bed that he described as the 'zig zags'. Her manual dexterity was exceptional, as her skill on the harp demonstrated. She was an extremely tactile woman, who often sat on his knee, caressed his face, ran her fingers through his hair. As in all areas of her life, her vocation was to please. She understood her husband and knew what delighted him. She knew he was an *odomane*, intensely sensitive to smells, and so she gave up perfumes that he disliked like musk, replacing them with scents imported from Martinique which he preferred. The important role of bodily odours in their sexual relationship is demonstrated in their correspondence, including the infamous letter in which Napoleon begged her not to bath before they met so he could enjoy all her natural aromas.

This olfactory sensuality was not her only weapon. Her artistry with maquillage and wardrobe was legendary. She was a woman who looked alluring, according to Napoleon, even when she first emerged from bed. She changed her appearance incessantly, giving her lovers the illusion of infinite variety. She also understood the importance of the mise en scène of love, the settings of her romantic encounters. She paid meticulous attention to the design of her bedrooms; some of her devices were worthy of the *grandes horizontales* themselves. Her fondness for mirrors, evident at the rue Chantereine and in later palaces, multiplied the images of their love, and created the illusion of an orgy. Her skills between the sheets brought Bonaparte back to the conjugal bed again and again. How heady it must have been for Josephine to inspire such passion! She had come a long way from the inexperienced bride who had endured sexual rejection by her handsome young husband.

It is bizarre, therefore, that Josephine is remembered for a moment of sexual rejection at Napoleon's hands – 'Not tonight, Josephine.' Maybe he did say those words on a weary, arduous night on campaign, but it is more likely a posthumous invention, a music-hall joke born out of a desire to impugn Bonaparte's reputation by evoking his wife's supposedly rapacious sexuality. The joke turns precisely on the unlikeliness of such a rejection. When Josephine became Empress these kinds of attacks escalated, particularly in Britain. It was a strategy that her predecessor Marie Antoinette would have recognized. Like many famous women, Josephine's sexuality was both her strength and her vulnerability. Women who are desirable are blamed for the power they wield over men, and so they must be punished.

By 23 November Napoleon was back in green-eyed mode:

I no longer love you. On the contrary I detest you. You are hateful, clumsy, stupid, mean! You never write me! You no longer love your husband! Even though you know the pleasure your letters give him, you will not send him six quick lines! What do you do all day, Madame? What important business is it that gives you no time to write to your adoring husband? What affection has stifled and cast away the love, the constant and tender love, that you once promised me? Who can this wonderful new lover be who claims all your time, monopolizes your days, and stops you from giving your husband any attention? Beware, Josephine! Some fine night the door will burst open and I shall stand before you! Seriously, my darling, I am disturbed at not hearing from you. Write me quickly, four pages of those loving words which will fill my heart with love and pleasure. I hope that in a few days you will be in my arms, and cover you with a million kisses as burning as the equator.[38]

When Napoleon returned from Milan on 27 November, Josephine was not there. She was in Genoa, enjoying the company of Hippolyte Charles. Napoleon – who had bounded up the stairs and burst into her rooms – was so distraught at finding her absent he almost fainted. In fact, he fell ill, and his condition provoked such anxiety that his officer Berthier summoned Josephine back: 'Come, he is afflicted and gravely upset.' A pair of letters demonstrated his hurt and sense of betrayal:

> *I get to Milan; I fling myself into your room; I have left everything in order to see you, to clasp you in my arms . . . You were not there . . . do not concern yourself with the happiness of a man who lives only in your life, rejoices only in your pleasure and happiness . . . When I expect from you a love like my own I was wrong; why expect lace to weigh as heavy as gold? . . . nature has not given me attractions with which to captivate you; but what I do deserve from Josephine is her regard and esteem, for I love her frantically and uniquely. Farewell, beloved wife; farewell, my Josephine. May fate concentrate in my breast all the griefs and troubles, but may it give Josephine happy and prosperous days . . . I reopen my letter to give you a kiss . . . Ah! Josephine! . . . Josephine!*[39]

This was a watershed moment in their relationship. Napoleon's subsequent letters to Josephine, though still loving and even passionate, were shorter and more restrained than they had been in the past. Whether this was the result of romantic disillusionment or of increasing demands on his time remains conjecture. Certainly the pace of military events had greatly accelerated at the end of 1796. After an eight-month siege, Mantua finally succumbed. By February 1797 Napoleon was finally in a position to obey his standing order from the Directoire in Paris, to invade Austria from the south and meet up with Generals Hoche, Josephine's former lover, and Jourdan and the French Army of the Rhine. By the end of March he was only ninety miles from Vienna and on 26 March offered an armistice to the hard-pressed Austrians. In April, without consulting the Directoire, he signed a preliminary treaty with the enemy at Leoben.

As a result of the triumphant conclusion of the Italian campaign, in May 1797 Napoleon relocated from Milan to the castle of Mombello, ten miles away. It was an elegant place to spend the hot summer months. Its vast rooms were lavishly decorated and ornamented with frescoes, in a style that mixed the baroque with elements of the antique. The French diplomat Miot de Mélito painted an intimate picture of the young conqueror and his circle during that momentous summer. He reported that Napoleon was surrounded by a brilliant court rather than 'the headquarters of an Army': 'Strict etiquette already reigned around him; his aides-de-camp and his officers were no longer received at his table, and he had become fastidious in the choice of the guests whom he admitted to it. An invitation was an honour eagerly sought, and obtained with great difficulty.' Napoleon had also acquired the habits of a monarch. 'He dined, so to speak, in public, the inhabitants of the country were admitted to the room in which he was eating and allowed to gaze at him with a keen curiousity . . . His reception rooms and an immense tent pitched in front of the palace were constantly full of a crowd of generals, administrators and big contractors; besides members of the highest nobility, and the most distinguished men in Italy, who came to solicit the favour of a momentary glance or the briefest interviews.'[40]

Despite the encroaching formality, it was nonetheless a wonderful time for many in Napoleon's circle. 'One of the remarkable things about this period', wrote Marmont, 'was the admirable spirit and the ardent zeal of all those who surrounded him. Each one of us had the sense of a future without limits . . .' This was never truer than during their sojourn in Mombello. The beautiful sunny days, the enchanted location, cast a 'unique spell' over the party. Indeed, Marmont felt that that summer had 'a character of its own which no later circumstances could recreate'. Summing up the mood of youthful optimism that surrounded the gathering, he wrote, 'There was grandeur, hope, and gaiety. In those days our ambition was altogether sec-ondary; our glory and our pleasures alone occupied us; a bold and cordial spirit reigned amongst us and no circumstances, no event, seemed to carry the slightest threat.'[41]

At the centre of this new court, Josephine's impeccable ancien-régime manners brought elegance and etiquette to the barrack-room style of the French Republican Army. When she was not indulging her passions for gardening or collecting birds for her new aviary, she presided over a ceaseless round of pleasures and diversions: balls and dinners, luncheons and boar hunts. Mme Grassini, the great prima donna of La Scala – who would eventually become Napoleon's mistress – was invited to sing; there were picnics, soirées and amateur theatricals. Miot de Mélito recalled that on one of these pleasure jaunts, a trip to Lake Maggiore, Berthier and Mélito sat frozen with embarrassment as, beside them in the coach, Napoleon took 'conjugal liberties' with his wife.

Although their days were devoted to pleasure, they were carefully structured. Dinner was always at three, followed by coffee and ices on the terrace. Josephine presided over the company with pleasure and ease. She always wore white, often with a cameo choker that had been presented to her by the Pope. She had 'an angelic face . . . [with] dazzling skin and a ravishing voice', noted one visitor. Her wonderful eyes were particularly alluring: 'dark blue, always half closed under heavy lids, fringed by the longest eyelashes in the world . . .' She possessed 'an unusually perfect body'. There was 'a suppleness, an incredible lightness in all her movements'. Her walk 'both aerial and majestic' particularly entranced him.[42]

The poet Carrion de Nisas, also present that summer, was less impressed: 'Mme de Bonaparte is neither young nor pretty, but she is extremely modest and engaging. She frequently caresses her husband and he seems devoted to her. Often she weeps, several times a day, for very trivial reasons . . .'[43] Indeed there was cause for heartache that summer. Fortuné, the hideous creature who had ousted Napoleon from his honeymoon bed, finally met his nemesis in the unattractive form of the cook's dog, a large and vicious mongrel who – tired of the pug's daily assaults – one day turned on him. To console Josephine, Hippolyte Charles covertly gave her a replacement. Not long after, Napoleon spotted the cook skulking in the shrubbery. Asking him why, he received the answer that the cook was frightened because his dog had killed Mme Bonaparte's beloved pug, adding that the offending creature was no longer allowed in the park. 'Bring him back,' demanded Bonaparte, 'perhaps he will rid me of the new one too.'

Josephine also wept for Hippolyte Charles. It was a bittersweet summer for their illicit love. Promoted to the rank of captain and decorated for gallantry, he was part of the Bonaparte entourage and so Josephine saw him daily. But there was no opportunity for intimacy or romance; she was under too much scrutiny for that. If this made her miserable, one of the great joys of the summer was the arrival of Eugène. After fifteen months apart, Josephine was desperate to see him. While Josephine had good relationships with both her children, the one with Eugène was special. Their strong mother–son bond expanded into friendship as he grew up. At fifteen and a half he was growing into a handsome young man: always good natured, extremely loyal and a testament to her skills as a parent.

It was at Mombello that Josephine met the majority of the Bonaparte family for the first time. Their party included the clever and capable eldest daughter, Élisa, and young Louis, whose health was a constant worry, as well as the two youngest, Jérôme and Caroline, who were at school with Eugène and Hortense. Then there was Pauline, Napoleon's favourite sister, whose beauty 'was near perfection'. The two women had a great deal in common: they both loved fashion and frivolity, and Pauline's reputation as a *femme galante* would in time outstrip even that of Josephine. But Pauline detested her sister-in-law, regarding her as a competitor. She made faces behind Josephine's back and insisted on referring to her as '*la vieille*', the 'old one'. Pauline was, according to the poet Antoine Arnault, 'the prettiest and worst behaved person imaginable'. He described her 'chattering away without pause . . . contradicting the most eminent personages, sticking out her tongue at her sister-in-law behind her back, nudging my knee when I wasn't paying her sufficient attention, and drawing upon herself from time to time the most terrifying looks of reproof from her brother'.

But the pivotal figure in the Bonaparte clan was Napoleon's formidable mother, Mme Letizia. She had been a handsome woman in her youth and maintained a pristine bone structure well into old age. An old-fashioned matriarch, it had been she, rather than her mercurial husband, who had sustained the family during its travails. Mme Bonaparte's resistance to her son's marriage was, she claimed, not personal. Josephine was simply too old – older than her son – a widow who already had two almost grown children. More than that, Josephine was everything that Mme Letizia loathed: a decadent aristocrat of dubious morals and extravagant spending habits. Despite the Bonapartes' claims to noble birth, they were steeped in solid bourgeois values: modesty, chastity and an almost obsessive frugality. (No doubt, it is precisely because she was so different from his mother that Napoleon desired Josephine so much. Despite his avowed admiration for Mme Letizia, all his life Napoleon would despise women who, like her, were strong-willed and forceful.)

Not many people enjoyed the experience of meeting the Bonapartes en masse. Prince Eugène's ravishing wife Princess Augusta-Amalia of Bavaria remarked in a letter to her brother on her only visit to Paris, in 1810: 'when one has known [the Bonapartes] at close quarters one can only despise them. I could never conceive anything so abominable as their ill-breeding. It is torture for me to have to go about with such people'. Josephine, largely unaware of her mother-in-law's hostility, did not anticipate the family's attitude when they met. She treated Mme Letizia with the careful courtesy and charm that most found so beguiling. But the Bonapartes made their feelings very clear. Josephine intimidated them. She was an elegant Parisian, a public woman, a woman of fashion, a celebrity. They resented the spell that she had cast over Napoleon. They closed ranks against her in a feud that would endure till her death.

Almost any woman Napoleon had chosen would have been in for a rough ride. He was the breadwinner for the entire family and anyone else who had a claim on his funds would be watched like a hawk. The Bonaparte clan was insular and instinctively hostile to outsiders. They thrived on feuds, interminably falling out with each other and then closing ranks on any outsider who got in their way. With the arrival of the Bonapartes there was a natural struggle for dominance in Napoleon's salon. Until then Josephine had reigned unthreatened, her regality, charm and grace eliciting an instinctive loyalty and affection. But Mme Bonaparte felt that as mother of the conqueror she was due the greater deference. Josephine gracefully stepped aside – so that when Madame Mère entered a room she was given precedence.

That summer Josephine commissioned a portrait of Napoleon to immortalize his success during the Italian campaign. The artist was an up-and-coming young painter, Antoine-Jean Gros. His intention was to paint Bonaparte clutching the colours and rallying his soldiers at the bridge of Arcola. But Napoleon simply could not sit still, and the young artist was too overawed by his illustrious subject to order him to stop fidgeting. Josephine solved the problem with her usual charm. She accompanied Bonaparte to the studio, seated him on her lap, and wrapped her arms tightly around him until Gros could complete his draft. The result was a legendary portrait depicting Napoleon in all his youthful glory: gripping the flag, his face framed with battle-blown hair, his intense gaze looking off into the distance as if contemplating some as yet indecipherable future.

As the Bonapartes relaxed in Mombello, another political explosion was building in France. Although Napoleon's victories were applauded by the populace, none of his popularity had rubbed off on the Directoire, and the elections of 1797 had reflected a massive anti-Jacobin backlash. But many of those in power, particularly the regicides Barras and Talleyrand (the new Foreign Minister), could not countenance a royalist revival. Napoleon was approached to support a coup d'état. (Had he not been willing, his rival in love and work, Hoche, was the next in line to be asked.) Napoleon decided to lend his support; a Bourbon restoration did not suit his plans either. But having done the job of suppressing the popular will once before at Vendémiaire, it would not be politic for him to do it again. So he delegated the job to one of his subordinates, Pierre Augereau, the most fervently Jacobin of his generals. As Augereau mobilized his troops, the most left-wing of the

Directors, led by Barras and Talleyrand, circulated rumours that a monarchist coup was imminent. Late in the evening of 17 Fructidor (3 September) Augereau's troops arrested the newly elected deputies and annulled the results of the recent elections. In a brief resumption of the Terror, scores of political opponents were imprisoned and over 150 people were condemned to the 'dry guillotine' – deportation to Guiana. The coup of Fructidor, as it came to be known, had manifold repercussions. It repressed the first real democratic expression by the nation and reinforced the general notion that, in Augereau's words, 'the sword is king'. Most importantly, the Government was now indebted to Napoleon and he could dictate the terms he wanted in negotiations with Austria. Without realizing it, the Directoire had sold the future to Bonaparte.

As the long summer days came to a close the Bonapartes went to Passeriano, taking up residence in the doge's summer palace. Here the business of the Italian campaign returned. Determined to conclude the peace treaty with Austria, Napoleon entered into stormy negotiations with the Austrian envoy Graf Ludwig von Cobenzl. Sometimes he raged and shouted at the Austrian negotiator, on other occasions he tried to charm him into submission. In this endeavour he elicited the skills of his wife, whom Cobenzl described as 'amiability personified'. She hosted dinner parties and organized *déjeuners sur l'herbe* for the Austrian delegation. Cobenzl felt that Napoleon was somewhat in awe of his wife. He described a dinner for the French and Austrian delegates where Napoleon childishly bombarded Josephine with pellets of bread. But at one reproachful look, according to Cobenzl, he 'hung his head and stopped'. Josephine was so helpful in facilitating the talks that the diplomat wrote to her on his return to Vienna, expressing his profound gratitude. He also sent her a team of magnificent stud horses.

Despite her gracious behaviour, Josephine was profoundly unhappy during these weeks. She had heard a rumour that Hippolyte Charles had begun an affair with an Italian woman. She had also been saddened by the news of the death of Lazare Hoche at only twenty-nine years of age. The official cause of death was pneumonia, but there were persistent rumours that he had been poisoned. In addition to her grief and loss, she was also worried about the fate of the love letters she had sent him. He had long since requested the return of her letters to him but had not returned the favour.

By the middle of October, the terms of the treaty with Austria were finally ironed out and the peace was signed at Campo Formio, a village near

Udine. The eventual loser was a third party, the Republic of Venice. In a secret clause of the preliminary treaty at Leoben, France had agreed to 'concede' this independent and neutral state to Austria, in exchange for Belgium and Lombardy. Not realizing that its fate was already sealed, the Venetian Republic invited Napoleon to visit. Since he had already betrayed the republic, Napoleon was reluctant to go himself and sent Josephine in his stead. It was an intimidating diplomatic mission for her to tackle on her own. But Josephine took it on with determination and a formidable armoury of gowns and other feminine accoutrements, paid for by the Army of Italy. Indeed, so exorbitant was her toilette that one observer remarked it would have served to pay for two or three months of the military campaign.

The Venetians were eager to placate Napoleon, on whom they believed their fate depended so the wife of the conqueror received an extravagant welcome. As she entered this 'elegant and voluptuous' city, 150,000 Venetian citizens greeted her, hanging out of windows, waving banners and throwing flowers. The following day there were water excursions and a picnic at the Lido, where Josephine's vessel was followed by hundreds of boats decorated with garlands of flowers and serenading her with Italian music. On the third night a ball at the doge's palace was preceded by fireworks and a procession along the Grand Canal, which particularly impressed Napoleon's friend General Marmont. 'A multitude of gondolas, themselves covered with different coloured lights', gave the appearance of 'a whole city in movement'.[44]

Josephine's mission was judged a great success. She charmed her hosts so effectively that after her return to Passeriano a Venetian delegation, led by the great patriot Dandalo, offered her 100,000 ducats if she could convince her husband to act in Venice's interest. The following night Josephine, who had fallen in love with the republic, responded by speaking enthusiastically on Venice's behalf at a gala dinner. To encourage her continued support a member of the delegation slipped a beautiful diamond ring on her finger as they walked through the grounds. But the fate of Venice had long since been sealed, so Josephine never received her ducats; but there is no evidence that she returned the ring.

In October the Italian campaign was officially wrapped up. In November Napoleon left Italy to attend conferences at Rastadt about the reorganization of Germany. Josephine stayed behind in Italy to wind up her affairs, leaving for Paris in late November. Her journey home was interrupted by numerous tributes to her illustrious spouse. The towns of both Lyon and Moulins were illuminated in her honour and she was fêted at various balls and parties. A verse was recited to her glory: 'Companion of the hero admired by every nation / In thee our hearts acclaim his source of inspiration.' Josephine's speech in response was gracious, and when she left huge crowds gathered to speed her on her way. But once again she had acquired a travelling companion: Hippolyte Charles.

Twelve

EGYPT

*The unique and supreme pleasure of love lies
in the certainty of doing wrong.*

BAUDELAIRE

WHILE JOSEPHINE ROMPED THROUGH THE countryside in the company of her lover Hippolyte, Napoleon returned alone to the rue Chantereine on 5 December 1797. But his little 'temple of love',[1] as one of his aides had dubbed it, was changed beyond all recognition. Josephine had mentioned that she was doing a bit of redecorating; after all, the modest little house was no longer suitable for the 'conqueror of Italy'. What she did not say was that she had instructed her friend the architect Vautier to oversee a full refurbishment 'in the latest elegance'. So Napoleon was totally unprepared for the splendour that confronted him. Two decades later his astonishment was still apparent when he recalled the cost of Josephine's vision: 'all the suites of furniture were specially designed, that for the salon alone cost 130,000 francs'.[2]

There was a new entrance to the house itself: a monumental door decorated with martial motifs, which was all but obscured by a striped canvas vestibule so that visitors no longer entered straight into the antechamber. On the ground floor the dining room was paved in mosaics, while in the salon Josephine had retained the friezes that the previous owner had commissioned from the artist David, and added beautiful mahogany furniture designed by Marie Antoinette's favourite cabinet-makers, the Jacob brothers. Works of art 'liberated' from Italy hung throughout the house.

But it was the refurbishment of the first floor that was the pièce de résistance. Josephine's dressing room was hung with mirrors and panelled with arches supported by slender pillars. The boudoir was a melange of the martial and the antique: a reproduction of a soldier's tent, with white-and-blue striped canvas draped and billowing from the ceiling. The casement windows were curtained in muslin embroidered with gold, and a forest-green pile carpet covered the floor. The twin beds, painted bronze in the ancient Roman style, were linked by an ingenious spring mechanism which at the touch of a button could snap them together or push them apart. Eleven small seats in the shape of drums, upholstered with fringed muslin, were scattered around the room, which was further embellished by a porphyry vase and a taffeta-covered screen embroidered with Josephine's initials and a bouquet of flowers.[3]

And, much to Napoleon's dismay, the work was far from complete. The Jacob brothers' journal notes a further delivery a few days after his arrival: 'a writing desk made of mahogany, satinwood, purple-wood and ebony, in the antique style . . .', followed by 'a mahogany commode four feet wide . . . a pedestal table in mahogany and canary-wood, with an octagonal top made of white marble . . . two cylindrical oval bedside tables and a large mahogany folding screen with six panels and another folding screen with six panels and copper hinges, the bottom with solid panels and the top with stretchers.'[4] Josephine had thought of everything. But the revamped house was not just breathtaking to look at; it was also colossally extravagant. A quarter of a century later, Napoleon would still recall the bills with shock and disbelief. The total cost of the refurbishment was an incredible 300,000 francs, almost ten times the worth of the house, which he would purchase some months later for a mere 40,000 francs.

Napoleon had little time to brood over his wife's extravagance. He was the man of the hour and everyone wanted to share in his triumph. So euphoric was the response of the populace to their returning hero that Napoleon was virtually besieged in his own home. Even Hortense, who went to visit him a few days after his return, found it difficult to gain entrance. 'All Paris rang with his name,' she wrote. 'The people thronged in such vast numbers to cheer "The Conqueror of Italy" that the sentries stationed at the gateway to the house on the rue de la Victoire [as the rue Chantereine was renamed in his honour] could hardly hold them back . . . Finally, in spite of the crowds, we managed to get through to the General, who was breakfasting, surrounded by his general staff. He greeted me with the tenderness of a father.'[5]

But Bonaparte was not deluded by the crowd's excitement. 'The people would flock just as eagerly to see me if I were on the way to the guillotine,' he remarked. In order to avoid this unpleasant fate, all too possible in the tumultuous politics of the time, Napoleon had to play down his popularity and his military victories. His position was delicate. The Directors knew that they were as unpopular as he was acclaimed; and he represented a real threat to them. Talleyrand counselled prudence, and so Napoleon played down his ambition and achievements, going abroad infrequently and receiving only his most intimate circle of family and friends. His determination to shun society, 'to fly from all eyes and withhold himself from all tributes', was noted by everyone. On the few occasions when he indulged his passion for the theatre, he responded to the audience's cheers by withdrawing into the shadows of his box.

On one of his few forays into the outside world, Bonaparte attended a rather morose ceremony held in his honour at the Palais du Luxembourg on 10 December 1797. Against the backdrop of the severe and noble architecture of the palace, an altar to the fatherland had been erected and covered with captured flags. In front of this sat the Directors, dressed in their red-and-gold robes and plumed hats, ready to receive the hero. Napoleon appeared in a simple uniform, standing immobile and apparently timid. Talleyrand gave the address, praising Bonaparte's 'insatiable love of the fatherland and humanity'. Referring to Napoleon only as 'citoyen', never as 'general', he reassured his jittery audience: 'Far from fearing what some would call his ambition, I feel the time will perhaps come when we will find it necessary to tear him from his studious retreat.'

In order to consolidate his new image as a man of peace, Napoleon accepted election to the Institut de France, declaring that there was nothing he desired more than a life devoted to intellectual endeavour: 'I am only too conscious that before becoming their equal I must long remain their pupil . . . I shall bury myself in a retreat and labour to deserve one day the honour of being a member of the Institut.' His performance as apolitical scholar was beginning to convince. On 20 December a writer for Le Moniteur, who had clearly never been inside Napoleon's newly refurbished residence, created an idealized portrait of his republican modesty and rectitude. He described Bonaparte 'staying at his wife's house in the rue Chantereine, which is small, modest and unpretentious. He goes out rarely and when he does, it is alone in a carriage pulled by two horses. He can be seen frequently walking in his little garden.'

At the end of December, Napoleon made an exception to his virtual ban on public appearances to attend a ball hosted by Charles-Maurice de Talleyrand-Périgord, the Directoire's Minister of External Relations.

Talleyrand was a descendant of one of France's oldest families and a crucial new ally of Napoleon's. A fall in early childhood had left him with a severe limp, and this disability was a source of embarrassment to his family who had kept him out of sight whenever possible. His relationship with his parents was so distant that he claimed that he had never, throughout the years of his childhood, slept under the same roof as them. Later they pressured him into renouncing his rights of primogeniture in favour of his younger brother and nudged him towards a career in the Church. The young Talleyrand had emerged from these misfortunes with a cynicism and adaptability that would serve him all his life.

Talleyrand dutifully followed his parents' suggestion to enter the Church. However, he never allowed his religious path to get in the way of more worldly pursuits: money, women and politics. By the onset of the Revolution he had completely allied himself with the revolutionary cause. As the situation radicalized, however, he managed to find himself in America before the worst excesses of the Terror engulfed his country. On his return to France in 1796 he marshalled his old contacts – especially his old flame, Germaine de Staël – in order to kick-start his political career. Despite the hostility of Directors like Reubell, who dismissed him as 'a powdered lackey of the ancien régime' and 'a collection of every vice, a model of betrayal and corruption', he nonetheless manoeuvred himself into the position of Minister of External Relations.

Aware that his revolutionary allegiance was regarded by his class as the ultimate treachery, Talleyrand's great fear was that the political chaos of the Directoire might spawn a royal restoration. Convinced that a political coup d'état backed by a 'sword' was the only viable alternative, he fixed his hopes on Napoleon Bonaparte. His courtship of his elected hero was both graceful and assiduous. He had started writing to him during the Italian campaign – letters that were both flattering and intelligent, cultivating an epistolary relationship of some intensity. On the night of Napoleon's return to the city, Talleyrand was his first visitor.

Soon after, he started planning a ball to honour Bonaparte and cement his allegiance. With his unerring political judgement Talleyrand decided to dedicate the ball to Mme Bonaparte rather than to her illustrious husband. This avoided making an overt political commitment to any one faction, while simultaneously touching Napoleon on his emotional Achilles heel: his love for Josephine.

But of course the evening was designed to flatter the aspirations of its real guest of honour. Through word of mouth Talleyrand made it clear that this would be no vulgar Directoire affair. His only sop to prevailing revolutionary attitudes was a slip enclosed with the invitations which read, 'You will, I feel sure, find it appropriate to abstain from wearing fabrics manufactured in England.' So 'unpatriotic' – that is, unrevolutionary – was the event rumoured to be, that some individuals decided to boycott the affair. Director La Revellière-Lepeaux declined without giving a reason, Reubell because he had a horror of 'those people'. A couple of other official representatives decided to attend in plain clothes in protest at the decadent spirit of the occasion.

Talleyrand had designed an evening reminiscent of the luxurious but dignified galas of the ancien régime. No effort or expense were spared to create a spectacular effect. The architect Bellanger, creator of the Bagatelle Pavillon, was hired to style the event. He in turn delegated tasks to an army of carpenters, painters, decorators, florists and caterers, who set about transforming the beautiful Hôtel Gallifet on the rue Grenelle, abandoned by its aristocratic owner during the Terror and subsequently requisitioned to serve as the official residence of the Minister of External Relations.

The notoriety of the event guaranteed that the Parisian elite awaited the great day, 25 December (5 Nivôse), with bated breath. The only problem was that Josephine was nowhere to be found. She had still not returned to the city. Talleyrand hastily cancelled the ball and a new set of invitations were issued for three days later. At great effort and expense the food was reordered, the decorations stripped and replaced and 903 flowering trees and shrubs removed and repositioned. But the 28th dawned and still no Josephine. Talleyrand was forced to move the event yet again.

Finally, on the third attempt, the ball went ahead. On the evening of 3 January queues of carriages stretched back from the Hôtel Gallifet to the Seine. When the elegantly dressed guests finally alighted in front of the residence they were sprinkled with light, powdery snow. Passing between the Doric columns that framed its entrance, they found themselves inside the first of the courtyards, where Talleyrand, in obvious tribute to Napoleon, had recreated a military camp, complete with tents, fires and soldiers in their multi-coloured uniforms. All the armies of the French in Italy were represented. In the second courtyard Talleyrand had built a mock antique shrine dominated by a bust of that Jacobin idol Brutus, as if to say, 'Look, here he is amongst us.'

When they finally entered the reception rooms the guests were enveloped in a spell of light, fragrance and soft music. On every available surface Talleyrand displayed artworks that Napoleon had 'liberated' in Italy and laid at the feet of the Republic. At the top of a majestic double staircase draped in myrtle stood the host, impeccably dressed, leaning on his cane. Those in favour received a firm handshake, the less important, two limp fingers. To complete the perfect aesthetic effect Talleyrand had also invited 'a multitude of charming women, to astonish, to enchant all beholders', and his female guests played their part to perfection, providing their own delicious diversion as they circulated in diaphanous pink-and-gold ensembles, the colours of the event.

The evening was in full swing when the Bonapartes entered at half past ten. At the first sight of the conqueror and his wife, the guests fell quiet. The hushed, nearly religious silence was more impressive and unsettling than any amount of applause or bravos. Both Napoleon and Josephine had struck exactly the right note of restraint: he in his unobtrusive dark coat buttoned up to the chin, she in a deceptively simple gown and a small gold cap with a diadem of antique cameos. Hortense, who had accompanied them, was all virginal innocence, her golden hair piled on her head to frame her soft blue eyes. So obvious was the crowd's awe that even Napoleon was intimidated, grabbing the arm of his friend Arnault so that he could avoid having to talk to anyone else.

The only false note in Talleyrand's impeccably orchestrated evening was struck by Germaine de Staël. For several months she had nurtured an infatuation for Napoleon, and had written him numerous letters while he was on campaign. According to Napoleon, these letters (now lost) compared him with both 'Scipio and Tancred, uniting the simple virtues of the former with the brilliant deeds of the latter'.[6] In response Napoleon had murmured to an aide, 'This woman is mad!' and refused to reply. Magnificently unaware that she was the sort of intellectual, assertive woman that Napoleon found most offputting, she continued to bombard him. Believing that she was a more suitable match for the young hero than Josephine, she offered herself to him, urging Napoleon to discard 'that little insignificant Creole', because 'to unite his genius' with someone like her 'was nothing short of a monstrosity since she could never appreciate him'.[7] According to Bonaparte, she had even attempted to storm the house in rue Chantereine on his return to Paris.

Informed by the butler that the general was naked in the bath, she nonetheless attempted to barge past, crying, 'No matter, genius has no sex!'[8]

Napoleon was eager to elude her advances, and so had declined an invitation to another great ball held in his honour. At other events he had avoided speaking to her. But now there was no escape. Germaine, much to Talleyrand's fury, insisted on being presented to him. She then proceeded to bombard him with questions. 'General, which woman could you love the most?' Napoleon answered immediately, 'My wife.' 'Of course, but which woman, alive or dead, do you most admire?' She clearly expected him to say something polite or elegant, but he replied brutally, 'The one who has borne the most children.' On which retort he turned on his heel and walked away. Utterly taken aback, Germaine could only remark, 'Extraordinary man.'[9]

Dinner was announced at 11 p.m. It was to be a meal worthy, according to the host, ' . . . of those Romans who had conquered Asia, just as we have conquered Italy'. The guests formed a procession and slowly advanced into the great banqueting room, where gleaming crystal sparkled like diamonds in the candlelight. Talleyrand began the meal with a toast 'to the citoyenne who bears the name most dear to glory!' The guests were then informed that, for this evening only, Talleyrand had revived the old court custom in which only the women were seated, while the men remained standing behind them in order to serve their partner. With great ceremony the host took up his place behind Mme Bonaparte where he remained throughout the repast, serving her with a care and gallantry that impressed everyone. Not a single gesture betrayed any annoyance he might have felt about her costly delays. Indeed the *grand seigneur* and the lovely Josephine made a beautiful tableau.

After dinner, the 'queen of the fête' was serenaded by the celebrated singer Lays. The song, composed by Despreaux and specially commissioned in her honour, was received 'amid transports', and an encore was requested:

> Of the warrior, of the conquering hero,
> Oh dear companion!
> You who possess his whole heart,
> Alone with the fatherland,
> Pay the immense debt
> Of a great people to its defender;
> By tending to his happiness,
> You acquit the obligation of France.[10]

★

The Bonapartes departed just after 1 a.m., but many guests stayed until dawn, enraptured by the grandeur of the event. A new dance called the waltz had been introduced for the first time that evening. Despite Mme de Staël and the massive expense he had incurred, Talleyrand counted the evening a complete success. The ball was what one writer described as one of those 'gestures more decisive than battles'.[11] Through the style of the event Talleyrand gave a subtle message about what he could contribute to Napoleon. His role would be that of a sort of 'master of ceremonies', cultivating 'the past and its rituals and making them fruitful in the new age'.[12]

One person who did not enjoy the splendour of the ball at the Hôtel Gallifet was its guest of honour, Josephine. Some observers remarked that she looked 'distracted', others thought she seemed positively out of sorts. Perhaps she was missing Hippolyte. Certainly she had been quarrelling with Napoleon. He was livid about the cost of the redecoration and resented her late return, however she might justify her delay by claiming that she was just being a good wife, accepting accolades on his behalf.

This little storm soon passed and Josephine settled into her role as dutiful wife and helpmate. The core of their social circle remained the same: Barras, the Talliens and new allies like Talleyrand. The Bonapartes withdrew from those who might damage their reputation, such as the more flamboyant of the *merveilleuses*, while assiduously cultivating those who reflected well on their new image. Josephine entertained her husband's new friends: the academics of the Institut de France, artists, scientists, poets like Arnault and Chénier, and the painter David. Occasionally the ever-eager Germaine de Staël was included in their gatherings because of her political influence. The newspapers continued to marvel at Napoleon's lack of ambition and at his retired life. As one wrote, he 'avoids anything which might draw attention to himself. His wife too has adopted a way of life as retiring as his own'. Whatever tension may have lingered between the Bonapartes, they appeared to be happy.

Behind his charade of reticence Napoleon was developing his own plans. These had nothing to do with the Directoire's ideas for an invasion of England. But he played along with them, pretending to explore a proposal he had already privately dismissed as unfeasible, while he pursued his own dreams. One particular dream had bewitched him since adolescence: the conquest of Egypt. As early as 1769 the duc de Choiseul – Louis XV's Foreign Minister – had proposed this as a way to compensate France for the loss of her American colonies. His was an ambitious plan that involved cutting a canal through the isthmus of Suez and planting cotton, indigo and sugar alongside more traditional Egyptian crops, thereby bringing about a revolution in world trade that would give France a stranglehold over the route to India. The plan had been shelved for a number of decades. But Napoleon felt that the moment was now opportune. England had withdrawn her fleet from the Mediterranean in 1796 and Europe was at peace.

Napoleon saw the Egyptian project as essential to his long-term ambitions. 'I realize that if I stay [in Paris] my reputation will soon be gone. All things fade here, and my reputation is almost forgotten; this little Europe affords too slight a scope; I must go to the Orient; all great reputations have been won there . . .' In his campaign to convert those sceptical about his plans, Josephine was Napoleon's secret weapon. On his instructions she laid siege to those most hostile to the oriental project. The Directors Barras and Reubell were her particular targets. The latter was the greater challenge, until she discovered that he had known her first husband when he had been fighting with the Revolutionary Army in Mainz. She took advantage of her special relationship with Barras by organizing candlelit dinners and sending him conspiratorial notes: 'I need, my dear Barras, to talk to you. I want to see you alone. I wait in the hope that our friendship prompts you to sacrifice a quarter of an hour to come and see me, where you will find me absolutely alone. I hope, my dear Barras, that you will not refuse this mark of interest by a woman whom you care for . . .'[13]

Despite this unity of political purpose, a storm was brewing in the love nest at no. 6 rue de la Victoire. On her return from Italy, Josephine had dismissed her chambermaid, Louise Compoint, when she discovered that the girl had been sleeping with Napoleon's aide Junot. The vengeful Compoint sought an appointment with Napoleon and she told him that a young soldier, Charles, 'a little whorish creature' he remembered from the Italian campaign, had followed Josephine on her return from Italy, shared her carriage and stayed in the same inns. Bonaparte confronted Josephine: 'Tell me the truth, after all there is no great wrong in sleeping in the same auberge, or making the journey together . . .'

'No, it isn't true!' she immediately replied and dissolved into tears.[14]

Weeping always disarmed her husband and the squall passed. Complaining to her lover, she wrote, 'Yes, my Hippolyte, my existence is a continual torture. You alone give me any happiness. Tell me that you love me and only me. I will be the happiest of women.' Business briefly interrupted these romantic outpourings when she requested that Charles send her 50,000 livres by Blondin, one of the Bonaparte servants, but the letter ended passionately: 'Goodbye, I send a million tender kisses. All for you.'[15]

Over the following weeks a lull fell over the Bonaparte household. Then Napoleon departed for the coast to inspect military dispositions for the proposed invasion of England. In his absence Josephine got herself embroiled with the Bodin company, one of the firms of speculators that had mushroomed during the period in order to exploit army contracts. These activities had made politicians like Barras and bankers like Ouvrard immensely rich. Significantly, Hippolyte Charles was also involved with the Bodin brothers; indeed he had abandoned his army commission to work more closely with them.

Josephine's motivation for becoming involved in this rather shady set-up was more than greed or a desire to be near her beloved; she had acquired a taste for entrepreneurial activity out of necessity – her marriage to Alexandre and the deprivations of the Revolution had left her in persistent financial insecurity. But taking advantage of a country at war was not a pretty business. A newspaper scandal erupted. The company was accused of providing the army with poor-quality horses, requisitioned from farmers whom it then neglected to pay. Rumours of Josephine's entanglement with the Bodin company reached her brother-in-law, Joseph Bonaparte, who loathed her.

The 'Catastrophe', as Josephine dubbed it, erupted in the middle of March. Joseph was only too delighted to convey to his brother details of Josephine's debts and her involvement with the Bodin company. He also confirmed Louise Compoint's accusations about Charles. Bonaparte listened to the sordid story and entered his wife's boudoir in a rage. Josephine recounted to her lover, Hippolyte, the details of the subsequent argument.

> *Joseph had a long conversation with his brother yesterday. Afterwards he asked me if I knew citoyen Bodin, if it was me who procured the contract with the Army of Italy; he was told that Charles lived at the home of citoyen Bodin, no. 100 faubourg Saint-Honoré, and asked if it was there that I went every day. I responded that I didn't know anything about what he was saying, that if he wanted to divorce, he had only to say so, he did not need to resort to such accusations, and I was the most unfortunate of women and the most unhappy. Yes, my Hippolyte, they have my complete hatred; you alone have my tenderness and my love. They must see now how I loathe them by the terrible state I have been in for several days. They can see my disappointment – my despair at being deprived of the*

*chance of seeing you as often as I wish. Hippolyte, I shall kill myself —
yes, I wish to end a life that henceforth would be only a burden if it could
not be devoted to you. Alas! What have I done to these monsters? But they
are acting in vain, I will never be a victim of their atrocious conduct . . .*

But Josephine also had practical matters to address:

*Tell Bodin to say that he doesn't know me; that it was not through me
that he got the contracts for the Army of Italy; tell him to instruct the
porter at no. 100 to tell anyone who asks if Bodin lives there, to say that
he doesn't know him. Tell Bodin not to use the letters which I have given
him for Italy until some time after his arrival in that country and only
when he needs to . . . Ah, they torment me in vain; they will never separate
me from my Hippolyte; my last sigh will be for him . . . I will do everything
I can to see you today. If I am unable to, I will go to Bodin's tonight
and tomorrow morning, I will send Blondin to you to tell you what time
to meet me in the garden of Monceau. Adieu, my Hippolyte, a thousand
kisses, as burning as is my heart, and as amorous . . .*[16]

Josephine's behaviour expressed a deep-seated ambivalence. Her letters to
Charles display passionate feelings, but there is also good evidence that she
was settling very happily into the role of Bonaparte's helpmate at this time
and was becoming more and more attached to her husband. Cynics have
suggested that she supported Napoleon's military activities simply so that she
could get rid of him in order to spend time alone with Hippolyte. Others
believe that it was the relationship with Hippolyte that was the lie, since the
only proof of its existence lies in these letters, which turned up unexpectedly
in the twentieth century and could so easily be forgeries (though most
historians now accept them as genuine). It is possible, of course, that Josephine
was torn between two loves, each of whom satisfied different aspects of her
personality.

Surprisingly, however, Napoleon did not pursue the accusations against
Josephine. His secretary, Bourrienne, put this down to 'his love for his wife,
his inspection tours of the coast, and his preoccupation with plans for the
Egyptian campaign'. Napoleon and Josephine were reconciled and life settled
back into a semblance of normality. It is possible that Napoleon did not yet
feel confident enough to do without his wife's formidable political influence.
This was the view of some of his contemporaries. However absurd it may
seem in retrospect, it was still being said during these years that 'It is his

wife's influence that upholds him,'[17] according to the duchesse d'Abrantès. Certainly one reason for Napoleon's apparent docility would have been the oriental project, around which Josephine had been – and continued to be – both very useful and supportive. The Directoire had finally accepted that the invasion of England was a non-starter, as Napoleon had always thought, and reluctantly gave the go-ahead for the Egyptian expedition.

Whether their assent was motivated by enthusiasm for the idea, or by the fear of having such a popular and ambitious character at a loose end in the city, is not clear. But Napoleon was delighted. He had realized months before that his fame was a diminishing asset: 'Paris has a short memory. If I remain longer doing nothing I am lost. In this great Babylon one reputation quickly succeeds another.' Besides, inactivity did not suit him; it made him melancholy. Josephine expressed her desire to accompany her husband to Egypt; but before that project they had one closer to home to accomplish: like all affluent Parisians she wanted to purchase a country house. Josephine dragged Napoleon to view Malmaison, the exquisite chateau that she had first seen four years earlier from the windows of her rented house in Croissy. It had been love at first sight for Josephine, who had coveted it ever since, but Napoleon felt it was too expensive, and the matter seemed closed.

There was also family business to settle before the departure to Egypt. Napoleon discovered that his younger brother, Louis, was in love with Josephine's niece, Émilie de Beauharnais. Napoleon didn't approve of the match: her father, Alexandre's brother François, was a royalist; and for years her mother had lived out of wedlock with a black man from the Caribbean. Instead, Napoleon decided to fix Émilie up with one of his aides-de-camp. Sadly Antoine Lavalette was not the sort of man to turn a young girl's head. A porcine young man with abnormally short limbs, he had a red, round face dominated by small squinty eyes, and a nose like a pea. His hair was so sparse that his colleagues had nicknamed each individual strand. Only too aware of his shortcomings, Lavalette was nonetheless kind-hearted, and had no intention of pressuring the teenager into marriage. But the wedding went ahead, and against all expectations the union proved enduring and happy.

By the end of April 1798 the secret plans for the Egyptian campaign were complete. On 4 May the Bonapartes – travelling in separate vehicles – left Paris. Five days later the large Berlin conveying Josephine, Napoleon's secretary Bourrienne and Eugène in his smart aide-de-camp uniform lumbered into Toulon. They were confronted by an awe-inspiring sight: the entire

French fleet, 'whose masts resembled a huge forest', at anchor in the city's harbour, its ships spreading almost a mile out to sea. On board were over 30,000 troops, 1,000 civilians and 700 horses. Napoleon, surrounded by his generals, took his place on the admiral's barge to review the fleet. Every gun on every vessel and in the port's fortresses fired a salute, while every ship broke out its flags. It must have been an intensely satisfying sight for the young general who had arrived in this same harbour as a poverty-stricken unknown five years before.

Forced to wait six days for a storm to pass, Josephine was given the opportunity to inspect Napoleon's flagship, the *Orient*. It was meant to be the greatest battleship of its time and was certainly one of the biggest: more than 6,000 great oak trees would have been felled in its creation. Home to 2,000 soldiers, sailors, scholars and craftsmen, the ship was so vast its inhabitants called it 'the wooden world'. Nearly sixty metres long, it had three gun decks, with 120 cannon. Despite its size, however, it was terribly overcrowded. Later, when supplies ran out, the inhabitants would suffer even more as they battled with heat, dysentery and tainted water.

Josephine was awed by the ship's size and the cavernous darkness and silence of the lower depths, like that of a Gothic church. She was astonished too by the luxury of her husband's quarters. His bed was set on casters in an attempt to lessen the seasickness that always plagued him. Their friend the poet Arnault had assembled a comprehensive library of 287 volumes of history, politics, philosophy, poetry, travel writing, literature and science. There was even a printing press on which Napoleon would prepare his declarations to the Egyptian population. The wine cellar was stocked with 800 bottles of the finest wines and a carriage was on board for his use in Egypt. Josephine also met a number of the 150 savants, the scientists and intellectuals who were also part of the expedition. Of these, only a select few knew the armada's true destination; the rest spent their time speculating and dreaming.

Despite the ship's many amenities, Napoleon did not want Josephine to risk the journey. Instead he decided that she should visit Plombières, a spa famous for sulphur baths that were said to boost fertility. Determined to accompany her husband, Josephine spent much of her time trying to change his mind. One morning one of Napoleon's generals, Alexandre Dumas, the handsome black giant whose son would write *The Three Musketeers* and *The Count of Monte Cristo*, walked in on the couple, only to discover Josephine in tears. 'She wants to go to Egypt,' Napoleon explained. 'Are you taking your wife, Dumas?' 'Gracious, no!' he replied. 'It's traditional for soldiers' wives to follow later.' Napoleon agreed. 'If we are there for several years, we will send for our wives.' He punctuated these remarks, according to Dumas, with a resounding smack on Josephine's bare and shapely buttocks.[18]

In a letter to Hortense Josephine seemed reconciled to Napoleon's decision: 'I have been in Toulon for five days. I was not tired en route but quite unhappy to have had to leave so quickly, without having told you goodbye, much less to my dear Caroline. But my dear daughter, I am a little consoled by the hope that I will soon embrace you. Napoleon doesn't want me to make the trip to Egypt. He will send for me in two months. And so, my Hortense, I will have the pleasure of pressing you to my heart and to assure you that you are much loved.' In reality though she was still hopeful that her husband would change his mind. She might have succeeded in changing it for him had not a number of vessels, believed to be English, been sighted on 18 May. It proved to be a false alarm, but the scare only strengthened Napoleon's resolve that Josephine should stay behind.

At daybreak on the morning of 19 May Napoleon gave his final orders and boarded the *Orient*. After an intensely emotional parting, Josephine, along with the other officers' wives, repaired to the balcony of the marine intendancy, which overlooked the bay. One hour later the sails were raised. But as the ships moved out of the harbour, the overloaded *Orient* dragged along the bottom and listed sharply. The spectators gasped in alarm. Josephine's heart in particular must have skipped a beat: both her husband and her son were on board. Mercifully the ship soon righted itself and pulled out into the open sea. The fleet finally departed in the brilliant sunshine, accompanied by a fanfare of brass bands, cannon fire and singing. Josephine stood amongst the cheering crowds waving farewell to what seemed, 'the most spectacular expedition since the crusades'.

Towards the end of May Josephine and her companions, Mme de Cambis and Mme de Krény, began travelling north to Plombières, a spa town nestling in the pine forests of the Vosges mountains. They arrived in the resort, famous since Roman times for its sulphur baths, on 14 June. Josephine was lodged in the Pension Martinet, a 'very respectable house', as she explained in a letter to a friend, run by an elderly couple whose devotion to each other reminded her of Ovid's Philemon and Baucis.

Two days after her arrival she wrote to her daughter:

*I have received no news from you, my dear Hortense. What keeps you so
busy that you can't write to the mother who loves you. I began my
treatment today. I will stay for one month, then return to Paris for a few
days and then go on to join Bonaparte. I've news of him. He asked me to
write to you and to Caroline to tell you he loves you both and to write
him often . . . I am sending you and Caroline dresses of taffeta of the
latest fashion. Hug her for me, tell her that I love her . . . I had a letter
from your brother, he is well. Hug Mme Campan for me and write often.
I love you to the point of idolatry.*[19]

At Plombières, as Josephine recounted in a letter to Barras, she had 'no social
life'. She saw virtually no one but her 'water doctor' and concerned herself
solely with her health. Teasingly she went on to ask him whether he wished
to join her in taking the cure, then pleaded for news of Bonaparte.

*I have need of it. I am unhappy to be separated from him; I'm overcome
with a sadness that I can't conquer. Besides, his brother, with whom he
frequently corresponds, is so horrible about me that I am always worried
when I am far from Bonaparte. I know what he [Joseph] has told friends,
one of whom repeated it to me, that he is only happy as long as he is
getting me into trouble with my husband. It is a vile existence, abominable,
a fact that you will understand one day . . . I send you a letter for Bonaparte
that I beg you to pass on to him quickly. I will send you all my letters
to him. I beg you, be very punctual in delivering them to him. You know
how upset he gets with me when he receives no news. The last letter
which he wrote to me was very tender and emotional. He told me to come
and join him quickly, that he cannot live without me. So I work diligently
to improve my health so I can leave as quickly as I can to join Bonaparte,
whom I love in spite of his little faults.*[20]

Her pleasant stay in the sedate little resort was rudely interrupted on 20 June
1798. The morning began innocuously enough, with Josephine and her
companion Adelaide de Cambis sitting hemming the madras headkerchiefs
that Creole women tied around their hair and chatting with their two
morning callers: General Colle and citoyen Latour. Mme de Cambis
wandered out onto the balcony and called to her friend to come and see a
sweet little dog that was passing on the street below. Ever the animal lover,
Josephine rushed to join her and was followed by her visitors. Overwhelmed
by their collective weight, the fragile balcony gave way and the entire party

fell twenty feet to the street below. The two men landed on their feet but the women fell more awkwardly. Adelaide broke her leg, while Josephine was badly hurt. The faithful Euphémie was immediately dispatched to Paris to fetch Hortense, and all the notables in the area rushed to her sickbed.

Hortense arrived to discover Josephine with a suspected broken pelvis and spinal paralysis. Her bruises were so severe, especially on her arms, that she could not even lift a fork and had to be fed like a baby. Delighted to find himself with such an illustrious patient on whom to display his medical prowess, her doctor subjected Josephine to such an esoteric series of treatments that it is a miracle she survived. In the bulletins he sent daily to Barras, Dr Martinet gleefully recounted how, when called to the scene, he immediately bled her, administered an enema and plunged her into a hot bath. The noxious herbal teas, enemas and scalding baths continued and – on the advice of a number of specialists – the doctor added leeches, camphor compresses and topical remedies made of boiled potatoes to his medical repertoire. There was even talk of a sheep being skinned so that she could be wrapped in its bloody pelt.

The treatment was in danger of being more lethal than the accident. But despite the gravity of her injuries and the eager ministrations of Dr Martinet, Josephine's health began to slowly improve. On 28 June the doctor wrote to Barras: 'Good news. There is still some pain in the lumbar region but that does not prevent the patient sleeping and having an appetite. I hope that tomorrow she will go out for a walk.'[21] The same day a delegation of notables came to present their regards 'to the wife of the Liberator of Italy'. They proceeded to invite her on behalf of the municipality of Épinal to a reception they wished to hold in her honour. She responded graciously, avowing 'the esteem and attachment' she felt for the inhabitants of Épinal, and assuring them that she would visit as soon as her health allowed it.

Despite her doctor's optimism and her own determination to keep up appearances, she was still feeling dreadful. She told Barras, ' . . . I've suffered a great deal of pain. I still can't walk. My body aches horribly. I have to take the baths every day. I have to be a bit stronger to take the showers, the only thing, the doctors tell me, that will cure me . . . I suffer cruelly.'[22] Almost three weeks later Josephine was still in profound discomfort, unable to sit or stand for more than ten minutes without pain in the small of her back and her lower stomach. Extremely discouraged, her depression was only exacerbated by Napoleon's loving letters begging her to join him, which she longed to do.

By the end of July Josephine's health had rallied sufficiently for her to make the promised trip to Épinal. Her arrival was heralded by the music of a military band and the sound of cannon. Accompanied by Hortense and Mme Beurnonville, the wife of a general on whose behalf she intervened during the Revolution, she was ushered through streets festooned with greenery and thronged by adoring crowds. The National Guard escorted her through a triumphal arch to the town hall, in front of which stood a statue of liberty with an inscription honouring Napoleon. There Josephine was presented with a large bouquet and subjected to a lengthy speech by the president of the municipal council. The celebrations were crowned that evening by a grand supper, followed by a magnificent fireworks display. Josephine summarized the day in a letter to François de Neufchateau, the Minister of the Interior: 'I received for Bonaparte all the vows of esteem and affection imaginable . . . My only regret on this enchanting day was that my health did not permit me to fully throw my heart into the celebrations . . .'

Meanwhile, there was good news from Egypt. After his triumphant departure, Napoleon had taken Malta on 12 June, following a day's token fighting. Ten days later, back at sea, he issued a stirring proclamation to his army: 'Soldiers!' he declaimed. 'You are about to attempt a conquest, the effect of which will be incalculable on civilization and the commerce of the world!'[23] On 1 July the French armada sighted Alexandria. Two thousand years earlier the city had been known as the warehouse of the world; the place where papyrus, ebony and spices came from. But by the time the French landed, its importance had declined and there were only 6,000 inhabitants. Napoleon audaciously landed his troops in the dangerous reefs of the west bay and by 11 a.m. they had taken the city. His proclamation to the Egyptian people was couched in the liberatory rhetoric typical of the Revolutionary Army: ' . . . Henceforth, with God's help, no Egyptian shall be excluded from high office . . . Those who are the most intelligent, educated and virtuous shall govern and thus the people shall be happy.'[24]

Three weeks later at Embaba, in a confrontation he dubbed the Battle of the Pyramids, Napoleon took on Murad Bey's army. The enemy, the 10,000 Mamelukes, were more formidable opponents than the French had anticipated. Each of them, according to one French officer, was 'a mounted one-man arsenal and had at least two servants-at-arms at foot'. Their usual equipment consisted of a musket, a brace of pistols, several javelins, a scimitar of Damascene steel 'and an assortment of battle-axes, maces and daggers'.

When the Mamelukes burst upon the weary French troops at dawn on 13 July, the latter were awestruck. Recalling the spectacle in his memoirs, an officer wrote:

> In the background, the desert under the blue sky; before us, the beautiful Arabian horses, richly harnessed, snorting, neighing, prancing gracefully and lightly under the martial riders, who are covered with dazzling arms, inlaid with gold and precious stones. Their costumes are brilliantly colourful; their turbans are surmounted by a crest of feathers, and some wear gilded helmets. This display produced a vivid impression on our soldiers by its novelty and richness. From that moment on, their thoughts were set on booty.[25]

Despite their panache and reckless courage, the Mamelukes' lack of organization meant they were relatively easy to defeat and the French Army got its booty. It was here that Napoleon is credited with uttering the immortal words, 'Soldiers, 40,000 centuries look down upon you . . .' Although it was not a decisive victory, it was a highly evocative one; 'linking Napoleon's name with the magic of the pyramids produced an impression worth several victories.'[26] Almost overnight everything Egyptian was à la mode in France, and Bonaparte more exalted than ever.

The glorious stories of these victories obscured a much more sordid reality: the Egyptian campaign was up to its elbows in mud, blood and disease. Far from receiving their liberators with delight, the Egyptian people 'were seized by unimaginable terror'.[27] The French troops were suffering too. After enduring a six-week crossing, sustained only by rotten salt meat, wormy biscuits and fetid water, they landed in Alexandria sick, starving and exhausted. Had they not taken Alexandria so quickly, they would have died of thirst. When the French Army resumed its tortuous march towards Cairo, water was so scarce that 'thirty men were trampled to death in a stampede for a few drops of brackish water . . . scores of men lost their wits and shot themselves'.[28]

However, on 19 July Napoleon's military duties were interrupted by a personal cataclysm. His secretary Bourrienne told the story:

> I noticed Bonaparte walking alone with Junot . . . the general's pale face had turned paler than ever. His features were suddenly convulsed, a wild look came into his eyes, and several times he struck his head

with his fists! . . . Some fifteen minutes later, he left Junot and came towards me. I had never seen him so distraught and preoccupied . . . he burst out: 'You are not genuinely devoted to me, or you would have told me what I have just learned from Junot. There's a true friend for you. Josephine! And I six hundred leagues away! You should have told me! Josephine – thus to have deceived me! Damn them, I shall exterminate that whole breed of fops and coxcombs! As for her, divorce! Yes, divorce – a public divorce – open scandal! . . .'

   . . . Unless one is familiar with the violence of the wrath of which Bonaparte was capable when roused, it is impossible to imagine what he was like during this terrible scene.[29]

His secretary nonetheless stood his ground. He explained how easily rumours were fabricated and circulated and how unfair it was 'to accuse a woman who was not there to justify or defend herself'. Why should any friend, he argued, 'add domestic anxieties to those already confronting a commander at the outset of a hazardous military exercise'. Napoleon responded, 'Oh what would I not give to discover that what Junot has told me is untrue! So deeply do I love that woman! But if she is guilty, then divorce must separate us forever. I will not be the laughing stock of Paris! I will write to Joseph and tell him to have the divorce pronounced.'[30]

Bourrienne persuaded Napoleon to calm down, arguing that divorce was something that he could think about later, 'after due consideration'. Bonaparte agreed but nonetheless remained distraught. In a letter to his brother he wrote, 'I am undergoing acute domestic distress, for the veil is now entirely torn. It is a sad state when one and the same heart is torn by such conflicting sentiments regarding one and the same person . . . I am disgusted with human nature. I have need of solitude and isolation. Grandeur palls on me. My emotions are spent, withered. I am weary of glory. At the age of 29, I have exhausted everything; life has nothing more to offer . . .'[31]

In the same dispatch pouch, Eugène sent a letter to Josephine that displayed a delicacy and maturity that belied his seventeen years:

My dearest mother . . . For the last five days Bonaparte has appeared exceedingly sad, and this came about as the result of a talk he had with Junot and Jullien – even Berthier joining in . . . From the few words I could catch, it all goes back to Charles, to the fact that he returned with you [from Italy] in your carriage . . . that you have seen him since in Paris, that you have been going with him to the Italiens [the Théâtre Italien],

to the fourth-balcony loges [the discreet upper private boxes]; that it was he
who gave you your little dog; that he is with you even at this moment . . .
  . . . As you can imagine, Maman, I do not believe a word of this, but
what is certain is that the general is deeply affected by it. Still, he
redoubles his kindnesses to me; he seemed to be saying, by his actions, that
children cannot be held responsible for their mothers' frailties. But your son
tells himself that all this gossip has been fabricated by your enemies, and
he loves you no less, no less yearns to embrace you. I only hope that by
the time you arrive here all this will be forgotten . . .[32]

Josephine arrived back in Paris on the night of 15 September to be met by
bad news. The French fleet had been destroyed at Aboukir. As a result
Napoleon was cut off from France, unable to receive supplies of men, arms
and materials, and in grave danger. Josephine's letter to Barras hints at her
alarm: 'I arrived last night late. My first thought was to send a messenger to
know your news. I learned that you were in the country and that you would
only be arriving back very late. I am so disturbed by the news which I've
received via Malta that I must ask to see you alone tonight at 9 p.m. Please
give orders that no one else be admitted.'[33]

At this meeting with Barras, Josephine would have been apprised of the
details of the battle that would decide who had control of the Mediterranean
and effectively put an end to France's empire-building in the east. In the
early afternoon of 1 August Vice Admiral Nelson had surprised the French
fleet anchored in Aboukir Bay. Caught off guard and badly unprepared, the
French commander Vice Admiral Brueys attempted to rally his troops, but
one-third of his men were stranded on land collecting supplies and he could
not receive advice from Napoleon, who was also on the mainland.

Caught unawares by Nelson, Brueys was paralysed by the Englishman's
innovative attack. Within a couple of hours the ships of the French vanguard
and centre, under fire from the British guns, were reduced to so much
kindling. At ten that evening the battle reached its climax when the *Orient*,
the armada's flagship, was blown up. The explosion shook everything within
a twenty-five-kilometre radius; sixteen kilometres distant in Alexandria it
illuminated the night sky, and it could be heard fifty kilometres away. After
the smoke had dissipated all that was left of the *Orient* was a burning shell.
The bay itself was an awful sight, littered with French bodies, mangled,
wounded and scorched. In an age before weapons of mass destruction and

mass killing, this sight so shocked the combatants that it provoked a ten-minute hiatus in the battle. But then fighting resumed and continued unbroken for several hours.

At the end of this long, fateful night of carnage, Brueys was dead and Nelson was wounded. Eleven French battleships had been captured or destroyed and 1,700 of their sailors were dead. The terrible fate of the *Orient*'s captain, Louis Casabianca, and his son – 'the boy who stood on the burning deck' – was immortalized in the poem by Mrs Henman.

Napoleon played down what he called the Battle of the Nile, as did the Directoire, much to the fury of the French press. But the battle nonetheless had wide-ranging political repercussions. By cutting off Napoleon's troops from the homeland, the defeat meant that the French Army in Egypt was effectively doomed. It also generated a storm internationally. Yielding to English and Russian pressure that September, Sultan Selim III declared war on France. Tsar Paul of Russia, who had declared war after the French seizure of Malta, dispatched his Black Sea fleet to the Mediterranean where, after a long siege, it took Corfu and the other French-held Ionian islands, while King Ferdinand of Naples, personally encouraged by Nelson, attacked the French forces in Italy. Thus the entire foreign policy plan, of which the Egyptian campaign was a cornerstone, had gone profoundly awry.

Despite her anxiety about Napoleon in Egypt, the whirl of Parisian life swept Josephine away. There were visits to return, dates to juggle and gossip to catch up with. The most juicy surrounded her dear friend Thérésia Tallien. Just as Barras had once handed over Josephine to Bonaparte, he was now matchmaking for Thérésia. The transfer was made public at a grand hunting party at Barras's country house, Grosbois. Under his indulgent eye, Thérésia arrived with her new beau, the great financier Ouvrard. The arrangement was cemented when the couple appeared at the theatre in Ouvrard's box; and later moved, courtesy of the millionaire, to a new house at 685 rue de Babylone.

As ever, Josephine was besieged with requests for assistance. One of the most singular of these came from a rather eccentric friend, Caroline Wuiet. An infant prodigy, who at the age of five had played the piano for Marie Antoinette, she had subsequently become a writer who celebrated Josephine's 'generosity and enchanted spirit' in one of her poems. When she fell on hard times she decided that the expense of being a woman was such that it was cheaper to dress in men's clothes. Her habit of dressing *en travesti* attracted the negative attention of the police and Wuiet begged Josephine to intervene. Josephine obligingly requested and received permission from the authorities for her 'to sometimes wear men's clothes'.[34]

Once Josephine had settled back into city life she reopened her salon. Her extensive female circle – Mmes Visconti, de Kreny, Hamelin, Récamier, de Lameth and de Castellane – were invited to provide the prerequisite elegance and beauty. Eccentrics were there to add drama: Pindar, who went around with his pockets stuffed with verse which he read to everyone; Hoffman, who was, in spite of his stammer, a brilliant polemicist; and Aunt Fanny, just about to celebrate her sixty-first birthday. They mingled with the most celebrated cultural figures of Directoire society: musicians such as Méhul and Cherubini; artists like Gérard and Girodet; the actor Desaugiers; and the writer Bernardin de Saint-Pierre whose book *Paul et Virginie* had so influenced Napoleon's ideas about his wife; as well as poets like Ducis and Arnault – the latter had accompanied Napoleon as far as Malta only to discover that battle was not to his taste and hastily returned to France. The cast of characters was so scintillating that Parisians begged to be admitted into her circle.

Since Josephine's finances were controlled by Napoleon's brother Joseph, who quibbled over her every request, she struggled to remain on good terms with the family. Madame Mère, who was living in Paris with cardinal Fesch, occasionally deigned to dine with her. The rest of the family declined her invitations. So Josephine did not see much of the Bonaparte clan. However, she could not avoid the gossip about them that circulated in the city. That October Joseph bought one of the most famous properties in France. Once the residence of the banker Durey, whose heirs had been guillotined for consorting with émigrés, the chateau and estate of Mortefontaine encompassed almost 700 acres of meadow land, woods, gardens and ponds. The purchase price was 258,000 francs and Joseph spent roughly the same amount again on renovations. Having been told in no uncertain terms that Malmaison was too expensive, Josephine must have smarted at this extravagance – especially since Joseph's wealth was largely generated by her husband's success.

She decided to visit Malmaison once again. This time she was accompanied by Hortense and the painter Isabey. She discovered that the property she coveted had a venerable history; as early as the eleventh century records existed of a fortified grange on the site. By the seventeenth century it was a fully fledged manor house whose owner, a counsellor in the Parlement de Paris, carried the title of 'seigneur de La Malmaison'. Despite its name, 'Malmaison', which evokes the idea of a bad, even fatal, stay, the property was always attractive; situated on the outskirts of the pretty hamlet of Rueil. The visit only whetted her desire for the chateau and she put the purchasing process in motion. In the middle of October 1798 she contacted her old friend Chanorier, the mayor of Croissy, and asked him to act as an intermediary between the Bonapartes and the du Moley family in the purchase of Malmaison. The negotiations took close to six months.

In the middle of that October the Parisian newspaper *La Clef du Cabinet* reported on a rumour then making the rounds in England. It claimed that a French mail ship had been captured at Aboukir with a cargo of correspondence from the French Army – including some written by its leader. Despite Vice Admiral Nelson's faithful assurance 'that all non-military communications – letters of a confidential, personal or romantic nature – would be released and forwarded to their addresses', the letters were published in November. An editorial in the *Morning Chronicle* complained that publication did 'little credit to the ethics of our Cabinet'. Despite horror at this 'scandal-mongering', the author nonetheless detailed that 'one of the confiscated letters is from Bonaparte to his brother, a lament on his wife's coquetries; another, from young Beauharnais, expresses the hope that his *chère maman* is less of a coquette than she had been depicted . . .'[35] Barras persuaded most of the French journals not to reprint the two letters, but since the French edition of the *Chronicle* was already available, the damage was done. By December all of France knew that Napoleon was aware of his wife's relationship with Charles. The Bonapartes' marital rift was a public scandal.

Napoleon's revenge was as public as his humiliation. He immediately began an affair with another woman. With his secretary Bourrienne as his co-conspirator, a 'half-dozen Asiatic women most highly recommended for their beauty were summoned up for the general's inspection'.[36] Their opulent charms did not appeal to Bonaparte. He preferred a woman who was 'slender and graceful, in the palest gowns, walking on shadowy garden paths'. In other words: Josephine. The closest approximation came in the form of Pauline Fourès. Recently married to one of Bonaparte's lieutenants, she had stowed away at Toulon disguised in the uniform of her husband's regiment in order to stay close to him. Despite this impulsive act, her relationship with her husband was rocky and so the young blonde was receptive to Napoleon's charms when she met him at a dinner party. Her husband was quickly dispatched overseas on a mission for the Directoire and Pauline was established in a palace adjoining Napoleon's own.

'Gossip about the affair set headquarters buzzing',[37] according to Bourrienne. It was so widespread that when Pauline's unfortunate husband was captured by an English captain, he was quickly set free and returned to Egypt, just for sport. Napoleon had no option but to organize a divorce for the pair. Freed from any marital restraints the twenty-year-old Pauline – now nick-named 'Our Lady of the Orient' – brazenly revelled in their relationship. To the glee of his troops, she accompanied Bonaparte on a matching white Arabian horse, dressed in form-fitting white breeches, gold-braided sky-blue coat and plumed bonnet. The flagrant display of this illicit union was difficult for Josephine's son, Eugène, who also happened to be Napoleon's aide-de-camp. He was forced to ride escort on the couple's carriage on a number of occasions, until, 'no longer able to endure the situation',[38] he applied for a transfer. This precipitated a heated scene with his stepfather, but resulted in Napoleon tempering his 'public promenades with the lady in question'.

Napoleon remained in Egypt until one year and a fortnight after the defeat of Aboukir. 'Despite all its dramatic happenings and heroic accomplishments,' the historian Christopher Herold characterized this as 'a year of make believe'.[39] Napoleon claimed to control Egypt when in fact he never controlled more than a few key cities, and he pretended that he was in Egypt with the approval of the sultan for a full three months after the sultan had declared war on him. In a letter to the Directoire he wrote reassuringly: 'We lack nothing here. We are bursting with strength, good health and high spirits.'[40] This despite the fact that one-third of his troops were afflicted with 'the Egyptian eye disease', many had contracted syphilis and gonorrhea and that in December bubonic plague had struck.

His decision to conquer Syria was also ill-fated. It began monstrously when the town of Jaffa was sacked in an orgy of rape and murder. Two thousand or more citizens – including children – who had surrendered were taken to the beach and shot, bayoneted or drowned. The siege of Acre ended in defeat after two desperate months. Of his 13,000 men, at least 2,200 had been killed in action or by plague and more than 2,000 were crippled or ill. Napoleon nonetheless saw to it that his return to Egypt looked like a triumph. Trophies and prisoners of war were sent to Cairo along with bulletins of glory. One civilian member of the expedition, writing to describe the horrors of the campaign, concluded, 'The report of the commander-in-chief which I enclose will prove to you how much a man must lie to be in politics.'[41]

Napoleon's last engagement of the Egyptian campaign proved the letter-writer's point. On 15 July the Turkish Army (the same one that he had already claimed in his bulletins to have destroyed) landed at Aboukir. Ten days later, with a force of about 10,000 men, he attacked the Turks still ensconced near the beach and drove a large number of them into the sea where they drowned – a sight he described as both terrible and beautiful. By wildly exaggerating the number of his foe, Napoleon's report turned a 'foregone conclusion into a spectacular victory'.[42]

It was shortly after this battle, during a routine exchange of prisoners, that Napoleon was given a set of European newspapers. The news they recounted was explosive. Austria had declared war in March; her armies were driving the French out of Germany. The Russians and the Austrians meanwhile, under Field Marshal Alexander Suvorov, were routing the French in Italy. Napoleon realized instantly that, at last, the 'fruit was ripe'. Confiding in only his most intimate circle, he planned his covert departure for France. On 18 August 1799 he slipped out of Cairo with a few of his closest aides. When the coast was clear of English vessels he departed from Alexandria, stopping briefly in his native town of Ajaccio – the last time he would see the land of his birth. His arrival in Fréjus was preceded by news of his latest victory.

Just before Napoleon departed for Egypt he said, 'The true conquests, the only ones that leave no regret, are those that have been wrested from ignorance.' This remark neatly summed up the Egyptian campaign. Though the military domination of Egypt endured for only two years after his departure, it was in the areas of learning and discovery that the campaign could be judged an unequivocal success. Napoleon's scientific commission, which included engineers, cartographers, physicists, chemists, mathematicians, astronomers, geologists and archeologists, found that – freed from the distractions of the French capital – their work flourished. The result of their labours was the magnificent twenty-four volumes of text and plates that make up the *Description of Egypt*, published between 1809 and 1828.

But it was in the arena of archaeology that Napoleon's Egyptian campaign provided its most enduring legacy. When a French captain stumbled on a granite block featuring a proclamation in three languages – Greek, a demotic script and hieroglyphics – he had uncovered the Rosetta stone, dating from the second century BC, which was to provide the key to deciphering Egyptian hieroglyphics, and a new science was born. Another catalyst for the science of Egyptology was provided by Bonaparte when he ordered General Desaix to pursue Murad Bey and conquer Upper Egypt as far south as Aswan. This epic campaign lasted eleven months and covered over 3,000 miles. It opened up the ruins of Dendera, Luxor, Karnak and the Valley of the Kings, as well as the awe-inspiring sight of Thebes – which moved an entire division to spontaneously applaud and strike up the band. These sights and others were captured in the famous sketches and drawings by the erstwhile pornographer, Vivant Denon, whose work would give Europeans their first glimpse of an ancient culture that would continue to fascinate until the present day.

In Josephine's life, meanwhile, scandal followed scandal. This time it was her involvement with the Bodin company that was causing a stir. A War Ministry enquiry into the company had resulted in serious financial difficulties for the firm and the imprisonment of Bodin himself. In a drama that unfolded over six months, newspapers were filled with details of the company's shoddy practices: horses unfit for service and meat – maggoty and rotten – totally unfit for human consumption. To make matters worse, unpaid suppliers were now threatening legal action. To have his wife embroiled in a profiteer's scandal would have enraged Napoleon even further, especially since he had once described army speculators as 'the scourge and leprosy of the services'. Unwilling, and perhaps unable, to turn to Napoleon, she once again reached out to Barras. In a letter dated 21 June 1799 she wrote, 'A report on the Bodin company is to be made today to the Directoire, and I implore you to intervene in their favour. I hesitate to distract you from your weightier duties, but the firm is in such dire straits that it cannot survive without powerful sponsorship.'[43]

But not even Barras could save the Bodin company from bankruptcy. The financial anxiety and public embarrassment this caused Josephine precipitated something of a rift between herself and her co-director and lover, Hippolyte Charles. In one of the letters she wrote to him, discovered among his business papers, she concludes on a surprisingly practical note: ' . . . So now I am asking you to grant me a moment of your time to speak to you on a matter of importance to me. You may rest assured that after this interview, which will be the last, you will be no further annoyed by either my letters or my presence. A self-respecting woman finding herself the victim of deceitful practices quietly withdraws, without a word . . .'[44]

Charles's response to this unhappy missive has never been discovered, but it provoked such misery in Josephine that she sent this indignant letter to her Creole confidante, Mme de Krény:

*Please do me the favour, darling, of reading the enclosed letter, which has
been handed to me this very moment — and then ask this person to come
to you, and try to discover what motives could have prompted such a
message. I find it so unreasonable, so unmerited, that I am not even
taking the trouble to reply. Of course, I have done nothing with which to
reproach myself, it is obvious to me that the intention is to bring about
an open breach. I have the feeling that such has been the intention for quite
a while, but methods more straightforward, less hypocritical, than these
should have been employed. Forgive me, darling, for upsetting you with
this, but you can imagine how horribly distressed I am to impose my
distress on you. It is proof, as well, of how greatly I rely upon your
friendship. I am so unhappy!*[45]

There was one consolation in Josephine's scandal-ridden life: Malmaison. Just
how she had put together the money for the 50,000 franc deposit (of a
272,000 franc bill of sale) remains something of a mystery, especially since
Joseph continued to short-change her on her allowance. It seems likely that
she sold some of her jewellery and borrowed the rest from either Barras or
the financier Ouvrard. However it was achieved, raising the money was an
enormous struggle that would have discouraged a less tenacious creature than
Josephine. Malmaison was more than a passing whim. This, the first home
that she would own in France, would prove to be one of the great loves of
her life, a haven of security and stability, her heart's home.

In many ways Malmaison was reminiscent of La Pagerie. Situated ten
miles downriver from Paris, near the village of Rueil, the property was three
hundred acres of rolling lawns, woodlands, vineyards and farmlands, bordered
by the silvery ribbon of the Seine. Over the years Josephine would expand
and embellish Malmaison beyond all recognition, but when she first purchased
it, it was a modest property full of rustic charm. Unlike the ostentatious
estates that the Bonaparte brothers were gobbling up in the fashionable
countryside, it was more a manor house than a chateau. Malmaison was in
fact a working farm, home to numerous tenant families and replete with
wheat fields and stables, a dozen cattle and 150 wool-producing sheep, as
well as assorted pigs and poultry. It was potentially as self-sufficient as her
childhood plantation, except that its most important crop was wine, not
sugar, which it sold at respectable prices to local dealers.

Since all the furniture was included in the purchase price, she could move in immediately, and she did so that April, when the property was at its most beautiful. As the year passed, Josephine found that she was spending more and more time there, especially since Paris was becoming less hospitable. The negative press was taking its toll. At a fashionable dinner in the capital Talleyrand had snubbed her, much to her chagrin. Fearing that he would never have dared to do this if he had not had some indication that Napoleon was going to put her aside, she became increasingly paranoid. She retreated to Malmaison where she cocooned herself with her family; and rather dangerously with Charles, with whom she had been reconciled. The pair, mistaken by one observer for mother and son, were often seen promenading in the grounds.

Feeling herself besieged from all sides, Josephine's behaviour during the latter part of 1799 was erratic in the extreme. While recklessly flaunting her affair with Charles, she simultaneously attempted to safeguard her political position. To this end she began assiduously to court the next president, Louis-Jérome Gohier. An ardent Republican, this tall, dignified fifty-four-year-old probably hoped that Josephine's overtures offered more than friendship. After all, she was something of an erotic trophy and Gohier, under his serious exterior, considered himself something of a Casanova. She flirtatiously kept him at bay that summer and when she asked his advice on her romantic life, he advised her – undoubtedly with ulterior motives – to give up her relationship with Charles. When she reassured him that they were simply friends, he insisted that 'it compromises you in the eyes of the world'. If she was not willing to give up Charles, he argued, then she must divorce Bonaparte.

But Josephine could not or would not clarify her situation. She continued to flounder around, trying desperately to shore up her position. Once again she reached out to Barras:

> Since I have been living in the country, I have become such a rustic, so much of a recluse, that the great world frightens me. Besides, I am so unhappy that I prefer not to be an object of pity to others. I want to see only you, my dear Barras – you who love your friends even in adversity. So please tell me which day you will offer me luncheon. I will come in expressly from Malmaison and can be with you as early as nine in the morning. I must talk to you. I need your counsel. You owe it to the wife of Bonaparte as well as to our own friendship, yours and mine . . .[46]

Barras and his circle were still faithful to her, and Josephine took refuge with them whenever she was in the capital. One observer recollected seeing her at the Luxembourg around this time:

> An extremely elegant woman of medium height walked by, leaning on Gohier's arm: it was Mme Bonaparte – Josephine – who would later be Queen of France! She bowed deeply to Mme de Staël as she passed her. As soon as she entered Barras's salon he got up, went to meet her and, taking her by the hand, led her to an armchair . . . Mme Tallien came and sat beside her. They were very close friends then, and there was nothing to indicate that only a few months later she would be a sovereign in the very salons where Mme Tallien now reigned.[47]

Early in October 1799 Hortense's wrote to Eugène. Clearly crafted with the possibility of it being read by others – including Napoleon – it recounts the virtuous existence that she and her mother were leading in town and country:

> *Maman has bought Malmaison near Saint-Germain. She lives a very*
> *retired life there, seeing only Mme Campan and her nieces Mlles Auguiés,*
> *who often go with me. She has only given two big dinner parties since you*
> *both left. The Directors and the Bonaparte family were invited but the*
> *latter always refuse. Even Louis refused to stay with us and never comes to*
> *see us. Of them all, only Madame Bonaparte is amiable to us, and we*
> *of course show her every attention . . . Maman is, I assure you, very*
> *distressed that the family won't live on friendly terms with her, which I*
> *know must vex her husband whom she loves very much. I am certain that*
> *if Maman could have been sure of reaching him she would have gone,*
> *but you know how impossible that would be now . . .*[48]

Josephine added a rather cryptic postscript to this letter, explaining how much she was looking forward to seeing them: 'I love you with all my heart, my dear Eugène; I think of you without ceasing. I await the moment which will reunite me with all I love. I should have nothing more to wish for if only I could have Bonaparte back as he was when he left me, and he should always have been towards me. Think, my dear Eugène, of all I have suffered by the absence of both of you. Take care of yourself for the sake of your mother and your sister, both of whom adore you.' Whatever she meant by the remarks concerning herself and Bonaparte – whether she was in denial of the precariousness of their marriage, or whether it was a veiled request for a truce – was immaterial because neither Bonaparte nor Eugène would receive these letters in Egypt. On the day they were written, the pair were already en route to France.

On 10 October Josephine was at a dinner at President Gohier's when a telegraphic dispatch was delivered announcing Napoleon's arrival at Fréjus. After telling the president to 'have no fear that Bonaparte comes as an enemy of liberty',[49] she departed hastily, not even finishing her meal and exclaiming, 'I am going to meet him. It is important for me to reach him ahead of his brothers, who have always hated me.' By daybreak the following morning Josephine, accompanied only by Hortense, without so much as a maid, was speeding to meet her husband. But as precipitous as her departure was, Napoleon's brothers were faster. In the race to intercept Bonaparte on the road to Lyon, they were ahead of her, so the journey was a desperate and anxious one.

Despite their personal concerns, Hortense nonetheless noted the rapture that news of Napoleon's arrival evoked in the French populace.

> At that time France was in such a sorry plight that all arms were stretched out to the General and every hope was in him . . . in every city and in every village triumphal arches had been erected. When we stopped to change horses the people would gather round our carriage to ask whether it was really true that the saviour (for that was the name that all France had given him) had returned. With Italy lost, the finances exhausted, the Directorate without energy or authority, the return of the General was accounted a favour from heaven. The road from Fréjus to Paris was a series of ovations which showed him, as well as his enemies, what France expected of him.[50]

The enthusiasm that greeted his arrival confirmed Napoleon's belief that the time was 'ripe'. In a masterly public-relations gesture designed to reinforce his image in the collective consciousness, he took the time on his journey to attend a performance of a play entitled *The Return of the Hero*. As news of his landing spread, crowds gathered, despite the unseasonable cold and fog, with torches to light his way to the capital. At each stage-stop, cheering villagers fêted him with bunting and music. As he approached Paris the frenzy increased. His entry into the capital was marked by fireworks and by an excitement that was reminiscent of the early days of the Revolution. Regimental bands promenaded down the street with swarms of soldiers and civilians following them. Theatrical performances were interrupted by cries of 'Long live the Republic! Long live Bonaparte!' In the streets, complete strangers embraced and one unfortunate citizen was so overcome by joy that he reputedly dropped dead of a heart attack.

Unluckily for Josephine, Napoleon and his travelling companions trans-ferred to a faster vehicle in Lyon, so that he could arrive in Paris more quickly. To make matters worse, he took the westerly route through the Bourbonnais, while Josephine had taken the easterly Burgundy route, with the unfortunate result that he arrived in Paris two days ahead of her. So when Napoleon's post-chaise pulled up at the house on the rue de la Victoire at 6 a.m. on 16 October, Josephine was not there. 'The effect upon him of that homecoming was profound and terrible', wrote Laure Junot. He inter-preted his wife's absence as 'an admission of her unworthiness to come into the presence of his mother and sisters, an admission of her fear to face the man she had wronged'.[51]

Much to Eugène's despair, Josephine's delay was exploited by her enemies, the Bonaparte family: 'They turned it to their advantage, seizing on the opportunity of her absence to further injure her in her husband's estimation, to poison his mind, to turn him against her.'[52] Which is precisely what Letizia Bonaparte, her daughters Pauline Leclerc and Eliza Bacciochi, and her available sons proceeded to do, playing on Napoleon's fears that Josephine had run off to join Charles, that she no longer loved him and perhaps never had. Bonaparte, who had earlier shown signs of wanting to forgive his wife, became profoundly agitated, remarking bitterly to his friend Pierre-François Réal, 'The warriors returning from Egypt have this in common with the warriors who returned from the siege of Troy: their wives demonstrate the same species of fidelity.'[53]

So decisive and sure-footed in most areas of his life, Napoleon was uncharacteristically indecisive about his relationship with Josephine. As one historian wrote, 'Napoleon's obsession with Josephine, his love and his passion for her, were not susceptible to the analysis or the logic of which he was the master . . . She still haunted his flesh.'[54] On the night of his arrival, as was the duty of a returning army general, Napoleon presented himself to Barras and President Gohier, the representatives of the Directoire. Eternally the pragmatist, Barras recommended simply that Napoleon 'be philosophical about the matter'.[54] Gohier dwelt less on Josephine's behaviour than on the political consequences of divorce. 'The law permits divorce but society disapproves. Divorce is a black mark against the record of a man in public office; his public conscience is judged by his private life, his personal morals. The marital status is simply one more guarantee to be offered to society by a prominent political figure.'[55]

The following day Napoleon sought advice from other members of his circle. First he visited Josephine's friend and fellow Creole Mme Hamelin. If he had been expecting her to betray her old friend he was much surprised; instead she defended Josephine's virtue and reminded him of the advantages of being married to her: 'the enemies disarmed by her exquisite *politesse*, the noble rebels who had become reconciled, the young dissidents she had attracted to his side'.[56] Bourrienne also defended Josephine, as did Napoleon's friend the financier Jean-Pierre Collot. When Napoleon remarked that Josephine deserved to be divorced, Collot replied,

> I cannot answer that question, but I ask you another: is this the proper time for it? Think of France! Her eyes are on you. France expects you to consecrate all your time and thought and energies to her safety. If she sees you embroiled in domestic squabbles, your grandeur will suffer; you will become instead just another comic husband out of a Molière farce. Overlook your wife's shortcomings for the moment; put them out of your mind. If you continue to be dissatisfied with the situation, you can send her packing later . . . you are too familiar with our moral climate not to realize how important it is for you not to make your political debut on the national scene in a role that verges on the ridiculous.[57]

Unable to contain himself, Napoleon interrupted his friend: 'No! My mind is made up – she shall never set foot in this house again! . . . Tongues will wag for a day or two; on the third it will be forgotten. In the light of the momentous events that are brewing, of what significance is another broken marriage? . . . My wife will go to Malmaison. I'll stay here. The general public knows enough about what has gone on not to be deceived as to the reason for the separation.' Collot continued to preach moderation, to which Napoleon responded with a stream of invective and abuse. 'Such violence on your part', remarked Collot, 'convinces me that you are still in love with her. She will make her appearance, make her excuses, you will forgive her and peace will be restored.' 'I forgive her?' Napoleon bellowed. 'You should know me better than that! If I were not sure of myself, I would tear this heart out of my bosom and hurl it into the fire!' Almost choked with rage, Bonaparte clutched at his breast as if to tear it open, a gesture which

Bourrienne felt poignantly demonstrated his heartache and his impassioned state.

That very night, at around midnight, Josephine arrived back at the rue de la Victoire. At the porter's lodge she was confronted with her own possessions, boxed and packed away in trunks. The embarrassed porter told her that he had been given orders not to admit her. After much urging, he eventually let her in. She emerged from her carriage into the arms of her son. After this brief embrace she ran up the stairs, only to discover that her bedroom was empty. Her maid told her that the general was in his study. But when she crossed the hall she found the door locked and bolted against her. According to Mme de Rémusat, who claimed that Josephine had related to her the dramatic tale of that night, 'She called out to Bonaparte, beseeching him to open. Through the closed door, the general replied that it would never be opened to her again. Then she fell to her knees and wept, imploring his pardon in her name and that of her children. But silence was the only answer. The house was hushed about her, and the long hours of the night went by in that same deathly stillness and suspense, broken only by her sobs.'[58]

'Ah! Tears!' declared Napoleon. 'Woman's only weapon.'[59] He was partially correct. While tears were certainly not Josephine's 'only weapon', they were her most formidable. And she certainly cried frequently and copiously. One companion on the Italian campaign described her as crying two or three times a day. Today we would be cynical about such an easy resort to tears, but Josephine was the product of a lachrymose age. In the eighteenth century, weeping was not just an expression of grief but a social skill, a sort of *art de vivre*. 'Tears were mighty orators' that told a multitude of stories. Encouraged by Rousseau's belief that to cry brings us back 'to the body and nature', the eighteenth-century cult of sensibility demanded that men and women cry when they were happy, when they were sad, when they were in love and when they had fallen out of love. Voltaire could not hear a sad tale without dissolving into weeping. The novels of the period, from Rousseau to Goethe, were drenched in tears, the Enlightenment elite wept together in the salons after hearing a good story, while in the theatre it was 'de rigueur to weep' and a play was judged a failure if it did not elicit tears. It was important not just to cry but to be seen to cry. Even in Britain – later so famed for its stiff upper lip – weeping was widespread. During one altercation in the House of Commons the two protagonists, Messrs Fox and Burke, burst into tears, while Wordsworth's first published poem was entitled 'On Seeing Miss Helen Maria Williams Weep at a Tale of Distress'.

This sensibility was considered to be particularly developed in women. Indeed, weeping was such an accomplishment that women resented those who could better them at it. The otherwise sweet-natured English writer Fanny Burney – who recorded with relish her tear-stained stint at court – was positively catty about a woman who could weep more impressively. Tears were part of the mystery, the emotionality, that was woman. Nothing was as enticing to the men of the era as a weeping woman. One writer exalted, 'How ravishing and adorable are the eyes of a lover when they are filled with tears.'[60] The sincerity of a woman's weeping was less significant than her ability to produce tears. As the abbé Galiani declared, 'their tears whether true or false tear at our hearts'.[61] Weeping demonstrated sensitivity and was an intrinsic part of the theatrical spectacle of love and desire.

Weeping was not just esteemed but also eroticized. The marquis de Sade's heroine Justine found her tears served to inflame the lust of her rapists. Napoleon, who possessed a sadistic streak of his own, once remarked that nothing embellished a woman better than 'rouge and tears'. Like most of his generation, brought up on the tear-stained novels of Goethe and Rousseau, Napoleon was moved and sometimes aroused by the spectacle of his lover crying. And thus Josephine and her perpetual weeping represented to him the quintessential woman; her tears an intrinsic expression of her femininity. As the abbe Prévost wrote, tears had 'an infinite sweetness'. Knowing what a beguiling picture she made when her large, long-lashed eyes filled with tears, when they spilt delicately onto her porcelain face, it was no wonder Josephine had developed an entire strategy of crying, the success of which Napoleon himself conceded when he remarked, '. . . she thinks she has carried her point when she begins to cry'.[62]

But to Josephine's immense shock, for the first time in the three years of their marriage, her tears failed her. After a night lying prostrate on the ground, weeping, pleading and begging, Josephine was finally ready to admit defeat. At dawn she got to her feet and made her way down the stairs. She was met by her maid who suggested one final assault on the obdurate Napoleon, but this time she should take Hortense and Eugène with her. 'The children's pleas', according to Mme de Rémusat, 'shook Bonaparte in his iron resolve. With a grim visage, but with reddened eyes that betrayed that he too had been weeping, the general opened his arms to embrace Eugène. Josephine and Hortense clung to his knees. Shortly afterward, all was forgiven.'

In a conversation with Collot, taken down by Bourrienne, Bonaparte gave his version of events:

> Never think that I have forgiven her. I swear to you I have not! I ordered her out of the house when she arrived – but what could I do, Collot? Just as she was leaving, going down the stairs in tears, I saw Hortense and Eugène go after her, sobbing too. I was not born with a heart in my bosom that would be able to endure the sight and sound of weeping. Eugène accompanied me to Egypt; I have come to look upon him as my adoptive son. He is so brave, such a fine young man! And Hortense is just about to make her debut in the world; everyone who knows her sings her praises. I admit, Collot, I was profoundly stirred. I could not bear the sobs of these two children. I asked myself, should they be made the victims of their mother's failings? I reached out, caught hold of Eugène's arm and drew him back to me. Then Hortense came back up the steps with her mother. I said nothing. What was there to say? One cannot be human without being heir to human weaknesses.[63]

Arriving at the house early the following morning, Napoleon's brother Lucien was confronted by the sight of his brother and his sister-in-law in bed together, bodies entangled, in a state of 'unmistakable, total reconciliation'.

The dramatic tale of this watershed episode in the Bonapartes' marriage – undoubtedly embellished by all who memorialized it – contained one profound truth: this reconciliation was indeed a turning point in the couple's relationship. Bonaparte's ability to resist her tears and entreaties, that terrible night on the stairs, had shaken Josephine to the core. She knew that she had come to within a hair's breadth of losing Napoleon, and with him the status and security that their marriage provided. The power balance in their relationship had irrevocably shifted. Each had become a slightly different person and their partnership was henceforth renegotiated on different terms, more in his favour. Napoleon was perhaps less romantic and indulgent; Josephine could no longer take him for granted. The man who had once 'worshipped her as if she was a divinity' no longer put her on a pedestal. From that point on she would have to labour to sustain his love. The terms of his surrender were clear; she would never again be unfaithful. It was a sacrifice that Josephine was willing to make.

Thirteen

BRUMAIRE

With Bonaparte, patriotism was only the cloak for ambition . . .

THIÉBAULT

AFTER THE ROLLERCOASTER RIDE OF their reconciliation the Bonapartes barely had time to draw breath before they were confronted by their greatest challenge yet: Napoleon's bid for power. Threatening though this was for the equilibrium of France, the Government and Napoleon's own fortunes, it proved a stabilizing influence on the Bonaparte union. In the intense days leading up to Napoleon's coup, the couple, working together for the same political objective, had little time to brood on past mistakes. Josephine was denied the opportunity to indulge her grief over losing Hippolyte. She had always enjoyed power and the buzz of business and was now forcefully reminded about what Napoleon offered as a husband. Napoleon, in his turn, watching his wife busy charming and networking, found any residual doubts about her swiftly banished. Reminded of what a tremendous political and social asset she was, he could congratulate himself on making the right choice.

The epic political drama that would culminate in the coup d'état of Brumaire unfolded over an action-packed three weeks. In contrast to the elation of the populace, the Directoire had received the news of Napoleon's arrival with profound ambivalence. True, they had requested his return, but Napoleon had departed Egypt of his own volition long before his orders had arrived. Rather carelessly he had left behind his troops, which, as he was commander-in-chief, meant he had deserted his army. It was an act of treason that – on paper at least – warranted a firing squad.

So it was no surprise that Napoleon was a little nervous when he paid his official visit to the Luxembourg on 17 October. Despite being a popular hero, he did not look very threatening. He appeared before them a thin, exhausted young man, skin bronzed by the sun, dressed in a civilian coat and breeches. His only flamboyant touch was provided by a silk sash from which hung a Turkish sabre. Reassured by his unassuming manner and appearance, the Directoire decided to overlook Bonaparte's behaviour and his stuttered excuses, which clearly held no water. (The one deputy who suggested he should be shot was shouted down.) His popularity was such that it would have been political suicide to do otherwise.

Having salvaged this rather tricky situation, Napoleon once again assumed the role of reclusive and apolitical soldier that had served him so well on his previous stay in Paris. In the evenings he could be found playing backgammon alone with his wife: a picture of republican rectitude. His days were spent receiving, with scrupulous impartiality, visitors from every group and faction – all of whom hoped to embroil him in their schemes. The Jacobins wanted to claim him as their own, as did the republicans. The royalists – aware of his penchant for the ambiance of the old regime, so clearly illustrated by his feelings for Josephine – also hoped to solicit his support. Napoleon skilfully manipulated them all, making them feel that he wanted what they wanted, that he could be and would be the man of the hour.

Meanwhile he kept his ear firmly to the ground. He discovered that there were not one but several plots afoot to overthrow the corrupt Government. He realized he had to move swiftly. His natural inclination to work with Barras was thwarted when the latter made it clear that he did not take his young protégé seriously as a political leader. Instead Napoleon would choose to fatally betray his mentor by pretending to collude with him while making other arrangements behind his back. The next alliance he considered was that led by the apostate priest Emmanuel-Joseph Sieyès, a member of the Directoire and author of the pamphlet *Qu'est-ce-que le Tiers État?* ('What is the Third Estate?') which had helped to kickstart the Revolution. Sieyès had already enlisted the support of Napoleon's brother Lucien, president of the Five Hundred, and his mentor, Talleyrand.

This faction of what might be described as moderates aimed not to destroy the Republic but to consolidate it. However, Sieyès still lacked a 'sword'. No coup d'état could hope to succeed without the support of the army, which had now replaced the insurrectionary mobs called up by the Government in the early days of the Revolution. He needed a military man who would enforce the shift of power, but who would not be tempted to seize it for himself. The stumbling block was that Napoleon and Sieyès loathed each other. Napoleon could not abide the intellectual pretensions of 'that cadaverous priest'. Sieyès in his turn both feared and distrusted Bonaparte. Their mutual dislike meant that neither would make the first move. Childish games ensued. Bonaparte enraged Sieyès by ignoring him at a dinner, then Sieyès slighted Bonaparte by ignoring a messenger who had been sent to arrange a meeting. Raging egos were eventually soothed by Talleyrand, who intervened because time was growing short. An accommodation was finally reached. And Napoleon was in.

It was an uneasy alliance. Every player had his own agenda; each was somewhat antagonistic to the others. Sieyès pictured himself as the leading light of the conspiracy, while Barras smugly thought himself the major player. Fouché and Talleyrand were in it for the money, the power and the love of intrigue itself. Bonaparte watched them deceiving each other and deceived them all. As one historian concluded: 'There can never have been a conspiracy in which the leading conspirators had so little in common, trusted each other so little and cloaked their own intentions so carefully beneath vague phrases of collaboration.'[1]

Since the rue de la Victoire was the headquarters for the conspiracy, Josephine was inevitably enmeshed in the plot. As two historians wrote: 'The Directoire was murdered under the chandelier glow of Josephine's dinners.'[2] Her salon provided perfect cover for the surreptitious toing and froing of the various conspirators, who shuttled from the Bonapartes' home to Sieyès's apartments at the Luxembourg and on to Talleyrand's residence. Since her gatherings attracted all the great and the good it was easy for Bonaparte to use these occasions to convert significant players who needed convincing, siphoning them quietly off into his study where the big deals were being done while the usual conversations of fashion and gossip in the salon allayed the suspicions of those who must remain ignorant. But Josephine offered much more than cover, as Philippe de Ségur noted: 'her discretion, her grace, her gentle manner, her cool composure, her ready ingenuity and wit were of great service'. She justified Bonaparte's renewed confidence in her.

Josephine, like all the conspirators, was assigned specific objectives. Bonaparte needed her help in charming General Bernadotte (who was now married to Désirée Clary, Napoleon's spurned first love). Rivals in both romance and politics, the two men disliked each other intensely. Bonaparte thought Bernadotte a blustering buffoon, while Bernadotte took every opportunity to remind all who would listen that Napoleon was a traitor who had abandoned his army. As Bernadotte rapidly became what Napoleon described as 'the obstacle man', Josephine's 'grace and tact' were mobilized. It was a formidable task, and Josephine cannot be criticized for having only limited success.

A meeting was engineered on 7 Brumaire (29 October) when the two couples were invited to a gala at Joseph Bonaparte's chateau, Mortefontaine. Seizing an opportunity to spend time with the Bernadottes on their own, Bonaparte arranged for them to share the same vehicle. It was going to be an uneasy journey, given the men's mutual antipathy and the fact that Désirée had not seen Bonaparte since he had jilted her. So Josephine was instructed by her husband to deploy all 'the resources of her charm and coquettishness', which she dutifully did. Despite her efforts and Napoleon's forced conversation, the journey was plagued by heavy silences. Désirée was not won over. Reunited with her sister Julie that evening, she recounted the day's events — laughing, and mimicking Josephine's lash-fluttering efforts.

Gohier was a simpler task. He remained infatuated with Josephine and was easily taken in by her charms. He was kept busy by frequent invitations to the rue de la Victoire, where Josephine distracted him with gentle flirtation while subtly eliciting his views on the future Government. She played her role prettily, as events would soon prove. It was one of the nightly gatherings at the Bonapartes' home, which included men of every possible faction; most were blissfully ignorant of what was afoot. Gohier was there at Josephine's feet when Fouché arrived. 'Well, citizen minister,' said Gohier to Fouché, 'and what's the latest news?' 'News?' repeated Fouché. 'Oh, there's no news.' 'But surely,' said Gohier in his innocence. 'Just the little tittle-tattle, you know; rumours.' 'About what?' 'The conspiracy,' said Fouché lightly. Now Josephine knew that Gohier was completely ignorant of the whole business, and she therefore wondered what game Fouché was playing. She gave a little gasp — 'The conspiracy!' 'Yes,' said Fouché in an offhand manner, 'the conspiracy.' 'Conspiracy!' repeated Gohier with a shrug, as though to say, 'What foolish talk!' 'I know just how much to believe,' continued Fouché. 'I know what I'm about, citizen Director. Leave it to me. I'm not one to be caught napping. If there'd been any conspiracy we should have given proof of it on the place de la Révolution or in the plain of Grenelle.' And he laughed loudly. Josephine pretended to be frightened. 'Citoyen Fouché,' she said, 'shame on you! How can you make a jest of such things?' Gohier, delighted to have a chance of consoling Josephine, said: 'But don't be distressed, citoyenne Bonaparte. The mere fact that he talks like that in front of the ladies proves that there's no need for him to carry out his threats. Be like the Government, citoyenne. Don't worry yourself about such rumours. Don't let them disturb your sleep.'[3] All the while Bonaparte listened with a smile.

The plot, such as it was, can be described thus: on the appointed day, 18 Brumaire, the Ancients (otherwise known as the Council of Elders) would, prompted by a fabricated Jacobin uprising, declare a state of emergency. Bonaparte would be given command of the troops in the Paris region and the seat of both houses would be transferred to Saint-Cloud. There, 'protected' from undue influence, they would be encouraged to vote in the new Government.

On the night of 17 Brumaire Josephine opened the attack on the Directoire. Shortly after 8 p.m. she gave Eugène, who was on his way to the theatre, a note to be delivered to Gohier at the Luxembourg. It read, 'Please come, my dear Gohier, with your wife to breakfast with me tomorrow at eight o'clock. Don't fail to come. I have some very interesting matters to discuss with you. Adieu, my dear Gohier, and count always on my sincere friendship. Lapagerie Bonaparte.'[4] In case this failed to lull him into a false sense of security, Napoleon also sent him a separate note inviting him to dine the following evening. It was this gesture, Gohier confessed later, that assuaged his concerns about the rumours that were circulating: 'How could I believe in such black perfidy?'[5]

With Gohier neutralized by this pre-emptive strike, plans for the following morning unfolded, initially as planned. The day began long before dawn, when the deputies were roused from their beds for an emergency meeting. Since those senators who were present were largely sympathetic to the plot, the vote was assured anyway. But they listened attentively as Coronet, another Bonaparte ally, reported on the imaginary plot. Indeed, he painted such a perilous picture that the vote to transfer the legislative body to Saint-Cloud was easily carried. The only article which caused some to hesitate was the one that illegally conferred the command of the military district to Bonaparte. But the vote was won and the senators remained in their seats to await Bonaparte's reply.

By the time the emissaries of the Elders reached the rue de la Victoire, they found a gathering of military men so vast that even the garden was filled. Bonaparte had sent each a separate summons, and each had expected a private interview. Those who seemed put out were taken to see Bonaparte in his study, but most of those present realized immediately what was going on: the Government was to be overthrown. Since they, like Bonaparte, despised the 'bunch of lawyers' that had been mismanaging the country, most cared little how it was done.

At about nine that morning Bonaparte appeared on the steps outside his house. At the sight of him, bathed in the pale morning sunshine, cheers erupted, swords were drawn and he was acclaimed by troops and sightseers alike. Announcing that the Republic was in danger, he mounted his horse and set out at the head of this formidable procession. Huge crowds gathered to watch the saviour for whom France had been waiting.

At the Tuileries, Bonaparte made his first speech to a public assembly. He spoke of the sacred principles of national representation but neglected to swear loyalty to the constitution. Afterwards, reviewing the troops in the gardens of the Tuileries, he was out of sorts. Despite the cheering of his troops and the congratulations of the senators, he knew his performance had been mediocre. In order to recover the situation, he turned on Botot, Barras's secretary, and delivered the famous words, 'What have you done with the France I left you so glorious? I left you peace – I return and find war. I left you victories – I find reverses. I left you the millions of Italy – I find rapacious laws and misery throughout!' His words, the music, the uniforms, all came together to create a profound effect on the gathered crowds, who were already reading the bills and leaflets that the conspirators had circulated earlier. In these they took great pains to reassure the public that Bonaparte had no thought of tyranny and was only there to salvage the Republic; above all there must be no suggestion that he was seizing power for his own ends.

Meanwhile, at the house on the rue de la Victoire, Josephine waited for Gohier. Alarmed by events, he stayed away, sending his wife in his stead. But as time passed Mme Gohier also grew fearful. So when Bonaparte asked her to write a note encouraging Gohier to visit, she instead wrote and sealed a warning for him to stay away. Thoroughly alarmed by his wife's missive, Gohier called a Directors' meeting. But of the five Directors, three had already been nobbled. Thus Sieyès, Ducos and Barras claimed to be indisposed. Only the idiotic Moulin was left, and he and Gohier decided to go to the Tuileries to find out what was afoot. But Gohier was still not seriously alarmed. Had Josephine not stressed in what high regard Bonaparte held him? And was he not dining with the man that very evening?

It was suggested to Gohier that the conspirators simply wanted to make some minor alterations to the Directoire, so Gohier signed the decree that empowered the transfer of the Government to Saint-Cloud and gave

Bonaparte control of the Paris garrison. Gohier was then informed in no uncertain terms that there was no Directoire. Moulin and Ducos obstinately refused to resign. Back at the Luxembourg sentries were posted at all the entrances and nobody was allowed in or out. As the conspirators reviewed the day's achievements and worried about what would follow, the betrayed Gohier went to bed, with a soldier stationed at the foot of the bed as he slept. At the rue de la Victoire Josephine awaited Bonaparte anxiously. When he arrived late that night he reassured her and said to Bourrienne, 'Today went well. We shall see about tomorrow.' Despite this apparent confidence, when Bonaparte climbed into bed beside Josephine she could not help but notice that he placed two loaded pistols beside his pillow.

The following day began positively enough. Just before sunrise bugles sounded from barracks all over Paris, while in the rue de la Victoire Bonaparte, surrounded by his generals, was, despite the tension in the air, in high spirits. Just as he was about to depart, Josephine sent a message requesting he come upstairs to see her. 'Still more in love than he wished to admit', the general appeared pleased. 'I will go up,' he said, 'but this is not to be a day for women. This business is far too serious.'[6] After kissing his wife one more time, Bonaparte drove to Saint-Cloud with an escort of cavalry. As they crossed the place de la Concorde, where the guillotine had once stood, Bourrienne remarked to Bonaparte's aide-de-camp Lavalette, 'Tomorrow we shall sleep in the Luxembourg or else we shall finish up here.'

But progress on the roads was slow. Their journey was impeded by parties of sightseers, in carriages and on horseback, who, alerted that something momentous was about to happen, had also set out for Saint-Cloud. Along the route the taverns and cafes were full of laughing men and women, while in Saint-Cloud itself, despite the chill, people were picnicking in the open air or in their carriages.

Inside the palace the atmosphere was less celebratory. It had been arranged that the two Chambers would sit in different halls, to prevent them from comparing notes and rallying themselves. The Senate was to be in the great Gallery of Apollo which Mignard had decorated for Louis XIV, while the Five Hundred were to meet in the Orangery, a gloomy hall looking on to the garden. But Saint-Cloud had not been inhabited since 1790 and the rooms were not ready. So members of the two Chambers went out into the garden and had the opportunity to mingle and talk; precisely what the conspirators had hoped to avoid. As Napoleon paced in an adjoining room the deputies had the opportunity to ask difficult questions. What were Bonaparte's intentions? Why were all these troops needed so far from the anarchist plot in Paris?

When the Chambers finally reconvened a couple of hours later, the result was not what Bonaparte had hoped for: the Elders simply passed a resolution calling for the election of a new Directoire. Enraged, Napoleon stormed into the Gallery of Apollo accompanied by Bourrienne and a few of his officers. The address that followed was by turns incoherent and intimidating. He told them that they were in peril, that he and his comrades had hurried to their rescue only to be met with slander and accusations of a military conspiracy. 'Had I wanted a military government, should I have come here to offer support to the representatives of the nation? . . . As soon as these dangers pass . . . I will abdicate all power . . . Let us save liberty . . .' But the senators were in no mood to listen to vague tales about some plot. 'Names!' they demanded, 'Names!' Unable to persuade, he tried to bully them. 'Remember', he said ill-advisedly, 'that I go my way accompanied by the god of victory and the god of war . . .' The implied threat only enraged the Elders further and a sea of red togas confronted him. Bourrienne, tugging his sleeve, whispered, 'Leave, General, you don't know what you are saying.'[7]

Curiously, Napoleon genuinely did not seem to realize what a blunder he had made. He sent a message to Josephine to say that all had gone well and went straight into the Orangery to address the Five Hundred. There he was immediately turned on, with cries of '*Hors la loi!*' ('Outlaw, Outlaw!'), 'Down with the tyrant. Kill him! Out with the dictator!' As the members clambered over benches to get to him, Napoleon was surrounded, jostled and pummelled. To increase the confusion, spectators outside the hall were trying to push their way in. A woman expressed the popular view when she cried out, 'Vive Bonaparte!' Then scuffles broke out and Bonaparte, overwhelmed by the claustrophobia crowds always induced in him and on the point of fainting, was half carried, half dragged through the mass of deputies into the fresh air.

All would have been lost were it not for the cool head of his brother. As Bonaparte recovered his composure outside, Lucien took to the floor, pointing out that they had not even let Bonaparte speak and therefore did not know his intentions. He succeeded in stalling long enough for the deputies to begin to quarrel among themselves. Then Lucien, still wearing his red toga, left the tumultuous session, leapt onto a horse and rallied the troops. He told them that a handful of armed deputies, 'brigands in the pay of

England', were terrorizing the other deputies and refusing to accepting Bonaparte's appointment. Pointing to the blood-stained face of his brother (who had scratched his own face in his nervous agitation), he declared operatically, 'See where the daggers of these ruffians have drawn the blood of your general.'[8]

Murat, Napoleon's faithful aide-de-camp, immediately placed himself at the head of a column and roared, 'Throw these people out of here!' To the insistent beat of drums, the hall was cleared. There was no bloodshed. Some of the officials retreated slowly in an attempt to maintain their dignity; others dashed for the doors. Those who refused to move were firmly carted out. Of the deputies who managed to escape, some wandered about the gardens and the woods until darkness fell and then crept into town to seek shelter. Those trying to return to Paris found the gates of the city closed by order of Fouché. The next day their tricolour sashes and scarlet robes were found caught up on thickets or lying soiled and torn on woodland paths.

Although any hope of a purely parliamentary coup had now vanished, it was Lucien again who salvaged the appearance of legality, rounding up a few dozen shivering deputies and a few remaining Elders to recognize the end of the Directoire and then making them swear an oath of loyalty to three provisional Consuls: Sieyès, Ducos, and, of course, Napoleon Bonaparte.

At the Feydeau Theatre Mme Letizia, Pauline Leclerc and Laure Permon, oblivious to the day's momentous events, saw the performance interrupted by an actor who declared, 'Citzens! General Bonaparte has nearly been assassinated by traitors to our country!'[9] Madame Mère emitted a piercing shriek and the trio immediately left the performance and set out for the rue de la Victoire in search of news. They discovered a frantic Josephine, who had been waiting at home all day, terrified by rumours that Bonaparte had been killed. Somewhat reassured by the reports of the women, her anxiety was finally assuaged when a messenger arrived with a note that read, 'The General has saved the threatened Republic, and the spirit of the Republic has saved the General!'[10] Four troopers were immediately dispatched to Mme Campan's school to reassure Hortense and Bonaparte's sister Caroline.

At two o'clock that morning Lucien read the oath to the three Consuls and they swore as requested. Bonaparte immediately issued a proclamation reassuring the public that he was not a plaything of any faction and that the time had come to restore order and a way of life dear to moderate men. He also included his version of what happened at the Orangery, insisting that 'twenty armed assassins fell upon me, seeking my heart with their daggers'. Napoleon need not have bothered; the populace was not overly concerned with the legality of the issue, they simply wanted the Directoire out.

Meanwhile Barras, who thought that he was at the centre of the conspiracy, waited in vain in his empty Luxembourg apartments for the message from Bonaparte that would summon him to power. After many hours Talleyrand arrived instead to request his resignation. Barras, the great survivor, realized just how cruelly he had been deceived. Whether by bribery or by blackmail his signature was obtained. Barras repaired to his country property, Grosbois, where he remained in bitter exile, abandoned by the hangers-on who had only days before flocked to his side. Josephine had lost an ex-lover, friend and ally, and acquired in their stead her most implacable enemy.

At dawn Bonaparte arrived back in Paris. He comforted the distraught Josephine who had been waiting up for him and remarked to Bourrienne, ' . . . tomorrow we sleep at the Luxembourg'. And so began what the duc de Broglie called one of the greatest periods of French history: the four years of the Consulate.

Fourteen

THE CONSULATE

The time of Fable is over, the time of History has begun.

JOSEPHINE

THE CONSULATE WAS A WATERSHED both in France's history and in Josephine's life. After a decade of disorder and uncertainty, the news of Bonaparte's ascension was greeted with enormous enthusiasm and relief. A police report of 21 November stated that 'peace and Bonaparte's re-establishment of the Republic are viewed as a happy prospect' and the newspaper *Le Moniteur* reported that the coup d'état was greeted by 'long lines of people marching to cheers of, "Long live the Republic; long live peace!" '

Within a few months Napoleon had translated the gains of Brumaire into the unequivocal leadership of France. Parisians noted that there 'was nothing but Bonaparte' in the Constitution of Year VIII. His ally–rival Sieyès was sidelined into the Senate; and the other provisional Consul, Ducos, agreed to step aside, conceding, 'It is clear that the nation wants to be commanded by a general.'[1] (The pair were later replaced by two new consuls, the altogether more cooperative and deferential Cambacérès and Lebrun.) As a consequence of these machinations Napoleon was appointed First Consul in December 1799. The result was the establishment of a virtual constitutional monarchy in France. Such was Bonaparte's confidence in his new position that he issued a proclamation on 24 December 1799 that closed one historical chapter and heralded a new age. It read simply, 'Citizens, the Revolution is now established on the principles on which it was founded. The Revolution is finished.'

Thus, in the first year of the new century, Josephine found herself in a new role: that of the wife of a head of state. It was a role with an entirely new set of expectations and rewards. While the status, admiration and attention were gratifying, she was now under constant scrutiny. As Napoleon's consort, she assumed a leading role on both the national and international stage and was confronted with a rigorous timetable of official appearances, ambassadorial receptions and foreign visits. At all times her behaviour and appearance were expected to epitomize the values and reflect the priorities of her illustrious husband. This transition from private citizen into public figure occurred very swiftly and Josephine, now thirty-seven, quickly had to learn the attitudes and manners required by her new position. Despite its challenges, however, the Consulate was to be the most settled period of Josephine's life and, many believe, the happiest.

Five days after the coup of Brumaire Josephine and Napoleon departed their 'temple of love' in the rue de la Victoire for the last time and moved into the Luxembourg. They were both already familiar with this splendid palace, having frequently visited their betrayed former friends Barras and Gohier there. The Bonapartes installed themselves in the sombre apartments that had belonged to Gohier, in the wing to the right of the main entrance known as the Petit Luxembourg. Built nearly two centuries earlier at the behest of Marie de Medici, the Italian wife of Henri IV, the Luxembourg had been much improved since its stint as a revolutionary prison (Alexandre de Beauharnais had spent the early days of his incarceration here), but it wasn't without its own grim memories. The Bonapartes' apartments overlooked the rue Vaugirard, on which stood the Carmelite prison where Josephine had been imprisoned only six years before.

Their time at the Luxembourg was short. With Napoleon's appointment as First Consul he considered his power sufficently established to acquire a new official residence: the Tuileries. Determined to 'dazzle the Parisians with a brilliant ceremony', Napoleon ensured that his official installation on 19 February was marked by a magnificent parade. It was his first ceremonial appearance since his advent to power and he wanted to make an impact. Josephine travelled to the Tuileries in advance of the procession to install herself in the upper windows of the Pavillon de Flore. Accompanied by Hortense and her coterie of ladies, she was beautifully dressed *à la grecque*. All the women carried brightly coloured handkerchiefs with which to salute the soldiers.

At 1 p.m. precisely the procession set off to the thunder of cannon and the sound of fanfares. The route between the Luxembourg and the Tuileries was lined by the garrison of Paris, while the capital's populace, 'clinging like human bunches of grapes to windows',[2] watched the display. The first part of the procession – the civilian contribution – was somewhat disappointing. Since the grand coaches of the ancien régime had long since disappeared, the ministers and senators were forced to travel in a succession of dilapidated hackney carriages on which the licence plates had been hastily concealed with brown paper.

The spectacle improved with the arrival of the First Consul himself. Travelling in his private carriage, he was escorted by six magnificent horses that had been presented to him by the Austrian Emperor after the Treaty of Campo Formio. He was escorted by a cavalry guard, brilliantly uniformed and perfectly drilled. When they reached the Pavillon de Flore, Napoleon – dressed in his new official uniform of red velvet laced with gold – alighted. Before mounting, 'or rather *leaping* onto his horse',[3] he looked up and saluted his beloved Josephine who waved her handkerchief proudly back. Then, accompanied by the roars of the crowd, the drums beating and the bugles sounding, Napoleon saluted the regimental colours, some faded and weather-beaten, others scorched by gunpowder or torn by bullets. The sight of these souvenirs of his victories so overwhelmed Napoleon that he took off his hat and bowed his head, an action that moved many in the the crowd to tears.

What followed was the first of the military reviews that became a staple visual symbol of Napoleon's rule. It was a dashing sight: military bands, precision marching and meticulously choreographed cavalry manoeuvres. That day Napoleon also introduced his new Consular Guard, an elite corps, most over six feet tall, with their own striking uniform. According to an official report, the entire spectacle inspired profound enthusiasm in Parisians: 'Joy was at its height and hope and happiness shone on every face', while 'the crowd shouted tirelessly, "Long live the First Consul! Long live Bonaparte!" '[4]

After the review the Bonapartes took an official tour of their new apartments. That night, their first in the Tuileries, Napoleon, alone at last with Josephine, was in an exultant and playful mood. Picking his wife up in his arms, he carried her into the bedroom, with the words 'Come on, little Creole, get into the bed of your masters.'

Some days after the installation there was a reception at the Tuileries for the diplomatic corps. These evening gatherings allowed Josephine to display her brilliance as a hostess and did much to bolster her popularity and public profile. Though the 'etiquette of the event was simple', according to Napoleon's valet Constant, these gatherings around the couple were already being called a court:

> At 8 o'clock in the evening, the apartments of Mme Bonaparte were crowded with people. There was an incredible wealth of plumes, diamonds and dazzling formal dress. The crowd was so great that it was found necessary to throw open the bedroom of Mme Bonaparte, as the two salons were so full there was not room to move. When, after much embarrassment and difficulty, everyone had found a place as they could, Mme Bonaparte was announced, and entered, leaning on the arm of Talleyrand. She wore a dress of white muslin with short sleeves, and a necklace of pearls. Her head was uncovered; and the beautiful braids of her hair, arranged with charming negligence, were held in place by a tortoiseshell comb. The flattering murmur which greeted her appearance was most gratifying to her; and never, I believe, did she display more grace and majesty.[5]

Contrary to appearances, however, Josephine was not enjoying life in the Tuileries. Despite its majesty and fame, the palace was not a pleasant place to set up house. A long grey building, which stretched between what are now the two westward protruding wings of the Louvre, the palace was commissioned by Catherine de Medici in 1563 and subsequently enlarged by Henri IV. It was completed by Louis XIV in 1672, who abandoned it when he moved his court to Versailles. Since then the Tuileries had been a principal residence of every subsequent French ruler. But its recent history had been unhappy. It was in this palace that Louis XVI and his family were kept under virtual house arrest after their ill-fated flight to Varennes. Its walls were still scarred with bullet and cannon shot from the uprising of 10 August 1792, which marked the establishment of the first French Republic. Inside, some of its floors and staircases were still stained with the blood of the Swiss Guards butchered there during that historic uprising, while in its gardens all the trees had been destroyed except for a couple of slim poplars, spared because they resembled 'trees of liberty'.

After the royal family's removal to the Temple, all semblance of regal splendour disappeared. The Tuileries turned into an ad hoc office building-cum-shopping mall. The Committee of Public Safety had its first meeting in Marie Antoinette's apartments, while the theatre was used by the Convention until 1795. The revolutionary bureaucrats who worked in the building (including Napoleon, who, in the run up to the Italian campaign, had toiled in the topographical bureau on the fifth floor of the Pavillon de Flore) were serviced by a series of lemonade stands, tobacconists and pastry shops. Beggars took advantage of the revolutionary throng to ply their trade. The famous red cap of liberty was everywhere, painted or stencilled on the whitewashed walls. Napoleon ordered the architect Lecomte to 'get rid of all this. I don't like to see such filth.'

For Napoleon the palace represented a challenge. As he said to Bourrienne, 'It's not enough to be here, the problem will be to stay.' But Josephine, always sensitive to ambiance, found the Tuileries haunted and unbearably sad. 'I shall never be happy here,' she told Hortense. 'I felt gloomy forebodings from the first minute I entered.'[6] She was particularly uncomfortable with her private apartments, which felt oppressive despite the refurbishments made as soon as she moved in. According to the duchesse d'Abrantès, her apartments were now, 'furnished with taste, but without ostentation. The large reception room was hung with yellow silk draperies, the furniture standing against the walls covered with damask, the fringes of silk and the wood of mahogany. Gilt was not used anywhere. The other rooms were furnished as simply, their decoration was new and elegant, but this was all.'[7]

These refurbishments, however, could not transform the atmosphere of the palace, a dark warren-like place with confusingly connected rooms and dark corridors. Josephine's apartments, located on the ground floor on the southern side of the palace, overlooked the gardens and the Champs-Élysées and were conveniently situated for access to Napoleon's apartments directly above. They had once served as the meeting place for the dreaded Committee of Public Safety and before that they had belonged to Marie Antoinette. For a superstitious Creole like Josephine, this was horrible. With misery in her voice, she told Hortense, 'I have dark misgivings . . . I feel as if the shadow of the queen is asking me what I am doing in her bed. There is an air of monarchy about this palace that one cannot breathe with impunity and I am still disturbed by it.'

Perhaps Marie Antoinette haunted Josephine in other ways, too. As the previous consort of a ruler of France – and one executed by her subjects – she remained imprinted on the nation's collective memory. 'The Austrian's' personal independence, her rumoured sexual licentiousness and her reputation as a 'petticoat ruler' who intervened in politics had irrevocably undermined her husband's authority, emasculating him in the nation's consciousness. She was blamed for her own downfall, and for that of her husband, her family and her entire caste. As a result, both Josephine and Napoleon were acutely mindful of the need to create a new image for the nation's first lady. Initially Napoleon was anxious about allowing any women to apppear at public functions, declaring firmly, 'There is no feminine of the function of Consul.' As a result, Josephine's public position was rather tentative. At first she was hardly ever seen with her husband at official events. He was the strong man, the son of the Revolution, and it was important to him to show that the Citoyenne Générale, sometimes referred to as the Consuless, 'in no way shared her husband's rank'.

In order to distance his regime even further from the decadence and sexual laxity of the ancien régime and the Directoire, the First Consul was determined that it acquire an aura of respectablity. Or, as the writer Stendhal put it, 'Napoleon, this great man with his will of iron . . . wishing to inspire respect for his infant court, declared that it should be moral and moral it was.'[8] He instructed the authorities to clean up the most visible excesses of the capital's prostitution, intervened in the theatrical profession, where he discouraged productions 'that offend good taste', and curbed the more licentious publications of the press. A new mood descended over public life, one that was more formal and reticent than hitherto. Revolutionary terms like *citoyen* and *citoyenne* were slowly replaced by *monsieur* and *madame; vous* replaced the familiarity of *tu*.

Knowing that her behaviour and appearance were expected to embody the new tone of public life, Josephine felt under pressure to regulate her rather disreputable financial affairs. Her first move was to discreetly extricate herself from companies supplying equipment to the army. When rumours of the immense sums she owed the city's merchants reached the ears of her husband, she also reluctantly set about confronting her debts. Napoleon ordered Bourrienne to collect the bills from her in order to discover the full amount. 'I can't do it, Bourrienne,' she protested. 'I know how violent he is and I couldn't face his rage.' The sum was so large – 1.2 million francs – that Josephine decided she would confess to only half the amount. Knowing that even that sum would outrage Napoleon, his secretary encouraged her to be honest. But she would not agree. When they went through the bills, Napoleon's and Bourrienne's amazement was compounded. How could she have ordered thirty-eight summer hats in one month in retirement at Malmaison while Napoleon was in Egypt? Napoleon agreed to pay exactly half the merchants' bills and Bourrienne successfully negotiated with

Josephine's creditors, most of whom had overcharged her outrageously in the first place.

Josephine's social behaviour was also expected to change. Much to her grief, Napoleon now actively discouraged her friendship with fellow *merveilleuses* like Mme Hamelin and Mme Tallien, whom he deemed inappropriate confidantes for his consort. He was also perhaps motivated by revenge. These women had discounted and rejected him during the Directoire. A couple of years later, suspecting that Josephine might be in touch with Thérésia on the sly, Napoleon made his feelings explicit: 'I forbid you to see Madame Tallien, under any pretext whatsoever. I will not accept any excuse. If you wish to remain high in my estimation and if you wish to please me, do not ever transgress this present order.'[9] Josephine tearfully attempted to change her husband's mind, but Napoleon remained obdurate and she was eventually forced to acquiesce. Thérésia's pain at being abandoned was evident in a letter to Josephine. Addressing her as 'you who were once my friend', she writes bitterly that 'time, events and your own heart have undeceived me'. Thérésia concluded her letter on a guilt-inducing note. Despite her betrayal, she declared, writing to Josephine afforded her 'an opportunity of reminding you that my friendship for you is proof against everything and that it will end only with my life'.[10]

Josephine was also expected to preserve her own reputation from any possible charge of sexual impropriety. Never averse to a bawdy joke or risqué conversation, Josephine now had to behave in a more modest manner. Napoleon became enraged if men were alone with her in her apartments. She was encouraged to be punctual and, somewhat against her own inclination, her social arrangements became more formal. A letter of invitation was now necessary before guests could be received at the palace. In all ways she was expected to play the dutiful wife, delighted to accommodate her husband's every whim.

Although she had never been one of the more racy dressers of the Directoire, an incident shortly after the Bonapartes' move to the Tuileries made it clear that Josephine was also expected to modify her style of dress. One evening Napoleon, after staring at a group of *merveilleuses* in their transparent gowns, walked over to the fireplace and began throwing logs onto the fire. When someone asked what he was doing, Bonaparte replied loudly, 'We must have more heat! Don't you see that these ladies are naked?' The gesture was not subtle, but his point was effectively made; the flimsy Directoire fashion was not becoming to the dignity of the new state. As Napoleon's representative, whether at his side or alone, Josephine realized she now had to consider her public persona and choose her clothes accordingly.

Led by her example, fashion, the visual symbol of Directoire decadence, was gradually transformed. The spirit of fashion took a temperate turn, as the excesses of the recent past were rooted out. The outrageous Grecian costumes, with their clinging contours, transparent materials and bare breasts went out of vogue and women's dress became more modest. Sleeves, which had been completely abandoned during the Directoire, made a comeback. As one historian wrote: 'for the sake of politics, fashion was gradually abandoning that impalpable lightness that had been so charming'.[11] In order to avoid shocking people's sensibilities too much or making too definitive a break between the styles of the Directoire and those approved by the Consulate, Josephine chose a new style of close-fitting dress 'that would have been at home in the days of Hadrian'.[12] The waist was so high that there was only space for two fingers between the 'belt' and the top of the dress, which gently compressed and lifted the breasts. To it she added a back panel, belted high and forming a train which suited her natural grace.

Napoleon made his own efforts to influence fashion. He was particularly keen to encourage the use of French silks and velvets, rather than the popular muslin, which was imported via England. He instructed the newspapers to report that 'Women are wearing silk again, not because of the cold but because both decency and fashion demand it.' He expected his wife to lead the way, but she was reluctant, addicted to the sheer, light fabric that had become her trademark. But Napoleon matched her stubbornness with his determination, as Hortense illustrated in her memoirs: 'When my mother and I were dressed, his first question was always, "Are you wearing muslin?" Sometimes our smiles betrayed us, and then he would rip our dresses in two.'[13]

The vogue for shawls was another example of the Consulate push for female propriety. Popularized by Josephine, who was reputed to be the most elegant shawl-wearer in France, the shawl replaced the fan as the must-have accessory of the period. A shawl allowed an elegant woman to hint at her charms without compromising her modesty, thus adding to her mystery. Originally of oriental origin, the shawl came to France by way of the Egyptian campaign. It was usually handmade from cashmere, and it became an essential luxury item that could cost a fortune. One beautiful shawl that the First Consul presented to Josephine, for example, cost over 10,000 francs.

Napoleon provided ample opportunities to display these fashions, reinstating some of the grand social traditions of earlier years. On 25 February 1800 Josephine was present at the first masked ball to be held in the city for a decade. She also presided over her own balls and these, according to Hortense, were models of their kind. The phrase *bon chic, bon genre* (well dressed, well born) could have been coined to describe her guest list, which included the younger representatives of ancien-régime society: the Noailles, Choiseul-Praslin, Gontaut and others. The painter Élisabeth Vigée-Lebrun noted the profound change in attitude. She 'saw once again a kind of magnificence and bearing that the younger generation had not known before then. For the first time the young twenty-year-old men and women saw liveries in the antechambers, in the salons, and met ambassadors and important foreigners richly dressed and displaying stunning decorations.'[14]

Josephine's transformation from decadent Directoire goddess into virtuous, restrained statesman's wife seemed complete. But her scandalous past continued to haunt her. That summer the naughty little satire *Zoloé et ses Deux Acolytes*, depicting the 'saturnalia of the Palais du Luxembourg', was published. Within Josephine's own circle, too, memories were not so short nor tongues so discreet that her affairs and adventures were forgotten. Having pressured Talleyrand to marry his mistress, Cathérine Grand, a woman with a rather tarnished reputation, Napoleon finally allowed her to be presented at the Tuileries. In the spirit of despotic paternalism that was rapidly coming to dominate in his character he remarked to her, 'I hope that the good conduct of the Citoyenne Talleyrand will soon cause the indiscretions of Madame Grand to be forgotten.' Citoyenne Talleyrand promptly replied, her wide blue eyes innocently staring into Bonaparte's own, 'In that respect, I surely cannot do better than follow the example of Citoyenne Bonaparte.'[15] This reproof enraged Napoleon and proved that Mme Grand was not quite as stupid as everyone had assumed.

The restrictions that Napoleon placed on his wife were soon extended to all women. As if determined to eliminate the freedoms that had made the emergence of a woman like Josephine possible, Napoleon's Civil Code comprehensively eliminated the legal progress that women had made during the Revolution and Directoire years. Indeed, women emerged even less well protected than they had been during the latter part of the ancien régime. Drafted in 1800, but not passed until March 1804, Napoleon's Civil Code (known later as the *Code Napoléon*) remains the basis of law in Belgium and Luxembourg and has left its mark on the civil laws of Holland, Switzerland,

Italy and Germany. Then and now, it embodied many of the liberal and enlightened views of the Revolution: equality for all before the law, an end to feudal rights and duties, freedom of conscience and the inviolability of property. Only in respect to women are its ideas retrogressive. The misogynistic attitudes of its architect resonate throughout the code. In discussions during its drafting he stoutly defended his belief that a wife should be subject to her husband. Marriage, he wrote, should contain a promise of obedience and fidelity by the wife. 'She must understand that in leaving the guardianship of her family, she is passing to that of her husband . . .' In a clear reference to his wife and her friends, he added, 'We need the notion of obedience in Paris especially, where women think they have the right to do as they like. I don't say it will have an effect on them all, only on some.'[16]

In the field of education, a particular preoccupation of Napoleon's, he argued that the state secondary schools should be for boys only. Later he said, 'I do not think we need trouble ourselves with any plan of instruction for young females: they cannnot be better brought up than by their mothers. Public education is not suitable for them, because they are never called upon to act in public.'[17] Napoleon partially reversed the Revolution's legalization of divorce, which many believed had led to the delinquency of women. Considering 'a couple bent on divorce as being subject to passion and requiring guidance . . .' he therefore suggested that the couple must get approval from their parents. He also proposed that divorce could occur only after two years and before twenty years of married life. The impact of the Civil Code reduced the divorce rate in Paris from one in five marriages in 1799–1800 to one in sixty during the later years of Napoleon's rule. But observers noted that Napoleon had not rescinded altogether the right to divorce and wondered if he was keeping his own options open.

It is possible that Josephine considered these constraints a small price to pay for the security and affluence of her new life. For the first time in many years, there were no financial worries and the fate of her children was secure. But if Josephine preserved this new-found stability by appearing more submissive, more acquiescent to her husband's formidable will, she did not surrender her autonomy so much as channel it into areas that were separate and containable. The side of her that was less governable, the initiative, determination and entrepreneurial flair that had sustained her during the turbulent years, was now channelled into her passionate relationship with Malmaison. She had initially purchased the chateau as insurance, a place of her own should things go awry with Napoleon. After all, her previous marriage had not lasted; and her new husband was a warrior who could easily be killed in battle or decide to divorce her because of her inability to have children. Josephine shared her Creole forefathers' faith in land; Malmaison represented security. It would always be there, her little kingdom, a world where she was safe and in charge. More and more, she devoted her leisure time to improving and modernizing the chateau, the one place where her vision and imagination could reach their full expression. Thus it is Malmaison, her favourite home, that provides the clearest picture of her taste and desires. It is here that she amassed and exhibited her collections of art, furniture, animals and plants. Over the years she would transform an agreeable but modest property into a haven of delights and of enchantment, more than worthy of the designation *Palais impérial de Malmaison*, alongside those famous royal residences, Fontainebleau and Compiègne.

In these early years of the Consulate, Josephine – her finances revitalized – was finally free to realize her dreams for Malmaison. She set to work immediately. The architects Fontaine and Percier, who would eventually create the plans for the Arc de Triomphe, were put in charge of refurbishments. The former noted in his journal on 27 September 1800, with just a hint of exasperation, that 'Madame Bonaparte takes the greatest interest in the work in hand and is constantly requesting new improvements. She wants us to see to the ornamental lake, the hothouses, indeed everything that can embellish a property which she regards as her personal home.'[18] The pair were also responsible for renovations to the chateau itself. Their budget was half a million francs. They built a pavilion in the shape of a tent in the entrance of the chateau, which opened onto a vestibule with stucco columns, giving it the appearance of the atrium of a Roman villa. To the right of the entrance hall they created a billiard room, a drawing room and a gallery which doubled as a music room. To the left were the dining room and Napoleon's much admired library, with its vaulted ceilings. On the first floor there were seven bedroom suites, with ten smaller ones on the second floor.

Fontaine and Percier employed the most celebrated decorators of the day for the interior design. Soon Malmaison was brimming with competing fancies: the classical embellishments of Greece and Rome were found alongside sphinxes, scarabs and other symbols of Egyptian antiquity. Louis Lafitte decorated the walls of the dining room with graceful Pompeian dancers, S. F. Moench, guided by Percier's drawings, executed for the dome of the First

Consul's library a delicate decoration *à l'antique*, with scrolls and arabesques and medallions of the great writers in profile, and in Josephine's bedroom a delightful allegorical frieze enlivened the walls.

Although she was happy with the work that Percier and Fontaine had done on the chateau, Josephine was dissatisfied with the changes that were being made to the park, and her relationship with them soon soured. Fontaine, complaining about her constant changes of mind, wrote that 'Projects are continually discarded, as she expresses a new wish and we cannot get her to adopt any plan or consistent scheme which would allow her to realize her ambitions . . .'[19]

In the spring of 1800 these pleasant domestic diversions were interrupted by a new military campaign. England, Russia and Austria – the Second Coalition – had been defeated by France before Napoleon departed for Egypt, but the Austrian Army now had the French pinned down in Genoa. Bonaparte came up with an audacious and spectacular plan to relieve his nation's besieged compatriots: like Hannibal, he would lead his reserve army across the snowy Saint Bernard Pass and surprise the enemy. On 5 May, after months of clandestine preparations, Napoleon, disguised in civilian clothes, departed secretly for Switzerland to join the Army of Reserve in the canton of Valais. Five days later he led 40,000 troops, including field and baggage trains, on their epic crossing. In contrast to David's celebrated painting, however, Napoleon crossed the Saint Bernard not on a glorious white charger, but on a mule.

But this campaign was very different from the previous Italian one. This time it was Josephine who insisted on accompanying him, and Napoleon who was reluctant. In his first letter sent from Lausanne, dated 15 May, he appeared to finally concede to her requests to join him, but he was less interested in her arrival than he was concerned that spies might watch her movements and so discover his secret dispositions. 'I see no reason why in ten or twelve days you should not join me here; but you must travel incognito and not mention where you are going, because I want no one to know what I am about to do.'[20]

The tone of his correspondence was different too. Gone were the romantic, erotic meanderings of yesteryear; in their stead were brief, irrregular letters, such as the one he sent two weeks later: 'The enemy is thoroughly demoralized; he cannot even yet understand us. I hope within ten days to be in the arms of my Josephine, who is always very good when she is not crying or flirting.'[21] It was now her turn to worry about whether he loved her and was being faithful. Especially when she received a curt missive saying, 'I am at Milan . . . I don't encourage you to come here. I shall be home in a month. I trust to find you flourishing. I am just starting for Pavia and Stradella. We are masters of Brescia, Cremona and Placentia.'[22]

During Napoleon's absence from France, the capital was in a ferment; the streets bristled with tension and buzzed with rumours of defeat and of Bonaparte's capture and death. There was even talk of a coup being engineered by Fouché and Talleyrand, an unlikely event since the two were such rivals. During this period of terrible uncertainty, and much to Napoleon's pride, Josephine kept her head. At a reception held on 20 June for the diplomatic corps and sundry government ministers, she presided over matters with a beatific calm designed to inspire confidence in the nervy throng. Not a single word or action revealed any grief or concern for her supposedly dead husband.

Just as the reception was finishing, a messenger burst in and dramatically laid two bullet-torn Austrian flags at Josephine's feet. The envoy informed the gathering that on 14 June Bonaparte's army had met the Austrians in Piedmont, near the town of Marengo. After an epic struggle in which the French initially appeared defeated, General Desaix had swept in and the Austrians were comprehensively beaten. The next morning Austrian emissaries appeared at Bonaparte's tent to beg for an armistice. It was granted, on condition that the Austrian Armies immediately withdraw from Mantua, Piedmont and Lombardy. 'I hope', Napoleon wrote from Milan, 'that France will be pleased with its army.'

France was more than pleased; it was ecstatic. In Paris *Le Moniteur* reported that 'the cabarets were full until eleven o'clock at night, and not a single glass was drunk except in honour of the Republic, the First Consul, and the army'. According to the duchesse d'Abrantès, there were 'outbursts of rejoicing everywhere, everyone congratulated everyone else and toasted the day of their deliverance and glory'. In the provinces – even in the still-rebellious Vendée – joy was as universal as it was in Paris. This was what the regime needed, and, more precisely, it was what Bonaparte needed. As Hyde de Neuville, a royalist agent, wrote: 'Marengo was the baptism of the personal power of Napoleon.' After the string of defeats that had characterized the latter years of the Directoire, Marengo appeared to the people to be the symbol of change. In a few short months Bonaparte had succeeded to a large extent in pacifying the country, establishing some order in France's chaotic finances and now he had given his people a taste of that military glory for which they had yearned. As a result his hold on France was immeasurably strengthened, and the cheers that greeted him upon his return to Paris were, he told Bourrienne, 'as sweet to me as the sound of Josephine's voice'.

On 2 July, at around two o'clock in the morning, the 'hero of Marengo' pulled up in front of the Tuileries. As word spread, the courts and garden filled with people, who pressed their faces to the palace windows and illuminated the area with torches. To celebrate her husband's victory and safe return, 'Madame Bonaparte', according to Fontaine, 'gave a supper under the trees in the garden at Malmaison. We were seated under a tent made by Lecomte and we were confronted with a delicious spread that covered the tables. That day, Josephine would plant a young cedar near the chateau.' This gesture, designed to commemorate her husband's victory and mourn the death in action of his dear friend General Desaix, would be an enduring one – as Fontaine points out: 'the cedar of Marengo is there still, majestic'.[23]

Napoleon's latest campaign had brought one unpleasant legacy: a mistress. Pauline Fourès was no longer the problem; although she had long since returned from Egypt and Napoleon had given her money and arranged a marriage for her, he had made no effort to see 'the Cleopatra of the Nile'. But a new threat had emerged in the ample form of the celebrated Italian singer, Giuseppina Grassini. She had attempted to seduce Napoleon during the first Italian campaign but he, blinded by his desire for Josephine, had not been interested. She renewed her assault when Napoleon was in Milan after the victory of Marengo, and this time she succeeded. That was why he had been so unwilling to let Josephine join him. After the fighting was concluded Napoleon installed Grassini in a house not far from the 'old temple of love' in the rue de la Victoire. The reverberations of her presence in Paris were felt immediately. Confiding in her close friend Mme de Krény, Josephine wrote, 'I am so unhappy, my dear. Every day there are scenes generated by Bonaparte, with no apparent reason . . . Searching for the cause, I discovered that for the last eight days, *la Grassini* has been in Paris. It appears she has been the cause of all my suffering . . . Will you find out where that woman is living and whether he goes to her or she comes to him here . . .'[24] Josephine need not have fretted. Grassini was soon unfaithful to Napoleon and was swiftly discarded. (She went on several years later to have an affair with Bonaparte's arch-enemy, Wellington.)

There were other women – Mme Branchu of the Paris Opéra, actresses including Thérèse Bourgoin and Mlle Duchesnois, as well as others less famous who passed through his private apartments, distracting him for a few hours or nights. But they were no real threat to Josephine. Napoleon clearly saw mistresses as a prerequisite of power, and one that usefully demonstrated that he, unlike the monogamous Louis XVI, was not excessively in thrall to his wife. At the same time he was determined not to have a *maîtresse en titre*, as so many earlier rulers of France had done; he did not want to be seen to be overly influenced by any woman, even one not his spouse. Indeed there was often something rather half-hearted about his affairs. Napoleon was more turned on by power than by sex: 'My only real mistress is France', he once said. He often treated his dalliances with appalling disregard, summoning them peremptorily, keeping them waiting for hours and then completing the act within minutes or not bothering to see them at all. The Napoleonic historian Frédéric Masson, in his book *Napoléon et les Femmes*, has excused his hero's behaviour by blaming the women themselves: 'Unfamiliar with courteous phrases, and not hiding sufficiently the contempt he felt for women who came to him on the message of a valet. . . . he could speak brutally and his manner would have been cynicism in any other. Yet in fact no one was less cynical than he was.' A less sympathetic reading of Napoleon's behaviour would accuse him of misogyny; one of his contemporaries claimed that he 'despised women'.[25] Certainly his behaviour smacks of vindictiveness – the revenge of a man who, once dismissed by women, now had the power to treat them badly.

Napoleon had affairs because he could, because it suited his image and flattered his self-esteem and because, quite simply, that was what men of his rank and time did. ('Love is a warrior's recreation,' he once remarked.) But his attitude to the women he dallied with illustrates the extent to which his sexual and emotional needs were still largely met by Josephine. According to his valet, Napoleon still 'slept with his wife like any respectable citizen'.[26] They had managed to transcend the shattering confrontation over Charles and were both intensely happy in their married life. Napoleon was still sexually enamoured with his wife and spent virtually every night in her bed. Josephine too was happy, a fact confirmed in a letter to her mother dated 18 October 1801: 'You will really love Bonaparte, he makes your daughter truly happy; he is good, amiable, in all ways a charming man, who really loves your Yeyette.'[27]

So, little peccadillos aside, the Bonapartes' marriage had never been more solid. Napoleon was in love with his wife, and 'full of consideration' for her, according to his valet, 'taking the utmost pains that no whisper of his infidelities ever reached her ears'.[28] She in her turn was falling ever deeper in love with her husband. This was more than pragmatism on Josephine's part. The Napoleon of the Consulate was a very different man from the gauche youth she had met in 1796. That spindly, undernourished creature with long, greasy hair had been replaced by a young man with a slim, healthy body, and impeccably cut and curled locks. This was the Napoleon depicted on all the medallions. To her excitement, and possible alarm, he was expanding and developing before her eyes. The man once dismissed as undignified and insignificant was now the focus of every gaze. Now Josephine's friends envied her, and every woman in Paris thought the First Consul infinitely attractive and desirable. It was as if Napoleon had grown into himself. 'A great ambitious spirit, formerly cramped and repressed,' wrote one historian, 'was now free from its chains and shackles and shone triumphantly through the mortal frame.'[29]

As a couple they genuinely complemented each other. In public life his lack of savoir faire was compensated for by what the Austrian ambassador Metternich described as Josephine's 'unique social tact'. He relied on her to charm and attract doubters to him. Never snobbish, she was warm and bounteous with a directness of address rarely found amongst the high born. She had an ability to intuit what others were thinking, feeling, needing and wanting and an amazing talent for pleasing, bending her lovely face to one then the other, enthralling bores, listening attentively. If someone was taciturn and shy, she endeavoured to bring them out. She elicited confidences easily and confided, if anything, too trustingly in others, sometimes evoking outpourings by the display of her own feelings. Her empathy was such that the emotional or physical distress of others moved her intensely, and she felt immediately that she must do something to remedy it. Her most consistent sentiments were admiration, loyalty and sympathy.

These social skills were invaluable for Napoleon, while Josephine enjoyed the gratifying sense of being a helpmate to France's most powerful man. Alexandre had made her feel useless and redundant, but Napoleon clearly valued her. Indeed, his reliance on his wife bordered on superstition. He believed she was essential to his success and wanted her with him as much as possible. In their private life too he relied on her. Her past as a kept woman had created its own positive legacy. She had become a wife without abandoning the attentiveness and charms of a mistress. Where he was mercurial, she was even-tempered and convivial. She knew when to talk and when to listen; she soothed him when he was tired and calmed him when he was angry. Josephine's 'habitual gentleness gave him repose . . .'[30] remarked a contemporary. In later years Napoleon would recall that 'Josephine possessed an exact knowledge of all the intricacies of my character', and she in her turn would defend him against charges of brutality: 'They don't know Bonaparte. He is harsh but he is good.'[31] She helped him not just as a wife but as a collaborator. He found peace in her company and pleasure in her appearance. She continued to work hard to please his eye, constantly renewing herself and her surroundings so that he would never tire of her, never grow indifferent.

Josephine fulfilled Napoleon's needs in a manner that no other woman could have done. She pandered to his whims and appeared bereft whenever he left her. Loving and warm, she smothered him with affection, and in her letters and utterances she stressed her faith in him and the adoration she felt for him. She maintained a lavish household which she festooned with monuments to his glory. He thrived in the warm glow with which she surrounded him. Josephine reinforced Napoleon's triumphant vison of himself and provided the stability and and confidence he needed to sustain it.

Josephine's genius lay in the *art de vivre*: those ephemeral and indefinable areas that leave no trace but without which life is not worth living. She was a solicitous lover, warm and kind; she loved the arts and music, had impeccable taste and knew how to create harmony and beauty around her. She provided the *douceur* in Napoleon's life. It was a word which then had a much more multifaceted meaning than it does today. The writer Robert Calassos defines it thus: '*Douceur* from sweetness to delight to pleasure to softness to mildness to languor to tenderness to civility to smoothness.'[32] It was a concept associated with Josephine throughout her life. In the court and in the country her generosity and sweetness provided an essential counterbalance to Napoleon's strong-man image. Without her his reign would be perceived as brutal rather than strong, intransigent rather than firm. Napoleon was well aware of this and appreciated Josephine's popularity and the symbolic role she played for the nation. Together, Napoleon and Josephine had created a highly charismatic partnership: she impeccably dressed, eternally graceful and endlessly kind; he the steely, dynamic, young general who would lead his country into a brave new future.

Napoleon now sought to exploit Josephine's qualities in the political sphere.

The émigré situation had been a thorn in the side of the Consulate since its inception. Many French people still regarded émigrés as traitors who had abandoned their country and plotted against its best interests. Bonaparte knew that any relaxation of policy towards them would be highly unpopular and regarded as a betrayal of the legacy of the Revolution. Something had to be done, however, as the émigrés were a fulcrum of dissent and revolt: their resentments reverberated within the boundaries of France and endangered his rule. In an attempt to neutralize this threat, since the Italian campaign Bonaparte had quietly stopped exercising 'sanctions against émigrés that tumbled into his hands'. His motivation, as Pasquier, Josephine's old neighbour in Croissy and now a member of Napoleon's administration, explained, was entirely pragmatic: 'The First Consul did not have any hatred towards them [émigrés]; he never felt either hatred or love, his feelings were commanded by self-interest, and at that moment it was very evident that what suited the country was to liquidate this source of internal division and to take away from foreign powers these allies who continually provided them with the means of acquiring intelligence, of great or lesser danger, about the internal affairs of the country.'[33] Napoleon hoped that by favouring émigré demands to be struck off the list of 'the enemies of the Republic', and restoring to them properties that had not been sold, he could stop their conspiring.

Josephine's role in this was crucial. The aristocrat Mme de la Tour du Pin, an émigré herself, wrote, 'I saw clearly that the First Consul had left her to deal with the feminine side of the Court, trusting her to win it over to his cause whenever opportunity arose.'[34] This wasn't difficult, she opined, for all 'were beginining to turn to the rising sun – Mme Bonaparte – who was living at the Tuileries in apartments that had been entirely redecorated as if by the wave of a wand. She already bore herself like a queen, but a very gracious one. Although not outstandingly intelligent, she well understood her husband's plan: he was counting on her to win the allegiance of the upper ranks of society.' When the women met during these months, Josephine paid her 'a thousand pretty compliments' and reassured her about the fate of the émigrés.[35]

Without appearing to have softened the official stance, Napoleon covertly encouraged Josephine to intervene on the émigrés' behalf, and made it known amongst his ministers that Josephine's protégés should be supported. It was a role that suited her perfectly. 'Madame Bonaparte had since the earliest days been a helpful and zealous intermediary for requests of this kind,' said

Pasquier. 'Her naturally good heart and the policies of her husband combined very well . . . Appearing to give in to his wife's influence suited Napoleon completely, satisfying all interests, appeasing hatreds, and sending a positive message to all of France.'[36]

In her famous Yellow Salon Josephine was deluged with petitioners. Literally hundreds of people sent her letters; almost as many sought an audience. She would listen tirelessly and sympathetically to the terrible stories of those who came before her, then inundate ministers and government officials with her recommendations. On 13 April 1800, for example, she wrote to the Minister of Justice: 'You would oblige me, *citoyen* minister, by expediting the affair of *citoyen* Michon de Vougy, in his attempt to be removed from the list of proscribed émigrés.'[37] Just over a week later, she wrote to the Ministry of Police to intervene on behalf of her friend Mme Pasquier, for *citoyen* Serre Saint-Roman Combret, whose family had endured numerous 'injustices at the hands of the past government', and who therefore had even more 'right' to the interest of the present Government.[38] This assertive request was followed by a letter to *citoyen* Lesage at the Commission des émigrés, on behalf of Joseph Martin who was also seeking to be struck from the list. She made it clear that she would be 'infinitely grateful' if 'very prompt' action could be taken in this matter, adding efficiently that his papers were in carton 34e and had been passed on to the commission.

Josephine was particularly determined when battling on behalf of family and friends. Notably, she intervened on behalf of her first husband's elder brother, the royalist François de Beauharnais, who had emigrated during the Revolution and joined the army of princes. Not only did she succeed in removing him from the list, she also managed to send money, through an intermediary, to defray his expenses as he travelled back to France: 'I hope that you will not be tardy in rejoining us and that I will soon have the pleasure of expressing to you in person the warm feelings that I have always felt for you, which distance hasn't altered.'

The 'Josephine strategy',[39] as one historian described it, was successful: in the year 1801, over 40,000 émigrés returned to France. By encouraging the émigrés to return, and providing support and succour in the person of Josephine, their gratitude was secured and many émigrés were willing to assimilate into the ruling strata. By providing them with jobs in his administration and his armies, Bonaparte gave them access to power and money, thereby neutralizing them further. Thus Josephine was invaluable in facilitating Bonaparte's ultimate goal: to refashion 'a head on France', which he hoped to create by bringing together the 'ancient nobility and the young revolutionary elite, the legitimate powers with the wealthy, the just and the powerful, old monarchical traditions and our existing government'. He acknowledged Josephine's contribution to his 'policy of assimilation': 'The circumstances of my marriage to Mme de Beauharnais', he recalled from St Helena, 'allowed me some contact with a whole party necessary for my system of fusion, one of the principal and most important points of my administration . . . Without my wife, I would not have had a natural rapport with that party.'

Josephine's sympathy and support for the émigrés gave some the impression that she was pro-royalist. Indeed, some of her biographers have suggested that she may have acted as a sort of royalist agent. But Josephine was kind, not stupid. She may have had a weakness for her old aristocratic circle, but her loyalty was to her husband. A royalist restoration would have threatened not just Bonaparte but her own interests and those of her children. Above all, it would have been disloyal to a man she had come to genuinely love and admire.

Her intimacy with the nobility served her husband rather than under-mining him. Josephine was Napoleon's eyes and ears within this essentially hostile group. Her guise as an apolitical clothes horse made her seem harmless, so people were careless around her. This, allied to her acute social sensitivity and ear for gossip, made her the ideal information-gatherer. So Bonaparte encouraged her friendships amongst the former nobility, while the royalist factions, who had been trying to open a channel to Bonaparte for years, actively cultivated her. Her own noble origins, and the contacts she had acquired during her first marriage, provided her with a considerable network amongst the aristocracy that had ruled the ancien régime. The toing and froing of the émigrés now widened that circle, allowing her to act as a conduit between her husband and the royalists. Some of her most useful royalist contacts, however, came from her own past – like François Hue, with whom she had become friendly in Fontainebleau. He had served Louis XVI faithfully while the sovereign had been imprisoned in the Temple, and was now *commissaire général* at Mitau and a close ally of the comte de Lille. She even maintained contact with advocates for restoration of the monarchy, like Pierre-Étienne Regnaud who proposed that Bonaparte give the throne to the duc d'Angoulême (son of the comte d'Artois) in exchange for the role of regent and governor of France. Josephine duly transmitted these messages to her husband who, impervious to the solicitations, was happy to be so well informed.

The grand hopes of royalists received a blow in autumn 1800. Louis XVIII – after months of reflection and debate with his advisors – had sent a letter to the First Consul. (The success of the 'Josephine strategy' had perhaps finally given him enough confidence in Bonaparte's sympathy to make this overture.) Dated 20 February, it arrived in Paris at the beginning of June; Bonaparte had already departed for the Italian campaign, and did not receive it for a number of months. His reply, written on 7 September, was, as one historian wrote, both 'abrupt and definitive': 'You must abandon all hope of returning to France, for you would then have to walk over the corpses of a hundred thousand men. Therefore, sacrifice your self-interest to the peace and happiness of France, and history will honour you for it.' (In private he remarked to Bourrienne, 'If I recall the Bourbons, they will erect a statue to me – and then bury me under it.')[40] His response provoked bitterness amongst the hard-core royalists who now lobbied the sympathetic ears of Europe's legitimate sovereigns against 'the usurper' Bonaparte, who they argued was 'the enemy of legitimacy and religion, the double foundation on which every throne of Europe was built'.

The repercussions of these events were felt months later. On Christmas Eve 1800 Haydn's *Creation* made its French debut at the Opéra, featuring the legendary singers Garat and Mme Barbier-Walbonne. It was one of the events of the season and all of fashionable Paris was to be there, including the First Consul and his family. At 8 p.m. Napoleon entered his carriage and departed. Josephine, wearing a beautiful new shawl over her evening dress, prepared to enter the carriage behind, when Napoleon's aide-de-camp Rapp suggested that she wear her wrap in the Egyptian style. Josephine, famous for her elegant and innovative ways of draping her shawls, was intrigued and asked him to demonstrate. Rapp folded the shawl and arranged it over her chestnut curls: Josephine could not know it then, but her enduring interest in fashion would save her life.

Realizing that Napoleon had already left, Josephine – accompanied by Rapp, Hortense and Napoleon's sister Caroline, who was now married to Murat – entered their carriage and set out behind him. As the first coach, in which Napoleon sat dozing, approached the rue Saint-Nicaise, his coachman, César, noticed that the street was partially blocked by a mare and cart. He drove swiftly into the next street, just as a violent explosion occurred. It was so forceful that the grenadiers who preceded the carriages were almost blown off their horses. Had the second carriage not been delayed it would have been blown to pieces; as it was, the horses bolted, windows were shattered and the smell of gunpowder laced the air. Flying glass cut Hortense's wrist and Josephine screamed and fainted. Only the heavily pregnant Caroline remained calm. The entire street was devastated, houses were destroyed, nine innocent people died and twenty-six were injured.

Profoundly shaken, the quartet nonetheless continued on to the Opéra, where they found Napoleon already ensconced in their box. The party was met with wild cheers from the audience. Napoleon, perusing the programme, maintained his sangfroid throughout, while Josephine sat pale and shaking behind him. Back at the Tuileries, however, the First Consul's mask cracked. Summoning Fouché, he raged that the Jacobins responsible for this atrocity must be hunted down. The Minister of Police vainly attempted to explain that the assassination attempt was the work of royalists, not Jacobin terrorists. Napoleon ignored Fouché and had almost one hundred former Jacobins deported. But it was Fouché who was proved right and in the end two Chouans − the royalist guerrillas in the west of France − were guillotined, while a third escaped to America, where he became a priest. According to one contemporary, the timing of this assassination attempt could not have been less favourable to the conspirators' designs, swaying public opinion strongly in Napoleon's favour. Pamphlets and songs condemning the plotters and praising the First Consul appeared soon afterwards. But the incident reminded the nation how very fragile the politicial equilibrium of France was; the entire regime depended on one man.

With better security precautions put in place (at Fouché's insistence, barracks six times larger than the chateau itself were built at Malmaison), life for the Bonapartes eventually settled back to normal. Time was divided mainly between the Tuileries, where they spent most of the working week, and Malmaison, where they went every decadi eve. Josephine still felt oppressed by the haunted atmosphere at the Tuileries and disliked the lack of privacy there, so their weekend retreat to Malmaison was a source of relief and pleasure to her. Surprisingly, the workaholic Napoleon also anticipated their visits with alacrity. One of his servants commented that he looked forward to visiting Malmaison as much as 'a schoolboy looked forward to his holidays'.

'Except on the field of battle,' Bourrienne said, 'I never saw Bonaparte as happy as he was at Malmaison.' The couple spent the happiest days of the

Consulate there. Malmaison's charms were numerous. Firstly it was convenient, only five miles' drive from the capital. It was also very comfortable.
The renovations undertaken by Percier and Fontaine had made the chateau
a much more pleasant place to live, and the grounds were unfolding beautifully under Josephine's exacting eye. The atmosphere of the property had
been sweetened by the spirit of its mistress. Impossible to achieve in a cold,
formal palace like the Tuileries, life at Malmaison was intimate and homely.
Its drawing rooms were pretty and feminine, its guest suites were cosy.
'Society there', according to Napoleon's valet Constant, 'was refined and
unpretentious, equally as far removed from the vulgarity of the Republic as
from the luxury of the Empire.'[41]

A visitor meandering through the property's gently undulating hills and
valleys would encounter a beautifully laid-out English garden amid acres of
perfectly manicured lawns. These were interrupted by leafy forests, amongst
which were artistically scattered temples of love, statues and over-sized
Etruscan vases. This beautiful landscape was criss-crossed by a network of
little brooks and streams that were forded by pretty stone or wooden bridges.
Some of these ran into a miniature lake on which swam the swans that
Josephine had chosen as her emblem because they mated for life. Throughout
the grounds the medley of flowers, both exotic and native, that Josephine
had meticulously collected and nurtured, were planted to great aesthetic
effect. These were contrasted against trees whose height provided the property
with wonderful views.

These riches nourished an impressive menagerie collected from all over
the world: kangaroos, emus and flying squirrels from Australia, Egyptian
gazelles, African antelopes, ostriches and zebras, South American llamas and
Scottish ponies – all roaming at semi-liberty in the park. This menagerie was
supplemented by the animals she kept in the house: rabbits, monkeys and
her beloved dogs. The chateau's waiting room bristled with birdsong,
including that of parakeets and cockatoos, one of which cried incessantly the
one word 'Bonaparte'. Josephine even acquired a female orang-utan, which
sometimes joined guests at table, beautifully dressed in a white cotton chemise,
munching delicately at her favourite food: turnips.

Josephine's children and their friends came regularly. They were an intense
source of pride and joy to both Josephine and her husband. Hortense, now
around seventeen years old, had grown into a very attractive young woman.
According to the duchesse d'Abrantès, she was as 'fresh as a rose' and as
slender 'as a palm tree' and very graceful, with blue-violet eyes and blonde

hair, her appearance a perfect fusion of both her parents. But her manner – soft, graceful and affable – was all Josephine. She was more intellectual than her mother, however, and notably gifted in all the arts: painting, acting, dancing and music ('all Paris sang the delicious love songs that she composed', according to Mlle Avrillon) – gifts which had been nurtured and developed by Mme Campan. Her air of innocence and goodness was so palpable that the duchesse d'Abrantès observed that Napoleon would not 'use indecent expressions in her presence'.

Her brother Eugène had much in common with her, sharing her love of music and theatre. One contemporary wrote, 'His figure was graceful, he was skilled in all bodily exercises, and he inherited from his father those fine manners of the gentleman of the *vieille cour* in which perhaps the vicomte de Beauharnais had himself given him his earliest lessons. To these attributes he added simplicity and kindheartedness; he was neither vain nor presumptuous; he was sincere without being indiscreet and could be silent when silence was necessary.'[42] Despite his style and sociability, Eugène was – much to his step-father's delight – a warrior. Promoted to lieutenant in Egypt, he had risen through the ranks and was now a captain in the Consular Horse Guards. His prowess on the battlefield was equalled by his style in the drawing room and, in his dashing uniform of dark green coat with red cuffs and facings, he was a welcome visitor at the most select gatherings. Charming, good-natured and fun loving, the dark, handsome young man was linked romantically with a number of the capital's beauties including the Italian *danseuse* Bigottini. But these dalliances were no cause for concern, nothing that wasn't considered perfectly normal for a spirited young man of his age.

Josephine's two children contributed greatly to the youthful and optimistic atmosphere of life at the chateau. They thrived in the 'Republican simplicity' and fresh pastoral atmosphere. According to the duchesse d'Abrantès, who stayed at Malmaison frequently during the Consulate, life there was 'exactly like that lived in any country chateau when there are a lot of visitors staying'. Hortense commented that, 'It was not difficult to be entertained' there, what with 'promenades, picnics by the lake, card parties, all these were charming'. As for Josephine, her passion for flowers occupied a large part of her day: inspecting her myriad plants and shrubs, discussing plans for the grounds with her gardeners and corresponding about seeds and plants she hoped to acquire.

Napoleon always brought work with him, but was sometimes tempted to abandon it. He played games and leapfrog with his nephews and nieces, and sometimes joined in games of prisoners' base, at which he cheated by failing to give the warning shout of 'Barre!' He also cheated at blind man's buff by peeking. Meals were sometimes taken out of doors, served at tables set amongst the flowers and plants. The relaxed atmosphere at the chateau did not suit everyone. On one visit to Malmaison, Talleyrand found the entire party sitting on the grass of the bowling green. 'It was nothing to him with his camp habits, his riding boots and his leather breeches,' recounted Napoleon's outraged minister, 'but I, in my silk breeches and silk stockings! Can you picture me sitting on that lawn? I'm crippled with rheumatism as it is. What a man! He always thinks he is camping out!'

At Malmaison the most pleasant activities took place out of doors. If the weather permitted, Josephine enjoyed taking an early afternoon ride around the grounds in her little barouche. Sometimes, especially during these early years of the Consulate, Bonaparte stole an opportunity to be alone with her and joined her on these little rides, driving the vehicle himself, rather brutally, or riding alongside her on his horse. When Bonaparte was too busy, Josephine and some of her female entourage took the ride, with Josephine sitting in the front vehicle under a giant parasol to protect her skin from the sun. One of her favourite routes was towards the Butard, a handsome hunting pavilion acquired in 1802, via the dairy, where she would taste the milk products prepared by Swiss herders in Bernese uniforms. Sometimes Josephine liked to take her guests rowing on the 'rivière anglais' in the small, light boats that she moored there. Or they walked around the chateau grounds as Josephine talked knowledgeably about the plants, flowers and exotic fruits that she had collected.

In the evenings Malmaison was the only place where the family and their intimates dined together, without formality. The conversation was lively and sometimes loud. As always, Napoleon complained about the abundance of the food, ate distractedly and found the dinner drawn out if it lasted longer than a quarter of an hour. Coffee was served in the salon. If dinner was finished by half past six, Napoleon often returned to his office to attend to urgent matters, then rejoined Josephine for an after-dinner walk along the sinuous paths that networked the grounds. They were reunited indoors with a lively and predominantly young crowd, consisting largely of Bonaparte's coterie of army friends and Hortense's school friends. The Consul and his wife hoped that this free fraternization would prepare for happy marriages between the two groups. Although the matchmaking efforts of Napoleon and Josephine were not always successful, Malmaison nurtured many a nascent love affair. Marshal Ney, Lannes, Macdonald and Bessières all met their wives at Malmaison.

As night fell the guests played cards, very occasionally for money. Josephine enjoyed games like vingt-et-un, reversi, and tric-trac. Napoleon played nervously, getting bored quickly, cheating constantly; he hated losing, and always made excuses for his failures. Sometimes he lectured the gathering loudly on one of his pet themes, or read poorly from one of the great tragedies by Corneille, Voltaire or Racine. New novels were sometimes introduced; Hortense remembered with anguish being forced by Napoleon to read the first few pages of *Atala* to the assembled company. Conversation often turned into a a monologue in which Bonaparte recounted his memories, or he spoke about science, history or literature with Monge, Denon and Arnault, saving his ideas about politics for others. Sometimes he would tell ghost stories in an eerie voice, to great effect. The chateau had numerous pianos by Erard and harps by Cousineau; although Josephine swiftly abandoned the singing and harp playing that she had once done in front of close friends and family, she encouraged her children to perform in her stead, since both had rather sweet voices.

Sometimes the Bonapartes held society evenings, when actors, like the elderly Mlle Clairon, Mlle Racourt, Talma and Michaud, and esteemed members of the former aristocracy, like Mme Montesson, were admitted to dine with the Consul. Sometimes a more important dinner was held, bringing together forty or fifty guests from the elites of political and military life. They gathered in the dining room, the grand vestibule and the billiard room, all of which were connected by large double doors. Ambassadors were invited if important negotiations were under way. These larger gatherings were often followed by elaborate entertainments: balls, musical concerts and theatrical productions.

Since both Josephine and Napoleon adored the theatre, and since private theatricals were very much à la mode, drama had an essential place at Malmaison. At first the productions staged there were short one-act plays, which required virtually no props or scenery and demanded the minimum of effort from the players. But quite quickly they became more ambitious, evolving into a Malmaison troupe that aimed to perform spectacles akin to those undertaken by the professionals. With the construction of Malmaison's own theatre in 1802, the players had a proper place to develop their art. They were determined to outdo their great rivals, Lucien Bonaparte's troupe at Neuilly. Napoleon, a committed impresario, chose the plays, assigned the roles, provided the best costumes and press-ganged the most illustrious teachers, including the immortal Talma, to coach his players. Everyone was roped in, including the painters Isabey, who had been Hortense's teacher at Mme Campan's, and Denon.

The Malmaison troupe mastered a number of contemporary plays that were already classics. Hortense became one of the stars when she played Rosine in Beaumarchais's *The Barber of Seville* in the first grand performance given by the company. Eugène was also an enthusiastic thespian, as were Bourrienne and Napoleon's sister Caroline. So young and attractive were the players that, one observer noted, 'Few Paris theatres could have boasted such pretty actresses.'[43] After the play, the crowd gathered on the ground floor, according to the duchesse d'Abrantès. 'There everyone was served with every possible choice of refreshment and Josephine did the honours, making the introductions with her usual amiability, so that each was made to think that she was interested in them and only them. After these delicious evenings, which ended usually around midnight, we took the road back to Paris.'

It may seem strange, considering their mutual love of theatre, that neither Napoleon nor Josephine themselves took roles in these private theatricals. It would certainly not have been considered unfitting. Previous rulers had often enjoyed treading the boards. History has recorded the great performances of the Sun King, Louis XIV, in the private theatricals at Versailles and Marie Antoinette's bewitching turn as a shepherdess. Maybe both felt that it was not prudent to display their theatrical talents on a stage, lest people began to doubt the sincerity with which they played their greatest roles: that of Napoleon and Josephine.

Historians have made much of Napoleon's theatricality. They stress his fondness for the theatre, the frequency with which he visited it and his friendships with theatre folk, especially Talma. During the Consulate years Napoleon would spend whole nights in the thespian's company discussing acting, even presuming on occasion to give the great actor advice on how to play his roles. When Talma was playing Caesar in Corneille's *Mort de Pompée*, and delivered the line 'I who regard the throne as infamous', Napoleon informed him that he was being too sincere. 'Here,' he explained, 'Caesar is by no means expressing his real feelings. He says this only because he wishes the Romans to believe that he holds the throne in detestation.'[44] It was no wonder Chateaubriand said of Napoleon that he was 'at once a model and a copy, a real person and an actor playing that person; Napoleon was his own mime; he would not have believed in himself as a hero if he had not dressed himself in a hero's costume.'[45]

Josephine was just as stage-struck as her husband. She visited the theatre as regularly as he did and also cultivated friendships within the acting profession. As a young woman she had found her niche in France by acting the part of a Parisienne. Since then she had negotiated the world through a series of roles: the abandoned wife, the patriotic citoyenne, the courageous widow, the carefree courtesan. In each case she had meticulously studied her role, learning a new set of gestures and mannerisms, assembling the right wardrobe and accessories. Now in her greatest part, that of the nation's impeccable first lady, she was just as engaged as her husband in gauging reactions and manipulating responses. Even Napoleon's valet, Constant, who was used to his master's indefatigable work ethic, was impressed with the diligence with which Josephine learned the 'scripts' for her public appearances, rehearsing in her mind her entrances and exits, memorizing names and speeches. As her friend-turned-enemy Barras remarked (accurately for once), Josephine 'was a true actress who knew how to play several parts at one time'.[46] But it was in her starring role as Napoleon's consort that she was transcendent. As first lady of France Josephine was indeed incomparable, never making a false move. In the carrying out of her official duties the mask did not slip for so much as a minute; she was never haughty or dismissive, her face never betrayed boredom or tiredness and she never shirked the most tedious of ceremonies.

In that beautiful summer of 1801 Josephine made her second spa visit to Plombières, still hopeful that she could remedy her infertility and give Napoleon an heir. The party set off on 7 July escorted by Bonaparte's aide-de-camp Rapp, and including Hortense, Mme de Lavalette and Napoleon's mother. Mercifully it was a more pleasant visit than her previous one, when she had endured her terrible fall. Josephine met old friends, like the comtesse Alex, Mme de Sourdis and Mme de Talhouët, who accompanied her to various fêtes and balls and on excursions. Left behind, Napoleon was not so happy. In a letter to Josephine he wrote morosely, 'The weather is so bad here that I have remained in Paris. Malmaison, without you, is too sad . . . Some plants have come for you from London, which I have sent to your gardener. If the weather is as bad at Plombières as it is here, you will suffer severely from floods.'[47] But the weather in the spa town was much better than in the capital and Josephine diligently continued her cure.

When she returned to Paris that autumn, Josephine was compelled to attend to an issue that had been looming for a couple of years: Hortense's marriage. Ever since Napoleon's elevation to Consul the girl had been besieged by potential suitors: there had been one of Germaine de Staël's cast-offs, the rich and witty comte de Mun, whom Hortense dismissed as a social climber; there had been the sons of two of the erstwhile Directors, Gohier and Reubell, as well as talk of proposals from foreign dignitaries: the duke of Cumberland and the Archduke Charles. Hortense even had that scourge of modern celebrities: a stalker. This deranged young man hung about the gates of Malmaison and ran alongside her carriage when she drove out, passing her flowers, verses and locks of his hair. On one occasion he even flung himself at her feet when she emerged from the theatre.

But the golden-headed Hortense was a romantic young lady with an 'aversion to marriages of expediency', and so none of these had yet come to anything. But she could not be indulged for ever. She was now seventeen, an age at which her mother had already borne two children. And pressure had begun to build. Napoleon was particularly interested in securing the right match, as he had been so disappointed in his sisters' marriages: Élisa's to the lumpen Corsican Bacciochi, Pauline's to General Leclerc and now Caroline's to Joachim Murat. Hortense recounted how he had said to Mme Campan, 'I hope that this one [pointing to me] will let herself be married properly.'[48] According to Hortense, her stepfather had had high hopes for his faithful army comrade, General Desaix, whose death in Italy 'much depressed' him. Another potential suitor was Napoleon's favourite aide, General Duroc. While not in love with him, the prospect of marriage to Duroc 'was not displeasing' to Hortense. Napoleon had no objections, but Josephine vetoed it, remarking, 'I could never get used to hearing you called Madame Duroc.'[49]

The one candidate upon whom both Napoleon and Josephine could agree was Bonaparte's brother Louis. For Josephine it seemed to solve the thorny problem of the succession. Her continued childlessness meant that she was coming to terms with never bearing Napoleon an heir. But if Hortense married amongst the brothers, any child produced could be adopted and would have both her blood and that of her husband running in its veins. This would make it unnecessary for Napoleon to put her aside. For Bonaparte too it was an attractive proposition. Louis was his favourite sibling, 'having', Bonaparte once commented to one of his secretaries, 'none of the defects of his brothers and all their virtues'.

Bourrienne offered to approach Hortense with the proposition and explained to her the advantages of the match: 'He is kind and affectionate.

His tastes are simple. He will appreciate you to the fullest degree and is the only suitable husband for you . . . No one until now has appealed to you. You love France. Do you want to leave it? Your mother cannot bear the thought of your being the wife of some foreign prince. You know it is her great sorrow no longer to hope to have a child. You can remedy this. I assure you intrigues are constantly being formed to persuade the First Consul to obtain a divorce. Only your marriage can strengthen those bonds on which depends your mother's happiness.'[50]

But Hortense was still reluctant. In her memoirs she played down her personal feelings about the matter, but her ambivalence towards Louis was evident. She saw him 'as a brother', not a suitor, and feared that he was a bit of a misogynist. Her feelings were not without justification. In himself, Louis was not a tempting prospect. His appearance was blighted by a mild paralysis on one side of his body, and his personality was no more attractive. A depressive and moody young man, he had a penchant for wallowing in the melancholy sentiments of novels like Goethe's *Werther* and Rousseau's *La Nouvelle Héloïse*. Mentally unstable, he was given to bouts of intense self-pity and rampant paranoia and he suffered from a myriad of neurotic symptoms including vertigo, constrictions of the throat and recurring headaches.

Mme Campan was drafted in to convince the reluctant bride. She wrote to Hortense to defend arranged marriages. 'Young people are too often swayed by emotion to choose wisely,' she argued. 'In marriage, love was a passing illusion. When gone, no affection, no community of interest, to take its place.' She herself had rejected a man she loved and happily married the man her parents chose. This missive was soon followed with a visit to see her 'dear angel' at Malmaison. Hortense explained to her former headmistress that she did not like the disdain with which Louis looked upon women. Would it not be a source of sorrow to his wife? Explaining that Louis had grown up as a soldier and that he therefore knew few good women, Mme Campan felt it was natural that he had a poor view of them. 'You will change his opinion.'

Eventually Hortense relented. In her memoirs she recalled, 'It was a question of sacrificing my romantic fantasies for my mother's happiness. I could not hesitate between the two.'[51] The wedding took place in January 1802 in a civil ceremony at the Tuileries, where an altar had been erected in the drawing room on the ground floor. The witnesses included the two Consuls, Cambacérès and Lebrun, as well as Generals Bessières and Lavalette. The service was to be conducted by Cardinal Caprara. The otherwise dutiful bride allowed herself one small act of rebellion. Instead of the magnificent embroidered gown and diamonds that Josephine had given her, she chose to wear a simple white crêpe dress, adorned only by a single string of pearls. At the sight of her pale sacrificial lamb, Josephine burst into tears.

At the time it seemed that the marriage would safeguard not just Josephine's own interests but those of the entire Beauharnais family. But it is hard to believe that Josephine would have encouraged the union if she could have anticipated its outcome, whatever benefits accrued to her. It was with some justification that Mme de Rémusat described Hortense as 'the most unhappy person of her time'. It was a desperately unhappy relationship from the start. The couple's intrinsic incompatibility degenerated quickly into constant strife. Josephine was forced to watch helplessly as Hortense bravely bore the brunt of her husband's jealousy and paranoia. Their marital difficulties were exacerbated by cruel slander, nurtured in Britain, that Napoleon was himself the father of Hortense's child. The couple plodded on for years in abject misery until they finally separated. It would have been scant consolation to her mother that Hortense's third child, born in 1808 and baptized Charles-Louis-Napoleon, would one day become Napoleon's heir, the Emperor Napoleon III.

As these domestic dramas unfolded, great political events were being played out on the world stage. Shifting relations between France and the other nations of Europe persuaded Napoleon reluctantly to pursue peace with England. After months of negotiations the final treaty was signed at Amiens in March 1802. It was a triumph for France. England surrendered virtually all that it had won since hostilities began in 1792. France got back Martinique and Guadeloupe; Surinam and the Cape of Good Hope went back to the Dutch; and Minorca to Spain. Of all its conquests England retained only Trinidad and Ceylon. Although the harshness of this settlement doomed it to ultimate failure, at the time France was exultant and Napoleon triumphantly claimed the credit for creating the peace. His popularity soared even further a few months later with the signing of the Concordat which recognized Roman Catholicism as the religion 'of the great majority of the French people' and permitted 'its free exercise'. The re-establishment of religion was, Talleyrand wrote, 'an act not only of justice but one of great cleverness'.

To the general public, Napoleon seemed 'like a second Augustus, a demigod who not only restored the world to order and peace, but was also proof incarnate that greatness had finally come back to dwell on earth'. Under his rule France had made incredible strides forward, both at home and abroad. He had inherited a country in total disarray, with a bankrupt treasury and the stock market at an all-time low, but now industry prospered and the bourse thrived. The threat from the Jacobins had been largely neutralized and all but the most extreme royalists had been appeased by the administration's treatment of the émigrés. Napoleon's goal to make Paris 'something fabulous, colossal and entirely new' was well on the way to being achieved. A programme of public works was in full swing, and water supplies, bridges, roads and sewers had been improved. The public gardens had gained enormously in magnificence and charm. The Louvre overflowed with master-pieces that aroused the admiration of all who saw them. 'Paris', wrote the duchesse d'Abrantès, 'had indeed realized the First Consul's dream for his great city – that it be the capital of the civilized world.'[52]

Confidence in the Government had never been greater, and France was enjoying a more dominant position in the world than it had done for many years. 'It can be said without exaggeration', Talleyrand wrote, 'that at the time of the Peace of Amiens France was, in its foreign relations, possessed of a power, a glory and an influence as great as any that could have been desired for her by the most ambitious minds. And what rendered this situation even more astounding was the rapidity with which it had been accomplished. In less than two and a half years, France has passed from the humiliating depths into which the Directoire had plunged her, to the first rank of Europe.'[53]

These magnificent achievements were celebrated by a Te Deum held at Notre-Dame on Easter Sunday 1802. The mile-long procession was announced by sixty cannon shots. The First Consul rode to the ceremony in a coach drawn by eight Arab horses. He was dressed in a scarlet velvet coat, black breeches and a ceremonial sword, in whose hilt glittered one of the most famous French crown jewels, the Regent diamond. Josephine, 'in a blaze of diamonds', created a sensation. The whole event was a wonderful piece of pageantry. Gold and crimson shone in the streets as they had not done since the days before the Revolution; great bells broke a silence of ten years and in the cathedral decorated with Gobelins tapestries two orchestras played under Cherubini and Mehul. Napoleon, the hero, the peacemaker, the defender of religion, took his place beneath a draped canopy of crimson and gold surmounted with plumes of white feathers. After the service, when Napoleon and his entourage returned to the Tuileries in carriages escorted by footmen in his new livery of green and gold, the crowds cheered, and one eyewitness exclaimed, 'Oh how beautiful it is, how we love it! It is like the old days, at last our country is itself again!'[54]

In that notable year some 10,000 English visitors flocked into the rejuvenated capital. Amongst them were such illustrious figures as Lord Erskine, the prince of Wales's sister-in-law the duchess of Cumberland, and Georgiana, duchess of Devonshire and her entourage. A notable beauty, Lady Devonshire danced elegantly with Josephine's son Eugène and sparked a frisson of delicious gossip. Although much struck by 'the beauty and the bustle' of the city, these visitors were chagrined to discover that all the clothes they possessed seemed, according to one, 'hideously old fashioned, or comically rustic'.[55] Once they had ascertained that French fashions were not quite as shocking as reports in England had led them to believe, they rushed to the fashionable milliners and dressmakers, like Josephine's favourite designers, Leroy and Mlle Despeaux, where they discarded their numerous petticoats, chemises and stays in favour of the light drapery and cashmere shawls of the *costume français*.

Armed with a new wardrobe and clutching the essential *permis de séjour*, on which was written the name, profession and personal description of the bearer, they went to see the sights. As well as the normal Parisian distractions of balls, receptions and gaming houses, they went to the Louvre to see the *Apollo Belvedere* and the *Venus de Milo*. Or crowded into one of the city's dozens of theatres to see Vestris dancing or Talma declaiming. They took their pick of the city's three thousand cafés: chess players chose the Régence, while intellectuals preferred the Café Cheron and those in search of luxury went to the *Café des Mille Colons*. Those travellers with deeper pockets frequented the exclusive restaurants, where they were treated to marvellous spun-sugar or pastry follies in the shape of classical temples, bridges and rotundas inspired by the great chef Carême. The most devoted gourmets prayed for an invitation to dine at the palatial home of Consul Cambacérès, for whom food was a virtual religion. He once silenced a chattering guest with the words, 'Pray be quiet, I cannot hear what I am eating.'

All fashionable souls wanted to see Mme Récamier's new house on rue du Mont Blanc, 'millionaires' row', whose bedroom one Englishman described as being decorated 'in the highest degree of fairy-like beauty'. They visited the site of the Bastille, now a woodyard of which only 'fragments of its mossy walls, and two or three dungeons remain'. Then there was the infamous Palais Royal, that 'Paris within Paris', which provoked one shocked visitor to comment, 'a man may pass his life here with every gratification of low sensuality and vice. Perhaps there is not anywhere else on earth such a

concentration of wickedness, so much compressed within so small a com-
pass . . .'[56] Some also wanted to see the 'wild child' of Aveyron, an enfant
sauvage who had been discovered living in the woods and was now invited,
accompanied by his benefactor Itard, to numerous grand homes to gratify
the curiosity of the gentry.

One of the most thoughtful portraits of Paris was provided by the great
politician Charles Fox, whose heavy jowls and drayman's shoulders made him
seem, to the duchesse d'Abrantès, less like a statesman and more like an
English farmer. Remarking that it was hard not to feel 'almost breathless
expectation at the thought of seeing so celebrated a city', he found the
appearance of Paris pleasing despite the 'narrowness of the streets, and the lack
of foot-ways'. He visited one of the big amusement places in Paris, 'an
illuminated garden, which seemed decked by the hand of fairies . . .' He met
Talleyrand but found his countenance lacking in that which 'is noble and
elevated'. He attended one of Bonaparte's troop reviews, which he felt was
a 'brilliant and animating spectacle'. But it was at the Parisian theatre that
'the character of the people is truly displayed'. Here, he noticed, 'tears flowing
profusely and unchecked, from male and female spectators at every pathetic
and affecting passage of the piece'. But Fox noted that the city's new lease
of life had been purchased at some cost. The capital had military guards
everywhere and 70,000 troops were stationed nearby. He noted that the
system of espionage was developed to an intense pitch, 'making suspicion of
the slightest indisposition to Government sufficient cause for individuals to
be hurried away at night.'[57]

But the most popular tourist attraction was Napoleon and Josephine
themselves. Virtually to a man, visitors struggled to obtain an invitation to
the Tuileries or admission to one of the First Consul's military reviews. The
writer Fanny Burney has left us with a unique portrait of one such encounter.
Despite the extremely large crowd collected at the Tuileries, she was very
impressed that the French observers kindly gave her a prime viewing place:

> At length, the two human hedges were finally formed, the door of
> the audience chamber was thrown wide open with a commanding
> crash, and a vivacious officer – sentinel or I know not what . . . called
> out in a loud and authoritative voice, 'The First Consul!' . . . not a
> soul either spoke or stirred as he and his suite passed along . . . I had
> a view so near, though so brief, of his face, as to be very struck by
> it. It is of a deeply impressive cast, pale, even to sallowness, while

not only in the eye but in every feature – care, thought, melancholy, and meditation are strongly marked with so much of character, nay, genius, and so penetrating a seriousness, or rather sadness, as power-fully to sink into an observer's mind.[58]

Josephine was as much of a draw as her esteemed husband. (Lord Morpeth, later the Sixth Earl of Carlisle, was definitely in a minority when he refused to let his wife be presented to her, presumably because of the international scandal that had surrounded Josephine while Bonaparte was in Egypt.)[59] One visitor – Bertie Greatheed, a Warwickshire squire – described the business of being presented to Josephine as, 'very fine and princely . . . We were shewn into her apartments in the Tuileries which are not very large rooms but most beautifully furnished. The ladies between 20 or 30 in number were seated round and both splendidly and elegantly dressed . . . Her person is good and manners elegant and pleasing.' Bonaparte was, according to Greatheed, 'more easy than he is at his own audience'.[60] He commented that 'Bonaparte's superstition about his wife is very extraordinary . . . though quite ill one night she came with him to satisfy his feelings'.[61] Despite his great achievements and acclaim, Bonaparte still regarded Josephine as a sort of talisman and was much more comfortable when in her company.

If these foreign visitors were largely impressed with Paris and the First Consul, the British press remained determinedly – even virulently – anti-Bonaparte. It viciously lampooned Napoleon as 'Boney', the ridiculous Corsican upstart with sickly yellow skin, thin knobbly legs and greasy lank hair. It also inflated him as a monstrous spectre, Bonaparte the bogeyman, who featured in a popular children's lullaby of the time: 'Hush your squalling, then I say or maybe Bonaparte will pass this way . . . and he limb from limb will tear you just as pussy tears a mouse . . .'

These attacks often extended to Josephine. In February 1803 a British visitor to Paris – Trotter, secretary to the politician Charles Fox – wrote about the First Consul's reaction to derogatory press coverage of his wife: 'Bonaparte is extremely out of humour with the articles in the *Morning Post* and *Chronicle*; it seems to me very blaggard and illiberal to attack a woman for faults which every woman would willingly get rid of if she could – viz. being neither young nor handsome. I think it worse in this instance because she is already oppressed enough and yet generally beloved for her extreme goodness and humility.'[62]

The most malevolent attacks came from the pen of the cartoonist Gilray, described by one historian as the only man that Napoleon genuinely feared. His most famous caricature of Josephine, printed in the year of the coronation, played on her disreputable past by depicting her and Thérésia Tallien dancing naked for Barras, with a wolfish Napoleon peeping at the spectacle from behind a curtain. Josephine's age and her sexual history were not her only points of vulnerability; Gilray also impugned her Caribbean origins, depicting her family not as plantation owners but as dirt-poor field workers of dubious racial origin. As she grew older, Gilray most frequently depicted Josephine as a blowsy drunken old strumpet, with red cheeks and an enormous stomach.

Nothing, according to Mme de Rémusat, upset Napoleon as much as these attacks by the English press. 'How many times when we saw him gloomy and out of sorts did Mme Bonaparte tell us it was because of some article against him in the *Courier* or the *Sun*.' Napoleon was no champion of press freedom; when slurs appeared in the French media he avenged himself swiftly and ruthlessly. But the British press was largely outside his influence. He did, according to his secretary Bourrienne, once approach the English Chancellor of the Exchequer to demand legislative measures against licentious writings that targeted him and his wife, but the chancellor advised him to simply treat the papers with contempt. Bourrienne added, 'I believe that this nervous susceptibility to the libels of the English papers contributed as much as, and perhaps more than, the consideration of great political interests, to the renewal of hostilities.'[63]

Around this time something happened that would permanently tarnish Josephine's reputation in her homeland: the re-establishment of slavery. In the Treaty of Amiens France had regained control of many of its former colonies, including Martinique and Guadeloupe. As a result, Napoleon was forced to rethink his colonial strategy and decided to reimpose slavery in the French islands. This was a complete volte-face from the early stance of the Consulate which, determined to be seen to uphold Republican principles, had proclaimed to Santo Domingo (now Haiti) in December 1799: 'The Consuls declare that the sacred principles of the liberty and equality of the black peoples will never undergo any threat or modification among you . . . if there are any who maintain relations with the enemy powers, remember, brave blacks, that the French people alone recognize your freedom and the equality of your rights.'

Along with the reintroduction of slavery in the Caribbean, Napoleon authorized the importation of more African slaves to the islands. He also brought back the racial legislation of the ancien régime. In Guadeloupe and Martinique the freedmen were discriminated against and were refused entry into France, as they had used to. Miscegenation was strictly forbidden; indeed, Napoleonic regulations ordered the deportation from Santo Domingo of any white woman who had sexual contact with black men.

It is not clear how much influence Josephine had over this brutal reversion of revolutionary policy. Historians are divided. Some argue that, as a Creole whose family wealth was the product of slave labour, and whose mother still lived in the islands, Josephine would inevitably have encouraged the re-establishment of slavery. Others felt that Napoleon had more pressing motivations to make this decision. He was not, after all, the sort of man to act out of such sentimental motives as the protection of his wife's family; nor indeed was he a man who set much store by ideals. His reasoning was probably pragmatic: Napoleon thought slave production the best means of ensuring the wealth of France's restored Caribbean empire.

It was, at the time, a popular decision. In the minds of many in France, the massacres in Santo Domingo were due to the failure to control the blacks and to keep them in subjugation. Although these slave uprisings had finally led to emancipation, it was generally believed that events had occurred the other way round, that emancipation had led to the slaughter in the colonies. The bloodshed confirmed the popular belief in black savagery that was so prevalent among the proponents of slavery. Freedom for blacks was anathema to Napoleon, who asked, 'How could I grant freedom to Africans, to utterly uncivilized men who did not even know what a colony was, what France was?'[64]

Napoleon had also been extremely embarrassed by the failure of his military forays in the region; later in St Helena he would describe the expedition to Santo Domingo as 'one of my greatest errors'. The island had remained unconquerable and managed to preserve its independence, despite a French incursion led by Napoleon's brother-in-law, General Leclerc, who died there of yellow fever, leaving Napoleon's favourite sister, Pauline, a widow at twenty-three. It was said that she cut off her long raven hair and strewed it on her husband's bier, in accordance with Corsican tradition. Napoleon's irritation was only exacerbated by what he saw as the arrogance of Toussaint-L'Ouverture, elected Life-Governor of Santo Domingo. Toussaint wrote to him in July 1801, with the provocative introduction: from 'The First of the Blacks to the First of the Whites'. In this letter Toussaint declared,

'I am the Bonaparte of St. Domingo, and the Colony cannot exist without me . . .' Napoleon would make 'the sable chieftain' suffer for his hubris. Tricked into capture, Toussaint was deported to France, where he died of cold and neglect in his prison cell.

But Napoleon may have had other reasons for re-establishing slavery. Indeed, the vindictiveness of his handling of the issue of slavery suggests a motivation that was at least partly personal. Economic advantage alone can explain the re-establishment of slavery; it is harder to understand why Napoleon felt it necessary to order the École Polytechnique in Paris to dismiss its black students, or to forbid black people from the Antilles and Senegal to enter France, a law that remained in effect until 1818. Always acutely sensitive to his portrayal in the press, both national and foreign, Napoleon may have been haunted by jibes such as that in the *Morning Post* on 1 February 1803, which described him as 'an unclassifiable being, half-African, half European, a Mediterranean mulatto'.[65] When the British embassy's chaplain met Napoleon he was amazed to find him 'well-proportioned and handsome', rather than the yellow-skinned pygmy portrayed by English cartoonists. The purity of Josephine's blood was often suspected, too; as a Creole she was tainted by dint of proximity. Napoleon did not just reject the idea of equality and fraternity with black people, then; he acted as though determined to distance himself from the merest idea of connection.

Later, in exile at St Helena, when Napoleon was actively building his reputation as an enlightened liberal ruler, he maintained that he had considered ways of creating racial equality in the plantation colonies. He claimed to have discussed the idea of allowing planters to have two wives – one black, one white – so that their children would feel close to each other and racial antagonism would dissipate.[66] The reality of his rule tells a different story, however.

Josephine's racial attitudes also seem contradictory to a twenty-first century observer, although they would have been perfectly normal and acceptable to her contemporaries. Like many colonials she felt comfortable around black servants and treated them with great kindness and affection. That she also understood the cruelty of slavery is demonstrated by the efforts she put into freeing those slaves of whom she was fond. But on other occasions she displayed the racial paranoia of her colonial forefathers. Thus, in a letter to her mother in 1803 she wrote reassuringly, 'Bonaparte is very attached to Martinique and is counting on the support of the planters of that colony; he will use all means possible to preserve their position.'[67] Perhaps as a legacy of her childhood, she was capable of great compassion on a personal level but did not have the imaginative vision to extend it beyond the norms of her kind and time. It was a flaw that she shared with Napoleon who, while capable of random acts of kindness, thought little of squandering millions of lives on the battlefields of Europe.

Riding the wave of his enormous popularity, Napoleon Bonaparte was appointed 'Consul for Life' on 2 August 1802. The decision was ratified by an overwhelming majority. Of the 3,500,000 Frenchmen who voted, fewer than 9,000 opposed the life Consulate. Even the strongly royalist province of the Vendée voted overwhelmingly in Bonaparte's favour: only 6 citizens out of the 17,000 who voted were against the proposed extension of the Consul's term. Now all state powers were concentrated exclusively in Napoleon, and he had the authority to name his successor. One historian wrote, 'He had, in other words, become a king, and greater than a king in all but name, and there was no doubt either in his mind or in that of others, that the life Consulate was but an intermediate step to grander things.'[68]

Napoleon was exhilarated, but Josephine was filled with foreboding. Writing to Hortense that summer she confessed, 'I feel that I was not born, my child, for such grandeur, and I would be happier in retirement, surrounded by those I love.' Napoleon's new position had once again raised the dreaded issue of the succession, and her inability to produce an heir was at the forefront of everyone's mind. As the city celebrated Napoleon's appointment with a reception serenaded by 300 musicians, followed by fireworks, Bourri- enne noticed her sadness: 'Josephine's melancholy presented a striking contrast to the prevailing gaiety. She had to receive a host of dignitaries and officials on that evening and did it with her customary grace, despite the profound depression that weighed down her spirits. She believed that every step towards the throne was one step away from her.'[69]

Napoleon's elevation transformed Josephine's life. The first change came in September, when Napoleon decided that Malmaison, which had symbol- ized the relaxed style of the early Consulate and had been the scene of such happiness for both of them, was no longer sufficiently grand to act as his official second residence. It was forsaken in favour of the palace of Saint- Cloud. The palace was convenient, being somewhat nearer to Paris than Malmaison, located in a pretty valley dominated by the Seine. The residence, built by Mansard, had been acquired and refurbished by Louis XIV early in his reign but devastated during the Revolution. Napoleon hoped to remodel it cheaply, but by the time Percier and Fontaine had finished the bill was more than three million francs. The refurbishment was partially successful, clearing the grounds, replacing statues and fixing the fountains. While never regaining its original lustre, the property had its charms, but for Josephine the move was something of a cause for grief, since it meant that she would spend less time at Malmaison, the place that bore her stamp and her essence.

Napoleon also set about establishing a court. Many believed that this had been his intention from the beginning, when he acquired what Mme Campan described as 'the most famous palace in the universe' – the Tuileries – and created that essential military accessory, his elite Consular Guard. Since then Napoleon had been surreptitiously increasing the rituals and formality that surrounded his rule. As early as September 1801 the Prussian ambassador had observed that 'the household of the First Consul is increasingly taking on the appearance of a court'. By the end of that year Bonaparte was holding regular receptions for foreign ambassadors and the élite of the Republic, and by March 1802 official visitors began to be presented formally to Mme Bonaparte and formal dress (elaborate gowns for women, breeches for men) was made mandatory for receptions at the Tuileries. An Irish visitor noted that 'the etiquette of a Court and Court dress are strictly observed; and everyone agrees that the splendour of the court of the Tuileries is much greater than ever was the old court of France.'[70]

It was a development that suited both Napoleon's own personal inclination towards grandeur and that of the French people. A splendid court had been intrinsic to French national identity for centuries, impacting on manners and customs, social structures and the economic and artistic developments of the nation. Napoleon believed that many would find the old traditions reassuring and hoped that a splendid court might seduce the old ruling classes, who still hadn't accepted him as ruler. It would also demonstrate that he was different from his discredited predecessors of the Republic and the Directoire. He instinctively understood that visual splendour, one of the basic components of a court, was as necessary for a government in 1800 as a positive media image is for today's politicians. It was a view shared by Bonaparte's astute mother, who wrote to her son, 'You know how much external splendour adds to that of rank, or even of personal qualities in the eyes of public opinion.' By October 1802 one of Louis XVIII's agents reported, 'Every day Bonaparte adds to the etiquette of his household and to its representation.'

Josephine was his main advisor in this endeavour. She in turn consulted her friend Mme Campan. A former First Lady of the Bedchamber to Queen

Marie Antoinette, she was a mine of information about the habits and etiquette of the court of Versailles. She also helped former servants of the Queen and King to find positions in the Bonapartes' household. Another figure from the past whom Josephine consulted was Mme de Montesson, the morganatic widow of a Bourbon prince, the duc d'Orléans. A devotee of the old ways, it was in her drawing rooms that men first resumed wearing silk stockings and buckled shoes after ten years of the boots and trousers of the Revolution.

The establishment of a court had a profound impact on Josephine's public role. Her official position was augmented and she now took precedence over the Second and Third Consuls, an alteration which implied that a personal connection to Bonaparte was becoming more important than a position in the service of the state. Just as Napoleon had acquired four prefects of the palace, Josephine soon had four ladies-in-waiting. Their selection was a perfect example of Napoleon's policy of fusion, or assimilation, since most were from aristocratic backgrounds. In the official letter each woman received requesting they serve at the embryonic court, it was stated that 'The First Consul's personal knowledge of your character and of your principles makes him confident that you will acquit yourself of the honours with the politeness that distinguishes the ladies of France and the dignity that becomes the Government.'

The ladies-in-waiting were expected to live at the various palaces and to travel everywhere with Josephine. The two least known of them had husbands on the Consular staff: Mme de Luçay, whom Constant described as 'stingy but otherwise good-natured and obliging', was married to a prefect of the palace and Mme Lauriston's husband was one of Napoleon's aides-de-camp. History may have forgotten them, but they were both ideally suited to their role: thoughtful, efficient and discreet. The third had none of these qualities. Mme de Talhouët was beautiful and well bred, the descendant of an old Britanny family, whose husband would become a count during the Empire. But she would betray Josephine in numerous ways. She was reputedly a royalist spy and in later years wrote very unpleasant portraits of Napoleon and Josephine, despite their pivotal role in her family's advancement.

The fourth lady-in-waiting was the one who would grow closest to Josephine. She was Mme de Rémusat and at twenty-two she was the youngest to enter Josephine's service. Born Claire (known as Clari) de Vergennes, she was a descendant of Louis XVI's famous Foreign Minister. She first crossed Josephine's path as the little girl who befriended Hortense in Croissy, where the family had taken refuge during the Terror. The Revolution left her future in tatters; her father was guillotined the day before Alexandre de Beauharnais, and the family's finances were destroyed. She eventually married Augustin de Rémusat who, sixteen years her senior, like her had a great name and a small fortune. Despite her youth, the terrible experiences of the Revolution produced a precociously sensible, mature young girl, with a sensitive observant nature. This was put to great use in her wonderful memoirs, which are among the most interesting and complete representations of the Napoleonic age.

Her portrait of Josephine is one of the most balanced and insightful we have:

> Without being precisely pretty she possessed many personal charms. Her features were delicate, her expression was sweet; her mouth was very small and concealed bad teeth; her complexion was rather dark but with the help of skilfully applied rouge and powder she remedied that defect; her figure was perfect . . . she dressed with impeccable taste, enhancing the beauty of what she wore; and with these advantages . . . she contrived to avoid eclipse by the youth and beauty of many of the women by whom she was surrounded . . . She was not a person of remarkable intellect . . . but she was aware of her deficiences and never made blunders in conversation. She possessed true natural tact; she readily found pleasant things to say . . . To all this . . . she added extreme kindness of heart, a remarkably even temper and a great readiness to forget any wrong that had been done to her.[71]

As the years of the Consulate unfolded, Napoleon was metamorphosing into the legend he would become. Now he looked less like the young republican hero as painted by Gros and more like the full-faced, implacable despot captured in Ingres's famous portrait of the Emperor dressed in his coronation robes. But it was not just his physiognomy that was changing, so too was his personality. Those close to him had grown to fear him, not only because of his terrible rages but also because of the frightening and ruthless strength that emanated from him. 'The terror he inspires is inconceivable,' Mme de Staël wrote to her father after spending a weekend with the Bonapartes at Joseph Bonaparte's estate. 'One has the impression of an imperious wind blowing about one's ears when one is near that man.'

Many began to suspect that Napoleon's boundless ambition was nowhere near being satisfied. He began referring to himself by his first name, Napoleon, as kings habitually did, and he took up monarchical pursuits, like the royal hunt. As ceremony around him continued to be embellished, many, including Talleyrand, believed he would be happy with nothing less than a crown. Josephine was apprehensive about her husband's ambition for the throne. One day she came into his office while he was dictating to his secretary and attempted to dissuade him from making any such moves. 'Approaching him in her gentle and beguiling way,' wrote Bourrienne, 'and setting herself on his knee, she caressed him and brushed her fingertips softly across his cheek and through his hair. Her words came in a tender rush. "Bonaparte, I implore you don't go making yourself a king. It's that horrible Lucien who puts you up to such schemes. Please, oh please, don't listen to him." ' Bonaparte simply smiled and replied, 'You must be out of your mind, Josephine, you could only have heard such wild tales in the Faubourg Saint-Germain.' But Josephine knew her husband well enough not to trust this denial.

In October the Bonapartes went on a triumphal tour through Normandy, the first of a number of official visits that the newly minted Consul for Life and his consort would take through his territories. Josephine was privately reluctant to go, as Hortense had just given birth to her first child, a plump little boy who immediately became the apple of the family's eye. Nonetheless she acceded to her husband's wishes and played her part prettily. As always in her official life, she was perfect: attentive, kind, always ready with the right remark and the appropriate gesture. She was always alert to ways of improving her performance: in Dieppe, she was provided with a bracelet to give to the little girl who would present her with a bouquet. Having received the bracelet, the child put out her other arm and Josephine took off one of her own bangles to give to her. Noticing how much more delighted the child and the collected onlookers were with this second, more personal gesture, ever after she would put on before the ceremony any jewellery she had to distribute, so that she could take it from her own wrist, neck or finger.

On their return to Saint-Cloud, the elaboration of protocol continued. Gone was the informal conviviality of the early days of the Consulate: Napoleon and Josephine dined alone in state in the evenings, joined a couple of days a week by one of her ladies-in-waiting or one of his ministers. At Sunday Mass, with the bishop of Versailles officiating, Bonaparte, with his

Napoleon, General-in-Chief of the Italian campaign. This victory heralded the dawn of almost unprecedented power for Napoleon and his associates: 'Each one of us had the sense of a future without limits.'

Josephine and her entourage fleeing from gunfire in Italy.

Hortense de Beauharnais. Her marriage to Louis Bonaparte made her 'the most unhappy person of her time'.

right: The coronation.

below right: Josephine was famed for her love of children, which was an important part of her public image. Here she is shown with a group of foundlings whom she helped to support as part of her charitable activities.

left: Eugène de Beauharnais. Josephine's son was steadfast in his loyalty to both his mother and his stepfather. He had 'simplicity and kindheartedness; he was neither vain nor presumptuous'.

Empress Josephine –
'a woman in the fullest
meaning of the word:
capricious and alive, and
with the best of hearts'.

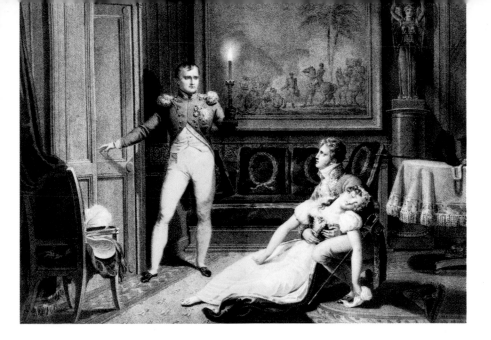

A popular lithograph showing Josephine's reaction to the news of her divorce.

A depiction of Josephine commending her children and grandchildren to Tsar Alexander for his protection.

The death of Empress Josephine.

Josephine and her ladies at Malmaison, painted after her death.

two Consuls behind him and Josephine at his side, took the place in the chapel box that had once been occupied by Louis XVI. He remained standing, in a martial posture with his hands folded on his breast; she knelt gracefully, in a gesture that showed off her elegant figure to perfection.

Despite the ever-encroaching ritual, the first couple – according to Mme de Rémusat – nonetheless settled into a comfortable routine that demonstrated just how integral Josephine was to Napoleon's life and how much pleasure he took in her company. Whether at Saint-Cloud or at the Tuileries, the couple always slept together. Napoleon left his wife's bed early to begin his arduous day. If he was in Paris he joined her later for breakfast; if in Saint-Cloud he dined alone on the terrace that abutted his study. Josephine rose an hour later and, after her long toilette, received endless streams of visitors: merchants trying to induce her to buy, individuals soliciting her help, others hoping she could remove loved ones from the list or get restitution of their property. Her days were frequently interrupted by visits from her husband. 'If he had as much as a few free moments, he came to spend them with Josephine,' Mme de Rémusat recounted, racing to his wife's apartments between appointments so that they could share a few moments together talking or relaxing. At six the couple dined, after which Napoleon often returned to his office for more work and went to bed early while Josephine – who preferred to go to bed late – whiled away the evenings with her household. The day ended as it began – in the shared marital bed, a symbol of their passion and enduring partnership.

But this domestic peace was soon threatened by another woman: the fifteen-year-old actress Marguerite-Josephine Weimer, known as Mlle George. What must have been particularly galling to Josephine was that she had welcomed this particular rival into her home and befriended her. Her friend Mlle Racourt had brought the young actress to Saint-Cloud to meet Josephine just before she made her theatrical debut. In her memoirs Mlle George recalled the profound impact 'the beautiful and gracious' Josephine made on her: 'Her eyes were so soft and so attractive! She was so amiable! She put you at your ease, but with a distinction, with that elegant simplicity that was intrinsic to her person. She had about her a charisma that magnetized you. It was impossible not to succumb in the face of that soft, mysterious charm. I liked her before I even heard her speak, one sensed that she was good-natured.'[72]

Her admiration for Josephine did not stop Mlle George from becoming

Napoleon's mistress. Her motives were probably twofold: glory and necessity. Her theatrical debut – witnessed by Josephine and Napoleon – was a great success, and her fame was further boosted by her notorious rivalry with another young actress, Mlle Duchesnois, which so divided Parisians that audiences frequently came to blows. But the 'Venus of Paris', as the newspapers had dubbed her, needed a protector; it was impossible to live in a fitting style without one. Numerous wealthy men, including Lucien Bonaparte, were more than willing to fill the role. Whether Napoleon's interest was piqued by that of his brother, or by George's voluptuous beauty, or the cachet of having a mistress from the Comédie Française, he sent for her.

As Mlle George breathlessly recollected in her memoirs, she was transported to the First Consul's apartments at Saint-Cloud, which were lit by huge candles in massive candelabra. She waited alone 'in this great room with its enormous bed and heavy curtains of silk'. After a show of 'timid resistance', which whetted Napoleon's appetite, she gracefully succumbed to his attentions. As was his wont, he rechristened her, saying, 'I am very fond of the name Josephine [her middle name] but I shall call you Georgina, if you'll allow me.'[73] If it is true, as Mlle Georges claimed years later, that 'in order to know this great man, one had to see him in intimacy',[74] their loveplay revealed a hitherto unseen side to Napoleon. It was a curiously childlike relationship. Their love-making was interspersed with games of chase and hide-and-seek and gossip about the theatre. On one occasion Napoleon grabbed a floral wreath she was wearing and pranced about with it perched on his own head. At another time he pretended to be an actor parodying popular songs, until they collapsed in a heap of laughter. This playfulness brought the pair together. It was a very different kind of relationship from the intense and passionate bond Napoleon shared with Josephine, and no doubt it was a relaxing respite for him.

Quite quickly Josephine noticed that her husband was less attentive: sometimes cold and irritable, sometimes distracted and dreamy. More tellingly, there were now nights when he pleaded too much work and did not join her in bed until very late, if at all. The realization that her husband's manner towards her had changed prompted scenes of weeping and accusations. Napoleon's first line of defence was denial. This gossip of an affair, he argued, was spread by those who wished to cause unhappiness in their marriage. She knew that he loved her exclusively, but he was far too busy to spend every waking moment in her company. He begged her not to harass him with hysterical scenes; she knew how much they disturbed him.

But the rumours escalated, and soon Paris was alive with talk of the First Consul's infatuation with the young actress. At one performance she delivered the line 'If I have charmed Cinna, I shall charm other men as well', and the audience cheered frenziedly and looked from the stage to the Consular box. 'Everyone', the actress realized, 'knew what I wanted so much to hide.'[75] If 'everyone knew', Josephine's spies only confirmed her suspicions. Humiliated and distraught, she confronted her husband again. Napoleon was no longer able to deny the affair, so now he attempted to justify it. He was weighed down by the cares of the world, he explained, and Mlle Georges lightened his spirits. If Josephine loved him she would be more understanding; she would be happy for him, even allow him to confide in her about his mistress once in a while.

Napoleon thought Josephine's distress was ridiculous. 'She troubles herself a great deal more than is necessary. Josephine is always afraid I shall fall seriously in love. Does she not know then, that I am not made for love? For what is love? It is a passion which balances the entire universe against the person loved and finds it lighter. You surely don't think I'm the sort of man to give myself up to any such exclusive passion? What do my little distractions matter, since love doesn't enter into them?' On another occasion he excused his infidelities with the remark, 'I am not like other men, and the ordinary laws of morality and rules of propriety do not apply to me.'[76]

Josephine was not mollified by such arguments. Her weeping and accusations exasperated Napoleon, and more violent arguments followed. One night, according to Mme de Rémusat, the green-eyed monster provoked Josephine to some extremely rash behaviour. It was one o'clock in the morning and a profound silence reigned in the Tuileries. ' "I can't rest," she suddenly said to me. "Mlle George is up there, I feel sure. I'm going up to see if I can take them by surprise." Not a little worried by this sudden resolve, I did what I could to dissuade her, but without success. "Follow me," she said. "We'll go up together." ' The nervous pair crept silently up a secret staircase that led to Bonaparte's rooms.

> Halfway through our journey, however, the stillness was interrupted by a small sound. Mme Bonaparte turned to whisper to me. 'Perhaps it's Roustan,' she said, referring to Bonaparte's black servant, who usually guarded the door. 'The brute is perfectly capable of cutting both our throats!' At this, I was seized with panic. Without reflecting

that I was leaving Mme Bonaparte in absolute darkness, I turned and rushed downstairs with the candle I was carrying, precipitating myself back into the salon with the utmost speed. She followed me a few minutes after, astonished at my sudden flight. When she saw my startled face, she began laughing and this set me laughing too. So our enterprise ended. I left her, saying that I believed the fright she had thrown me into had served her well and that I had been right to give way to it.[77]

Josephine felt profoundly threatened by Mlle George. No other woman had seriously engaged Napoleon's affections, and this young beauty – a fresh sixteen as opposed to Josephine's forty – was charming as well as beautiful. Josephine feared that she would no longer be indispensable to him and that once he realized that he might rethink their marriage, and perhaps her inability to bear him a child would become even more significant. Her anguish reached a climax when Napoleon suggested for the first time that they sleep in separate rooms. She temporarily managed to dissuade him but she was badly frightened.

Her fears however had little impact on him. He complained to Mme de Rémusat that Josephine's tears and reproaches bored him. He continued to entertain Mlle Georges in his private apartments and to see her frequently at the theatre. 'No doubt he came too often,' she admitted in her memoirs. But Napoleon felt justified and self-righteous, and refused to give ground to his wife. 'Bonaparte', says Mme de Rémusat, 'was by turn imperious, hard, defiant to excess; then suddenly he would show some feeling; he would relent and become almost sweet-tempered, repairing with a good grace the harm he had done – although he showed no sign of mending his ways.'[78]

Only time and the march of events would dampen Napoleon's ardour for his Georgina. As 1803 unfolded he was increasingly preoccupied with military plans and diplomatic efforts. France's relations with its foreign allies had begun to sour almost as soon as the peace of Amiens had been signed. Both sides were responsible for breaking the treaty. Britain had announced its intention to retain Malta, claiming that Bonaparte's retention of Piedmont in September 1802 and his refusal to evacuate Holland as promised at Lune-ville broke the terms of the treaty. In February 1803 this action prompted a terrible scene at the Tuileries, when Napoleon – in the presence of Talleyrand and the whole diplomatic corps – roundly abused the British ambassador, Lord Whitworth. As the envoys of Europe listened, 'mute with astonishment and fear', Bonaparte slammed out of the room with a final word for Whitworth: 'We shall be fighting in two weeks. Malta – or war!'

Concluding that Napoleon must be mad, the British Foreign Secretary, Hawkesbury, to whom Whitworth had reported the incident, set about issuing an ultimatum of his own. Despite intense diplomatic efforts to mend the breach, war became inevitable. On the morning of 2 May, Bonaparte summoned Junot, the governor of Paris, and instructed him to issue an order that read, 'All Englishmen from the age of eighteen to sixty or holding any commission from His Britannic Majesty, who are at present in France, shall immediately be constituted prisoners of war.' He concluded the conversation with the words, 'I am resolved that tonight not an Englishman shall be visible in the most obscure theatre in Paris.' And on 20 May 1803, after only fourteen months of peace, France formally declared war on Great Britain.

In order to rally and reassure the country, Napoleon decided to take a six-week tour of the coastal regions and the Low Countries, accompanied by his wife. On 24 June Napoleon and Josephine departed Saint-Cloud in a procession that included several carriages, a couple of generals, numerous aides-de-camp and two prefects of the palace. Josephine was accompanied by two of her ladies-in-waiting: Mme de Talhouët and Claire de Rémusat. Eugène's regiment formed part of the escort. The first night of their journey was spent at Joseph Bonaparte's country seat, Mortefontaine, where a revealing incident took place. That evening, at a gathering that included most of the Bonaparte clan, Napoleon insisted for the first time that Josephine take the place of honour, rather than his mother. It was a gesture that only served to increase the family's enmity towards her.

The rest of the trip was a triumph. In Amiens, the retinue was showered with garlands of flowers as they travelled through streets decorated by triumphal arches. The townspeople were so overcome at the sight of their legendary ruler and his beautiful consort that they insisted on unhitching the horses to pull their carriage themselves. In Picardy, in accordance with an ancient custom usually reserved for kings, Bonaparte was presented with a pair of swans. These were immediately sent back to Paris and settled in a pool at the Tuileries, to demonstrate to the capital the royal homage he had received. As they passed through other towns, including Lille, Ostend, Bruges, Brussels and Liège, the delirious reception was repeated. But behind the scenes Josephine was decidedly underwhelmed by these attentions. Missing her family intensely, she wrote to Hortense: 'Since my departure from Paris, I have been constantly occupied in receiving compliments. You know me;

so you can judge how much all this bores me. Happily, the company of my women has compensated for my noisy life.'[79] In public, however, she was all graciousness. According to Mme de Rémusat, Josephine left 'memories of her generosity and grace that fifteen years later would not be effaced'. She was a perfect match for her husband, who, dreaming all the while of planting a flag on the Tower of London, had on this occasion mustered all his charm, joking with the rank and file and, as was his custom, playfully pinching the cheeks of the most favoured.

The trip brought the Bonapartes back together again, reminding Napoleon how enormously popular his wife was and what an asset she was to him. When they returned to Paris in the middle of August, Napoleon did not send for his mistress immediately. When they did meet, he was distracted and distant. Mlle Georges realized that the intensity of their passion was gone for ever. The separation had made him realize that he did not need her; his peacetime pursuits of love had been replaced by the even more engaging lust for war. But Josephine was unaware that his ardour for the actress was swiftly cooling and was still insecure. In October, according to Mme de Rémusat, her jealousy provoked another quarrel.

Before everything could be smoothed over, Napoleon was gone again; this time to Boulogne to oversee military arrangements. An exchange of letters between them culminated in one addressed from Josephine to Napoleon dated November 1803. It is one of the very few surviving authenticated letters Josephine sent him:

> *All my sorrows have disappeared on reading the good, touching letter which contains such loving expressions of your feelings for me. How grateful I am to you for giving so much time to your Josephine. If you could know, you would applaud yourself for being the means of causing so much joy to the wife whom you love.*
>
> *A letter is the portrait of the soul, and I press this one to my heart. It has done me so much good! I will keep it always! It will be my consolation during your absence, my guide when I am near you, I wish to to be always in your eyes the good, the tender Josephine, occupied only with your happiness . . .*
>
> *You will not have a feeling that I do not share.*
>
> *There is my desire, my wish, to limit all that does not please you and make you happy . . .*
>
> *Adieu Bonaparte, I will never forget the last phrase of your letter.*

I keep it in my heart. How deeply it is engraved there! With what emotion mine has responded! Yes, my wish is also to please you, to love you, or, rather to adore you.[80]

There was little time for the newly reconciled couple to spend together. On 13 January 1804 a conspiracy was uncovered that had an enormous impact on Napoleon's rule. The prime mover was a man named Georges Cadoudal, a former émigré in the pay of the English. It was not entirely clear whether it was Bonaparte's abduction or his assassination that was planned. But in either case the managing agent was Charles Pichegru, the former leader of the Council of Five Hundred, who back in 1797 had been deported to Cayenne for plotting with Louis XVIII. He had subsequently escaped and made his way to London, where he offered his services to the British Government and the Bourbons. Pichegru's illegal re-entry into France was immediately reported to Bonaparte, who ordered that he, Cadoudal and their fellow conspirator Moreau be arrested. Thanks to the efficent police network organized by Fouché (who had been reinstated as Minister of the Police) the three men were soon in prison, where they revealed all. 'I came to Paris', Cadoudal said, 'to assassinate the First Consul . . . I was not supposed to assassinate him until there was a prince in Paris and so far none has arrived.' When the interrogator asked whether the plot had been conceived and was to be executed 'in cooperation with a French prince of the ancien régime,' Cadoudal answered simply, 'Yes'.[81]

When the news of Cadoudal's confession was brought to Bonaparte he was more angry than shocked. 'Am I a dog to be killed in the streets while my murderers are safe from punishment?' (The murderers obviously being the Bourbon princes.) 'The head of the guilty man will be my revenge.' Somehow Bonaparte convinced himself that the 'guilty man' behind the plot was the duc d'Enghien, a member of the Condé family and a prince of the blood, and that he was the 'French prince' expected in Paris. Enghien lived in Ettenheim in the duchy of Baden, near the French frontier, and it was rumoured (falsely) that he sometimes crossed the Rhine secretly into France. This was what Bonaparte seemed to have in mind when he swore that 'the first of these princes who comes within reach will be shot without mercy'.[82]

On the night of 14 March, under orders from Bonaparte and in violation of all international law, the duc d'Enghien was seized in the neutral territory of the state of Baden and taken back across the frontier to Barrier de la Villette and then to Vincennes. There, on the night of 20 March, after an interrogation and a trial that produced only the most circumstantial of evidence, the duc was executed and his body buried in a grave that had been dug earlier beside the moat of the chateau. The murder of the undoubtedly innocent duc, his abduction from neutral foreign territory and his trumped-up trial all constituted a crime that even Bonaparte's staunchest supporters found difficult to explain and that the most assiduous cultivators of the Napoleonic legend are still hard put to justify.

Josephine herself reprimanded the First Consul for the deed, and he dismissed her saying, 'You are a child in these matters! You don't understand.' Nonetheless he later felt called upon to explain in her salon, 'I have caused blood to be shed because it was necessary for me to do so.' And at table that night he shouted angrily, in reply to the silent accusations of his wife and his guests, 'At least we have shown them what we are capable of! Perhaps now they will leave us in peace.' Napoleon would maintain the wisdom of his decision right to the end of his life, asserting that 'I had the duc d'Enghien arrested and tried because it was necessary for the security, tranquillity and honour of the people of France . . . Under similar circumstances, I would do the same thing today.' But others were less understanding. Fouché concluded, 'It was worse than a crime, it was a mistake.'[83]

Despite his bravado, Napoleon was nervous about how the execution would be received by the French public. As he so often did, he tested public opinion by taking a visit to the theatre. Normally on these visits, according to one of their entourage, Napoleon did not wait for Josephine but passed 'rapidly up the staircase' to take his place in the box. 'On this occasion, however, he waited in the little ante-room adjoining it, until Mme Bonaparte arrived. She was trembling terribly and he was excessively pale; he looked round at us all, as if mutely asking us how we thought he would be received, and then he went forward at last like a man marching to face a firing squad.' To Napoleon's great relief, he was greeted with the usual accolades and applause.[84]

If the French public had been convinced by the cleverly manipulated version of events presented to them in the tightly controlled national press, people abroad were not. The impact of the conspiracy and the execution of the duc d'Enghien was felt across the Channel and in Europe, where there was widely expressed dismay and revulsion. France's sense of isolation engendered a paranoia of which Napoleon took immediate advantage. He had finally found the pretext he needed to reach for the crown. In the guise of being his nation's only friend and protector, Napoleon decided to consolidate his power by declaring himself Emperor of the French.

Fifteen

CORONATION

May God establish you upon this throne of Empire and may Jesus Christ, King of Kings . . . make you to reign with Him to all eternity.

POPE PIUS VII

THE EMPIRE WAS PROCLAIMED ON 18 May 1804. The guns in Paris were still roaring out a twenty-one-gun salute when the entire senate, escorted by a large body of troops, arrived at Saint-Cloud. Napoleon – in military uniform, and surrounded by his generals – received the contingent calmly, accepting his exaltation as if he had possessed 'the right all his life'. Then the president of the senate, Consul Cambacérès, turned to Josephine and used her new title for the first time:

> It rests to the senate to fulfil a very pleasant task; that of offering to Your Imperial Majesty the homage of our respect, and an expression of the gratitude of the French people. Yes, Madame, you are publicly renowned for the good that you never cease to do. It is said that you are always accessible to the unfortunate . . . and that you are always pleased to help . . . It is this sweet and kindly disposition that means the name of the Empress Josephine will eternally be an emblem of consolation and hope.[1]

'She replied', remarked an onlooker, 'with the natural grace which always raised her to the level of any position, however lofty, in which she might be placed.'[2]

At a family dinner the next evening, the triumphant mood of the day deteriorated into a morass of vituperation and spite. Napoleon, thoroughly enjoying his new role, announced to the household certain changes in protocol. As Emperor and Empress, Napoleon and Josephine were now to be addressed as their 'Majesties'. But of his siblings only Joseph and Louis and their spouses were to have the titles of prince and princess conferred on them. His sisters Élisa and Caroline were furious and humiliated. Why were those two outsiders, Hortense and Joseph's wife Julie, to become princesses, while they received nothing – no new title, no position? How could they, his own blood, be slighted like this? Napoleon raised the temperature of the evening by teasing them, constantly referring to Hortense as 'princess'. Caroline burst into frustrated and envious tears.

Napoleon's behaviour had a long history. His family had annoyed him intensely with a series of marriages that he considered inappropriate and demeaning. His disapproval of his sisters' liaisons was already well known. This disappointment was only compounded when his younger brother Jérôme married an American girl called Elizabeth Patterson in Baltimore. This decision so enraged Napoleon that he forbade Jérôme to return to France. His discovery that Lucien intended to marry Mme Jouberthon, the woman he had lived with since the death of his wife several years earlier, revived his fury. He attempted unsuccessfully to block the wedding, but the entire family had mutinied and the marriage went ahead. Now, with the proclamation of the Empire, he had the chance to bring his recalcitrant family to heel.

The following day a violent argument broke out, with Caroline demanding to know why she and her sisters were to be condemned 'to obscurity and contempt while strangers were to be loaded with honours and dignity'. Equally angry, Napoleon answered that he was master and he would distribute honours as he pleased. It was on this occasion that he uttered the memorable retort, 'Really, *mesdames*, to hear your pretensions, one would think we hold the crown for your father the late king.'[3] A dramatic attack of the vapours on Caroline's part put an end to Napoleon's wrath. A few days later it was arranged that courtesy titles should be given to the sisters of the Emperor and that they were to be addressed as their 'Imperial Highnesses'.

This victory should have won Josephine at least a short oasis of peace. But if there was one thing that brought the perpetually feuding Bonaparte family together, it was hatred of *la Beauharnais*. They knew perfectly well that Josephine ardently longed for her coronation, which she believed would 'establish her rank and her security', and they were also aware that Napoleon was undecided about whether to crown her. They redoubled their efforts to unseat the usurper, playing on Bonaparte's indecision in numerous ways: raking up old rumours about Josephine's infidelities, suggesting that her children's affection for him was 'forced' and dwelling on the chance of his acquiring a direct heir, Joseph pointing out 'the advantage of an alliance with some foreign princess or . . . [even] the heiress to a great name in France'.[4]

This muck-raking and Napoleon's continued silence alarmed Josephine more and more. But she continued to behave as normally as she could, throwing herself into her duties and the routine of court life. She was approached by the duchesse de Polignac, the elderly mother of one of the conspirators in the recent royalist plot against Napoleon, who begged Josephine to intervene on her son's behalf. Twelve other plotters had already been executed and the duchesse feared that her offspring would be next. After a six-hour audience, Josephine arranged to have the distressed woman secreted in Napoleon's office, where she promptly fainted at the Emperor's feet. Confronted with the prostrate woman and his own weeping wife, Napoleon relented and a pardon was granted. 'Josephine's intervention', according to Mme de Rémusat, 'made a great sensation in Paris, and gave rise to renewed praise of her kindness of heart, which had obtained almost universal recognition.' After this, other wives, mothers and sisters besieged Josephine with requests for an audience in the hope of enlisting her support for their own imperilled relatives. With the Empress's help, numerous capital sentences were commuted to imprisonment. Napoleon realized that 'a dark shadow might be cast by too many executions' and at this time, with the coronation approaching, it was politic to be seen to temper justice with mercy.[5]

At first Josephine's new role cannot have seemed very different from her previous one as *Consulesse*. The changes in procedure and protocol unfolded gradually. But they were to inexorably transform every area of her life. While the new title, 'Empress', still felt a bit unreal to Josephine, she would soon hear it used in an official context for the first time. On 14 July, at a mass held at Notre-Dame to celebrate the inauguration of the Légion d'Honneur, the newly created Empress Josephine made her first official appearance. Napoleon had told her that he wished her 'to be dazzling in jewellery and richly dressed' and Josephine was happy to oblige. That day she was particularly radiant, noted one observer. 'She appeared in bright sunshine attired in a robe of rose-coloured tulle, spangled with silver stars and cut very low, according to the fashion of the day. Her headdress consisted of a great number of diamond wheat-ears and this brilliant attire, the elegance of her bearing, the charm of her smile, the sweetness of her countenance, produced such an effect that I heard many persons who were present at the ceremony say that the Empress outshone all the ladies of her suite.'[6]

Ten days later Josephine departed on her annual spa visit, this time to Aix-la-Chapelle. (Napoleon – with a view to invading England – had already gone off to inspect naval dispositions in Boulogne.) As befitted her new station, she travelled with great ceremony. Her Imperial retinue numbered over fifty people, including a Master of the Horse, two chamberlains, a lady of honour, three ladies-in-waiting, two ushers, ten footmen, plus sundry maids and kitchen staff. But the new ceremony and her cumbersome entourage meant everything took twice as long. At each town she passed through, a detachment of cavalry rode out to escort her and the garrison fired a twenty-five-gun salute as she entered and left. In addition, there were beneficences to be distributed wherever she went, money, rings, brooches and bracelets. Writing about the people's reaction to Josephine on this trip, her maid Mlle Avrillon declared, 'I will not try to paint a picture of the enthusiasm that erupted at the sight of the Empress in the towns through which she passed: I will only say that the welcome she received from all that knew of her visit, showed how true it was that her reputation for goodness had preceded her, and demonstrated the belief, which had long been popular in France, that she was the inspiration for the good luck of her august spouse.'[7]

The trip was not without incident. On one miserable night the party attempted to negotiate the mountainous paths between Sedan and Liège; Napoleon had marked out their route for them and had mistaken a road under construction for one that was completed. Since nobody in the party had the courage to disobey the Emperor's instructions, the carriages had to be hauled with ropes along the treacherous path he had indicated. Josephine became so frightened and so ill with one of her migraines that she eventually got out and walked in the mud and rain. On another occasion, a visit to Charlemagne's tomb, she behaved with a resourcefulness that pleased Napoleon when it was reported back to him (as every detail of her trip was). Presented with a bone said to be from the legend's arm, she refused without any sign of distaste, explaining that she had 'for her own support an arm as strong as Charlemagne's'.

Josephine was relieved to reach Aix, despite the unprepossessing appearance of the town and the pervasive stink of sulphur from its springs. The weather was beautiful, the populace ecstatic. Entertainment in the spa town was appropriately sedate: suppers, card parties and performances provided by a Parisian acting troupe and a group of German singers. Napoleon's letters were particularly loving and warm: 'I trust soon to learn that the waters have done you much good. I am sorry to hear of all the vexations you have undergone. Please write me often . . . I cover you with kisses.' The following day he wrote, 'I am longing to see you. You are always necessary to my happiness.'[8]

So when Napoleon wrote charmingly, 'I am rather impatient to see you', and to inform her that he was to join her at Aix and stay with her during an official visit to the Rhine, Josephine was overcome by happiness. But when he arrived she discovered – much to her chagrin – that the person he was really impatient to see was one of her ladies-in-waiting, Mme de Vaudey. Her unhappiness was exacerbated by his boorish behaviour: as always when he was involved with another woman, he was bullying and unkind to Josephine. One night in Mainz, when Josephine was ill, he barged into her room and literally dragged her out of bed, demanding she get dressed immediately.

Much to Josephine's relief, when they returned to Paris that October Mme de Vaudey, who had proved a little too acquisitive for her own good, was quickly put aside. Almost immediately, however, another candidate was dangled before Napoleon. She was Adèle Duchâtel, a twenty-five-year-old blonde with a much older husband. This affair caused Josephine paroxysms of jealousy. In her memoirs Mme de Rémusat relates the story of one dramatic morning when Josephine noticed Adèle surreptitiously leave the room. Convinced that she was going to meet Napoleon, Josephine took Mme de Rémusat aside and said. 'I am going to clear up my doubts this very moment; stay here with all these people, and if you are asked where I have gone say that the Emperor sent for me.' Her lady-in-waiting tried to dissuade her, feeling it was not a good idea to furnish Napoleon with any 'pretext for a quarrel', but Josephine was not to be deterred. And she made her way up a back staircase to the small suite of rooms that communicated with his apartments.

When Josephine returned to the drawing room she was extremely agitated. Unable to suppress her feelings a moment longer, she beckoned Mme de Rémusat into her bedroom.

All is lost . . . I went to look for the Emperor in his office, he was not there. Then I went up the back stairs to the upper room. I found the door shut, but I could hear Bonaparte's voice and also that of Mme Duchatel. I knocked loudly at the door, and called out that I was there. You may imagine the start I gave them. It was some time before the door was opened; and when at last I was admitted, though I know I ought to have been able to control myself, it was impossible and I reproached him bitterly. Mme Duchâtel began to cry, and Bonaparte flew into so violent a passion that I hardly had time to fly before him and escape his rage. I am still trembling at the thought of it. I did not know to what excess his anger might have gone.'

A few minutes afterwards, we heard a great noise in the apartment of the Empress, and of course I knew that the Emperor was there and that a violent quarrel was taking place. Mme Duchatel called for her carriage and at once left for Paris.

Later, Josephine tearfully recounted the scene to Mme de Rémusat. Bonaparte, 'after having insulted her in every possible way, and smashed some of her furniture in his rage', had ordered her to quit Saint-Cloud at once. Weary of her jealous spying, he declared that he was 'determined to shake off this yoke and to listen henceforth only to the counsels of his policy, which demanded that he should take a wife capable of giving him children.'[9]

That evening the Emperor summoned Eugène to inform him that he intended to divorce Josephine. Making no attempt to interfere, Eugène impressed Bonaparte by refusing the personal favours that he offered, declaring that 'the moment such a misfortune should befall his mother', it would be his duty to follow her wherever she was to go, even Martinique.[10] Hortense, too, refused to intervene on her mother's behalf. 'I cannot interfere in any way,' she said to Mme de Rémusat. 'My husband has positively forbidden me to do so. My mother has been very imprudent. She is about to forfeit a crown, but at any rate she will have peace. Ah! believe me there are women more unhappy than she.' Hortense spoke with such profound sadness that Mme de Rémusat, Josephine's lady-in-waiting, knew she was speaking of her own personal situation. 'And besides,' she concluded, 'if there is to be any chance at all of setting this matter right, it is the influence over Bonaparte of my mother's tears and her gentleness. Believe me, it is better to leave them to themselves – not to interfere at all between them . . .'[11]

Hortense proved correct. Two days later the couple were reconciled. 'Her submission and her tears had in fact disarmed Bonaparte', reported Mme de Rémusat. But a few days later he was still entertaining the idea of divorce: 'I have not the courage', he said to Josephine, 'to come to a final resolution; and if you let me see that you are too deeply afflicted – if only you can render me obedience – I feel that I shall never have the strength to oblige you to leave me. I tell you plainly, however, that it is my earnest desire that you shall resign yourself to the interest of my policy, and yourself spare me all the difficulties of this painful separation.'[12] The Emperor wept bitterly as he uttered these terrible words. But Josephine adopted a strategy that totally disarmed him. Declaring that she would 'await a direct order from Napoleon to descend the throne', she assumed the attitude of a resigned and submissive victim. 'Yielding, sad . . . entirely obedient, but also skilful in wielding her power over her husband, she reduced him to a condition of agitation and indecision from which he could not escape.'[13]

Napoleon's continued ambivalence about the divorce was evident in a conversation with his comrade Pierre-Louis Roederer, in which he revealed how much his family's perpetual jockeying for position irritated him: 'They are jealous of my wife, of Eugène, of Hortense, of all that is near to me.' Their behaviour was, he noted, in stark contrast to that of his stepchildren who had earned his love and respect by never asking for anything – rather like Josephine during these difficult weeks. Despite the profound anxiety she harboured, Josephine had been 'considerate of everybody' and unfailingly sweet to him. As he admitted, 'she is always the butt of their persecutions. My wife is a good wife who never does anyone any harm . . . It is from a sense of justice that I will not divorce her! I am above all a just man. If I was thrown in prison, instead of mounting a throne, she would share my misfortune. How can I put away this excellent woman just because I am becoming great? No, that is beyond me. I have the heart of a man . . . Yes, she shall be crowned! She will be crowned,' he concluded strangely, 'if it costs me 200,000 men!'[14]

Thus it was the Bonapartes' bad behaviour, as much as Josephine's virtues, that decided Napoleon. Resentful of his family's 'premature air of triumph', he went to Josephine's apartments. He told her that the Pope was about to arrive in Paris, that he would crown them both, and that she should begin at once to prepare for the great ceremony. Her months of 'mortal anguish and suspense' were at an end.

The news that Josephine was to be crowned provoked a new wave of hostility from the Bonaparte clan, particularly when they discovered that Napoleon expected his sisters to carry her train. Once again the revolt was led by Caroline, who categorically refused – on behalf of all of them – to play such a subservient role to Josephine. Since the train was twenty-five yards of crimson velvet embroidered with golden bees and lined with Russian ermine, its weight demanded that someone carry it. After six sleepless nights, Napoleon finally found a solution that was acceptable to his disgruntled family. In a piece of semantic wizardry he decreed that instead of 'carrying the train', his sisters would merely be 'supporting the mantle', and they would have their own trains carried by chamberlains.

Josephine threw herself into preparations for the coronation with enthusiasm. 'The Empress', wrote Claire de Rémusat, 'called in the greatest artists and artisans of the day to confer with her on the design of the official costume for the court ladies as well as for herself. Deciding not to resurrect the hoop, Josephine and her advisors 'chose the long mantle to cover our dresses, the gold- or silver-embroidered lace or tulle ruff, called a cherusque, rising high from the shoulders to frame the neck and face . . .'[15] According to one observer, in the 'run-up to the coronation, a large part of the commerce of Paris was involved in creating brilliant and futile creations for the women'.[16]

In anticipation of the coronation, people flocked to the capital from the provinces and from overseas. During these weeks the population of the city seemed to double as establishments like the cafes and theatres profited from the influx of visitors. According to Bourrienne, business also flourished: 'The revival of old customs gave occupation to tradespeople who could get no employment under the Directoire or Consulate, such as saddlers, carriage-makers, lace-makers, embroiderers and others.'[17] Troops were mobilized to deal with the crowds, but the atmosphere in the city was benign, dominated by an air of curiosity and excitement. 'All was bustle and activity', said one Parisian, as everyone rushed around buying new outfits and lavishly entertaining friends. The poet Chénier was ordered to compose a tragedy in honour of the occasion and the Opéra was commissioned to put on a number of splendid ballets. It is impossible, according to Laure Junot, 'to imagine the excitement, the gaiety and the revelry that prevailed in Paris at that time'.

The coronation was to be the ultimate spectacle of Napoleon's rule and he wanted to dazzle the world with its majesty and grandeur. In order that everything should run smoothly, the Emperor instructed the painter Isabey, who was overseeing the organization of the event, to prepare a series of elaborate drawings depicting various stages of the ceremony. But the time-pressed painter chose instead to trawl through the shops of Paris, buying up all the toy figures he could find. These he dressed up in various costumes and placed inside a model of Notre-Dame. With these dolls, Josephine and Bonaparte were able to enact and re-enact every detail of the ceremony. This unorthodox manner of rehearsing was effective. According to Mlle Avrillon, the coronation 'was absolutely like a theatrical performance where all the roles had been studied in advance'.[18]

Another significant duty fell to Josephine during these weeks. On 25 November she was delegated by Napoleon to receive Pope Pius VII at the palace of Fontainebleau. It must have seemed strange to stand there as sovereign, when years before she had been too lowly even to be presented in the palace. Now she was mistress of all France, greeting a papal retinue that included sixteen cardinals and bishops and 100 lesser clerics. Whatever her thoughts, Josephine played her part prettily and charmed the pontiff, who referred to her fondly as 'my daughter' throughout his stay.

Josephine had reasons of her own to charm the Pope, as he would discover when he and his boisterous party arrived in Paris and were put up in the elaborate fifty-six-room quarters reserved for them in the Tuileries. On the day before the coronation she requested a private audience with His Holiness. Propelled by the fear that her childless union might be annulled, she confided the fact that her marriage to Napoleon was solely a civil union. Soothing her tears, Pius VII reassured her that the situation would be remedied. There was no possibility of his crowning a couple who were effectively living in sin. Napoleon attempted to change his mind but the Pope remained obdurate. He had made numerous concessions about the nature of the service, but there would be none made about this. Unwilling to have the coronation delayed or cancelled, Napoleon had no choice but to give in. That night, in a secret service, Cardinal Fesch married Napoleon to a triumphant Josephine before an altar erected in the Emperor's study.

Hours before daybreak on 2 December 1804 the Tuileries were awake and alive with activity. In order to stick to the strict timetable the Emperor had drawn up, some courtiers had decided against going to bed; others had had their hair done the previous evening and had slept sitting up in chairs until it was time to finish dressing. By dawn crowds were gathering on the bitterly cold streets. Snow had turned to rain, and both troops and public were soaked by the icy slush churned up by the procession.

At six o'clock Isabey had arrived to paint Josephine's face and to oversee her robing. After her meticulous make-up, her hair was transformed by her *coiffeurs* into a mass of shining chestnut ringlets, and a diadem of pearls interlaced with diamond leaves was perched atop. Then her ladies helped her into a long-sleeved gown of white satin, embroidered with gold and silver.

Its bodice was cut in a low square on the bosom, with a small collar of lace rising from the shoulders and encircling the neck, and its full skirt and long train were embroidered with golden bees. Her necklace and earrings were carved gems set in diamonds and on her finger she wore a ring with a ruby, the symbol of joy. The transformation complete, Josephine – a vision of diamonds and gold – waited patiently for Napoleon. He had awoken in high spirits and begun dressing, according to his valet, whistling tunelessly. But soon the great warrior, overwhelmed by a mass of jewellery and unfamiliar garments, was completely flustered and running late.

At seven a contingent of officials, dressed in their official robes, made their stately way on foot from the Palais de Justice to Notre-Dame and joined the first guests in the freezing interior of the church. (Percier and Fontaine's redecorations had so altered the appearance of the church that one observer noted, 'So much work has been done that God Himself would lose His bearings.') Promptly at nine, the Pope set out from the Tuileries. His state carriage, topped with a large papal tiara, was escorted by four squadrons of dragoons and preceded by a papal chamberlain riding a mule and carrying a large wooden cross. The incongruity of the sight prompted laughter from some of the spectators but a surprising number, overwhelmed by long-suppressed religious feeling, dropped to their knees in awe. The pontiff was followed by the rest of the cortège, including Marshal Murat, governor of Paris, and his staff, four squadrons of carabineers, four squadrons of cuirassiers and the chasseurs of the Guard, as well as numerous carriages carrying various ministers, visiting dignitaries and the princes and princesses.

Almost two hours behind schedule, at 10 a.m., the Imperial coach set out from the palace, announced by a gun salute. Escorted by twenty squadrons of cavalry, the carriage had been designed by Fontaine especially for the occasion. A 'great gilded and painted cage', it was drawn by eight magnificent horses with white head plumes and plaited manes and tails, with a footman walking at the head of each. On its roof was set a giant crown borne by four eagles; the rest of the coach, lined with white velvet embroidered in gold, was embossed by the eagles, bees and laurel that were the Empire's new emblems. Through its eight great glass windows Napoleon and Josephine could be seen clearly as they sat opposite Joseph and Louis Bonaparte. It was 'an amazing sight', recounted Napoleon's former mistress Mlle George. Noting merely that the Emperor was 'calm and smiling', her attention – like that of most of the crowd – was fixed on his wife. 'The Empress Josephine looked "regal" as always', displaying 'perfect taste in her dress' and blessed with that 'benevolent manner that so attracted you to her'.

At a quarter to twelve the Imperial coach arrived at Notre-Dame. As the Bonapartes descended from the carriage, the crowd caught its breath at the sight of the Empress, 'her expression of bliss, of her graceful majesty and simplicity'. The Imperial couple entered the tent that had been erected beside the cathedral to serve as a robing room. Napoleon attached his purple velvet mantle embroidered with bees over his long satin garment, while Josephine covered her robe of white satin with the Imperial mantle of purple velvet lined with ermine and exchanged her diamond diadem for one dominated by amethysts. When she emerged from the robing room Josephine was breathtaking. 'She carried the diadem she was wearing as if it was weightless,' one observer remembered later. 'Acknowledging her entourage with all the goodness and encouraging warmth that was intrinsic to her . . . Ah! it is true she was really good, that wonderful woman! The elevation of her position had not changed her: she was a woman of spirit and of heart.'[19]

The procession passed through the wooden passage into Notre-Dame, where many had been waiting in the draughty church for several hours, sustained only by the sausage-filled buns that were being surreptitiously peddled amongst them. At the head of the procession were the heralds, the pages, the ceremonial aides and the grand master of ceremonies. In front of Josephine walked Murat, bearing the Imperial crown on a velvet cushion. To the right and left of her were the chamberlain and first equerry. Behind her in sequence walked Napoleon's sisters, then Napoleon and behind him his brothers Joseph and Louis. Conspicuous by their absence were the banished Jérôme, the self-exiled Lucien and Mme Letizia who had gone to join him. (In order to keep up appearances, the artist David later added her to his painting of the occasion.)

The duchesse d'Abrantès described the moment when Josephine descended from the throne and advanced towards the altar, where the Emperor awaited her:

> One of the chief beauties of the Empress Josephine was not merely her fine figure, but the elegant turn of her neck, and the way in which she carried her head; indeed, her deportment altogether was conspicuous for dignity and grace. I have had the honour of being presented to many real princesses, to use the phrase of the faubourg Saint-Germain, but I never saw one who, to my eyes, presented so

perfect a personification of elegance and majesty. In Napoleon's countenance I could read the conviction of all I have just said. He looked with an air of complacency at the Empress as she advanced towards him; and when she knelt down – when the tears which she could not repress fell upon her clasped hands, as they were raised to Heaven, or rather to Napoleon – both then appeared to enjoy one of those fleeting moments of pure felicity which are unique in a lifetime, and serve to fill up a lustrum of years. The Emperor performed every action required of him during the ceremony with peculiar grace; but his manner of crowning Josephine was most remarkable: after receiving the small crown surmounted by the cross, he had first to place it on his own head, and then to transfer it to that of the Empress. When the moment arrived for placing the crown on the head of the woman whom popular superstition regarded as his good genius, his manner was almost playful. He took great pains to arrange this little crown, which was placed over Josephine's tiara of diamonds; he put it on, then took it off, and finally put it on again, as if to promise her she should wear it gracefully and lightly.'[20]

Fittingly it was this image of Josephine kneeling before her husband, having the crown placed on her head, that David chose to make the centrepiece of his representation of the coronation.

With the sacred element of the ceremony over, the Bonapartes began to return to their thrones. As Josephine descended the precarious steps, the Bonaparte sisters seized an opportunity to take their revenge on their loathed sister-in-law, dropping her heavy mantle. Josephine stumbled and would have fallen if a deadly look and a sharp hiss from Napoleon had not brought his sisters to heel. But not even this mishap could tarnish the day for Josephine. As they drove through the cheering crowd, she was wreathed in smiles. Indeed, Mlle Avrillon remarked, 'Never have I seen on any face an expression of joy, of contentment, of good fortune, to compare with that which animated the figure of the Empress; she was radiant.'[21] Back at the Tuileries, whose palace and gardens were illuminated by thousands of lights, the magic continued. Decreeing that he and his new Empress would dine tête-à-tête, Napoleon insisted that Josephine wear her crown throughout the meal, 'because it was so becoming, because she looked so pretty', and because 'no one could wear a crown with more grace'.

Sixteen

EMPIRE

Grandeur has its constraints . . .

NAPOLEON

THE ROLE OF IMPERIAL CONSORT shaped Josephine's life from this point until her death. It was a role that she had not been born into, trained for, nor aspired to, but it was nonetheless her fate. The old Martiniquan soothsayer had proved correct, she was indeed 'greater than a queen': she was an empress or, as her official title put it, 'Empress of the French'. It was a demanding position and a frustrating one, involving as it did a life of constraint and constant scrutiny. Although Napoleon was determined that she wasn't seen to have any official political power, she was expected to play a central role in the social, cultural and ceremonial life of the nation. Above all, she was expected to symbolize the Napoleonic regime in all its power and grandeur.

Since Josephine had no significant experience of court life, she had to acquire the skills entirely 'on the job', learning from her mistakes and picking up what she could as she went along. Her upbringing amongst the intricate hierarchies and internecine squabbles of plantation life may have provided some oblique preparation for this new life, but in the main it was Josephine's own adaptable, sensitive and charismatic personality that steered her through.

Her role was a particularly important and difficult one in these whirlwind years when the face of Europe was transformed by cataclysmic successions of war and peace. Her reign took place against a backdrop of legendary battles: Austerlitz, Jena, Eylau, Essling, Wagram. During this tumultuous period 'Austria was twice conquered, Prussia was destroyed and Russia subdued. Spain was invaded, Italy constituted, Germany confederated, and Poland regenerated.'[1] Despite these challenges, and the overwhelming fear of being put aside, Josephine excelled at a role that defeated many who were born to it, putting her own elegant stamp on the queenly function and emerging as one of France's most beloved female sovereigns.

For several weeks after her coronation Josephine was swept up in a stream of celebrations. Paris was *en fête*, its streets alive with fair-shows, dancing-booths, maypoles, merry-go-rounds and travelling musicians. The populace was enriched by the Emperor's heralds-at-arms throwing coronation medals to the crowd, and excited by a number of balloon launches. The first of these official events, the fête of the 'Distribution of the Eagles', was literally a wash-out, when a relentless downpour mingled with snow, turning the ground at the Champs de Mars into 'a lake of mud' and forcing the spectators to flee in their ruined court dresses and uniforms. (A belief that Napoleon could control even the weather led some to claim, rather implausibly, that 'the rain did not wet them'.) More successful were subsequent events: the 'colossal feast' given by the City of Paris in the Hôtel de Ville; the ball held by the Ministers of War and the Navy at which the supper alone – prepared by the famous chef Véry – cost an exorbitant 60,000 francs; the concert held in Josephine's honour at an Opéra decorated with silver gauze and wreaths of flowers; and the opening of the legislative body attended by the city's most elegant citizens, where the Empress was serenaded by what was rapidly becoming the sovereign's signature tune: Gluck's *Iphigénie*.

Once these events began to die down, Josephine had a few months to come to terms with the challenge of being Empress. In this new life every move she made, every item of clothing she wore and almost every word she uttered were circumscribed by a maze of ceremony, convention and protocol. The elaborate structure of court etiquette was compiled by the comte de Ségur, in a publication entitled *Étiquette du Palais impérial*. This document effectively laid out the ceremonial required for all occasions and explained in minute detail the protocol of the Imperial day, whether Napoleon and Josephine were in residence in Paris or travelling abroad. It explained who could be presented at court and how close the differing categories of guests were allowed to get to the Imperial couple. It stipulated the disposal and use of the various rooms in the Imperial residences. It dictated the appropriate number of Imperial dignitaries and attendants required to attend court, explaining their precise duties and describing the exact spot where each was to be stationed. Many of these rules were of Byzantine complexity. Chapter II, which was headed 'On the Arrangement of Apartments and on the

Rights of Entry into Each One of Them', had forty-eight precisely detailed paragraphs. Chapter V, 'On the Meals of Their Majesties', had forty-three paragraphs and included information on etiquette such as 'when Their Majesties eat in Public'. Chapter XII, 'Court Mourning', covered in detail every possible eventuality.

Every moment of Josephine's daily routine was dictated by an immutable code of etiquette. Unlike Marie Antoinette, whose household was virtually independent from those of her husband and the other members of the royal family, Josephine's household was not separate from that of Napoleon. As a regulation of 1804 explained, 'His Majesty has decided to have only one household and only one administration.' So the chief of each department in the Empress's household was under the authority of the chief of the equivalent department in the household of the Emperor.

Thus the Empress's apartments, like the Emperor's, were divided between the *service d'honneur* and the *service des besoins* – the official and the private. In the former, where Josephine received, the rooms were arranged virtually identically whatever the palace, including an ante-chamber, a first salon, a second salon and the Empress's own salon. Her private apartments comprised a bedroom, a library, a dressing room, a boudoir and a bathroom. In both sets of rooms careful rules regulated who was allowed to enter and into which rooms they could go, as well as how the Empress and her visitors should conduct themselves. Ladies of higher rank were allowed chairs, while those of lower rank were provided with stools on which they were expected to perch, their legs always crossed. Josephine was not permitted to receive into her inner sanctum any man who was not in her service.

Whenever Josephine travelled she had escorts of infantry and cavalry. At every town border she was met by the appropriate official, whether prefect or mayor, as all the bells tolled. According to the Napoleonic historian Masson, the ceremonial was even more complicated when Josephine entered a fortified town. Then 'the entire garrison was under arms; the cavalry went forward to meet her at the distance of half a league, the trumpets sounded the march; the officers and the standards saluted . . . and the soldiers presented arms; the drums beat a salute and the artillery of the fortress fired three salvos'.[2] Her place of abode was guarded by a battalion of infantry with a flag, commanded by the colonel; before the door stood two sentries, sword in hand. If she drove through the town the troops on guard presented arms and the drums beat a salute, on both her arrival and departure. When she visited a port she was similarly received. And when she went on board a vessel, the Imperial flag was hoisted and saluted with seven shouts of '*Vive l'Empereur!*' as the guns were fired. Then, when she returned to Paris after a prolonged absence, her arrival was announced by cannon, and all the constituted bodies came to give homage as she sat on her throne surrounded by her household.

Aware that Marie Antoinette's informality had facilitated some of the lurid speculations about her, Napoleon demanded that Josephine live as formally as possible, even when he was away from Paris. He wrote to her from Poland that she should be surrounded by 'an appropriate splendour' when in Paris. If she went to the Opéra she should always use the Imperial box: 'Grandeur has its constraints: you cannot go where a private person can.' In another letter he wrote, 'I desire that you never dine except with persons who have dined with me.' The message was always the same: 'Live as you do when I am in Paris ... If you do differently, you will displease me.' Aware that her illustrious husband received detailed information about her every move, Josephine knew that she would be called to order for any infraction of procedure and endeavoured to comply.

The price Josephine paid for her obedience was high: she was never alone and there was virtually no time when she could relax and be herself. Her life, wrote one of her biographers, was that of a 'favourite Sultana'.[3] Like her cousin, the unfortunate harem conscript Mlle de Rivery, she endured a guarded, closed palace life, the torture of perpetual jealousy and the incessant fear of being repudiated. It was a miracle in this claustrophobic, oppressive atmosphere that Josephine 'was able somehow to accept and carry out these stifling routines with skill, sympathy, invariable elegance, and at least outward pleasure'.[4]

Josephine's new life was highly peripatetic. During the following five years she spent only twelve months in Paris. Two years were spent travelling abroad and within France: she passed thirteen months at Saint-Cloud, eight months at Malmaison, three and a half months at Fontainebleau and one month at Rambouillet. But even these periods were deceptive, since none of them represented a continuous sojourn: her months at Saint-Cloud, for example, covered seven separate trips. These did not include her annual spa visits to Plombières or Aix-la-Chapelle. In this period she also visited the borders of the Rhine, spent nearly six months at Strasbourg and four months at Mainz, visited Germany, Italy, Belgium and north, south and central France. Since Napoleon acquired more palaces than any contemporary European or French monarch – forty-four in total – her time was spread very thin.

Some stability was provided by the regular manner in which the Empress's life was ordered. Whatever the names of the palaces through which she passed, they all looked uncannily the same. Protocol required that they were laid out almost indentically and decorated in the sumptuous Empire style with its Beauvais or Gobelins tapestries, heavy gilded seats ranged against the wainscoting, and big console tables supporting heavy crystal vases. In these familiar, if rather impersonal surroundings, Josephine was accompanied by her faithful retinue who went with her virtually everywhere. The personnel of her household was extensive, composed of roughly one hundred people. At its head was the first almoner, Ferdinand de Rohan, a bishop and member of one of the most powerful families in France, who attended her on all public appearances. The most important figure in her household was the *dame d'honneur*, or principal lady-in-waiting. She organized the Empress's household, supervised the servants, kept an eye on Josephine's expenditure and was responsible for deciding on presentations and invitations. For the duration of most of her reign, this role was played by la comtesse Alexandre de La Rochefoucauld, a distant cousin of Alexandre de Beauharnais, who had been imprisoned as a suspect during the Terror and met Josephine soon after both had been released. A *grande dame* with a haughty manner and a vicious tongue, she was heartily disliked by the Emperor, who described her as 'a little cripple, as stupid as she is ugly'. She would, in the end, betray Josephine.

Under the principal lady-in-waiting were a number of *dames du palais*, or ladies-in-waiting. The Empress had twenty, while Marie Antoinette had had only sixteen. Josephine also had seventeen ladies of the palace, rising to thirty by 1807. Amongst these were ladies of the wardrobe, ladies of the bedchamber and a *lectrice* (reader). Among her male staff, there was a first equerry in charge of her stables and a first chamberlain whose duty it was to present ambassadors to her. Beneath him were four 'ordinary' chamberlains who assisted him in carrying out his duties. She also had three more equerries and a private secretary. Lower down the scale were a number of *huissiers* (ushers), who stood guard with halberds at the entrances to her two salons and decided whether one or both wings of the door should be flung open. There were four personal *valets de chambre*, two footmen and two pages, one preceding her and the other carrying Josephine's train whenever she left her apartments. As the court grew, so did the number of attendants – by 1809 there were six ushers, seven *valets de chambre* and twenty-six footmen. These were the people directly serving the Empress and did not include the menials necessary for routine housekeeping. These people – with whom Josephine passed every day, all day – or at least a select coterie of them, became her inner circle, something of a surrogate family. They provided an emotional anchor for her in her nomadic and hermetic Imperial life, and she lavished attention on those whose interests she championed.

Josephine's daily routine provided another anchor in her turbulent life. Wherever she was, it hardly varied. At eight o'clock in the morning one of her maids (*les femmes de garde-robe*) opened the shutters and gently awakened her mistress, presenting her with an infusion of herbal tea or lemonade. Josephine lazed a moment in bed, nestling in her sheets of embroidered cambric with their matching pillowcases trimmed in Mechlin lace. The door was opened and one of her beloved dogs – the successors to Fortuné – was let into the room, yapping ecstatically. These were usually pugs, but were sometimes fluffy little Pomeranians or at one time a pair of Alsatians. However, none of them enjoyed the privilege of sharing her bed as Fortuné had; instead they slept on a chair in the room of the lady-in-waiting on duty.

After a cuddle and caress of the beloved animal, she slipped out of her embroidered lace dressing gown and muslin nightcap and took a long bath, aromatic with oils and scents. She then put on a corset, a petticoat, a silk dressing gown and a pair of morning shoes made of kid, silk or satin. Crossing to her dressing room, she settled in front of her beautiful mahogany dressing table designed by Biennais, where she began her meticulous toilette. (Her tools – hairbrushes, combs and scissors – were silver, part of a beautiful toilet-set contained in a cabinet made of inlaid wood with steel engravings, and decorated with a miniature of the Emperor.) This included the skin preparations she had invented for herself. Then she put on her make-up. Rouge and powder played a big part in her maquillage, if her expenditure on them was anything to go by; she always had enough to supplement the other women in her entourage.

Josephine then decided what to wear. This was not a simple task. Her extensive wardrobe was kept in a large room, and each morning her maids brought up a selection of dresses in large baskets for her to consider. Josephine, who often changed three or four times daily, nonetheless took these decisions very seriously, often soliciting the opinions of her ladies-in-waiting or of Hortense if she were in residence. In summer her gowns were muslin or batiste; in winter they were made of velvet or a woollen material like cashmere. After this she chose her accessories. Since Josephine's collection of shawls, jewels, hats and gloves was as extensive as her wardrobe of frocks this could take some time. Then the resident hairdresser, usually Herbault, presented himself to dress her hair. For more elaborate events she would summon the celebrity *coiffeur* Duplan from Paris.

Dressed and made-up, one of her ubiquitous little hats perched on her head, Josephine received the bevy of merchants who came regularly to tempt her to purchase their wares, which she bought without considering the price. After this enjoyable retail therapy, she began on her correspondence, dictating recommendations, bills, charitable contributions and letters to those businessmen and officials from whom she obtained the plants, buds and cuttings for her botanical collection. Josephine wrote her more intimate correspondence to her husband, children and family herself. Over the years she had developed a direct and eloquent style that would have elicited praise even from that hard taskmaster, Alexandre. During this time her secretary briefed her about forthcoming state events. Josephine took these meetings very seriously, meticulously learning the names, titles and personal details of those she would encounter. Her efforts were rewarded. People were astonished that she was so well informed about everything; they were flattered by her knowledge of them and went away charmed.

At eleven, Josephine was finally ready for breakfast, served by her maître d'hôtel, Richaud, in her apartments. Bonaparte did not join her, usually breakfasting alone in his office, a meal he polished off with his customary despatch. But Josephine's meal was often shared with Hortense and five or six friends or *dames de service*. The menu seems formidable to modern eyes, including a soup, hors d'oeuvres, entrées, roasts, entremets and sweet dishes. These were accompanied by numerous bottles of Burgundy and followed by coffee and liqueurs. Josephine, like her husband, was not a gourmet, and ate lightly, preferring the gossip to the food. Occasionally the Emperor decided to join them, but he sulked if he did not approve of those present and was often inadvertently rude, teasing people mercilessly and rendering the occasion altogether less relaxed than usual.

After the morning repast Josephine received in the salons on the ground floor. As the guests gradually arrived, she passed her time playing billiards, embroidering or tinkling on the harp. Among her visitors were the spouses or children of émigrés whose cause she had championed, individuals soliciting help and the legion of people who appeared claiming some familial connection. If the weather permitted, at around two o'clock she would take a walk around the grounds. (This was not possible at the Tuileries, since the park was public and she was mobbed wherever she went.) On other occasions she would go for a brief ride. Very occasionally, the Emperor decreed that the court go hunting. Josephine would accompany him dressed in a white satin robe and purple velvet jacket embroidered with gold, and a hat of the same colour decorated with a white plume. Each royal household had its own colours: Hortense wore blue and silver; Caroline pink and silver; Pauline lilac and silver. With its grand costumes and bugles, the hunt was an impressive event. But it was a torture for Josephine, although she enjoyed riding. Much to Napoleon's exasperation, she could barely suppress her tears as they closed in on the unfortunate prey, while the actual kill made her sick.

Josephine then retired to her apartments to begin the evening's grand toilette, a far more intricate affair than the morning's preparations. Despite his quibbling about money, Napoleon expected his wife to appear in full dress every evening. So she changed all her clothes: new lingerie was slipped into; grander, more ostentatious jewellery was selected; a more elaborate hairstyle was created, often incorporating pearls, precious stones, flowers, plumes, combs and a diadem. The selection of gowns from which she chose came in every design and material – gauze, velvet, satin and tulle – and were embroidered in gold and silver and trimmed with lace or braid or fur. Napoleon sometimes came to disrupt the peace of this ritual, teasing his wife, giving instructions to the domestics. Sometimes he would pinch her or ruffle her hair, or tweak her cheeks until she cried out, 'Stop it, Bonaparte! Stop it!' But usually Josephine remained serene throughout his childish boisterousness, using the time alone together to cement their relationship and intercede on behalf of others, obtaining favours and deflecting his constant remarks about her expenses.

Once her toilette was completed, Josephine waited to be summoned to dinner by the prefect of the palace. The meal was scheduled for six o'clock but it was sometimes delayed by one, two or even three hours while Napoleon worked. When he finally arrived the pair usually dined alone; Napoleon would get through his courses in a speedy fifteen or twenty minutes. If dinner was finished by half past six, Napoleon usually returned to his office to attend to urgent matters. For Josephine, who never went to bed before midnight, this was the time to go to her salon and meet with the rest of the court.

Around 10 p.m. Bonaparte retired to bed, often asking Josephine to come in and read to him. He loved listening to her melodious voice, with its languid Creole accent. After he fell asleep she returned to the drawing room, where tea was served at around eleven. Josephine then played patience or billiards or did puzzles before going upstairs. When she was alone with her household the conversation was more free and light, focusing on family goings-on and gossip about the court. Eventually she returned to her apartments. Chatting about the events of the day with her ladies, she began the process of undressing, removing her make-up, applying her night creams and putting her hair up in a fetching little nightcap. Her bedtime toilette was almost as long as the earlier ones and the result was just as becoming. 'She was equally elegant in it,' remarked Napoleon. 'She even got into bed gracefully.'

No matter what intrigues or dramatic events punctuated her life, Josephine always made time for her grooming routine. She had to: she had always relied on her attractiveness to charm others, and by the time the Empire was declared she was forty-one years old, a grandmother, with a husband several years younger than herself who also happened to be the most sought-after man of his age. In addition, the Napoleonic court was a youthful one, replete with young comely beauties, the wives of his precocious military colleagues. Despite this her efforts were very successful; at court and in society Josephine appeared as a goddess of elegance and taste. Napoleon – who, according to Hortense, 'believed that the great affair of women was and should be their toilette' – saw Josephine's interest in fashion as evidence of her intense femininity. No one admired her artistry more than him. He loved watching her dressing and making-up, seeing his wife as the epitome of feminine beauty and elegance, a miraculous outcome of all 'the arts and graces'.

Her beauty routine was long and meticulous. Like Napoleon, Josephine was very particular about cleanliness, bathing daily in an age which considered such behaviour dangerously excessive. She took care of the beautiful hands and feet that Napoleon worshipped with regular pedicures and manicures. There was a part of her toilette that one of her servants described as being 'very secret', in which she used the skin preparations that she concocted herself. (Josephine was something of an amateur cosmetician.) She had discovered the moisturizing properties of glycerine – still the key ingredient in most moisturizers, whatever their price – and she used it in the aromatic oils, skin creams, emollients, astringents, powders, rouge and skin-whiteners that she lavished on her face and body. Her 'pleasant and youthful appearance' continued to attract compliments even into her fifties.

Josephine's preoccupation with beauty and fashion has led some of her biographers to accuse her of being vain and shallow. But there is nothing narcissistic about the process of making-up. To create Josephine's type of polished glamour a woman must be able to see herself dispassionately, she must be honest with herself. In order to create the perfect canvas, she must be aware of every blemish, wrinkle and flaw, so that she can efface them. She must be able to assess which of her features should be emphasized and which she would prefer the observer not to notice. Thus Josephine focused her efforts on her eyes and skin to distract from her bad teeth. She added so much colour to her face that Napoleon could not find a woman beautiful without it. ('What is the matter, madame?' he once asked a woman who appeared without rouge. 'Just up from childbed?') Josephine skilfully created a vision of groomed beauty, a charm enhanced by means of illusion.

No one understood the importance of surfaces better than Josephine. It had been through transforming her appearance and style at the convent that she had made herself into a *Parisienne*. Her skill at these feminine 'arts' had kept her afloat during those terrible times after the Revolution. Now it was these same beauty routines that helped her to metamorphose into an empress. The significance of these rituals was more than physical, they were psychological too. These times were healing interludes, whose repetitive actions, like words chanted during a meditation, allowed her the space to collect herself, so that she could carry on being the equanimous, eternally good-natured woman everyone expected her to be. Josephine at her dressing table was like an actress before a mirror, making herself up for a part. The ceremony of preparing her face and putting on her make-up gave her the time and the confidence – liberated the energy – to 'become' someone anew. Once applied, the same make-up that gave her courage also gave her a sense of protection, providing a mask, a 'decorative barrier' between herself and society.

As one of history's great style icons, Josephine's influence on the way an entire generation wanted to look, dress and behave cannot be overstated. She was the wife of the world's most powerful man, and the most visible female figure of her era. Her every action and nuance of appearance were followed eagerly by newspapers and journals in France and abroad. She was the high priestess of style, and fashion-conscious women the world over idolized her. They pored over fashion journals like *Le Journal des Dames et de la Mode*, the era's version of *Vogue*, in order to see what Josephine was wearing, and attempted to copy her style. Josephine reinforced Paris's position as fashion capital of the world, which in turn boosted French industry.

It is ironic, therefore, that the fashion of the Empire, which Josephine did so much to popularize, was not really to her taste at all; she found all the lace and embroidery too fussy and formal. Her own inclination was towards simplicity, but she understood that her preferences did not coincide with Napoleon's priorities. So she evolved a style that supported the value he placed on promoting France's luxury trades, as well as reinforcing his belief in the power of conspicuous display to strengthen public awareness of the confidence of his new regime. The result was a melange of Greek purity and European sumptuousness, mingling the neoclassical aesthetic which had been so dominant since the Revolution with the revival of interest in the Middle Ages, known as the 'troubadour style'. Hence the preference for embroidery and the raised lace collar, or cherusque, that had become part of court dress. The grace with which Josephine wore these grand costumes belied just how uncomfortable they were: stiff and heavy and often overlaid by a cumbersome manteau.

Her 'look' was created in collaboration with the dressmaker Leroy, who had become one of the most important men in her life. He was a rather unpleasant man who managed to combine, according to Josephine's maid Mlle Avrillon, 'fatuity and affectation'. He was a horrible snob: 'haughty with the humble, unctuous and craven with the well born', but nonetheless a genius with the scissors. Leroy's designs showed Josephine off to the best possible advantage. She was his most important client: her position, income and impeccable taste enabled him to create his most original toilettes. In time he became something of a confidant, one of the few men who had entry to her *cabinet de toilette*. She stood as godmother to his granddaughter Finette, and the closeness of their relationship enhanced his stature. Their intimacy was such that Leroy once took it upon himself to speak to Napoleon about allowing Josephine more money for her wardrobe. According to Napoleon's account of this meeting, he was so outraged at Leroy's audacity that he silenced the dressmaker with his famous 'look'.

The allure of Josephine's celebrity enhanced Leroy's fame and attracted new clients. Under her patronage he became the leading *marchand de modes* of the early nineteenth century and a celebrity in his own right. Women flocked to his prestigious address in the rue de Richelieu, where they were waited upon by servants in liveries of light blue edged with black velvet. His prices were astronomical; his clientele was made up of those men and women who formed the European elite. His trademark was gold embroidery, revived during the Directoire because it was associated with the old regime and reflected new attitudes towards luxury.

Josephine's wardrobe, her styling, her hostessing, her entertaining, her conversational skills and her interest in and knowledge of arts and culture were all part of the job, and she invested prodigally in their upkeep. An inventory of her wardrobe taken in 1809 listed 49 grand court dresses, 676 dresses, 60 cashmere shawls, 496 other shawls and scarves, 498 blouses, 413 pairs of gloves and over 200 pairs of silk stockings. It did not include 533 items that she had given away to her friends and family.

Her jewels were just as formidable. The young girl whose baubles could fit in a single pocket was long gone. Now her collection of gems was too vast to fit into Marie Antoinette's jewel chest. An inventory taken after her death revealed 'a dazzling treasure': 'her jewellery collection', according to one of her ladies-in-waiting, 'could have figured in a tale of Arabian Nights'.[5] It included rubies from the East and from Brazil, emeralds, opals, sapphires, turquoises, mosaics, corals, agates and cameos, ten necklaces of real pearls and a superb necklace of twenty-seven diamonds that would eventually be purchased by Tsar Alexander I. One of the tiaras, which she had worn on the day of the coronation, was composed of 1,049 diamonds, weighed 200 carats and was mounted in platinum. On her death this astonishing piece was bequeathed to her daughter and is now part of the Van Cleef & Arpels collection in New York.

It is no wonder that the only area of consistent conflict between Napoleon and Josephine was finances. Despite the pride he took in her appearance, and his frequent requests that she appear at her 'dazzling best in jewellery and costume', Napoleon constantly grizzled about paying her bills. When he went through her accounts in 1805 (and again she confessed to only half of her debts) Napoleon forbade her entire household to receive any items from retailers and instructed that any visiting tradesmen be diverted to her comptroller. But determined merchants still flocked to the palace and Josephine still managed to see them. When Napoleon found the old milliner, Mlle Despeaux, sitting in the blue salon at Saint-Cloud, he bellowed for the guards to imprison her. (He soon relented and she was released before she reached the palace gates.)

Mme de Rémusat astutely argued that Napoleon 'liked people to contract debt because it kept them in a state of dependence. His wife gave him complete satisfaction in the latter particular, and he would never put her affairs in order so that he might reserve the power of alarming her.'[6] There is no doubt, however, that Josephine was one of the great shoppers of all time, who bought for the sheer joy of buying. Bourrienne, who often had to act as a buffer between the Imperial couple over these matters, was shocked by the amount of money she could fritter away on nonsense. Merchants often overcharged her, knowing that she would pay whatever they asked and also that they would have to wait a long time for their money. Her mania for spending 'was almost the sole cause of her unhappiness', said Bourrienne. Today we would probably describe her shopping as an addiction and send her into therapy.

Despite these little squabbles, Josephine's style and beauty could still enrapture Napoleon. Laure Junot described Josephine's dress one night at Saint-Cloud and its impact on her husband: 'Josephine was a vision in misty-white Indian muslin, with a narrow lamé border like a rivulet of gold around the hemline of the pleated skirt, a gold-and-black enamelled lion's head at each shoulder and another as a clasp for the golden belt. Her coiffure was like that of an antique cameo, curls spilling out of a golden circlet, and she wore a golden serpent for a necklace, with matching earrings and bracelets.' If there was a striking simplicity in her costume, it was simplicity of the most artful kind; if it was tremendously becoming, it was because Josephine always adapted the mode to her person – one explanation for her reputation as the most elegant of women. ' "It was clear that the Emperor was as struck as I by her charming ensemble, for he went to her as he entered the room, kissed her on the shoulder and the brow, and led her to the mirror over the mantel, so that he might see her from all sides at the same time." '[7]

Josephine's royal status was confirmed in 1805, when she became Queen of Italy. Earlier that year a delegation from Lombardy had arrived at the Tuileries requesting that Napoleon become their king. His first thought was to offer the crown to his brother Joseph. Since one of the terms of Napoleon's offer was that Joseph would have to renounce his position as heir to the French throne, he refused. Bonaparte then offered the kingdom to his grandson Napoleon-Charles. But the child's father, Louis, also refused. Louis did not want to see his son elevated above him, nor was he willing, he wrote, to give any credence to the unpleasant rumours being circulated in 'the English slander sheets' about the child's paternity.

Reluctantly, Napoleon accepted the crown for himself and informed the Italians that he would go to Milan to be crowned. By early April the Imperial party was on its way, arriving in Lyon on 10 April, where they were fêted with the prescribed ceremonies and celebrations. After a week they once again set off, this time on mules for the arduous journey over the Mount

Cenis Pass. On 24 April they arrived in Turin, where they had a meeting with the Pope and his large and noisy entourage. On 8 May the Imperial party arrived in Milan where they were received rapturously with cannon fire and pealing church bells. They were lodged at the Monza Palace, where Josephine was assigned an Italian household of the noblest Milanese ladies.

The coronation was held at the gleaming marble cathedral opposite the palace, in front of cheering crowds and with great pageantry. Although Josephine took her place in the procession, this time she was not an active participant in the ceremony. Instead, she sat in the gallery attended by her sister-in-law Élisa, who had nagged Napoleon into giving her the small Italian principality of Piombino. They watched Napoleon being honoured with the famous iron crown – actually a circle of faded gold, decorated with irregular jewels and enamelwork, and enclosing a slender band of metal believed to have been a nail of the True Cross brought by the Empress Helena from Jerusalem. Napoleon took the crown, placed it on his own head and said loudly in Italian, 'God gives it to me; woe to him who touches it.'

Napoleon made it clear that he wished the celebrations to be reminiscent of those of Imperial Rome. So the next day games and chariot races were held in the arena of Castello. That evening, in sharp contrast to this homage to antiquity, a very modern display was presented: a female aeronaut made a balloon ascent, scattering flowers over Napoleon and Josephine. 'In one day', reported *Le Moniteur*, 'the Italians combined what to the ancients was most spectacular and what to modern science was most daring, in the presence of a hero who surpasses both the ancients and the moderns.'

On 7 June Napoleon summoned the legislative assembly and announced that Eugène was to be his viceroy, to govern Italy in the absence of its king. His stepson immediately took an oath of fealty and made plans to settle in the country. Josephine's feelings were ambivalent: pleased and proud for her son, desperately upset at being forced to live so far from him. On the day they were scheduled to depart she wept. Napoleon's response, according to Mlle Avrillon, was brutal: 'You are crying, Josephine. That is insensitive of you. You cry because you must part with your son. If the absence of your children causes you so much pain, guess what I must always feel. The affection which you display for them makes me feel bitterly the unhappiness of having none myself.'

Shortly after, Napoleon left Josephine to inspect the major fortified cities of northern Italy while she went to visit the Italian lakes. His letter addressed from Brescia was much more good natured: 'I have received your letter, my good little Josephine, and I learn with pleasure that bathing is doing you good . . . Lake Como will be good for you . . . Be sensible, gay and happy. Such is my will.'[8] Soon the couple were reunited in Genoa, where they were received with grandeur. Before an enormous crowd they were installed on a barge designed as a floating temple, which was then rowed out to the middle of the bay. Four huge rafts decorated with trees, flowers, statues and fountains were towed alongside them. Magnificent fireworks illuminated the town and the boats assembled on the water. When they reached Turin they received news that made it clear they should return to Paris immediately – war loomed again.

Talleyrand had uncovered intelligence that Austria was again on the warpath. Napoleon's decision to crown himself king of their former possession, Italy, was the final provocation. Napoleon received incontrovertible proof of this from his Foreign Minister while at Boulogne, where he had gone directly from Italy to inspect his army in advance of the proposed invasion of England. Although preoccupied with matters of strategy, Napoleon's letters to Josephine, who was now at Plombières taking her annual spa treatment, were warm and teasingly affectionate: 'I have a fine army here and a fine fleet, everything I need to pass the time agreeably; only my sweet Josephine is missing, but I should not say that, in matters of love women are better kept in suspense, uncertain of their power.'[9] Napoleon's conciliatory tone was in part prompted by guilt. He had taken an attractive Italian companion with him to Boulogne and it was with her that he was 'passing the time agreeably'. But Josephine held her tongue, as she had promised her family and friends she would. In a letter to Eugène, she confessed this new strategy was working well: 'The Emperor is always very sweet to me and I also do everything in my power to make things agreeable: no more jealousy, my dear Eugène, I really mean it. He is happier that way and I am happier as well.'[10]

   Napoleon's plan was audacious: he would lead his army across Europe and confront the Austrians and Russians. Then he would swing back to the Channel and invade England. Not wishing to be parted from her husband for any longer than necessary, Josephine lobbied to accompany him, at least as far as Strasbourg. She won the day and on 24 September they departed the Tuileries in the Emperor's sleeping coach. After fifty-eight hours of travelling non-stop – according to Constant, buckets of water had to be splashed over their steaming wheels at every relay – they arrived at Strasbourg. There they were housed in the splendid episcopal palace of a great French noble family, the Rohans. This residence had claimed its place in history as the house where the fourteen-year-old Marie Antoinette spent her first night on French soil. Until recently it had housed a hotchpotch of offices, archives and even a few prisoners. But Napoleon had dispatched his architect Fontaine to put it in order for their arrival, and within a couple of weeks the apartments were restored. Fourteen rooms were at the disposal of the Empress and her retinue.

The first four days of the couple's stay were taken up with receptions and audiences. But after Napoleon's departure on 1 October Josephine settled down to life on her own. She was deluged with invitations to balls, dinners and concerts, all of which were replete with requests for presentations. First came the authorities of the department and eighty young ladies of the first families of Strasbourg; then Marshal Kellerman and his staff; then the great deputation from the Tribunate, who were to have gone to the Emperor at his headquarters with the army, but then received orders to stay in Strasbourg and 'make it a centre of society'. They were followed by the mayors from Paris, who were on their way to congratulate the Emperor, and then, with the rising tide of her husband's success, the arrival of sundry German royals: the prince of Baden, the prince of Hohenlohe, the hereditary prince of Hesse-Darmstadt.

During these events Josephine's 'royal face' did not slip for a single moment. She was unfailingly punctual and did not miss a ceremony. She greeted each newcomer with a seemingly endless stream of charming small talk, and when she encountered those whom she had met before, she miraculously remembered the names of their wives or daughters or grandchildren. She remained to the end of all the balls, and smiled graciously and continuously. As well as hosting numerous events of her own, she invited performers to come to Strasbourg to entertain them there. The most famous of these was the composer Spontini, whose way she paid from Paris to give performances of *La Vestale*, which he had dedicated to her, and his new composition, *O Salutaris*. To relax, Josephine did what she always did: shop. She bought paintings, china, seeds, plants, animals, toys, bonbons. The amount of money that she injected into the economy was so substantial that the merchants of Strasbourg were inconsolable when she left.

One of the activities that filled her time during this sojourn was a renewal of her interest in freemasonry. At the Orient lodge of Strasbourg, 'franc chevaliers' held a lodge of admission under the direction of Mme de Dietrich, titular grand mistress and wife of Strasbourg's mayor; Josephine presided.

Since she had been initiated alongside Alexandre many years earlier she was in a position to propose a number of new members; the result was that Josephine became very popular with brethren all over the world. Lodges in Paris and Milan took her name and claimed her patronage. This masonic activity was undoubtedly undertaken with Napoleon's blessing (her son Eugène was also a mason); with his policy of fusion, the Emperor cultivated contacts in all circles, especially ones that attracted such illustrious members as that era's freemasons.

Ensconced in her comfortable apartments, Josephine waited for news from Napoleon. His letters, written almost daily, were tender and reassuring, those of a long-standing but still loving married couple. On 2 October he wrote, 'Great operations are now in progress . . . I am well placed for the campaign and I love you.'[11] Two days later, with nothing of interest to report, he wrote, 'Keep well, and believe in my entire affection.' From a town near Stuttgart he wrote explaining, 'You will, my darling, be five or six days without hearing from me; don't be uneasy.'[12] Then he instructed her to purchase a wedding present for the marriage of the son of the Elector to a niece of the king of Prussia. Five days later he wrote to her from Augsbourg, 'The campaign has been successful enough so far . . . Events are unfolding rapidly. I have sent 4,000 prisoners, eight colours to France and captured 14 enemy cannon.'[13]

On 12 October, despite exhaustion and illness brought on by incessant wet weather, he wrote triumphantly, 'My army has entered Munich . . . The enemy is beaten, has lost its head, and everything points to a most glorious campaign, the shortest and most brilliant yet.'[14] On 19 October he concluded, 'My goal has been accomplished; I have destroyed the Austrian army by marches alone; I have captured 60,000 prisoners, taken 120 pieces of cannon, more than 90 colours, and more than 30 generals. I am about to fling myself on the Russians; they are lost men. I am satisfied with my army. I have only lost 1,500 soldiers, of whom two-thirds are but slightly wounded.'[15]

Josephine's celebrations in Strasbourg for her husband's magnificent victories were restrained: she attended a Te Deum in the cathedral and threw a party for the ladies of the town. Meanwhile Napoleon's victorious march continued; on 26 October he started for Munich. Despite his success, Josephine was still desperately anxious. Hearing this, he wrote, 'I received your letter . . . I was grieved to see how needlessly you have made yourself unhappy. I have heard particulars which have proved how much you love me, but you should have more fortitude and confidence . . . You need not think of crossing the Rhine for two or three weeks. You must be cheerful, amuse yourself, and hope that before the end of the month we shall meet.'[16]

On 3 November he wrote briefly, 'My campaign proceeds satisfactorily; my enemies must have more anxieties than I. I wish to hear from you and to learn that you are not worrying yourself.'[17] On the fifteenth he wrote, 'I have been at Vienna two days ... I have not yet seen the city by day; I have traversed it by night. Tomorrow I receive the notables and public bodies. Nearly all my troops are beyond the Danube, in pursuit of the Russians. Adieu, Josephine; as soon as it is possible I will send for you.'[18] What he did not mention was the news he had received about the annihilation of the Franco-Spanish fleet at Trafalgar on 21 October. This defeat was a bitter blow to Napoleon, since it unequivocally put paid to his dreams of invading England. He had once written to Josephine, 'I will take you to London, I intend the wife of the modern Caesar to be crowned at Westminister.'

The following day Josephine received the orders that would allow her to rejoin her husband. She was to travel to Baden, then to Stuttgart, where she was to present the wedding present to Princess Paul, and from there on to Munich. Napoleon instructed her to take enough money to give presents to the ladies and gentlemen who were waiting on her: 'Be civil, but receive full homage; they owe everything to you, and you owe nothing save civility.'[19] With full ceremony, Josephine departed immediately, visiting all the German courts on her way. At Karlsruhe the grand duke of Baden stationed himself at the door of his own palace to receive her while the bells pealed and cannon roared. At Stuttgart, the Elector refused to let her or her entourage pay a single bill in any coffee house or inn. He was a man of such redoubtable proportions that a concave circle had to be cut out of the dining table in order to accommodate his epic belly. His wife, the daughter of George III, was also formidably stout and tall and rather downtrodden. Her only pleasure was in wearing her ill-fitting crown jewels at every opportunity. She was much taken by Josephine, who was kindness itself to the dowdy woman. Napoleon was not surprised when it was reported that she charmed all she encountered: 'I win battles,' he said, 'but Josephine wins hearts.'

In the interim weeks Napoleon fought the most important battle of the campaign. Though he was outnumbered by the Austro-Russian forces two to one, Napoleon believed he could defeat them if he could control when, where and how the engagement took place. The site that Napoleon selec-ted for the confrontation was some land near a village called Austerlitz, a few miles from Brunn. There he hatched a plan to outwit the young and inexperienced Russian commander, the Tsar Alexander. Abandoning the strongest position, the Heights of Pratzen, Napoleon instead stationed the greater part of his troops behind the heights and ostensibly made preparations for a rearguard action designed to protect his retreat. The enemy behaved exactly as he had hoped, and on the night before the battle a gratified Napoleon, watching from the height of his bivouac, declared, 'Before tomorrow night this army will be mine.'

On the day of the battle, 2 December, the first anniversary of the Emperor's coronation, the sun rose, promising a beautiful day. It was the famous sun and sky of Austerlitz, so poignantly described in Tolstoy's *War and Peace*, under which Andrei Bolkonsky lies on his back, wounded, gazing up serenely, at peace with life and death. Napoleon sprung his trap and the enemy was completely wrong-footed. 'Finding themselves attacked, when they thought that they were the attackers,' Napoleon wrote, 'they looked upon themselves as half defeated.' Within five hours the battle was over. The Austro-Russians lost some 26,000 men and the French 9,000, and Napoleon had won what was, beyond any doubt, the most brilliant victory of his career. 'This is the finest evening of my life,' he told an aide.

On 5 December Josephine arrived in Munich. There she received the news of her husband's great victory. Napoleon wrote, 'The Russians have gone, the Battle of Austerlitz is the grandest of all those I have fought. Forty-five colours, more than 150 piece of cannon, the standards of the Russian Guard, 20 generals, 30,000 prisoners, more than 20,000 slain – a horrible sight . . . I look forward with much pleasure to the moment when I can once more be near you.'[20] On 7 December he wrote, 'I have concluded an armistice; within a week peace will be made . . . Goodnight, my darling, I am very anxious to see you again.'[21] In France the victory was the cause of wild rejoicing; peace, they felt, was finally assured.

Josephine was too busy celebrating her husband's victories and charming the Elector of Bavaria and his court to find time to respond. But Napoleon was elated by his success and could not find it in his heart to be annoyed with her. His next couple of letters were uncharacteristically jovial and teasing: 'It is a long time since I had news of you. Have the grand fêtes at Baden, Stuttgart and Munich made you forget the poor soldiers, who live covered with mud, rain and blood?'[22] A week later, he still had not heard from her: 'Great Empress – not a single letter from you since your departure from Strasbourg . . . This is neither very kind nor very affectionate . . .

Deign from the height of your grandeur to concern yourself a little with your slaves.'[23]

His mock annoyance over, Napoleon confirmed his intention of marrying Eugène off to the daughter of Josephine's host, the Elector of Bavaria. This had been mooted several weeks earlier, and one of Josephine's letters to her daughter reveals that she was aware of the plan. Now Napoleon was on his way. On his arrival the reunited Imperial couple discovered that all was not well with the nuptial arrangements. As the Elector explained, his daughter had long been promised to the crown prince of Baden and as a matter of honour he did not wish to betray this agreement. Nor was he thrilled with the prospect of Eugène as a son-in-law. Neither of royal blood nor a head of state, Eugène was merely a 'French gentleman', not nearly good enough for his royal offspring. Could Napoleon not divorce Josephine and marry Princess Augusta himself? The Emperor solved the problem swiftly by making Maximilian of Bavaria a king, adopting Eugène officially and making him 'Imperial Highness', Viceroy of Italy.

In a letter dispatched to Eugène, Napoleon wrote, 'I have arrived at Munich. I have arranged your marriage with Princess Augusta. This morning the princess paid me a visit. She is very pretty. You will find her portrait on a teacup which I am sending you, but really she looks much better.' Josephine too was impressed with her future daughter-in-law, describing her as having a 'charming personality and the beauty of an angel'. When Napoleon instructed Eugène to 'set out with all speed to Munich', his dutiful son-in-law obeyed, making the journey in a record-breaking four days. On his arrival Josephine nagged Eugène to shave off his huge moustache – fashionable amongst the military – in case it repelled the young bride. A wedding contract was swiftly negotiated and on 13 January 1806 the wedding went ahead, with a bare-lipped Eugène. Much to her sadness, Hortense was not present: her quixotic husband had forbidden her to attend. Against the odds, the hastily arranged marriage was successful. As charming and easy-going as always, Eugène was gratified that his eighteen-year-old bride was both beautiful – 'fashioned like a nymph' – and sweet-natured. Largely through their progeny Josephine's blood would eventually be disseminated through most of the royal families of Europe.

Eugène was not the only member of Josephine's family whose fate was decided by Napoleon's foreign policy. The Pressburg Treaty had made Napoleon virtual master of western Europe: the Coalition had been dismantled,

Austria had been rendered innocuous and the Holy Roman Empire was dismembered. Germany was reorganized by the treaty signed on 27 December. Napoleon, now the pivotal player in Europe, set about distributing its component parts to family and allies so as to create a buffer state around France. By this method, and by a series of arranged marriages linking his family with the legitimate dynasties of the continent, he hoped to safeguard his territory. By the end of 1806 two of Josephine's relatives had followed her son into arranged marriages: Stephanie Tascher was offered to the German prince the duc d'Arenberg, while Fanny's granddaughter – pretty Stephanie de Beauharnais, whom Napoleon had officially adopted alongside Eugène and Hortense – was married off in Augusta's stead to the crown prince of Baden.

Napoleon's largesse did not end there. His eldest sister, Élisa, whose bossiness was legendary, was given the principality of Lucca to rule, alongside the Tuscan seaport of Piombino that she had acquired early in 1805. The Kingdom of Naples, which Napoleon had declared extinct on the day the treaty was signed, was given to his brother Joseph. Much to their vexation the Murats were 'only' given the duchy of Berg, rather than a kingdom. But the decision that would have the greatest impact on Josephine was the appointment of Louis Bonaparte to the throne of Holland, which meant that Hortense had to accompany him to the Hague. The idea of being separated from her daughter, who was still desperately unhappy with her husband, was difficult to bear.

Despite these promotions, the Bonaparte family was still not happy. With few exceptions they were disappointed by the titles they had received: either because they were not sufficiently elevated, or because the territory was not sufficiently vast. They were also annoyed on behalf of those brothers who had been excluded from the honours list: Lucien, because he still refused to abandon the mistress with whom he now had four children, and Jérôme, who was still at that time (if not for much longer) with the pretty American wife of whom Napoleon so disapproved. Most of all they were furious at the extent to which Josephine's family had benefited from Napoleon's largesse. The ongoing problem of the succession was also a cause for dissent. Eugène was still in the running, especially now that he had been officially adopted by Napoleon, much to the resentment of Napoleon's brothers, who felt the honour should fall to them. Louis still refused to relinquish his claim in favour of his son, Napoleon-Charles, declaring that he would leave France rather than be 'disinherited'. The only thing that united this feuding clan was their resentment of Josephine and the rest of the Beauharnais and their desire to get rid of them.

Josephine arrived back in Paris on 26 January 1806 and was immediately engulfed by court life with its lengthy rituals and lavish entertainments. In a letter to Eugène dated 13 February she begged his forgiveness for not writing earlier, but explained that, 'the life I lead here is as fatiguing as it is possible to be: never a moment for myself, I go to bed very late and wake up early. The Emperor, who is very strong, copes very well with this busy life, but my health and my soul are suffering a little.'[24] The experience of the Germanic courts, which they had both visited, had whetted Napoleon's appetite for even greater pomp and circumstance. He returned to France determined to further embellish the visual splendour of his palaces and to increase the rituals of the court. At the Tuileries those essential props of court life, a chapel and a theatre, were restored. Rich silk brocade was ordered for the upholstery and wall hangings. The Imperial symbols, already frequent, became ubiquitous: the letter N everywhere, the draperies covered with bees and many furniture items surmounted by an Imperial eagle. Josephine tempered Napoleon's excess somewhat with the decorations she chose for her own apartments. But her taste – which so many admired – displeased Napoleon, who dismissed it as that of a 'kept woman'.

Napoleon regarded the Imperial court as a useful political tool, a vehicle through which he could win over opponents to his regime. He created a new nobility, including dukes, counts and barons, whom he endowed with revenue-producing property. He used the court to raise his own prestige as the nation's ruler and to satisfy his own ambition, vanity and love of splendour. As the writer Stendhal explained, 'If [Napoleon] wanted to be a king, a court was necessary to seduce the feeble French people over whom the word "court" is all-powerful.'[25] The court reinforced a sense of national pride and contributed significantly to national identity. Napoleon made sure that it reinforced his policy of fusion: it included nobles and non-nobles and was much more international than other courts.

If Napoleon's prime motivation in creating a court was pragmatic, his love of splendour and luxury certainly played a part. The Napoleonic court was dazzling. Visually the palaces were mesmerizing: luxurious and grandly appointed. Courtiers glistened with gold and silver embroidery everywhere and medals and ribbons pinned on every chest – while the women circulated in glorious dresses, embellished by diamonds and flowers. At the centre of all this, as both impresario and star, was the Emperor. 'One had to see Napoleon', wrote the duchesse d'Abrantès, 'in the midst of his fabulously luxurious court, himself directing festivities, masked balls, a whole host of pleasures in such good taste that for seven years they made the Court of France the most consummately beautiful in the whole world.'

The excitement of life at court was enhanced by many diversions. For the court was the social centre of Paris; its entertainments – balls, concerts, operas and plays – were the best the country had to offer. 'The sound as well as the sight of the court', according to one historian, 'was intoxicating. The military marches played in the palace courtyards were almost as impressive as the terrified silence which fell on each room when the Emperor entered.'[26] Indeed court life was very dramatic, providing far greater opportunities and risks than private life; and many courtiers found it intoxicating, even addictive. They could not imagine any other life, as Metternich noted when he arrived in Paris as Austrian ambassador in 1806. After presenting his credentials to the Emperor he wrote that 'The whole court together presents a very imposing spectacle and the richness of the costumes is less astonishing than the air of permanence it has acquired: the household functions as if everybody had been doing the same job for a hundred years.'[27]

This air of confidence and outward magnificence obscured darker realities, for the court was not always a pleasant place to be. Napoleon's formidable reputation, the splendour and formality of the costumes, the constellations of courtiers and the officers in full uniform rendered the court so intimidating that women regularly fainted from fear when they were presented. In addition, life at court was 'devoured by ambition', as Stendhal put it. The atmosphere was intensely competitive and, according to Mme de Rémusat, the courtiers were constantly jostling for position: 'A ribbon, a slight difference in dress, permission to pass through a particular door, an entrance to such-and-such a salon – these are the pitiful causes of a constantly recurring vexation.'[28] Alongside this, a pervasive paranoia reigned amongst the courtiers because of the strict surveillance that prevailed. 'Every day', wrote Mme de Rémusat, 'people are more reserved and distrustful. They hardly dare talk about the most harmless matters.' The picture she paints of court life is one of competitiveness, backbiting and anxiety; she concluded, gloomily, that 'Pleasure does not inhabit palaces.'

To a large extent Napoleon was responsible for this strained atmosphere. His perfectionism fostered anxiety in his courtiers, who always worried that they were playing their roles correctly. According to Mme de Rémusat, the

Emperor 'enforced etiquette with the strictness of martial law. Ceremonies gone through as though by the beat of a drum. Everything was done at double-quick time, and the perpetual hurry, the constant fear that Bonaparte inspired, added to the unfamiliarity of a good half of his courtiers with formalities of that kind, rendered the court dull rather than dignified.'[29] The other problem was Napoleon's manner, for if there was an award for the rudest monarch in history, he would probably have won it. Mme de Rémusat wrote, 'Those *grand seigneurs* who fondly believed that they might conduct themselves as they had been accustomed to do in those same palaces, where all but the masters remained unchanged', were swiftly disabused of this notion when 'a harsh word, a peremptory order, the pressure of an arbitrary will soon reminded them roughly that everything was new in this unique court.'[30]

Napoleon could be impatient and irascible with his staff when they irritated him. His tirades against his ministers were also legendary; during one outburst he described Talleyrand as 'shit in a silk stocking'. Even when in a good mood, one of his favourite games was to stir things up amongst his courtiers, suggesting for example that their spouses were having affairs. At an audience in 1806 he quizzed the crown prince of Bavaria about his mistress. When the prince denied having one Napoleon erupted with the words, 'Nonsense, tell me.' He saved his most offensive comments for women, however. His female courtiers ran a gauntlet of abuse. To one he would say, 'What an ugly hat!'; to another, 'Good heavens, how red your arms are.' On one occasion he offered, 'Madame, I heard you were ugly, they did not exaggerate.' Taken aback by these extraordinary attacks, most women were rendered speechless. The exception was the spirited Amy de Coigny, to whom he addressed the ill-mannered query, 'Do you still fancy men as much as ever, Madame?' 'Yes,' she replied, totally unabashed, 'when they are polite.'

His rudeness was in part mitigated by Josephine's tact and charm. Despite the malice and intrigue endemic to court life, she never made any enemies other than the Bonapartes. Napoleon's discourteous behaviour, however, placed an additional burden on her. Josephine's legendary diplomacy was often strained to the limit as she followed in his wake attempting to soothe hurt feelings and smooth ruffled feathers. In contrast to her husband's cavalier attitude to his courtiers, Josephine was kindness itself. She understood the ambitions and anxieties of those surrounding her and wanted to support them. She wrote to Eugène about her desire to do 'something for the people who surround me and contribute every day to making my life agreeable', and she put her words into practice, arranging marriages and helping advance careers.[31]

There were some enjoyable distractions during these months. Early in April 1806 2,500 guests were invited to the Tuileries to celebrate the nuptials of Josephine's niece Stéphanie de Beauharnais and the crown prince of Baden. The guests were treated to a dazzling two-day exhibition of Napoleonic pageantry. The civil ceremony and the signing of the marriage contract took place in the Gallery of Diana and the religious ceremony the next day in the new chapel at the Tuileries. On that day the guests watched as a glittering forty-person parade – including Bonaparte in Spanish costume, the bride in her gown of white tulle starred with silver, and a host of ladies-in-waiting dressed in silk and velvet, their hair crowned with garlands of flowers interspersed with diamonds – processed solemnly to the altar. The facade of the palace sparkled with lanterns and shimmering glass and the skies were lit up by a huge firework display. That day the Empress looked particularly beautiful, wearing 'a gown entirely covered with gold embroidery of different shades and wore, besides the Imperial crown, pearls in her hair, to the value of a million francs.'

The rest of the time, Josephine's routine focused on her pet projects: Malmaison, her botanical collection and her charitable work. Josephine's charitable giving grew exponentially every year: 72,000 francs in 1805, rising to 120,000 francs the next year and 180,000 francs in 1809. As in every other area of her life she overspent considerably, constantly returning to the treasury for funds. Her nickname, 'Our Lady of Bounty', was well deserved. Quite apart from the sums she gave to those now forgotten supplicants who wrote requesting her help, she also dispensed considerable amounts as alms on her official travels. The charities to which she contributed were diverse, but many supported mothers and children: the Charitable Society for Mothers, the maternity hospital in Paris and numerous orphanages. She also gave substantial sums to religious charities and those for the old and infirm.

Josephine's interest in art predated her marriage, and she was responsible for introducing into the Napoleonic court many of the artists who shaped the Empire style. She had befriended the painter Isabey after the Revolution, when he was a teacher at Mme Campan's school. During the Directoire she encountered many of the creative circle – like the artist Prud'hon – that she would later cultivate. With Napoleon's appointment as First Consul she had the financial means to commission and purchase works, and her interest in the arts expanded.

As Empress, Josephine saw her patronage of the arts as part of her role as consort. She understood the importance of cultural endowment in forging a national identity and creating a commercial market, and made it her business to keep abreast of developments in the art world by subscribing to the *Cours historique et élémentaire de peinture ou galerie complète du Muséum central de France*. In 1806 she bought the thirty-two issues of *La Galerie de Florence et du Palais Pitti*, illustrated by Wicar and with notes by Mottez. She had numerous advisors: Mlle Avrillon recalled Josephine's long conversations with Vivant Denon, a rakish survivor of the ancien régime who was responsible for those immortal illustrations of Egypt. He was particularly fond of modern art and Josephine helped him to secure a number of commissions for his protégés. There was also Guillaume Constantin, a failed painter who was the curator of her paintings; Toussaint Hacquin, who restored her pictures; and Alexandre Lenoir, who advised her about objets d'art and sculpture. With their support Josephine developed an eclectic but formidable art collection that included Italian masters like Perugino and Titian as well as contemporary French works.

If Josephine had done nothing but nurture the career of Pierre-Joseph Redouté, she would have deserved her reputation as a patron of the arts. She first met the famous flower painter at the Louvre in the year before she purchased Malmaison, and he visited there a few months after the purchase. From then on, until just hours before she died, he was part of her life. Both had loved plants since childhood. Through his books they would be connected forever, his art immortalizing the garden she had created. Without the security and financial support she provided, Redouté would never have been able to carry out his work. It was Napoleon and Josephine who financed his books as well as popularizing them; buying copies for themselves, encouraging others to buy them and giving them as presents to eminent guests. Redouté's work is today amongst the most expensive botanical art in the world.

Just as much as Napoleon, Josephine understood the importance of cultivating and controlling her popular image, which largely explains what Mme de Rémusat called her 'mania for having her portrait painted'. In these collaborations between artist and sitter, Josephine is captured in all her myriad guises. One of the earliest, a profile sketch by Isabey (1797), depicts her as a model of republican simplicity, in a white dress and matching headkerchief. Five years later there was Andrea Appiani's portrait of her in full Roman splendour, a shawl draped artistically over her arm, the ideal consort for the young Caesar. But her favourite portrait was that by Prud'hon, now hanging in the Louvre, which represents her in meditative mood, lounging in her perfumed garden at Malmaison.

These portraits satisfied Josephine's vanity and allowed her to chart the evolution of her life, much as we do today with photographs, but their chief purpose was propaganda. They were often presented to foreign courts as presents and disseminated within France as reproductions, in prints and on products like commemorative cups, plates, shawls and cards. Collectively they acted as a corrective to the vicious caricatures of her propagated in Britain, as well as contributing to her desired image as Napoleon's consort.

Between wars, more and more of Josephine's time was taken up with the welfare of her vast family, who besieged her with requests for support. The first beneficiary of her generosity was not surprisingly her mother, for whom she provided an annual pension. Despite repeated suggestions that she sell the plantation and buy a property in France, her mother refused to leave her beloved Martinique, preferring instead to live in virtual solitude in a few rooms of the great house at La Pagerie. Others on the island like Aunt Rosette, who had accompanied her to France for her first marriage, also received financial support. Although the one person Josephine really wanted to see refused to come to the metropolis, the rest of her family were more than willing. Her uncle Robert Tascher arrived in France with five of his nine children, also a number of her maternal cousins, the Vergers de Sannois. All of these needed to be housed and supported. The Beauharnais family also benefited from her bounty. Aunt Fanny received an annual pension of 24,000 francs, while her daughter received regular financial support. Other members of the family also profited from their association with Josephine. Alexandre's brother, the royalist François, was named Minister Plenipotentiary in Etruria and later ambassador to Spain. His daughter Émilie, wife of Napoleon's aide-de-camp Lavalette, became one of Josephine's ladies-in-waiting. They joined a growing army of dependants that Josephine acquired, almost 150 in total. These included Euphémie, the loyal half-sister and slave who had followed her to France; Hortense's old governess, Mlle de Lannoy; her first husband's wet-nurse; and his various illegitimate children. There was nothing partisan about these endowments. She gave financial aid to the widow of the deceased revolutionary Collot d'Herbois, when she was dying of cancer, as well as to numerous impecunious royalists. Most telling of all was the pension that she granted to her old enemy, Alexandre's mistress Laure de Longpré. When confronted with the request, Josephine instantly forgave all the wrong this woman had done her, writing in the margins of her recommendation, 'this lady is now very infirm'.

The other side of the family continued to cause problems. In their ongoing campaign against their hated sister-in-law, the Bonaparte clan had found another female morsel to tempt Napoleon away from her. This one was a former pupil of Mme Campan's called Eleonore Dénuelle de La Plaigne, who was currently employed as *lectrice* to Caroline Murat. According to Constant, she was 'tall, well-shaped, dark with fine black eyes, lively and a great coquette'. Her husband was conveniently absent, in prison for forgery. The affair began in February 1806 and the lovers initially met in the suite of small rooms above the Emperor's private apartments in the Tuileries. If visitors arrived, the Emperor's valet was instructed to inform them that he was in a meeting with a minister. Once the relationship had 'taken', however, the Murats conspired to have the girl moved to an isolated cottage, in the hope that she would get pregnant, proving that Napoleon was capable of fathering a child. What passion existed between the pair was one-sided; Eleonore was so bored by Napoleon's company that she would put the clocks forward to hasten his departure.

Josephine had grown resigned to these affairs, and, on the advice of family and friends, she again attempted to curb her jealousy. She took consolation from Mme de Rémusat, who explained to her that to be Napoleon's mistress would always be 'unsatisfactory . . . He was not of a nature to compensate a weak and loving woman for the sacrifices she would have to make for him, nor to afford an ambitious one the means of exercising power.' Being his wife was a better deal, because at least Josephine had 'a grand and enviable position, gratifying to one's pride at least'. Josephine knew that her husband still had strong feelings for her and regarded her as his talisman, 'one of the rays of his star'. Her only real problem would occur if one of his mistresses were to confirm his fertility by becoming pregnant: then, she knew, her fate would be precarious indeed.

By autumn 1806 the Emperor was again preparing for war, this time against Prussia, a nation with a formidable military reputation. Josephine was installed at Mainz where she could more easily follow the campaign and was easier to reach should Napoleon be able to get away. She arrived in the city on 28 September, not realizing that she would be there until mid-January and would not see her husband again for ten months, a separation that would prove fatal for their marriage.

During these months Josephine was accommodated in the chateau of the Electors, which dated from the twelfth century. It was convenient for visits to Hortense and Stephanie, now princess of Baden. But Josephine was miserable during her stay. She missed Napoleon and her family and friends, and found it hard to cope with the uncertainty of war. On 5 October the Emperor wrote, 'I cannot think why you weep; you do wrong to make yourself ill.' Two days later his tone was more reassuring: 'All goes well. My health is perfect.'[32]

On 8 October Prussia, assisted by Saxony, Russia and England, declared war against France. The following day the campaign started. Napoleon swiftly won the battles of Jena and Auerstadt, heaping disaster on the enemy. As he wrote the next day, 'Never was an army more thoroughly beaten and more entirely destroyed.' Prussia was reduced to a fraction of its original territory, occupied, humiliated and liable to a huge war indemnity. Expecting Josephine to be delighted, Napoleon was exasperated to discover that not even his victories had lifted her mood. On 1 November he wrote, 'Talleyrand has just arrived and tells me, my dear, that you do nothing but cry. What on earth do you want? You have your daughter, your grandchildren, and good news; surely these are sufficent reasons for being happy and contented.'[33]

But Josephine was not contented. She had discovered that Eleonore Dénuelle was pregnant, apparently with Napoleon's child. Almost as if she had had a premonition of the future, her letters resonated with anxiety about being separated from her husband. In an uncharacteristically exasperated letter to Talleyrand, dated 11 November, she wrote, 'It is not secrets of state that the Empress Josephine is asking of you, but just what you think about the return of the Emperor. Tell me frankly, what I can hope for. You know how I suffer being away from him.'[34] Two days later in a letter to Berthier, she wrote how 'extremely touched' she was by his reassuring remarks about the Emperor's feelings for her, adding: 'I need to be valued by him and to see that he has not forgotten me; that is my only consolation during his absence, and I see with a great deal of chagrin that his return is less near than I had thought . . .'[35]

Napoleon kept dangling the possibility of reunion, but somehow the moment was always delayed. Josephine grew increasingly anxious and agitated, provoking his irritation and compassion in equal measure. He wrote to reassure her that 'there is only one woman for me', but he was already involved with one of the fair Polish beauties Josephine so feared. The encounter has been as mythologized as everything else about Napoleon. One snowy day towards the end of 1806 Napoleon, returning from his winter quarters in Warsaw, stopped at a posting house to change his carriage horses. There he was met by a volley of cheers from enthusiastic Poles who regarded him as their liberator. Amongst the throng eager to catch a glimpse of him was a blonde girl with pink cheeks. General Duroc declared to his master, 'Sire, look, here is a woman who has braved the dangers of the crowd to see you.' She approached the carriage and (in impeccable French) expressed her gratitude for saving her homeland. In return he handed her one of the bouquets the crowd had tossed him and drove off.

Back in Warsaw, the great conqueror could not get the young woman out of his mind. Duroc was instructed to track down the mysterious stranger. Within days he had discovered that she was the wife of an ageing Polish aristocrat and her name was Countess Marie Walewska. After a reunion at a ball held in his honour, Napoleon decided he must have her. That night he sent her a note that read, 'I saw only you. I admire only you. I desire only you. Answer me at once, and calm the impatient ardour of your N.'[36] But married, virtuous and pious, Marie was reluctant. The next day she received another missive: 'Have I displeased you, Madame? I had hoped otherwise. Was it a delusion on my part? Your ardour has cooled, while mine burns more and more fiercely. You have destroyed my peace! Oh, give some little joy and happiness to the poor heart that longs to worship you! Is it so difficult to get an answer from you? You owe me two.'[37]

Over the following days he continued to besiege her. His seduction strategy was more rape and pillage than hearts and flowers: 'I want to force you, yes *force* you to love me,' he wrote. When she continued to resist him he thundered, 'If you persist in refusing me I'll grind your people into the dust . . .' Walewska continued to resist until her own countrymen, even her husband, hinted that succumbing to Napoleon was her patriotic duty.

In reality the couple's meeting was probably much more prosaic than this story suggests; it may have been engineered by Talleyrand in the hope of sweetening Napoleon's attitudes towards Poland. But there was nothing fabricated about the couple's affair; this relationship was to be one of the longest and most passionate of Napoleon's extramarital liaisons.

Napoleon's letters to Josephine no longer talked of reunion; instead he argued that for her own good she should avoid the journey. On 7 January he wrote, 'the season is cold, the roads very bad and not at all safe, I cannot consent to expose you to so many fatigues and dangers. Return to Paris in order to spend the winter there.'[38] The next day he wrote, 'Paris reclaims you; go there, it is my wish. I am more vexed about it than you. I should have liked to spend the long nights of this season with you, but we must obey circumstances.'[39]

Josephine returned to Paris. Court life resumed as normal and she performed her duties, keeping up appearances by making official visits to manufacturers and monuments, receiving presentations, attending diplomatic receptions, operas and balls. But she was still unhappy. On 16 January her husband wrote, 'Everyone who writes tells me of your unhappiness . . . Why the sadness, the upset? Do not tell me that you lack courage? I sincerely hope not. Do not doubt my feelings, and if you still want to be dear to me in the future, rally your strength and your force of character.'[40] Two days later he was just as stern. 'I hear you are always weeping. Shame! How unbecoming it is! . . . Be worthy of me; display more fortitude. Cut a suitable figure at Paris and, above all, be contented . . . I do not love cowards, an Empress should be brave.'[41]

But it was military matters that preoccupied Napoleon. The Battle of Eylau was a victory, but one that came at a very high price: 25,000 Russians and 18,000 French soldiers perished in the blood-soaked snow. 'To visualize the scene', Napoleon wrote in his victory bulletin, 'one must imagine within the space of three square miles, nine or ten thousand corpses; four or five thousand dead horses . . . the ground covered with cannon balls, shells and other ammunition . . . A sight such as this should inspire rulers with the love of peace and the hatred of war.' He wrote to Josephine, 'This country is covered with dead and wounded. It is not the glorious side of warfare; one suffers, and the mind is oppressed at the sight of so many victims.'[42]

Enmeshed in continued warfare, Napoleon dug in until spring – first in the 'wretched village' of Osterode, and then in the Château de Finckenstein near Koenigsberg. Despite his military preoccupations and the company of the delectable Marie Walewska, his letters to his wife were as controlling as ever. 'If you really wish to please me, you must live exactly as you live when I am in Paris,' he wrote in late March. 'Then you were not in the habit of visiting the second-rate theatres or other places.'[43]

Determined to obey her husband, Josephine attempted to curb her public displays of unhappiness. But her despair remained evident in letters to her children. She wrote to her son, 'Adieu, my dear Eugène. My health is all right, but my heart is very sad because of the Emperor's long absence.' On 7 March, attempting to put on a brave face, she told Hortense that she received news from the Emperor, 'sometimes twice daily; this is a great consolation but does not replace him'.[44] A week later she wrote to Eugène in the same vein: 'I receive the Emperor's letters freqently. His health, as always, is good, but I am really sad about his absence and if it goes on much longer, I do not know if I will find the courage to bear it.'[45]

Then a tragedy befell the entire family. Late in the night of 4 May 1807 Josephine's grandson, the eldest child of Hortense and Louis, died. He had suffered a brief but violent illness, perhaps diphtheria, whose symptoms included a rash and high temperature. The four-year-old's death was, according to one observer, a 'harrowing scene'. He died in his mother's embrace, and Hortense was so distraught that she hooked her arms through the chair and couldn't be removed from him. When she eventually fainted, her unconscious body was removed to her own apartment still seated in the chair she clutched compulsively. When she came round, her piercing shrieks could be heard around the palace. In her hysteria Hortense became delirious, calling for her son, begging for death, unable to recognize those who approached her. As time passed, her condition deteriorated into a catatonic state. For days on end she sat paralysed by grief, her eyes fixed in a dull, glassy stare, her lips grey and her countenance deadly pale. One observer recalled, 'I never beheld grief so painful to witness.'

The death of little Napoleon-Charles was a source of grief to everyone. He had been a charming child, whose friendliness and curiosity had even endeared him to the querulous Bonaparte family. Napoleon adored the little boy, whom he called '*petit chou*' and who referred to him as 'oncle Bibiche'. On every visit to the little boy he hid presents in his pockets and delighted the child by conjuring them up for him. Josephine too was inconsolable. He was her first grandchild and he was Napoleon's heir; with his death, she felt, divorce was inevitable. Napoleon would feel that having his own child was the only possible option.

Despite his undoubted grief, Napoleon's reaction to the loss of his grandson was brusque. On 14 May he wrote to Josephine, 'I realize the grief this death . . . must cause; you can imagine what I am enduring . . . You have had the good fortune never to lose children; but it is one of the pains and conditions attached to our miseries here on earth.'[46] Her distressed response must have displeased him, because six days later he wrote, 'I am sorry to see that you have not been rational. Grief has bounds which should not be passed.'[47] Four days after that he wrote again, 'I am sorry to see your grief undiminished and that Hortense has not yet come . . . she is unreasonable, and does not deserve our love, since she loves only her children. Try to calm her and do not make me wretched.'[48]

Josephine travelled to meet her daughter at Laeken, a chateau in the Brussels countryside. As time passed, under Josephine's maternal care, Hortense slowly began to regain her equilibrium. United in their grief, and their fear for Hortense's health, the family rallied round. Eugène came to visit and his sweet-natured optimism had its usual soothing effect on his sister. He and his wife Augusta had recently had their first child, a girl whom they had christened Josephine. Even Louis, Hortense's husband, rushed to her side. Mme de Rémusat related that he had been 'terrified and grieved' at the state of his wife, and her breakdown brought about a sincere, if temporary, reconciliation. Eventually Hortense recovered enough to take the waters in the Pyrenees, where Louis joined her. There she slowly returned to herself and conceived her third child, the little boy who was destined to become her stepfather's only real heir apparent: Napoleon III.

Another bereavement befell Josephine that summer: the death of her mother. Initially Napoleon ordered that the terrible news be withheld from her, as she was still overcome with grief for her grandson, but eventually she found out. Mme de La Pagerie had remained at Trois-Îlets right to the end, surrounded by her slaves and accompanied by her curate, who had become the devout woman's closest confidant. As befitted 'the mother of the Empress', she was buried with full Imperial ceremony. On 10 June the funeral procession, signalled by cannon fire, crossed the harbour and arrived at the little church in Trois-Îlets, which had been richly decorated for the occasion. There the ceremony, conducted by an imposingly large contingent of clerics, unfolded before the great and the good of the island. At its end the body was interned in an ornate tomb to the sound of a full military salute. And thus the final member of Josephine's birth family was consigned to the grave.

If the summer of 1807 was full of sadness for Josephine, it was one of triumph for her husband. On 14 June he achieved a decisive victory over the Russian Army at the Battle of Friedland. The Tsar quickly saw the wisdom of meeting with Napoleon and their historic three-hour encounter took place at the end of June in the middle of the Niemen, the river that marked the boundary between Russia and Europe. Josephine, who had received eyewitness accounts from Napoleon's household, recounted to Hortense that 'it was a magnificent spectacle. The two armies were ranged on the right and left banks of the Niemen. The Emperor arrived first on a magnificent raft in the middle of the river. The craft of the Tsar was slightly slower in its approach . . . They told me that the moment when the two Emperors embraced was met by universal acclamations from those on both sides of the river.'[49]

Napoleon was much taken with the Tsar. In a letter to his wife dated 25 June he wrote, 'I have just seen the Emperor Alexander. I was much pleased with him. He is a very handsome, young and kind-hearted Emperor; he has more intelligence than people usually give him credit for.'[50] Their treaty was signed on 7 July in the nearby town of Tilsit and ratified two days later. Its terms were a triumph for Napoleon. He had acquired nearly half the territory and population of Prussia. The Tsar also agreed to evacuate the Ionian Islands and the part of Dalmatia held by Russian troops. In addition Alexander undertook to act as mediator between England and France, while Napoleon would do the same between Russia and the Ottoman Empire. Napoleon was jubilant; he had in rapid succession vanquished Austria, Prussia and Russia, and now most of Europe was under his rule.

After ten months away, Napoleon arrived back at Saint-Cloud in July 1807. But the man who returned from Tilsit was very different from the one who had gone away. The conquest of Austria, Russia and Prussia was such an extraordinary achievement that Napoleon now believed he could accomplish almost anything. He saw himself as virtually infallible, protected by destiny – his famous star. He was, according to Talleyrand, 'intoxicated with himself'. His Empire stretched from the Atlantic coast to the steppes of Russia; from the North Sea to the Mediterranean. At thirty-eight years old he ruled over 70 million people, including French, Dutch, Italians, Germans and Poles; it was an Empire unequalled since the days of Rome.

But, as Napoleon himself once remarked, 'Ambition is never content even on the summit of greatness.' Over the following six months he remade the map of Europe: Prussia was dismembered, and a new Poland created; Italy underwent further reorganization. On 1 September the Ionian Islands became part of the French Empire and in the middle of November Napoleon created the Kingdom of Westphalia, appointing his brother Jérôme as king. Now, suspecting that he could father children, Napoleon wished to take his place as head of a dynasty of the crowned heads of Europe, and the right marriage could achieve this for him. All of this, as those surrounding him argued, was predicated on divorce.

Josephine reported these alarming developments to her children. She wrote to Eugène of her suspicions that Murat was coaxing Napoleon into divorce. 'As for me,' she continued:

> *you know that I aspire for nothing but his heart. If they should succeed*
> *in separating me from him, it is not the loss of rank I should regret . . .*
> *sooner or later he would discover that those who surround him are more*
> *interested in themselves than in him, and he would know how he has*
> *been deceived. However, my dear Eugène, I have nothing to complain*
> *of in him, and I am happy to count on his justice and his affection.*
> *As for you, my dear son, continue to behave with the same zeal for the*
> *Emperor; you will command general respect and even the greatest favour*
> *cannot give you this.*[51]

In his reply Eugène confirmed that he had 'heard much about divorce, from Munich and Paris'. But he was reassured by the conversations she had had with the Emperor. If the worst should happen, Eugène argued, 'He must treat you well, give you an adequate settlement and let you live in Italy with your children. The Emperor then will be able to make the marriage which his policy and his happiness demand. We shall remain no less attached to him, for there is no need for his sentiments towards us to change, even though circumstances should have obliged him to separate from our family. If the Emperor wishes to have children who are truly his there is no other way.'

Eventually Napoleon decided it was time to broach the subject of divorce with his wife. Lacking the courage to approach Josephine directly, he elicited Fouché's help. In a private audience with the Empress, Fouché was blunt. Arguing that the nation would never be safe until Napoleon had an heir, he declared that it was her duty to sue for divorce. She immediately demanded to know whether he spoke on behalf of her husband. 'No, of course not,' he replied, 'but my devotion to the dynasty forces me to speak to your Majesty as I do now.' 'It is not a matter that I will discuss with you,' said Josephine. When she spoke to her husband, he denied any knowledge of the conversation and promised to punish Fouché for his 'excess of zeal'.

Napoleon knew he had to talk to his wife himself. Fearing her tears, he raised the subject hypothetically. Speaking with some emotion, according to Mme de Rémusat, he said, 'If such a thing should happen, Josephine, it will be for you to help me to make the sacrifice. I shall count upon your love to save me from all the odium of a forced rupture. You would take the initiative, would you not? You would enter into my position, and you would have the courage to withdraw?' Josephine's answer made it clear that she would obey his orders but never anticipate them. 'Sire,' she said, 'you are the master, and you shall decide my fate. If you should order me to quit the Tuileries, I will obey on the instant, but the least you can do is to give me that order in a positive manner. I am your wife; I have been crowned by you in the presence of the Pope. Such honours at least demand that they should not be voluntarily renounced. If you divorce me, all France shall know that it is you who send me away, and shall be ignorant neither of my obedience nor of my profound grief.'[52] Her calm then cracked, and Josephine broke into fits of weeping; he clutched her to him and his own eyes were damp.

Napoleon was moved by Josephine's response. Mme de Rémusat reported that whenever the subject was revived he wept and was 'genuinely agitated by his conflicting feelings'. Sometimes it seemed that Napoleon was almost as miserable as Josephine, but the uncertainty was taking a terrible toll on her mental health. She wept even more frequently and behind the scenes railed against her husband's behaviour. She recalled that when they had married he had been 'highly honoured' by their alliance and claimed it was ignoble of him to abandon her in his greatness when she had been willing to share his life when his fortunes were uncertain.

As the weeks went on, there was less talk of divorce. Napoleon's problem was that he could only sustain his decision to divorce Josephine when he was away from her. When they were reunited and he was reminded again of the pleasures of her company, his resolve crumbled. As he lamented to Talleyrand, 'I would be giving up all the charm she has brought to my private life . . . She adjusts her habits to mine and understands me perfectly . . . I would be showing ingratitude for all she has done for me.' He would also be losing the perfect consort, as Mlle Avrillon confirmed: 'Josephine was invariably, unfailingly sweet with the Emperor, adapting herself to his every mood, every whim with a complaisance such as I have never seen in anyone else in the world. By studying the slightest change in his expression or tone she offered him the only thing he now required of her.'

That November Napoleon decided to visit Italy. Ominously he chose not to take Josephine with him, ostensibly because of the poor weather. What she did not know was that her husband was leaving with a list of twenty eligible princesses in his pocket. His formidable itinerary took him all through the region, where he 'was received with unbounded adulation by all the towns of Italy . . . He was Redeemer of France, but the Creator of Italy'.

While he was away the rumours of divorce persisted. A police report dated 4 December noted:

The moralizing ladies of the Faubourg St Germain [the aristocratic neighbourhood of Paris] are raising holy hands of horror about the divorce. Mme Hamelin repeats in public what she says Her Majesty the Empress confided to her in private. This woman and several others of her kind take it upon themselves to comment daily, to encourage and exaggerate the Empress's complaints and distress. They say they know exactly what on such-and-such a day the Emperor said to the Empress, what conversations were held before and after the coronation and what quarrels there are in the Imperial family. They claim to know that the Empress's sterility is not her fault; that the Emperor has never had any children; that his majesty's relations with several women have never borne fruit but that as soon as these ladies were married they became pregnant.[53]

The new year dawned full of anxiety for Josephine. She wrote to Eugène on 10 February 1808:

You can easily guess that I have had much reason for anxiety and still have. The rumblings that circulated during the Emperor's absence haven't ceased on his return, and at this moment there is more gossip than ever . . . Well, I entrust myself to Providence and to the will of the Emperor. My only defence is my conduct, which I endeavour to make irreproachable. I do not go out any more, I have no pleasures. People are amazed that I can endure it, accustomed as I have been to such a sociable life . . . How unhappy do thrones make people, my dear Eugène! I would resign mine tomorrow, without any pain. For me the love of the Emperor is everything. If I should lose that, I would have little regret about anything else.[54]

Much to Josephine's relief, Napoleon was far too busy over the next few months to dwell on divorce. The latest hot spot in his empire was Spain, and he set off in early spring determined to heal this 'running sore'. Finding the Spaniards recalcitrant, Napoleon swiftly summoned Josephine, in the hope that her charm would prove useful. Josephine departed with a glad heart, travelling to Bayonne where Napoleon was meeting with the Spanish Prime Minister and royal family. She proved as useful a helpmate as ever, smoothing things over after the stormy sessions and befriending the mad, ill-kempt Queen Maria Luisa, to whom she gave clothes and jewellery. Reminded again of what an asset his wife was, Napoleon's feelings for her were resurrected and the couple were inseparable. Observers watched in amazement as the Imperial couple played like children on the Atlantic shores, Napoleon throwing Josephine's shoes into the sea and tumbling her in the sand.

Despite these activities abroad, divorce was still the main topic of conversation at home, as Fouché reported to Napoleon on 26 May: 'Everyone here believes there will be a divorce. They quote letters from Bayonne, one of which declares that it will be soon. They talk of a diadem recently bought in Paris for the new Empress. The need for a divorce is fully understood. No one in France or abroad is not convinced that the dynasty's life and prosperity is linked with the fruitfulness of the Emperor's marriage. The Parisians also believe that if he had had children, he would . . . be more careful.'[55]

But Napoleon was still deeply ambivalent about the divorce and was irritated by Fouché's meddling in his domestic affairs. On 17 June he wrote to Cambacérès, 'I am told that the wildest things are being said at Fouché's. Ever since divorce was rumoured they say it is constantly a subject of discussion in his salon . . . I have no doubts about Fouché's loyalty but I do fear this frivolity which by spreading these ideas engenders others to suppositions which later his duty obliges him to contradict.'

Napoleon and Josephine returned to Paris in July. Immediately they arrived back at Saint-Cloud, it became clear that Napoleon would have to leave again soon. The stitches that held his empire together were strained to breaking point. Revolts in Spain continued and there were problems in Portugal. Napoleon needed to ensure that his alliance with the Tsar would hold; with his rear protected by the Russians he could march into Spain to command his army there. A date was set for a meeting with the Tsar in September. The interim weeks were a time of mutual tenderness between the estranged Emperor and Empress.

Josephine wrote to Eugène, 'You know how much anxiety I have been suffering; I have paid for it with terrible headaches . . . which have made me suffer horribly . . . the Emperor has proved his attachment to me by the concern he has displayed; waking up, sometimes as often as four or five times a night to see how I have been feeling. For the last six months he has not ceased to be perfect to me. Thus when I saw him depart this morning it was with pain but without any anxiety about our relationship on my part.'[56]

Josephine was unaware that amongst the many matters that Napoleon intended to discuss with the Tsar at the Congress of Erfurt was the possibility of obtaining permission to marry one of his sisters. His letters to her, however, were still reassuring. On 9 October, pleased to see the Tsar again, Napoleon remarked in his letter to Josephine, with rare self-deprecation, that at the balls they both attended, 'The Emperor Alexander dances; but not I. Forty years are after all, forty years.'[57] In his next letter he wrote, 'My dear, I write you seldom; I am very busy. Conversations which last whole days, and which do not improve my cold. Still all goes well. I am pleased with Alexander; he ought to be with me. If he were a woman, I think I should make him my sweetheart. I shall be back to you shortly; keep well and let me find you plump and rosy.'[58]

Napoleon arrived back in Paris at the end of October, but observers noted that his relationship with his wife appeared strained. Napoleon didn't know if she was aware of the proposal he had made to the Tsar, while Josephine did not dare enquire about what was going on. Their reunion lasted only ten days before Napoleon had to leave to attend to the troubles in Spain. He remained there until March 1809; during this time Josephine's anxiety once more reached fever pitch.

Napoleon's return from Spain was, once again, short-lived. On the evening of 12 April 1809 he received dispatches that the Austrians had opened hostilities. At around 2 a.m. he attempted to depart without disturbing the Empress, but – according to Constant – 'she heard the sounds of departure and sprang out of bed and down the steps into the courtyard in her bedroom slippers and without stockings. Crying like a child, she threw herself into his carriage. She was so lightly dressed that His Majesty threw his fur-lined [cloak] over her shoulders and then issued orders for her luggage to be sent on to her.' It was to be their last journey together. Almost as soon as they had arrived, Napoleon was off and Josephine settled once again into the palace of the Rohans and held court there, awaiting news from her husband.

This campaign was not as straightforward as many in the past had been. With a significant portion of his army still pinned down in Spain, the battle at Eckmuhl lasted a ghastly five days. Then at Ratisbonne there was a rumour that Napoleon had been wounded, perhaps killed. He wrote to Josephine to reassure her: 'The ball that touched me has not wounded me; it barely grazed my Achilles tendon.'[59] The Battle of Essling, which took place over 21 and 22 May, was a near disaster in which the French Army was initially forced to retreat before the tide turned. During these terrible days Napoleon's old comrade the valiant General Lannes had both legs blown off and eventually died of his wounds. The campaign culminated a month and a half later in the great Battle of Wagram. Unfolding over two bloody days, this was the most formidable artillery battle ever fought, with over 900 guns in action. Napoleon ultimately prevailed, but his victory came at a terrible price, with 50,000 men left dead or dying in the mud.

With Napoleon's encouragement, Josephine left for her annual spa visit to Plombières in June and then went on to Malmaison. Napoleon, meanwhile, travelled to Vienna – accompanied by Marie Walewska. Perhaps fuelled by guilt, during this period his letters were very affectionate. On 26 August he wrote, 'I have your letters from Malmaison. They bring me word that you are plump, florid and in the best of health. I assure you Vienna is not an amusing city. I would rather be back again in Paris.'[60] On 31 August, 'I have had no letter from you for several days; the pleasures of Malmaison, the beautiful greenhouses, the beautiful gardens, cause the absent to be forgotten. It is, they say, the rule of your sex. Everyone speaks only of your good health; all this is very suspicious . . .' On 25 September he added, 'Be careful, and I advise you to be vigilant, for one of these nights you will hear a loud knocking.'[61]

This disingenuous act as the jealous lover did not fool Josephine. By this time she would have known that Marie Walewska was with him and pregnant. (His previous mistress Eleonore Dénuelle had also given birth to a child, a son, but when it was discovered that there had been other gentleman callers at the little cottage, the 'experiment' was regarded as contaminated and Napoleon disallowed the baby as proof of his fertility. Later the child's uncanny resemblance to Napoleon would make him claim it as his own.) The countess genuinely loved Napoleon and was of unimpeachable virtue; there was no doubt that the child was his. Josephine confessed to the duchesse d'Abrantès, 'I who have never known envy have truly suffered when any of you brought one of your children to me. I know I will be shamefully dismissed from the bed of the man who crowned me, but God is my witness that I love him more than my life, and much more than the throne.'

By the middle of October the Treaty of Vienna was finally concluded. Although Napoleon departed the city knowing that he intended to divorce Josephine and pursue a speedy remarriage, his letters to her were still full of false bonhomie. On 21 October he wrote from Munich on his way to Paris, 'I shall make a celebration when we are reunited and I impatiently await this moment.'[62] But Josephine was not fooled; she must have known her fate was sealed. So when she received a message to meet him in Fontainebleau 'on the 26th or 27th', her heart must have been full of foreboding. But she did as she was instructed, gathering her ladies and setting out immediately.

When Napoleon arrived back at Fontainebleau on the evening of 26 October, Josephine had not yet arrived. Although she turned up not long after him, she received a frosty reception. Napoleon was apparently annoyed at her tardiness; for the first time he did not come to meet her, instead remaining crouched over his desk. When she went up to his study to see him he greeted her only with the words, 'Ah, here at last.' Of course Napoleon's bad mood had nothing to do with her being late: he was torn apart by guilt. He had decided to divorce her, but he did not have the courage to tell her. Over the following agonizing weeks, Josephine endured terrible treatment as he searched for every spurious excuse he could to put her in the wrong and thus justify the action he had already decided to take. As Hortense wrote, 'No more kindness, no more consideration for my mother . . . He became unjust and plaguing.'[63] The dinners *à deux* which the couple used to enjoy were now miserable, silent affairs. Napoleon refused to utter a word to his wife, instead preferring to eat with his family and ignoring Josephine who sat excluded from the merriment at the table.

In this horrible atmosphere, scene followed scene. The very sight of his wife sometimes enraged Napoleon, at other times reduced him to tears. Josephine was unable to sleep or eat; she lost weight and wept incessantly. Eventually, after begging numerous other people – Cambacérès, Eugène, even Hortense – to do his dirty work, Napoleon finally worked up the courage to tell his wife that he was abandoning her. It was a terrible scene. According to the comte de Bausset, the prefect in attendance, her piercing cries could be heard throughout the palace. When Bausset arrived Josephine was collapsed on the floor. The two of them – Napoleon carrying a candle, Bausset tripping over his ceremonial sword – half carried, half dragged the fainting woman to her apartments. But Josephine was not as desperately overcome as Bausset first feared. On the way to her chambers she whispered to him, 'You are holding me too tightly.'

Hortense was sent for to comfort her mother. When Josephine told her daughter what had happened, Hortense's reply must have surprised her: 'Well, so much the better. We will all go away and you can live in peace.' 'But you, my children, what will become of you?' Josephine asked. 'We will go away with you. My brother will feel as I do. For the first time in our life, far from the crowd, we can really know what it means to be happy.'[64] This bracing conversation seemed to calm her mother, and Hortense left her resigned to her fate and went to join Napoleon, who grew agitated. He began the conversation defensively: 'You have seen your mother. She has spoken to you. My decision is made. It is irrevocable. All France desires a divorce and claims it loudly. I cannot oppose my country's will. So nothing will move me, neither prayers nor tears.' Hortense's reply, in a calm, cold tone, completely threw him: 'You are free to do as you think fit. No one will try to oppose you. Since your happiness requires this step, that is enough; we shall know how to sacrifice ourselves. Do not be surprised at my mother's tears; it would be more surprising if after fifteen years of married life she shed none. But she will submit, I am convinced; and we shall all go, remembering only the kindness you have shown us.'[65]

It was as if Hortense's words made Napoleon finally confront the enormity of what he was losing: not just a loving wife but two good and dutiful children whom he had come to regard as his own. He burst into tears. 'Hardly had I finished when abundant tears started from his eyes and in a voice broken by sobs he exclaimed: "What! All of you leave me! You will desert me! Don't you love me any longer? If it were my happiness I would sacrifice it to you. But it is the good of France. Pity me rather for being obliged to sacrifice my most cherished affections." ' Weeping herself, Hortense attempted to comfort him while he continued to justify himself and protest against their leaving him. In the end, though, Hortense held firm, concluding, 'Sire, my duty is towards my mother. She will need me. We can no longer live near you. That is a sacrifice that we must make. We are prepared to make it.'[66]

Eugène, summoned from Italy, realized immediately what was taking place. His first words to his sister were, 'Has my mother courage to face it?' When Hortense replied in the affirmative, he replied, 'Well then. We will all go away quietly and end our days more peaceably than we began them.' But his meeting with his stepfather was a painful one. A tearful Napoleon was so overwhelmed by grief that he seemed willing to revoke the idea of the divorce itself. But Josephine's offspring assured him 'that the time for that was passed, now that we knew what was in his mind, that the Empress could no longer be happy with him'. Refusing all favours, the honourable Eugène would accept 'no advantage that might seem bought by his mother's misfortune'.[67]

Josephine, despite her grief, was determined to negotiate a situation that protected herself and her children. Playing on the tremendous 'sacrifice' she was making for the nation, she set to work on Napoleon. Her reasoning was sensible. She knew Napoleon better than anyone, and she knew that she must strike while the iron was hot; as time passed, his sense of obligation would wane. As it was, Napoleon pledged to remain a protector to her children and expressed his desire to keep them near him. He promised her, she told Mlle Avrillon, 'that he would come to see me frequently during my retreat. He has given me permission to live at Malmaison; he wishes that I should continue to be regarded in very high favour and that I will receive a considerable settlement.' His only condition was that she should never leave France. Any thoughts of returning to her homeland were obliterated. Josephine accepted his terms.

Once Napoleon's intention to divorce Josephine was made public, her life at court was made a misery. The Bonapartes in particular, as Hortense recollected, could not hide their joy. In truth they did not try very hard to repress their glee at what they saw as their ultimate victory against *la Beauharnais*. 'Every time they turned towards us of whom they had always been so jealous,'[68] Hortense remembered, 'they betrayed themselves by their satisfied and triumphant manner.' Napoleon too was cruel. Determined to make his intentions clear, before the official announcement of the divorce he removed his protection from Josephine, ignoring her and instructing that the Empress should no longer be treated as per Imperial protocol. On 3 December, at a Te Deum to celebrate the fifth anniversary of the coronation, he insisted she arrive in a separate coach and sit apart from him. That night, at a banquet held by the city, Laure d'Abrantès revealed that the Empress was neither met at the entrance nor escorted to the dais. 'Seating herself quickly, her legs almost giving way beneath her, she must have wanted to sink through the floor, yet somehow she managed to smile.'

During these difficult days Josephine displayed 'her own unique brand of heroism', according to Mlle Avrillon. Despite all the slights and humiliations, she never publicly allowed her feelings to show, remaining charming and gracious with everyone. On 14 December she made her last public appearance at a dinner at the Tuileries. Pasquier, her old neighbour from Croissy, recalled, 'I will never forget the last evening at which the Empress did the honours at her court.' He was struck by the 'perfect composure she maintained', despite it 'being the last time, since in a few hours she would be descending the throne and leaving the palace never to return . . . I doubt whether any other woman could have acted with such perfect grace and tact. Napoleon's own bearing was less impressive than that of his victim.'[69]

The divorce ceremony was a public affair, held in the throne room at the Tuileries. The entire family assembled there: Murat, king of Naples, and Queen Caroline; Jérôme, king of Westphalia, and Queen Catherine; Louis, king of Holland, and Queen Hortense; Pauline, princess Borghese; Julie, queen of Spain; Madame Mère. Josephine was escorted by her children. Composed and calm, dressed in a simple white gown, Josephine looked beautiful – though all her artistry with make-up could not entirely obscure the redness of her eyes. Of all of them, Constant felt that Eugène looked the most tragic: he trembled so violently that his old valet thought he might fall at any moment.

After a quarter of an hour of superfluous formalities, Napoleon opened proceedings by reading from a prepared statement, but swiftly pushed it aside. Tears springing to his eyes, he said, 'God alone knows what this resolve has cost my heart. But there is no sacrifice beyond my courage if it is in the best interests of France. I need to add that far from ever having any complaints . . . I have only gratitude to express for the devotion and tenderness of my well-beloved wife. She has adorned thirteen years of my life; the memory of which will remain forever engraved on my heart.'[70] Unable to contain his weeping, he ended with the words 'I would like her to continue to hold the privileges and title of Empress, and, above all, never to doubt my feelings for her; she will always be my best and my dearest friend.'

It was then Josephine's turn to speak. Consulting the tear-stained document that she had spent the previous night painstakingly rewriting, she announced, 'With the permission of my dear and august husband, I declare that, no longer preserving any hope of having children to satisfy the political need for an heir in France, I proudly offer him the greatest proof of love and devotion ever given to a husband on this earth . . .'[71] Overcome, she took a full minute of silence and passed the statement to an official who began reading it himself, weeping openly. '. . . But the dissolution of my marriage will change none of the feelings of my heart: the Emperor will always be my dearest love. I know how much this act, demanded by politics and wider interests, has crushed his heart; but both of us nonetheless glory in the sacrifice that we have made for the good of the country.'

All that was left was for Napoleon and Josephine to sign the proceedings, whereupon the Emperor kissed her and escorted her back to her apartments. As soon as they left the room Eugène, the seasoned, decorated warrior, fainted. (The pathos of the ceremony, like a scene from some Greek tragedy, was such that – as for all the crucial moments of his life – Napoleon commissioned the artist David to commemorate the event.)

That night Josephine took comfort in Napoleon's arms for the last time. According to Constant, she came to the Emperor's bedroom, 'her hair in disarray and her face contorted. She fell onto the bed, put her arms around His Majesty's neck and lavished upon him the most touching caresses . . . The Emperor too began to weep; he raised himself to a sitting position and pressed Josephine to him saying, "*Allons*, my dear Josephine, be brave. I will always be your friend." There followed a silence lasting several minutes, while their tears and sobs mingled.'[72]

Seventeen

SECLUSION

Age could not wither her, nor custom stale her infinite variety.

SHAKESPEARE

THIS WAS JOSEPHINE'S LAST NIGHT at the Tuileries. On 15 December 1809 she awoke alone in the apartments which only that year had been redecorated to her specifications. Eventually the door opened and the Emperor, still in his dressing gown and followed by his new secretary Mèneval, who had replaced Bourrienne after his dismissal for embezzlement, walked into the room. At the sound of his entry, she leapt from her bed and threw herself against his chest. He pulled her to him, embracing her tenderly, until she fainted. White as a sheet, the anguished Napoleon transferred her limp body into Mèneval's arms and left the room rapidly, retreating to his rooms on the first floor. Noticing when she revived that he was no longer there, Josephine's cries and sobs redoubled. She grasped Mèneval's hands and tearfully begged him to tell the Emperor not to forget her, to send her news from the Trianon palace and to make sure that the Emperor wrote to her.

Meanwhile, a convoy of carriages had pulled up in the courtyard and was being loaded with her belongings. Amongst all of the expected cargo, a huge quantity of dresses, shawls, hats and shoes, boxes of cosmetics and accessories, were a number of more esoteric items: a parrot in a cage, two wolfhounds that she had been presented with in Strasbourg and their newborn puppies. At around 2 p.m., when the packing was complete, Mèneval notified Josephine that it was time to go. Napoleon had already left the palace, unable to bear the sight of her leaving. After some prevarication, Josephine adjusted a heavy veil over her face and walked out of the Tuileries for the final time, past the amassed household in the foyer, many of whom were openly weeping.

Accompanied by Hortense and Eugène, she entered the *Opale*, her travelling coach, and pulled away into the gloomy December afternoon, the rain falling incessantly as if heaven itself was weeping at her departure.

According to Hortense, 'We were sad and silent all the way to Malmaison. Her heart was heavy as she entered this place she loved so much. "If he is happy," she said, "I shall not regret it", and her eyes filled constantly with tears.'[1] The small party arrived at Malmaison late that afternoon. For the first time, the chateau and its beautiful grounds failed to raise Josephine's spirits. Instead the sight 'of this place that she had shared so long with the Emperor' reduced her to tears.

The following day was even more difficult. Everything saddened her: the season, the cold, the memories. The rain was merciless; it did not cease for a moment. Nor did her tears. These began falling afresh first thing in the morning when a messenger arrived from the Emperor inquiring how she was, and only increased when friends arrived offering their sympathy and support. At the Trianon Napoleon's gloating family attempted to distract him from his grief. His agitation was such that he could barely sit still. The rain made matters worse; it meant that he couldn't go hunting, or even for a walk, and was therefore reduced to playing cards.

Unable to contain his tension, Napoleon called for his carriage and went over to Malmaison, where her retinue watched through the windows as the pair walked in the rain hand in hand. On his return that evening he wrote to her:

> *My dear, I found you today weaker than you ought to be. You have shown courage; it is necessary that you should maintain it and not give way to a doleful melancholy. You must be contented and take special care of your health, which is so precious to me. If you are attached to me, and if you love me, you should show strength of mind and force yourself to be happy. You cannot question my constant and tender friendship, and it would be very wrong of you to doubt the great affection I have for you or to imagine that I can be happy if you are unhappy, and contented if you are ill at ease. Adieu, my dear. Sleep well; dream that I wish it.*[2]

This tender missive reinforced Josephine's sense of loss, prompting yet another restless and miserable night. The following morning the continuing downpour meant that even if she had wanted to walk around the grounds and distract herself with her plants and blooms, she could not. Instead she was forced to stay indoors, where Eugène tried in vain to distract her with silly jokes and his unwavering optimism. Throughout the day there was a steady stream of visitors. Some were there on the prompting of the Emperor, who greeted all his circle with the words, 'Have you gone to see the Empress yet?' But many had come of their own volition, motivated by genuine affection. They thought her courageous and admired her sacrifice. Josephine greeted them all with her customary grace and sweetness, but with each new expression of condolence and sympathy she was moved yet again to tears.

The duchesse d'Abrantès was one such visitor:

> The Empress received anyone who wanted to pay their respects. The drawing room, billiard room and gallery were full of people . . . As for the Empress, she had never looked better: she sat on the right of the fireplace, under the fine painting by Girodet, very simply dressed with a wide green hood on her head which could serve when necessary to hide her tears . . . She raised her eyes on each person who entered and smiled at them . . . but if this person was one of her old friends, tears flowed at once down her cheeks, effortlessly, without any of the contractions which make a woman's face so ugly when she cries . . . All the crowned heads, majesties, highnesses who were in Paris during that winter of 1810, came to Malmaison to bow to the Empress. These visits were painful, yet they made her happy because they proved that the Emperor desired she should still be honoured as his *chosen wife*; at least that was my impression . . .[3]

At the chateau, visitors discovered that memories of the past were carefully cultivated. According to the countess de Kielmansegge, the Empress 'took me into the library which had once been the Emperor's bedchamber and in which every object was still exactly in the place he had left it. Her emotion grew as she showed me one thing after another. The last object she pointed out was the worn armchair of black morocco leather which he had slashed all over with his penknife. Then unable to contain herself any longer, she burst into tears.' The account of Georgette Ducrest, a member of her circle, was a little more reserved:

> The Empress had kept a veritable cult for the Emperor and would not allow so much as a chair to be moved in the apartment he had occupied: and rather than sleep in it herself, she preferred to be very uncomfortably lodged on the first floor. Everything remained just as it was when the Emperor took leave of his study; a book of history

on his writing table was marked at the page where he left off reading . . . a globe, on which he used to show his confidants the lands he planned to conquer, bore the marks of certain impatient movements . . . Josephine herself dusted what she called 'his relics' and she seldom allowed anyone to enter this sanctuary.[4]

Josephine's grief and loss were exacerbated by the disloyalty of some of her entourage. Already a number of her attendants had disappeared. Aware of these defections and determined to stop them, Napoleon ordered the circulation of a notice that read, 'The Empress's Household will continue to carry out their duties with Her Majesty the Empress Josephine until 1 January.' He had bestowed on her a substantial 'establishment': the comtesse d'Arberg as chief lady-in-waiting, nine ladies attached to the palace, a chaplain, chamberlains, including the charming painter Turpin de Crissé, equerries, a knight of honour, a *lectrice*, a doctor, a head secretary, a superintendent-general and four ladies of the bedchamber; at least thirty-six persons, not counting the servants.

On 18 December the Emperor dispatched three couriers to find out how she was. The following day, 19 December, he sent an aide to enquire after her and collect her reply. His report upset the Emperor. He wrote, 'My dear, I have just received your letter. Savary tells me that you are always crying; that is not good . . . I trust that you have been able to go for a walk today . . . I shall come to see you when you tell me you are reasonable, and that your courage has the upper hand . . . Adieu my dear. I also am sad today; I need to know that you are satisfied and to learn that your equilibrium is restored. Sleep well.'[5] The following day a planned visit by the Emperor was thwarted by his workload. But he wrote that evening instructing her to 'go and see her plants', if the weather allowed. In the end she did go for a walk, escorted by a concerned Claire de Rémusat. Hollow-eyed, exhausted and grief-stricken, Josephine told her friend, 'Sometimes, it seems as if I am dead and all that remains is a sort of faint sensation of knowing that I no longer exist.'

Josephine was in deep shock. While talk of separation had dragged on between the couple for ages, the reality had taken place over a very short time. It was a mere month and a half from the moment Napoleon informed her of his decision to seek a divorce to her tear-drenched departure from the Tuileries. The pace of events had been so swift that Josephine had had no time to come to terms with such a radical change in her life. Napoleon too was unreconciled, as his overbearing and self-pitying notes demonstrate. He seems to have convinced himself that he too was a victim and that the divorce was not his responsibilty, but rather an act of God imposed on them both equally.

This stance, many felt, simply prolonged the agony. Mme de Rémusat, witness to Josephine's daily torment and sleepless nights, suggested via her husband that Napoleon should rethink his letters to the Empress. Rather than nurturing Josephine's sense of loss by dwelling on his own, she suggested that he should attempt, on paper at least, to 'moderate his grief'. He heeded her advice as much as he was able, and his subseqent letters are less self-indulgent. On Christmas Eve he went to visit Josephine at Malmaison, and on Christmas Day invited her, Eugène and Hortense to dine with him at the Trianon. On both occasions he was kind and considerate but, mindful that he was already in negotiation for a new wife, he made sure that there could be no accusations of impropriety. His conduct was scrupulous; he did not embrace Josephine, nor did he take her into his apartments, making sure that he remained in public view throughout her visit.

Undoubtedly one of the topics for discussion during this Christmas lunch was his forthcoming marriage. Although Napoleon claimed that he remained undecided, the most likely candidate was rumoured to be the Archduchess Marie Louise of Austria. On 1 January Josephine sent a messenger to Mme de Metternich, the wife of the Austrian ambassdor, requesting she visit her at Malmaison. The following day Mme de Metternich arrived for a charming grilling at the hands of the Empress, who explained that only the success of the negotiations with Austria could redeem 'the sacrifice that she had made'.[6] The marriage negotiations probably did not need her help, but this assertive act of direct intervention made it clear that, even now, Josephine was determined to play an active political role and remain at the centre of affairs.

As the marriage-brokering went on, Napoleon and Josephine continued to wear out the couriers that travelled between Malmaison and the Trianon, ferrying endless letters and little presents. After one visit to see her, Napoleon wrote – heavy with grief – 'you know what charm your company has for me'. Missing him terribly and bored at Malmaison, where the flow of visitors had slowed to a meagre trickle, Josephine lobbied him for permission to move to the Élysée Palace, the other residence he had promised her in the settlement. The move would make it easier to see each other more frequently. Despite his charming letters, Napoleon was ambivalent about this prospect. He did not want his former wife in Paris when his new bride arrived. But

Josephine prevailed and she moved into the Élysée in early February. Four days later Napoleon signed the treaty of marriage between himself and the Archduchess Marie Louise. The capital erupted in joyous celebration of the forthcoming nuptials.

In her isolation at Malmaison Josephine had longed for the social whirl the city offered, but when she got there she was terribly disappointed. Unbeknownst to her, Napoleon had made it clear that he would be seriously displeased if affection for the former Empress in any way overshadowed the devoted attention he felt was due the new one. So whilst the rest of the city distracted themselves with the celebratory balls, concerts and dinners that filled this brilliant winter season, Josephine was left out in the cold; receiving neither invitations nor visitors. Effectively imprisoned at the Élysée, she was plunged into despair, all her fears of obsolescence and loneliness crowding in on her. Her abandonment was harder to endure in Paris, where all else was happy and convivial, than it had been at Malmaison, and she returned there just five weeks after she had left. Even the brief mention in the press of her departure from the capital brought Fouché a sharp rebuke from Napoleon: 'I have told you to see that the newspapers do not mention the Empress Josephine. Yet they do nothing else.'

Now Napoleon felt that even Malmaison was too close for comfort. Sifting through the multitude of possible alternative residences for Josephine, he came up with a near-perfect option: Navarre. Situated in the beautiful Normandy countryside, the chateau – which had once belonged to the queen of Navarre – had the invaluable benefit of being neither too near nor too far away from Paris. With its forests, farms and lawns it was an impressive property; the only drawback was the chateau itself, which had been empty for a substantial period of time. After initiating hurried renovations Napoleon wrote to Josephine on 12 March: 'I trust that you will be pleased with what I have done for Navarre. You must see from this how anxious I am to make myself agreeable to you. Get ready to take possession of Navarre; you will go there on 25 March, to pass the month of April.'[7]

Running a few days behind schedule, Josephine left for Navarre late on the evening of 28 March. After travelling through the night she arrived in Evreux at nine in the morning. She was met in the town square – fittingly named the place Bonaparte – by the entire population, cannon fire, a speech by the mayor and a gun salute from a contingent of the National Guard, who then escorted her to the property. But what confronted the newly coined 'duchesse of Navarre' was something of a shock. The chateau was hideous: a big two-storey stone building on which was perched a dome truncated by a big platform covered in lead. Designed by the nephew of the great architect Mansard, the aesthetic of the house had been entirely compromised by a random folly of the duc de Bouillon. He had dreamed of erecting a colossal statue of his uncle, the illustrious Marshal Turenne, astride the dome, but the king's hostility to the project meant that it had never been completed. Thus Josephine's new home had remained for decades neither a chateau nor a monument. So hideous was the building's appearance that the region's inhabitants, making a play on its shape and the owner's name of Bouillon, had nicknamed it *la Marmite* ('the cooking pot').

Four great columns framed the entry to the chateau. Its foyer led to a huge round reception room paved in marble, the height of which reached right up through two storeys to the roof. This gloomy hall was lit only by the windows of the vestibule and the slits cut into the dome far above. The chateau was not only dark by virtue of its curious design, but also impossible to heat. Despite the tons of wood that were delivered to feed its huge fireplaces, in the huge draughty hall around which its triangular rooms were organized, cold air circulated relentlessly.

Damp was a huge problem, too. The chateau was situated at the bottom of a valley between two hillsides of forests, so all the rain flowed downwards into the depression where the house stood and collected in stagnant pools around it. The problem was exacerbated by the landscaping of the grounds. Laid out in the Chinese style, intersected by a network of artificial canals and streams that were crossed by rickety little bridges and fringed by dilapidated oriental pavilions and temples of love, there was water everywhere. This meant that the chateau's wooden-framed windows were irrevocably warped and unwilling to budge, able neither to open nor close.

The depressing conditions took their toll on Josephine's household. They had not wanted to leave Paris, where the celebrations for the Emperor's nuptials were in full swing. Malmaison was out of the way, but at least it was near enough to the heart of things that one could come and go, and it was warm and comfortable. But this cold, damp and isolation led to an acceleration in defections. Mme de Rémusat's excuse was a poor one: she claimed that she could not find appropriate transport. Josephine's gentleman-in-waiting, the comte de Beaumont, provided a more credible reason in his election to the Legislative Corps. But the most wounding defection of all was that of Mme Ney, a protégé of Josephine's since her childhood. She was Mme Campan's niece and Hortense's school friend; Josephine had promoted her marriage to Marshal Ney and stood as godmother to her eldest son. Now she announced that her husband did not wish her to continue in Josephine's service. Josephine's response was so gracious and helpful that one can only hope it shamed her disloyal friend. She agreed that it is 'the first duty of a wife to submit to the wishes of her husband' and added, 'I will convey to the Emperor, and do my best to support, your husband's desire that you should obtain a position with the Empress.'[8]

If Josephine resented the disloyalty of those whom she had treated so kindly, she did not show it. Instead she rallied herself, mobilizing those who remained faithful to her and supervising the refurbishment of the house. It was something of a challenge. The furniture that came with the chateau was scant and broken down. When new furnishings arrived the desperate members of the household descended upon them like vultures, claiming chairs and tables for their own apartments and frustrating the efforts of Pierlot, the comptroller, to carry out an inventory. Eventually some order was restored and Josephine turned her attention to the grounds.

Isolated in this uncomfortable castle with her disgruntled staff, Josephine strived to adjust to her new provincial life. She spent her days walking in the grounds, if the weather permitted, and her evenings playing backgammon with the seventy-six-year-old bishop of Evreux. Meanwhile she fretted over the rumours that had been relayed to her from Paris. These claimed that she was to be exiled permanently in Navarre, that Malmaison was to be sold and that the new Empress had developed such an aversion to Josephine that she did not want her anywhere in the vicinity of Napoleon or herself. In addition, she was worried about Hortense; under pressure from the Bonapartes she had returned to her husband, Louis, in Amsterdam, but the reunion had brought her to the brink of despair. Fearing for her health and sanity, Josephine wrote to reassure her: 'As long as I have anything, you will be mistress of your own fate. Sorrows and happiness – you know that I will share them all with you. Try to find a little courage, my dear daughter, you know that we have great need of it, both of us. Often mine is weak but I have faith in time and our own efforts.'[9]

Josephine's gloom was lifted temporarily by a visit from Eugène. The Emperor had sent him to bring a personal reply to a letter she had sent. Eugène was charged to say that Napoleon was indeed willing to pay for the necessary restorations at Navarre and, much to Josephine's relief, he grudgingly gave her permission to return to Malmaison while they were completed. Her son's playful personality brought some fun to life at Navarre, charades replaced billiards and impromptu plays replaced monotonous lectures. But Josephine was still deeply unhappy. She was hurt that Napoleon cared so little for her that he would banish her to such a miserable place, and she resented the fact that since his marriage he had not bothered to send her any letters expressing either concern or interest in her new life.

In her letter dated 19 April 1810 she ostensibly gave thanks for his permission to return to Malmaison, but reproach resonates from every line:

> *Sire, I have received, by my son, the assurance that your Majesty consents*
> *to my return to Malmaison, and grants to me the advance as requested,*
> *in order to make the chateau of Navarre habitable. This double favour,*
> *Sire, dispels to a great extent the uneasiness, nay, even the fears which*
> *your Majesty's long silences had inspired. I was afraid that I might be*
> *entirely banished from your memory; I see that I am not. I am therefore*
> *less wretched today, and even as happy as henceforth it will be possible for*
> *me to be.*
>
> *I shall go at the end of the month to Malmaison, since your Majesty*
> *sees no objection to it. But I ought to tell you, Sire, that I should not so*
> *soon have taken advantage of the latitude which your Majesty left me in*
> *this respect had the house of Navarre not required, for my health's sake*
> *and for that of my household, repairs which are urgent. My idea is to stay*
> *at Malmaison a very short time; I shall soon leave it in order to go to*
> *the waters. But while I am at Malmaison, your Majesty may be sure that*
> *I shall live there as if I were a thousand leagues from Paris. I have made*
> *a great sacrifice, Sire, and every day I realize more its full extent. Yet*
> *that sacrifice will be, as it ought to be, a complete one on my part.*
> *Your Highness, amid your happiness, shall be troubled by no expression*
> *of my regret.*
>
> *I shall pray unceasingly for your Majesty's happiness, perhaps even*
> *I shall pray that I may see you again; but your Majesty may be assured*
> *that I shall always respect our new relationship. I shall respect it in silence,*
> *relying on the attachment that you had for me formerly; I shall call for no*
> *new proof; I shall trust to everything from your justice and your heart.*
>
> *I limit myself to asking from you one favour: it is that you will deign*
> *to find a way of sometimes convincing both myself and my entourage that*
> *I have still a small place in your memory and a great place in your esteem*
> *and friendship. By this means, whatever happens, my sorrows will be*

mitigated without, as it seems to me, compromising that which is of permanent importance to me, the happiness of your Majesty.[10]

Napoleon's reply was reassuring and loving, that of an affectionate husband rather than a distant sovereign who had put her aside:

My dear, I have received your letter of 19 April; it is written in a bad style. I am always the same; people like me do not change. I know not what Eugène has told you. I have not written to you because you have not written to me, and my sole desire is to fulfil your slightest inclination.

I see with pleasure that you are going to Malmaison and that you are contented; as for me, I shall be so likewise on hearing news from you and in giving you mine. I say no more about it until you have compared this letter with yours, and after that I will leave you to judge which of us two is the better friend. Adieu dear; keep well, and be just for your sake and mine.[11]

It was as if a weight had been lifted from her heart. Josephine's relief and gratitude is evident in every line of her reply:

A thousand thousand loving thanks for not having forgotten me. My son has just brought me your letter. With what impetuosity I read it, and yet I took a long time over it, for there was not a word which did not make me weep; but these tears were very pleasant ones. I have found my whole heart again – such as it will always be; there are feelings which are life itself, and which can only end with it.

I was in despair to find my letter of the 19th had displeased you; I do not remember the exact expressions, but I know what torture I felt in writing it – the grief at having no news from you. I wrote you on my departure from Malmaison, and since then how often have I wished to write to you! But I appreciated the causes of your silence and feared to be importunate with a letter. Yours has been the true balm for me. Be happy, be as much so as you deserve; it is my whole heart which speaks to you. You have also just given me my share of happiness, and a share which I value the most, for nothing can equal in my estimation a proof that you still remember me. Adieu dear; I again thank you as affectionately as I shall always love you.[12]

That spring Josephine returned to Malmaison: her citadel, her retreat, her stage. It was at its most beautiful at this time of the year, the flowers in full bloom, the foliage at its most luxuriant. In the years since its purchase she had made an indelible mark on this place. Just as her forefathers had carved La Pagerie out of the tropical wilderness and shaped it to their will, so she had done with Malmaison. This was *her* place, the product of her vision, and she had painstakingly overseen its creation, expansion and embellishment. If she could never return to her island home, it did not matter; she had recreated it here and more: Malmaison was her own little kingdom, her Eden, with all that she loved, coveted and found lovely. As she herself exulted in 1813, 'My garden is the most beautiful thing in the world.'

From the days of Napoleon's appointment as First Consul, Josephine had worked ceaselessly to improve Malmaison. With patience, tenacity and good judgement, she had developed new areas of her botanical collection and acquired new sections of land. In 1802 she had built the orangery, where she grew the pineapples which assuaged the duchesse d'Abrantès's cravings in pregnancy. In 1803 the property had acquired a dairy, like Marie Antoinette's garden at Le Petit Trianon. Josephine's cowherd was Swiss and her attendants, too, wore Swiss costume. The butter and cheese that were produced there were served daily on the tables of the chateau. The estate also had a menagerie and an aviary. In 1805 Josephine built her famous greenhouse. When the king of Spain sent her a herd of sheep in 1808 she created a sheep farm. In 1810 she acquired the neighbouring property of Bois-Preau, which she had coveted for many years. By 1811 Malmaison was almost three times its original size; it covered 726 hectares and stretched from the outskirts of Rueil and the woods of Saint-Cucufa to the banks of the Seine at Bougival.

Josephine was not a gardener; she did not spend hours crouched over the earth, digging and planting. Hers was the role of the collector, the connoisseur, and she took it very seriously. She read extensively on the subject of horticulture, subscribed to journals that would supplement her knowledge, and was in constant dialogue with specialists in the field. She had initially entrusted the design of the park to the architects employed to renovate the chateau, Percier and Fontaine, but their plans did not correspond with her own vision. They were succeeded by Morel, who had become famous before the Revolution. Ageing and irascible, he was replaced by the architect and landscape artist Louis Berthault, whose vision coincided with that of Josephine; his layout of the gardens at Malmaison made him famous. Finally there was the explorer–botanist Bonpland, who shared his predecessors' ability to seize the suggestions of the Empress and convert them into reality. But these are only a sample of the veritable army of landscape artists, gardeners, supervisors and botanists who worked at the property.

In the beginning, in a property where she felt free to reflect her imagination, Josephine revisited her Caribbean childhood for inspiration. The first plants that she actively pursued were from Martinique. In a letter to her mother she asked Mme de La Pagerie to send her the 'trees and seeds of as many species as possible'. In those days her botanical collection was dominated by exotic varieties such as orchids, magnolias and cherries from St Lucia. Very quickly, however, her interests broadened and rhododendrons, violets and roses mixed with the more exotic plants. She shared Redouté's belief that 'flowers are the stars of the earth and should be handled with tenderness and love'.

Josephine displayed a remarkable tenacity of purpose in putting together her botanical collection. She was in regular correspondence with individuals and institutions that would be useful to her, including the professors at the Jardin des Plantes and André Thouin, professor of horticulture at the National Museum of Natural History. In the voluminous correspondence Josephine conducted with these experts, she always wrote the letters herself, in a warm and gracious style. She also took advantage of her husband's position, besieging his various commercial attachés, diplomats and ambassadors posted abroad with horticultural requests. As a result she was sent seeds and cuttings from places as disparate as Africa, South America, Constantinople and the Far East.

The quality and diversity of Josephine's botanical collection received a major boost when she acquired plants from the Baudin expedition to Australia. Nicolas Baudin, a self-taught botanist, had made his name with a fruitful trip to the Caribbean in 1796–98. His next expedition, approved by the First Consul (undoubtedly at Josephine's urging), left Le Havre in October 1800 and returned to France in 1803. It brought with it floral specimens including ficus, hibiscus, acacias and mimosas, and unfamiliar animals like kangaroos, emus and cockatoos. The shipment also brought the black swans that would become Josephine's unofficial emblem. Today these can be found in any important zoological park, but Josephine was the first, certainly in France, to succeed in raising these elegant birds in captivity. The division of the spoils Baudin brought to France was hotly contested between Josephine and the Museum of Natural History. But Chaptal, the Minister of the Interior – no doubt under pressure from Josephine – directed the museum officials to give her first choice.

Josephine was not a grasping collector, however. 'Her joy', affirmed Bourrienne, 'was to acquire, not to possess.' Josephine did not guard the riches of Malmaison jealously; she loved to make them known and to popularize her discoveries; she stimulated public interest and galvanized people's good will; she exchanged plants, cuttings and information with botanical gardens in many provinces. In 1804 she wrote, 'For me it is a great happiness to see more and more foreign vegetation in our gardens . . . I would like in 10 years that each department possess a collection of rare plants, offshoots of my nurseries.'[13]

In 1805 the hothouse built by Jean-Thomas Thibaut and Barthélemy Vignon was completed. One of the largest outside Kew Gardens, it was 155 feet long and the object of general admiration. Her rare tropical plants now had a purpose-built home, and with patience and perseverance her policy of selection, hybridization and grafting eventually proved very effective. Beautiful species of dahlia, amaryllis and tropical fruit like tangerines thrived there. Pride of place was given to a statue of Rousseau, one of Josephine's gardening inspirations. She had instructed her superintendent to ensure 'that the vines and foliage may play around his head. This will be a natural crown, worthy of the author of *Émile*.'[14]

Josephine did not allow the Napoleonic Wars to stand in the way of her developing horticultural collection. Despite her apparent desire to be acquiescent to Napoleon's every wish, in this area she consistently ignored his edicts, ordering plants to be shipped across the Channel from the Hammersmith-based Lee & Kennedy, one of the largest plant-dealers in England. In this climate of conflict it seems extraordinary that plants from Britain and her colonies should find their way into Josephine's hands. Britain and France were at war for the fifteen years that she was at Malmaison, with the exception of the thirteen months that followed the signing of the Treaty of Amiens in 1802, but Josephine's botanical pursuits continued through peace and war. Knowing that she was incorrigible in this regard, Napoleon gave instructions that her plant orders be allowed through his continental blockade, and her deliveries from England arrived undisturbed.

After 1810 the repudiated Empress's botanical fervour reached new heights. It was Josephine's great consolation, and her botanical ambitions at Malmaison and Navarre occupied an ever-increasing share of her attention. Napoleon understood this and assigned her a generous budget for the Malmaison gardens. Josephine knew that her park could not hope to compete with the grand official gardens, but she hoped to create a melange that would be uniquely attractive. She was entirely successful, creating a harmonious natural world that resembled her Martiniquan birthplace as far as this was possible under different skies. In her world the trees were free to grow and spread, and the animals lived unfettered. Visitors to the property were fulsome in their praise: the prince de Clary wrote, 'Malmaison is the most attractive park that I have visited in France. It is huge, designed with great taste, covering an entire hill and extending as far as you can go . . . It is made up of great forests, very well-designed lawns, magnificent waterways and a long canal on which float beautiful boats and the fashionable black swans.'

Although Josephine is now primarily remembered for her roses, she was not initially interested in this kind of flower at all; the first Malmaison plantings did not contain any roses. It was not until 1804, under the influence of her botanists and gardeners, that roses began to appear in the Malmaison gardens. After this, Josephine's enthusiasm grew into a genuine passion. Over a relatively short period of time she managed to collect and grow over 250 different species, including varieties with such evocative names as 'Rouge formidable', 'Belle Hébé', 'Beauté touchante', 'Parure des Vierges', 'Cuisse de nymphe émue' and 'Rire niais'. Josephine's fabulous rose gardens encouraged the French nation's enthusiasm for cultivating the species, and the 500,000 roses now found in public parks in Paris are part of her legacy. Her role as First Lady of the Rose is captured in Vital Dubray's statue, which depicts Josephine standing proudly, holding a single rose. After her death Redouté's most famous work, *Les Roses*, provided his testament to her passion for roses and for plants in general. Indeed, no one did more to increase the fame of Malmaison than this middle-aged Belgian with his large, fleshy hands. His beautiful illustrations in numerous books attracted a great deal of attention to Josephine's collection.

That awareness of Josephine's contribution to horticulture has faded does not diminish its genuine impact. Recent reseach has revealed, according to the curator of the Musée de Malmaison and Bois-Preau, 'that she played an essential role in natural history in France at the beginning of the nineteenth century'.[15] Hers was the greatest private horticultural collection in France at that time. Nearly two hundred species that were new to the country were first grown at Malmaison. Some of these plants are now forgotten, but were named in honour of their protectress. Who today plants the 'Lapagerie Rosea', dedicated by Spanish horticulturalists to the wife of the Emperor? However, the sumptuous red 'Amaryllis Josephinae' exists still under the appellation 'Brunsvigia Josephinae'.

Josephine's botanical work was enshrined in two magnificent publications: *Le Jardin de Malmaison* and *Les Plantes rares cultivées à Malmaison et à Navarre*. In the former's foreword, Ventenat summed up her overall achievement: 'You have gathered around you the rarest plants growing on French soil. Some, indeed, which have never before left the deserts of Arabia or the burning sands of Egypt have been domesticated through your care. Now, regularly classified, they offer to us, as we inspect them in the beautiful gardens of Malmaison, an impressive reminder of the conquests of your illustrious husband and most pleasant evidence of the studies you have pursued in your leisure hours.'[16]

After Josephine's death and Napoleon's defeat the contents of Malmaison were sold or dispersed, and sections of the grounds were sold off in lots. In subsequent years Malmaison passed through many hands and the gardens fell into neglect and decay. During the Franco-Prussian War of 1870 they were almost completely destroyed. But in 1904 Malmaison's fate took an upturn when a philanthropic Frenchman, Daniel Osiris, bought the chateau and gave it to the nation. Subsequently turned into a museum, Malmaison was revived and protected. Today we can enter the chateau and wander through the grounds where Josephine and Napoleon walked 200 years ago. Only a few of the enormous variety of plants that once flourished there still remain, but the charm and beauty of the place still lingers; and Josephine's spirit is everywhere.

Malmaison also housed Josephine's famous art collection. This was a product both of her own passion and of her belief that, as Empress, it was her duty to patronize the arts. The result was an extensive and eclectic collection that was regarded as being of significant cultural value. It was housed predominantly in the grand gallery built by Louis Berthault and inaugurated in 1809. Almost 100 feet long, the gallery was designed with skylights and console tables for the display of Josephine's many works of art. Inspired by her love of the Troubadour style, it was decorated with white silk curtains, green upholstered furniture and thirty stools designed by Jacob *frères*, covered in red morocco leather.

The collection she displayed there was impressive. The inventory made after her death revealed 360 paintings and innumerable other objets d'art. Many of these were purchased by the Tsar Alexander and are now in the Hermitage. Since some of them were presented to her as gifts or were booty acquired through her husband, they did not necessarily represent her personal taste. She had acquired thirty-six paintings from the collection of the Elector of Hesse-Cassel, for example; these had been captured by General Lagrange after the Battle of Jena in 1807. They included Claude's *The Hours*, a Rembrandt, a Rubens, and Potter's *Farm near Amsterdam*. Josephine's collection also included a number of Italian Renaissance paintings by Bellini, Ghirlandaio, Titian and Veronese. In addition she owned a Dürer, various Spanish works and several pieces by French seventeenth- and eighteenth-century artists like Nattier, Greuze and Carle van Loo.

It was in her collection of contemporary paintings that Josephine's own preferences were most evident. Her taste was decidedly feminine: there were a substantial number of portraits of family and loved ones; flower paintings, such as the gouaches and watercolours by her protégé Redouté; animal portraits, such as the painting of *Lioness Feeding Her Cubs* by the Flemish artist J. B. Berre, which depicted the cats that had been born in the Jardin des Plantes and had become one of the sights of Paris. Her collection also included a few gently erotic works, such as *Venus Asleep* and its pendant, *The Torch of Venus*, painted by Prud'hon's pupil Constance Mayer. She loved gentle landscapes. Of the fifty or so such paintings, there were a number of historical landscapes and pastoral scenes by B. P. Ommeganck and J. B. Kobell, which depicted the peaceful Dutch landscape with its distant horizons.

The female painters of the period were virtually all represented. These included a rather sentimental painting entitled *Young Girl Feeding the Chickens* by Mme Jeanne-Élisabeth Chaudet, the wife and pupil of the celebrated sculptor. Josephine was also one of the first to collect paintings that memorialized the Middle Ages, such as those of Duperreux and Lecomte, whose vast canvases included *The Crusaders Consecrating Their Arms to the Virgin* and *Bayard at Prayer*. As a devotee of the Troubadour style, she also enjoyed the intimate domestic scenes depicted in the manner of Pieter de Hooch and Gerard Dou. A perfect example of this was a pair of paintings by Antoine Laurent, *The Woman with a Lute* and *The Oboe-player*, which were displayed in the recess of a casement window. Her favourite painter in this category was François-Fleury Richard, a pupil of David. She owned seven of his pictures, including *Respect Paid by St Louis to His Mother*, which had been the triumph of the Salon of 1810. She appointed him '*peintre de l'Impératrice*' in 1808. The Troubadour style that Josephine helped to popularize would pave the way for artists like Decamps and Delaroche and precipitate the triumph of the Romantic movement.[17]

Malmaison also housed Josephine's collection of sculpture. Many were displayed in the grand gallery; others were scattered with an air of contrived negligence around the grounds or displayed in the other rooms of the chateau. These works reveal Josephine's preference for alabaster and marble. Displayed alongside 215 antique vases, these sculptures included the works of Bosio and Chinard, and Antoine-Denis Chaudet's *Cyparissus Mourning His Faun*. Her collection was dominated, however, by her favourite sculptor, Canova. She eagerly sought out his works and managed, with some difficulty, to obtain two versions of *Hébé* and his *Standing Cupid and Psyche*. She also commissioned from him two original works: *Dancer with Her Hands on Her Hips* and a marble statue of *Paris*. She was such an enthusiastic and supportive patron that after the divorce, when Canova was in Paris to make a bust of the new Empress, he insisted on coming to Malmaison to pay his respects.[18]

This formidable collection of art, placed alongside the glorious botanical display in the chateau's grounds, made the aesthetic pleasures of visiting Malmaison virtually incomparable. It also provides a revealing insight into Josephine's personality. The temperament of a collector is an interesting one; after all, necessity is never the raison d'être of a collection. And since a collection can never be complete – there is always another item or a better version available – its creation requires a predatory love of objects and an endless appetite. Despite the acquisitiveness associated with collection (and this was a quality for which Josephine was justly famous) it is not a traditionally female occupation. Good collectors are aggressive and enjoy the chase. They also need to have a ruthless business sense, the ability to assess value and the hard-headedness to negotiate a good price. They must be able to dissemble: to act interested but not too interested, lest they be taken advantage of.

The abundance of her collections might have helped to compensate Josephine for the terrible days of deprivation; they certainly provided a refuge from the tumult of war and politics that often surrounded her. That Josephine so excelled as a collector exposes a repressed side of her personality: a desire for excess and profusion that was incompatible with the restraint and moderation required by a royal consort. As a collector, Josephine invented her own legacy and revealed a desire to be remembered that was not dissimilar to Napoleon's. If she failed in this, because of the death of many of her plants and the dispersal of many of her paintings, her legacy as a style innovator and taste-maker has endured. Above all, her collection revealed her own inner story, one of longing, passion and insatiable desire. It is no wonder that Napoleon once said of Josephine, 'My wife wants to have everything!'

★

On 13 June, much to Josephine's delight, Napoleon came to visit her at Malmaison. Their main topic of conversation was Hortense, whose situation continued to worry them. Under pressure from her in-laws, she had dutifully returned to Holland; there she was at the mercy of Louis's precarious mental state, which grew more depressed and paranoid each day. The misery of Hortense's life was made worse by her ill health: she had contracted consumption and had begun to spit blood. Unable to improve her condition, her doctors advised her to visit Plombières. She had arrived back in France early that June and appealed to Napoleon to allow her to stay there. Now she was awaiting his decision on her fate. In a letter to her daughter Josephine explained, 'I spoke to him about your situation . . . he listened with interest. He advises that you do not return to Holland, the king's [Louis's] conduct has not been what it should be . . . The advice of the Emperor is that you take the waters for the necessary time and that you write your husband to tell him that the doctors have advised you that you need to live in a warm climate for a while, so you will go to Italy to be near your brother. Once you are with your sibling, the Emperor will give the order that you don't have to return to France.'[19]

But Louis took them all by surprise by abdicating his throne on 1 July. Much to Napoleon's chagrin, he had always taken his role as sovereign of Holland more seriously than his loyalty to his brother, whose continental blockade was ruining Dutch merchants. When Napoleon assembled a French army on the Dutch frontier, Louis even briefly contemplated opening the dykes and resisting his brother's aggression, but he knew that this would inflict even greater misery on Holland. So he chose instead to abdicate, leaving Hortense as regent to her eldest son, the duke of Berg, who was not yet six years old. She reigned for all of eight days before Napoleon incorporated Holland into the French Empire. This decision, he wrote to Josephine, 'has the advantage of setting the Queen at liberty'. It meant that Hortense had lost a throne and, now that Napoleon was hoping for an heir, her children were likely to be superseded by his successors.

But Hortense did not care. Envisaging a new life of peace and happiness with her lover, Charles de Flahaut, Talleyrand's son whom Hortense had met in Savoy, her health slowly began to improve. When she rejoined her mother late that summer to take the waters in Aix, Hortense – though thin and drawn – had begun to recover something of her earlier joie de vivre.

That August Josephine was preoccupied as she set off on her tour of Switzerland. Rumours circulated that Marie Louise might be pregnant, and

Josephine was worried about whether she would be allowed to return to Paris at the end of summer as Napoleon had promised. The Swiss received her graciously; she was guest of honour at the Festival of the Lake, where she was enthroned in a customized boat drawn by two swans. When the authorities insisted that the other craft pull back to give her precedence, she protested sweetly, 'I wish to let the people see how much I am delighted by everything around me, and how pleased I am with the reception I have been given. It is so gratifying to be loved.'

As September rolled on, Josephine continued her tour, passing through Lausanne, Geneva and Berne. On her way she received confirmation of Marie Louise's pregnancy, followed by a letter from Mme de Rémusat that confirmed her worst fears. Carefully her friend made it clear that it would be best if she did not return to Malmaison:

> *At the time of the birth of a child awaited with such impatience, amid the noise of the festivals that will follow that event, what will you do, Madame? What will the Emperor do, whose first duty must be to care for the young mother and who will be still affected by the memories of the fondness that he retains for you? He will suffer, although your feelings of delicacy will not permit you to demand anything of him; but you will suffer too: you will not without grief listen to the sound of so much rejoicing, relegated as you may be to oblivion by the whole nation, or rendered an object of pity by those who will perhaps commiserate with you out of partisan spirit. Gradually your situation will become so burdensome that only a complete withdrawal could set matters right.*[20]

The threat was veiled but it was nonetheless there; if Josephine did not stay away she was in danger of provoking dismissal into permanent exile. The sentiments of the letter were clearly influenced by Napoleon himself, who knew that his pregnant wife was desperately jealous of Josephine and did not want to endure any more scenes. Mme de Rémusat concluded that there remained one last sacrifice for Josephine to make, and that was not to wait for a letter from the Emperor, but to be 'courageous and determined' and write to him immediately explaining that she would prolong her trip and spend the winter in Italy and the spring at Navarre.

This plan was not dissimilar to the one Josephine had proposed to Napoleon some months earlier, when she had requested permission to return to Malmaison. But she was nonetheless worried; the oblique threat in Mme de Rémusat's letter did not bode well. She wrote to the Emperor, 'Bonaparte, you promised that you would not abandon me. Here is a circumstance where I really need your advice. I have no one but you in the world, you are my only friend, talk to me frankly. Should I return to Paris or stay here? . . . Decide what you would like me to do, and if you prefer not to write, tell the queen [Hortense] to pass on the details of your intentions. Ah! . . . do not refuse to guide me. Counsel your poor Josephine; this will be proof of your affection and will console me for all my sacrifices.'[21]

The letter, and Hortense's pleas, had their impact on Napoleon. But he was still under pressure from his wife. 'I am obliged to consider my wife's happiness,' he told Hortense.

> *Things have not developed as I hoped they would. She is alarmed by your mother's attractiveness and the hold that people know she has on me. I know this for a fact. Recently I wanted to go out driving with my wife to Malmaison. I do not know whether she thought your mother was there, but she began to cry and I was obliged to turn round and go somewhere else. However, no matter what happens, I will never oblige the Empress Josephine to do anything that she does not want to do. I shall always remember the sacrifice she has made for me. If she wishes to settle at Rome, I will have her appointed governor of the city. At Brussels she could hold a brilliant court and at the same time do good for the country. It would be still better and more suitable if she were to go and live with her son and grandchildren.*[22]

Eventually he gave way completely: 'Write to tell her that if she prefers to return to Malmaison, I shall do nothing to stand in her way.'

Josephine was reassured. She decided to depart for Geneva on 1 November and tour around the parts of the country she was not familiar with. From there she would spend one day at Malmaison en route to Navarre. She arrived on 22 November and had a much more enjoyable sojourn than her previous one. The architect Berthaut had, during her absence, restored the property to the highest standard of which he was capable, considering the building's limitations. But it was in the garden that the greatest expense had been incurred. Under the eagle eye of Aimé Bonpland, an explorer and naturalist, the gardens had been laid out afresh, and plants and flowers had been brought over from Malmaison to brighten up the melancholic winter months.

Josephine's entourage was larger and much more content than on her previous trip. It included Mme d'Arberg, who reprised her role as supervisor of the household, her dear friend Annette de Mackau and two pretty but impoverished young girls whose musical talent had distinguished them at Mme Campan's. The party also included Mlle Ducrest and her mother, with whom she had become acquainted in Switzerland. The former would in time write a rather unreliable memoir of her time with Josephine. Amongst the rolling cast of visitors was her niece Stéphanie Tascher, now the princesse d'Arenberg, and Hortense and Eugène when they could get away.

Josephine's routine was as regular as always. She did not make her appearance until eleven o'clock after she had breakfasted; then, despite the distance from Paris, she received the merchants who still besieged her door. After this she dealt with her correspondence. The local residents had quickly discovered that she could not resist a worthy cause and she was deluged with requests for funds or to lend her name to their causes. Josephine also maintained a commitment to all her old charities and continued to lobby ministers and officials on behalf of others. After lunch there was reading or needlework in the reception room. If the weather was good there were walks around the grounds or drives in an open-topped barouche. At four o'clock the party went their own way, only to regroup at six for dinner, which often included local dignitaries. Then they listened to music or performed little skits and played billiards or card games. Mme de Rémusat, remembering the leisurely rhythms of these days in Navarre, wrote, 'The time passed there in a singular manner; we were always together, we did not do anything much . . . but we were never bored.'

After the turmoil that preceded, accompanied and followed the divorce, nothing could have been better for Josephine than this calm, regular lifestyle. Her health improved and her migraines became much less frequent. She fattened up to such an extent that she was obliged to put whalebones in her corsets, for firmer control of her more ample curves. Her mellowness spread to her entourage, who gradually abandoned the rigid decorum of the past. This more relaxed, less hierarchical style of living had always suited her Creole soul but Napoleon, who had his spies at Navarre, was disapproving. He insisted on a return to full protocol, instructing that etiquette was to be observed as if she was still at the Tuileries. So Josephine, who had allowed the chamberlains and equerries to wear a simpler and cheaper uniform, was now instructed to demand that they return to their dress uniforms at all times. And when she dismissed the escort that clattered beside her carriage every time she took a drive into the woods, he immediately ordered that it be restored. Josephine did, however, succeed in winning a simpler life for the women of her household by permitting them to wear any style of dress they chose so long as it was green, the household colour.

In this peaceful atmosphere Josephine may have had the chance to assess exactly what she had lost in the divorce from the Emperor. Yes, she loved Napoleon and the status and security he brought to her life; but, as his edicts on etiquette must have reminded her, her former husband was also an intensely controlling autocrat who allowed her little autonomy. Josephine had never – despite appearances – enjoyed court life; in a rarely expressed moment of frustration she once claimed that an Empress was nothing but 'a bejewelled slave'. The Imperial palaces were, in the main, impersonal and uncomfortable. She found the constant travel exhausting and missed the company of those she genuinely cared for. She hated the court's contrived etiquette, the endless internecine squabbles amongst the courtiers and the perpetual need to mask her real feelings.

On the eve of Josephine's saint's day, 19 March, the villagers created a presentation in her honour. Young girls in white paraded past Josephine carrying her bust on a dais of flowers, and then recited verse and distributed presents. On the day itself Josephine threw a ball for the town in the great salon, whose marble flooring was boarded over for the occasion. It was all done in great style, with food and dancers brought in from Paris much to the delight of the inhabitants of Evreux. To prolong the celebrations, the next night the mayor of the town held a dinner for her. But she was tired and a little depressed; she sent her household in her stead and remained at the chateau with Mme d'Arberg. Just after the pair had completed their meal a messenger from the town's prefect arrived with an official dispatch. As he handed over the note the women heard the peal of the village bells and then a salute of forty cannon: Marie Louise's son had been born.

Josephine's reaction was, as always, impressively acted. 'After a brief constriction of her features', a witness recalled, 'she resumed the gracious manner which was habitual for her and said, "The Emperor will not doubt the real pleasure that I take in an event that gives him such joy; as you know, I am inseparable from his destiny and I will always be happy for his good fortune." ' She immediately dispatched a courier with a message of congratulations. On 22 March a note from the Emperor arrived: 'My dear, I have your letter. I thank you for it. My son is fat, and in excellent health. I trust he may continue to improve. He has my chest, my mouth, and my eyes. I hope he may fulfil his destiny. I am always well pleased with Eugène; he has never given me the least anxiety. Napoleon.' This mention of Eugène was a sensitive touch, his tacit way of reassuring her that despite the birth of a bloodchild he would continue his patronage.[23]

Napoleon's happiness resulted in a new largesse towards Josephine, and he gave her permission to return to Malmaison. She arrived at the end of April, only to be confronted by yet another financial crisis. Montlivault, her new comptroller, discovered that money had been embezzled from her accounts. The problem was particularly acute in the stables, which were under the control of the son of the prince of Monaco, who had sold off top-quality horses cheaply and bought knackered old mounts to replace them. He had falsified the accounts and 40,000 francs had disappeared. His records showed that there were sixty horses but Josephine herself attested to the fact that there were never more than fifty. Josephine's soft heart and the young man's prominent family saved him from prosecution.

But Napoleon was still anxious about the state of Josephine's finances and wrote her a warning letter:

> *Put some order into your affairs. Spend only 1,500,000 francs and save as much every year; that will make a reserve of 15 million francs in ten years for your grandchildren. It is pleasant to be able to give them something, and be helpful to them. Instead of that, I hear you have debts, which would be really too bad. Look after your affairs, and don't give to everyone who wants to help himself. If you wish to please me, let me hear that you have accumulated a large fortune. Consider how ill I must think of you, if I know that you, with 3 million francs a year, are in debt. Adieu, dear; keep well.*[24]

Napoleon's reproach was only partially justified. Josephine was a dreadful spendthrift who never did learn to manage her finances. However, a substantial proportion of her expenses were as a result of his determination that she should maintain herself in the Imperial manner. He dispatched the State Treasurer, Mollien, to visit her to discover the full extent of the problem. Reporting back to his master, Mollien concluded that matters were not as dire as they could have been, but he did confess that in the course of the interview Josephine had been reduced to tears. At this news Napoleon exclaimed, 'You musn't make her cry!' Somewhat abashed, he sent her a soothing note: 'I send to know how you are . . . I was annoyed with you about your debts. I do not wish you to have any; on the contrary, I wish you to put a million francs aside every year, to give to your grandchildren when they get married. Nevertheless, never doubt my affection for you, and don't worry any more about the present embarrassment. Adieu, dear. Send me word that you are well. They say that you are as fat as a good Normandy farmer's wife.'[25]

Over the following months Josephine did make some attempts to get her financial affairs in order. She took an active interest in her comptroller's efforts to cut expenses and increase revenue at Malmaison. He attempted to curtail the wild spending on plants by demanding a budget from Bonpland, and he let out some of the estate's uncultivated land. He also attempted to reclaim funds owed from her properties in Martinique, but this was difficult, since the island had been taken back by the British in 1809. Getting into the spirit of things, Josephine sent him her own suggestions on cost-cutting, remarking, 'You will find this letter rather serious, but I notice that every day I am becoming more of an economizer, if not an economist.' She probably believed it, too, although she still could not resist purchasing beautiful things to keep or to give away as presents.

Fiscal difficulties aside, Josephine was indeed plump and happy, throwing herself into life at her beloved Malmaison. Writing to her daughter, she described the tranquillity of her life there: 'It is perfectly calm and I am finding it very good for me.' The only interruptions to her repose were delightful ones, when Hortense's children twice arrived to stay during the summer of 1811. Josephine was a devoted grandmother who spared no effort to amuse her beloved grandchildren, spoiling them not just with toys and sweets, but also with visits from clowns and magic-lantern shows. A letter to her daughter makes plain her delight in seeing them:

> *I wanted also to reassure you about your children; their health is perfect, their colour is very good, and they seem to be as pleased to be here as I am happy to see them. They really are charming, and very gallant towards me. On Sunday, I asked Oui-Oui [the nickname for little Louis-Napoleon] who I looked like . . . He looked all around the table and he responded that I looked like the most beautiful woman in Paris. An answer which proves that he sees me more with his heart than he does with his eyes . . . They enliven everything around me; you see how happy you have made me by leaving them with me.*[26]

These summer visits from her grandsons were repeated each subsequent year till Josephine's death. It is clear from some fragments of Napoleon III's autobiography, entitled *Souvenirs de ma vie*, that these visits to his grandmother provided him with some of his earliest and clearest memories, the most 'precious relics' of his childhood.

> Then my memory carries me to Malmaison. I can still see the Empress Josephine in her salon on the ground floor, covering me with her caresses, and even then flattering my vanity by the care with which she repeated my childish bons mots. For my grandmother spoiled me in every sense of the word, whereas my mother, from my tenderest years, tried to correct my faults and develop my good qualities. I remember that once arrived at Malmaison, my brother and I were masters, to do as we pleased. The Empress, who loved flowers and conservatories passionately, allowed us to cut the sugar canes to suck them, and she always told us to ask for everything we wanted.[27]

Josephine found that life at Malmaison had improved greatly since the days following the divorce. Then the initial rush of visitors had soon trickled away into bereft isolation. Now, it was 'the height of fashion to visit *L'impératrice* Josephine at Malmaison.' The hospitality at Malmaison was so enjoyable that even courtiers-in-waiting at Saint-Cloud or the Tuileries visited and dined with her. Would-be guests inundated her *dame d'honneur* with requests for permission to visit her, as protocol required, and when they arrived they would be taken on a tour of her works of art or treated to music concerts in the gallery. If the weather was good they went for a tour around the garden, where she showed off her knowledge on botanical subjects and her menagerie of exotic animals: black swans, gazelles and kangaroos.

Josephine had always been a considerate hostess and Malmaison, despite her personal indifference to cuisine, laid a fine spread on tables elegantly decorated with exotic flowers and gorgeous porcelain. Visitors were indulged with the best food and wine; Josephine even had her own ice-cream maker, a man she had imported from Italy who pioneered a raisin and liqueur ice-cream known as 'glace Malmaison'. Those who did not share her passion for ice cream were treated to exotic fruits from her greenhouse, like bananas and pineapples. There were other delicacies provided by an English *femme de chambre*, who served up the alien delicacies of Cheshire cheese and English muffins. In tribute to Josephine, le comte Turpin de Crissé wrote that she held a court 'where dignity, grace, wit, talents and good conversation made a seat of exile into a place of enchantment and a queen without a crown into a woman surrounded by real friends'.[28]

When not entertaining guests, Josephine turned her attention to her own household. An incurable romantic, she could not resist matchmaking and meddling in the love lives of those around her. When she discovered that M. de Pourtales had begun corresponding with Mlle de Castellane, she immediately intervened. He was something of a roué and had already had an affair with Mlle Gazzani, one of Josephine's *lectrices*, with whom Napoleon had had a brief fling. Determined that he should not take advantage of the rather innocent and sweet-natured Mlle de Castellane, Josephine took them both for a turn around the grounds, where she informed them that she was aware of their burgeoning romance. Then, with a wiliness worthy of her husband, she said to Mlle de Castellane, 'You possess nothing but your name . . . M. de Pourtales is very rich; you cannot believe that he intends to marry you.' Embarrassed, Pourtales interrupted, piping up in his own defence that he would be very happy to do so. Before he had finished uttering the words, Josephine announced, 'I give a dowry of a hundred thousand francs and the trousseau.' When it was discovered that the couple were of different faiths, Josephine also smoothed this complication away by organizing one service by a pastor in the salon and another by a cardinal in the chapel.

She also facilitated the marriage of Annette de Mackau, offering the same dowry as she had done to Mlle de Castellane. Her beloved maid Mlle Avrillon chose to marry a M. Bourgillon and Josephine gave her a dowry and trousseau. Another of her servants hoped to marry a black man and Josephine obtained special permission from Napoleon for the interracial union. When one of her black maids, Malvina, fell in love with a local black man, Jean-Baptiste Julien, she also promised a financial gift.

And what of Josephine's own romantic life? There was no real obstacle to a new relationship. She was an attractive divorcee, in good health and with a joie de vivre that belied her years. Some of her biographers have maintained that her chamberlain, the artist Turpin de Crissé, was also her lover. It is a pleasant thought; Josephine deserved romantic consolation after what she had endured during the end of her marriage. But there is no evidence to substantiate an affair. The handsome painter clearly adored Josephine but she, like many women who had enjoyed a robust and tumultuous romantic life, seemed happy to retire from sexual involvement and absorb herself in the love of family and friends. Turpin de Crissé wed in 1813 with Josephine's complete blessing, and if his relations with her had ever gone beyond friendship, he never revealed it.

When not marrying off her entourage, Josephine invested much of her energy in her family. In May 1812 she spent a short but 'enchanting' visit with Hortense and her children in Saint-Leu, before they went off to Aix for the summer. In July she received permission from the Emperor to visit her heavily pregnant daughter-in-law, Augusta, in Milan. Travelling incognito, Josephine arrived laden down with presents and delicacies for her son's family: designer dresses for the beautiful Augusta and innumerable toys for the children. Her daughter-in-law had arranged a wonderful reception in the form of a great fête and she was lodged very comfortably in the villa Bonaparte. Her grandchildren were adorable: the boy was, she recounted in a letter, 'very strong; he is a Hercules-baby; his sisters are extremely pretty; the eldest is a beauty; she resembles her mother in the nobility of her features. The second girl has attractive looks, is lively and intelligent; and she will be very pretty.'[29] During Josephine's stay Augusta's fourth child was born. There had been much worry about her beloved daughter-in-law's health, but she was fine and the baby girl, 'a little kitten', was also well. Josephine stayed with Augusta until September and then went first to Aix-le-Bains and then on to Pregny for three weeks.

On 25 October Josephine returned to a capital in the midst of a political storm. Two days earlier there had been an attempted coup. The ringleader, an ex-army officer called Malet, asserted that Napoleon had been killed in Moscow and he moved to claim power. He failed; Napoleon was not dead. But for a while Paris was demoralized and frightened, reminded again of how much its fortunes hung on the fate of one man. If this was true for France, it was even truer for Josephine. Her fate was still intertwined with his, despite the divorce, and she wrote anxiously to Eugène: 'The audacity or even more the folly of the three monsters who created this trouble is truly incredible. Watch carefully over the Emperor's safety; for these evil men are capable of anything. Tell him from me that he is wrong to live in palaces without knowing whether they are mined.'[30]

The Russian campaign had been a debacle from start to finish. Napoleon had invaded in the spring of 1812, prompted by Russia's unwillingness to continue taking part in his continental blockade against Britain. The army that accompanied him was the largest assembled in living memory: 600,000 men, from all corners of his Empire, including Italians, Poles, Portuguese, Germans, Dalmatians, Danes, Dutch, Saxons and Swiss, all with their own uniforms and marching songs. Napoleon had rashly prophesied that the campaign would be over in twenty days, but as they trudged slowly across the vast spaces of the Russian plains it became clear that this would not be the case. The Russians, outnumbered two to one, refused to confront him. But as they retreated to avoid him, they inadvertently weakened Napoleon's forces. The heat of the Russian summer took its toll (some old veterans compared conditions on the march with those in Egypt) and thousands of soldiers were lost to sickness, heat and exhaustion. After two months, before a single battle had been fought, 150,000 of Napoleon's men were out of action. Many of them had simply deserted.

In early September the Empire's forces finally met the Russians south of the village of Borodino, and the ensuing battle was long and brutal. At its end 44,000 Russians were dead and wounded, while the French had lost 33,000, including a large number of Napoleon's senior officers – among them forty-three generals. The French claimed victory, but the Russians refused to make peace. Napoleon continued on to Moscow and on 15 September 1812 he entered the city. That night Moscow began to burn, set alight by its own citizens. Remembering the sight, Napoleon said, 'mountains of red, rolling flames, like immense waves of the sea. Oh, it was the most grand, the most sublime, the most terrifying sight the world had ever seen!'

From the quarters he had occupied in the Kremlin, Napoleon wrote to the Tsar, still hoping to negotiate an armistice. He received no reply and in the middle of October, on a warm autumn day, he led his army out of the city. Within three weeks it began to snow: the legendary Russian winter had come early. Soon temperatures were as low as twenty-two degrees below zero and Napoleon's troops were freezing in the open countryside. 'Our lips stuck together, our nostrils froze,' recalled one soldier, 'we seemed to be marching in a world of ice.' The suffering of the Russian retreat was indescribable: the food ran out, horses died in their thousands and the soldiers perished from starvation, cold, fatigue and disease. The Cossack army harried Napoleon's troops, picking off the weakened French soldiers as they moved through the glacial countryside. By the campaign's end, only 93,000 of the 600,000 troops were still alive. It was, as Talleyrand concluded, 'the beginning of the end'.

Josephine was frantic with worry about her son. She had had no contact with either Eugène or the Emperor; in fact there had been no news from the army in Russia at all. Finally a letter arrived from Eugène early in November; Josephine immediately sent it on to his worried sister, with a relieved note: 'I read these with such avidity. I have passed from anxiety to the most vivid sense of good fortune. My son is alive!' But no more news came. Josephine knew that Eugène had suffered during the campaign and that his leg was wounded. Her worry intensified. 'Why haven't I heard from him?' she pleaded to Hortense. Moved by their collective suffering, Marie Louise showed Hortense the letters she had received from the Emperor, knowing that she would pass the information on to her mother. Josephine was grateful. With these snippets of news, she managed to maintain her equilibrium until she finally received confirmation that Eugène was safe and recuperating well.

Rumours of a coup reached Napoleon, and he returned to Paris on 19 December in advance of his troops. Deeply shaken by his army's terrible losses, and fearing the impact on his reputation for infallibility, the Emperor insisted that the court maintain a positive front, with frequent entertainments and lavish balls. The winter season of 1812–13 passed in a curious state of denial: so many of those invited to court festivities had lost limbs in the fighting that these events were nicknamed the *'bals des jambes de bois'* (the 'wooden-leg balls'). For Josephine this season was particularly melancholy; she had remained at Malmaison instead of going to Navarre, but she was not included in the festivities. Many of her regular visitors were, however, so Josephine spent these dark, cold months alone just a stone's throw away from the diversions that absorbed her social circle.

By the beginning of 1813 the fighting had resumed. Prussia again joined Russia in an alliance against France, and Napoleon hastily scraped together an army and departed for Germany, leaving Marie Louise as regent.

This was not a good idea. Despite Napoleon's best efforts, his second wife had never been popular. The French distrusted her for being an Austrian and a relative of the hated Marie Antoinette. In addition, Marie Louise did not have Josephine's charm. Despite her royal birth – or perhaps because of it – she did not possess Josephine's desire or talent to please. When the Emperor sent her to Cherbourg in 1813 to raise morale and launch a ship, the Minister of Police wrote a revealing letter to the commander of her Imperial Guard escort. He begged le comte Caffarelli to ensure that the Empress would be punctual, that she would smile, that she would speak kindly to those who were presented to her and that she would show confidence; 'For God's sake, my friend, no ice . . . you understand', he added.[31]

It was becoming evident that Napoleon's Empire was an edifice that was slowly crumbling, besieged from without, eaten away by dissent from within.

In part this was because of its sheer size. The Grand Empire was a vast, bloated, unwieldy thing, difficult to control, impossible to police. By 1812 the Inner Empire included not only France proper but Westphalia, Berg, Baden, the Swiss Confederation, Bavaria and the Kingdom of Italy. The Intermediate Zones of the Empire included the grand duchy of Warsaw and the Kingdom of Naples, while the Outer Empire comprised Spain, Bremen, Rome and the Illyrian provinces including Dalmatia, Croatia and part of the Tyrol.

Whether these states were ruled directly as French departments, by proxy in his satellite kingdoms, or by indirect pressure as in the case of independent states like the Confederation of the Rhine, Napoleonic rule engendered discontent in many places. The grievances were numerous. Chief among them was the misery of conscription. Compulsory military service had existed in many of the states of eighteenth-century Europe, but in practice few men were actually taken, so the extraordinary demands of the Napoleonic Empire came as a terrible shock. As well as the horror of having their menfolk plucked from their towns often never to return, the loss of a youthful workforce generated great economic hardship. Attacks on religion also engendered much ill-feeling. Despite the provisions of the Concordat recognizing Catholicism as the religion of most French people, Napoleon's determination that the Church should be completely subordinate to the state led to appropriation of Church property and the closing of orders. The pitiful sight of nuns begging in the streets in some parts of the Empire did not inspire goodwill for the Napoleonic regime.[32]

These miseries were exacerbated by the other hardships of war. Many Europeans' first experience of Napoleon's Grand Army was brutal: these were violent, battle-hardened troops who raped, pillaged and ravaged their way across occupied lands. In addition, their victims were forced to pay high taxes and financial levies to compensate for the costs of occupation. It was no surprise that there was popular resistance in many parts of the Empire. Major revolts broke out in Calabria in 1806, Portugal in 1808 and the Tyrol in 1809. But the most spectacular example was that of Spain, where French rule provoked massive popular resistance. The word for this genuine war of liberation, *guerrilla,* gave its name to a style of warfare still used today. Napoleon massively misjudged the threat of Spanish resistance and never really treated it with the seriousness it merited; the Spanish problem remained a running sore for the Empire, bleeding it of valuable troops and giving heart to other resistance movements.

Napoleon's Empire was dependent on a series of alliances that could not be sustained or relied upon. Denmark, Saxony and Mecklenburg were trustworthy, but others, like the Kingdom of Prussia and the Austrian Empire, offered only a facade of loyalty. This was largely because Napoleon insisted on treaties that were so disadvantageous to his allies' interests that they eventually felt it necessary to renege on them. The Russian campaign was a case in point. With the Treaty of Tilsit in 1807 Tsar Alexander had tacitly conceded French domination of Europe. Yet Napoleon did not invest in sustaining this massive compromise. Instead of nurturing his relationship with the Tsar, he jeopardized this vital alliance by developing the grand duchy of Warsaw, which he knew would make Russia insecure (Polish weakness had long been seen as a precondition of Russian strength). This action fuelled Russian distrust and made it easier for the Tsar to abandon the continental system, which was proving calamitous for the Russian economy, at the end of 1810. This act of independence was a provocation; Napoleon had the option of a conciliatory response – he and the Tsar had once enjoyed a good relationship – but instead he moved instantly to prepare for war. When his former ally made diplomatic approaches towards him, he did not respond positively. His closest advisors counselled against going to war; they felt that France should conserve its resources for its real enemies, like England. But Napoleon could not be deterred: he put together a massive coalition and attacked in 1812. The ensuing disaster proved to the rest of Europe that continued Napoleonic power would entail ceaseless war and, simultaneously, that France could be contained, even beaten. Napoleon meant war, but not always victory. His fall was now inevitable.

Even those alliances that Napoleon had built on blood ties were proving unreliable. Of his siblings, only Élisa had proved a natural ruler – a firm and conscientious adminstrator with a definite vision for her domain. Joseph had been a major disappointment in Spain, unable to impose any kind of order on the country's domestic upheavals, his incompetence and inconsistencies only exacerbating resentment. Meanwhile, in the Kingdom of Westphalia, Jérôme was playing at being king with little enthusiasm or efficacy. Indeed, the loyalty of some of Napoleon's siblings seemed to be wavering. Louis had been the first to renounce his position, unwilling to be a puppet ruler and sacrifice what he felt was the well-being of his kingdom for that of his brother. In Naples, where his sister Caroline ruled with her husband Joachim Murat, the motivation for turning away from Napoleon was fuelled by ambition rather than principle. Determined to hang on to his throne come what may, within the year Murat made a secret pact with Vienna against the brother-in-law who had nurtured his career and been responsible for his elevation.

Napoleon too had changed. He was growing increasingly divorced from reality, insulated by his flattering, servile court. As early as 1807 Josephine had written to Eugène expressing her worry abut the impact of the court and its constant toadying: 'The Emperor is too grand for anybody to tell him the truth, everybody who surrounds him flatters him all day long.'[33] Napoleon's tendency to surround himself with sycophants had grown worse since the divorce. Without Josephine's moderating influence he had grown more autocratic and isolated. He no longer accepted advice; he had confidence only in himself and his 'star'. This problem was exacerbated by the size of the court, which had grown exponentially in the years immediately after the divorce. Its scope and its grandeur now absorbed more of his time and his interest.

The young military genius who felt alive only in combat had disappeared; Napoleon was now a plump, middle-aged man who would rather remain at home with his new wife and child, enjoying court life. He had always believed that his powers would decline when he reached the age of forty, and he was now forty-two, his stomach swollen to a paunch. The prospect of field life, with its discomforts and deprivations, haunted him rather than excited him. As he told an aide: 'The late hours, the hardships of war, are not for me at my age. I love my bed, my repose, more than anything, but I must finish my work.'

But, above all, the reason why the Grand Empire was destined to end was because Europe – including the population of France – was profoundly tired of war. Napoleon had ascended to power in 1799 with the promise of bringing peace to the nation. Since then every subsequent campaign was promised as the last, the one that would finally bring about the cessation of war. Now the populace was increasingly sceptical about Napoleon's claims to desire reconciliation. People in France were beginning to say, one contemporary claimed, that 'Every year wars grow worse, fresh conquests force him to seek out fresh enemies. Soon Europe will not be enough for him, he will hanker after Asia.'[34]

This loss of faith was underpinned by the realities of life under Napoleonic rule, with its ceaseless conflicts and annual haemorrhaging of hundreds of thousands of young men. In his memoirs, Chateaubriand described the conscription notices pasted on street corners, the crowds gathered in front of those huge death warrants: 'looking in consternation, for the names of their children, their brothers, their friends, their neighbours'. Now, he noted, every criticism of Bonaparte that escaped the censor's pen was met in the theatres with rapture. He concluded that 'the people, the court, the generals, the ministers and Napoleon's relatives were weary of his tyranny and his conquests . . . because of the impossibility of peace'.[35] The novelist Alfred de Musset in his memoirs presented a vivid picture of what it was like growing up under Napoleon: 'Never were there so many sleepless nights as in the time of this man; never were to be seen, leaning over the ramparts of town walls, such a nation of sorrowing mothers; never did such silence envelop those who spoke of death.'[36]

There was a brief interlude of peace in spring 1813, and Josephine's visitors returned along with the beautiful weather. In May she spent a few days in Saint-Leu; in June she joined Hortense and her children for their annual three-month stay in Aix. But this tranquillity lasted only until August, when Austria joined forces with France's enemies. Hortense had taken the boys to Dieppe, and Josephine had nothing to distract her from her obsessive worrying about the fates of Eugène and the Emperor. In October Wellington advanced from Spain into France, and Eugène's father-in-law, the king of Bavaria, who was now an ally of the Austrians, wrote to him offering the opportunity to sign an armistice. Eugène responded warmly and respectfully, but affirming his complete devotion to the Emperor; it was his duty, he said, not to accept this proposal. His wife Augusta also wrote to her father. With touching nobility she asked him to protect her children, should the need arise, but declared that out of loyalty to her husband she could no longer communicate with him.

Eugène's fidelity to the Emperor was a source of great pride to Josephine. His honourable behaviour was in striking contrast to that of the Bonaparte clan. Both Murat and Bernadotte had shown themselves willing to collude with Napoleon's enemies. Only the abdicated Louis was faithful; he wrote to Napoleon asking that in this 'time of misfortune' their quarrels be put aside so that he could return to France and serve beside him. When she heard this, and despite the misery of their marriage, Hortense commented, 'My husband is a good Frenchman, he has proved it by returning to France at the point when all of Europe has turned against it. He is an honest man and, if our characters were incompatible, it was because we each had faults that could not be reconciled.'[37]

On 22 November Eugène was offered a chance to change his mind when an aide-de-camp of the king of Bavaria, disguised as an Austrian officer, demanded to see him. He proposed that Eugène should desert Napoleon, in exchange for which the king would protect his interests in Italy and guarantee him a crown. Eugène was steadfast: 'I am sorry to have to refuse the king, but this is impossible . . . It is not to be denied that the Emperor's star is beginning to wane, but that is only another reason why those who have received so much from him should remain faithful.' He then wrote to Napoleon to reassert his fidelity:

> *I did not need to reflect for long to be able to assure the king of Bavaria that his son-in-law was too honest a man to commit such a despicable act; that I would, until my final breath, remain true to the oath that I made to you and that I repeated, to serve you faithfully; and that the fate of my family is, and always will be, in your hands; and that even if misfortune was poised above our heads, that finally, I had a sufficiently high opinion of the king of the Bavaria to be sure in advance that he would prefer to find his son-in-law an honest man rather than a king and a traitor.*[38]

But the situation had moved beyond such lofty issues as loyalty; Napoleon was fighting for his very survival. Battles were now taking place on French soil. The mercurial shifts in the army's fortunes – this battle won, that lost – meant that communication lines were totally disrupted. No one really knew what was going on, and this exacerbated national anxiety. In lieu of any concrete information, rumours and questions reverberated across the country. Having trampled across much of Europe, occupying its lands and mistreating its peoples, France was now fearful of retribution being wreaked on its soil. At Malmaison, where all that was left of the guard was sixteen wounded soldiers, Josephine was desperately frightened. All was crumbling around her – the Emperor, the Empire – and her children were far away: Eugène in Italy and Hortense ordered to stay with Marie Louise.

She spent her days worrying about the Emperor and wondering whether she should flee the capital, as so many had done already. She divided her time between lobbying her formidable network of contacts for information and making lint for the hospitals. On the night of 28 March she received a messenger from Hortense informing her that Marie Louise was leaving Paris the following morning. The Empress's flight was a turning point in French morale. The city read it as a sign that all was lost. After much agonizing

Josephine decided to abandon her beloved Malmaison, where her black swans had just had their first cygnets. She fled to Navarre on 29 March. It was a cold, rainy morning and she travelled with all her horses and carriages, and with some of her valuable jewellery sewn into her petticoat. By the time she arrived she was despondent. She wrote to Hortense, 'I don't know if it is possible to express how unhappy I am. I have had courage in the many sad situations in which I have found myself; I can bear these reversals of fortune; but I do not know if I have enough strength to bear the absence of my children and the uncertainty of their fate.' Two days later Hortense and her children joined her with the news that Paris had capitulated. Napoleon was under virtual house arrest at Fontainebleau.

As soon as he arrived in Paris for meetings with the other allied leaders to conclude the peace and celebrate the victory, Tsar Alexander wrote to Josephine requesting to see her. Her instinctive response was to refuse him; she had no desire to fraternize with the enemy. But Napoleon himself advised her to return, suggesting that ' . . . the future of your children depends upon it'. On 14 April Josephine journeyed back to Malmaison, profoundly tired and depleted, unsure whether she could rally her strength to face such an emergency. Like an actress coming to the end of a long run, she dug deep within herself to find the energy to once again play the role of the 'incomparable Josephine'. She fell back on the weapons that had always served her in the past: her charm and her attractiveness. She ordered an exquisite new wardrobe of beautiful diaphanous dresses from Leroy and redoubled her efforts at the make-up mirror. When Hortense joined her a couple of days later, her mother was immersed in her part, strolling arm in arm with the Tsar in the garden while the courtyard bristled with Cossacks. Hortense recalled, 'I arrived at Malmaison at one o'clock. I was astonished to see the courtyard full of Cossacks and great activity everywhere, and I asked the reason. I was told that my mother was walking in the garden with the Emperor of Russia. I went to join them and met them near the hothouse. My mother was pleased and surprised to see me. She kissed me tenderly and said to the Emperor, "Here is my daughter with my grandsons. I commend them to you".'[39]

Hortense was cold and brusque with the Tsar, until Josephine reprimanded her sharply. She reminded her daughter that without Alexander's intervention Napoleon would have been forced to accept even harsher terms. She also pointed out that, despite Napoleon's attempt to protect them in the act of abdication he had negotiated, the Beauharnais's situation was still vulnerable. Eugène's fate in particular remained uncertain. Hortense eventually thawed out; and Alexander continued to visit and eventually won her over. The Tsar's fondness for Malmaison started a fashion amongst the allied leaders, who flocked there to meet Josephine and tour her famous gardens. After time spent in her delightful company, enjoying her wonderful table and perusing her art collection, they left utterly enchanted and beguiled.

In a letter to his sister Sophia dated 25 April the future Leopold I of Belgium wrote,

> *This evening, I am to dine with the grand duke at Malmaison; I hope you*
> *will be pleased with me when you read the following: though everyone*
> *loves poor Josephine and Queen Hortense, they are in a very difficult*
> *position. Though they asked nothing of me, I arranged an interview with*
> *the 'Cesar' at Malmaison which had the happiest consequences for them.*
> *There was no one but me who could talk to the Emperor on this subject,*
> *and I did not hesitate to make things right for them. Now, I can congratulate*
> *myself on this point. They were very friendly to me at the time of their*
> *prosperity, and now that nobody cares about them and I can no longer hope*
> *for any protection from them, I have acted in such a way as to show them*
> *my gratitude and have protected them in my turn.*

But underneath Josephine's apparent gaiety and charm, the anxiety and turmoil of the preceding months had taken a profound toll. She confided in Mlle Cochelet: 'I'm suffering from a terrible sadness that I cannot conquer . . . The thought of my children in distress! The very idea will kill me.'[40] She also grieved incessantly for her ex-husband, worrying about how he was and what the future would hold for him. She said to one of Hortense's household, 'Sometimes I feel so melancholy that I could die of despair; I cannot be reconciled to Bonaparte's fate.'[41] Her daughter recalled, 'the picture of the Emperor cast down from his throne and confined to the island of Elba was constantly before her eyes, and tore her heart'.[42]

On 14 May 1814 Hortense, accompanied by her mother and Eugène, received Alexander at Saint-Leu, at his own request. While out walking with him Josephine caught a chill, which she assured everyone would clear up of its own accord. On 23 May she had a visit from the king of Prussia and the Grand Duke Constantine. 'My mother was already ill and made an effort to come down to welcome them', Hortense remembered. 'She seemed to me to have a mere cold and her health was usually so good that I was not at all alarmed.'[43] Josephine had to spend the next day in bed, but her doctor,

Horeau, professed not to be too worried. So the following day she insisted on hosting a gathering and opening the dancing with the Tsar. She then linked arms with Alexander and took a long walk around the grounds, exacerbating her condition further. She made light of her illness but by Wednesday her arms and chest were covered with a rash. By Thursday night her condition had deteriorated even further: her tongue was swollen and the fever had climbed. Horeau prescribed blistering for her shoulders and mustard plasters for her feet, but none of these treatments improved the situation.

Her condition had clearly developed into something serious. On the 27th, according to Hortense, 'The Emperor of Russia sent his chief doctor. Though she was very tired she said to him in her usual gracious way: I hope his [the Tsar's] interest will bring me luck.' Indeed, the Tsar Alexander was expected for dinner the following day. Despite her illness, Josephine supervised every detail for his reception and intended to get up to welcome him. Her doctor suggested she stay in bed but Josephine dissented; there were influential people to entertain and win over. 'When he left her,' recalled Hortense, 'the doctor's anxious face prepared us for what he had to say: he found her very ill.' Terrified, Hortense sent for the best doctors in Paris: Bourdois de la Motte, Lamoureux and Lasserre.

To distract and cheer her, Redouté brought Josephine the paintings he was making of the plants in her greenhouse. She smiled gratefully but waved him away from the bed, in case her illness was contagious. That evening, 28 April, Alexander was expected for dinner again and, according to legend, an unexpected guest arrived – her childhood sweetheart, 'William', who had never ceased to love her. But Josephine received neither of them for she was now almost completely unable to speak. Horeau, and the team of doctors he had hurriedly consulted, admitted that there was little hope. Josephine was having trouble breathing, her pulse was faint and a purple patch at the back of her throat had darkened. The terrible pain she suffered was relieved somewhat by her receding consciousness. More blisters were induced, and that night Hortense stayed with her.

At one point she brought her children in to wish their grandmother goodnight. Josephine sent them away at once, saying, 'The air here is bad; it might harm them.'[44] She wanted to send Hortense away too. To keep her calm, Hortense left, but stayed near her mother's apartment throughout the night. 'My waiting-woman told me not to worry, that she was peaceful, that she sometimes murmured a few words: "Bonaparte . . . island of Elba . . . the king of Rome".'[45] But by eight o'clock the following morning, when

Hortense and Eugène went to see her, it was clear that nothing could save her. 'When she saw us, she held out her arms with great emotion and uttered something we could not understand.' At eleven o'clock the abbé Bertrand was brought to administer the last rites while her children wept at her bedside. At noon, attired in a rose silk peignoir and bedecked with rubies, she died. Some doctors ascribed her end to diphtheria, others to septicaemia of the throat. Whatever the presenting cause, there can be no doubt that, at nearly fifty-one, Josephine was worn out. She was simply too burdened by exhaustion and sorrow to reinvent herself, to make the transition into a new life under a new regime. Her maid Mlle Avrillon suggested a different diagnosis, one that may offer a deeper truth: 'she died of grief'.

For three days Josephine lay in state in the stucco-pillared foyer at Malmaison. An estimated 20,000 members of the public paid their final respects. Slowly they filed past the sentries of the Imperial Guard, down the long driveway that intersected the beautifully manicured grounds, into the courtyard and past the coffin of lead and mahogany on the black-draped catafalque. There lay their Lady of Victory – 'as if sleeping', whispered one mourner – her long-lashed eyelids peacefully closed and her mouth set firm, haunted by just the ghost of a smile. The bells of the surrounding parishes tolled continuously and the local curates prayed for her soul.

In the capital the public grief was as evident as at Malmaison. On the streets of the city pamphlets entitled 'The Last Will and Testament of the Empress Josephine' were being sold despite the fact that she had died intestate. There was public demand for her to retain her title into death, even though the Emperor had been deposed. In part in response to the public outcry, in part to quash the rumours of poisoning that circulated whenever someone famous died, the new Louis XVIII was forced to publish a bulletin which read, 'The news of the death of Mme de Beauharnais has provoked general sadness. This woman was born with sweetness and something genuinely good in her manner and in her spirit. Sadly, during the terrible times of the rule of her husband she was forced to take refuge against his brutalities in her love of horticulture . . . She alone amongst the milieu of this Corsican upstart spoke the language of the French and understood their hearts.'

At noon on Thursday 2 June the coffin was closed and the cortège set out for the church at Rueil. Directly behind the hearse were the local representatives carrying the parish banners. They were escorted by a detachment of the Imperial Guard, in full dress uniform, their drums draped in black crêpe. Behind them, a solitary footman in a mourning cloak carried a cushion with a small silver casket perched on top: this contained the heart of the Empress. On both sides of the hearse were the four pall-bearers: the grand duke of Baden, whose genuine affliction was evident; the marquis and the comte de Beauharnais (Alexandre's brother François and uncle Claude); and the comte de Tascher. Behind the hearse were the chief mourners, Eugène and Hortense, the faithful Mme d'Arberg and Josephine's grand-children. They were accompanied by the governor of Paris, the aide-de-camp of the Tsar and official representatives of the king of Prussia.

Along a route lined by the National Guard they walked, followed by a long, snaking procession which included numerous personalities of the old Imperial regime, foreign dignitaries and diplomats, as well as local celebrities in the arts and sciences. Amongst the mourners were twenty muslin-clad girls singing canticles, and two thousand workers and peasants whose weeping was clearly audible despite the muffled beat of the drums and the tolling of the bells. On arrival at the church, which was entirely draped in black, they were met by the archbishop of Tours, the bishops of Evreux and Versailles and the choir of the Madeleine, who waited to commence the service. The crowd was so large that only those with written invitations could hope to enter the church, but the rest settled outside, straining to hear what they could of the proceedings.

There was no emblem or symbol of her past rank evident at the service, though the tributes to Josephine were fulsome, even florid. But no eulogy, however articulate, could capture the whirlwind that was her life: her child-hood in the heat of the Caribbean; the rejection and isolation of her first marriage; the misery of life in the Revolution and the terror of imprisonment in the shadow of the guillotine; that hasty marriage to a young general who would usher her onto the world stage and transform her into the Empress of the French.

Seven hundred miles away, on the island of Elba, Napoleon eventually received the news of Josephine's death. Utterly devastated, he retired to bed for three days in a darkened room, alone and without food. During the Hundred Days, when he returned to France to make a final attempt to recapture his empire, and before the ill-fated battle at Waterloo, he made a pilgrimage to Malmaison. There he interviewed all those who had been with Josephine during her final hours, attempting to discover her last thoughts. He then wandered through the house and grounds disconsolately, saying, 'I still seem to see her walking along the paths and collecting the flowers that she loved so much. Poor Josephine! She was truly more full of charm than any other person I have ever known. She was a woman in the fullest meaning of the word: capricious and alive, and with the best of hearts.' When Napoleon died, in the spring of 1821, the last word to leave his lips was the name he had given her: 'Josephine'.

NOTES

I CHILDHOOD

1 Frédéric Masson, *Joséphine de Beauharnais* (Paris, 1913), p. 28.
2 Robert Rose-Rosette, *Les Jeunes Années de L'Impératrice Joséphine* (Les Trois-Îlets, 1992), p. 30.
3 François Girod, *La Vie quotidienne de la société créole* (Paris, 1972), p. 29.
4 Sidney Daney, *Histoire de la Martinique* (Fort-Royal, 1846), p. 252.
5 Ibid., p. 254.
6 M. A. Le Normand, *The Historical and Secret Memoirs of the Empress Josephine*, vol. I (London, 1895), p. 6.
7 Lafcadio Hearn, *Esquisses Martiniquaises* (Paris, 1887), p. 72.
8 Dr Jones quoted in James Walvin, *Black Ivory* (London, 1992), p. 94.
9 Victor Schoelcher quoted in *Vivre, survivre et être libre* (Fort de France), 22 May–22 July 1998, p. 33.
10 This anecdote is related by numerous sources, including C. L. R. James, *The Black Jacobins* (London, 1980), p. 56.
11 For details of accusations of poisoning, see Françoise Wagener, *L'Impératrice Joséphine* (Paris, 1999), p. 424.
12 Le Normand, *The Historical and Secret Memoirs*, p. 32.
13 Quoted in William B. Cohen, *The French Encounters with Africans* (Bloomington, Indiana, 1980), p. 104.
14 C. L. R. James, *The Black Jacobins*, p. 57.
15 J. B. T. de Chanvallon, *Voyage à la Martinique* (Paris, 1763), p. 38.
16 Girod, *La Vie quotidienne*, p. 74.
17 See Evangeline Bruce, *Napoleon and Josephine: An Improbable Marriage* (London, 1996), p. 1.
18 Masson, *Joséphine de Beauharnais*, p. 56.
19 Ibid., p. 56.
20 Quoted in Ernest Knapton, *Empress Josephine* (London, 1969), p. 16.
21 Rose-Rosette, *Les Jeunes Années*, p. 30.
22 Joseph Aubenas, *Histoire de l'Impératrice Joséphine*, vol. I (Paris, 1857), p. 77.
23 Ibid., p. 78.
24 Ibid., p. 84.

25 Le Normand, *The Historical and Secret Memoirs*, p. 8.
26 Moreau de Saint-Méry quoted in Girod, *La Vie quotidienne*, p. 31.
27 L. Garaud, *Trois Ans à la Martinique*, 2nd edn (Paris, 1895), p. 54.
28 J. G. M. de Montgaillard, *Souvenirs* (Paris, 1895), p. 277.
29 C. A. Tercier, *Mémoires politiques et militaires* (Paris, 1891), p. 15.
30 Le Normand, *The Historical and Secret Memoirs*, p. 19–20.
31 See *Le Thé*, 30 Mai 1797.
32 Lafcadio Hearn quoted in Liliane Chauleau, *Les Antilles au temps de Schoelcher* (Paris, 1990), p. 242.
33 Masson, *Joséphine de Beauharnais*, p. 29.
34 Ibid., p. 67.
35 Ibid., p. 73.
36 Ibid., p. 75.
37 Jean Hanoteau, *Le Ménage Beauharnais: Joséphine avant Napoléon – d'après des correspondances inédites* (Paris, 1935), p. 80.

2 ARRIVAL

1 Quoted in François Girod, *La Vie quotidienne de la société créole* (Paris, 1972), p. 32.
2 Frédéric Masson, *Joséphine de Beauharnais* (Paris, 1913), p. 10.
3 Jean Hanoteau, *Le Ménage Beauharnais: Joséphine avant Napoléon – d'après des correspondances inédites* (Paris, 1935), p. 76.
4 Ibid., p. 28.
5 Ibid., p. 28.
6 Ibid., p. 54.
7 Ibid., p. 78.
8 Ibid., p. 78.

3 MARRIED LIFE

1 Mme de La Tour du Pin, *Memoirs*, ed. and tr. Felice Harcourt (London, 1969), p. 72.
2 Arthur Young, *Travels in France during the years 1787, 1788 & 1789*, ed. Constantia Maxwell (Cambridge, 1950), p. 90.
3 Quoted in Evelyn Farr, *Before the Deluge* (London, 1994), p. 22.
4 Mercier quoted in Alain Corbin, *The Foul and the Fragrant: Odour and the Social Imagination* (London, 1996), p. 54.

5 Gouverneur Morris, *The Diary and Letters of Gouverneur Morris*, ed. A. C. Morris (London and New York, 1889), p. 57.

6 F. K. Turgeon, 'Fanny de Beauharnais: Bibliographical Notes and Bibliography' in *Modern Philology*, August 1932, p. 62.

7 Ibid., p. 64.

8 Prince de Ligne quoted in Evelyn Farr, *Before the Deluge*, p. 121.

9 Jean Hanoteau, *Le Ménage Beauharnais: Joséphine avant Napoléon – d'après des correspondances inédites* (Paris, 1935), p. 85.

10 Ibid., p. 87.

11 Alicia M. Annas, 'The Elegant Art of Movement' in *An Elegant Art: Fashion and Fantasy in the Eighteenth Century*, organized by Edward Maeder (New York and Los Angeles, 1973), p. 48.

12 William Howard Adams, *The Paris Years of Thomas Jefferson* (New Haven, Conn. and London, 1997), p. 298.

13 L. S. Mercier, *The Picture of Paris Before and After the Revolution* (London, 1929), p. 103.

14 J. Christopher Herold, *Mistress to an Age: A Life of Madame de Staël* (London, 1959), p. 165.

15 Ibid., p. 58.

16 Ibid., p. 69.

17 Adams, *The Paris Years*, p. 212.

18 See Dr. G. Valensin, *Le Lit de Joséphine* (Paris, 1971).

19 de La Tour du Pin, *Memoirs*, p. 342.

20 Ibid., p. 342.

21 Hanoteau, *Le Ménage Beauharnais*, p. 43.

22 Ibid., p. 103.

23 Frédéric Masson, *Joséphine de Beauharnais* (Paris, 1913), p. 12.

24 Ibid., p. 10.

25 Hanoteau, *Le Ménage Beauharnais*, p. 102.

26 Ibid., p. 87.

27 Ibid., p. 90.

28 Ibid., p. 91.

29 Ibid., p. 92.

30 Ibid., p. 95.

31 Ibid., p. 106.

32 Ibid., p. 58.

33 Ibid., p. 103.

34 Ibid., p. 104.

35 Ibid., p. 115.

36 Ibid., p. 124.

37 Ibid., p. 125.
38 Ibid., p. 130.
39 Ibid., p. 137.
40 Ibid., p. 14.

4 ALEXANDRE IN MARTINIQUE

1 Jean Hanoteau, *Le Ménage Beauharnais: Joséphine avant Napoléon – d'après des correspondances inédites* (Paris, 1935), p. 149.
2 Ibid., p. 151.
3 Ibid., p. 152.
4 Ibid., p. 156.
5 Ibid., p. 155.
6 Ibid., p. 158.
7 Ibid., p. 160.
8 Ibid., p. 162.
9 Frédéric Masson, *Joséphine de Beauharnais* (Paris, 1913), p. 117.
10 Hanoteau, *Le Ménage Beauharnais*, p. 173.
11 Ibid., p. 171.
12 Ibid., p. 186.
13 Masson, *Joséphine de Beauharnais*, p. 115.
14 Ibid., p. 116.
15 Hanoteau, *Le Ménage Beauharnais*, p. 124.
16 Masson, *Joséphine de Beauharnais*, p. 118.
17 Hanoteau, *Le Ménage Beauharnais*, p. 183.

5 THE CONVENT

1 Explored in Virginia Swain, 'Hidden From View: French Women Authors and the Language of Rights', in *Intimate Encounters: Love and Domesticity in Eighteenth-Century France*, ed. Richard Rand (Hanover, N. H. and Princeton N. J., 1997), p. 22.
2 Jean Hanoteau, *Le Ménage Beauharnais: Joséphine avant Napoléon – d'après des correspondances inédites* (Paris, 1935), p. 201.
3 Ibid., p. 194.
4 Ibid., p. 197.
5 Ibid., p. 197.
6 Alicia M. Annas, 'The Elegant Art of Movement' in *An Elegant Art: Fashion*

and Fantasy in the Eighteenth Century, organized by Edward Maeder (New York and Los Angeles, 1973), p. 47.

7 Hanoteau, *Le Ménage Beauharnais*, p. 199.

6 FONTAINEBLEAU

1 Quoted in Francine du Plessix Gray, *At Home with the Marquis de Sade* (London, 1999), p. 255.
2 Mercier quoted in William Howard Adams, *The Paris Years of Thomas Jefferson* (New Haven, Conn. and London, 1997), p. 38.
3 Ibid., p. 41.
4 L. S. Mercier, *The Picture of Paris Before and After the Revolution* (London, 1929), p. 135.
5 Simon Schama, *Citizens: A Chronicle of the French Revolution* (London, 1989), p. 131.
6 See Chantal Thomas, *The Wicked Queen: The Origins of the Myth of Marie-Antoinette*, tr. Julie Rose (New York and London, 1999).
7 Quoted in Adams, *The Paris Years*, p. 47.
8 Ibid., p. 215.
9 Impératrice Joséphine, *Correspondance 1782–1814*, eds. Bernard Chevallier, Maurice Catinat and Christophe Pincemaille (Paris, 1996), p. 14.

7 RETURN OF THE NATIVE

1 Queen Hortense, *The Memoirs of Queen Hortense*, vol. I, ed. Prince Napoleon, tr. Arthur K. Griggs and F. Mabel Robinson (London, 1929), p. 31.
2 Source unknown.
3 Queen Hortense, *Memoirs*, vol. I, p. 30.
4 Queen Hortense, *Memoirs*, vol. I, p. 32.
5 See, for example, Jacques Petitjean Roget, *J'ai Assassiné la Sultane Validé* (Fort-de-France, 1990).
6 Armand Nicolas, 'La Résistance des esclaves à la Martinique à la veille de la Révolution de 1789 – Spécial Révolution 1789', *Les Cahiers du patrimonie* (Martinique, n.d.), p. 111.
7 Jacques Janssens, *Joséphine de Beauharnais et son temps* (Paris, 1963), p. 86.
8 David P. Geggus, 'Slavery, War and Revolution in the Greater Caribbean, 1789–1815', in *A Turbulent Time*, eds. David B. Gaspar and David P. Geggus (Indiana, 1997), p. 3.

9 Marquise de Sade quoted in Francine du Plessix Gray, *At Home with the Marquis de Sade* (London, 1999), p. 292.

10 Armand Nicholas, 'La Résistance des esclaves', *Les Cahiers du patrimonie* (Martinique, n.d.), p118.

11 Ibid., p. 117.

8 REVOLUTION

1 William Howard Adams, *The Paris Years of Thomas Jefferson* (New Haven, Conn. and London, 1997), p. 266.

2 Gouverneur Morris, *The Diary and Letters of Gouverneur Morris*, ed. A. C. Morris (London and New York, 1889), p. 35.

3 Richard Holmes, *Footsteps* (London, 1995), p. 74. The author is speaking of his feelings regarding 1960s student politics but it seems entirely appropriate here.

4 Ibid., p. 80.

5 Marquis de Bouillé, *Souvenirs et fragments pour servir aux mémoires de ma vie et de mon temps: 1769–1812*, vol. I (Paris, 1906–11), pp. 53–4.

6 Baron de Frénilly, *Recollections of Baron de Frénilly, Peer of France*, tr. Frederic Lees (London, 1990), p. 81.

7 Germaine de Staël quoted in Marilyn Yalom, *Blood Sisters: The French Revolution in Women's Memory* (London, 1995), p. 25.

8 Lezay-Marnesia quoted in Evangeline Bruce, *Napoleon and Josephine: An Improbable Marriage* (London, 1996), p. 42.

9 Aileen Ribeiro, *Fashion in the French Revolution* (London, 1988), p. 75.

10 Jean Hanoteau, *Le Ménage Beauharnais: Joséphine avant Napoléon – d'après des correspondances inédites* (Paris, 1935), p. 201.

11 Frédéric Masson, *Joséphine de Beauharnais* (Paris, 1913), p. 163.

12 Queen Hortense, *The Memoirs of Queen Hortense*, vol. I, ed. Prince Napoleon, tr. Arthur K. Griggs and F. Mabel Robinson (London, 1929), p. 33.

13 Baron de Frénilly, *Recollections*, p. 91.

14 Ibid., p. 95.

15 Germaine de Staël quoted in Marilyn Yalom, *Blood Sisters*, p. 146.

16 André Gavoty, *Les Amoureux de l'Impératrice Joséphine* (Paris, 1961), p. 78.

17 Source unknown.

18 Simon Schama, *Citizens: A Chronicle of the French Revolution* (New York, 1989), p. 631.

19 Ibid., p. 615.

20 Impératrice Joséphine, *Correspondance 1782–1814*, eds. Bernard Chevallier, Maurice Catinat and Christophe Pincemaille (Paris, 1996), p. 16.

21 William B. Cohen, *The French Encounter with Africans* (Bloomington, Indiana, 1980), p. 115.

22 Masson, *Joséphine de Beauharnais*, pp. 186–7.

23 Ibid., p. 208.

24 Schama, *Citizens*, p. 788.

25 Claye quoted in Alain Corbin, *The Foul and the Fragrant* (Leamington Spa, 1994), p. 196.

26 Fabre d'Eglantine quoted in Simon Schama, *Citizens*, p. 771.

27 Mme de Rémusat, *Memoirs of Madame de Rémusat 1802–1808*, vol. 1 (London, 1880), tr. Mrs. Cashel Hoey and John Lillie, p. 34.

28 Élisabeth Vigée-Lebrun quoted in Marilyn Yalom, *Blood Sisters*, p. 25.

29 Quoted in Ewa Lajer-Burcharth, *Necklines: The Art of Jacques-Louis David after the Terror* (New Haven, Conn. and London, 1999), p. 17.

30 Source unknown.

31 Masson, *Joséphine de Beauharnais*, p. 201.

32 Ibid., p. 209.

33 Ibid., p. 210.

34 Queen Hortense, *Memoirs*, vol. I, p. 34.

9 IMPRISONMENT

1 Grace Dalrymple Elliott, *Journal of My Life During the French Revolution* (London, 1859), p. 189.

2 Source unknown.

3 Quoted in André Gavoty, *Les Amoureux de l'Impératrice Joséphine* (Paris, 1961), p. 115.

4 Queen Hortense, *The Memoirs of Queen Hortense*, vol. I, ed. Prince Napoleon, tr. Arthur K. Griggs and F. Mabel Robinson (London, 1929), p. 38.

5 Quoted in Dorinda Outram, 'The Guillotine, the Soul and the Audience for Death', in *The Body and the French Revolution* (New Haven, Conn. and London, 1989), p. 113.

6 Ibid., p. 111.

7 Impératrice Joséphine, *Correspondance 1782–1814*, eds. Bernard Chevallier, Maurice Catinat and Christophe Pincemaille (Paris, 1996), p. 82.

8 Grace Dalrymple Elliott, *Journal of My Life*, p. 188.

9 Quoted in André Castelot, *Joséphine* (Paris, 1964), p. 81.

10 Castelot, *Joséphine*, Paris 1964, p. 79.

11 Frédéric Masson, *Joséphine de Beauharnais* (Paris, 1913), p. 216.

12 Queen Hortense, *Memoirs*, vol. I, p. 38.

13 Oliver Blanc, *Last Letters: Prisons and Prisoners of the French Revolution* (New York, 1987), p. 46.

10 THERMIDOR

1 Quoted in Minnigerode Meade, *The Magnificent Comedy* (London, 1932), p. 92.
2 Baron de Frénilly, *Recollections of Baron de Frénilly, Peer of France* (London, 1909), tr. Frederic Lees, p. 154.
3 Impératrice Joséphine, *Correspondance 1782–1814*, eds. Bernard Chevallier, Maurice Catinat and Christophe Pincemaille (Paris, 1996), p. 20.
4 Meade, *The Magnificent Comedy*, p. 246.
5 Paul Barras, *Memoirs of Barras: Member of the Directorate*, vol. II, ed.George Duruy, tr. Charles E. Roche (London, 1895–6), p. 62.
6 Impératrice Joséphine, *Correspondance*, p. 23.
7 Ibid., p. 26.
8 Ibid., p. 28.
9 Baron de Frénilly, *Recollections*, p. 130.
10 Ibid., p. 129.
11 Ibid., p. 136.
12 Ibid., p. 136.
13 François Furet and Denis Richet, *French Revolution*, tr. Stephen Hardman (London, 1970), p. 232.
14 Étienne Denis Pasquier, *Histoire de mon temps: Mémoires du Chancelier Pasquier*, part 1 (Paris, 1893–5), p. 14.
15 Both letters quoted in Lillian Faderman, *Surpassing the Love of Men* (London, 1981), p. 71.
16 Christian Gilles, *Madame Tallien* (Biarritz, 1999), p. 206.
17 Edmond and Jules de Goncourt, *Histoire de la société française pendant le Directoire*, 4th edn (Paris, 1879), p. 295.
18 Margaret Trouncer, *Madame Récamier* (London, 1949), p. 23.
19 Ibid., p. 24.
20 Impératrice Joséphine, *Correspondance*, p. 32.
21 Meade, *The Magnificent Comedy*, p. 217.
22 Larevellière-Lepeaux quoted in Henri d'Alméras, *Barras et son temps* (Paris, 1930), p. 205.
23 Carnot quoted in Christian Gilles, *Madame Tallien*, p. 248.
24 Pasquier, *Histoire de mon temps*, part I, p. 118.
25 Guy Breton, *Histoires d'amour de l'histoire de France*, vol. VII (Paris, 1955), p. 16.
26 Barras, *Memoirs*, vol. II, p. 67.

27 Ibid., p. 66.

28 Francine du Plessix Gray, *At Home with the Marquis de Sade* (London, 1999), p. 371.

29 Anon., *Zoloé et ses Deux Acolytes* (Paris, 1800).

30 Joanne Richardson, *The Courtesans: The Demi-Monde in Nineteenth-Century France* (London, 1967), p. 1.

31 Simone de Beauvoir, *The Second Sex* (New York, 1969), p. 435.

32 Grimod quoted in Venetia Murray, *High Society in the Regency Period 1788–1830* (London, 1998), p. 176.

33 Letter from Josephine to Mme Tallien.

34 Duc Victor de Broglie, *Souvenirs, 1785–1870* (Paris, 1886), p. 23.

35 Aileen Ribeiro, *Fashion in the French Revolution* (London, 1988), p. 127.

36 Ibid., p. 134.

37 Meade, *The Magnificent Comedy*, p. 145.

38 Gabriel Girod de L'Ain, *Désirée Clary* (Paris, 1959), p. 48.

39 Ibid., p. 51.

40 G.-J. Ouvrard, *Mémoires de G.-J. Ouvrard*, vol. I (Paris, 1827), p. 20.

41 Girod de L'Ain, *Désirée Clary*, p. 73.

42 Impératrice Joséphine, *Correspondance*, p. 32.

43 Napoléon I, *Lettres d'amour à Joséphine*, presented by Jean Tulard (Paris, 1981), p. 45.

44 Ibid., pp. 46–7.

45 Girod de L'Ain, *Désirée Clary*, p. 88.

46 Duc de Raguse, *Mémoires de Maréchal Marmont*, vol. I (Paris, 1857), p. 93.

47 Queen Hortense, *The Memoirs of Queen Hortense*, vol. II, ed. Prince Napoleon, tr. Arthur K. Griggs and F. Mabel Robinson (London, 1929), p. 43.

48 Freud to Thomas Mann, November 1936.

11 ITALY

1 Napoléon I, *Lettres d'amour à Joséphine*, presented by Jean Tulard (Paris, 1981), pp. 49–50.

2 Ibid., pp. 51–2.

3 Ibid., pp. 54–5.

4 Ibid., pp. 58–9.

5 Jean Savant, *Napoléon et Joséphine* (Paris, 1960), p. 53.

6 Ibid., p. 53.

7 Napoléon I, *Lettres d'amour*, p. 63–4.

8 Duc de Raguse, *Mémoires de Maréchal Marmont*, vol. I (Paris, 1857), p. 187.

9 Ibid., p. 188.

10 François Furet and Denis Richet, *French Revolution*, tr. Stephen Hardman (London, 1970), p. 330.

11 See Gilray's cartoon of Mme Tallien.

12 Françoise Wagener, *L'Impératrice Joséphine* (Paris, 1999), p. 143.

13 Louis Hastier, *Le Grand Amour de Joséphine* (Paris, 1955), p. 70.

14 Ibid., p. 70.

15 Napoléon I, *Lettres d'amour*, pp. 74–5.

16 Ibid., p 78.

17 Ibid., pp. 78–9.

18 Savant, *Napoléon et Joséphine*, pp. 66–70.

19 Napoléon I, *Lettres d'amour*, p. 80.

20 Ibid., pp. 85–6.

21 Ibid., pp. 90–2.

22 A. R. Hamelin, 'Douze ans dans ma vie', *Revue de Paris*, November 1926, pp. 14–15.

23 Ibid., p. 14.

24 Impératrice Joséphine, *Correspondance 1782–1814*, eds. Bernard Chevallier, Maurice Catinat and Christophe Pincemaille (Paris, 1996), p. 45.

25 Ibid., p. 41.

26 Ibid., p. 45.

27 Napoléon I, *Lettres d'amour*, p. 95.

28 Ibid., pp. 96–7.

29 Ibid., p. 101.

30 Hamelin, 'Douze ans dans ma vie', p. 19.

31 Ibid., p. 22.

32 Napoléon I, *Lettres d'amour*, pp. 112–13.

33 Ibid., pp. 113–14.

34 Impératrice Joséphine, *Correspondance*, pp. 45–6.

35 Ibid., p. 47–48.

36 Napoléon I, *Lettres d'amour*, pp. 123–4.

37 Dr. G. Valensin, *Le Lit de Joséphine* (Paris, 1971).

38 Napoléon I, *Lettres d'amour*, pp. 124–5.

39 Ibid., p. 127–130.

40 Miot de Mélito, *Memoirs of Count Miot de Mélito*, vol. I, ed. General Fleischmann, tr. Cashel Hoey and John Lillie (London, 1881), p. 184.

41 Duc de Raguse, *Mémoires de Maréchal Marmont*, vol. I, p. 282.

42 Baron Coston quoted in Evangeline Bruce, *Napoleon and Josephine: An Improbable Marriage* (London, 1995), p. 195.

43 Fonds Masson, Bibliothèque Thiers, no. 223, I, 81.

44 Duc de Raguse, *Mémoires de Maréchal Marmont*, vol. I, pp. 293–5.

12 EGYPT

1 Duc de Raguse, *Mémoires de Maréchal Marmont*, vol. I (Paris, 1857), p. 313.
2 Quoted in Denise Ledoux-Lebard, 'Josephine and Interior Decoration', *Apollo*, July 1977, p. 16.
3 Ibid., pp. 16–17.
4 Ibid., p. 16.
5 Queen Hortense, *The Memoirs of Queen Hortense*, vol. I, ed. Prince Napoleon, tr. Arthur K. Griggs and F. Mabel Robinson (London, 1929), p. 48.
6 J. Christopher Herold, *Mistress to an Age: A Life of Madame de Staël* (London, 1959), p. 172.
7 Andrew C. P. Haggard, *Women of the Revolutionary Era* (London, 1914), p. 278.
8 Herold, *Mistress to an Age*, p. 176.
9 Jean Orieux, *Talleyrand ou Le Sphinx incompris* (Paris, 1998).
10 Ibid., p. 28.
11 Roberto Calasso, *The Ruin of Kasch* (London, 1995), p. 9.
12 Ibid., p. 12.
13 Impératrice Joséphine, *Correspondance 1782–1814*, eds. Bernard Chevallier, Maurice Catinat and Christophe Pincemaille (Paris, 1996), pp. 56–57.
14 André Gavoty, *Les Amoureux de l'Impératrice Joséphine* (Paris, 1961), p. 271.
15 Ibid., p. 270.
16 Ibid., p. 272.
17 Duchesse d'Abrantès, *Memoirs of Madame Junot, Duchesse d'Abrantès*, vol. I (London, 1883), p. 203.
18 Vincent Cronin, *Napoleon* (London, 1994), p. 146.
19 Impératrice Joséphine, *Correspondance*, p. 66.
20 Ibid., pp. 66–67.
21 André Castelot, *Joséphine* (Paris, 1964), p. 199.
22 Impératrice Joséphine, *Correspondance*, p. 68.
23 J. Christopher Herold, *The Age of Napoleon* (Boston, 1981), p. 65.
24 Ibid., p. 65.
25 Ibid., p. 67.
25 Ibid., p. 68.
26 Ibid., p. 63.
27 Ibid., p. 64.
28 Louis-Antoine-Fauvelet de Bourrienne, *La Vie privée de Napoléon, par Bourrienne, son secrétaire intime* (Paris, 1910), p. 66.

29 Ibid., p. 66.

30 Frances Mossiker, *The Biography of a Marriage* (London, 1965), p. 181.

31 Ibid., p. 182.

32 Impératrice Joséphine, *Correspondance*, p. 73.

33 See Georges Maugin, *L'Impératrice Joséphine: anecdotes et curiosités* (Paris, 1954), pp. 34–40.

34 Mossiker, *Biography of a Marriage*, p. 183.

35 Ibid., p. 185.

36 Ibid., p. 185.

37 Ibid., p. 187.

38 Herold, *The Age of Napoleon*, p. 71.

39 Ibid., p. 71.

40 Ibid., p. 73.

41 Ibid., p. 74.

42 Impératrice Joséphine, *Correspondance*, p. 86.

43 Gavoty, *Les Amoureux*, p. 279.

44 Impératrice Joséphine, *Correspondance*, p. 93.

45 Ibid., p. 89.

46 Quoted in Evangeline Bruce, *Napoleon and Josephine: An Improbable Marriage* (London, 1995), p. 268.

47 Carola Oman, *Napoleon's Viceroy* (London, 1966), p. 99.

48 Ibid., p. 99.

49 Queen Hortense, *Memoirs*, vol. I, p. 52.

50 Duchesse d'Abrantès, *Memoirs*, vol. I, p. 265.

51 Mossiker, *Biography of a Marriage*, p. 201.

52 Ibid., p. 201.

53 Ibid., p. 201.

54 Ibid., p. 202.

55 Maurice Lescure, *Madame Hamelin* (Paris 1995), p. 54.

56 Mossiker, *Biography of a Marriage*, p. 203.

57 Ibid., p. 204.

58 Ibid., p. 204.

59 Mme de Rémusat, *Memoirs of Madame de Rémusat 1802–1808*, vol. I (London, 1880), tr. Mrs. Cashel Hoey and John Lillie, p. 247.

60 Baculard d'Arnaud quoted in Anne Vincent-Buffault, *The History of Tears* (London, 1991), p. 52.

61 Ibid., p. 49.

62 de Rémusat, *Memoirs*, vol. I, p. 247.

63 Mossiker, *Biography of a Marriage* (London, 1965), p. 205.

13 BRUMAIRE

1 J. B. Morton, *Brumaire: The Rise of Bonaparte* (London, 1948), p. 216.
2 Impératrice Joséphine, *Correspondance 1782–1814*, eds. Bernard Chevallier, Maurice Catinat and Christophe Pincemaille (Paris, 1996), p. 192.
3 Morton, *Brumaire*, pp. 221–2.
4 Ibid., p. 223.
5 Ibid., p. 223.
6 Evangeline Bruce, *Napoleon and Josephine: An Improbable Marriage* (London, 1995), p. 292.
7 Ibid., p. 293.
8 Morton, *Brumaire*, p. 260.
9 Duchesse d'Abrantès, *Memoirs of Madame Junot, Duchesse d'Abrantès*, vol. I (London, 1883), p. 273.
10 Bruce, *Napoleon and Josephine*, p. 295.

14 THE CONSULATE

1 Thierry Lentz, *Le Grand Consulat 1799–1804* (Paris, 1999), p. 99.
2 Maurice Guerrini, *Napoleon and Paris*, tr. Margery Weiner (London, 1970), p. 37.
3 Evangeline Bruce, *Napoleon and Josephine: An Improbable Marriage* (London, 1995), p. 309.
4 Guerrini, *Napoleon and Paris*, p. 37.
5 Louis Constant, *Memoirs of Constant, the Emperor Napoleon's head valet*, vol. I, tr. Percy Pinkerton (London, 1896), pp. 41–2.
6 Queen Hortense, *The Memoirs of Queen Hortense*, vol. II, ed. Prince Napoleon, tr. Arthur K. Griggs and F. Mabel Robinson (London, 1929), p. 56.
7 Duchesse d'Abrantès, *Memoirs of Madame Junot, Duchesse d'Abrantès*, vol. I (London, 1883), p. 441.
8 Stendhal, *Selected Journalism from the English Reviews*, ed. Geoffrey Strickland (London, 1959), p. 170.
9 Napoléon I, *Lettres d'amour à Joséphine*, presented by Jean Tulard (Paris, 1981), p. 179.
10 Source unknown.
11 Philippe Seguy, 'Costume in the Age of Napoleon', in *The Age of Napoleon:*

Costume from Revolution to Empire, 1789–1815, ed. Katell le Bourhis (New York, 1989), p. 76.

12 Ibid., p. 73.

13 Queen Hortense, *Memoirs*, vol. I, p. 56.

14 Élisabeth Vigée-Lebrun quoted in Seguy, 'Costume in the Age of Napoleon', p. 72.

15 Quoted in J. F. Bernard, *Talleyrand: A Biography* (London, 1973), p. 240.

16 Vincent Cronin, *Napoleon* (London, 1994), p. 199.

17 Ibid., p. 203.

18 Quoted in Denise Ledoux-Lebard, 'Josephine and Interior Decoration', *Apollo*, July 1977, p. 17.

19 Ibid., p. 17.

20 Napoléon I, *Lettres d'amour*, p. 148.

21 Ibid., pp. 151–2.

22 Ibid., p. 153.

23 Source unknown.

24 Impératrice Joséphine, *Correspondance 1782–1814*, eds. Bernard Chevallier, Maurice Catinat and Christophe Pincemaille (Paris, 1996), p. 101.

25 Mme de Rémusat, *Memoirs of Madame de Rémusat 1802–1808*, vol. 1 (London, 1880), tr. Mrs. Cashel Hoey and John Lillie, p. 11.

26 Constant, *Memoirs*, vol. I, p. 27.

27 Impératrice Joséphine, *Correspondance*, p. 115.

28 Constant, *Memoirs*, vol. I, p. 73.

29 Edith Saunders, *Napoleon and Mademoiselle George* (London and New York, 1958), p. 50.

30 de Rémusat, *Memoirs*, vol. I, p. 79.

31 Queen Hortense, *Memoirs*, vol. II, p. 59.

32 Roberto Calasso, *The Ruin of Kasch* (London, 1995), p.58. The author explores the concept of *douceur* in relation to Talleyrand but it applies equally well to Josephine.

33 Étienne Denis Pasquier, *Histoire de mon temps: Mémoires du Chancelier Pasquier*, part 1 (Paris, 1893–5), p. 149.

34 Mme de La Tour du Pin, *Memoirs*, ed. and tr. Felice Harcourt (London, 1969), p. 343.

35 Ibid., p. 341.

36 Pasquier, *Histoire de mon temps*, part 1, p. 149.

37 Impératrice Joséphine, *Correspondance*, p. 99.

38 Ibid., p. 99.

39 Lentz, *Le Grand Consulat*, p. 247.

40 Bernard, *Talleyrand*, p. 232.

41 Constant, *Memoirs*, vol. I, p. 25.

42 Marie Avrillon, *Mémoires de Mlle Avrillon, première femme de chambre de l'impératrice, sur la vie privée de Joséphine, sa famille et sa cour*, ed. Maurice Dernelle (Paris, 1969), p. 137.

43 Constant, *Memoirs*, vol. I, p. 29.

44 Stendhal, *Selected Journalism*, p. 139.

45 Chateaubriand, *Memoirs*, tr. Robert Baldick (Harmondsworth, 1965), p. 327.

46 Paul Barras, *Memoirs of Barras: Member of the Directorate*, vol. II, ed. George Duruy, tr. Charles E. Roche (London, 1895–6), p. 74.

47 Napoléon I, *Lettres d'amour*, p. 155.

48 Queen Hortense, *Memoirs*, vol. I, p. 55.

49 Ibid., p. 69.

50 Ibid., p. 73.

51 Ibid., p. 73.

52 Guerrini, *Napoleon and Paris*, p. 96.

53 Bernard, *Talleyrand*, p. 245.

54 Philip Mansel, *The Court of France 1789–1830* (Cambridge, 1988), p. 52.

55 Fanny Burney, *Diary and Letters of Madame D'Arblay*, vol. II, ed. Sarah Woolsey Chauncey (Boston, 1880), p. 416.

56 Bertie Greatheed, *An Englishman in Paris: 1803 – The Journal of Bertie Greatheed*, ed. J. P. T. Bury and J. C. Barry (London, 1953), p. 34.

57 Charles James Fox, *Memoirs of the Latter Years of the Right Honourable Charles James Fox* (London, 1811), pp. 188–285.

58 Burney, *Diary and Letters*, vol. II, p. 427.

59 Venetia Murray, *High Society in the Regency Period 1788–1830* (London, 1998), p. 176.

60 Greatheed, *An Englishman in Paris*, p. 55.

61 Ibid., p. 144.

62 Bruce, *Napoleon and Josephine*, p. 341.

63 Ibid., p. 341.

64 William B. Cohen, *The French Encounter with Africans* (Bloomington, Indiana, 1980), p. 119.

65 *Morning Post*, 1 February 1803, quoted in Cronin, *Napoleon*, p. 231.

66 Cohen, *The French Encounter with Africans*, p. 119.

67 Impératrice Joséphine, *Correspondance*, p. 138.

68 Bernard, *Talleyrand*, p. 246.

69 Bruce, *Napoleon and Josephine*, p. 327.

70 Philip Mansel, *The Court of France*, p. 49.

71 de Rémusat, *Memoirs*, vol. I, p. 34.

72 Marguerite Joséphine Weimer, called Mlle George, *Mémoires inédits de Mademoiselle George*, 2nd edn (Paris, 1908), p. 29.

73 Saunders, *Napoleon and Mademoiselle George*, p. 55.

74 Ibid., p. 63.

75 Ibid., p. 69.

76 de Rémusat, *Memoirs*, vol. I, p. 91.

77 Ibid., p. 93.

78 Ibid., p. 91.

79 Impératrice Joséphine, *Correspondance*, p. 135.

80 Ibid., p. 137.

81 Bernard, *Talleyrand*, p. 250.

82 Ibid., p. 251.

83 Ibid., p. 251.

84 de Rémusat, *Memoirs*, vol. I, p. 214.

15 CORONATION

1 Bernard Chevallier and Christophe Pincemaille, *Impératrice Joséphine* (Paris, 1998), p. 227.

2 Mme de Rémusat, *Memoirs of Madame de Rémusat 1802–1808*, vol. 1 (London, 1880), tr. Mrs. Cashel Hoey and John Lillie, p. 232.

3 Ibid., p. 255.

4 Ibid., p. 255.

5 Ibid., p. 281.

6 Ibid., p. 297.

7 Marie Avrillon, *Mémoires de Mlle Avrillon, première femme de chambre de l'impératrice, sur la vie privée de Joséphine, sa famille et sa cour*, ed. Maurice Dernelle (Paris, 1969), p. 69.

8 Napoléon I, *Lettres d'amour à Joséphine*, presented by Jean Tulard (Paris, 1981), p. 167.

9 de Rémusat, *Memoirs*, vol. I, pp. 305–8.

10 Ibid., p. 308.

11 Ibid., pp. 308–9.

12 Ibid., p. 309.

13 Ibid., p. 311.

14 Napoléon I, *In the Words of Napoleon: The Emperor Day by Day*, ed. R. M. Johnston with new material by R. M. Haythornthwaite (London, 2002), p. 141.

15 de Rémusat, *Memoirs*, vol. I, p. 313.

16 Avrillon, *Mémoires*, p. 73.

17 Bourrienne quoted in J. Christopher Herold, *The Age of Napoleon* (London, 1963), p. 136.

18 Avrillon, *Mémoires*, p. 74.

19 Marguerite Joséphine Weimer, called Mlle George, *Mémoires inédits de Mademoiselle George*, 2nd edn (Paris, 1908), p. 151.

20 Duchesse d'Abrantès, *Memoirs of Madame Junot, Duchesse d'Abrantès*, vol. II (London, 1883), pp. 347–8.

21 Avrillon, *Mémoires*, p. 75.

16 EMPIRE

1 Frédéric Masson, *Josephine, Empress and Queen*, tr. Mrs Cashel Hoey (London, 1899), p. 2.

2 Ibid., p. 156.

3 Ibid., p. 170.

4 Ernest Knapton, *Empress Josephine* (London, 1969), p. 272.

5 Mme de Rémusat, *Memoirs of Madame de Rémusat 1802–1808*, vol. 1 (London, 1880), tr. Mrs. Cashel Hoey and John Lillie, p. 40.

6 Ibid., p. 23.

7 Quoted in Norman Hartnell, *Royal Courts of Fashion* (London, 1971), p. 117.

8 Napoléon I, *Lettres d'amour à Joséphine*, presented by Jean Tulard (Paris, 1981), p. 174.

9 Ibid., p. 175.

10 Impératrice Joséphine, *Correspondance 1782–1814*, eds. Bernard Chevallier, Maurice Catinat and Christophe Pincemaille (Paris, 1996), p. 156.

11 Napoléon I, *Lettres d'amour*, p. 182.

12 Ibid., p. 183.

13 Ibid., p. 184.

14 Ibid., p. 185.

15 Ibid., p. 186.

16 Ibid., p. 190.

17 Ibid., p. 192.

18 Ibid., p. 194.

19 Ibid., p. 195.

20 Ibid., p. 198.

21 Ibid., p. 200.

22 Ibid., p. 201.

23 Ibid., p. 202.

24 Impératrice Joséphine, *Correspondance*, p. 173.

25 Philip Mansel, *The Court of France 1789–1830* (Cambridge, 1988), p. 53.

26 Philip Mansel, *The Eagle in Splendour* (London, 1987), p. 104.

27 Ibid., p. 106.

28 de Rémusat, *Memoirs*, vol. I, p. 294.

29 Ibid., p. 295.

30 Ibid., p. 297.

31 Mansel, *The Eagle in Splendour*, p. 99.

32 Napoléon I, *Lettres d'amour*, p. 204.

33 Ibid., p. 211.

34 Impératrice Joséphine, *Correspondance*, p. 185.

35 Ibid., p. 186.

36 Napoléon I, *Napoleon's Letters*, ed. J. M Thompson (London, 1998), p. 145.

37 Ibid., p. 145.

38 Napoléon I, *Lettres d'amour*, p. 235.

39 Ibid., p. 237.

40 Ibid., p. 239.

41 Ibid., p. 240.

42 Ibid., p. 252.

43 Ibid., p. 267.

44 Impératrice Joséphine, *Correspondance*, p. 199.

45 Ibid., p. 200.

46 Napoléon I, *Lettres d'amour*, p. 283.

47 Ibid., p. 285.

48 Ibid., p. 286.

49 Impératrice Joséphine, *Correspondance*, p. 216.

50 Napoléon I, *Lettres d'amour*, p. 297.

51 Impératrice Joséphine, *Correspondance*, p. 217.

52 de Rémusat, *Memoirs*, vol. I, pp. 409–10.

53 Maurice Guerrini, *Napoleon and Paris*, tr. Margery Weiner (London, 1970), p. 183.

54 Impératrice Joséphine, *Correspondance*, p. 219.

55 Guerrini, *Napoleon and Paris*, p. 199.

56 Impératrice Joséphine, *Correspondance*, p. 229.

57 Napoléon I, *Lettres d'amour*, p. 312.

58 Ibid., p. 313.

59 Ibid., p. 331.

60 Ibid., p. 347.

61 Ibid., p. 348.

62 Ibid., p. 353.

63 Queen Hortense, *The Memoirs of Queen Hortense*, vol. I, ed. Prince Napoleon, tr. Arthur K. Griggs and F. Mabel Robinson (London, 1929), p. 208.

64 Ibid., p. 209.

65 Ibid., p. 210.

66 Ibid., p. 210.

67 Ibid., p. 212.

68 Ibid., p. 215.

69 Étienne Denis Pasquier, *Histoire de mon temps: Mémoires du Chancelier Pasquier*, part 1 (Paris, 1893–5), p. 371.

70 Frédéric Masson, *Joséphine répudiée, 1809–1814*, 6th edn (Paris, 1901), p. 80.

71 Ibid., p. 81.

72 Evangeline Bruce, *Napoleon and Josephine: An Improbable Marriage* (London, 1995), p. 446.

17 SECLUSION

1 Queen Hortense, *The Memoirs of Queen Hortense*, vol. I, ed. Prince Napoleon, tr. Arthur K. Griggs and F. Mabel Robinson (London, 1929), p. 215.

2 Napoléon I, *Lettres d'amour à Joséphine*, presented by Jean Tulard (Paris, 1981), p. 359.

3 Duchesse d'Abrantès, *Memoirs of Madame Junot, Duchesse d'Abrantès*, vol. III (London, 1883), pp. 230–3.

4 Mme Ducrest, *Memoirs of the Empress Josephine*, vol. I (London, 1894), p. 295.

5 Napoléon I, *Lettres d'amour*, p. 360.

6 Frédéric Masson, *Joséphine répudiée, 1809–1814*, 6th edn (Paris, 1901), p. 123.

7 Napoléon I, *Lettres d'amour*, p. 381.

8 Impératrice Joséphine, *Correspondance 1782–1814*, eds. Bernard Chevallier, Maurice Catinat and Christophe Pincemaille (Paris, 1996), p. 255.

9 Ibid., p. 254.

10 Ibid., pp. 255–6.

11 Napoléon I, *Lettres d'amour*, p. 382.

12 Impératrice Joséphine, *Correspondance*, p. 257.

13 Ibid., p. 154.

14 Jill Douglas-Hamilton, Duchess of Hamilton and Brandon, *Napoleon, the Empress and the Artist* (London, 1999), p. 48.

15 Bernard Chevallier, *L'Impératrice Joséphine et Les Sciences Naturelles* (Paris, 1997), p. 8.

16 Douglas-Hamilton, *Napoleon, the Empress and the Artist*, p. 22.

17 My account of Josephine's art collection is taken largely from Nicole Hubert, 'Josephine and Contemporary Painting', *Apollo*, July 1977, pp. 25–33.

18 My account of Josephine's sculpture collection is taken largely from Gérard Hubert, 'Josephine, a Discerning Collector of Sculpture', *Apollo*, July 1977, p. 43.

19 Impératrice Joséphine, *Correspondance*, p. 262.

20 Masson, *Joséphine répudiée*, pp. 199–201.

21 Impératrice Joséphine, *Correspondance*, p. 274.

22 Queen Hortense, *Memoirs*, vol. II (London, 1929), pp. 17–18.

23 Napoléon I, *Lettres d'amour*, p. 395.

24 Ibid., p. 396.

25 Ibid., p. 397.

26 Impératrice Joséphine, *Correspondance*, p. 296.

27 Fenton Bresler, *Napoleon III: A Life* (London, 2000), p. 48.

28 Philip Mansel, *The Court of France 1789–1830* (Cambridge, 1988), p. 121.

29 Impératrice Joséphine, *Correspondance*, p. 323.

30 Ibid., p. 340.

31 Mansel, *The Court of France*, p. 121.

32 Charles Esdaile, 'Popular Resistance in Napoleonic Europe', *History Today*, vol. 48 (2), February 1998, p. 37.

33 Impératrice Joséphine, *Correspondance*, p. 217.

34 Chateaubriand, *Memoirs*, tr. Robert Baldick (Harmondsworth, 1965), p. 269.

35 Ibid., p. 292.

36 Michael Broers, 'The Empire Behind the Lines', *History Today*, vol. 48 (1), January 1998, p. 28.

37 Masson, *Joséphine répudiée*, p. 306.

38 Ibid., p. 308.

39 Queen Hortense, *Memoirs*, vol. II, p. 83.

40 Bernard Chevallier and Christophe Pincemaille, *L'Impératrice Joséphine* (Paris, 1996), p. 423.

41 Evangeline Bruce, *Napoleon and Josephine: An Improbable Marriage* (London, 1995), p. 477.

42 Queen Hortense, *Memoirs*, vol. II, p. 102.

43 Ibid., p. 103.

44 Ibid., p. 106.

45 Ibid., p. 107.

BIBLIOGRAPHY

Abrantès, duchesse d', *Memoirs of Madame Junot, Duchesse d'Abrantès*, 3 vols (London, Richard Bentley & Son, 1883).

Adams, William Howard, *The Paris Years of Thomas Jefferson* (New Haven, Conn., and London, Yale University Press, 1997).

Alexander, R. S., *Napoleon* (London, Arnold, 2001).

Alméras, Henri d', *Barras et son temps* (Paris, Albin Michel, 1930).

– *La Vie Parisienne sous le Consulat et l'Empire* (Paris, Albin Michel, 1909).

Annas, Alicia M., 'The Elegant Art of Movement' in ed. Edward Maeder, *An Elegant Art: Fashion and Fantasy in the Eighteenth Century* (New York, Los Angeles County Museum of Art in Association with Harry N. Abrams, 1973).

Anon., *Zoloé et ses Deux Acolytes* (Paris, 1801).

Arnault, A. V., *Souvenirs d'un sexagénaire* (Paris, Dufey, 1833).

Arneville, Marie-Blanche d', *Parcs et Jardins sous le Premier Empire* (Paris, Librairie Jules Tallandier, 1981).

Aubenas, Joseph, *Histoire de l'Impératrice Joséphine*, 2 vols (Paris, 1857).

Avrillon, Marie, *Mémoires de Mlle Avrillon, première femme de chambre de l'impératrice, sur la vie privée de Joséphine, sa famille et sa cour*, ed. Maurice Dernelle (Paris, Mercure de France, 1969).

Banbuck, Cabuzel Andréa, *Histoire politique, économique et sociale de la Martinique sous l'ancien régime* (Paris, M. Rivière, 1935).

Barras, Paul, *Memoirs of Barras, Member of the Directorate*, 4 vols, ed. George Duruy, tr. Charles E. Roche (London, Osgood, McIlvaine and Co., 1895–6).

Basily-Callimaki, Mme de, *J.-B. Isabey: sa vie, son temps* (Paris, Frazier-Soye, 1909).

Baumer, Franklin, *Modern European Thought: Continuity and Change in Ideas, 1600–1950* (New York, Macmillan, and London, Collier Macmillan, 1977).

Bausset, Louis-François-Joseph, baron de, *Mémoires anecdotiques sur l'intérieur du palais et sur quelques événements de l'Empire depuis 1805 jusqu'au Ier mai 1814 pour servir à l'histoire de Napoléon*, 2nd edn, 2 vols (Paris, Baudouin Frères, 1827–29).

Beauvoir, Simone de, *The Second Sex*, tr. Howard Madison Parshley (London, Landsborough Publications, 1960).

Berlin, Isaiah, *The Age of Enlightenment: The 18th Century Philosophers* (New York, New American Library, 1956).

Bernard, J. F., *Talleyrand: A Biography* (London, Collins, 1973).

Bertrand, comte, *Napoleon at St. Helena*, deciphered and annotated by Paul Fleuriot de Langle, tr. Frances Hume (London, Cassell and Co., 1953).

Blanc, Olivier, *Last Letters: Prisons and Prisoners of the French Revolution*, tr. Alan Sheridan (New York, Andre Deutsch, 1987).

Blanning, T. C. W., *The French Revolution: Class War or Culture Clash?*, 2nd edn (Basingstoke, Macmillan, 1998).

Boigne, Louise-Eléonore-Charlotte-Adélaïde d'Osmond, comtesse de, *Mémoires de la comtesse de Boigne, née d'Osmond: récits d'une tante*, 2 vols, presented and annotated by Jean-Claude Berchet (Paris, Mercure de France, 1999).

Bonaparte, Napoléon, *In the Words of Napoleon: The Emperor Day by Day*, ed. R. M. Johnston (London, Greenhill Books, 2002).

Bouillé, Louis-Amour, *Souvenirs et fragments pour servir aux mémoires de ma vie et de mon temps: 1769–1812*, 3 vols (Paris, A. Picard et fils, 1906–11).

Bourhis, Katell le (ed.), *The Age of Napoleon: Costume from Revolution to Empire 1789–1815* (New York, Metropolitan Museum of Art, 1989).

Bourrienne, Louis-Antoine-Fauvelet de, *La Vie privée de Napoléon, par Bourrienne, son secrétaire intime* (Paris, Librarie Contemporaine, 1910).

Bresler, Fenton, *Napoleon III: A Life* (London, HarperCollins, 2000).

Breton, Guy, *Histoires d'amour de l'histoire de France* (Paris, Éditions Noir et blanc, 1955).

Broglie, Victor, duc de, *Souvenirs, 1785–1870*, 2nd edn (Paris, Calmann Lévy, 1886).

Brookner, Anita, *Jacques-Louis David* (London, Chatto & Windus, 1980).

Bruce, Evangeline, *Napoleon and Josephine: An Improbable Marriage* (London, Weidenfeld & Nicolson, 1995).

Burney, Fanny, *Diary and Letters of Madame D'Arblay*, 2 vols, ed. Sarah Chauncey Woolsey (Boston, Robert Brothers, 1880).

Calasso, Roberto, *The Ruin of Kasch* (London, Vintage, 1995).

Campan, Mme, *Correspondance inédite de Mme.Campan avec la reine Hortense* (Brussels, J. P. Meline, 1835).

Castelot, André, *Joséphine* (Paris, Perrin, 1964).

– *Napoléon et les femmes* (Paris, Perrin, 1998).

Chanvallon, Thibault Baptiste de, *Voyage à la Martinique* (Paris, 1763).

Chateaubriand, François-René, *Atala/René*, tr. Irving Putter (Berkeley, University of California Press, 1980).

Chauleau, Liliane, *Les Antilles au temps de Schoelcher* (Paris, 1990).

– *Dans les îles du vent: la Martinique (XVIIe–XIXe siècle)* (Paris, L'Harmattan, 1993).

Chaunu, Pierre, *La Mort à Paris: XVIe, XVIIe et XVIIIe siècles* (Paris, Fayard, 1978).

Chevallier, Bernard, *L'art de vivre au temps de Joséphine* (Paris, Flammarion, 1998).

– and Christophe Pincemaille, *L'Impératrice Joséphine* (Paris, Payot, 1988).

– , Maurice Catinat and Christophe Pincemaille (eds), l'Impératrice Joséphine, *Correspondance, 1782–1814* (Paris, Payot, 1996).

Christiansen, Rupert, *Romantic Affinities: Portraits from an Age, 1780–1830* (London, Vintage, 1994).

Cobb, Richard, *Death in Paris, 1795–1801* (Oxford, Oxford University Press, 1978).

– *The French and Their Revolution* (London, John Murray, 1998).

Cohen, William B., *The French Encounter with Africans: White Response to Blacks, 1530–1880* (Bloomington, Indiana University Press, 1980).

Cole, Hubert, *Josephine* (New York, Viking, 1963).

Constant, Louis, *Memoirs of Constant, the Emperor Napoleon's Head Valet*, 4 vols, tr. Percy Pinkerton (London, H. S. Nichols, 1896).

Cooper, Alfred Duff, *Talleyrand* (London, Phoenix, 1997).

Corbin, Alain, *The Foul and the Fragrant: Odour and the Social Imagination* (London, Papermac, 1996).

Coryn, Marjorie, *The Marriage of Josephine* (London, Hodder & Stoughton, 1945).

Cronin, Vincent, *Napoleon* (London, HarperCollins, 1994).

Daney, Sidney, *Histoire de la Martinique, depuis la colonisation jusqu'en 1815*, 6 vols (Fort Royal, 1846–47).

Dessalles, Pierre, *Sugar and Slavery, Family and Race: The Letters and Diary of Pierre Dessalles, Planter in Martinique, 1808–1856*, ed. and tr. Elborg and Robert Forster (Baltimore, John Hopkins University Press, 1996).

Douglas-Hamilton, Jill, Duchess of Hamilton and Brandon, *Napoleon, the Empress and the Artist: The Story of Napoleon, Josephine's Garden at Malmaison, Redouté and the Australian Plants* (East Roseville, New South Wales, Kangaroo Press, 1991).

Ducrest, Mme Georgette, *Memoirs of the Empress Josephine*, 2 vols (London, H. S. Nichols & Co., 1894).

Elias, Norbert, *The Civilizing Process*, vol. I: 'The History of Manners' (Oxford, Blackwell, 1978).

– *The Court Society*, tr. Edmund Jephcott (Oxford, Blackwell, 1983).

Elliot, Grace Dalrymple, *Journal of My Life During the French Revolution* (London, R. Bentley, 1859).

Ellis, Geoffrey, *The Napoleonic Empire* (London, Macmillan, 1991).

Erickson, Carolly, *Josephine: A Life of the Empress* (New York, St. Martins Press, 1998).

Faderman, Lillian, *Surpassing the Love of Men: Romantic Friendship and Love between Women from the Renaissance to the Present* (London, The Women's Press, 1985).

Fain, Agathon-Jean-François, baron, *Mémoires du baron Fain: premier secrétaire du cabinet de l'Empereur* (Paris, Plon-Nourrit et Cie, 1908).

Farr, Evelyn, *Before the Deluge* (London, Peter Owen, 1994).

Flake, Otto, *The Marquis de Sade* (London, Peter Davies, 1931).

Fontana, Biancamaria, *Benjamin Constant and the Post-Revolutionary Mind* (New Haven, Conn., Yale University Press, 1991).

Forster, Elborg and Robert (eds and trs), *Sugar and Slavery, Family and Race: The Letters and Diary of Pierre Dessalles, Planter in Martinique, 1808–1856* (Baltimore, John Hopkins University Press, 1996).

Fouché, Joseph, *Mémoires* (Paris, Tournon et Nouvelles, 1957).

Fox, Charles James, *Memoirs of the Latter Years of the Right Honourable Charles James Fox* (London, 1811).

Fraser, Antonia, *Marie Antoinette: The Journey* (London, Weidenfeld & Nicolson, 2001).

Frénilly, baron de, *Recollections of Baron de Frénilly, Peer of France*, tr. Frederic Lees (London, William Heinemann, 1909).

Furet, François, and Denis Richet, *French Revolution*, tr. Stephen Hardman (London, Weidenfeld & Nicolson, 1970).

Gallaher, John G., *General Alexandre Dumas: Soldier of the French Revolution* (Carbondale, Southern Illinois University Press, 1997).

Garaud, L., *Trois Ans à la Martinique*, 2nd edn (Paris, A. Picard et Kaan, 1895).

Gaspar, David Barry, and David Patrick Geggus, *A Turbulent Time: The French Revolution and the Greater Caribbean* (Bloomington, Indiana University Press, 1997).

Gautier, Arlette, *Les Soeurs de solitude: la condition féminine dans l'esclavage aux Antilles du XVIIe au XIXe siècles* (Paris, Éditions Caribbéennes, 1985).

Gavoty, André, *Les Amoureux de l'Impératrice Josephine* (Paris, Librairie Arthème Fayard, 1961).

Gay, Sophie, *Salons célèbres* (Paris, Michel-Lévy, 1864).

Genlis, comtesse de, *Mémoires* (Paris, 1828).

George, Mlle (Weimer, Marguerite Joséphine), *Memoires inédits de mademoiselle George* (Paris, Plon-Nourrit et Cie, 1908).

Gilles, Christian, *Madame Tallien: la reine du Directoire* (Biarritz, Atlantica, 1999).

Girod, François, *La Vie quotidienne de la société créole* (Paris, Hachette, 1972).

Girod de L'Ain, Gabriel, *Désirée Clary* (Paris, Hachette, 1959).

Goethe, Johann Wolfgang, *The Sorrows of Young Werther*, tr. Michael Hulse (London, Penguin, 1989).

Goldworth, John Alger, *Paris in 1789–94: Farewell Letters of Victims of the Guillotine* (London, George Allen, 1902).

Goncourt, Edmond and Jules, *Histoire de la société française pendant le Directoire*, 4th edn (Paris, G. Charpentier, 1879).

Gough, Hugh, *The Terror in the French Revolution* (London, Macmillan, 1998).

Gourgaud, Gaspard, baron, *The St Helena Journal of General Baron Gourgaud*, ed. Norman Edwards, tr. Sydney Gillard (London, John Lane, the Bodley Head, 1932).

Gouyé Martignac, Gérald, and Michel Sementéry, *La Descendance de Joséphine, impératrice des Français* (Paris, Christian, 1994).

Grandjean, Serge, *Inventaire après décès de l'Impératrice Joséphine à Malmaison* (Paris, Ministère d'État – Affaires culturelles, 1964).

Greatheed, Bertie, *An Englishman in Paris: 1803 – The Journal of Bertie Greatheed*, ed. J. P. T. Bury and J. C. Barry (London, Geoffrey Bles, 1953).

Gronow, Captain, *The Reminiscences and Recollections of Captain Gronow, 1810–1860*, abridged by John Raymond (London, Bodley Head, 1964).

Guerrini, Maurice, *Napoleon and Paris*, tr. Margery Weiner (London, Cassell, 1970).

Gulland, Sandra, *The Last Great Dance on Earth* (London, Review, 2001).

– *The Many Lives and Secret Sorrows of Josephine B* (London, Review, 1999).

– *Tales of Passion, Tales of Woe* (London, Review, 2000).

Haggard, Andrew C. P., *Women of the Revolutionary Era* (London, Stanley Paul & Co., 1914).

Hanoteau, Jean, *Le Ménage Beauharnais: Joséphine avant Napoléon – d'après des correspondances inédites* (Paris, Librairie Plon, 1935).

Hartnell, Norman, *Royal Courts of Fashion* (London, Cassell, 1971).

Hastier, Louis, *Le Grand Amour de Joséphine* (Paris, Chastel, 1955).

Hearn, Lafcadio, *Esquisses Martiniquaises* (Paris, 1887).

Herold, Christopher J., *The Age of Napoleon* (Boston, Houghton Mifflin, 1987).

– *Mistress to an Age: A Life of Madame de Staël* (London, Hamish Hamilton, 1959).

Hibbert, Christopher, *The French Revolution* (London, Penguin, 1982).

– *Napoleon: His Wives and Women* (London, HarperCollins, 2002).

Hobsbawm, E. J., *The Age of Revolution: Europe 1789–1848* (London, Abacus, 1962).

Honour, Hugh, *Neo-Classicism* (Harmondsworth, Penguin, 1968).

– *Romanticism* (London, Penguin, 1981).

Hortense, Queen, *The Memoirs of Queen Hortense*, 2 vols, ed. Prince Napoleon, tr. Arthur K. Griggs and F. Mabel Robinson (London, Thornton-Butterworth, 1929).

Hubert, Gérard, *Malmaison* (Paris, Réunion des musées nationaux, 1989).

Hurel, Roselyne, and Diana Scarisbrick, *Chaumet, Paris: deux siècles de création* (Paris, Musée Carnavalet, 1998).

Imbert de Saint-Amand, Arthur Léon, *La Citoyenne Bonaparte* (Paris, E. Dentu, 1883).
Iung, Thomas, *Bonaparte et son temps 1769–1799*, 3 vols (Paris, Charpentier, 1881).

James, C. L. R., *The Black Jacobins: Toussaint L'Ouverture and the San Domingo Revolution* (London, Allison and Busby, 1980).
Janssens, Jacques, *Joséphine de Beauharnais et son temps* (Paris, Berger-Levrault, 1963).
Johnston, R. M. (ed.), *In the Words of Napoleon: The Emperor Day by Day* (London, Greenhill Books, 2002).
Joséphine, l'Impératrice, *Correspondance, 1782–1814*, ed. Chevallier, Bernard, Maurice Catinat and Christophe Pincemaille (Paris, Payot, 1996).

Kahane, Eric H., *Un mariage parisien sous le Directoire* (Paris, Éditions le Carrousel, 1961).
Kauffmann, Jean-Paul, *The Dark Room at Longwood: A Voyage to St Helena* (London, Harvill Press, 1999).
Keates, Jonathan, *Stendhal* (London, Minerva, 1995).
Kelly, Linda, *Women of the French Revolution* (London, Hamish Hamilton, 1987).
Kielmannsegge, comtesse de, *Mémoires de la comtesse de Kielmannsegge sur Napoléon 1er*, 2 vols, tr. Joseph Delage (Paris, Éditions Victor Attinger, 1928).
Knapton, Ernest John, *Empress Josephine* (London, Penguin, 1969).
Kunstler, Charles, *La Vie privée de l'impératrice Joséphine* (Paris, Hachette, 1939).

Laclos, Choderlos de, *Les Liaisons Dangereuses*, tr. P. W. K. Stone (London, Penguin, 1961).
Lacroix, Paul, *The XVIIIth Century: Its Institutions, Customs and Costumes: France, 1700–1989*, (tr.), (London, Bickers and Son, 1870)
Laing, Margaret, *Josephine & Napoleon* (London, Sidgwick & Jackson, 1973).
Lajer-Burcharth, Ewa, *Necklines: The Art of Jacques-Louis David after the Terror* (New Haven, Conn., and London, Yale University Press, 1999).
Las Cases, Emmanuel-Auguste-Dieudonné, comte de, *Le Mémorial de Sainte-Hélène*, 2 vols, ed. Gérard Walter (Paris, Gallimard, 1956).
La Tour du Pin, Mme de, *Memoirs*, ed. and tr. Felice Harcourt (London, Harvill, 1969).
Lavalette, Antoine-Marie Chamans, comte de, *Memoirs of Count Lavallette, written by himself*, 2nd edn, 2 vols (London, H. Colburn & R. Bentley, 1831).

Laver, James, *The Age of Illusion: Manners and Morals, 1750–1848* (London, Weidenfeld & Nicolson, 1972).

Lenôtre, G., *La Maison des Carmes* (Paris, Librarie académique Perrin, 1933)

Lentz, Thierry, *Le Grand Consulat: 1799–1804* (Paris, Fayard, 1999).

Lever, Evelyne, *Marie Antoinette; The Last Queen of France*, tr. Catherine Temerson (London, Piatkus, 2000).

Lutz, Tom, *Crying: The Natural and Cultural History of Tears* (New York, Norton, 1999).

Lyons, Martyn, *France under the Directory* (Cambridge, Cambridge University Press, 1975).

Mackau, Annette de, *Correspondance d'Annette de Mackau, comtesse de Saint-Alphonse, dame du palais de l'impératrice Joséphine, 1790–1870*, ed. Chantal de Toutier-Bonazzi (Paris, S.E.V.P.E.N., 1967).

Mallet du Pan, Jacques, *Mémoires et correspondance pour servir à l'histoire de la Révolution Française* (Paris, Amyot et Cherbulliez, 1851).

Mansel, Philip, *The Court of France 1789–1830* (Cambridge, Cambridge University Press, 1988).

– *The Eagle in Splendour: Napoleon I and His Court* (London, George Philip, 1987).

Mantel, Hilary, *A Place of Greater Safety* (London, Penguin, 1993).

Marbot, Jean-Baptiste de, *The Exploits of Baron de Marbot*, ed. Christopher Summerville (London, Constable, 2000).

Marchand, Louis-Joseph, *In Napoleon's Shadow: Being the First English Language Edition of the Complete Memoirs of Louis-Joseph Marchand, Valet and Friend of the Emperor, 1811–1821*, ed. Proctor Jones (San Francisco, Proctor Jones Publishing, 1998).

Marmont, Auguste Frédéric, *Mémoires du maréchal Marmont, duc de Raguse, de 1792 à 1841*, 6 vols (Paris, Perrotin, 1928).

Marquiset, Alfred, *Une Merveilleuse (Mme Hamelin), 1776–1851* (Paris, H. Champion, 1909).

Martin, Andy, *Napoleon the Novelist* (Cambridge, Polity, 2000).

Masson, Frédéric, *Joséphine de Beauharnais* (Paris, Librairie Paul Ollendorff, 1913).

– *Josephine, Empress and Queen*, tr. Cashel Hoey (London, Simpkin, Marshall, Hamilton, Kent & Co., 1899).

– *Joséphine répudiée* (Paris, Paul Ollendorff, 1901).

– *Mme Bonaparte: 1796–1804* (Paris, Albin Michel, 1945).

Maugras, Gaston, *Delphine de Sabran, marquise de Custine* (Paris, Plon-Nourrit et Cie, 1912).

Mauguin, Georges, *L'Impératrice Joséphine: anecdotes et curiosités* (Paris, J. Peyronnet, 1954).

Mélito, Miot de, comte, *Memoirs of Count Miot de Melito*, 2 vols, tr. Cashel Hoey and John Lillie (London, Sampson Low, Marston, Searle & Rivington, 1881).

Mercier, Louis-Sébastien, *The Picture of Paris: Before and After the Revolution*, tr. Wilfrid and Emilie Jackson (London, Routledge, 1929).

Montgaillard, Maurice, comte de, *Souvenirs du comte de Montgaillard* (Paris, Paul Ollendorff, 1895).

Morris, Gouverneur, *The Diary and Letters of Gouverneur Morris*, ed. Anne Cary Morris (London, Kegan Paul, Trench, & Co., 1889).

Morton, J. B., *Brumaire: The Rise of Bonaparte* (London, T. Werner Laurie Ltd, 1948).

Mossiker, Frances, *Napoleon and Josephine: The Biography of a Marriage* (London, Victor Gollancz, 1965).

Murray, Venetia, *High Society in the Regency Period, 1788–1830* (London, Penguin, 1998).

Napoléon I, *In the Words of Napoleon: The Emperor Day by Day*, ed. R. M. Johnston (London, Greenhill Books, 2002).

– *Lettres d'amour à Joséphine*, presented by Jean Tulard (Paris, Fayard, 1981).

Ober, Frederick, *Josephine, Empress of the French* (New York, Grafton, 1901).

Oman, Carola, *Napoleon's Viceroy: Eugène de Beauharnais* (London, Hodder & Stoughton, 1966).

Orieux, Jean, *Talleyrand ou Le Sphinx incompris* (Paris, Flammarion, 1998).

Ouvrard, G.-J., *Mémoires de G.-J. Ouvrard*, 4th edn, 2 vols (Paris, Moutardier, 1827).

Paine, Thomas, *Rights of Man* (London, C. A. Watts, 1954).

Pasquier, Étienne Denis, *Mémoires du Chancelier Pasquier*, 2 parts, 6 vols (Paris, Plon-Nourrit et Cie, 1893–95).

Petitjean Roget, Jacques, *J'ai assassiné la Sultane Validé* (Fort-de-France, Société d'histoire de la Martinique, Imprimerie Pierron, 1990).

Plessix Gray, Francine du, *At Home with the Marquis de Sade* (London, Chatto & Windus, 1999).

Rand, Richard (ed.), *Intimate Encounters: Love and Domesticity in Eighteenth-Century France* (Hanover, N. H., Hood Museum of Art, Dartmouth College, and Princeton, N. J., Princeton University Press, 1997).

Rémusat, Mme de, *Memoirs of Madame de Rémusat 1802–1808*, 2 vols, tr. Cashel Hoey and John Lillie (London, Sampson Low, Marston, Searle & Rivington, 1880).

Ribeiro, Aileen, *Dress and Morality* (London, Batsford, 1996).

- *Fashion in the French Revolution* (London, Batsford, 1988).

Richardson, Frank, *Napoleon: Bisexual Emperor* (London, Kimber, 1972).

Roberts, Andrew, *Napoleon and Wellington* (London, Weidenfeld & Nicolson, 2001).

Roederer, Pierre-Louis, *Autour de Bonaparte: Journal du comte P.-L. Roederer, ministre et conseiller d'état* (Paris, H. Daragon, 1909).

Rose, J. H., *The Revolutionary and Napoleonic Era, 1789–1815*, 7th edn (Cambridge, Cambridge University Press, 1815).

Rose-Rosette, Robert, *Les Jeunes Années de l'Impératrice Joséphine* (Les Trois-Îlets, publié avec le concours de la Fondation Napoléon, 1992).

Rousseau, Jean-Jacques, *La Nouvelle Héloïse* (Paris, 1763).

- *The Social Contract* (London, Penguin, 1972).

Rude, George, *The French Revolution* (London, Weidenfeld & Nicolson, 1988).

Russell, John, *Paris* (New York, Abrams, 1983).

Saunders, Edith, *Napoleon and Mademoiselle George* (London, Longmans, 1958).

Savant, Jean, *Napoléon et Joséphine* (Paris, Fayard, 1960).

Schaeffer, Neil, *The Marquis de Sade: A Life* (London, Hamish Hamilton, 1999).

Schama, Simon, *Citizens: A Chronicle of the French Revolution* (New York, Knopf, 1989).

- *Landscape and Memory* (London, Fontana, 1996).

Schom, Alan, *Napoleon Bonaparte* (New York, HarperCollins, 1997).

Selinko, Annemarie, *Désirée*, tr. Arnold Bender and E. W. Dickes (London, Heinemann, 1953).

Sergeant, Philip Walsingham, *Empress Josephine*, 2 vols (London, Hutchinson, 1908).

Stendhal, *Selected Journalism from the English Reviews*, ed. Geoffrey Strickland (London, John Calder, 1959).

- *The Life of Henry Brulard*, tr. John Sturrock (London, Penguin, 1995).

Sydenham, M. J., *The First French Republic, 1792–1804* (London, Batsford, 1974).

Tercier, C. A., *Mémoires politiques et militaires*, ed. C. de La Chanonie (Paris, 1891).

Thibaudeau, A. C., *Mémoires sur la Convention et le Directoire*, 2 vols (Paris, Baudouin Frères, 1824).

Thiébault, Paul Charles, baron, *The Memoirs of Baron Thiébault*, 2 vols, tr. and condensed by John Arthur Butler (London, Smith, Elder & Co., 1896).

Thomas, Chantal, *The Wicked Queen: The Origins of the Myth of Marie-Antoinette*, tr. Julie Rose (New York, Zane Books, 1999).

Tocqueville, Alexis de, *The Ancien Régime and the French Revolution* (Manchester, Fontana, 1966).

Tomalin, Claire, *Mary Wollstonecraft* (London, Penguin, 1992).

Trouncer, Margaret, *Madame Récamier* (London, Macdonald, 1949).

Tulard, Jean (presented by), Napoléon I, *Lettres d'amour à Joséphine* (Paris, Fayard, 1981).

Tussaud, Marie, *Memoirs and Reminiscences of France, forming an abridged history of the French Revolution*, ed. F. Hervé (London, Saunders & Otley, 1838).

Valensin, Dr Georges., *Le Lit de Joséphine* (Paris, La Table ronde, 1971).

Vigny, Alfred de, *The Servitude and Grandeur of Arms*, tr. Roger Gard (London, Penguin, 1996).

Vincent-Buffault, Anne, *The History of Tears: Sensibility and Sentimentality in France*, tr. Teresa Bridgeman (Basingstoke, Macmillan, 1991).

Wagener, Françoise, *L'Impératrice Joséphine* (Paris, Flammarion, 1999).

Walvin, James, *Black Ivory: A History of British Slavery* (London, HarperCollins, 1993).

Warner, Marina, *Monuments & Maidens: The Allegory of the Female Form* (London, Picador, 1987).

Weimer, Marguerite Joséphine (Mlle George), *Memoires inédits de mademoiselle George* (Paris, Plon-Nourrit et Cie, 1908).

White, T. H., *The Age of Scandal* (London, Jonathan Cape, 1950).

Yalom, Marilyn, *Blood Sisters: The French Revolution in Women's Memory* (London, Pandora, 1995).

Young, Arthur, *Travels in France during the years 1787, 1788 & 1789*, ed. Constantia Maxwell (Cambridge, Cambridge University Press, 1950).

PERIODICALS

This book relied on information from scores of articles. These are just a few I found particularly useful:

Castel-Çagarriga, G., 'Fanny de Beauharnais et ses amis', in *Revue des deux mondes*, August 1959.

Clouzot, Henri, 'Un soir de Ventose an IV à l'hôtel de Mondragon', in *Revue des études napoléoniennes*, July 1935.

Hamelin, Antoine R., 'Douze ans de ma vie', in *Revue de Paris*, November 1926 and January 1927.

History Today, 48 (1), January 1998.

– 48 (2), February 1998.

– 48 (3), March 1998.

– 48 (6), June 1998.

Macey, David, 'Fort de France', in *Granta* 59, autumn 1997.

'Spécial Révolution 1789', in *Les Cahiers du patrimoine* (Martinique, n.d.).

Sutton, Denys, 'The Empress Josephine and the Arts', in *Apollo* 185, July 1977.

Turgeon, F. K., 'Fanny de Beauharnais: Bibliographical notes and a Bibliography', in *Modern Philology*, August 1932.

Vivre, survivre et être libre, 22 May–22 July 1998 (Fort de France).

INDEX